Perspectives
on the American Past

VOLUME I ■ 1620-1877

About the Author

Michael Perman teaches American history at the University of Illinois at Chicago and is the author of *Reunion Without Compromise: The South and Reconstruction, 1865–1868* (1973); *The Road to Redemption: Southern Politics, 1869–1879* (1984); and *Emancipation and Reconstruction, 1862–1879* (1987). The winner of three book prizes for *The Road to Redemption,* Professor Perman has been awarded fellowships by the Guggenheim Foundation and the Charles Warren Center at Harvard University.

Perspectives
on the American Past

VOLUME I ▪ 1620-1877

READINGS AND COMMENTARY
ON ISSUES IN AMERICAN HISTORY

MICHAEL PERMAN
University of Illinois at Chicago

Scott, Foresman and Company
Glenview, Illinois
London

Acknowledgments are listed at the back of the book on page 352, which constitutes a legal extension of the copyright page.

Cover Photo

Samuel Finley Breese Morse: THE OLD HOUSE OF REPRESENTATIVES. In the collection of The Corcoran Gallery of Art, Museum Purchase, Gallery Fund, 1911.

Library of Congress Cataloging-in-Publication Data

Perman, Michael.
    Perspectives on the American past.

    Bibliography: p.
    Contents: v. 1. 1620–1877—v. 2. 1865 to the
present.
        1. United States—History.   I. Title.
E178.6.P47   1989   973   88-30610
ISBN 0-673-18616-4 (v. 1)
ISBN 0-673-18617-2 (v. 2)

1 2 3 4 5 6-MVN-93 92 91 90 89 88

Preface

Perspectives on the American Past is intended to introduce students to some of the central problems in American history as well as to the different, and often divergent, ways in which historians have recently approached and interpreted them. Although the anthology is most suitable for undergraduate survey courses, it also provides a valuable compilation of influential articles for American history majors. It is also appropriate for advanced placement courses in high schools.

The need for a reader of this kind has become apparent over the past decade because textbooks in American history have become so comprehensive that they have assumed a position of dominance and authority in the teaching of United States survey courses. To offset the definitiveness of the text, students need to be aware that the meaning of history and the explanation of events and developments in the past are still matters of controversy and conjecture. This anthology enables students to join in and discuss the problems that confront historians as they try to understand the past. In this sense, the anthology *engages* the text, and not simply supplements it with additional information, as so many have done in recent years.

The Topics

The major issues and episodes in American history are the focus of *Perspectives on the American Past*. Twenty-three topics have been chosen, divided evenly between the Colonial and Revolutionary eras, the nineteenth century, and the twentieth century. Among other things, this means that the subject of Early America, where much existing work is now being done, is not slighted, as too often happens in anthologies.

The Selections

Two or three articles, or extracts from books, have been selected for each topic. Sometimes, these pieces present sharply contrasting opinions on the topic in question; but usually they simply represent differing perspectives that approach the subject from a different angle or with a different emphasis.

The exact nature of the difference between the selections in each set varies. There is no predetermined set of categories throughout the book that differentiates all the contributions. For instance, there is no overarching dualism separating them as elitist or democratic, conservative or liberal, or consensus- or conflict-oriented. Because no such sharp alternatives are presented, students are not forced to go to one or the other extreme, or to settle for a compromise between diametrically opposite positions; both of these options are pedagogically unsatisfactory. Equally, because there is no set pattern or predictability about how and why these selections differ, students have to approach each topic on its own terms, critically and without prior conceptions.

There are three more criteria used in the choice of each reading. First, the piece had to be a significant contribution to the particular topic or problem. Hence, the historian who wrote it is likely to be a leading figure in the field. Second, the quality of the writing had to be superior. And third, it had to have a recent publication date. Although one or two selections appeared before 1970, most were written within the last decade or so.

The Format

Each topic or chapter consists of the readings and a brief introduction that sets the scene, recounts something about the topic, and indicates the ways in which historians have approached and understood it. The introduction also identifies the historians and their contributions.

Following the introduction are three questions to help focus a student's thoughts before embarking on the readings. These questions are intended to get the student to think about the argument or viewpoint of each selection and the way the piece is constructed. Comprehension and analysis are therefore the objectives. The third question generally requires the student to compare and relate the readings for each topic.

At the end of the text, there is a short reading list, sufficient to prepare a term paper or to satisfy an inquiring student's urge to go a little further into the subject. It is purposely limited to about a dozen items so that it will not overwhelm students, which is often the effect of exhaustive, and therefore exhausting, bibliographies.

Acknowledgments

Many of my colleagues at the University of Illinois at Chicago were helpful in appraising this anthology and offering valuable suggestions about the selection of articles. I am very grateful to Gerald Danzer, Richard Fried, George Huppert, Richard Jensen, Gregg Roeber, Leo Schelbert, and Daniel Scott Smith. Especially valuable were Stephen Wiberly's editorial comments.

I also want to thank the academic reviewers to whom the proposal and its table of contents were sent for evaluation. A number of them took the assignment very seriously and submitted perceptive reports that led to constructive changes. I appreciate the comments of the following: Philip J. Avilo, York College of Pennsylvania; Christopher Collier, University of Connecticut; Jerald Combs, San Francisco State University; Thomas Dublin, State University of New York at Binghamton; Barbara J. Fields, Columbia University; George Forgie, University of Texas at Austin; David Katzman, University of Kansas; Paul R. Lucas, Indiana University; Fred Olsen, Northern Virginia Community College; Leonard Richards, University of Massachusetts at Amherst.

The staff of my publisher, Scott, Foresman and Company, provided significant support; I am particularly indebted to Bob Johnson, whose interest in my ideas about American history readers initiated the project, and to Charlotte Iglarsh, whose editorial experience and her knowledge and understanding made it a delight to work with her.

Finally, I want to thank my seventeen-year-old son, Benjamin, for his comments on the Introduction and my daughter of twelve, Sarah, for helping me by just being herself.

Michael Perman

Contents

Perspectives
on the American Past

VOLUME I ▪ 1620-1877

The Past in Perspective

The purpose of this anthology is to let students of American history in on a secret. It is not exactly a closely guarded one but, all the same, it seems not to be widely known. Or, if known, its implications are rarely understood. The secret is that historians seldom, if ever, agree over the main problems and features of the American past. In fact, differences of opinion and viewpoint are the norm among American historians, rather than the exception.

Many readers may find this revelation startling and perhaps unsettling. Some might already be muttering to themselves, "If they haven't yet decided why there was a civil war, then what have historians been doing all these years?" Others might be wondering, "If it's all up for grabs, then what's the point of studying American history? All we learn may turn out to be wrong." A third reaction might be: "If there's so much disagreement, how do we know what to believe?" Expressing a mixture of annoyance and anxiety, these reactions are quite understandable. They spring from a sense of betrayal because the authoritative certainty that the study of history is expected to provide has been questioned. But, in fact, the student might more appropriately look forward with anticipation to the prospect of a lively course in American history. Let me explain why.

The idea that historians should agree rests on the assumption that the purpose of studying history is to find out exactly what happened in the past. Since past events presumably took place at a specific time and place and in a precise and singular way, it seems reasonable that the task of the historian is to find out what exactly these events were. So there is only one past to reconstruct—the one that actually happened. Any other version of the past is simply inaccurate. The historian who suggests that a particular event occurred in a way that it did not, or for reasons that turn out to be erroneous, needs to get his facts straight. Once this error is corrected, the account will be accurate and all disagreement will end. In other words, disagreement occurs only because a particular historian is inaccurate or is careless with the facts.

At the end of the nineteenth century, the leading historians in Europe and America held a similar view about history. They were convinced that if all the available evidence about a particular event or episode were collected together, the historical actuality of it could be discovered. In the words of the great German historian, Leopold von Ranke, this was history *wie es eigentlich gewesen*, that is, as it really happened. The mass of data that had been assembled would simply tell the story by itself. The historian functioned merely as archivist and editor, whose task was to allow the accumulated facts to speak for themselves—to tell it like it was. This kind of historical literalism, usually referred to as *historicism,* sounds convincing. It seems to be reasonably scientific in its method and likely to produce results that are objective and as accurate as it is possible to be. Furthermore, disagreement will be cut to a minimum because the evidence itself, rather than historians' personal views, will be the ultimate arbiter, determining what did or did not happen.

Many people, if not most, assume that this is how historians go about studying the past. But the fact is that they do not proceed in this fashion—nor should they. In the first place, this kind of history would soon become quite dreary. Historians would be little more than antiquarians rummaging around for as many details from the past as they could find. They would then write histories narrating the lives of people in earlier times and describing what life was like, keeping strictly to the data and rarely, if ever, speculating beyond what was contained within the evidence. Essentially the history that resulted would be descriptive, detailed, detached and, to continue the alliteration, deadly dull.

Historians do not function like this for a second reason. Quite frankly, it is because they cannot. To assume that once all the evidence is collected, the past can be reconstructed with accuracy is simply fallacious. The past cannot be retrieved in anything like its actuality, as any lawyer or judge can attest. Every day in courts of law, witnesses to crimes are called to testify under oath about what happened. Even though a crime may have been committed just a few weeks or months earlier, each witness remembers the incident differently. Yet they were all actually present and saw, or even participated in, the event itself. If people who were at the scene cannot agree on what happened, how realistic is it to expect historians to be accurate about something in the distant past of which they can have no first-hand knowledge? Indeed, the historian may not even have been alive when it occurred.

A third, and last, observation concerns the evidence that historians use. The accuracy with which the past can be reconstructed depends on how complete the record is. From the confidence with which those late nineteenth-century historians approached the data, one might imagine that the evidence was so massive and so comprehensive that everything that was needed to be known was available. In truth, however, the documentary record that is at hand is simply whatever has survived. As time passes, more and more of the historical record gets lost or destroyed. The disappearance of the evidence actually begins even earlier when the participants in the events decide themselves to discard records not thought to be of historical value or interest. So the historical record that a particular era leaves is what it selects and chooses to bequeath. In this sense, each generation—as well as the groups and individuals that compose it—writes its own historical ticket. Confronted by this selectivity, historians' hands are tied. All they have to go on is the surviving evidence, and this limits the content and scope of their knowledge of the past. Anything that is not in the record either did not take place, or else historians do not *know* that it happened even if it did.

So it turns out that the definitive, factual history that historians have been presumed to write is not feasible. What then do historians do? For a start, they might simply concede that all they can hope to offer is a vague approximation of the past. This would be an admission of the limitations of both the evidence and historians' claims to recreate the past with any accuracy. But this is not the way they react. Instead, in a remarkable display of perversity and self-confidence, they take the evidentiary record, acknowledge its shortcomings, and then proceed to impose even greater demands on it than those of their historicist forebears. They are not content to restrict themselves to the question of what happened and answer it with a tentative description of the event or episode involved. Rather, they consider the question "what?" to be merely basic and preliminary, neither very interesting nor very challenging. Two other questions that historians want to move on to and deal with are more intriguing.

The *Why?* Question

The first of these is the query *why*. Why did things in the past happen? How and why did they occur when they did? This is a far more complex question than *what* and requires historians to delve into the tricky problem of causation. Because causation is so problematic, many people, including teachers of history, often try to get around it by citing a list of items called causes that brought about the event in question. Just exactly how they do this is often left unexplained. For this reason, their baffled students may respond to a typical question such as "What were the causes of the American Civil War?" by asking in return, in a state of puzzlement, "How many causes are enough? Five, six, a dozen?" A playful student ostensibly asking about a point of information, might inquire, "How many causes does it take to start a civil war?" But the point is that a list of causes, which are in reality only contributing factors somehow related to the outcome, does not account for or explain what finally occurred. What is needed instead is a formulation that relates all causal factors to each other as well as to the ultimate event, in this case the outbreak of a civil war. The causal relationship that emerges is called an explanation.

This explanation, not an assortment of undifferentiated causes, constitutes the *why* of the Civil War.

Constructing an explanation is a complicated procedure. Actually, it involves several steps. First, causal factors that operated in the short run have to be distinguished from those that were long-term. Factors that were "proximate" and were simply incidents that tipped the scale then have to be differentiated from the "necessary" causes that created the situation where a spark or "proximate" cause could ignite the conflagration and produce an outcome, such as the Civil War. In the case of the Civil War, Lincoln's election in 1860 was a "proximate" cause—and even then, not the only one—whereas the institution of slavery was, in some way or other, a "necessary" cause. Lastly, causal factors come in different forms—some are economic, some political, some cultural—and the historian has to categorize them. So causal factors have to be defined, weighed, assessed, and finally related to each other before an explanation can be derived. Because each explanation contains so many constituent parts and interrelationships, it is highly unlikely that any two of them will be the same in all, or even most, respects. That leaves much room for disagreement over the composition and construction of the explanation; and consequently, much to debate concerning why and how the Civil War, or any other event, occurred.

The *So What?* Question

After *what* and *why* there arises a question that is even more intriguing and more difficult to respond to; it occasions even more discussion and difference of opinion. This is the query *so what.* In a sense, this is the reverse of the question of causation because it deals with results and consequences, the repercussions of an event rather than its antecedents. The question therefore pushes historical inquiry forward in time from the origins of the incident to its aftereffects. What happened as a result? What did the event achieve? What impact did it have? What was its significance? This is what is involved in the question *so what.* As with the problem of causation, one can measure consequences over the short term or within a longer time-frame. Consequences are of different kinds—political, social, or economic. But what mainly differentiates the two phenomena are the contrasting ways in which they operate. The causes of an event flow toward an objective—the event itself—whereas the impact and consequences scatter—away from the event in different directions.

Like a stone that is thrown into a pond creating ever-widening ripples, an event's consequences can be assessed in many ways, depending on the context or level at which their impact is to be measured. For example, the impact of the American Revolution could be estimated in terms of how it shaped and influenced the later development of the United States. Alternatively, the inquiry could be given a narrower focus by asking how it affected the lives and prospects of one group in the American population, such as black slaves.

Did they, in fact, gain from the Revolution, or was it a setback for them? At the same level, one might inquire whether the break with Britain resulted in damage or improvement to the economy of its former colonies. Of course, the question could become parochial in scope if a historian pondered what the effect of the Revolution was on Boston or on a particular county in Virginia. Needless to say, in each of these examples, a cutoff date beyond which the investigation will not be pursued also has to be determined by the historian. For example, it would be sensible to terminate the study of the Revolution's impact on the slaves around 1800 rather than to go on until slavery is ended altogether in 1865. These hypothetical questions simply indicate the numerous contexts and time-frames for assessing an event's impact. Indeed, there are countless possibilities of this type, and the limits are set only by the historian's sense of what is worthwhile and reasonable. Although an assessment of the Revolution's effect on early American manufacturing is conceivable, a study of the impact of the American Revolution on the twentieth-century automobile industry would, it may safely be assumed, fail to pass the historical feasibility test.

Besides its almost limitless possibilities, estimating the impact of a historical phenomenon also involves an extremely complicated and rather inexact procedure. This requires historians to go beyond the existing documentary evidence about the event itself, both in the use of sources and in the delineation of the problem. In the first place, the participants in the episode who created the evidence about it do not, indeed cannot, know what the consequences will be. Only later will the outcome be evident; by that time those who were present may not be alive to see the results. A helpful analogy might be the comparison of the record of a historical event with the record of a baseball game, as described in a newspaper the following day. The story by the sports reporter states that the game was lost by the home team. That is what happened. But there is nothing in the report about the game's consequences and significance. As it turned out, this loss was to be the first in a disastrous losing streak that denied the team the league pennant. The game may have triggered this consequence, but the account of the game could not have referred to it. In the same way, the significance or the consequences of a historical event will not be included in the contemporary record, that is, in the evidence. Instead, it will have to be supplied by the historians who will have to go to other historical sources that they themselves will have to select and locate, in order to find out what happened later. So the historians will, in a real sense, know more about the totality of the episode than the participants who were there at the time.

The second reason why historians trespass beyond the record of the event itself is that they, not the people in the past, determine the significance of what was experienced as well as the criteria by which it is to be measured. That is to say, historians choose the time-frame, the context, and the standard or yardstick for assessing the impact and consequences of past events. They decide the rules by which the past is appraised. To demonstrate what is involved, let us take a question often asked of historians: how a particular president will "go down in history." If Harry S Truman is the President in question, the historian will first try to determine what Truman did and said while in office. After that is more or less established, the method for evaluating President Truman's reputation in history is entirely a matter for the historian as an individual to decide. Perhaps those features will be selected from Truman's total record that are considered central to, and typical of, Truman's presidency and the question will be asked, "What happened to them years later after he left office?" The investigator will also bring to this assessment some ideas about what successful and effective Presidents have done. After all this is assembled and evaluated, it will be time to draw conclusions about President Truman's legacy. With the exception of the first phase in which the details of Truman's presidency were established, this entire procedure was conceptualized and carried out at the discretion of each individual historian. Thus, sources and criteria outside, actually beyond, the record of Truman's term in office were the basis for determining its lasting consequences. Inevitably, therefore, the method one historian chooses for deciding the significance of the Truman presidency will differ fundamentally from those of others, and so too, most likely, will the conclusions.

The question *so what* allows the historian a good deal of latitude in framing and defining an inquiry and also gives the authority to decide what effect people and events in the past have had on their own and later generations and eras. This authority has sometimes been called historical judgment. And it is true that historians can assign blame or confer approval. They can say, for instance, that this war was justified because it had beneficial consequences or that king was unjust because his subjects rose up against him. Handing down such judgments on the past has not been unknown among historians, but besides being moralistic and rather arrogant, it is usually not helpful. Although historians should avoid crude judgments in assessing people and events in history, they are, nonetheless, inescapably involved in some kind of judging whenever they attempt to answer the *so what* question. For, in doing so, they have to measure impact and attribute significance. Perhaps *evaluation* might be more appropriate than judgment to describe what historians do in this context. But, however described, the entire procedure is, quite evidently, subjective and far from exact. Indeed, this facet of the historian's analysis is the least precise and the most discretionary, even speculative, of them all. Compared to description and explanation, where exactitude and certainty are, as we have already seen, difficult to obtain, the process of evaluation is even more open to speculation. This leaves more room than ever before for differences of opinion and disagreement to emerge.

The Historian's Selection of a Topic

No matter what questions historians ask or what analytical procedures they employ, dispute and debate will always permeate the study of history. By its very nature, history is argumentative. This is because historians do not study the past out of some obligation simply to know and be informed about some particular historical subject. Historians do not suffer from a historical compulsion to study the past as if it were Mt. Everest, just "because it is there." Rather, they bring to their investigations of the past specific concerns or interests. The topic they decide to explore holds some particular fascination for them. They do not embark on a project as if they are going on a fact-finding tour, employed as impartial observers with no interest in the outcome.

Although choice of topic may stem from a purely personal curiosity about the subject or some aspect of it, it is much more likely that a historian will be influenced by an awareness of prevailing intellectual currents and public concerns. Moreover, the historian's own thoughts and preoccupations are bound to be shaped profoundly by contemporary events. Hence, the preoccupations of the historian in the present play a profound role in the choice of what to study in the past. They will also shape, to some extent, the perspective or approach that the historian will bring to that investigation.

Some recent examples illustrate this point. Over the past twenty years, historical scholarship has changed dramatically with the emergence of an interest in the history of social groups that previously had been overlooked or even ignored—the respective roles of women, blacks, and native Americans, for instance. Since then so much has happened that each of these now constitutes a distinct field within American history. This has occurred because of changes in perception and understanding in contemporary America about these groups. Sharing in and responding to this shifting cultural, political, and social climate, historians have accordingly brought these changed attitudes to bear on the past. Of course, not every historian has decided to do research in these areas. But even those who have not approach their particular fields and topics of interest with a frame of mind considerably altered by current viewpoints and attitudes. One instance is the revival of interest in the history of American labor. Instead of focusing their attention on labor leaders and labor unions, as had been the case previously, historians nowadays examine with a great deal of care and insight the thoughts and behavior of working people themselves, both as individuals and as members of a class. This shift of emphasis away from an institutional and elitist perspective can be accounted for in several ways. But they all are part of a change in contemporary attitudes about the ordinary and powerless people of American society. Historians now assume that the attitudes of the masses of people cannot be dismissed but have to be understood. Those who once seemed to be insignificant are no longer seen as passive nonparticipants in history but are believed, in their own way, to have influenced and even shaped it.

These developments are particularly interesting because large numbers of people who were excluded from history have now become actors on the historical stage, and as they appear, the stage becomes filled with rather different characters, and so the play itself begins to change. In effect, history is changed. There is a further impact that is not obvious. As historians ask novel questions, they begin to look for historical information in unexplored places. Once the historians of American slavery, for instance, began to take slaves themselves seriously, as they did in the late 1960s and after, and started to examine their life and culture, they cast about for sources of information other than the plantation records of slaves' masters. Soon, they discovered documentation that had existed all along but had seldom, if ever, been used. In these sources, a remarkable amount of information about the thoughts and behavior of slaves was uncovered. Particularly revealing was the language of the slaves' spiritual and secular songs that gave historians access to their religious beliefs and popular culture. Despite the plausible assumption that illiterate slaves would leave no traces of themselves, a different perspective toward them, along with new questions and concerns, enabled historians to identify records thought to be nonexistent or valueless. Imagine how late nineteenth-century historians would react to all of this. Their history "as it really was" would not have included any of these overlooked and disadvantaged groups, and the records they considered definitive would not have contained evidence and sources such as these.

The Historian's Selection of Perspective

The historians' own consciousness has a formative impact, therefore, on the way they approach the past. It will determine the purpose of their investigation, the questions asked, the sources sought and consulted. Part of this outlook or consciousness is what might be called the approach or stance toward the phenomenon under investigation. Although this can take a number of forms, let us take just one example. A historian has decided to study a particular aspect of the history of black Americans. But from what vantage point will the subject be approached? It can be viewed from the perspective of how blacks were affected by the white-dominated wider society, or alternatively it can be looked at in terms of how blacks dealt with this situation. In the first case, the emphasis will be on the world that was imposed on blacks, the context in which they were forced to operate. In the second, the thrust of the investigation will be in the opposite direction, with the historian trying to discover what blacks did on their own and how they reacted to external restraints. The two alternative approaches could be labeled the perspectives of domination and of resistance. And a similar choice of approach would present itself in the cases of women, native Americans, working people, and other similar groups.

On a wider scale, this set of alternatives corresponds to a decision on whether to approach the history of any society "from the top down" or "from the bottom up." Is the focus to be on the elites and the ruling classes so as to discover how they dominated and molded the society, or is it to be on the masses, those who are ruled, to examine how they lived and how they reacted to their condition? The flow and thrust of the investigation could go in either direction, but the kind of study that emerges will be quite dramatically affected by the choice that is made. Even though the phrases describing the alternatives indicate that there is motion from the bottom up to the top, and vice versa, the emphasis will be on the point of departure and may not go much beyond it. Ideally, of course historians should be trying to integrate both approaches, since all parts of society are related to each other and, together, they form a single society. But few historians will want, or be able, to cover everything. Besides, they have to start somewhere, and wherever it is, the decision will be significant.

The Rules of the Discipline

With all these choices and decisions left to the individual historian to determine, the reader may have the impression by now that historical inquiry is entirely subjective. He or she may be concluding that "anything goes" and that "one view is as good as another." That, however, is not the case. "Anything goes" is not the motto or slogan of history. Although history does not generate proof as in mathematics or conduct controlled laboratory experiments as in physics and chemistry, it is nevertheless a discipline. And, as such, it has rules that are binding on its practitioners, similar to the Hippocratic oath of medical professionals. Two of these rules are of cardinal importance. The first requires that only evidence originating directly from the moment in time that is being examined be the basis for historians' deliberations and conclusions. This injunction prevents historians from making statements about an episode in the past for which they have no contemporary evidence—after all, historians are not novelists. They may use imagination and they may speculate somewhat, in order to interpret and understand the past. But their imagination and speculation are historically grounded. Historians do not write works of fiction that are merely embellished with historical characters and scenery. Books of this kind, such as Alex Haley's *Roots* and Gore Vidal's *Lincoln,* should not, for even a moment, be considered history.

The second rule is that historians must be historical. That sounds obvious. But there is more to it than is initially apparent. Although present concerns may well arouse a historian's interest in a particular aspect of the past, those current considerations may not determine the outcome of an investigation. In other words, the past must not be studied in order to produce a predetermined conclusion. Once again, the evidence has to intervene so as to prevent the historian from going to the past to vindicate preconceived notions. Someone who, for example, believes the present era to be most enlightened and advanced should not study the past in order to prove the benightedness of previous societies. Although an initial hypothesis may subsequently be confirmed, the evidence must not be twisted nor denied so as to derive certain conclusions. Just as historians may not use the past to sustain present viewpoints, so too they must never blur the distinction between past and present. The past is not interchangeable with the present. People who lived in earlier times were different from us; they faced different circumstances, and they had different views on many issues, not just the trivial. Therefore, historians must never assume that people in history are just like themselves and the people of their own era, nor may they blame them for those differences. Of course, that does not mean that historians condone everything that has happened in the past. Rather, they have to understand the historical context and circumstances before evaluating the actions of the people who lived in them. Abraham Lincoln, for example, should not be treated as if he were a contemporary of ours. Consequently, he should not be upbraided for moving cautiously against slavery, a social institution that is deemed morally reprehensible by Americans of the late twentieth century. If these precautions are not observed, the peculiarities of each epoch are lost, and the historian becomes present-minded and therefore unhistorical.

These are the cardinal rules that historians have to observe. The restrictions they impose require only that historians ground their arguments and formulations on the evidence, such as it is, and that they respect the past and ensure that it is not confused with the present. In other words, historians have to be imaginative and insightful about the past, but they cannot invent it or lift events and people from their historical context.

Once these ground rules are accepted, every historian is free to take any approach, pose any question, and follow any lead. Under such conditions, how can there be an authorized or true version of the past? Equally, how can there not be differences and disagreements of all kinds? Inconclusive though this state of affairs may be, it at least guarantees that the tour through American history that is about to begin will not be dull and routine. Instead, there is an excellent chance that it will be lively, challenging, even exciting.

Part One

The Encounter Between the Indians and the Europeans

An empty wilderness. A virgin land. Images like these have captured the imagination and convinced Americans that the settlement of the continent was providential and painless. Though comforting, these notions are unfortunately false. The area that became the United States was actually inhabited by roughly 4 million people, whose social organization and ways of life were diverse. At one extreme were nomadic hunters and gatherers, while at the other were sedentary societies engaged in agriculture and living in relatively settled communities. For this reason the arrival of the Europeans was tantamount to an invasion of their homelands. And it soon became conquest.

Even though the task of historians is to discover what actually happened in the past and explain how and why things happened the way they did, they too seem to have shared in the myth of an empty wilderness, for the presence of innumerable people native to American soil was frequently overlooked and even ignored. In actuality, the Indians had for the most part disappeared by the time modern historians came to examine the American past at the turn of this century. By extermination, by removal to reservations, and by the assimilation of the small number still remaining, they had vanished from Euro-American society and consciousness. As members of the dominant culture and society, historians too often had the same blind spots and lack of awareness that prevailed around them. So they allowed the Indians to disappear from their accounts of the American past.

It was impossible to expunge all trace of the Indians. Countless Indian wars were fought in the colonial era, and the contest for control of the plains has been immortalized in the drama of the cowboy and the Indian. Even so, the Indians were invariably depicted as obstacles to be removed and as primitives whose ultimate extinction was simply a matter of time. Only anthropologists treated them with seriousness and respect while studying their customs and cultures.

In the past generation or so, however, perceptions about Indians have changed quite dramatically. This is primarily because of an increasing national awareness about the experiences of minorities and other exploited segments of American society, both past and present. The upshot has been a remarkable outpouring of books and other publications about the institutions and culture of native Americans and about the effect they had on the centuries-long process of European settlement and domination of the continent. The tragic outcome and the terrible consequences of the contact between the Europeans and the Indians cannot be reversed and it should not be sentimentalized. But the critical influence and impact of the Indians is beginning to emerge, as well as an appreciation of who they were. The result has been a quite different and more accurate understanding of what happened when these two forces collided and interacted.

Although the contest between the native inhabitants and the European invaders continued for several hundred years, becoming in the process a constant and formative influence on the course of what is called American history the selections in this topic concentrate on the colonial era. The contribution by James Axtell of William and Mary College seems at first glance a departure from what historians normally do. He speculates on what American history might have been without Indians. This is called *counterfactual* history because it is ahistorical and challenges the known facts. But it is interesting to explore, since it enables the historian to discover insights and detect implications that are overlooked when things are taken for granted. Indeed, when trying to explain why particular events turned out as they did, historians frequently have to ponder why they did not happen differently. Without this imaginary dimension, they would simply be accepting past occurrences as inevitable, so that the task of explaining them would just be a matter of chronicling and recounting the causal sequence that brought them about. For example, wars cannot be fully explained without some conjecture about whether they could have been avoided. Because he ponders the alternatives Professor Axtell is able to dramatize the significance of native Americans to the course of American historical development.

The study by James H. Merrell of Vassar College is an arresting example of what has emerged from the recent awareness about the history of native Americans. The title reveals at the outset how far such recognition can take the historian, since the article suggests that the experience of a "new world" was not one appreciated only by the Europeans. This idea reverses the customary perspective on the settlement of America by describing the unfamiliar world introduced by the arrival of the Europeans.

By focusing on the impact of the Indians on the society and culture of the dominant Europeans, James Axtell's essay contrasts with that of Professor Merrell, who is concerned with the impact that the Europeans had on the Indians' culture and way of life. In their different ways, both contributions deepen our understanding of this encounter.

■

QUESTIONS TO CONSIDER

1. How did the Indians contribute to what Axtell calls the Americanization of the Europeans?

2. Merrell says that the Catawbas were able to "play the hand dealt them well enough to survive." How did they do this, and what was the price they paid?

3. What insights into the encounter between the Indians and the Europeans do these two articles together provide?

Colonial America Without the Indians: Counterfactual Reflections

James Axtell

It is taking us painfully long to realize that throughout most of American history the Indians were "one of the principal *determinants* of historical events." A growing number of scholars understand that fact, but the great majority of us still regard the native Americans—if we regard them at all—as exotic or pathetic footnotes to the main course of American history.

This is patently clear from American history textbooks. As Virgil Vogel, Alvin Josephy, and most recently Frederick Hoxie have shown in embarrassing detail, "Indians in textbooks either do nothing or they resist." In their colonial and 19th-century manifestations, they are either "obstacles to white settlement" or "victims of oppression." "As victims or obstacles, Indians have no textbook existence apart from their resistance." In short, the texts reflect our "deep-seated tendency to see whites and Indians as possessing two distinct species of historical experience" rather than a mutual history of continuous interaction and influence.

Attempts to redress the balance have suffered from serious flaws. Some observers have exaggerated and oversimplified the Indian impact. We certainly ought to avoid the fatuity of the argument that "what is

Axtell, James, "Colonial America without the Indians: Counterfactual Reflections," *Journal of American History,* 73 (March 1987), 981–96. Copyright © 1987 Organization of American Historians. Reprinted by permission.

distinctive about America is Indian, through and through" or that Americans are simply Europeans with "Indian souls." Historians have been more drawn to other, less sweeping, approaches. Robert Berkhofer described four well-meaning but unproductive remedial approaches to "minority" history, especially the history of American Indians. They are the "great man" or "heroes" approach (the "devious side of treaty-making"), the "who-is-more-civilized" approach ("barbarities committed by whites against Indians" contrasted with the "civilized" contributions of Indians), the "crushed personality" and "cultural theft" approach ("change only destroys Indian cultures, never adds to them"), and—by far the most important—the "contributions approach" ("long lists of the contributions Native Americans made to the general American way of life"). The first two approaches offer variations on the theme of Indian heroism and resistance. The third presents Indians as victims. None of the three gives much help in analyzing processes in which both Indians and whites played varying and evolving roles. At best they alert us to the moral dimensions of Indian-white history.

The contributions approach, although flawed, is useful. We inevitably employ it when we seek to define the Indian role in American history, rather than the white role in Indian history. Since most scholars who refer to Indian history are primarily interested in the evolution of the dominant Anglo-American "core culture" and political nationhood, they will write in terms of Indian contributions. It is therefore essential to understand the pitfalls in the approach and to devise ways of avoiding them.

A relative disregard for chronology weakens the contributions approach. By focusing on the modern legacy of Indian culture, it usually ignores the specific timing of the various white adaptations and borrowings. Generic "Indian" contributions seem to have been made any time after 1492, it hardly matters when. Such cavalier chronology ought to offend historians not only because it is imprecise but also because it prevents us from determining causation with any accuracy. If we do not know *which* Indian group lent the word, trait, or object and *when,* we will be unable to measure the impact of the adaptive changes in Anglo-American culture at the time they occurred and as they reverberated.

An even more serious flaw is an almost exclusive focus on native material culture (and names of native or American objects and places) that neglects how those items were used, perceived, and adapted by their white borrowers. That focus and the neglect of chronology restrict discussion to a narrow range of additions to contemporary American "life" (i.e., material culture) rather than opening it up to the cultural and social fullness of American *history.* What the approach sadly ignores are the changes wrought in Anglo-American culture, not by borrowing and adapting native cultural traits, words, and objects, but by reacting negatively and perhaps unconsciously to the native presence, threat, and challenge. Without consideration of these deeply formative *reactive* changes, we can have no true measure of the Indians' impact on American history.

In seventeenth- and eighteenth-century Anglo-America, the adaptive changes whites made in response to their contacts with Indians significantly shaped agriculture, transport,

and economic life. The more elusive reactive changes significantly shaped the identity of a new people and the nation they founded.

One striking way to register the sheer *indispensability* of the Indians for understanding America's past is to imagine what early American history might have looked like in the utter *absence* of Indians in the New World. The emphasis should be on historical control, not the free flight of fancy. If we posited an Indian-less New World in 1492 and then tried to reconstruct the course of later history, we would end up in a speculative quagmire because each dependent variable could develop in many alternative ways, depending on the others. By the time we reached 1783 we might have a familiar historical product or, more likely, a virtually unrecognizable one. Whatever the outcome, its artificiality would make it heuristically useless. But by following the historical course of events in America and at selected points imaginatively removing the Indians from the picture, we reduce the artificiality of the exercise and the opportunity for conjectural mayhem. Such a controlled use of the counterfactual can invigorate the search for historical causation.

The following series of counterfactual reflections is offered as a heuristic exercise. . . . "Had the European colonists found an utterly unpopulated continent," we ask, "would colonial American life have differed in any major respect from its actual pattern?"

To begin at the beginning, in the period of European discovery and exploration, we can say with confidence that if Christopher Columbus had not discovered the people whom he called *los Indios* (and they him), the history of Spanish America would have been extremely short and uneventful. Since Columbus was looking for the Far East, not America or its native inhabitants, it would not have surprised him to find no Indians in the Caribbean—the new continent was surprise enough. But he would have been disappointed, not only because the islands of the Orient were known to be inhabited but also because there would have been little reason to explore and settle an unpopulated New World instead of pursuing his larger goal. He would have regarded America as simply a huge impediment to his plan to mount an old-fashioned crusade to liberate Jerusalem with profits derived from his short-cut to Cathay.

If the Caribbean and Central and South America had been unpopulated, the placer mines of the islands and the deep mines of gold and silver on the mainland probably would not have been discovered; they certainly would not have been quickly exploited without Indian knowledge and labor. It is inconceivable that the Spanish would have stumbled on the silver deposits of Potosí or Zacatecas if the Incas and Aztecs had not set Spanish mouths to watering with their sumptuous gold jewelry and ornaments. Indeed, without the enormous wealth to be commandeered from the natives, it is likely that the Spanish would not have colonized New Spain at all except to establish a few supply bases from which to continue the search for the Southwest Passage.

It is equally possible that without the immediate booty of Indian gold and silver, the Spanish would have dismissed Columbus after one voyage as a crack-brained Italian and redirected their economic energies eastward in the wake of the Portuguese, toward the certifiable wealth of Africa, India, and the East Indies. Eventually, sugar cane might have induced the Iberians to colonize their American discoveries, as it induced them to colonize the Cape Verde, Madeira, and Canary islands, but they would have had to import black laborers. Without Indian labor and discovery, however, saltwater pearls and the bright red dye made from the cochineal beetle—the second largest export of the Spanish American empire in the colonial period—would not have contributed to Spain's bulging balance sheets, and to the impact of that wealth on the political and economic history of Europe in the sixteenth and early seventeenth centuries.

Perhaps most important, without the millions of native Americans who inhabited New Spain, there would have been no Spanish conquest—no "Black Legend," no Cortés or Montezuma, no brown-robed friars baptizing thousands daily or ferreting out "idolatry" with whip and fagot, no legalized plunder under the encomienda system, no cruelty to those who extracted the mines' treasures and rebuilt Spanish cities on the rubble of their own, no mastiffs mangling runaways. And without the fabulous lure of Aztec gold and Inca silver carried to Seville in the annual bullion fleets, it is difficult to imagine Spain's European rivals racing to establish American colonies of their own as early as they did.

Take the French, for example. As they did early in the sixteenth century, the cod teeming on the Grand Banks off Newfoundland would have drawn and supported a small seasonal population of fishermen. But without the Indians, the French would have colonized no farther. Giovanni da Verrazzano's 1524 reconnaissance of the Atlantic seaboard would have been an even bigger bust than it was, and Jacques Cartier would probably have made two voyages instead of three, the second only to explore the St. Lawrence River far enough to learn that China did not lie at the western end of Montreal Island. He would have reported to Francis I that "the land God gave to Cain" had no redeeming features, such as the greasy furs of Indian fishermen and the promise of gold and diamonds in the fabled Kingdom of the Saguenay, of which the Indians spoke with such apparent conviction.

If by chance Samuel de Champlain had renewed the French search for the Northwest Passage in the seventeenth century, he would have lost his backers quickly without the lure of an established fur trade with the natives of Acadia and Canada, who hunted, processed, and transported the pelts in native canoes or on native snowshoes and toboggans. And without the "pagan" souls of the Indians as a goad and challenge, the French religious orders, male and female, would not have cast their lot with Champlain and the trading companies that governed and settled New France before 1663. In short, without the Indian fur trade, no seigneuries would have been granted along the St. Lawrence, no *habitants, engagés* (indentured servants) or marriageable "King's girls" shipped out to Canada. Quebec and Montreal would not have been founded even as crude *comptoirs,* and no Jesuit missionaries would have craved martyrdom at an Iroquois stake. No "French and Indian" wars would mar our textbooks with their ethnocentric denomination. North America would have belonged solely to settlements of English farmers, for without the Indians and their fur trade, the Swedish and the Dutch would have imitated the French by staying home or turning to the Far East for economic inspiration.

Without the lure of American gold and the Elizabethan contest with Spain that it stimulated, the English, too, would probably have financed fewer ocean searches for the Northwest Passage. If no one thought that Indian chamber pots were made of gold, far fewer gentle-born investors and lowborn sailors would have risked their lives and fortunes on the coasts of America. Unless the Spanish had reaped fabulous riches from the natives and then subjected them to cruel and unnatural bondage, Sir Walter Ralegh would not have sponsored his voyages of liberation to Guiana and Virginia. If the Spanish bullion fleets had not sailed regularly through the Straits of Florida, English privateers would not have preyed on the West Indies nor captured the booty they used to launch permanent colonies in Ireland and North America. Arthur Barlowe's 1584 voyage to North Carolina would probably not have been followed up soon, if he had not discovered friendly natives able to secure a fledgling colony from Spanish incursions.

Sooner or later, the English would have established colonies in America as a safety valve for the felt pressures of population growth and economic reorganization and as a sanctuary for religious dissenters. Once English settlement was under way, the absence of native villages, tribes, and war parties would have drastically altered the chronology of American history. In general, events would have been accelerated because the Indian presence acted as a major check on colonial development. Without a native barrier (which in the colonial period was much more daunting then the Appalachians), the most significant drag on colonial enterprise would have been the lack of Indian labor in a few minor industries, such as the domestic economy of southern New England (supplied by Indians captured in the Pequot and King Philip's wars) and the whale fisheries of Cape Cod, Long Island, and Nantucket. Indians were not crucial to wheat farming, lumbering, or rice and tobacco culture and would not have been missed by the English entrepreneurs engaged in them.

Without Indians to contest the land, English colonists would have encountered opposition to their choice of prime locations for settlement only from English competitors. They would not have had to challenge Indian farmers for the fertile river valleys and coastal plains the natives had cultivated for centuries. Without potential Indian or European enemies, sites could be located for economic rather than military considerations, thus removing Jamestown, Plymouth, and St. Mary's City from the litany of American place-names. Boston, New York, Philadelphia, and Charleston would probably be where they are, either because Indian opposition did not much affect their founding or because they were situated for optimal access to inland markets and Atlantic shipping lanes.

In an empty land, English leaders would also have had fewer strategic and ideological reasons for communal settlements of the classic New England type. Without the military and moral threat of Indian war parties, on the one hand, and the puzzling seduction of native life, on the other, English colonists would have had to be persuaded by other arguments to cast their lots together. One predictable result is that New England "Puritans" would have become unbridled "Yankees" even faster than they did. Other colonies would have spread quickly across the American map. By 1776, Anglo-American farmers in large numbers would have spilled over the Appalachians, headed toward their "Manifest Destiny" in the West. Without Indians, Frenchmen, or Spaniards in the Mississippi Valley and beyond to stop them, only the technology of transportation, the supply of investment capital, and the organization of markets en route would have regulated the speed of their advance.

Another consequence of an Indian-less America would be that we could not speak with any accuracy of "the American frontier" because there would be no people on the other side; only where two peoples and cultures intersect do we have a bona fide frontier. The movement of one people into uninhabited land is merely exploration or settlement; it does not constitute a frontier situation. In fact, without viable Indian societies, colonial America would have more nearly resembled Frederick Jackson Turner's famous frontier in which Indians are treated more as geographical features than as sociological teachers. In Turner's scenario, the European dandy fresh from his railroad car is "Americanized" less by contact with palpably attractive human societies than by the "wilderness" or Nature itself. Moreover, the distinctively American character traits that Turner attributed to life on the edge of westering "civilization" would have been exaggerated by the existence of truly limitless cheap land and much less control from the Old World and the Eastern Establishment.

Not only would Turner's mythopoeic frontier really have existed in a non-Indian America, but three other common misunderstandings of colonial history would have been realities. First, America would indeed have been a virgin land, a barren wilderness, not home to perhaps four million native people north of Mexico. If those people had not existed, we would not have to explain their catastrophic decline, by as much as 90 percent, through warfare, injustice, forced migrations, and epidemics of imported diseases—the "widowing" of the once-virgin land, as Francis Jennings has so aptly called it.

Second, colonial history would be confined roughly to the eastern and midwestern parts of the future United States (which themselves would be different). Without Indians, we could ignore French Canada and Louisiana, the Spanish Southwest, the Russian Northwest (whose existence depended on the Indian-staffed seal trade), and the borderless histories of Indian-white contact that determined so much of the shape and texture of colonial life.

The Algonquin village of Secoton, located in present-day North Carolina. Historians have often overlooked the Indians' contribution to the viability of the early colonies.

And third, we would not have to step up from the largely black-and-white pageant of American history we are offered in our textbooks and courses to a richer polychromatic treatment, if the Indians had no role in the past. We would not even have to pay lip service to the roll call of exclusively male Indian leaders who have been squeezed into the corners of our histories by Indian militance during the last twenty years. Still less would we have to try to integrate into our texts an understanding of the various native peoples who were here first, remained against staggering odds, and are still here to mold our collective past and future.

To get a sharper perspective on an Indian-free scenario of colonial history, we should increase our focal magnification and analyze briefly four distinguishable yet obviously related aspects of colonial life—economics, religion, politics, and acculturation. The economy of Anglo-America without the Indians would have resembled in general outline the historical economy, with several significant exceptions. Farming would certainly have been the mainstay of colonial life, whether for family subsistence or for capitalist marketing and accumulation. But the initial task of establishing farms would have required far more grubbing and clearing without the meadows and park-like woods produced by seasonal Indian burning and especially without the cleared expanses of Indian corn fields and village sites. Many colonists found that they could acquire cleared Indian lands with a few fathoms of trading cloth, some unfenced cows, or a well-aimed barrel of buckshot.

There would have been no maize or Indian corn, the staple crop grown throughout the colonial period to feed people and sometimes to fatten livestock for export. If Indians had not adapted wild Mexican corn to the colder, moister climates of North America and developed the agricultural techniques of hilling, fertilizing by annual burning, and co-planting with nitrogen-fixing beans to reduce soil depletion, the colonists would have lacked a secure livelihood, particularly in the early years before traditional European cereal crops had been adapted to the American climate and soils. Even if traditional crops could have been transplanted with ease, colonial productivity would not have benefitted from the efficiency and labor savings of native techniques, which were often taught by Indian prisoners (as at Jamestown) or by allies like Squanto at Plymouth. So central was maize to the colonial economy that its absence might have acted as a severe brake on westward settlement, thereby somewhat counteracting the magnetic pull of free land.

The colonial economy would also have been affected by the lack of Indian trade, whose profits fueled the nascent economies of several colonies, including Massachusetts, Rhode Island, New York, Pennsylvania, Virginia, and South Carolina. Without fortunes made from furs, some of the "first families" of America—the Byrds, Penns, Logans, Winthrops, Schuylers—would not have begun to accumulate wealth so soon in the form of ships, slaves, rice, tobacco, or real estate. Nor would the mature economies of a few major colonies have rested on the fur trade well into the eighteenth century. New York's and Pennsylvania's balance of payments with the mother country would have been badly skewed if furs supplied by Indians had not accounted for 30 to 50 percent of their annual exports between 1700 and 1750. A substantial portion of English exports to the colonies would not have been sent to colonial traders for Indian customers, whose desire for English cloth and appetite for West Indian rum were appreciated even though throughout the colonial period furs accounted for only .5 percent of England's colonial imports, far less than either tobacco or sugar.

The lack of Indians and Indian property rights in America would have narrowed another classic American road to wealth. If the new land had been so close to inexhaustible and "dirt cheap," the range of legal and extralegal means to acquire relatively scarce land for hoarding and speculation would have been markedly reduced. Within the unknown confines of the royal response to a huge, open continent, every man, great and small, would have been for himself. If the law condoned or fostered the selective aggrandisement of colonial elites, as it tended to do historically, unfavored farmers and entrepreneurs could simply move out of the government's effective jurisdiction or find leaders more willing to do their bidding. The proliferation of new colonies seeking economic and political independence from the felt tyranny of an Eastern Establishment would have been one certain result, as would a flattening of social hierarchy in all the mainland colonies.

Finally, in an America without Indians the history of black slavery would have been different. It is likely that, in the absence of Indians, the colonial demand for and use of African slaves would have begun earlier and accelerated faster. For although the historical natives were found to be poor workers and poorer slaves, the discovery took some time. Not only would the rapid westward spread of settlements have called for black labor, perhaps more of it indentured, but the rice and tobacco plantations of the Southeast probably would have been larger than they were historically, if scarce land and high prices had not restricted them. In a virgin-land economy, agricultural entrepreneurs who wanted to increase their acreage could easily buy out their smaller neighbors, who lacked no access to new lands in the west. Greater numbers of black laborers would have been needed because white indentured servants would have been extremely hard to get when so much land and opportunity beckoned. The slaves themselves would have been harder to keep to the task without surrounding tribes of Indians who could be taught to fear and hate the African strangers and to serve the English planters as slave catchers. The number of maroon enclaves in the interior would have increased considerably.

While most colonists came to the New World to better their own material condition, not a few came to ameliorate the spiritual condition of the "godless" natives. Without the challenge of native "paganism" in America, the charters of most English colonies would have been frankly materialistic documents with pride of motive going to the extension of His (or Her) Majesty's Eminent Domain. Thus, American history would have lost much of its distinctively evangelical tone, though few of its millenarian, utopian strains. Without the long, frustrated history of Christian missions to the Indians, there would have been one less source of denominational competition in the eighteenth century. And we would lack a sensitive barometer of the cultural values that the European colonists sought to transplant in the New World.

Without Indian targets and foils, even the New England colonists might not have retained their "Chosen People" conceit so long or so obdurately. On the other hand, without the steady native reminder of their evangelical mission in America, their early descent into ecclesiastical tribalism and spiritual exclusiveness might have been swifter. The jeremiads of New England would certainly have been less shrill in the absence of the Pequot War and King Philip's War, when the hostile natives seemed to be "scourges" sent by God to punish a sinful people. Without the military and psychological threat of Indians within and without New England's borders, the colonial fear of limitless and unpredictable social behavior would have been reduced, thereby diminishing the harsh treatment of religious deviants such as Roger Williams, Anne Hutchinson, the Quakers, and the Salem witches. Finally, the French "Catholic menace" to the north would have been no threat to English Protestant sensibilities without hundreds of Indian converts, led by "deviously" effective Jesuit missionaries, ringing New England's borders. The French secular clergy who would have ministered to the handful of fishermen and farmers in Canada would have had no interest in converting Protestant "heretics" hundreds of miles away and no extra manpower to attempt it.

Colonial politics, too, would have had a different complexion in the absence of American natives. Even if the French had settled the St. Lawrence Valley without a sustaining Indian fur trade, the proliferating English population and European power politics would have made short work of the tiny Canadian population, now bereft of Indian allies and converts in the thousands. In all likelihood, we would write about only one short intercolonial war, beginning much earlier than 1689. Perhaps the English privateers, David and Jarvis Kirke, who captured New France in 1629, would not have given it back to the French in 1632. Without the Catholic Indian *reserves* (praying towns) of Lorette, Caughnawaga, and St. François to serve as military buffers around French settlements, Canada would quickly have become English, at least as far north as arable land and lumber-rich forests extended.

Without a formidable French and Indian threat, early Americans would not have developed—in conjunction with their conceit as God's "Chosen People"—such a pronounced garrison mentality, picturing themselves as innocent and holy victims threatened by heavily armed satanic forces. If the English had not been virtually surrounded by Indian nations allied with the French and an arc of French trading forts and villages from Louisiana to Maine, the Anglo-American tendencies toward persecuted isolationism would have been greatly reduced.

As the colonies matured, the absence of an Indian military threat would have lightened the taxpayers' burden for colonial defense, lessening the strains in the political relations between governors and representative assemblies. Indeed, the assemblies would not have risen to political parity with the royal administrators without the financial crises generated by war debts and defense needs. Intercolonial cooperation would have been even rarer than it was. Royal forces would not have arrived during the 18th century to bolster sagging colonial defenses and to pile up imperial debts that the colonies would be asked to help amortize. Consequently, the colonies would have had few grievances against the mother country serious enough to ignite an American Revolution, at least not in 1776. On the other hand, without the concentration of Indian allies on the British side, the colonists might have achieved independence sooner than they did.

Indeed, without the steady impress of Indian culture, the colonists would probably not have been ready for revolution in 1776, because they would not have been or felt sufficiently Americanized to stand before the world as an independent nation. The Indian presence precipitated the formation of an American identity.

Without Indian societies to form our colonial frontiers, Anglo-American culture would have been transformed only by internal developments, the evolving influence of the mother country, and the influence of the black and other ethnic groups who shared the New World with the English. Black culture probably would have done the most to change the shape and texture of colonial life, especially in the South. But English masters saw little reason to emulate their black slaves, to make *adaptive* changes in their own cultural practices or attitudes in order to accommodate perceived superiorities in black culture. English colonial culture changed in response to the imported Africans largely in *reaction* to their oppositional being, and pervasive and often virulent racism was the primary result. Other changes, of course, followed from the adoption of staple economies largely but not necessarily dependent on black labor.

English reactions to the Indians, on the other hand, were far more mixed; the "savages" were noble as well as ignoble, depending on English needs and circumstances. Particularly on the frontier, colonists were not afraid or loath to borrow and adapt pieces of native culture if they found them advantageous or necessary for beating the American environment or besting the Indians in the contest for the continent. Contrary to metropolitan colonial opinion, this cultural exchange did not turn the frontiersmen into Indians. Indian means were simply borrowed and adapted to English ends. The frontiersmen did not regard themselves as Indians nor did they appreciably alter their basic attitudes toward the native means they employed. But they also knew that their American encounters with the Indians made them very different from their English cousins at home.

While the colonists borrowed consciously and directly from Indian culture only on the frontier, English colonial culture as a whole received a substantial but indirect impress from the Indians by being forced to confront the novel otherness of native culture and to cope with its unpredictability, pride, and retaliatory violence. Having the Indians as adversaries sometimes and contraries at all times not only reinforced the continuity of vital English traits and institutions but also Americanized all levels of colonial society more fully than the material adaptations of the frontiersmen. The colonial experience of trying to solve a series of "Indian problems" did much to give the colonists an identity indissolubly linked to America and their apprenticeship in political and military cooperation. In large measure, it was the *reactive* changes that transformed colonial Englishmen into native Americans in feeling, allegiance, and identity, a transformation without which, John Adams said, the American Revolution would have been impossible.

What identity-forming changes would *not* have taken place in colonial culture had the continent been devoid of Indians? The adaptive changes are the easiest to describe. Without native precedent, the names of twenty-eight states and myriad other place-names would carry a greater load of Anglophonic freight. The euphonious Shenandoah and Monongahela might well be known as the St. George and the Dudley rivers. We might still be searching for suitable names for the *moose, skunk,* and *racoon,* the *muskellunge* and *quahog,* the *hickory* tree and marshy *muskeg.* It would be impossible, no doubt, to find *moccasins* in an L. L. Bean catalog or canned *succotash* in the supermarket. We would never refer to our children playfully as *papooses* or to political bigshots as *mugwumps.* Southerners could not start their day with *hominy* grits.

Without Indian guides to the New World, the newly arrived English colonists could not have housed themselves in bark-covered wigwams and longhouses. Not only would their diet have depended largely on imported foods, but even their techniques for hunting American game and fowl and coping in the woods would have been meager. Without native medicines, many colonists would have perished and the *U.S. Pharmacopeia* would lack most of the 170 entries attibutable to Indian discovery and use. Without Indian snowshoes and toboggans, winter hunting and travel would have been sharply curtailed. Without the lightweight bark canoe, northern colonists would have penetrated the country on foot. English hunters probably would have careered around the woods in gaudy colors and torn English garments much longer, unaware that the unsmoked glint of their musket barrels frightened the game. And what would Virginia's patriotic rifle companies have worn in 1775 as an alternative to moccasins, leggings, fringed hunting shirts, scalping knives, and tomahawks?

Without native opponents and instructors in the art of guerilla warfare, the colonists would have fought their American wars—primarily with the British—in traditional military style. In fact, without the constant need to suppress hostile natives and aggressive Europeans, they might have lost most of their martial spirit and prowess, making their victory in the now-postponed Revolution less than certain. Beating the British regulars at their own game without stratagems and equipment gained from the Indians would have been nearly impossible, particularly after the British gained experience in counterinsurgent warfare in Scotland and on the continent.

The absence of such adaptive changes would have done much to maintain the Anglicized tone and texture of colonial life; the absence of Indians would have preserved more fundamental cultural values that were altered historically. The generalized European fear of barbarism that colonial planners and leaders manifested would have dissipated without the Indian embodiment of a "heathenism" that seemed contagious to English frontiersmen or the danger of Englishmen converting to an Indian way of life in captivity or, worse still, voluntarily as "apostates" and "renegades." Without the seduction of an alternative lifestyle within easy reach, hundreds of colonists would not have become white Indians.

More generally, the Anglo-Americans' definition of themselves would have lacked a crucial point of reference because the Indians would no longer symbolize the "savage" baseness that would dominate human nature if man did not "reduce" it to "civility" through government, religion, and the capitalist work ethnic. Only imported Africans, not American natives, would then have shown "civilized men [what] they were not and must not be." Because the settlers were "especially inclined to discover attributes in savages which they found first but could not speak of in themselves," they defined themselves "less by the vitality of their affirmations than by the violence of their abjurations." All peoples define themselves partly by contrast with other peoples, but the English colonists forged their particular American identity on an Indian anvil more than on a (non-English) European or African one.

The Indians were so crucial to the formation of the Anglo-American character because of the strong contrasts between their culture and that of the intruders, which the English interpreted largely as native deficiencies. While English technology had reached the Age of Iron, Indian technology was of the Stone Age, without wheels, clocks, compasses, cloth, iron, glass, paper, or gunpowder. While the English participated in a capitalist economy of currency and credit, the natives bartered in kind from hand to hand. While the English were governed by statutes, sheriffs, parliaments, and kings, the Indians' suasive politics of chiefs and councils seemed to be no government at all. While the English worshipped the "true God" in churches with prayer books and scripture, native shamans resembled "conjurers" who preyed on the "superstitious" natures of their dream-ridden, "devil-worshipping" supplicants. While the English enjoyed the benefits of printing and alphabetic literacy, the Indians were locked in an oral culture of impermanence and "hearsay." While the English sought to master nature as their religion taught them, the natives saw themselves as part of nature, whose other "spirits" deserved respect and thanks. While English men worked in the fields and women in the house, Indian women farmed and their menfold "played" at hunting and fishing. While English time shot straight ahead into a progressive future, Indian time looped and circled upon itself, blurring the boundaries between a hazy past, a spacious present, and an attenuated future. While the English lived in permanent towns and cities, the Indians' annual subsistence cycle of movement seemed aimlessly "nomadic." While the English waged wars of state for land, crowns, wealth, or faith, Indian warriors struck personally for revenge, honor, and captives. While English society was divided into "divinely sanctioned" strata of wealth, power, and prestige, Indian society fostered an "unnatural" sense of democratic individualism in the people. And while English ethnocentrism was based on a new religion, technology, social evolution, and ultimately race, the Indians' own strong sense of superiority, color-blind and religiously tolerant, could not be undermined except by inexplicable European diseases.

For the whole spectrum of colonial society, urban and rural, the Indians as cultural contraries were not so frustrating, alarming, or influential as the Indian enemy. As masters of an unconventional warfare of terror, they seared the collective memories, imaginations, and even subconscious of the colonists, leaving a deep but blurred intaglio of fear and envy, hatred and respect. Having the American natives as frequent and deadly adversaries—and even as allies—did more to "Americanize" the English colonists than any other human factor and had two contradictory results. When native warfare frustrated and humbled the English military machine, its successes cast into serious doubt the colonists' sense of superiority, especially when the only recourse seemed to be the hiring of mercenaries from other tribes. At the same time, victorious Indians seemed so insufferably insolent—a projection of the Christians' original sin—that the colonists redoubled their efforts to claim divine grace and achieve spiritual and social regeneration through violence. One of the pathetic ironies of early America is that in attempting to exterminate the wounding pride of their Indian enemies, the colonists inflated their own pride to sinful proportions.

The Indians' brand of guerilla warfare, which involved the "indiscriminate slaughter of all ranks, ages and sexes," torture, and captivity for adoption, gave rise to several colonial reactions. The first reaction was a well-founded increase in fear and paranoia. The second reaction was the development of a defensive garrison mentality, which in turn reinforced the colonists' sense of being a chosen if momentar-ily abandoned people. And the colonists' third response was a sense of being torn from their own "civilized" moorings and swept into the kind of "savage" conduct they deplored in their enemies, motivated by cold-blooded vengeance. Without Indian enemies, it is doubtful if the colonists would have slaughtered and tortured military prisoners, including women and children, taken scalps from friends and enemies to collect government bounties, encouraged the Spanish-style use of dogs, or made boot tops and tobacco pouches from the skin of fallen foes. It is a certainty that non-Indian enemies would not have been the target of frequent if unrealized campaigns of genocide; it is difficult to imagine English settlers coining an aphorism to the effect that "the only good Dutchman is a dead one."

It is both fitting and ironic that the symbol chosen by Revolutionary cartoonists to represent the American colonies was the Indian, whose love of liberty and fierce independence had done so much to Americanize the shape and content of English colonial culture. It is fitting because the Indians by their long and determined opposition helped to meld thirteen disparate colonies into one (albeit fragile) nation, different from England largely by virtue of having shared that common history of conflict on and over Indian soil. It is ironic because after nearly two centuries of trying to take the Indians' lives and lands, the colonists appropriated not only the native identity but the very characteristics that thwarted the colonists' arrogations.

The Indians' New World:
The Catawba Experience

James H. Merrell

In August 1608 John Smith and his band of explorers captured an Indian named Amoroleck during a skirmish along the Rappahannock River. Asked why his men—a hunting party from towns upstream—had attacked the English, Amoroleck replied that they had heard the strangers "were a people come from under the world, to take their world from them." Smith's prisoner grasped a simple yet important truth that students of colonial America have overlooked: after 1492 native Americans lived in a world every bit as new as that confronting transplanted Africans or Europeans.

The failure to explore the Indians' new world helps explain why, despite many excellent studies of the native American past, colonial history often remains "a history of those men and women—English, European, and African—who transformed America from a geographical expression into a new nation." One reason Indians generally are left out may be the apparent inability to fit them into the new world theme, a theme that exerts a powerful hold on our historical imagination and runs throughout our efforts to interpret American development. From Frederick Jackson Turner to David Grayson Allen, from Melville J. Her-

skovits to Daniel C. Littlefield, scholars have analyzed encounters between peoples from the Old World and conditions in the New, studying the complex interplay between European or African cultural patterns and the American environment. Indians crossed no ocean, peopled no faraway land. It might seem logical to exclude them.

The natives' segregation persists, in no small degree, because historians still tend to think only of the new world as the New World, a geographic entity bounded by the Atlantic Ocean on the one side and the Pacific on the other. Recent research suggests that process was as important as place. Many settlers in New England recreated familiar forms with such success that they did not really face an alien environment until long after their arrival. Africans, on the other hand, were struck by the shock of the new at the moment of their enslavement, well before they stepped on board ship or set foot on American soil. If the Atlantic was not a barrier between one world and another, if what happened to people was more a matter of subtle cultural processes than mere physical displacements, perhaps we should set aside the maps and think instead of a "world" as the physical and cultural milieu within which people live and a "new world" as a dramatically different milieu demanding basic changes in ways of life. Considered in these terms, the experience of natives was more closely akin to

From "The Indians' New World: The Catawba Experience" by James H. Merrell, *The William and Mary Quarterly*, Vol. 41, October 1984. Reprinted by permission of the author.

that of immigrants and slaves, and the idea of an encounter between worlds can—indeed, must—include the aboriginal inhabitants of America.

For American Indians a new order arrived in three distinct yet overlapping stages. First, alien microbes killed vast numbers of natives, sometimes before the victims had seen a white or black face. Next came traders who exchanged European technology for Indian products and brought natives into the developing world market. In time traders gave way to settlers eager to develop the land according to their own lights. These three intrusions combined to transform native existence, disrupting established cultural habits and requiring creative responses to drastically altered conditions. Like their new neighbors, then, Indians were forced to blend old and new in ways that would permit them to survive in the present without forsaking their past. By the close of the colonial era, native Americans as well as whites and blacks had created new societies, each similar to, yet very different from, its parent culture.

The range of native societies produced by this mingling of ingredients probably exceeded the variety of social forms Europeans and Africans developed. Rather than survey the broad spectrum of Indian adaptations, this article considers in some depth the response of natives in one area, the southern piedmont (see map). Avoiding extinction and eschewing retreat, the Indians of the piedmont have been in continuous contact with the invaders from across the sea almost since the beginning of the colonial period, thus permitting a thorough analysis of cultural intercourse. Moreover, a regional approach embracing groups from South Carolina to Virginia can transcend narrow (and still poorly understood) ethnic or "tribal" boundaries without sacrificing the richness of detail a focused study provides.

Indeed, piedmont peoples had so much in common that a regional perspective is almost imperative. No formal political ties bound them at the onset of European contact, but a simi-

lar environment shaped their lives, and their adjustment to this environment fostered cultural uniformity. Perhaps even more important, these groups shared a single history once Europeans and Africans arrived on the scene. Drawn together by their cultural affinities and their common plight, after 1700 they migrated to the Catawba Nation, a cluster of villages along the border between the Carolinas that became the focus of native life in the region. Tracing the experience of these upland communities both before and after they joined the Catawbas can illustrate the consequences of contact and illuminate the process by which natives learned to survive in their own new world.

For centuries, ancestors of the Catawbas had lived astride important aboriginal trade routes and straddled the boundary between two cultural traditions, a position that involved them in a far-flung network of contacts and affected everything from potting techniques to burial practices. Nonetheless, Africans and Europeans were utterly unlike any earlier foreign visitors to the piedmont. Their arrival meant more than merely another encounter with outsiders; it marked an important turning point in Indian history. Once these newcomers disembarked and began to feel their way across the continent, they forever altered the course and pace of native development.

Bacteria brought the most profound disturbances to upcountry villages. When Hernando de Soto led the first Europeans into the area in 1540, he found large towns already "grown up in grass" because "there had been a pest in the land" two years before, a malady probably brought inland by natives who had visited distant Spanish "posts." The sources are silent about other "pests" over the next century, but soon after the English began colonizing Carolina in 1670 the disease pattern became all too clear. Major epidemics struck the region at least once every generation—in 1698, 1718, 1738, and 1759—and a variety of less virulent illnesses almost never left native settlements.

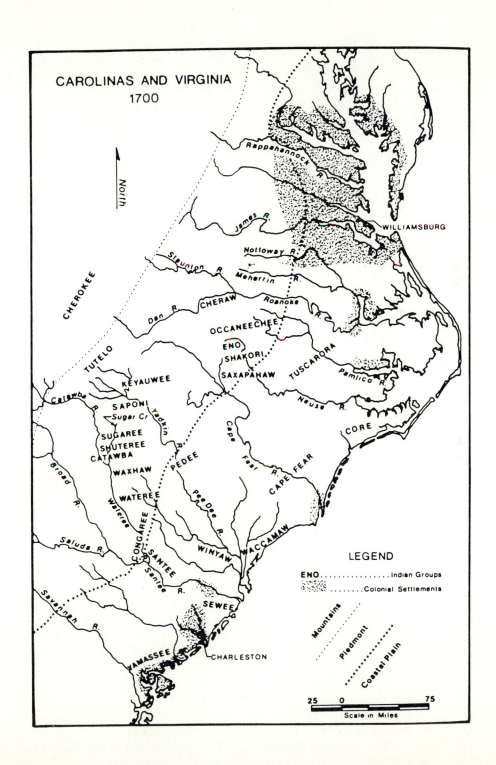

CAROLINAS AND VIRGINIA
1700

North

Rappahannock R.

James R.

WILLIAMSBURG

Staunton R.

Nottoway R.

Meherrin R.

CHEROKEE

Dan R.

CHERAW

Roanoke R.

OCCANEECHEE

ENO

SHAKORI

SAXAPAHAW

TUSCARORA

Pamlico R.

TUTELO

KEYAUWEE

Neuse R.

Catawba R.

SAPONI

Sugar Cr.

Yadkin R.

CORE

SUGAREE

SHUTEREE

CATAWBA

PEDEE

Cape Fear R.

CAPE FEAR

WAXHAW

Pee Dee R.

WATEREE

Broad R.

Wateree R.

Saluda R.

CONGAREE

SANTEE

WINYAW

WACCAMAW

Savannah R.

Santee R.

SEWEE

YAMASSEE

CHARLESTON

LEGEND

ENO . . . . Indian Groups

. . . . . . Colonial Settlements

Mountains

Piedmont

Coastal Plain

25   0   75
Scale in Miles

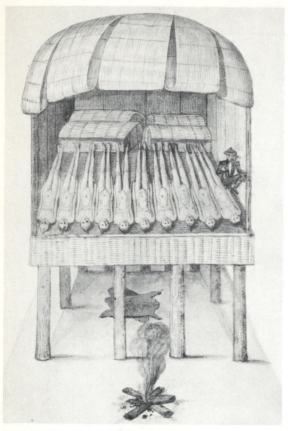

Burial House of the chief lords of the North Carolina Indians. European colonization exposed the Indian population to new strains of bacteria and virulent disease.

Indians were not the only inhabitants of colonial America living—and dying—in a new disease environment. The swamps and low-lands of the Chesapeake were a deathtrap for Europeans, and sickness obliged colonists to discard or rearrange many of the social forms brought from England. Among native peoples long isolated from the rest of the world and therefore lacking immunity to pathogens introduced by the intruders, the devastation was even more severe. John Lawson, who visited the Carolina upcountry in 1701, when perhaps ten thousand Indians were still there, estimated that "there is not the sixth Savage living within two hundred Miles of all our Settlements, as there were fifty Years ago." The recent smallpox epidemic "destroy'd whole Towns," he remarked, "without leaving one *Indian* alive in the Village." Resistance to disease developed with painful slowness; colonists reported that the outbreak of smallpox in 1759 wiped out 60 percent of the natives, and, according to one source, "the woods were offensive with the dead bodies of the Indians; and dogs, wolves, and vultures were . . . busy for months in banqueting on them."

Survivors of these horrors were thrust into a situation no less alien than what European immigrants and African slaves found. The collected wisdom of generations could vanish in a matter of days if sickness struck older members of a community who kept sacred traditions and taught special skills. When many of the elders succumbed at once, the deep pools of collective memory grew shallow, and some dried up altogether. In 1710, Indians near Charleston told a settler that "they have forgot most of their traditions since the Establishment of this Colony, they keep their Festivals and can tell but little of the reasons: their Old Men are dead." Impoverishment of a rich cultural heritage followed the spread of disease. Nearly a century later, a South Carolinian exaggerated but captured the general trend when he noted that Catawbas "have forgotten their ancient rites, ceremonies, and manufactures."

The same diseases that robbed a piedmont town of some of its most precious resources also stripped it of the population necessary to maintain an independent existence. In order to survive, groups were compelled to construct new societies from the splintered remnants of the old. The result was a kaleidoscopic array of migrations from ancient territories and mergers with nearby peoples. While such behavior was not unheard of in aboriginal times, population levels fell so precipitously after contact that survivors endured disruptions unlike anything previously known.

The dislocations of the Saponi Indians illustrate the common course of events. In 1670 they lived on the Staunton River in Virginia and were closely affiliated with a group called Nahyssans. A decade later Saponis moved toward the coast and built a town near the Occaneechees. When John Lawson came upon them along the Yadkin River in 1701, they were on the verge of banding together in a single village with Tutelos and Keyauwees. Soon thereafter Saponis applied to Virginia officials for permission to move to the Meherrin River, where Occaneechees, Tutelos, and others joined them. In 1714, at the urging of Virginia's Lt. Gov. Alexander Spotswood, these groups settled at Fort Christanna farther up the Meherrin. Their friendship with Virginia soured during the 1720s, and most of the "Christanna Indians" moved to the Catawba Nation. For some reason this arrangement did not satisfy them, and many returned to Virginia in 1732, remaining there for a decade before choosing to migrate north and accept the protection of the Iroquois.

Saponis were unusual only in their decision to leave the Catawbas. Enos, Occaneechees, Waterees, Keyauwees, Cheraws, and others have their own stories to tell, similar in outline if not in detail. With the exception of the towns near the confluence of Sugar Creek and the Catawba River that composed the heart of the Catawba Nation, piedmont communities decimated by disease lived through a common round of catastrophes, shifting from place to place and group to group in search of a safe haven. Most eventually ended up in the Nation, and during the opening decades of the eighteenth century the villages scattered across the southern upcountry were abandoned as people drifted into the Catawba orbit.

No mere catalog of migrations and mergers can begin to convey how profoundly unsettling this experience was for those swept up in it. While upcountry Indians did not sail away to some distant land, they, too, were among the uprooted, leaving their ancestral homes to try to make a new life elsewhere. The peripatetic existence of Saponis and others proved deeply disruptive. A village and its surrounding territory were important elements of personal and collective identity, physical links in a chain binding a group to its past and making a locality sacred. Colonists, convinced that Indians were by nature "a shifting, wandring People," were oblivious to this, but Lawson offered a glimpse of the reasons for native attachment to a particular locale. "In our way," he wrote on leaving an Eno-Shakori town in 1701, "there stood a great Stone about the Size of a large Oven, and hollow; this the *Indians* took great Notice of, putting some Tobacco into the Concavity, and spitting after it. I ask'd them the Reason of their so doing, but they made me no Answer." Natives throughout the interior honored similar places—graves of ancestors, monuments of stones commemorating important events—that could not be left behind without some cost.

The toll could be physical as well as spiritual, for even the most uneventful of moves interrupted the established cycle of subsistence. Belongings had to be packed and unpacked, dwellings constructed, palisades raised. Once migrants had completed the business of settling in, the still more arduous task of exploiting new terrain awaited them. Living in one place year after year endowed a people with intimate knowledge of the area. The richest soils, the best hunting grounds, the choicest sites for gathering nuts or berries—none could be learned without years of experience, tested by time and passed down from one generation to the next. Small wonder that Carolina Indians worried about being "driven to some unknown Country, to live, hunt, and get our Bread in."

Some displaced groups tried to leave "unknown Country" behind and make their way back home. In 1716 Enos asked Virginia's permission to settle at "Enoe Town" on the North Carolina frontier, their location in Lawson's day. Seventeen years later William Byrd II came upon an abandoned Cheraw village on a tributary of the upper Roanoke River and remarked how "it must have been a great misfortune to them to be obliged to abandon so beautiful a dwelling." The Indians apparently agreed: in 1717 the Virginia Council received "Divers applications" from the Cheraws (now living along the Pee Dee River) "for Liberty to Seat themselves on the head of Roanoke River." Few natives managed to return permanently to their homelands. But their efforts to retrace their steps hint at a profound sense of loss and testify to the powerful hold of ancient sites.

Compounding the trauma of leaving familiar territories was the necessity of abandoning customary relationships. Casting their lot with others traditionally considered foreign compelled Indians to rearrange basic ways of ordering their existence. Despite frequent contacts among peoples, native life had always centered in kin and town. The consequences of this deep-seated localism were evident even to a newcomer like John Lawson, who in 1701 found striking differences in language, dress, and physical appearance among Carolina Indians living only a few miles apart. Rules governing behavior also drew sharp distinctions between outsiders and one's own "Country-Folks." Indians were "very kind, and charitable to one another," Lawson reported, "but more specially to those of their own Nation." A visitor desiring a liaison with a local woman was required to approach her relatives and the village headman. On the other hand, "if it be an *Indian* of their own Town or Neighbourhood, that wants a Mistresss, he comes to none but the Girl." Lawson seemed unperturbed by this barrier until he discovered that a "Thief [is] held in Disgrace, that steals from any of his Country-Folks," "but to steal from the *English* [or any other foreigners] they reckon no Harm."

Communities unable to continue on their own had to revise these rules and reweave the social fabric into new designs. What language would be spoken? How would fields be laid out, hunting territories divided, houses built? How would decisions be reached, offenders

punished, ceremonies performed? When Lawson remarked that "now adays" the Indians must seek mates "amongst Strangers," he unwittingly characterized life in native Carolina. Those who managed to withstand the ravages of disease had to redefine the meaning of the term *stranger* and transform outsiders into insiders.

The need to harmonize discordant peoples, an unpleasant fact of life for all native Americans, was no less common among black and white inhabitants of America during these years. Africans from a host of different groups were thrown into slavery together and forced to seek some common cultural ground, to blend or set aside clashing habits and beliefs. Europeans who came to America also met unexpected and unwelcome ethnic, religious, and linguistic diversity. The roots of the problem were quite different; the problem itself was much the same. In each case people from different backgrounds had to forge a common culture and a common future.

Indians in the southern uplands customarily combined with others like themselves in an attempt to solve the dilemma. Following the "principle of least effort," shattered communities cushioned the blows inflicted by disease and depopulation by joining a kindred society known through generations of trade and alliances. Thus Saponis coalesced with Occaneechees and Tutelos—nearby groups "speaking much the same language"—and Catawbas became a sanctuary for culturally related refugees from throughout the region. Even after moving in with friends and neighbors, however, natives tended to cling to ethnic boundaries in order to ease the transition. In 1715 Spotswood noticed that the Saponis and others gathered at Fort Christanna were "confederated together, tho' still preserving their different Rules." Indians entering the Catawba Nation were equally conservative. As late as 1743 a visitor could hear more than twenty different dialects spoken by peoples living there, and some bands continued to reside in separate towns under their own leaders.

Time inevitably sapped the strength of ethnic feeling, allowing a more unified Nation to emerge from the collection of Indian communities that occupied the valleys of the Catawba River and its tributaries. By the mid-eighteenth century, the authority of village headmen was waning and leaders from the host population had begun to take responsibility for the actions of constituent groups. The babel of different tongues fell silent as "*Kàtahba,*" the Nation's "standard, or court-dialect," slowly drowned out all others. Eventually, entire peoples followed their languages and their leaders into oblivion, leaving only personal names like Santee Jemmy, Cheraw George, Congaree Jamie, Saponey Johnny, and Eno Jemmy as reminders of the Nation's diverse heritage.

No European observer recorded the means by which nations became mere names and a congeries of groups forged itself into one people. No doubt the colonists' habit of ignoring ethnic distinctions and lumping confederated entities together under the Catawba rubric encouraged amalgamation. But Anglo-American efforts to create a society by proclamation were invariably unsuccesful; consolidation had to come from within. In the absence of evidence, it seem reasonable to conclude that years of contacts paved the way for a closer relationship. Once a group moved to the Nation, intermarriages blurred ancient kinship networks, joint war parties or hunting expeditions brought young men together, and elders met in a council that gave everyone some say by including "all the Indian Chiefs or Head Men of that [Catawba] Nation and the several Tribes amongst them together." The concentration of settlements within a day's walk of one another facilitated contact and communication. From their close proximity, common experience, and shared concerns, people developed ceremonies and myths that compensated for those lost to disease and gave the Nation a stronger collective consciousness. Associations

evolved that balanced traditional narrow ethnic allegiance with a new, broader "national" identity, a balance that tilted steadily toward the latter. Ethnic differences died hard, but the peoples of the Catawba Nation learned to speak with a single voice.

Muskets and kettles came to the piedmont more slowly than smallpox and measles. Spanish explorers distributed a few gifts to local headmen, but inhabitants of the interior did not enjoy their first real taste of the fruits of European technology until Englishmen began venturing inland after 1650. Indians these traders met in up-country towns were glad to barter for the more efficient tools, more lethal weapons, and more durable clothing that colonists offered. Spurred on by eager natives, men from Virginia and Carolina quickly flooded the region with the material trappings of European culture. In 1701 John Lawson considered the Wateree Chickanees "very poor in *English* Effects" because a few of them lacked muskets.

Slower to arrive, trade goods were also less obvious agents of change. The Indians' ability to absorb foreign artifacts into established modes of existence hid the revolutionary consequences of trade for some time. Natives leaped the technological gulf with ease in part because they were discriminating shoppers. If hoes were too small, beads too large, or cloth the wrong color, Indian traders refused them. Items they did select fit smoothly into existing ways. Waxhaws tied horse bells around their ankles at ceremonial dances, and some of the traditional stone pipes passed among the spectators at these dances had been shaped by metal files. Those who could not afford a European weapon fashioned arrows from broken glass. Those who could went to great lengths to "set [a new musket] streight, sometimes shooting away above 100 Loads of Ammunition, before they bring the Gun to shoot according to their Mind."

Not every piece of merchandise hauled into the upcountry on a trader's packhorse could be "set streight" so easily. Liquor, for example, proved both impossible to resist and extraordinarily destructive. Indians "have no Power to refrain this Enemy," Lawson observed, "though sensible how many of them (are by it) hurry'd into the other World before their Time." And yet even here, natives aware of the risks sought to control alcohol by incorporating it into their ceremonial life as a device for achieving a different level of consciousness. Consumption was usually restricted to men, who "go as solemnly about it, as if it were part of their Religion," preferring to drink only at night and only in quantities sufficient to stupefy them. When ritual could not confine liquor to safe channels, Indians went still further and excused the excesses of overindulgence by refusing to hold an intoxicated person responsible for his actions. "They never call any Man to account for what he did, when he was drunk," wrote Lawson, "but say, it was the Drink that caused his Misbehaviour, therefore he ought to be forgiven."

Working to absorb even the most dangerous commodities acquired from their new neighbors, aboriginal inhabitants of the uplands, like African slaves in the lowlands, made themselves at home in a different technological environment. Indians became convinced that "Guns, and Ammunition, besides a great many other Necessaries, . . . are helpful to Man" and eagerly searched for the key that would unlock the secret of their production. At first many were confident that the "*Quera, or good Spirit*," would teach them to make these commodities "when that good Spirit sees fit." Later they decided to help their deity along by approaching the colonists. In 1757, Catawbas asked Gov. Arthur Dobbs of North Carolina "to send us Smiths and other Tradesmen to teach our Children."

It was not the new products themselves but the Indians' failure to learn the myster-

ies of manufacture from either Dobbs or the *Quera* that marked the real revolution wrought by trade. During the seventeenth and eighteenth centuries, everyone in eastern North America—masters and slaves, farmers near the coast and Indians near the mountains—became producers of raw materials for foreign markets and found themselves caught up in an international economic network. Piedmont natives were part of this larger process, but their adjustment was more difficult because the contrast with previous ways was so pronounced. Before European contact, the localism characteristic of life in the uplands had been sustained by a remarkable degree of self-sufficiency. Trade among peoples, while common, was conducted primarily in commodities such as copper, mica, and shells, items that, exchanged with the appropriate ceremony, initiated or confirmed friendships among groups. Few, if any, villages relied on outsiders for goods essential to daily life.

Intercultural exchange eroded that traditional independence and entangled natives in a web of commercial relations few of them understood and none controlled. In 1670 the explorer John Lederer observed a striking disparity in the trading habits of Indians living near Virginia and those deep in the interior. The "remoter Indians," still operating within a precontact framework, were content with ornamental items such as mirrors, beads, "and all manner of gaudy toys and knacks for children." "Neighbour-Indians," on the other hand, habitually traded with colonists for cloth, metal tools, and weapons. Before long, towns near and far were demanding the entire range of European wares and were growing accustomed—even addicted—to them. "They say we English are fools for . . . not always going with a gun," one Virginia colonist familiar with piedmont Indians wrote in the early 1690s, "for they think themselves undrest and not fit to walk abroad, unless they have their gun on their shoulder, and their shot-bag by their side." Such an enthusiastic conversion to the new technology eroded ancient craft skills and hastened complete dependence on substitutes only colonists could supply.

By forcing Indians to look beyond their own territories for certain indispensable products, Anglo-American traders inserted new variables into the aboriginal equation of exchange. Colonists sought two commodities from Indians—human beings and deerskins—and both undermined established relationships among native groups. While the demand for slaves encouraged piedmont peoples to expand their traditional warfare, the demand for peltry may have fostered conflicts over hunting territories. Those who did not fight each other for slaves or deerskins fought each other for the European products these could bring. As firearms, cloth, and other items became increasingly important to native existence, competition replaced comity at the foundation of trade encounters as villages scrambled for the cargoes of merchandise. Some were in a better position to profit than others. In the early 1670s Occaneechees living on an island in the Roanoke River enjoyed power out of all proportion to their numbers because they controlled an important ford on the trading path from Virginia to the interior, and they resorted to threats, and even to force, to retain their advantage. In Lawson's day Tuscaroras did the same, "hating that any of these Westward *Indians* should have any Commerce with the *English,* which would prove a Hinderance to their Gains."

Competition among native groups was only the beginning of the transformation brought about by new forms of exchange. Inhabitants of the piedmont might bypass the native middleman, but they could not break free from a perilous dependence on colonial sources of supply. The danger may not have been immediately apparent to Indians caught up in the excitement of acquiring new and wonderful things. For years they managed to dictate the terms of trade, compelling visitors from Carolina and Virginia to abide by aboriginal codes of conduct and playing one colony's traders against the other to ensure an abundance of goods at favorable rates. But the natives' influence over the protocol of exchange combined with their skill at incorporating alien products to mask a loss of control over their own destiny. The mask came off when, in 1715, the traders—and the trade goods—suddenly disappeared during the Yamassee War.

The conflict's origins lay in a growing colonial awareness of the Indians' need for regular supplies of European merchandise. In 1701 Lawson pronounced the Santees "very tractable" because of their close connections with South Carolina. Eight years later he was convinced that the colonial officials in Charleston "are absolute Masters over the *Indians . . .* within the Circle of their Trade." Carolina traders who shared this conviction quite naturally felt less and less constrained to obey native rules governing proper behavior. Abuses against Indians mounted until some men were literally getting away with murder. When repeated appeals to colonial officials failed, natives throughout Carolina began to consider war. Persuaded by Yamassee ambassadors that the conspiracy was widespread and convinced by years of ruthless commercial competition between Virginia and Carolina that an attack on one colony would not affect relations with the other, in the spring of 1715 Catawbas and their neighbors joined the invasion of South Carolina.

The decision to fight was disastrous. Colonists everywhere shut off the flow of goods to the interior, and after some initial successes Carolina's native enemies soon plumbed the depths of their dependence. In a matter of months, refugees holed up in Charleston noticed that "the Indians want ammunition and are not able to mend their Arms." The peace negotiations that ensued revealed a desperate thirst for fresh supplies of European wares.

Ambassadors from piedmont towns invariably spoke in a single breath of restoring "a Peace and a free Trade," and one delegation even admitted that its people "cannot live without the assistance of the English."

Natives unable to live without the English henceforth tried to live with them. No up-country group mounted a direct challenge to Anglo-America after 1715. Trade quickly resumed, and the piedmont Indians, now concentrated almost exclusively in the Catawba valley, briefly enjoyed a regular supply of necessary products sold by men willing once again to deal according to the old rules. By mid-century, however, deer were scarce and fresh sources of slaves almost impossible to find. Anglo-American traders took their business elsewhere, leaving inhabitants of the Nation with another material crisis of different but equally dangerous dimensions.

Indians casting about for an alternative means of procuring the commodities they craved looked to imperial officials. During the 1740s and 1750s native dependence shifted from colonial traders to colonial authorities as Catawba leaders repeatedly visited provincial capitals to request goods. These delegations came not to beg but to bargain. Catawbas were still of enormous value to the English as allies and frontier guards, especially at a time when Anglo-America felt threatened by the French and their Indian auxiliaries. The Nation's position within reach of Virginia and both Carolinas enhanced its value by enabling headmen to approach all three colonies and offer their people's services to the highest bidder.

The strategy yielded Indians an arsenal of ammunition and a variety of other merchandise that helped offset the declining trade. Crown officials were especially generous when the Nation managed to play one colony off against another. In 1746 a rumor that the Catawbas were about to move to Virginia was enough to garner them a large shipment of powder and lead from officials in Charleston

concerned about losing this "valuable people." A decade later, while the two Carolinas fought for the honor of constructing a fort in the Nation, the Indians encouraged (and received) gifts symbolizing good will from both colonies without reaching an agreement with either. Surveying the tangled thicket of promises and presents, the Crown's superintendent of Indian affairs, Edmond Atkin, ruefully admitted that "the People of both Provinces . . . have I believe [sic] tampered too much on both sides with those Indians, who seem to understand well how to make their Advantage of it."

By the end of the colonial period delicate negotiations across cultural boundaries were as familiar to Catawbas as the strouds they wore and the muskets they carried. But no matter how shrewdly the headmen loosened provincial purse strings to extract vital merchandise, they could not escape the simple fact that they no longer held the purse containing everything needed for their daily existence. In the space of a century the Indians had become thoroughly embedded in an alien economy, denizens of a new material world. The ancient self-sufficiency was only a dim memory in the minds of the Nation's elders.

The Catawba peoples were veterans of countless campaigns against disease and masters of the arts of trade long before the third major element of their new world, white planters, became an integral part of their life. Settlement of the Carolina uplands did not begin until the 1730s, but once underway it spread with frightening speed. In November 1752, concerned Catawbas reminded South Carolina governor James Glen how they had "complained already . . . that the white People were settled too near us." Two years later five hundred families lived within thirty miles of the Nation and surveyors were running their lines into the middle of native towns. "[T]hose Indians are now in a fair way to be surrounded by White People," one observer concluded.

Settlers' attitudes were as alarming as their

numbers. Unlike traders who profited from them or colonial officials who deployed them as allies, ordinary colonists had little use for Indians. Natives made poor servants and worse slaves; they obstructed settlement; they attracted enemy warriors to the area. Even men who respected Indians and earned a living by trading with them admitted that they made unpleasant neighbors. "We may observe of them as of the fire," wrote the South Carolina trader James Adair after considering the Catawbas' situation on the eve of the American Revolution, "'it is safe and useful, cherished at proper distance; but if too near us, it becomes dangerous, and will scorch if not consume us.'"

A common fondness for alcohol increased the likelihood of intercultural hostilities. Catawba leaders acknowledged that the Indians "get very Drunk with [liquor] this is the Very Cause that they oftentimes Commit those Crimes that is offencive to You and us." Colonists were equally prone to bouts of drunkenness. In the 1760s the itinerant Anglican minister, Charles Woodmason, was shocked to find the citizens of one South Carolina upcountry community "continually drunk." More appalling still, after attending church services "one half of them got drunk before they went home." Indians sometimes suffered at the hands of intoxicated farmers. In 1760 a Catawba woman was murdered when she happened by a tavern shortly after four of its patrons "swore they would kill the first Indian they should meet with."

Even when sober, natives and newcomers found many reasons to quarrel. Catawbas were outraged if colonists built farms on the Indians' doorstep or tramped across ancient burial grounds. Planters, ignorant of (or indifferent to) native rules of hospitality, considered Indians who requested food nothing more than beggars and angrily drove them away. Other disputes arose when the Nation's young men went looking for trouble. As hunting, warfare, and other traditional avenues for achieving status narrowed, Catawba youths transferred older patterns of behavior into a new arena by raiding nearby farms and hunting cattle or horses.

Contrasting images of the piedmont landscape quite unintentionally generated still more friction. Colonists determined to tame what they considered a wilderness were in fact erasing a native signature on the land and scrawling their own. Bridges, buildings, fences, roads, crops, and other "improvements" made the area comfortable and familiar to colonists but uncomfortable and unfamiliar to Indians. "The Country side wear[s] a New face," proclaimed Woodmason proudly; to the original inhabitants, it was a grim face indeed. "His Land was spoiled," one Catawba headman told British officials in 1763. "They have spoiled him 100 Miles every way." Under these circumstances, even a settler with no wish to fight Indians met opposition to his fences, his outbuildings, his very presence. Similarly, a Catawba on a routine foray into traditional hunting territories had his weapon destroyed, his goods confiscated, his life threatened by men with different notions of the proper use of the land.

To make matters worse, the importance both cultures attached to personal independence hampered efforts by authorities on either side to resolve conflicts. Piedmont settlers along the border between the Carolinas were "people of desperate fortune," a frightened North Carolina official reported after visiting the area. "[N]o officer of Justice from either Province dare meddle with them." Woodmason, who spent even more time in the region, came to the same conclusion. "We are without any Law, or Order," he complained; the inhabitants' "Impudence is so very high, as to be past bearing." Catawba leaders could have sympathized. Headmen informed colonists that the Nation's people "are oftentimes Cautioned from . . . ill Doings altho' to no purpose for we Cannot be present at all times to Look after them." "What they have done I could not prevent," one chief explained.

Unruly, angry, intoxicated—Catawbas and Carolinians were constantly at odds during the middle decades of the eighteenth century. Planters who considered Indians "proud and deveilish" were themselves accused by natives of being "very bad and quarrelsome." Warriors made a habit of "going into the Settlements, robbing and stealing where ever they get an Oppertunity." Complaints generally brought no satisfaction—"they laugh and makes their Game of it, and says it is what they will"— leading some settlers to "whip [Indians] about the head, beat and abuse them." "The white People . . . and the Cuttahbaws, are Continually at varience," a visitor to the Nation fretted in June 1759, "and Dayly New Animositys Doth a rise Between them which In my Humble oppion will be of Bad Consequence In a Short time, Both Partys Being obstinate."

The litany of intercultural crimes committed by each side disguised a fundamental shift in the balance of physical and cultural power. In the early years of colonization of the interior the least disturbance by Indians sent scattered planters into a panic. Soon, however, Catawbas were few, colonists many, and it was the natives who now lived in fear. "[T]he white men [who] Lives Near the Neation is Contenuely assembleing and goes In the [Indian] towns In Bodys, . . ." worried another observer during the tense summer of 1759. "[T]he[y] tretton the[y] will Kill all the Cattabues."

The Indians would have to find some way to get along with these unpleasant neighbors if the Nation was to survive. As Catawba population fell below five hundred after the smallpox epidemic of 1759 and the number of colonists continued to climb, natives gradually came to recognize the futility of violent resistance. During the last decades of the eighteenth century they drew on years of experience in dealing with Europeans at a distance and sought to overturn the common conviction that Indian neighbors were frightening and useless.

This process was not the result of some clever plan; Catawbas had no strategy for survival. A headman could warn them that "the White people were now seated all round them and by that means had them entirely in their power." He could not command them to submit peacefully to the invasion of their homeland. The Nation's continued existence required countless individual decisions, made in a host of diverse circumstances, to complain rather than retaliate, to accept a subordinate place in a land that once was theirs. Few of the choices made survive in the record. But it is clear that, like the response to disease and to technology, the adaptation to white settlement was both painful and prolonged.

Catawbas took one of the first steps along the road to accommodation in the early 1760s, when they used their influence with colonial officials to acquire a reservation encompassing the heart of their ancient territories. This grant gave the Indians a land base, grounded in Anglo-American law, that prevented farmers from shouldering them aside. Equally important, Catawbas now had a commodity to exchange with nearby settlers. These men wanted land, the natives had plenty, and shortly before the Revolution the Nation was renting tracts to planters for cash, livestock, and manufactured goods.

Important as it was, land was not the only item Catawbas began trading to their neighbors. Some Indians put their skills as hunters and woodsmen to a different use, picking up stray horses and escaped slaves for a reward. Others bartered their pottery, baskets, and table mats. Still others traveled through the upcountry, demonstrating their prowess with the bow and arrow before appreciative audiences. The exchange of these goods and services for European merchandise marked an important adjustment to the settlers' arrival. In the past, natives had acquired essential items by trading peltry and slaves or requesting gifts from representatives of the Crown. But piedmont planters frowned on hunting and warfare, while provincial authorities—finding Catawbas less useful as the Nation's population declined and the French threat disappeared—discouraged formal visits and handed out fewer presents. Hence the Indians had to develop new avenues of exchange that would enable them to obtain goods in ways less objectionable to their neighbors. Pots, baskets, and acres proved harmless substitutes for earlier methods of earning an income.

Quite apart from its economic benefits, trade had a profound impact on the character of Catawba-settler relations. Through countless repetitions of the same simple procedure at homesteads scattered across the Carolinas, a new form of intercourse arose, based not on suspicion and an expectation of conflict but on trust and a measure of friendship. When a farmer looked out his window and saw Indians approaching, his reaction more commonly became to pick up money or a jug of whiskey rather than a musket or an axe. The natives now appeared, the settler knew, not to plunder or kill but to peddle their wares or collect their rents.

The development of new trade forms could not bury all of the differences between Catawba and colonist overnight. But in the latter half of the eighteenth century the beleaguered Indians learned to rely on peaceful means of resolving intercultural conflicts that did arise. Drawing a sharp distinction between "the good men that have rented Lands from us" and "the bad People [who] has frequently imposed upon us," Catawbas called on the former to protect the Nation from the latter. In 1771 they met with the prominent Camden storekeeper, Joseph Kershaw, to request that he "represent us when [we are] a grieved." After the Revolution the position became more formal. Catawbas informed the South Carolina government that, being "destitute of a man to take care of, and assist us in our affairs," they had chosen one Robert Patten "to take charge of our affairs, and to act and do for us."

Neither Patten nor any other intermediary could have protected the Nation had it not joined the patriot side during the Revolutionary War. Though one scholar has termed the Indians' contribution to the cause "rather negligible," they fought in battles throughout the Southeast and supplied rebel forces with food from time to time. These actions made the Catawbas heroes and laid a foundation for their popular renown as staunch patriots. In 1781 their old friend Kershaw told Catawba leaders how he welcomed the end of "this Long and Bloody War, in which You have taken so Noble a part and have fought and Bled with your white Brothers of America." Grateful Carolinians would not soon forget the Nation's service. Shortly after the Civil War an elderly settler whose father had served with the Indians in the Revolution echoed Kershaw's sentiments, recalling that "his father never communicated much to him [about the Catawbas], except that all the tribe . . . served the entire war . . . and fought most heroically."

Catawbas rose even higher in their neighbors' esteem when they began calling their chiefs "General" instead of "King" and stressed that these men were elected by the people. The change reflected little if any real shift in the Nation's political forms, but it delighted the victorious Revolutionaries. In 1794 the Charleston *City Gazette* reported that during the war "King" Frow had abdicated and the Indians chose "General" New River in his stead. "What a pity," the paper concluded, "certain people on a certain island have not as good optics as the Catawbas!" In the same year the citizens of Camden celebrated the anniversary of the fall of the Bastille by raising their glasses to toast "King Prow [*sic*]—may all kings who will not follow his example follow that of Louis XVI." Like tales of Indian patriots, the story proved durable. Nearly a century after the Revolution one nearby planter wrote that "the Catawbas, emulating the examples of their white brethren, threw off regal government."

The Indians' new image as republicans and patriots, added to their trade with whites and their willingness to resolve conflicts peacefully, brought settlers to view Catawbas in a different light. By 1800 the natives were no longer violent and dangerous strangers but what one visitor termed an "inoffensive" people and one group of planters called "harmless and friendly" neighbors. They had become traders of pottery but not deerskins, experts with a bow and arrow but not hunters, ferocious warriors against runaway slaves or tories but not against settlers. In these ways Catawbas could be distinctively Indian yet reassuringly harmless at the same time.

The Nation's separate identity rested on such obvious aboriginal traits. But its survival ultimately depended on a more general conformity with the surrounding society. During the nineteenth century both settlers and Indians owned or rented land. Both spoke proudly of their Revolutionary heritage and their republican forms of government. Both drank to excess. Even the fact that Catawbas were not Christians failed to differentiate them sharply from nearby white settlements, where, one visitor noted in 1822, "little attention is paid to the sabbath, or religeon."

In retrospect it is clear that these similarities were as superficial as they were essential. For all the changes generated by contacts with vital Euro-American and Afro-American cultures, the Nation was never torn loose from its cultural moorings. Well after the Revolution, Indians maintained a distinctive way of life rich in tradition and meaningful to those it embraced. Ceremonies conducted by headmen and folk tales told by relatives continued to transmit traditional values and skills from one generation to the next. Catawba children grew up speaking the native language, making bows and arrows or pottery, and otherwise following patterns of belief and behavior derived from the past. The Indians' physical appearance and the meandering paths that set Catawba settlements off from neighboring communities served to reinforce this cultural isolation.

The natives' utter indifference to missionary efforts after 1800 testified to the enduring power of established ways. Several clergymen stopped at the reservation in the first years of the nineteenth century; some stayed a year or two; none enjoyed any success. As one white South Carolinian noted in 1826, Catawbas were "Indians still." Outward conformity made it easier for them to blend into the changed landscape. Beneath the surface lay a more complex story.

Those few outsiders who tried to piece together that story generally found it difficult to learn much from the Indians. A people shrewd enough to discard the title of "King" was shrewd enough to understand that some things were better left unsaid and unseen. Catawbas kept their Indian names, and sometimes their language, a secret from prying visitors. They echoed the racist attitudes of their white neighbors and even owned a few slaves, all the time trading with blacks and hiring them to work in the Nation, where the laborers "enjoyed considerable freedom" among the natives. Like Afro-Americans on the plantation who adopted a happy, childlike demeanor to placate suspicious whites, Indians on the reservation learned that a "harmless and friendly" posture revealing little of life in the Nation was best suited to conditions in post-Revolutionary South Carolina.

Success in clinging to their cultural identity and at least a fraction of their ancient lands cannot obscure the cost Catawba peoples paid. From the time the first European arrived, the deck was stacked against them. They played the hand dealt them well enough to survive, but they could never win. An incident that took place at the end of the eighteenth century helps shed light on the consequences of compromise. When the Catawba headman, General New River, accidentally injured the horse he had borrowed from a nearby planter named Thomas Spratt, Spratt responded by "banging old New River with a pole all over the yard." This episode provided the settler with a colorful tale for his grandchildren; its effect on New River and his descendants can only be imagined. Catawbas did succeed in the sense that they adjusted to a hostile and different world, becoming trusted friends instead of feared enemies. Had they been any less successful they would not have survived the eighteenth century. But poverty and oppression have plagued the Nation from New River's day to our own. For a people who had once been proprietors of the piedmont, the pain of learning new rules was very great, the price of success very high.

On that August day in 1608 when Amoroleck feared the loss of his world, John Smith assured him that the English "came to them in peace, and to seeke their loves." Events soon proved Amoroleck right and his captor wrong. Over the course of the next three centuries not only Amoroleck and other piedmont Indians but natives throughout North America had their world stolen and another put in its place. Though this occurred at different times and in different ways, no Indians escaped the explosive mixture of deadly bacteria, material riches, and alien peoples that was the invasion of America. Those in the southern piedmont who survived the onslaught were ensconced in their new world by the end of the eighteenth century. Population levels stabilized as the Catawba peoples developed immunities to once-lethal diseases. Rents, sales of pottery, and other economic activities proved adequate to support the Nation at a stable (if low) level of material life. Finally, the Indians' image as "inoffensive" neighbors gave them a place in South Carolina society and continues to sustain them today.

Vast differences separated Catawbas and other natives from their colonial contemporaries. Europeans when the colonizers, Africans the enslaved, Indians the dispossessed: from these distinct positions came distinct histories. Yet once we acknowledge the differences, instructive similarities remain that help to integrate natives more thoroughly into the story of early America. By carving a niche for themselves in response to drastically different conditions, the peoples who composed to Catawba Nation shared in the most fundamental of American experiences. Like Afro-Americans, these Indians were compelled to accept a subordinate position in American life yet did not altogether lose their cultural integrity. Like settlers of the Chesapeake, aboriginal inhabitants of the uplands adjusted to appalling mortality rates and wrestled with the difficult task of "living with death." Like inhabitants of the Middle Colonies, piedmont groups learned to cope with unprecedented ethnic diversity by balancing the pull of traditional loyalties with the demands of a new social order. Like Puritans in New England, Catawbas found that a new world did not arrive all at once and that localism, self-sufficiency, and the power of old ways were only gradually eroded by conditions in colonial America. More hints of a comparable heritage could be added to this list, but by now it should be clear that Indians belong on the colonial stage as important actors in the unfolding American drama rather than bit players, props, or spectators. For they, too, lived in a new world.

Part Two

The Origins of Slavery

Within a generation after the establishment of the first European settlements in America, the newcomers began importing slaves into their midst. The first Virginians and Marylanders who embarked on this fateful course could not have imagined the long-term consequences of their actions. They could not have known the future would bring civil war and racial problems that would persist to the present and had no idea of the personal harm and deprivation that the slaves and their descendants would suffer as a result. But the early settlers did know two things. First, they were introducing a population that they themselves regarded as alien and unassimilable; second, they were inevitably tarnishing, even undermining, their own new world experiment in which conditions and prospects for individual men and women were intended to be different from, conceivably better than, the past they themselves had experienced in Europe. How could they have done such a thing knowingly and with so little hesitation?

Several decades ago, historians' interest in the origins of slavery was centered on a rather different question. In the 1950s and 1960s, a vigorous debate was raging about the relationship between slavery and racial prejudice: Did prejudice toward people of African descent arise *after* they were enslaved, or did a pattern of prejudice exist even *before* the blacks arrived as slaves? Because the surviving evidence on which historians could base their conclusions is both fragmentary and ambiguous, the question is difficult to answer definitively. Nevertheless, the motivations and attitudes of the colonists who began to import slaves continued to puzzle historians. But they shifted the emphasis to the more answerable question: Why did the settlers embark on the enterprise in the first place and why did they choose a people who lived thousands of miles away on a distant continent?

Examination of these questions revealed a startling truth about virtually every colony in mainland America; there existed a preoccupation with finding a supply of labor that could be closely controlled and made to work under compulsion. From the outset, the European settlers sought and employed labor that was, in some way, unfree. In early Virginia and Maryland, a large part of the labor force consisted of those who worked without remuneration for a period of years, usually seven, in return for having their passage to America paid by their employer. These were indentured servants. Concurrently, in the early seventeenth century, attempts were made to compel labor from Indians who had been captured in war or had been brought forcibly into the European settlements and villages. When neither of these sources of coerced labor proved sufficiently reliable or permanent, the search moved overseas to Africa. The need or desire for an unfree labor supply proved pervasive at the inception of North American settlement; it is therefore evident that enslavement was not so anomalous or unacceptable to the colonists as might have been assumed.

The two studies of this problem by Peter Kolchin and Edmund Morgan concur in the view that the original settlers were predisposed toward acquiring laborers that were far from free and independent, but they take rather different approaches to the question of why and how slavery became established. Peter Kolchin of the University of Delaware is the author of a recent important book comparing slavery in the United States with serfdom in Russia. It is called *Unfree Labor: American Slavery and Russian Serfdom* (1987), and the selection presented here is from the introductory chapter comparing the beginnings of the two systems. In this extract, Professor Kolchin discusses the economic considerations that he believes were the primary concern in the search for a coercible labor force, especially slave labor from Africa.

A rather different approach that produces a different explanation is pursued in Edmund Morgan's "Slavery and Freedom: The American Paradox" (1972), which was his presidential address to the Organization of American Historians and a preview of his influential book, *American Slavery, American Freedom: The Ordeal of Colonial Virginia* (1975). Although acknowledging the economic pressures for an unfree labor force, Professor Morgan sees the creation of an alien unfree population at the bottom of the social order as an answer to a pressing social and political problem in seventeenth-century Virginia. This means of resolving the short-term social crisis had repercussions Morgan considers to be, not just long-term, but fundamental and formative. Essentially, his extremely provocative claim is that black slavery provided the underpinning and justification for the subsequent expansion of the rights and liberties of free whites. In effect, black slavery was essential for white freedom. Besides being social and cultural rather than economic in approach, Morgan's piece also differs from Kolchin's in its discussion of the consequences of African enslavement, not merely its causes.

QUESTIONS TO CONSIDER

1. How does Kolchin explain why the American colonists imported slave labor from Africa?

2. How do you account for the different treatment in these two articles of the same problem of why slavery was so useful to the Virginians?

3. What do you think of Morgan's claim that slavery was a critical element in enabling whites to enjoy a broad degree of freedom?

The Economic Origins of Slavery

Peter Kolchin

A shortage of laborers plagued English settlers in the American colonies and . . . this situation led to the use of physical compulsion to secure workers. A vast abundance of virgin land together with a paucity of settlers defined the problem in all the mainland colonies; everywhere, land was plentiful and labor scarce. To attract laborers, the colonists consequently found it necessary to pay wages that in Europe would have been considered exorbitant. "Poor People (both men and women) of all kinds, can here get three times the wages for their Labour they can in *England* or *Wales*," reported an observer from Pennsylvania in 1698. In all the colonies complaints were rampant about the high cost of labor and about the resulting lack of submissiveness among the much-sought-after workers. The law of supply and demand rendered unsuccessful the early efforts of several colonial governments to legislate maximum wages, and both skilled and unskilled labor continued to command wages up to twice those prevalent in England.

The payment of high wages proved inadequate, however, to secure a sufficient number of workers, and in every colony highly paid free labor was supplemented by forced labor of one type or another. Like the Spaniards to the

south, although with less success, the English forced Indians to work for them. Indian slavery was most prevalent in South Carolina, where in 1708 the governor estimated that there were 1400 Indian slaves in a population of 12,580, but Indians also served as house servants and occasional laborers in the other colonies: New Jersey wills reveal the continued presence of small numbers of Indian slaves in that colony as late as the middle of the eighteenth century.

For a variety of reasons, however, Indian slavery never became a major institution in the English colonies. The proximity of the wilderness and of friendly tribes made escape relatively easy for Indian slaves. The absence of a tradition of agricultural work among East Coast Indian males—women customarily performed the primary field labor—rendered them difficult to train as agricultural laborers. Because they were "of a malicious, surly and revengeful spirit; rude and insolent in their behavior, and very ungovernable," the Massachusetts legislature forbade the importation of Indian slaves in 1712. Finally, there were not enough Indians to fill the labor needs of the colonists. In New England, for example, most of the natives present when the Puritans arrived died from illness and war during the next half-century. The policy of eliminating the threat of Indian attack by eliminating the Indians themselves proved in the long run incompatible with the widespread use of Indians as slaves and necessitated the importation of foreign laborers.

Excerpted by permission of the publishers from pages 10–17, 20–26, 30–31 of *Unfree Labor: American Slavery and Russian Serfdom* by Peter Kolchin, Cambridge, Massachusetts: The Belknap Press of Harvard University Press. Copyright © 1987 by the President and Fellows of Harvard College.

For the greater part of the seventeenth century the colonists relied on the most obvious source for their labor: other Europeans. Although more prevalent in some colonies than in others, indentured servants were common everywhere in seventeenth-century America. Most served between four and seven years in exchange for free passage from Europe to America, although some were kidnapped and others transported as criminals. All found themselves highly prized commodities. In many colonies, such as Virginia, settlers received a headright—often fifty acres—for every person they imported. But even without such incentives, colonists eagerly snapped up newly arriving stocks of servants, who performed vital functions as agricultural laborers, domestics, and artisans. These immigrant servants, as well as colony-born Americans bound out for poverty, debt, or crime, were virtually slaves during their periods of indenture, bound to do as their masters ordered, subject to physical chastisement, forbidden to marry without permission, and liable to be bought and sold. Like slaves, some were forcibly separated from their relatives. Although a few servants became prosperous and influential in later life, for most the future was decidedly less rosy. In the mid-seventeenth century close to half the servants in Virginia and Maryland died before their terms of indenture were complete; once freed, many males continued to labor for others, living in their households and often—because of the excess of men over women—remaining unmarried.

Finally, the colonists turned to Africa for labor. As early as 1619 the forced labor of blacks supplemented that of whites in Virginia, and by the middle of the seventeenth century blacks were to be found in all the existing English colonies. Nevertheless, what is most striking about the early American labor force is the length of time it took for slavery to replace indentured servitude: throughout most of the seventeenth century white laborers, not black, prevailed in the English mainland colonies, and it was only between 1680 and 1730 that slaves became the backbone of the labor force in the South (see Table 1). This pattern raises two interrelated questions: Why, despite the presence of some slaves, did the colonists continue for so long to rely primarily on indentured servants, and why, during the half-century beginning in the 1680s, did African slaves replace European servants in most of the colonies?

Despite the prevailing labor shortage, there were certain limitations on the colonists' demand for slaves. Very few could afford to buy them during the first three quarters of the seventeenth century. Most early settlers were people of fairly modest means for whom the purchase of a servant—at one third to one half the price of an African slave—represented a substantial investment. Even if one could afford the initial outlay, the high mortality rate among the inhabitants of the early southern colonies made the purchase of slaves risky, and servants who were held for only a few years may have represented a better buy. Not only were servants cheaper than slaves, but their successful management required smaller investments of time and effort. They usually spoke the language—at least in the seventeenth century, when most of them came from the British Isles—and were at least partially familiar with the agricultural techniques practiced by the settlers. Given the circumstances, as long as European servants were readily available, their labor continued to make sense to most colonists.

Precisely such conditions prevailed during the first three quarters of the seventeenth century, when the population of the colonies was small and the number of Englishmen anxious to come as servants was large. Readjustments in the English economy during the late sixteenth and early seventeenth centuries worked serious harships on many British subjects, who suffered through periodic depressions and famines. Vagabondage, crime, and destitution all increased markedly, as did public awareness of these problems. Increased concern was expressed both by greater attention to charity and by savage repression of the criminal, the rowdy, and the idle. Impoverished Britons were only too anxious to start anew in America, where radically different conditions promised some hope of success and where they were actually wanted rather than regarded as a burden, but so too were many skilled and semiskilled workers who saw their opportunities decline at home. Recent studies of servant immigrants in the seventeenth century suggest that they were overwhelmingly young and male but represented a wide diversity of occupations with perhaps as many as one half having some skill. The tide of immigration reached its peak in the third quarter of the seventeenth century when, spurred by a series of ten crop failures, political dislocations at home, and a strong colonial demand for labor, close to forty-seven thousand Englishmen came to Virginia alone.

If the supply of servants seemed abundant during most of the seventeenth century, that of slaves was limited at best. The English were latecomers to the African slave trade which, throughout the first two thirds of the century, was primarily in Portuguese and then Dutch hands. Only after the Anglo-Dutch war of 1664–67 was English naval superiority established; shortly thereafter, in 1672, the Royal African Company, with a (theoretical) monopoly of the English slave trade, was formed. Even then, the supply of Africans remained limited. Despite the anguished cries of British planters in the West Indies (where the most lucrative colonies were located), the Royal African Company was unable to supply a sufficient quantity of slaves. West Indian planters mounted a vigorous attack on the company's monopoly, and even before 1698, when the monopoly was formally lifted, private traders illegally supplied a large portion of the islands' laborers. If there were not enough Africans for the West Indies, where the need was greatest, the number available for export to the mainland, which was of relatively small

economic importance, was small indeed. Until the last third of the century, most of the slaves imported to the mainland colonies were probably bought from Dutch and other private merchants, so it is not surprising that New York, where the Dutch had early encouraged the importation of slaves, had a higher proportion of blacks in its population than any other English mainland colony except South Carolina as late as 1680.

During the half-century from 1680 to 1730 these conditions impeding the importation of slaves changed radically. The growing prosperity of many colonists meant that an increasing number of them were able to afford slaves. The growth in the number and wealth of large holdings was especially significant, because large planters, who could afford to make the initial investment and whose need for labor was greatest, were the principal purchasers of slaves. In Maryland, for example, the average net worth of the richest 10 per-

From 1680 to 1730 the importation of slaves to America increased greatly as demand grew for a large labor force.

cent of probated estates increased 241 percent between 1656–83 and 1713–19, far more than the increase among smaller estates; as a consequence the proportion of all wealth owned by the richest 10 percent increased from 43 to 64 percent.

Since servants were only temporarily bound and did not produce new servants, as the colonial population grew the number of servants imported would have had to increase sharply in order for them to form a constant proportion of the population. The 10,910 headrights issued in Virginia between 1650 and 1654 were the equivalent of more than 57 percent of the colony's estimated population in the former year; the 10,390 issued between 1665 and 1669 were only equal to about 29 percent of the population in 1670. Even if the number of immigrants had remained constant, they would have represented a continually decreasing percentage of the population and would soon have become inadequate to meet the colonies' labor needs.

In fact, the supply of English servants declined sharply at just the time that the demand for labor was increasing in many of the colonies. As the English social situation stabilized following the restoration of 1660 and the British government adopted a strongly mercantilist policy, Englishmen no longer complained, as they had formerly, about an excess population; instead, with increasing economic productivity and well-being, a large population now seemed an asset in Britain's struggle for supremacy with other European powers. Although conditions for the poor remained hard, they no longer experienced the continual crises, famines, and unemployment of the early and middle seventeenth century. Conditions within the colonies also acted to discourage immigration. By the late seventeenth century land was no longer so easily acquired as it had been earlier; furthermore, generally declining tobacco prices may have led merchants to reduce intentionally their importation of servants to Maryland and Virginia.

The result was a rather abrupt decline in the number of British immigrants to the colonies. In no five-year period between 1650 and 1674 did the number of headrights issued for whites in Virginia fall below 7900; in none between 1675 and 1699 did it rise above 6000:

1650–54:	10,910	1675–79:	3991
1655–59:	7926	1680–84:	5927
1660–64:	7979	1685–89:	4474
1665–69:	10,390	1690–94:	5128
1670–74:	9876	1695–99:	4251

The number of English servants thus declined precisely when more were needed. Although Britain continued to transport convict laborers to Maryland and a growing number of German and Irish servants settled in Pennsylvania, there simply were not enough Europeans willing to sell themselves into indentured servitude in America to continue filling the labor needs of the colonies.

At the same time that the supply of servants was decreasing, that of enslaved Africans was increasing, and it was this changing relative supply (and hence price) of labor in the face of high (indeed growing) demand that most simply explains the shift in the nature of the colonial labor force. With the founding of the Royal African Company in 1672, Britain became the foremost slave-trading country in the world. In 1713, by the Treaty of Utrecht, the English won the *asiento* or monopoly awarded by the Spanish government to supply the Spanish colonies with slaves. The eighteenth century was the golden era of the English slave trade, when British merchants provided slave labor for most of the world's colonies.

Given the heightened demand for labor and the new availability of Africans, planters who needed large, stable labor forces had good reason to prefer slaves to indentured servants even had the supply of the latter not begun to dwindle. For one thing, slaves were held permanently—as were their children—while servants were freed after a definite term. As a consequence, although slaves required a larger initial investment, a plantation using slaves became a self-perpetuating concern, especially by the early eighteenth century, when slave fertility rates increased markedly, mortality rates declined, and the black population began to grow through natural reproduction as well as importation. A plantation using indentured servants, however, required the continual replenishment of the labor force.

Equally important, servants tended to disrupt the efficient working of a farm or plantation by running away. Although slaves too attempted to escape, it was more difficult for them to succeed. Their color made them easily identifiable and naturally suspect. White servants, on the other hand, had little trouble pretending to be free, and the shortage of labor rendered it easy for fugitives to find employment. As a result, the flight of indentured servants was a common and widely lamented occurrence. The colonies adopted stringent penalties for fugitives, usually involving their serving additional time and, for subsequent offenses, branding or mutilation. Newspaper advertisements for fugitives give evidence of both the scope of the problem and the treatment of servants. A typical notice in the Pennsylvania *Gazette* of 18 June 1752 offered a five-pound reward for the return to his West Jersey master of "an Irish servant man, named Thomas Bunn, a thick well set fellow, of middle stature, full faced, a little pock mark'd and his hair cut off; he speaks pretty good English, and pretends to be something of a shoemaker, he has a scar on his belly, and is mark'd on the upper side of his right thumb with TB."

A comparison of the number of slaves and servants from New Jersey listed in newspaper advertisements with the number of slaves and servants listed in New Jersey wills suggests how much more often indentured servants escaped than did slaves. Although more than four times as many slaves as servants were listed in the wills of 1751–60 in 1753 and 1754 there were fifty-four notices of fugitive servants and

only seventeen of slaves. In other words, servants were apparently escaping at a rate about thirteen times as high as that of slaves. For planters this kind of discrepancy must have been a powerful argument in favor of using slaves.

Discontent with white laborers was not confined to the problem of fugitives. The prevalent labor shortage together with the availability of land encouraged an independent mode of thought on the part of supposedly subordinate white workers—who knew they would have little trouble finding employment no matter what their behavior that was extremely distasteful to employers. After complaining about the high price of blacks, New York planter-politician Cadwallader Colden noted that "our chief loss is from want of white hands. The hopes of having land of their own & becoming independent of Landlords is what chiefly induces people into America, & they think they have never answer'd the design of their coming till they have purchased land which as soon as possible they do & begin to improve ev'n before they are able to mentian [*sic*] themselves." That slavery did not allow for the development of this kind of independence among the laboring class was one more consideration in its favor.

*   *   *

The key determinant of the kind of labor system that emerged in the American colonies was the degree to which agriculture was geared to market. Although the increased availability of Africans made *possible* the widespread adoption of slave labor after 1680, slavery became the backbone of the economy in some colonies while in others it made little or no advance (see Table 1). Where a basic subsistence agriculture was practiced (as in most of New England), farms were small, the labor of a farmer and his family—and perhaps one or two extra hands at harvest time—was quite sufficient, and there was little need for forced labor. Where crops were grown for ex-

TABLE 1
Estimate of blacks as a percentage of the population in thirteen American colonies, 1680–1770

Colony	1680	1690	1700	1710	1720	1730	1750	1770
New Hampshire	3.6	2.4	2.6	2.6	1.8	1.8	2.0	1.0
Massachusetts	0.4	0.8	1.4	2.1	2.3	2.4	2.2	1.8
Rhode Island	5.8	5.9	5.1	4.9	4.7	9.8	10.1	7.1
Connecticut	0.3	0.9	1.7	1.9	1.9	1.9	2.7	3.1
New York	12.2	12.0	11.8	13.0	15.5	14.3	14.3	11.7
New Jersey	5.9	5.6	6.0	6.7	7.7	8.0	7.5	7.0
Pennsylvania	3.7	2.4	2.4	6.4	6.5	2.4	2.4	2.4
Delaware	5.5	5.5	5.5	13.6	13.2	5.2	5.2	5.2
Maryland	9.0	9.0	10.9	18.6	18.9	19.0	30.8	31.5
Virginia	6.9	17.6	27.9	29.5	30.3	26.3	43.9	41.9
North Carolina	3.9	4.0	3.9	5.9	14.1	20.0	25.7	35.3
South Carolina	15.7	38.5	42.9	37.7	70.4	66.7	60.9	60.5
Georgia	—	—	—	—	—	—	19.2	45.5

Source: Compiled from *Historial Statistics of the United States: Colonial Times to 1957* (Washington: Government Printing Office, 1960).

port, planters sought to maximize their production and extend the acreage planted. In such areas, which included much but not all of the southern colonies, the demand for labor was great, and the indentured servitude that characterized agricultural operations prior to the 1680s gave way to slave labor. Where commercial agriculture was practiced on a smaller scale, as in the middle colonies, the labor system was less uniform: In some places, such as Pennsylvania, indentured servitude remained widespread; in others, families augmented their own labor with that of occasional hired hands; and in still others—most notably parts of New York—slavery was an institution of some importance.

*   *   *

A brief examination of the geographic distribution of slaves and serfs illustrates the close connection between agricultural expansion and the spread of forced labor. In the British mainland colonies large-scale commercial agriculture developed first in the Chesapeake Bay region. As early as 1617 tobacco

was grown "in the streets, and even in the market-place of Jamestown"; a Dutch traveler reported of Maryland and Virginia in 1679 that "tobacco is the only production in which the planters employ themselves, as if there were nothing else in the world to plant." Spurred by a seemingly insatiable European demand for the new weed and blessed with good soil, a mild climate, and an excellent system of water routes, Chesapeake Bay planters produced increasing quantities of tobacco throughout the seventeenth century; the 20,000 pounds exported in 1619 swelled to 175,590,000 in 1672 and 353,290,000 in 1697, after which, despite annual fluctuations varying with tobacco prices, average yields stabilized for the next generation.

With an abundance of land and a shortage of labor, the amount of tobacco a planter could raise depended primarily on the number of workers he could command. Relying throughout most of the 17th century on a continual supply of fresh indentured servants, beginning in the 1680s, when the number of white immigrants had begun to decline sharply and African slaves had become more readily available, planters turned to slave labor. Wesley Frank Craven's computation of slave imports into Virginia, based on the number of black headrights granted, shows a marked increase beginning in 1690:

1650–54:	162	1675–79:	115
1655–59:	155	1680–84:	388
1660–64:	280	1685–89:	231
1665–69:	329	1690–94:	804
1670–74:	296	1695–99:	1043

He suggests, however, that "the greatly expanded number of black headrights in the 1690s . . . is substantially representative of postponed claims for Negroes reaching the colony somewhat earlier." Corroborative evidence comes from a calculation that in York county, Virginia, the ratio of servants to slaves plummeted from 1.90 in 1680–84 to 0.27 in 1685–89 to 0.07 in 1690–94; within a decade servants had virtually stopped coming to the county. By 1700, when more than one quarter of Virginia's population was black, the revolution in the composition of the colony's labor force had been largely completed. In Maryland, too, the number of slaves increased markedly, although because large parts of Maryland were unsuited for tobacco growing and because the colony continued to receive substantial shipments of convict servants, the change occurred slightly later than in Virginia and was less dramatic.

Even more heavily dependent on slave labor, although later in development, was South Carolina. First settled by Europeans in the 1660s, it grew slowly as colonists sought in vain to find a staple that would play for them the same role that tobacco did in Virginia. They raised cattle and hogs for sale to the West Indies and also exported deerskins and naval stores. Because of the large role played by West Indian planters in the settling of South Carolina, the colony from the beginning had a higher percentage of slaves than the other mainland colonies, although as elsewhere from Pennsylvania south

most of the early immigrants were white indentured servants.

Then, in the 1690s, Carolinians discovered rice, a crop that within a few years became as much a staple for them as tobacco was to planters of the Chesapeake. American rice shipments to England—almost all of which came from South Carolina (and from the middle of the eighteenth century, Georgia)—increased from less than 1 percent of the total value of American shipments to England in 1697–1705 to 12 percent in 1721–30 and 24 percent in 1766–75. Even more than in Virginia, South Carolina's commercial orientation created a society in which most heavy labor was coerced. With a population of only a little more than a thousand in 1680, the colony by 1740 claimed forty thousand residents, of whom approximately two thirds were slaves.

Slavery was much less central in the northern colonies and consequently proved relatively easy to abolish without serious social dislocations in the late eighteenth and early nineteenth centuries. . . . Nevertheless, it is worth noting that unfree labor was of some importance in parts of the North as late as the middle of the eighteenth century. In Pennsylvania, spurred in part by an active propaganda campaign waged by William Penn and his agents who sought to convince impoverished Europeans of the boundless opportunities that awaited them in the colony, tens of thousands of indentured servants, many of them German, continued to perform a significant share of the agricultural labor. By far the largest concentration of slaves outside the southern colonies, however, was located in New York: as late as 1760 about one of every seven New Yorkers was a black slave.

Although both the Dutch, who ruled the colony as the New Netherlands until 1667, and the British who came after them actively promoted the importation of Africans, this policy would have met with little success had not conditions there been conducive to their employment. Wherever water transportation was available, especially on Long Island, Staten Island, and along the banks of the Hudson River, large planters—beneficiaries of huge land grants from both the Dutch and the English—grew a variety of crops for sale. The most important of these was wheat. "Wheat is the staple of this Province . . ." explained New York's governor in 1734; "it's generally manufactured into flower [sic] and bread, and sent to supply the sugar collonys." Slaves appeared wherever large quantities of wheat or other crops were raised for export; on Long Island, for example, they increased from 14 percent of the population in 1698 to 21 percent in 1738. Of course, some New Yorkers, especially in the city, employed slaves as house servants, and others possessed slaves who performed various trades. The typical owner, however, was a farmer with one to five slaves, who used them to supplement his family's labor and increase the amount of its product available for sale.

Slavery was least important in New England, where small farms and a largely self-sufficient agriculture required little labor that a farmer's family could not provide. In the seventeenth century the New England colonies contained relatively few indentured servants, and those few more often served as domestics and artisans than as agricultural laborers. In the early eighteenth century blacks constituted about 2 percent of the population in Connecticut, Massachusetts, and New Hampshire, and few of them were farm workers. They were a luxury for those who could afford them rather than an essential part of the economy.

The one area of New England where extensive use of slaves prevailed nicely illustrates the impact of commercially oriented agriculture on the labor system of colonial America. In the fertile flatlands of the Narragansett region of Rhode Island there arose a system of large-scale stock raising and dairy farm-

ing. There, on soil ideally suited for grazing, planters bred the famed Narragansett racehorses, raised herds of sheep and dairy cows, and developed an aristocratic life-style similar to that of Virginia and Carolina planters. Estates of hundreds and sometimes thousands of acres required a large, steady laboring population, and it is no accident that "slavery, both negro and Indian, reached a development in colonial Narragansett unusual in the colonies north of Mason and Dixon's line." In 1730 about 10 percent of Rhode Island's population was black, but this figure conceals widespread variations. In the Narragansett country townships of South Kingston and Jamestown from one fifth to one quarter of the inhabitants were black, and including Indians about one third were slaves; in many other areas of Rhode Island blacks constituted no more than 3 or 4 percent of the population. As elsewhere in the colonies, slavery in Rhode Island was strong only where there was substantial market-oriented agriculture.

In the broadest sense, then, serfdom in Russia and slavery in America were part of the same historical process, despite the vastly differing societies in which they emerged. Both were products of geographic and economic expansion in areas of sparse settlement. In both countries there had been a long-term trend toward forced labor and experimentation with various forms of it: these included kholopstvo and the restriction of peasant movement in Russia and indentured servitude and Indian slavery in America. In both countries a crisis in the labor supply finally forced landholders and the governments that depended on them to make arrangements that led to the spread and institutionalization of new systems of unfree labor. Neither of these was an isolated development; both occurred in other areas of the Americas and eastern Europe.

Slavery and Freedom: The American Paradox

Edmund S. Morgan

American historians interested in tracing the rise of liberty, democracy, and the common man have been challenged in the past two decades by other historians, interested in tracinng the history of oppression, exploitation, and racism. The challenge has been salutary, because it has made us examine more directly than historians have hitherto been willing to do, the role of slavery in our early history. Colonial historians, in particular, when writing about the origin and development of American institutions have found it possible until recently to deal with slavery as an exception to everything they had to say. I am speaking about myself but also about most of my generation. We owe a debt of gratitude to those who have insisted that slavery was something more than an exception, that one fifth of the American population at the time of the Revolution is too many people to be treated as an exception.

We shall not have met the challenge simply by studying the history of that one fifth, fruitful as such studies may be, urgent as they may be. Nor shall we have met the challenge if we merely execute the familiar maneuver of turning our old interpretations on their heads. The temptation is already apparent to argue that slavery and oppression were the dominant features of American history and that efforts to advance liberty and equality were the exception, indeed no more than a device to divert the masses while their chains were being fastened. To dismiss the rise of liberty and equality in American history as a mere sham is not only to ignore hard facts, it is also to evade the problem presented by those facts. The rise of liberty and equality in this country was accompanied by the rise of slavery. That two such contradictory developments were taking place simultaneously over a long period of our history, from the seventeenth century to the nineteenth, is the central paradox of American history.

The challenge, for a colonial historian at least, is to explain how a people could have developed the dedication to human liberty and dignity exhibited by the leaders of the American Revolution and at the same time have developed and maintained a system of labor that denied human liberty and dignity every hour of the day.

*   *   *

Morgan, Edmund S., "Slavery and Freedom: The American Paradox," *Journal of American History,* 59 (June 1972), 5–29. Copyright © 1972 Organization of American Historians. Reprinted by permission.

Let us begin with Jefferson, this slaveholding spokesman of freedom. Could there have been anything in the kind of freedom he cherished that would have made him acquiesce, however reluctantly, in the slavery of so many Americans? The answer, I think, is yes. The freedom that Jefferson spoke for was not a gift to be conferred by governments, which he mistrusted at best. It was a freedom that sprang from the independence of the individual. The man who depended on another for his living could never be truly free. We may seek a clue to Jefferson's enigmatic posture toward slavery in his attitude toward those who enjoyed a seeming freedom without the independence needed to sustain it. For such persons Jefferson harbored a profound distrust, which found expression in two phobias that crop up from time to time in his writings.

The first was a passionate aversion to debt. Although the entire colonial economy of Virginia depended on the willingness of planters to go into debt and of British merchants to extend credit, although Jefferson himself was a debtor all his adult life—or perhaps because he was a debtor—he hated debt and hated anything that made him a debtor. He hated it because it limited his freedom of action. He could not, for example, have freed his slaves so long as he was in debt. Or so at least he told himself. But it was the impediment not simply to their freedom but to his own that bothered him. "I am miserable," he wrote, "till I shall owe not a shilling. . . ."

Though Jefferson's concern with the perniciousness of debt was almost obsessive, it was nevertheless altogether in keeping with the ideas of republican liberty that he shared with his countrymen. The trouble with debt was that by undermining the independence of the debtor it threatened republican liberty. Whenever debt brought a man under another's power, he lost more than his own freedom of action. He also weakened the capacity of his country to survive as a republic. It was an axiom of current political thought that republican government required a body of free, independent, property-owning citizens. A nation of men, each of whom owned enough property

to support his family, could be a republic. It would follow that a nation of debtors, who had lost their property or mortgaged it to creditors, was ripe for tyranny. Jefferson accordingly favored every means of keeping men out of debt and keeping property widely distributed. He insisted on the abolition of primogeniture and entail; he declared that the earth belonged to the living and should not be kept from them by the debts or credits of the dead; he would have given fifty acres of land to every American who did not have it—all because he believed the citizens of a republic must be free from the control of other men and that they could be free only if they were economically free by virtue of owning land on which to support themselves.

If Jefferson felt so passionately about the bondage of the debtor, it is not surprising that he should also have sensed a danger to the republic from another class of men who, like debtors, were nominally free but whose independence was illusory. Jefferson's second phobia was his distrust of the landless urban workman who labored in manufactures. In Jefferson's view, he was a free man in name only. Jefferson's hostility to artificers is well known and is generally attributed to his romantic preference for the rural life. But both his distrust for artificers and his idealization of small landholders as "the most precious part of a state" rested on his concern for individual independence as the basis of freedom. Farmers made the best citizens because they were "the most vigorous, the most independant, the most virtuous. . . ." Artificers, on the other hand, were dependent on "the casualties and caprice of customers." If work was scarce, they had no land to fall back on for a living. In their dependence lay the danger. "Dependance," Jefferson argued, "begets subservience and venality, suffocates the germ of virtue, and prepares fit tools for the designs of ambition." Because artificers could lay claim to freedom without the independence to go with it, they were "the instruments by which the liberties of a country are generally overturned."

In Jefferson's distrust of artificers we begin to get a glimpse of the limits—and limits not dictated by racism—that defined the republican vision of the eighteenth century. For Jefferson was by no means unique among republicans in his distrust of the landless laborer. Such a distrust was a necessary corollary of the widespread eighteenth-century insistence on the independent, property-holding individual as the only bulwark of liberty, an insistence originating in James Harrington's republican political philosophy and a guiding principle of American colonial politics, whether in the aristocratic South Carolina assembly or in the democratic New England town. Americans both before and after 1776 learned their republican lessons from the seventeenth- and eighteenth-century British commonwealthmen; and the commonwealthmen were uninhibited in their contempt for the masses who did not have the propertied independence required of proper republicans.

*   *   *

When Jefferson contemplated the abolition of slavery, he found it inconceivable that the freed slaves should be allowed to remain in the country. In this attitude he was probably moved by his or his countrymen's racial prejudice. But he may also have had in mind the possibility that when slaves ceased to be slaves, they would become instead a half million idle poor, who would create the same problems for the United States that the idle poor of Europe did for their states. The slave, accustomed to compulsory labor, would not work to support himself when the compulsion was removed. This was a commonplace among Virginia planters before the creation of the republic and long after. "If you free the slaves," wrote Landon Carter, two days after the Declaration of Independence, "you must send them out of the country or they must steal for their support."

Jefferson's plan for freeing his own slaves (never carried out) included an interim educational period in which they would have been half-taught, half-compelled to support themselves on rented land; for without guidance and preparation for self-support, he believed, slaves could not be expected to become fit members of a republican society. And St. George Tucker, who drafted detailed plans for freeing Virginia's slaves, worried about "the possibility of their becoming idle, dissipated, and finally a numerous banditti, instead of turning their attention to industry and labour." He therefore included in his plans a provision for compelling the labor of the freedmen on an annual basis. "For we must not lose sight of this important consideration," he said, "that these people must be *bound* to labour, if they do not *voluntarily* engage therein. . . . In absolving them from the yoke of slavery, we must not forget the interests of society. Those interests require the exertions of every individual in some mode or other; and those who have not wherewith to support themselves honestly without corporal labour, whatever be their complexion, ought to be compelled to labour."

It is plain that Tucker, the would-be emancipator, distrusted the idle poor regardless of color. And it seems probable that the Revolutionary champions of liberty who acquiesced in the continued slavery of black labor did so not only because of racial prejudice but also because they shared with Tucker a distrust of the poor that was inherent in eighteenth-century conceptions of republican liberty. Their historical guidebooks had made them fear to enlarge the free labor force.

That fear, I believe, had a second point of origin in the experience of the American colonists, and especially of Virginians, during the preceding century and a half. If we turn now to the previous history of Virginia's labor force, we may find, I think, some further clues to the distrust of free labor among Revolutionary republicans and to the paradoxical rise of slavery and freedom together in colonial America.

The story properly begins in England with the burst of population growth there that sent the number of Englishmen from perhaps three million in 1500 to four-and-one-half million by 1650. The increase did not occur in response to any corresponding growth in the capacity of the island's economy to support its people. And the result was precisely that misery which Madison pointed out to Jefferson as the consequence of "a high degree of populousness." Sixteenth-century England knew the same kind of unemployment and poverty that Jefferson witnessed in eighteenth-century France and Fletcher in seventeenth-century Scotland. Alarming numbers of idle and hungry men drifted about the county looking for work or plunder. The government did what it could to make men of means hire them, but it also adopted increasingly severe measures against their wandering, their thieving, their roistering, and indeed their very existence. Whom the workhouses and prisons could not swallow the gallows would have to, or perhaps the army. When England had military expeditions to conduct abroad, every parish packed off its most unwanted inhabitants to the almost certain death that awaited them from the diseases of the camp.

As the mass of idle rogues and beggars grew and increasingly threatened the peace of England, the efforts to cope with them increasingly threatened the liberties of Englishmen. Englishmen prided themselves on a "gentle government," a government that had been releasing its subjects from old forms of bondage and endowing them with new liberties, making the "rights of Englishmen" a phrase to conjure with. But there was nothing gentle about the government's treatment of the poor; and as more Englishmen became poor, other Englishmen had less to be proud of. Thoughtful men could see an obvious solution: get the surplus Englishmen out of England. Send them

to the New World, where there were limitless opportunities for work. There they would redeem themselves, enrich the mother country, and spread English liberty abroad.

*   *   *

Virginia from the beginning was conceived not only as a haven for England's suffering poor, but as a spearhead of English liberty in an oppressed world. That was the dream; but when it began to materialize at Roanoke Island in 1585, something went wrong. Drake did his part by liberating Spanish Caribbean slaves, and carrying to Roanoke those who wished to join him. But the English settlers whom Raleigh sent there proved unworthy of the role assigned them. By the time Drake arrived they had shown themselves less than courteous to the Indians on whose assistance they depended. The first group of settlers murdered the chief who befriended them, and then gave up and ran for home aboard Drake's returning ships. The second group simply disappeared, presumably killed by the Indians.

What was lost in this famous lost colony was more than the band of colonists who have never been traced. What was also lost and never quite recovered in subsequent ventures was the dream of Englishman and Indian living side by side in peace and liberty. When the English finally planted a permanent colony at Jamestown they came as conquerors, and their government was far from gentle. The Indians willing to endure it were too few in numbers and too broken in spirit to play a significant part in the settlement.

Without their help, Virginia offered a bleak alternative to the workhouse or the gallows for the first English poor who were transported there. During the first two decades of the colony's existence, most of the arriving immigrants found precious little English liberty in Virginia. But by the 1630s the colony seemed to be working out, at least in part, as its first planners had hoped. Impoverished Englishmen were arriving every year in large numbers, engaged to serve the existing planters for a term of years, with the prospect of setting up their own households a few years later. The settlers were spreading up Virginia's great rivers, carving out plantations, living comfortably from their corn fields and from the cattle they ranged in the forests, and at the same time earning perhaps ten or twelve pounds a year per man from the tobacco they planted. A representative legislative assembly secured the traditional liberties of Englishmen and enabled a larger proportion of the population to participate in their own government than had ever been the case in England. The colony even began to look a little like the cosmopolitan haven of liberty that Hakluyt had first envisaged. Men of all countries appeared there: French, Spanish, Dutch, Turkish, Portuguese, and African. Virginia took them in and began to make Englishmen out of them.

It seems clear that most of the Africans, perhaps all of them, came as slaves, a status that had become obsolete in England, while it was becoming the expected condition of Africans outside Africa and of a good many inside. It is equally clear that a substantial number of Virginia's Negroes were free or became free. And all of them, whether servant, slave, or free, enjoyed most of the same rights and duties as other Virginians. There is no evidence during the period before 1660 that they were subjected to a more severe discipline than other servants. They could sue and be sued in court. They did penance in the parish church for having illegitimate children. They earned money of their own, bought and sold and raised cattle of their own. Sometimes they bought their own freedom. In other cases, masters bequeathed them not only freedom but land, cattle, and houses. Northampton, the only county for which full records exist, had at least ten free Negro households by 1668. . . .

But a closer look will show that the situation was not quite so promising as at first it seems.

It is well known that Virginia in its first fifteen or twenty years killed off most of the men who went there. It is less well known that it continued to do so. If my estimate of the volume of immigration is anywhere near correct, Virginia must have been a death trap for at least another fifteen years and probably for twenty or twenty-five. In 1625 the population stood at 1300 or 1400; in 1640 it was about 8000. In the fifteen years between those dates at least 15,000 persons must have come to the colony. If so, 15,000 immigrants increased the population by less than 7000. There is no evidence of a large return migration. It seems probable that the death rate throughout this period was comparable only to that found in Europe during the peak years of a plague. Virginia, in other words, was absorbing England's surplus laborers mainly by killing them. The success of those who survived and rose from servant to planter must be attributed partly to the fact that so few did survive.

After 1640, when the diseases responsible for the high death rate began to decline and the population began a quick rise, it became increasingly difficult for an indigent immigrant to pull himself up in the world. The population probably passed 25,000 by 1662, hardly what Madison would have called a high degree of populousness. Yet the rapid rise brought serious trouble for Virginia. It brought the engrossment of tidewater land in thousands and tens of thousands of acres by speculators, who recognized that the demand would rise. It brought a huge expansion of tobacco production, which helped to depress the price of tobacco and the earnings of the men who planted it. It brought efforts by planters to prolong the terms of servants, since they were now living longer and therefore had a longer expectancy of usefulness.

It would, in fact, be difficult to assess all the consequences of the increased longevity; but for our purposes one development was crucial, and that was the appearance in Virginia of a growing number of freemen who had served their terms but who were now unable to afford land of their own except on the frontiers or in the interior. In years when tobacco prices were especially low or crops especially poor, men who had been just scraping by were obliged to go back to work for their larger neighbors simply in order to stay alive. By 1676 it was estimated that one fourth of Virginia's freemen were without land of their own. And in the same year Francis Moryson, a member of the governor's council, explained the term "freedmen" as used in Virginia to mean "persons without house and land," implying that this was now the normal condition of servants who had attained freedom.

Some of them resigned themselves to working for wages; others preferred a meager living on dangerous frontier land or a hand-to-mouth existence, roaming from one county to another, renting a bit of land here, squatting on some there, dodging the tax collector, drinking, quarreling, stealing hogs, and enticing servants to run away with them.

The presence of this growing class of poverty-stricken Virginians was not a little frightening to the planters who had made it to the top or who had arrived in the colony already at the top, with ample supplies of servants and capital. They were caught in a dilemma. They wanted the immigrants who kept pouring in every year. Indeed they needed them and prized them the more as they lived longer. But as more and more turned free each year, Virginia seemed to have inherited the problem that she was helping England to solve. Virginia, complained Nicholas Spencer, secretary of the colony, was "a sinke to drayen England of her filth and scum."

The men who worried the uppercrust looked even more dangerous in Virginia than they had in England. They were, to begin with, young, because it was young persons that the planters wanted for work in the fields; moreover, the young have always seemed impatient of control by their elders and superiors, if not downright rebellious. They were also predomi-

nantly single men. Because the planters did not think women, or at least English women, fit for work in the fields, men outnumbered women among immigrants by three or four to one throughout the century. Consequently most of the freedmen had no wife or family to tame their wilder impulses and serve as hostages to the respectable world.

Finally, what made these wild young men particularly dangerous was that they were armed and had to be armed. Life in Virginia required guns. The plantations were exposed to attack from Indians by land and from privateers and petty-thieving pirates by sea. Whenever England was at war with the French or the Dutch, the settlers had to be ready to defend themselves. In 1667 the Dutch in a single raid captured twenty merchant ships in the James River, together with the English warship that was supposed to be defending them; and in 1673 they captured eleven more. On these occasions Gov. William Berkeley gathered the planters in arms and at least prevented the enemy from making a landing. But while he stood off the Dutch, he worried about the ragged crew at his back. Of the able-bodied men in the colony he estimated that "at least one third are Single freedmen (whose Labour will hardly maintaine them) or men much in debt, both which wee may reasonably expect upon any Small advantage the Enemy may gaine upon us, wold revolt to them in hopes of bettering their Condicion by Shareing the Plunder of the Country with them."

Berkeley's fears were justified. Three years later, sparked not by a Dutch invasion but by an Indian attack, rebellion swept Virginia. It began almost as Berkeley had predicted, when a group of volunteer Indian fighters turned from a fruitless expedition against the Indians to attack their rulers. Bacon's Rebellion was the largest popular rising in the colonies before the American Revolution. Sooner or later nearly everyone in Virginia got in on it, but it began in the frontier counties of Henrico and New Kent, among men whom the gov-

ernor and his friends consistently characterized as rabble. As it spread eastward, it turned
out that there were rabble everywhere, and
Berkeley understandably raised his estimate
of their numbers. "How miserable that man is,"
he exclaimed, "that Governes a People wher
six parts of seaven at least are Poore Endebted
Discontented and Armed."

Virginia's poor had reason to be envious and
angry against the men who owned the land and
imported the servants and ran the government.
But the rebellion produced no real program
of reform, no ideology, not even any revolutionary slogans. It was a search for plunder,
not for principles. And when the rebels had
redistributed whatever wealth they could lay
their hands on, the rebellion subsided almost
as quickly as it had begun.

It had been a shattering experience, however, for Virginia's first families. They had seen
each other fall in with the rebels in order to
save their skins or their possessions or even to
share in the plunder. When it was over, they
eyed one another distrustfully, on the lookout for any new Bacons in their midst, who
might be tempted to lead the still restive rabble
on more plundering expeditions. When William
Byrd and Laurence Smith proposed to solve
the problems of defense against the Indians
by establishing semi-independent buffer settlements on the upper reaches of the rivers, in
each of which they would engage to keep fifty
men in arms, the assembly at first reacted favorably. But it quickly occurred to the governor and council that this would in fact mean
gathering a crowd of Virginia's wild bachelors
and furnishing them with an abundant supply
of arms and ammunition. Byrd had himself led
such a crowd in at least one plundering foray
during the rebellion. To put him or anyone else
in charge of a large and permanent gang of
armed men was to invite them to descend again
on the people whom they were supposed to be
protecting.

The nervousness of those who had property worth plundering continued throughout

the century, spurred in 1682 by the tobacco-
cutting riots in which men roved about destroying crops in the fields, in the desperate
hope of producing a shortage that would raise
the price of the leaf. And periodically in nearby
Maryland and North Carolina, where the same
conditions existed as in Virginia, there were tu-
mults that threatened to spread to Virginia.

As Virginia thus acquired a social problem
analogous to England's own, the colony began to deal with it as England had done, by
restricting the liberties of those who did not
have the proper badge of freedom, namely
the property that government was supposed to
protect. One way was to extend the terms of
service for servants entering the colony without indentures. Formerly they had served until twenty-one; now the age was advanced to
twenty-four. There had always been laws requiring them to serve extra time for running
away; now the laws added corporal punishment
and, in order to make habitual offenders more
readily recognizable, specified that their hair
be cropped. New laws restricted the movement
of servants on the highways and also increased
the amount of extra time to be served for running away. In addition to serving two days for
every day's absence, the captured runaway was
now frequently required to compensate by labor for the loss to the crop that he had failed to
tend and for the cost of his apprehension, including rewards paid for his capture. A three
weeks' holiday might result in a years extra
service. If a servant struck his master, he was
to serve another year. For killing a hog he had
to serve the owner a year and the informer another year. Since the owner of the hog, and the
owner of the servant, and the informer were
frequently the same man, and since a hog was
worth at best less than one tenth the hire of
a servant for a year, the law was very profitable to masters. One Lancaster master was
awarded six years' extra service from a servant who killed three of his hogs, worth about
thirty shillings.

The effect of these measures was to keep

servants for as long as possible from gaining their freedom, especially the kind of servants who were most likely to cause trouble. At the same time the engrossment of land was driving many back to servitude after a brief taste of freedom. Freedmen who engaged to work for wages by so doing became servants again, subject to most of the same restrictions as other servants.

Nevertheless, in spite of all the legal and economic pressures to keep men in service, the ranks of the freedmen grew, and so did poverty and discontent. To prevent the wild bachelors from gaining an influence in the government, the assembly in 1670 limited voting to landholders and householders. But to disfranchise the growing mass of single freemen

was not to deprive them of the weapons they had wielded so effectively under Nathaniel Bacon. It is questionable how far Virginia could safely have continued along this course, meeting discontent with repression and manning her plantations with annual importations of servants who would later add to the unruly ranks of the free. To be sure, the men at the bottom might have had both land and liberty, as the settlers of some other colonies did, if Virginia's frontier had been safe from Indians, or if the men at the top had been willing to forego some of their profits and to give up some of the lands they had engrossed. The English government itself made efforts to break up the great holdings that had helped to create the problem. But it is unlikely that the policy makers in

Virginia planters invested so heavily in slave labor that by 1700 slaves probably constituted a majority of the work force.

Whitehall would have contended long against the successful.

In any case they did not have to. There was another solution, which allowed Virginia's magnates to keep their lands, yet arrested the discontent and the repression of other Englishmen, a solution which strengthened the rights of Englishmen and nourished that attachment to liberty which came to fruition in the Revolutionary generation of Virginia statesmen. But the solution put an end to the process of turning Africans into Englishmen. The rights of Englishmen were preserved by destroying the rights of Africans.

I do not mean to argue that Virginians deliberately turned to African Negro slavery as a means of preserving and extending the rights of Englishmen. Winthrop Jordan has suggested that slavery came to Virginia as an unthinking decision. We might go further and say that it came without a decision. It came automatically as Virginians bought the cheapest labor they could get. Once Virginia's heavy mortality ceased, an investment in slave labor was much more profitable than an investment in free labor; and the planters bought slaves as rapidly as traders made them available. In the last years of the seventeenth century they bought them in such numbers that slaves probably already constituted a majority or nearly a majority of the labor force by 1700. The demand was so great that traders for a time found a better market in Virginia than in Jamaica or Barbados. But the social benefits of an enslaved labor force, even if not consciously sought or recognized at the time by the men who bought the slaves, were larger than the economic benefits. The increase in the importation of slaves was matched by a decrease in the importation of indentured servants and consequently a decrease in the dangerous number of new freedmen who annually emerged seeking a place in society that they would be unable to achieve.

If Africans had been unavailable, it would probably have provide impossible to devise a way to keep a continuing supply of English im-

migrants in their place. There was a limit beyond which the abridgment of English liberties would have resulted not merely in rebellion but in protests from England and in the cutting off of the supply of further servants. At the time of Bacon's Rebellion the English commission of investigation had shown more sympathy with the rebels than with the well-to-do planters who had engrossed Virginia's lands. To have attempted the enslavement of English-born laborers would have caused more disorder than it cured. But to keep as slaves black men who arrived in that condition *was* possible and apparently regarded as plain common sense.

The attitude of English officials was well expressed by the attorney who reviewed for the Privy Council the slave codes established in Barbados in 1679. He found the laws of Barbados to be well designed for the good of his majesty's subjects there, for, he said, "although Negros in that Island are punishable in a different and more severe manner than other Subjects are for Offences of the like nature; yet I humbly conceive that the Laws there concerning Negros are reasonable Laws, for by reason of their numbers they become dangerous, and being a brutish sort of People and reckoned as goods and chattels in that Island, it is of necessity or at least convenient to have Laws for the Government of them different from the Laws of England, to prevent the great mischief that otherwise may happen to the Planters and Inhabitants in that Island." In Virginia too it seemed convenient and reasonable to have different laws for black and white. As the number of slaves increased, the assembly passed laws that carried forward with much greater severity the trend already under way in the colony's labor laws. But the new severity was reserved for people without white skin. The laws specifically exonerated the master who accidentally beat his slave to death, but they placed new limitations on his punishment of "Christian white servants."

Virginians worried about the risk of having in their midst a body of men who had every reason to hate them. The fear of a slave insurrection hung over them for nearly two centuries. But the danger from slaves actually proved to be less than that which the colony had faced from its restive and armed freedmen. Slaves had none of the rising expectations that so often produce human discontent. No one had told them that they had rights. They had been nurtured in heathen societies where they had lost their freedom; their children would be nurtured in a Christian society and never know freedom.

Moreover, slaves were less troubled by the sexual imbalance that helped to make Virginia's free laborers so restless. In an enslaved labor force women could be required to make tobacco just as the men did; and they also made children, who in a few years would be an asset to their master. From the beginning, therefore, traders imported women in a much higher ratio to men than was the case among English servants, and the level of discontent was correspondingly reduced. Virginians did not doubt that discontent would remain, but it could be repressed by methods that would not have been considered reasonable, convenient, or even safe, if applied to Englishmen. Slaves could be deprived of opportunities for association and rebellion. They could be kept unarmed and unorganized. They could be subjected to savage punishments by their owners without fear of legal reprisals. And since their color disclosed their probable status, the rest of society could keep close watch on them. It is scarcely surprising that no slave insurrection in American history approached Bacon's Rebellion in its extent or in its success.

Nor is it surprising that Virginia's freedmen never again posed a threat to society. Though in later years slavery was condemned because it was thought to compete with free labor, in the beginning it reduced by so much the number of freedmen who would otherwise have competed with each other. When the annual increment of freedmen fell off, the number that remained could more easily find an in-

dependent place in society, especially as the danger of Indian attack diminished and made settlement safer at the heads of the rivers or on the Carolina frontier. There might still remain a number of irredeemable, idle, and unruly freedmen, particularly among the convicts whom England exported to the colonies. But the numbers were small enough, so that they could be dealt with by the old expedient of drafting them for military expeditions. The way was thus made easier for the remaining freedmen to acquire property, maybe acquire a slave or two of their own, and join with their superiors in the enjoyment of those English liberties that differentiated them from their black laborers.

A free society divided between large landholders and small was much less riven by antagonisms than one divided between landholders and landless, masterless men. With the freedman's expectations, sobriety, and status restored, he was no longer a man to be feared. That fact, together with the presence of a growing mass of alien slaves, tended to draw the white settlers closer together and to reduce the importance of the class difference between yeoman farmer and large plantation owner.

The seventeenth century has sometimes been thought of as the day of the yeoman farmer in Virginia; but in many ways a stronger case can be made for the eighteenth century as the time when the yeoman farmer came into his own, because slavery relieved the small man of the pressures that had been reducing him to continued servitude. Such an interpretation conforms to the political development of the colony. During the seventeenth century the royally appointed governor's council, composed of the largest property-owners in the colony, had been the most powerful governing body. But as the tide of slavery rose between 1680 and 1720, Virginia moved toward a government in which the yeoman farmer had a larger share. In spite of the rise of Virginia's great families on the black tide, the power of the council declined; and the elec-

tive House of Burgesses became the dominant organ of government. Its members nurtured a closer relationship with their yeoman
constituency than had earlier been the case.
And in its chambers Virginians developed the
ideas they so fervently asserted in the Revolution: ideas about taxation, representation,
and the rights of Englishmen, and ideas about
the prerogatives and powers and sacred calling
of the independent, property-holding yeoman
farmer—commonwealth ideas.

In the eighteenth century, because they
were no longer threatened by a dangerous, free
laboring class, Virginians could afford these
ideas, whereas in Berkeley's time they could
not. Berkeley himself was obsessed with the
experience of the English civil wars and the
danger of rebellion. He despised and feared
the New Englanders for their association with
the Puritans who had made England, however, briefly, a commonwealth. He was proud
that Virginia, unlike New England, had no free
schools and no printing press, because books
and schools bred heresy and sedition. He must
have taken satisfaction in the fact that when his
people did rebel against him under Bacon, they
generated no republican ideas, no philosophy
of rebellion or of human rights. Yet a century
later, without benefit of rebellions, Virginians
had learned republication lessons, had introduced schools and printing presses, and were
as ready as New Englanders to recite the apho-
risms of the commonwealthmen.

It was slavery, I suggest, more than any
other single factor, that had made the difference, slavery that enabled Virginia to nourish
representative government in a plantation society, slavery that transformed the Virginia of
Governor Berkeley to the Virginia of Jefferson,
slavery that made the Virginians dare to speak
a political language that magnified the rights of
freemen, and slavery, therefore, that brought
Virginians into the same commonwealth political tradition with New Englanders. The very
institution that was to divide North and South
after the Revolution may have made possible
their union in a republican government.

Thus began the American paradox of slavery and freedom, intertwined and interdepen-
dent, the rights of Englishmen supported on
the wrongs of Africans. The American Revolution only made the contradictions more glaring, as the slaveholding colonists proclaimed
to a candid world the rights not simply of Englishmen but of all men. To explain the origin
of the contradictions, if the explanation I have
suggested is valid, does not eliminate them or
make them less ugly. But it may enable us to
understand a little better the strength of the
ties that bound freedom to slavery, even in so
noble a mind as Jefferson's. And it may perhaps make us wonder about the ties that bind
more devious tyrannies to our own freedoms
and give us still today our own American paradox.

Part Three

Culture and Society in Seventeenth-Century New England

The colony of Massachusetts Bay, which after 1691 also included the Pilgrim settlement at Plymouth, was a most unusual society. The men and women who came to live there had encountered persecution in England for their religious beliefs and practices. Accordingly, their purpose in crossing the Atlantic to the New World was to establish the doctrinally pure and liturgically simple version of Protestantism that they had been forbidden to practice.

These religious refugees, who called themselves Puritans and whose aim was to live a life of purity and godliness, were fleeing from England, but they were not withdrawing from the world itself. They did not come to America to set up an exclusive, quietist community similar to those of the Shakers and the Amish several centuries later. Also far from their minds was the creation of a theocracy, a religious society that was ruled by the ministers and clergy. Instead, their intention was to create a "community of saints," consisting of people who today might be called born-again Christians. Nevertheless governmental institutions and economic activity would function in ways not unlike those of the secular society in England that they had left. At the same time, the religious life that was so vitally important to them was to be sustained by the church congregations and their ministers, through whose preaching and inspiration, the whole population, it was hoped, would be imbued with Puritan values and priorities. Although the success of the experiment depended on social stability, economic well-being and authoritative government, the Puritans' overriding concern was the creation of a godly community. When this priority was questioned later in the seventeenth century, a serious crisis over goals and identity ensued.

Because the Puritans' experiment was complex and unique, people in the twentieth century have had difficulty understanding them and their world. They have been measured too often according to norms and perceptions that make sense to us but would not to the Puritans. As a result, they have frequently been dismissed as strange, self-righteous fanatics or as insufferable killjoys. At other times, those characteristics that were unusual and distinctive about them have been attenuated, with the result that the Puritans have been viewed merely as earlier versions of modern Americans. For example, their emphasis on personal salvation and their introduction of the New England town-meeting are seen simply as precursors of the twentieth century values of individualism and democracy. These two approaches are insensitive to the Puritans and their times, and they cause considerable misunderstanding.

By contrast, an attempt to comprehend the Puritans on their own terms and to discover what shaped their material and spiritual world is far more likely to lead to an understanding of who they really were. And this is the perspective taken by the two historians whose writings have been selected for this topic. Both, in fact, take an approach that is widely shared by current students of early New England. The Puritans, so the argument goes, seem to have been influenced more by what they came from than by what they encountered on this side of the Atlantic. In effect, they did not start anew upon their arrival but transplanted their past beliefs and experiences without much alteration.

David Hall's essay was part of a guide to an exhibit at the Museum of Fine Arts in Boston called "New England Begins." In this succinct piece, Professor Hall of Boston University presents a portrait of the Puritans' literary world, a world strongly influenced by their religious concerns. The content of their thought and the style of their writing reflect their preoccupation with fulfilling their assigned mission in the New World as well as maintaining the values and beliefs they had brought with them from England. In other words, they embarked on a religious and cultural experiment that, ironically, was also quite conservative.

This theme is given greater stress by Timothy Breen of Northwestern University, though his focus is not Puritan cultural expression but the ways in which these settlers arranged their economy and social order. The maintaining of many English practices is what strikes Professor Breen most forcefully, and he shows why and how this may have happened. Because of a series of intrusions into the social and political life of England in the 1620's, he suggests, many segments of the population were severely disrupted. In the Puritans' case, this resulted in emigration in order to preserve what was threatened.

This depiction of the Puritans as conservers of traditional practices rather than dissenters and innovators is startling and provocative.

Although these two articles focus on different aspects of Puritan life, they nevertheless complement each other and thereby present a comprehensive portrayal of the religious and social world of the Massachusetts Bay colonists.

QUESTIONS TO CONSIDER

1. What, in Hall's view, were the most important features of the cultural and religious world of the Puritans?

2. How does Breen argue his case for "persistent localism" as the decisive element in the formation of New England society?

3. Do you agree that continuity with their English ways was a hallmark of the Puritans' life in Massachusetts? If so, then what was new about New England?

Persistent Localism and the Shaping of New England Institutions

T. H. Breen

The purpose of this investigation is to reconsider the relationship between ideas and institutions in seventeenth-century New England. . . . Without denying the centrality of Puritanism in the history of New England, this study suggests that the religious beliefs that the colonists carried with them to the New World cannot in themselves account for either the original form or subsequent development of specific institutions in Massachusetts Bay. Since there seems no reason to doubt the important role of ideas in the founding of that society, our goal will be to determine whether another set of ideas might not explain more adequately the peculiarities of the colony's social development.

It is the thesis of this essay that vague generalizations about the world the colonists left behind have obscured our understanding of the formation of New England institutions precisely because such generalizations neglect the colonists' institutional experiences in the mother country immediately prior to emigration. The towns and churches of Massachusetts were shaped by Charles I's ill-advised attempt to increase his authority by attacking

Matth.15.13. *Every plant which mine heavenly Father hath not planted should be rooted up.*

This satire of Archbishop William Laud reflects Puritan resistance to Laud's demand for conformity to the theology and rites of the Church of England.

local English institutions. The people who accompanied Gov. John Winthrop came from diverse regions within England, some from populous commercial centers such as London and Norwich, others from isolated rural communities, but regardless of where they originated, most had been affected in some personal way by the king's aggressive effort to extend his civil and ecclesiastical authority. Between 1625 and 1640 his government made what appeared to many Englishmen—not just Puritans—to be a

From "Persistent Localism: English Social Change and the Shaping of New England Institutions" by T. H. Breen, *The William and Mary Quarterly,* Vol. 32, January 1975. Reprinted by permission of the author.

series of arbitrary attempts to dominate county and local affairs, to assert the king's influence in matters that his predecessors had wisely left alone. Throughout the kingdom his subjects suddenly found themselves forced to defend what they had come to regard as traditional institutional forms.

The experience of having to resist Stuart centralization, a resistance that pitted small congregations against meddling bishops, incorporated boroughs and guilds against grasping courtiers, local trainbands against demanding deputy lieutenants, and almost everyone in the realm against the collectors of unconstitutional revenues, shaped the New Englanders' ideas about civil, ecclesiastical, and military polity. The settlers departed England determined to maintain their local attachments against outside interference, and to a large extent the Congregational churches and self-contained towns of Massachusetts Bay stood as visible evidence of the founders' decision to preserve in America what had been threatened in the mother country. And if the argument of this article is correct, it may offer a clue to disputes that divided the colonists as soon as they were safely out of Charles' reach. In fact, as we shall see, the settlers' English experience helps explain the bitter controversies between Winthrop and the local freemen who regularly elected him to office.

*   *   *

New England's social institutions appear in large part to have been shaped by Charles's efforts to expand his civil and ecclesiastical authority by curtailing the autonomy of local English institutions, an effort that forced people to think about protecting what they regarded as traditional rights from a meddling king. Charles became monarch in 1625, and Englishmen throughout the realm soon felt the impact of his policies upon their daily lives. What kind of society did the new king disturb? What were the institutions of the mother country like before he attempted to centralize his power? The answer, of course, would have been different depending on where one lived and what one's experiences had been. People felt local attachments to various levels of English society, to country villages, incorporated boroughs, religious groups, and county communities. To understand how these local bonds affected the settlement of Massachusetts Bay it is necessary to consider each level separately.

We know a good deal about the character of the English countryside, the hamlets and scattered manor houses. A thoughtful description has been offered by the English historian Alan Everitt, who contends that the three distinguishing attributes of much of seventeenth-century English country society were its diversity, its insularity, and its continuity. Everitt argues that the people living in what he calls, "local communities" throughout England had little interest in events that occurred outside their own immediate environment. National politics had no place in these agricultural villages, and the lives of most persons were bound up in the simple "affairs of buying, selling, making love, marrying, bringing up a family, and with all those thousand little concerns that tied together the bonds of family life." Each region developed its own special skills and crafts, its own unique farming practices.

Given the primitive state of communications in the early seventeenth century, one might attribute such strong local attachments solely to physical isolation. While isolation was certainly a major influence, there is evidence that the reign of James I was accompanied by a heightened sense of local loyalty or particularism. The Tudors had clipped the wings of over-mighty nobles but had neglected to establish a reliable centralized royal bureaucracy in the villages and country shires. In the absence of a strong national bureaucracy local leaders filled the vacuum, stressing as they did so the importance of local autonomy. And in those communities which possessed no "gentlemanly household," the yeomen or husbandmen were apt to run everything themselves. Almost everyone in the English countryside before 1625 had a stake in maintaining the customary routine of agricultural life.

Some seventeenth-century Englishmen lived in incorporated boroughs, small to middling size cities like Boston, Ipswich, Norwich, and Great Yarmouth, whose ancient royal charters gave them special rights of self-government. At the time Charles became king an incorporated borough might elect a mayor and burgesses, enforce local ordinances, hold fairs, and determine the qualifications for freemanship. Although these boroughs, usually regional trade centers, were less insular than the country villages, they were no less diverse in character. Some were narrow oligarchies; others allowed fairly broad participation in civil affairs. Many corporations also exercised ecclesiastical patronage and, as in the instance of Great Yarmouth, jealously guarded "the right of choosing their own minister." Because the boroughs, especially those engaged in foreign commerce, were often havens for nonconformists, the selection of ministers frequently fell to men of Puritan leanings—a fact that neither escaped nor pleased Charles and Archbishop William Laud. What is important to note here, however, is not the widespread nonconformity but the corporations' sense of their own continuity, their city was an "ancient borough" and "from time immemorial . . . a body corporate." Like their rural neighbors, the freemen of the boroughs had an obvious interest in preserving their autonomy from outside interference.

Charles also inherited a peculiar religious situation. Some of the ablest historians of this century have examined the origins of New England Congregationalism, and there is no need to review their work. One recent essay, however, merits special attention. Patrick Collinson has investigated what he calls the "popular protestantism" of pre-Civil War En-

gland, and some of his findings, tentative though they are, should cause historians to reconsider the adequacy of any interpretation that regards congregational polity as the invention of a few Cambridge-educated divines. Collinson argues that after the Hampton Court Conference of 1604 Protestant dissent split into a "fragmented sectarianism," characterized by scores of little religious groups that "agreed as to the *delenda* but not as to the *agenda* of the further reformation." Many of these bodies appear to have been voluntary organizations in which the members, not the ministers, decided matters of discipline and theology. Collinson recognizes that the Reformation contained other tendencies besides congregationalism. Nevertheless, as he observes, "it is hard to see how the movements generated within popular protestantism left to themselves, can have had any other end."

The important words here are "left to themselves." In the fifteen or so years before Laud decided to bring the nonconformists into line, dissenters had become better entrenched and more diverse, especially in the incorporated boroughs. During this period James I had done little to make good his threat of 1604 to harry the Puritans out of the land, and the sects may have grown accustomed to a certain measure of independence, of self-determination, and, perhaps it is fair to say, of congregationalism. Although the men and women involved probably composed only a small fraction of the English population, they would be disproportionately represented in the settlement of Massachusetts Bay. Charles's religious troubles resulted not only from his blundering efforts to punish dissenters, but also from his decision to institute such a policy after "popular protestantism" had had so many years to establish itself. The members of these little Protestant sects must have been as concerned as other Englishmen in the period before 1625 about the need to preserve local autonomy.

Another level of English society is also relevant to the specific background of Massachusetts Bay—the county communities. If town and country dwellers of the early 1620s felt a sense of political loyalty to anything beyond a few local institutions, it was likely to have been more to a county community than to the English nation as a whole. Within the shires a network of interrelated gentry families usually stood between the king and his subjects. Because the Tudors failed to replace the unpaid local gentry with salaried crown officials, "local particularism grew step by step with the growth of the central government." The gentry dominated county affairs, drilled the trainbands, sat on the quarter courts, served in Parliament, and by the time Charles became king it is difficult to imagine how any monarch could have successfully challenged their authority. They acted as mediators, rationalizing royal policies to farmers and borough freemen while simultaneously lobbying for county interests at court. If the monarch alienated these powerful gentry families, he lost effective contact with thousands of ordinary Englishmen living in places like Norfolk and Kent. Indeed, in the early decades of the seventeenth century the English body politic was composed of sets of loosely connected county elites, each of which placed its own rights and prerogatives before those of the crown. In some cases, provincial leaders self-consciously developed an idealized county history, a mythical heritage that provided all believers with a sense of regional identity.

It is difficult to establish how many men and women felt a part of these county communities; if a village had no resident gentry family or were extremely isolated, the county identification may have been small. Perhaps it was only the gentry themselves who perceived politics in this manner. The point is that the existence of county communities heightened the particularism that seems to have been present at other levels of English society. The natural instinct of the local ruling gentry was to preserve an independent heritage, a set of old customs and privileges, against all outside threats. It is important to remember that while few of the men who colonized Massachusetts Bay had been county leaders of the first rank, several dozen at least had been associated with the ruling gentry and carried to the New World political impressions formed within England's county communities.

Charles disrupted these local institutions. He came to power in 1625 determined to strengthen the court, curtail religious dissent, and build an efficient army—in short, to centralize his authority at the expense of the local and county communities. As Lawrence Stone has observed, the king's plans were in keeping with the growth of royal absolutism throughout Europe. In fact, if his actions are viewed from the perspective of the Continent, it appears that "the objectives and methods of Charles, Laud, and Strafford were precisely those in which the future lay." Although historians can now explain why Charles's dreams of absolutism were doomed from the start—why in the fact of deeply rooted traditions of common law and representative government he could never have become an English Louis XIV—his subjects feared he might succeed.

Charles went about his business with a humorless rigor disturbing to persons grown accustomed to James's easygoing ways. Even though the new king declared that he was defending his rightful prerogatives against parliamentary encroachment, his approach and methods looked, at least to some people, like radical innovations, and on all the levels of English society that we have examined his efforts to increase royal controls upset customary patterns of life. His policies threatened the autonomy of the county communities, the dissenting congregations, the incorporated boroughs, and the thousands of local communities that had formerly ignored national politics. Previous monarchs had sometimes been forced to remind excessively independent Englishmen of their responsibility to the throne. But Charles attacked across the board, and his ill-conceived reforms created more enemies than one king could handle.

Insufficient funds continually plagued Charles's government; all his plans seemed to require more money than Parliament was willing to grant. His disastrous military expeditions on the coast of France, his ever-growing number of court favorites, and his personal extravagance put tremendous strains on the exchequer. He asked his subjects for free gifts and, when that failed, for forced loans. By the 1630s the king was demanding ship money from areas traditionally exempt from such levies. Much has been written about the collection of these unconstitutional revenues, and there is no need to recount the bitter struggle between Charles and Parliament over this issue. What is important is that the king's unprecedented efforts to obtain money alienated Englishmen of all types. He unwittingly helped to break down the diversity and isolation of English society by creating a grievance that affected everyone.

The king's innovations were by no means restricted to unparliamentary taxation. He had the misfortune to rule during a period of general economic instability. Unemployment was high, especially in the textile regions. In the late 1620s serious food shortages developed, and groups of "lewde and dissolute persons" were reported wandering about the countryside. Charles and his advisers became convinced that unless something were done to relieve the suffering, rioting would spread throughout the depressed areas. Such fears were not without foundation. In 1629, for example, an Essex court hanged a woman and three male companions for breaking into a house in broad daylight and stealing some corn, "the woman saying 'come, by brave lads of Maldon, I will be your leader, for we will not starve.'" In an effort to preserve order, the Privy Council took control of local poor relief. It forbade the export of certain grains and directed justices of the

peace to levy rates that might be used to provide employment for indigent workers. While these orders were well intended, the Council's actions were without precedent. According to one historian of English poor relief, "the Central Authority set in motion the whole local machinery for the execution of the poor law." County officials resented the increased work load, and some of them even questioned whether they possessed constitutional authority to collect poor relief. The king's plans to pacify the poor, like his schemes to find additional revenue, were regarded by many Englishmen as another indication of growing absolutism, another assault on local independence.

The early years of Charles's reign brought disturbing efforts at religious innovation, both theological and institutional. Not only was the Arminianism of Laud offensive to England's Calvinists, but his ecclesiastical reforms aroused the antagonism of villagers and gentry alike in many parts of the realm. Laud was determined to force religious dissenters to conform to the Anglican service, and he urged his bishops to report any deviation from accepted ecclesiastical practice. Some bishops dragged their feet, but others were eager to please their superior. These men visited local congregations, broke up conventicles, and challenged respected ministers. Indeed, they attacked "popular protestantism" wherever they found it. In Hampshire angry villagers protested Laud's actions as "an unwonted, dangerous, and unwelcome innovation." People in other local communities agreed.

Laud's ecclesiastical officers also attempted to destroy "that ratsbane of lecturing" frequently found in the incorporated boroughs. Again, what men perceived as established local traditions were disturbed. According to one historian, when the king and his archbishop attacked the lectureships, "they were tampering not with a recent innovation but rather with an institution that in many places had been rooted in the life of the community for several generations." Laud's interference agitated people who wanted to preserve accustomed forms of worship and drove them into alliance with persons who resented the king's economic and political meddling.

Nothing created greater dislocation in the English countryside than Charles's military policies. Early in his reign the king decided to commit troops to the Continental wars. James had regarded overseas expeditions as an extravagance, but the wisdom of his position escaped Charles. He recklessly plunged ahead. Throughout the kingdom soldiers were pressed into service, marched to coastal cities, and dispatched to French battlefields from which few returned alive. The military companies consisted of the dregs of English society—misfits, troublemakers, men too poor to buy their way out of the army. The recruits often did not receive the "coat and conduct money" that might have sustained them on their journey to the port towns. The shortsightedness of this policy soon became apparent. Desperate bands of soldiers wandered from village to village disturbing the peace, assaulting people, and raping women. On one occasion at least, they attacked a community that failed to house them in the manner they desired. And even where no violence occurred, the dreaded visitors were forcefully billeted upon persons who could least afford the burden. . . .

Resentment against the king's interference in local affairs was by no means restricted to the poor and the humble. His policies steadily undermined the loyalty of the great gentry families that dominated England's county communities. He expected them as deputy lieutenants to develop what he termed a "perfect militia." He ordered them as justices of the peace to supervise poor relief. It was they who often ended up paying his illegal revenues, and when their spokesmen in Commons complained too strongly, Charles decided he could rule without Parliament's help.

The increased work load, the financial strain, even the constitutional crisis might

have been borne had not Charles's policies threatened to alter traditional social relationships within the county communities themselves. The gentry discovered that by putting the king's directives into effect they alienated local support. Suddenly in the late 1620s some of them found themselves in a defensive position before the very people from whom they had always received deference. The deputy lieutenants of Essex wrote plaintively that because of the crown's demands they had been deserted by many "of our Neighboures with whom wee were able to persuade much by love, and our tenents whom wee used to Command." Local loyalties were important, far too important to lose over a foolish "perfect militia" or some other royal scheme. Charles warned the county leaders that "ther remissnes in executing thes our commands geves encouragement to the inferior sort of people," but despite such admonishments, men of better quality—"the High sheriff, deputy Lieutenants and Justices of peace, and under them the constables and other inferior officers" —concluded that it was better to have friends at home than to try to please the king. . . .

In reaction to the king's continued interference in local affairs—his attacks on "popular protestantism," his disruption of the county communities, his assault on the corporate boroughs—a few thousand English men and women chose to leave the country. To these people Charles must have seemed perfectly capable of establishing himself as an absolute ruler: The future of local society appeared dark to those who followed John Winthrop in 1630, and to the emigrants of the mid-1630s the situation must have looked nearly hopeless. Their response was essentially defensive, conservative, even reactionary.

There is a substantial body of information about how other people—not necessarily Puritans—reacted to the disruption of local communities and traditional ways of life by some outside authority. Invariably, the beleaguered groups assumed a defensive stance, resisting, sometimes with force, any alteration of accepted routine. The historian J. H. Elliott discovered that the population of sixteenth- and seventeenth-century Europe deeply resented innovation. Indeed, the participants in violent risings seemed "obsessed by *renovation*—by the desire to return to old customs and privileges, and to an old order of society." England was no exception to the rule. In her comments on the Civil War, Joan Thirsk observes that "the great majority of the gentry and peasantry, in their almost morbid anxiety to preserve the traditional fabric of local society, generally stood side by side." It appears that the same local communities that resisted Charles ultimately defeated Oliver Cromwell, for he too tried to force them to change their ways—to make them integral parts of a centralized nation state. These examples suggest that the English countryside was filled with traditionally oriented men and women, who, like turtles, pulled back into the safe and familiar shell of local custom at the first sign of danger.

The results of this conservative response would appear in the social institutions of New England. The colonists' experiences under Charles had heightened their sense of tradition, and whether they came from small country villages or sizable corporate boroughs, whether they were humble yeoman or influential county leaders, they shared a desire to preserve a customary way of life. That they were willing to travel three thousand miles to achieve that goal reveals how strongly some of them felt about the disruptions of local institutions. Like the Catholic proprietors who in the late 1630s tried to create a vast feudal manor in Maryland, the Bay colonists looked to America as a place to escape the dislocating effects of social change.

These observations are not intended to imply that all colonists were of one mind about social institutions in the New World. They were not. The settlers' English background produced both unity and diversity. On the one hand, the people who transferred to New England during the 1630s were obviously influenced by the same general threats to local autonomy. This common experience helped to create broad areas of agreement about the character of New England society. On the other hand, the migration itself created diversity. New Englanders had crossed the Atlantic not as individual adventurers but as self-selected groups. Respected civil and religious leaders often recruited their neighbors, and it was not unusual for persons from the same small village to stay together once they reached Massachusetts. This type of migration, called "chain migration," meant that each group possessed separate and distinct memories of life in the mother country. Stuart policies had affected them in different ways. Habits and traditions, attitudes toward land division, town government, church membership—all these things were in part the product of a specific environment. While Massachusetts society was still in its formative stages, therefore, each community was forced to work out the relationship between its own particular English heritage and a more general English background that it shared with other Bay communities. Seen in this light, New England was not a single, monolithic "fragment" separating off from the mother country. It was a body of loosely joined fragments, and some of the disputes that developed in the New World grew out of differences that had existed in the Old.

The early migrants to Massachusetts Bay, men and women anxious to recapture a traditional way of life, had the good fortune to select a place inhabited by only a few Indians. Left behind were interfering Stuart officials and troublesome Anglican bishops. The very openness of New England made it possible for the colonists to transform social ideas into actual institutions. Each group of immigrants had an opportunity to create an independent community, a village in which local institutions might be safe from outside interference. The settlers' commitment to the preservation of local autonomy led almost inevitably to social diversity, and within a decade after Winthrop's arrival, a score of towns had taken root in Massachusetts, each developing institutions slightly different from those of its neighbors.

But the preservation of local institutions involved New Englanders in difficulties that no one anticipated. The immigrants were so obsessed with local autonomy that almost without being conscious of it, they created institutions that looked very little like those they had left behind in the mother country. The settlers realized that within a locality broad participation in civil, military, and ecclesiastical affairs would help to secure local independence from central authority, and voluntarism quickly became the hallmark of Massachusetts society. The colonists had no use for democracy, but they believed that anyone who possessed a voice in local concerns thereby acquired a responsibility to the community as a whole. Indeed, the person who enjoyed such a privilege would find it in his best interests to defend those elements that had been threatened in English—continuity, independence, and insularity.

The irony was that the New Englanders' social goals forced them unwittingly to accept significant social change. In elections of all sorts they opened the franchise to hundreds of men who would have been excluded in almost every English borough and town. In the early years of settlement the need for such alterations seemed perfectly obvious. Winthrop and the first assistants of the Massachusetts Bay Company could have legally become a narrow oligarchy selecting themselves anew year after year. But Winthrop encouraged a considerable expansion in the number of voters, a group that could and later did drop him from the governorship. The people who enlarged the franchise do not seem to have been as much concerned to create an ideal Puritan commonwealth as to avert absolutism. To appreciate how the settlers' English backgrounds influenced social institutions, one has only to examine the towns, churches, and trainbands established in Massachusetts Bay during the 1630s. In each case, forms developed which strongly suggest that sociocultural experiences in the mother country after 1625 were a major determinant in the way the colonists organized New England society.

Colonial historians have only recently come to appreciate the diversity of New England towns. Some evidence suggests that Winthrop wanted the settlers of 1630 to form one large fortified community, but whatever his ideas may have been, the colonists quickly went their separate ways. Historians who have traced the development of the early towns have been struck by local differences. Intensive studies of Andover, Dedham, Hingham, and Sudbury reveal how misleading it is to speak of *the* New England town. Some of the communities experienced bitter feuds; others were quite stable. Some were more commercially oriented than others. There was no uniform method of dividing lands, running town meetings, or laying out house lots. Edward Johnson surveyed the villages of Massachusetts Bay and discovered that while people in some places clustered around the meetinghouse, those in other communities were relatively dispersed. In Concord, for example, he found that the "buildings are conveniently placed chiefly in one straite streame [streete]. . . ." But in Newbury the "houses are built very scattering, which hath caused some contending about removall of their place for Sabbath-Assemblies." And when Johnson visited Salisbury he observed that "the people of this Towne have of late placed their dwellings so much distanced the one from the other, that they are like to divide into two Churches." In other words, even in the earliest years of settlement some towns allowed "out-livers" to erect homes away from the center of the village.

What the towns of Massachusetts Bay had in common was a desire to preserve their individual autonomy. New England villagers often bound themselves together by written covenants, promising to uphold certain clearly stated principles. Historians have analyzed these covenants, but few have seen them as an indication of the colony's reactionary origins. These voluntary agreements provided villagers with a sense of local identity, a rationale for excluding outsiders, and a means of achieving continuity between present and future generations. Moreover, the covenants served a more immediate function. By promoting harmony and homogeneity, they helped to ward off the kind of external interference that had been so troublesome in the mother country. Many town covenants contained a section specifically committing townsmen to settle their disputes through love and friendly arbitration. While this provision seems an expression of Christian charity, it also reduced the likelihood that colonial magistrates would intervene in local affairs. And by screening potential inhabitants—indeed, by accepting in some cases only those people who had emigrated from a particular English district—many towns avoided the contention that conflicting backgrounds and traditions might have bred. Each individual was under strong peer group pressure to give his first loyalty to the town, and, as one might expect, New England's local communities resisted anything that threatened established routine.

The Congregational churches were another institution that revealed the effect of the English background on the character of Massachusetts society. Historians have exaggerated the intolerance of the colony's ministers and magistrates. Although, to be sure, such outspoken critics of the New England Way as Roger Williams and Anne Hutchinson were exiled, Congregational orthodoxy, compared to other seventeenth-century religious systems, allowed a relatively wide range of opinion on questions of polity and theology.

Because the settlers insisted on local control over religious affairs, it is not surprising that significant differences developed among the churches. In fact, the Congregational system itself fostered diversity. New Englanders who had resented Laud's interference refused in America to recognize any ecclesiastical authority beyond the local community. Colony-wide synods could recommend—even cajole—but they could not order individual congregations to alter religious procedures. In the words of the Cambridge Platform of 1648, the churches were "distinct, and therfore may not be confounded one with another: and equall, and therfore have not dominion one over another." Only in the most extreme cases did the political leaders of Massachusetts involve themselves in local church matters, and then only reluctantly. Normally, the church members of a village selected their minister, set his salary, and determined ecclesiastical policy. One colonist, Thomas Lechford, described in 1642 some of the ways in which the churches varied. The Boston congregation, for example, was ruled "by unanimous consent," while in Salem decisions required only "the major part of the church." Moreover, Lechford found that "some Churches have no ruling Elders, some but one, some but one teaching Elder, some have two ruling, and two teaching Elders; some one, some two or three Deacons. . . ." It was not only in details of polity that congregations exercised their discretion. Even in the earliest years of colonization, some towns such as Newbury favored presbyterian forms of worship.

Some contemporaries in the mother country regarded the Bay colonists as religious innovators, experimenting with extreme types of separatism. These English critics were correct on one count. In the early 1630s there were few precedents for the ecclesiastical system that developed in Massachusetts. In 1644 one colonial minister, William Hooke, admitted, "It is a truth, we saw but little in comparison of what we now do, when we left our Native homes." But what the people back in England failed to understand was that the colonists regarded Congregationalism as a means to restore the Protestant faith and preserve true religion from outside interference.

Because they were safely beyond Laud's reach, they enjoyed an opportunity to do in the 1630s what was denied Englishmen until the 1640s. The New Englanders gave the church back to the local communities. And in so doing they were responding not only to the freedom of their new environment but also to specific conditions that they had experienced in England. New England's Congregational churches, like its towns, were the result of the general antipathy that the colonists felt toward Stuart centralism.

The colonists also created a system of defense. Military organizations by their very nature would seem to demand a highly centralized chain of command. If the New Englanders had been willing to compromise their desire for local autonomy, one might expect them to have done so in the formation of their militia. But the shape of this social institution was not so very different from that of the Congregational churches and the town governments. All of them stressed local control, even if that meant an unprecedented degree of popular participation in the selection of leaders.

In England it had been Charles's appointed officers, usually his deputy lieutenants, who had most frequently disrupted country life. They had been responsible for the king's "perfect militia," for the collection of unparliamentary levies, and for the billeting of unwelcome troops. With such experiences in mind the settlers of Massachusetts Bay insisted upon placing as many local controls on the military as security would allow. The colonial government could dispatch an army against the Indians, but the militia itself was a village institution. Not only did the townsmen drill together, they also chose their own officers. As early as 1632 Winthrop reported that "a proposition was made by the people, that every company of trained men might choose their own captain and officers. By the mid-1630s local trainband elections had become common practice throughout the colony. Although the Massachusetts General Court claimed ultimate authority in the selection of officers, the legislators seldom rejected a name, and local nomination amounted to final selection.

Some military men thought that the New Englanders had lost their good sense. One veteran of European campaigns complained that the Massachusetts system would destroy discipline. Voluntarism had no place in matters of defense, and the colony's organization appeared to this person, at least, a wrong-headed innovation. He reported with shock that the soldiers of Salem had selected a "Captaine, Lieutenant, and Ensigne . . . after such a manner as never was hearde of in any Schoole of warre; nor in no Kingedome under heaven." But the colonists were not concerned with winning Continental wars; they were far more conscious of the meddling deputy lieutenants who had made life so unpleasant in England. It was the king's appointed officers, not the elected New Englanders, who were viewed as the true innovators. The immigrants merely restored the trainbands to community control. Once the militia had been transformed into a local structure, it became highly unlikely that it could be used to oppress the settlers. And it is not surprising that a survey of Massachusetts records reveals no instance in which the colony's rulers attempted to employ the militia as a police force, as a tax collector, or as an instrument of social control.

The colonists' English background affected life in Massachusetts in another way that no one expected. Instead of promoting unity, it became a source of dissension, especially in political and ecclesiastical matters, and within a few years the settlers were forced to confront the unpleasant realization that they were not all interested in preserving the same things in the New World. Like their contemporaries in the mother country, a majority of the New Englanders seem to have been concerned primarily with what occurred in their own villages. They built homes, sowed crops, made love, and for the most part gave scant attention to the actions of the colony's central government. As one colonist explained, "Plantations in their be-ginnings have worke enough, and find difficul-ties sufficient to settle a comfortable way of subsistence, there beinge buildings, fencings, cleeringe and breakinge up of ground, lands to be attended, orchards to be planted, highways and bridges and fortifications to be made." But other men such as Winthrop appear to have re-garded Massachusetts Bay as a sort of Amer-ican "county community." These people nat-urally defined "local" in larger terms than did the other colonists, and when they were forced to curb the independence of certain local in-stitutions, they found themselves suddenly cast in the role of Charles I. Ironically, tensions be-tween central authority and local custom had followed the settlers to the New World.

The division was most apparent in politi-cal affairs. Indeed, at the same time that the colony's local institutions were taking shape, the central government was a continuous source of conflict. A year seldom passed with-out Bay rulers accusing each other of some abuse of power, and on one occasion at least jealousy and anger sparked an attempt to im-peach Winthrop. These political battles have been closely examined, and much is known about their intellectual content. So far, how-ever, no historian has adequately explained the social origins of these disputes. Since all the colonists involved presumably had similar re-ligious views, one is forced to look elsewhere for the roots of dissension. Why, indeed, did an elected governor and court of assistants find it so difficult to work in harmony with an elected house of deputies representing the towns of Massachusetts Bay? Had the local communities carried their contempt for external authority to such an extreme that they were unwilling to tolerate the slightest outside interference in their affairs?

In most of these controversies Winthrop and a small group of like-minded magistrates were pitted against an outspoken but loosely con-nected body of village representatives. The rea-sons for these fights were complex, but one

of them no doubt was the way in which the governor and his allies defined "local" inter-ests. Although Winthrop had not been a leader of the first rank in his native English county, Suffolk, he counted among his friends some of the most powerful gentry families in the shire. His business dealings carried him regularly from his home at Groton Manor to London, and he knew firsthand how a county commu-nity operated. The most influential members of the gentry (in Suffolk they would have been the Barnardistons and Barringtons) acted as mediators between England's central govern-ment and the specific interests of their county. When they spoke of preserving independence or complained of royal interference, they usu-ally had the shire in mind.

The actions of Winthrop and a few other men of similar experience suggest that they arrived in America intent on reproducing a county community. In this smaller New World pond they may well have regarded themselves as bigger fish and assumed the role and re-sponsibilities of the leading gentry of Massa-chusetts Bay. Although they were elected to office annually by the colony's freemen, they saw themselves as natural rulers—as persons prepared by God, training, and status to act in the colonists' best interests. The New En-gland county elite received advice from the people with ill grace, viewing any attempt to limit their discretionary powers as a personal insult. The Winthrops of Massachusetts be-lieved that the voters should trust the gen-try's judgment in much the same manner as in the mother country. These notions about the government and society grew out of a special English background, and to Winthrop's cha-grin they were challenged by groups within the colony who conceived of "local" autonomy in rather different terms.

Most settlers were willing to trust this self-styled county elite, but only up to a point. They had gone through too much in En-gland, traveled too far, raised their expecta-tions about local autonomy too high to do simply as Winthrop and his friends desired. In any case, the colonists found it difficult to regard these leaders as mere county gentry. The nature of this authority seemed quite different from that of the Barringtons and Barnardistons. They issued important executive orders, served in the highest courts, and claimed broad powers and privileges on the basis of a royal charter granted to the Massachusetts Bay Company. No one, of course, confused John Winthrop with Charles Stuart, but it seemed clear that the governor spoke for the central government as opposed to the local communities. Almost as soon as the migrants arrived in the New World, they sought ways to control the magistrates' discretionary powers and to ensure that civil rulers in Massachusetts understood that the ultimate source of political authority was a collection of independent corporate towns speaking through their elected delegates. . . .

The clash between local and county views of government authority reached a dramatic climax in 1645. In the spring of that year the militiamen of Hingham selected a West Country migrant, Anthony Eames, as their captain. For reasons that remain unclear, however, Eames fell out of favor with his neighbors, and the trainband held a second election, this time choosing Bozone Allen. At this point Winthrop, then the colony's deputy governor, stepped in and accused Allen's supporters of fomenting insubordination to lawful authority. Allen's followers countered in no uncertain terms that by intervening in a local affair Winthrop had exceeded his legitimate powers, and the disgruntled Hinghamites organized an unsuccessful attempt with the Massachusetts General Court

to impeach him. Throughout the controversy the inhabitants of Hingham insisted that they were defending local autonomy against unwarranted outside interference. One angry militiaman even protested that he would "die at the sword's point, if he might not have the choice of his own officers." Hingham reacted to what it perceived as a threat to its independence much as the English local communities reacted first to Charles and then to Cromwell. And like the members of Parliament, the village representatives serving in the Massachusetts legislature tried to assert their rights through impeachment. Winthrop came out of this trial with his reputation intact, but Hingham had served notice that civil power flowed up from the local communities, not down from a county elite.

By the 1650s the Bay colonists had sorted out their various English backgrounds. Unexpected problems had been confronted, and compromises made. But for most of them the trip to the New World had been an overwhelming success. The Massachusetts countryside at mid-century appeared remarkably like the traditional English society which they had sought to preserve from Stuart intervention. One historian has termed New England's little settlements "peasant utopias"—a description that captures their backward-looking character. Most of them went years without significant change in institutional forms or procedures. The townsmen regarded the village as the center of their lives; indeed, most were married and buried in the places of their birth. The vast undeveloped lands to the west had little appeal. Seldom has a conservative movement so fully achieved its aims.

Literacy, Religion, and the Plain Style

David Hall

The people who came to New England in the seventeenth century called themselves "English," and in their ordinary ways of life—the arrangement of their fields and villages, the food they ate, and the clothing they wore—they behaved like Englishmen. The transfer of culture was astonishingly complete. Very little changed, despite the differences of environment between old world and new. As the turmoil of the early years subsided, familiar patterns reappeared. A deep, instinctive conservatism prevailed.

Books were an essential strand in the web of continuity. The settlers were remarkably literate, and their libraries were precious to them. Space was scarce on the ships that brought supplies and people from old England, but even in the earliest cargoes there was room for books. Soon a printing press arrived, and by 1640 the first works in English published in the western hemisphere emerged from the Cambridge shop of Stephen and Matthew Day.

The act of reading could have deep significance. A Boston merchant, willing to his son a "little written book" on the Lord's Supper, spoke of it as "more precious than gold," and as something he had "read over I think 100 and 100 times. I hope he will read it over not less [and will] make it his constant companion. . . ." A woman held captive by Indians rejoiced when she came upon a Bible. Reading in its pages, she found comforts that eased the worst moments of her ordeal. Many colonists knew portions of the Bible by heart and could speak to each other in a shorthand of scriptural references. Many could recite a catechism, perhaps the Westminster, or a local product like John Cotton's *Spiritual Milk for Babes*. Indeed the very practice of reading was inextricably bound up with the practice of religion. The books that were most widely read—catechisms, psalm books and the Bible, almanacs and primers, captivity narratives and accounts of "remarkable" events—were always a means of absorbing certain themes and principles in Christianity. A verse in a schoolbook for young children made the connection explicit: "Thy life to mend/This book attend." No one in the seventeenth century needed to be told that mending one's life meant repenting of sin or that the book that taught this fundamental lesson was the Bible.

All this reading was surely conservative in its implications, a means of retaining traditional values. The colonists were conservative in wanting to re-create familiar ways of doing things. Books and literacy provided two kinds of reinforcement; they helped guarantee that the colonists would not succumb to the wilderness

"Literacy, Religion and the Plain Style" by David Hall from *New England Begins: The Seventeenth Century,* Vol. I: Introduction, Migration, and Settlement. Reprinted by permission of the Museum of Fine Arts, Boston and David Hall.

and lapse into barbarism, and they also perpetuated certain key values, like the importance of children's obedience to their parents. The *New England Primer* is classically conservative in this regard, for while teaching children to read, it also taught them to honor all superiors.

But to say that the *New England Primer* was conservative is not to exhaust its meaning. From another point of view, it is a radical document—radically Protestant, that is, by comparison with other primers of the seventeenth century. The same is true of most books circulated widely in New England. Some of these taught a particular version of Christianity. Others, like the Bible, were read in special ways. Altogether, the uses of literacy in seventeenth-century New England were complex, at once radical and conservative.

The reason for this mixture is the Puritanism of the immigrants. Puritanism is a complicated word. We read into it meanings that were not present in the seventeenth century, including sexual repression and extreme hostility to pleasure. (A twentieth-century critic once defined Puritanism as "the haunting fear that somewhere, someone might be happy.") As we have grown more secular ourselves, we have tended to forget that such fundamental doctrines as man's innate depravity and the sovereignty of God were the common stock of *all* Christians in earlier times. Much of what we find in Puritan writings is conventional Christianity or else a repetition of Calvinist Protestantism.

To the colonists themselves in the 1630s, as they were setting out for the New World, Puritanism meant three things above and beyond this common stock of Christian doctrine. It designated a group of people who regarded the Church of England as too "Catholic" in its rites and structure; Puritans wanted to reform it into something more stringently Protestant. The word also applied to persons who were "disciplined" in their way of life. Puritans did not dance or play games on Sunday and they attempted to curb their fondness for "worldly"

things. Finally, Puritanism designated persons who believed in a particular conception of history. To these Englishmen, the essence of history was God's plan for the redemption of mankind. This plan would culminate in the day of judgment, when faithful Christians—the "saints"—would join Christ in his kingdom. Puritans in the early seventeenth century believed that history was moving rapidly toward the day of judgment. It was everyone's duty to prepare for that event, whether by purifying the church or by strenuous self-discipline.

This conception of history was fundamental to the making of New England. We can follow its consequences in two of the most important books written by the colonists, William Bradford's "Of Plimoth Plantation" and John Winthrop's "Journal" or "History of New England". Bradford and Winthrop were leaders of their respective colonies. Bradford came over on the *Mayflower* and participated in the founding of Plymouth. Having survived the cruel winter of 1620–21, he was elected governor of the colony in 1621, a position he held almost without interruption until his death in 1657. Winthrop, a wealthy and educated man, became governor of the Massachusetts Bay Company, the joint stock company that was organizing the settlement of Massachusetts, in June of 1629. He crossed the ocean in 1630 as leader of the "Great Migration" and continued to serve as governor or deputy governor for most of the years before his death in 1649.

Winthrop started to keep a journal on board the *Arbella*, the ship that brought him to New England; Bradford began his narrative in 1630, ten years after his arrival, though he had earlier accounts by himself and other writers on which to base his chronicle. Both men wrote of public events, recording step by step the social, economic, political, and religious evolution of the settlements. Through their pages pass the overzealous and the self-seeking, many of them bent on damaging or destroying the Puritan communities. We hear of rebels such as Roger Williams and Anne Hutchinson, and watch as the colonists intimidate their Indian neighbors. There are ceremonies that draw the community together—like the first Thanksgiving at Plymouth in the fall of 1621—and those that separate the saints from the unregenerate—as in the gathering of new churches. Always, Winthrop and Bradford wrote from the perspective of leaders who place the welfare of the community before any personal advantage. Winthrop reported eating the same scanty food as the other colonists during the "starving time" of 1630–31 in Massachusetts, and Bradford praised Elder William Brewster for his selfless devotion to the sick and dying—Bradford himself among them—during the first winter at Plymouth. Valuing order and stability, the two historians exemplified the conservatism that enabled the fragile settlements to survive and mature.

The settling of New England meant an unsettling of traditional restraints. People who were strangers to each other had to cooperate, and individuals who lacked the special recognition that went with high social rank were thrust into positions of leadership. Civil government was often improvised under difficult conditions. Responding to the threat of mutiny among the passengers on board the *Mayflower,* the Pilgrims gathered all the adult males together to sign a special "compact" pledging everyone to obey the leaders of the expedition. In Massachusetts, John Winthrop faced a difficult situation in 1645. He had angered the deputies in the Massachusetts General Court by meddling in a local election of militia officers. After an inquiry had cleared him of wrongdoing, Winthrop spoke to the members of the General Court of the differences between "civil" and "natural" liberty. People who live together in civil society, he argued, give up some of their liberty, if only because they must obey rules that God himself has ordained. To live without rules and without regard for others in a state of "natural" liberty was to live, Winthrop declared, like "beasts" in the forest. That most New England communities sustained effective structures of authority and consensus during the seventeenth century suggests that the colonists agreed fundamentally with Winthrop on the importance of self-restraint and group regulation.

Bradford and Winthrop were realistic in describing the perils of colonization. Yet, as historians, they had a larger purpose in mind than merely to recount the struggle to survive. Both men believed that God ordered and arranged the ways in which things happened. God had a purpose in doing so, and the task of the historian was to make that purpose clear. Bradford and Winthrop wanted to uncover the *real* meaning of history, the "providential" meaning hidden in each event. One meaning of history as God directs is that faithful Christians are ultimately protected from their enemies. When a young sailor who taunted the passengers on the *Mayflower* suddenly fell ill and died, Bradford was confident that this was God's work. Deaths, fires, shipwrecks, good harvests and bad, all these are significant in terms of God's "providence," that is, as signs of his purpose and judgments.

The founding of the colonies had a special significance in itself. Why had these Englishmen ventured across the ocean? Did God have a particular purpose in the founding of New England? Winthrop answered this question directly in a sermon he preached on board the *Arbella:* God had entered into covenant with the colonists, commanding them to establish the "due form of government, both civil and ecclesiastical." The colonists were specially chosen, like the children of Israel, to be his people and to become a model of how God wanted all Christians to live. Reaching back to the New Testament for his figure of speech, Winthrop compared New England to Jerusalem, that "city upon a hill." We ourselves, he told the colonists, "must consider that we shall be as a city upon a hill, the eyes of all people are upon us. . . ." The colonists had embarked upon a mission that would help bring to completion the history of redemption. The task that Winthrop and

Bradford set themselves as historians was to fit everything that happened to the colonists into such a framework.

Living as they were in the shadow of the New Testament, Winthrop and Bradford believed that Christ would eventually return to earth and bring to an end the ancient struggle between good and evil, light and darkness. The events that led up to the Second Coming were foretold in various parts of Scripture; and the colonists, like many of their European contemporaries, puzzled over the meaning of the seals, trumpets, and vials mentioned in the Book of Revelation, trying to plot the exact chronology of the "last days." All this activity betokened their expectation that the Second Coming was not far off. They were heartened by recent history, and especially by the outbreak of the Protestant Reformation, which in their eyes seemed evidence that the forces of light had begun to prevail against the forces of darkness. In making the decision to immigrate, the leaders of the new colonies were swayed by the feeling that the American wilderness would serve not only as a refuge from storms of judgment breaking over Europe but also as the place where Christ's true followers would rebuild the Temple. New England would become another Zion, a New Jerusalem, a New Israel.

This frame of reference is always present in Winthrop's journal. Consider his description of an episode in 1646. A snake had crawled into the Cambridge meetinghouse, briefly disrupting an important session of ministers and magistrates who were discussing the nature of the Church. To us the episode might have no special meaning. But in the eyes of the colonists the snake was symbolic of larger things: "The serpent is the devil; the synod, the representative of the churches of Christ in New England. The devil had formerly and lately attempted their disturbance and dissolution; but their faith in the seed of woman overcame him and crushed his head." The saints, God's chosen, were at war with Satan. And the devil was especially enraged by the colonists' success at establishing the true Church. The symbolism transformed the mundane into the cosmic, enriching the history of New England with sacred meaning.

To William Bradford the founding of Plymouth was equally a special event. He began the story of the colony far back in time, locating its origins in the early history of the Christian Church, when the faithful were often martyred by their enemies. The struggle between light and darkness had gone on ever since; the persecution of Puritans in England was but the latest chapter in the everlasting war between Christ and Satan. The tiny group of persons who crossed on the *Mayflower* had mighty significance as soldiers in this battle. They could not have escaped their persecutors and found refuge in the wilderness without God's help. Their very survival betokened a special relationship between them and their Savior. In the magnificent passage that closes his account of the ocean crossing, Bradford summed up all of what they lacked in December 1620, ending with a question: "What could now sustain them but the spirit of God and his grace? May not and ought not the children of these fathers rightly say: Our fathers were Englishmen which came over this great ocean, and were ready to perish in this wilderness; but they cried unto the Lord, and he heard their voice, and looked on their adversity. . . ." In this, one of the three or four most famous passages in the entire literature of American Puritanism, Bradford resoundingly affirmed the extraordinary meaning of Plymouth.

The language of this passage touches on another theme in seventeenth-century Puritanism, the spirituality of true Christians. Bradford noted that Christians will cry out for help, so weak do they feel, so "overwhelmed" in their souls, and so utterly dependent on God. As he went on to indicate, this feeling of dependence is coupled with the rejection of "outward objects." The saint looks heavenward; he lives in this world of necessity, but he lives in it as a "pilgrim," always wary of distractions from the real business of gaining salvation. The figure of the pilgrim is basic to all of Puritanism—in no way is it peculiar to Plymouth—because it sums up an ethic of self-denial and self-discipline. This is the ethic that Puritans tried to exemplify in reordering their lives according to the will of God.

Thousands of people in 17th-century New England learned this code of self-denial from catechisms that they studied as children. A dozen ministers wrote catechisms to use in their own congregations, but only one of these, *Spiritual Milk for Babes,* became widely used in both old and New England. The author, John Cotton, was the minister of First Church, Boston, and an active figure in many areas of colonial life. But the role he preferred was that of preacher of the Word, a "means of grace" to persons seeking their salvation.

The purpose of Cotton's catechism was to teach the truths on which salvation depended. Learning these truths was the first and essential step in the process of conversion. *Spiritual Milk for Babes* lays out these truths in a simple question-and-answer form, like all catechisms of the period.

Q. Are you then born in sin?
A. I was conceived in sin, and born in iniquity.
Q. What are the wages of sin?
A. Death and damnation.
Q. How look you then to be saved?
A. Only by Jesus Christ. . .

This lesson is certainly explicit. Man by nature is corrupted by original sin and merits damnation. But God in his mercy offers free grace to some. Grace is free because man cannot win God's favor on his own. Like the archetypal pilgrim, the sinner must come to recognize his utter worthlessness: "So I come to feel my cursed estate, and need of a Savior. [I am convinced] of . . . my utter insufficiency to come to him; and so I feel myself utterly lost." No one who feels this way *is* really lost. Out of

despair springs faith, and faith is the act that completes rebirth into "new life" as a "visible saint." For the rest of his pilgrimage on earth the saint will seek to obey God's will.

This theology is Calvinism. John Cotton was notably fond of Calvin's theology—"Let Calvin speak for me," he once declared in responding to a challenge—but the Calvinism of *Spiritual Milk for Babes* was no different from the common faith of all Puritans in England and America, or for that matter the faith of Presbyterians in Scotland, Huguenots in France, and many other groups. When a convention of ministers in England published the Westminster Confession, a masterful summary of Calvinist doctrine, the colonists quickly adopted it as their own, and continued to regard it as the standard of orthodoxy far into the next century. Here, as in the architecture of their homes or the patterns of their fields, New England Puritans held on to tradition. *Spiritual Milk for Babes* retained its popularity even longer, reprinted more times in the eighteenth century than in the seventeenth, and often bound with the *New England Primer.*

Learning the principles of Calvinism from a catechism was one thing; acting on these principles was another. When Cotton asked that people *feel* their "cursed estate," he was asking a great deal of ordinary men and women. The struggle against pride and feelings of self-worth was intense and painful. It could never end in victory, for sinful impulses were always present, even in the best of saints. Anyone could fall into hypocrisy or spiritual "sloth." No wonder, then, that Puritans so often likened the progress of the soul to warfare.

Mary Rowlandson was thrust into a real war when Indians attacked her town in February 1676. Mary and her three children were among the captives carried off into the snowy, desolate woods. Ransomed three months later, she told the story of her experiences in all unpretentious narrative that became a bestseller in colonial new England, *The Soveraignty and Goodness of God Together With the Faithfulness of*

His Promises Displayed; . . . a Narrative Of the Captivity and Restauration of Mrs. Mary Rowlandson. It is a story rich in dramatic adventure, from the horrors of the original attack to her search for scraps of food. But the real adventure is inward and spiritual, the adventure of a soul who seeks to know God. Mary Rowlandson understood that God had willed her to suffer, as He also willed that Job would undergo afflictions. As the weeks of her captivity unfolded, Mrs. Rowlandson awakened to a new sense of God and what was expected of the Christian. She returned from the wilderness to civilization, stripped of all illusions about security and lasting comfort. While her family slept, she lay awake at night, mediating "upon the awful dispensation of the Lord toward us; upon his wonderful power and might, in carrying of us through so many difficults. . . . Oh! the wonderful power of God that mine eyes have seen, affording matter enough for my thoughts to run in, that when others are sleeping mine eyes are weeping." She had learned anew the "vanity [of] outward things. That they are the vanity of vanities, and vexation of spirit; that they are but a shadow, a blast, a bubble. . . . That we must rely on God himself, and our whole dependance must be upon him." Her terrible suffering had turned into a blessing: God afflicts, but for a purpose.

That afflictions were actually an expression of God's love is a theme another woman often used in her poetry and prose. Anne Bradstreet came to Massachusetts in 1630, the young wife of one of the colony's leaders. The verse she wrote and had published is sometimes formal and literary, its style and subject matter derivative of published verse by DuBartas and others. But it could also originate in incidents of daily life—the sickness of a child, her own pregnancies, the absence of a husband, the burning of her house in Andover. In these poems Anne Bradstreet is direct and moving: "If ever two were one, then surely we./If ever man were lov'd by wife, then thee;/If ever wife was happy in a man,/Compare with me ye woman if you can." But in keeping with the spirituality of "weaned affections," she comes to realize that nothing on earth is equal in value to her love of God. "He's mine, but more, O Lord, thine own,/For sure thy Grace on him is shown./No friend I have like thee to trust,/For mortal helps are brittle dust." It is to heaven she must look for lasting comfort and joy.

Like so many other Puritans, Anne Bradstreet spoke of herself as a pilgrim. Here on earth she must work to control the self-love and vanity that distract from knowing God. For her children she wrote out a series of "Meditations divine and moral" that express the wisdom gained from long years of this struggle. She puts homely images to good stead. "That house which is not often swept, makes the cleanly inhabitant soon loath it, and that heart which is not continually purifying itself, is no fit temple for the spirit of God to dwell in." "Prosperity" is dangerous because it makes the world too pleasant and attractive a place. She reminds her children once again that their real business lies elsewhere: "a christian is sailing through this world unto his heavenly country, and here he hath many conveniences and comforts; but he must beware of desir[ing] to make this the place of his abode, lest he meet with such tossings that may cause him to long for shore before he sees land. We must, therefore, be here as strangers and pilgrims, that we may plainly declare that we seek a city above. . . ." And the essential note of Calvinism is struck in a meditation on God, who in choosing some for salvation and others for damnation "will not be tied to time nor place, nor yet to persons but takes and chooses when and where and whom he pleases: . . . how unsearchable are his ways, and his footsteps past finding out."

Often, too, in growing older, Mrs. Bradstreet thought of death as bringing to an end her "weary" pilgrimage: "O how I long to be at rest/and soar on high among the blest." The frankness with which she spoke of death is characteristic of seventeenth-century New England. Even in the *New England Primer* death figures in the rhyme for the letter T: "Time cuts down all/Both great and small." The accompanying picture shows a skeleton holding an hourglass in one hand and a scythe in the other. The gravestones that began to appear in New England and burying grounds by the 1660s are among the most vigorous examples of Puritan art, with their extravagant winged skulls and hourglasses, coffins, skeletons, imps of death, vines, trumpets, and cherubs. Some of the images appear as decorations on printed broadside elegies. These poems, most of them printed on a single page, were a widely popular form of literature, written by many persons who had neither the wish nor the skill to be literary. Their intention is religious, to commemorate the goodness and piety of a friend or relative. In the twentieth century we focus our mourning on the qualities that make someone a distinctive individual. The colonists worked otherwise, assimilating the individual into a generalized, abstract figure of the saint.

This conflation of the general and the particular helped to reassure the living that those who died had entered heaven. The author of the Lydia Minot broadside moves quickly from describing her earthly situation to assuring us

of her ascent to heaven. "I dy to Husband, Children, Parents dear:/Mine they were once, I theirs: ('twixt hope and fear/No unmix'd Sweet I found) But now no more/These mine can be, as they were heretofore./My Interest's translated up on High/To things now mine, to which I ne're can dy./Then happy Death, my welcome I'le thee give,/'Cause now to God and Christ I ever live." In keeping with Christian teaching, the colonists could keep their grief in check by thinking of death as the doorway to a better life in the world to come. Death could even be an ecstatic moment, when at last the pilgrim found his rest in Jesus. Grief was out of place for another reason. Mrs. Bradstreet was never more authentically Puritan than in transforming deep sorrow at the death of a grandchild into the lesson that love for kin and family comes second to her love of God. Once again, affliction is a way of learning that the pleasures of this world do not last, and that only God's love is eternal.

Another kind of literature in wide use among the colonists was handbooks describing how to die, Puritan versions of the traditional *ars moriendi.* A popular example was James Janeway's *Token for Children,* an English book reprinted in Boston with additional text by Cot-

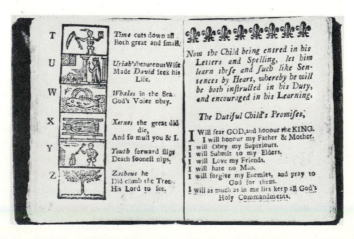

The New England Primer taught respect for authority and described death as the ultimate test of faith.

ton Mather. Janeway and Mather started from the assumption that death offers the supreme test of faith and self-discipline. Death is a summons to prepare for a final judgment, a summons from a Christ who is both just and merciful. Dying, the Puritan explored his conscience for the last time, searching out every vestige of pride and vanity. No one could approach the end feeling fully confident, but the people who watched the dying prepare themselves for judgment (dying in the seventeenth century was a highly public act) looked for expressions of joy and peace that betokened enduring faith in Christ. Janeway and Mather described a series of young people who die correctly, as in the example of a young girl who "spake with a holy Confidence in the Lord's Love to her Soul, and was not in the least daunted when she spake of her Death; but seemed greatly delighted in the Apprehension of her nearness to her Father's House: And it was not long before she was fill'd with Joy unspeakable in believing." The people watching her die ask that she "give them a particular account of what she saw" as she entered the last stages of life: "she answer'd *You shall know hereafter:* and so in an extacy of Joy and holy Triumph, she went to Heaven when she was about twelve Years old."

The importance of death as a final test of faith is summed up in a simple inscription on hundreds of gravestones: "Memento mori," remember (and think on) death. Puritan culture was saturated with memento mori—the iconography of gravestones, the broadsides with their printed borders, the mourning rings engraved with skulls, the dozens of sermons on how to die. Paintings such as Captain Thomas Smith's self-portrait use familiar icons to evoke the same warning. As if the skull in the painting did not make his meaning evident enough, Smith inserted a poem that emphasizes the classic distinction between *this* world and heaven: "Why why should I the world be minding/therein a World of Evils finding." Here, as in broadsides, sermons, and grave-

stone inscriptions, death becomes a warning against pride and vanity. All of these memento mori are a means of teaching and sustaining the self-discipline that was the core of Puritan spirituality.

If someone lapsed from self-discipline, as Mrs. Rowlandson confessed she did in becoming careless about the Sabbath, punishment was sure to follow. The colonists seemed to live through cycles of obedience and disobedience, zeal and carelessness. People experienced this cycle as individuals, some days feeling close to God, on others feeling "drowsy" or "slothful" in their faith. The cycle was also a matter of collective experience. The entire covenanted community had its good times and bad. In bad times God reached out to chastise the false-hearted—holding back the rains so that crops failed, or allowing Indians to win a battle.

To a young minister, Michael Wigglesworth, the signs of the times in the early 1660s were foreboding. People were too proud and too absorbed in money. Speaking like a prophet, he warned of what would happen unless the colonists repented: "Beware O sinful land, beware/And do not think it strange/That s'vere judgments are at hand/Unless thou quickly change." The same year he voiced this warning, Wigglesworth published *The Day of Doom,* a vivid description of the Last Judgment. *The Day of Doom* became undoubtedly the most widely read poem in 17th-century New England, and there were persons in the early 19th century who could still recite its 224 stanzas by heart. The poem owed its popularity to the high drama of the story being told, a tale of sinners surprised in their sleep by the "mighty voice" of God calling them to judgment: "They rush from Beds with giddy heads,/and to their windows run,/Viewing this light, which shines more bright/than doth the Noon-day Sun./Straightway appears (they see't with tears)/the Son of God most dread;/Who with his Train comes on amain/to Judge both Quick and Dead." The drama of Judgment

Day is strictly in accord with Wigglesworth's Calvinism. People who have not repented of their sins can expect no mercy. The afflicted, those, like Mary Rowlandson, "who by the Rod were turn'd to God, and loved him the more,/Not murmuring nor quarreling when they were chast'ned sore," ascend to heaven. Wigglesworth used all his powers as a theologian and a poet to dissect the many varieties of the reprobates and to apportion out the punishments awaiting them. His purpose in doing so was to reinvigorate the spirituality of the colonists. Like the memento mori, *The Day of Doom* played upon fears of death and judgment in endeavoring to restore the Puritan community to its former zeal.

Two strands of Puritanism are fused in *The Day of Doom,* the ethic of self-discipline and the understanding of history as God's plan for redemption. The structure of history and the structure of the spiritual life did indeed converge, in the sense that the individual pilgrim who entered into covenant with God spent his life thereafter fighting against darkness in the great war between Christ and Satan. The progress of the soul toward grace was exactly paralleled in the progress of the saints toward victory.

Into this grand drama of salvation the colonists fitted one other goal, the vision of a pure Church and a holy commonwealth that Winthrop expressed in his *Arbella* sermon. Their Puritanism included specific ideas about the nature of the Church, ideas they had never been able to act upon until they emigrated to New England. The church at Salem, the first to be established in the Massachusetts Bay, was radically different from the Church of England: the ministers were elected to office by the church members and the church itself was organized on the basis of a covenant open only to "visible saints," that is, persons who in the judgment of the community were true Christians. This type of organization came to be known as the "New England Way," or Congregationalism. In 1648 the ministers agreed on an official description of this system, published

the next year as *A Platform for Church Discipline Gathered out of the World of God.* Like the Westminster Confession of 1647, the Cambridge Platform, as this document was called, lasted into the eighteenth century as a standard of authority among the colonists. But to the great disappointment of John Cotton and his fellow ministers, it was never adopted as authoritative back in England, where Puritans in the 1640s and 1650s could not agree on how to reorganize the national church they had finally come to control.

The Cambridge Platform was a thoroughly Puritan document. The old ambition to purify the Church of England was carried out in two major respects: church membership was limited to persons whom the community recognized as regenerate, and all vestiges of Catholicism in the sacraments, the worship service, and the ministry were eliminated. Anti-Catholic feeling ran deep among the colonists. John Endicott, a magistrate in Salem, used his sword in 1635 to cut the red cross—to him a Catholic emblem—out of the English flag. Each November fifth, people lit bonfires in Boston streets celebrating the downfall of Guy Fawkes, a "popish" plotter. The *New England Primer* kept old stories of Catholic persecution alive with a picture of a Protestant martyr at the stake. The victories of the Protestant hero Gustavus Adolphus in faraway Germany were celebrated in Massachusetts in 1632, and at the end of the century, the folk prejudice against Catholics led the writer of an almanac to identify Louis XIV of France with the antichrist.

John Foster's portrait of the Reverend Richard Mather, one of the persons who helped draft the Cambridge Platform, shows the effects of this purifying zeal upon the dress of the minister. As a minister in the Church of England, Mather would (or should) have worn special vestments. In New England he dressed in a scholar's gown. Elsewhere, the zeal to purify was obvious in the Sabbatarianism of the colonists and in their calendar. New England almanacs contained no "red letter" saints' days or references to Christmas. "We under the New Testament," Samuel Danforth declared in 1646, "follow God's will in acknowledging no holy-days except the first day of the week only." Nor did the colonists like the traditional names for months and days, derived as they were from pagan sources. In Josiah Flint's *An Almanack or, Astronomical Calculations . . . For . . . 1666,* the traditional names were replaced with plain numbers: "1st month," "2nd month," and so forth.

We have already seen that Bradford and Winthrop spoke as though the colonists were a chosen people, commissioned to build a new Jerusalem in the wilderness. In fulfilling that commission, the colonists looked back to Scripture for guidance. It contained specific rules for many situations, from the nature of the church to the penalties for certain crimes. All of the colonists' efforts to purify the Church and Commonwealth can be understood as gestures aimed at sweeping away the corruptions that had crept in since the days of Moses and the Apostles. The ministers who designed the Congregational system were restoring the "primitive" or apostolic model of the Church. When John Cotton drafted a set of laws in 1636, he called them "Moses his Judicialls," and took much of the detail from sections of Leviticus. The same impulse to restore is embodied in the *Bay Psalm Book,* the informal title of the first book published in New England: *The Whole Book of Psalmes Faithfully Translated into English Metre.* It was a new translation of certain psalms, done by several ministers who kept to the original Hebrew as literally as possible. Occasionally, some colonists tried to carry the logic of this purism too far, as when John Eliot, better known for his missionary efforts among the Indians, argued on the basis of certain Scriptures that all societies should be organized in units of tens, hundreds, and thousands. The leaders of Massachusetts spurned this proposal, but certainly not the general ambition to model New England institutions as closely as possible on Scripture. This commitment was fundamental to the covenanted community, the Congregational Church, and the code of individual self-discipline.

Scripture had unique authority among the colonists, in part because the process of learning to read was so tied in with knowledge of the Bible. But the literacy of the colonists was not restricted to Scripture, and their world view incorporated many other elements. When Boston booksellers ordered stock from England, they specified a surprising variety of fare, from books that we would expect the colonists to be reading—devotional manuals and commentaries on Scripture—to ones that are decidedly unexpected, like fiction, jest-books, and erotica. If a little sensationalism crept into a story that was otherwise morally correct, so much the better. Colonial readers responded warmly to such a mixture, as in captivity narratives, descriptions of the final moments of criminals awaiting execution, or accounts of "strange and remarkable" phenomena.

Indeed the common reader in New England shared with his counterpart in England a taste for the bizarre and unusual. Puritanism per se had little to do with this taste, which is better understood as an aspect of English folk culture. Ordinary people regarded all sorts of natural phenomena as puzzling and mysterious: thunder and lightning, cloud shapes and comets, sickness and death. Anything that happened suddenly, that took persons by surprise, was disturbing. Beyond such mysteries lay another range of phenomena, the dreams, visions, and sounds that seemed to betoken the presence of invisible spirits among the living. People in Plymouth told stories of how, when a fire broke out on a ship in the harbor, "there was a voice heard (but from whence it came is uncertain) that bade them look well about them." Thanks to this warning, the colonists discovered and extinguished a fire in their storehouse. Urian Oakes, the president of Harvard, told his students of

A child that was born at Norwich last Batholomew Day being in the nurses arms last Easterday being about 30 weeks old spake these words (this is an hard world): the nurse when she had recovered herself a little from her trembling, & amazement at the extraordinariness of the thing, said Why dear child! thou hast not known it; the child after a pause, replied, But it will be an hard world & you shall know it; or words to this effect.

Here, as in so many other occurrences, the natural and spiritual words seemed immensely alive with elusive lines of force—elusive, yet tantalizingly visible in unexpected forces or "blazing stars" that shone briefly in the sky overhead.

As every colonist knew, the elusive forces of the universe encompassed the workings of Satan and his allies. It was entirely credible to persons living in seventeenth-century Europe and America that Satan could entice persons into covenant with him in exchange for the powers of black magic. The Bible referred to witches and in the sixteenth and early seventeenth century, many theologians and scholars in Europe reached the conclusion that the peculiar horror of witchcraft—a sin unlike most others—deserved the penalty of death. Ordinary people were familiar with "cunning folk" in the regular course of village life; their curses, spells and evil eyes were the reasons that milk turned sour in the churn, cows strayed from pasture, or someone broke his leg. Usually these cunning folk were the older women, the shrews, the impoverished, or the simple-minded of a community. In mid-seventeenth-century England, hundreds of such persons, were condemned and put to death; in New England, accusations of witchcraft occurred intermittently.

Then came the Salem witchcraft craze of 1692. Nineteen persons were executed by hanging in Salem—the actual location of the frenzy was Salem Village, later renamed Danvers—before the governor of Massachusetts intervened to stop the process. Eight more had been condemned to die and dozens had still to face their accusers. The special tragedy of Salem is that normal processes of communal reconciliation broke down, leaving the way open for the young girls who claimed they were tormented to make their accusations with abandon.

The minister of Salem-Village was Samuel Parris, whose own daughter and niece were among the first to accuse other townsfolk of covenanting with the devil. In early 1692 Parris was having problems in his ministry. The townspeople were not paying him his full salary, and he seemed unable to heal the feuds that had flourished for a decade. As fervently as anyone in all New England, Samuel Parris believed that Satan had organized a great plot against the saints of Salem-Village. Some of the sermons he preached during the crisis survive in his own handwriting as he had prepared them for delivery: the sermon for March 27, in which he associated the devil's work with deceit and covetousness among the townspeople, and the one for September 11, in which he spoke of "the war the Devil has raised amongst us by wizards and witches, against the Lamb and his followers."

A few years later, Parris would be forced out of Salem-Village by vengeful relatives of the victims. Had he been a person of more character, he might have benefited from the courage of Mary Easty. This fifty-eight-year-old woman lived in Topsfield, the town adjoining Salem-Village. Her husband had disputed the timber rights along the boundary line between the two villages, and this turmoil, no doubt, made Mary Easty's name familiar to the girls who were the chief accusers. In court they claimed that Goody Easty's apparition had tormented them with "such tortures as no tongue can express." Mary Easty was steadfast in declaring her innocence: "I will say it, if it was my last time, I am clear of this sin." When the magistrates ruled against her, she faced a terrible choice. By confessing and then testifying against others, she could save herself from execution. Or she could die, and in so doing perhaps spare others that same fare. The statement she left for the magistrates to read merits the praise of a nineteenth-century historian: "It would be hard to find, in all the records of human suffering and of Christian deportment under them, a more affecting production. It is a most beautiful specimen of strong good-sense, pious fortitude and faith, genuine dignity of soul. . . ." Mary Easty begged the judges that "no more innocent blood may be shed, which undoubtedly cannot be avoided in the way and course you go in," for she was certain that her accusers would continue to lie.

Mary Easty and six others who were executed on September 22 were the final victims of the panic. Or should we reckon Cotton Mather another victim? Mather shared the ministry of Second Church, Boston, with his father, Increase. Both men had described witchcraft as a genuine phenomenon. Increase, troubled by the procedures of the Salem Court, came to feel by midsummer of 1692 that the devil had brought matters to a state of complete confusion by impersonating innocent persons. How, he wondered, can we possibly tell the innocent from the guilty? Cotton was more supportive of the judges, who maintained that the Devil could not assume the shape of an innocent person.

When the witchcraft accusations began, Cotton interpreted them to mean that the Devil was making one last desperate attempt to subvert New England. Salem witchcraft became an episode in the history of redemption: the end was near, and New England must renew its purity by eliminating all witches. *Wonders of the Invisible World,* a compilation of sermons, commentary, and actual trial records, placed Mather in the position of vindicating the Salem affair. For this he was criticized by his own contemporaries, and his reputation was never the same again.

In justice to Cotton Mather, we should recognize that he was especially alert in the 1690s to portents of the future. Like Winthrop and Bradford before him, he found in every event a reflection of God's plan for redemption. Sim-

ilarly, Mather believed in the special mission of New England. But in the years between the founding of Plymouth and the outbreak of Salem witchcraft, much had occurred to weaken and erode the "city upon a hill." Looking around him, Mather could see that the colonists were not as zealous in observing the Sabbath or in limiting church membership as they once had been. Looking back into the past, he could trace certain changes that had carried the colonists away from their original errand. New England, he feared, was in "declension." The witches at Salem were a warning that the colonists must speedily repent and renew their covenant with God.

As we look back over the decades between 1620 and 1690 for evidence of change, we find that the most obvious lay in the political status of Massachusetts, Plymouth, and New Hampshire. Starting out as quasi-independent colonies, each came under the control of the English crown by the time Mather wrote about the trials at Salem. The holy Commonwealth of John Winthrop was now the "province" of an empire. As for Congregationalism, English Puritans had never used it as the model of the true Church and, after 1660, when Charles II assumed the throne in England, Puritans were even more discredited and remote from power than before the Great Migration. Was Cotton Mather foolish in continuing to assert that New England had a special mission?

The almanacs that once epitomized the zeal for purity were becoming more conventional in the late seventeenth century. After 1668, no one used numbers for the months any longer. An almanac in the traditional English style, its calendar marked for Christmas and Church holy days, appeared in 1687. In the sequel for 1688, there were references to "Oliver [Cromwell] the Tyrant" and "Charles I Murdered," references that contradicted conventional opinion among New England Puritans. Less tangible were the changes taking place in people's sympathy for signs and portents. The spiritual world was becoming less immediate, and there were persons in the 1690s who dared to suggest that witchcraft was not real.

Change came slowly in New England, for many worked to keep things as they were. Literature played a crucial role in keeping old values alive. *The Day of Doom* helped to sustain the immediacy of the spiritual world, as did Mary Rowlandson's captivity narrative. Richard Mather, feeling himself near death in 1657, warned with the special authority of the dying that the colonists must never depart from the principles of the founders. On his deathbed he urged his son Increase and all other second generation ministers to keep careful watch upon the "rising generation." John Foster's portrait of Richard Mather was undoubtedly understood by contemporaries as an icon of the founders and their zeal for purity. William Bradford wrote "Of Plimoth Plantation" for an audience of readers who had never suffered persecution in England or the perils of the ocean crossing; for them he sought to re-create in prose the heroism of the immigrants, elevating it to a legend that endures to this day.

The most dogged of the legend-makers was Cotton Mather. The burden of preserving the ideals of the founders passed to him by descent from his father, Increase, and his grandfather, Richard. A burden vastly swelled by his own literary and political ambitions, its outcome was the largest book written by any American colonist in the seventeenth century, the *Magnalia Christi Americana.* Superlatives surround Cotton Mather. He was the most prolific author in early America, and his library was the largest in New England. Quite likely, he was disliked more than any other person of his times. As for the *Magnalia,* it is large in size and in its grand design. It consists of seven "books," most of them cobbled out of previous publications and containing biographies of magistrates and ministers, civil and religious history, and accounts of portents and captivities. The opening sentence of the introduction, with its echo of Virgil's *Aeneid*—"I write the wonders of the Christian religion, flying from

the deprivations of Europe, to the American strand"—admits of no compromise with the vision of the founders. But within a few sentences the tone becomes uncertain. Excessive praise of England alternates with insecure assertions of New England's special errand. The contradictions lead to a paradoxically defiant sentence: "But whether New England may live anywhere else or no, it must live in our History!" A monument to the past, the *Magnalia* is actually a mirror of the 1690s, when all of the colonists were caught between their old identity as Puritans and their new identity as provincials.

The tension between old and new is apparent also in the history of Harvard College. The ministers and magistrates who somehow found resources in the 1630s to begin a college wanted to sustain the standards of learning familiar to them from the university training they received at Oxford and Cambridge. At the first commencement in 1642, proudly described for an English audience in *New Englands First Fruits,* the seniors carried on their debates in Latin, the international language of scholarship. Anyone who visited the college library that day could have browsed upon a substantial collection of books. Most of them were a legacy from John Harvard, a young minister who died soon after immigrating. He had brought with him from England a cosmopolitan library—commentaries on Scriptures by Dutch, German, and French scholars, the Greek and Latin classics, encyclopedias of knowledge, the writings of Thomas Aquinas. Harvard students had access to all the great monuments of Western culture.

Harvard was conservative in another respect. The founders wanted it to teach the truth, by which they meant the truth contained in Scripture. Truth was one, fixed, constant. The "veritas" that appeared in the college seal stood for an unchanging intellectual system, albeit a system that combined Scripture with scholastic Calvinism. Yet Harvard could not stay immune from change. Books continued to arrive from overseas, bringing with them fresh ideas. Popular and learned belief began to vary. When officers of the college realized in 1683 that commencement would coincide with an eclipse, they changed the date. "We are not superstitious in it, but reckon it very inconvenient," they explained, and in saying so revealed the distance that was opening up between superstitious and enlightened systems. First in science and then in philosophy, Harvard began to move into the age of reason. Young college graduates showed off some of their new learning in the almanacs. The Copernican system made its first appearance in the almanac for 1659, and the planets as described by modern science were diagrammed by John Foster in 1675. Tulley's almanac for 1693 offered purely natural explanations for earthquakes and thunderstorms, thereby lessening their significance as portents. Slowly but surely, some of the colonists moved down the road toward the Newtonian universe and its benevolent god.

Cotton Mather read all the new books and became a Copernican himself. He wanted to be up-to-date. Yet the pull of the past was strong. The literary style of the *Magnalia* is the same style in which his grandfather would have written half a century earlier—richly metaphoric, allusive, involuted. Within a few years of its publication, a young boy in Mather's Boston would begin to write in a wholly different way. Benjamin Franklin was as modern in the quality of his prose as Mather was old-fashioned in the qualities of his. Already Cotton sensed the difference; in the introduction he apologized that critics would not like the way he wrote. As the Puritan century ended, a literary and an artistic style was also dying.

Style, like Puritanism, is a complicated word, and the complications increase when we come to the issue of the colonists' own attitude toward art. Usually it is said that Puritans distrusted art. Did they not say that statues and stained glass violated God's commandment against "graven images"? Did they not prohibit

musical instruments in their churches and any plays from being performed? The answer to each of these questions is a qualified yes. But even if Puritans occasionally destroyed stained glass and statues in English churches, this does not mean that they were hostile or indifferent to beauty. Starting from certain premises about the differences between good and bad art, New England writers labored to create a literature that was rich in aesthetic achievement.

The initial premise of Puritan aesthetics is that art must teach the truth essential to salvation. The fundamental source of truth was the Word of God. The Word was truth, and the truth was to be understood plainly, not disguised or painted over with embellishments. No "fictions" or playful versions of reality could possibly be useful. Medieval literary theory had allowed for allegorical interpretation of Scripture. In rejecting this possibility, the Puritans also rejected any possibility of representing God in images. Many of the great traditions of Christian art were condemned as versions of "idolatry." Whether in sculpture, stained glass, or paintings, any "carved, painted [or] molten Images" of God were merely men's "Inventions." Eschewing all such physical representations of the holy in their churches and their art, the colonists sought in literature to close the distance between the written word and what it represented. In their discourse, as in the glass windows of the meetinghouse, they wanted the light of truth, unmediated and unadorned, to shine through clearly.

From William Bradford to Anne Bradstreet, every Puritan writer aspired to be "plain" in the sense of speaking truth. Bradford declared on his opening page that he would write "in a plain style; with singular regard unto the simple truth in all things." The translators of the *Bay Psalm Book* committed themselves to transmitting the Word in its literal unembellished sense. Earlier translators had varied from the originals, but the colonists, John Cotton declared in the preface, produced a "plain and familiar" text. They "have not so much as presumed to paraphrase or to give the sense . . . in other words . . . If therefore the verses are not always so smooth and elegant as some may desire or expect it; let them consider that Gods Altar needs not our polishings: . . . for we have respected rather a plain translation, than to smooth our verses with the sweetness of any paraphrase, and so have attended conscience rather than elegance, fidelity rather than poetry. . . ."

Similarly, Anne Bradstreet told her children that a diary of religious experiences she bequeathed them was plain for good reason: ". . . that you may gain some spiritual Advantage by my experience. I have not studied in this you read to show my skill, but to declare the Truth—not to sett forth myself, but the Glory of God." With this same plainness, finally, the ministers constructed their sermons, aiming to teach rather than to please, even if the Word became "painful" to their listeners. Richard Mather was exemplary in his style: "His way of preaching was plain, aiming to shoot his arrows not over his peoples heads, but into their hearts and consciences." In the woodcut of him by John Foster, Mather holds out to us an open Bible, emblem of his role as preacher of the Word.

Puritan writers who espoused truth and plainness as aesthetic principles wanted their art to be useful. Whatever they wrote or preached had to be easily understood by everyone if it were to have utility. Richard Mather, though trained in Greek and Latin, "studiously avoided obscure phrases, exotic words, or an unnecessary citation of Latin sentences" in his sermons. Out in Dorchester he preached to an audience of farmers and artisans, the same persons who paid him for being their minister in allotments of wheat, butter and wood. Living among these persons, and farming the land himself, Mather had every reason to use a widely shared vernacular in his sermons. He had no other audience except occasionally his fellow ministers, the students at Harvard, or some learned minister overseas. These were

circumstances to which most others are responsive. Michael Wigglesworth used a traditional ballad meter in *The Day of Doom;* John Cotton wrote as simply as he could in *Spiritual Milk for Babes.* No one in New England wrote esoteric prose and poetry.

In this respect, the relationship between writers and their audience in Puritan New England was consistent with a middle-class, provincial culture. Some writers and artists in seventeenth-century Europe depended upon the aristocracy and the court for patronage. A frequent consequence for these artists was a higher level of self-consciousness about one's art and a greater effort to create or imitate new styles. Court art was cosmopolitan, heroic, aggressive. Artists had substantial incomes and signed their work in order to confirm their individuality. Many painters in the Netherlands were, by contrast, persons of middling status equivalent to that of other artisans. They found their patrons among the wealthy merchants, magistrates, and officers who dominated the commercial society of the Dutch provinces. While history and allegorical paintings were executed in the Netherlands, particularly at the court of the Stadtholder, the Prince of Orange, most sophisticated merchant patrons preferred "lower" categories of genre painting such as still lifes, tavern scenes, and ship paintings. These patrons consciously demanded representations of themselves in a realistic style—comfortable in tone, convenient in size, and "provincial in the sense of being deliberately opposed to stylistic trends at royal and noble courts." Likewise Cotton Mather was provincial; he and most writers in New England were content with the plain style even as others in England and the colonies were experimenting in new directions.

To say that the colonists were provincial and utilitarian is not to say, however, that writers such as Bradford and Wigglesworth were inferior artists. Within certain self-imposed limitations, the colonists tried intentionally to achieve effective prose and poetry. They wanted their verse to be "smooth and elegant," as John Cotton and Anne Bradstreet inadvertently acknowledged in their statements about plainness. It would be astonishing if they felt otherwise, for the colonists knew and admired the literary accomplishments of European culture. The translators of the *Bay Psalm Book* had to confess that, after all, they had tinkered with the original Hebrew, inserting a "meeter" that made the psalsm more readable in English. The ambivalence in Puritan aesthetics is summed up in the dictum, "artis est eclare arteni" (art to conceal art). The colonists wanted plainness, but not at the expense of being dull or clumsy. Their errand into the wilderness was not a voyage that carried them away from civilization; in literature, as in the case of Harvard, they proudly boasted to an international audience of what they had achieved. The title page of Anne Bradstreet's book of poems, published in London in 1650, says it all: *The Tenth Muse, Lately Sprung Up in America.*

Provincial yet cosmopolitan, truthful and utilitarian—to this list of qualities we must add one more, a quality no less important than these others: symbolic. Puritan writers practiced symbolism in two ways. We have already observed how the colonists discovered cosmic meaning in everyday events. According to the Puritans and their European contemporaries, the structure of the universe was replicated in the structure of each particular object. Microcosm and macrocosm were conjoined. A language of ordinary description was a language, therefore, always ready to blossom into larger truths.

The other road to symbolism lay through Scriptures. In taking the Bible as their literary model, Puritan writers equipped themselves with an unending supply of metaphors and images. Moreover, the colonists could expand the supply by the way they read this language. For them, the person of David in the Old Testament was really a "figure" or "type" of Christ in the New Testament, and so on, ad infinitum. To make any use of biblical images and figures was immediately to evoke the many possibilities for meaning each one contained. Puritan writing was never plain, therefore, in the sense of avoiding the richness of symbolism. The opposite is true: every writer in the seventeenth century exploited these possibilities in marvelously intricate and compelling ways.

A few examples will suffice. Mary Rowlandson was one of many New England writers who played upon the symbolic possibilities of "wilderness." The literal wilderness of untamed forest to which the Indians carried her dissolves into the wilderness where Moses and the Children of Israel spent forty years in search of Canaan, and again into the wilderness where Christ had gone to meditate and suffer. The smoke arising from her burning village becomes the smoke of sacrifice and lamentation among the Jews of old. A scrap of meat blossoms into reflections on God's way of offering spiritual sustenance. The deeper patterns of symbolism, here and elsewhere in New England writing, are those that grow out of and express the history of redemption: the chosen people warring against Satan, the soul embarking on its pilgrimage to heaven. The Indians she encounters are agents of the devil, and her travels become a spiritual journey, a ritual cleansing of her soul. In such fashion, the literature of the period draws again and again upon the myths and symbolism of the Bible and, in doing so, proves beyond a doubt that imaginative art could triumphantly succeed in Puritan New England.

Part Four

The Great Awakening

*B*y the opening decades of the eighteenth century, the religious life of the American colonies had begun to assume a tone and pattern that caused considerable concern among ministers and other church leaders. But the remedy that arose in the 1740s, subsequently described as the Great Awakening, was not exactly what they had hoped for.

Colonial religion in the early eighteenth century had two characteristic features. The first was the decline of orthodoxy and dominance that had previously been enjoyed by the Puritan Congregationalists in New England, the Quakers in Pennsylvania, and the Anglicans in most of the South. Dissenting sects were arising whose existence was being tolerated and even accepted. Accompanying this lack of unanimity and weakening of authority was increasing evidence that the churches were not involving the masses. As a result, there was a vast segment of the population that was unchurched, a greater proportion perhaps than existed in western Europe at the time. This development was abetted no doubt by the disorganized state of society on the western frontier, where the necessities of daily existence took priority over spiritual and religious matters. Meanwhile, the decline in religious zeal was aggravated by the scepticism and rationalism that was becoming widespread throughout Europe and America in the eighteenth century.

This spiritual complacency was challenged in the late 1730s by a series of revivals whose purpose was to rekindle people's religious faith through an appeal to their hearts and emotions that would lead them through the experience of conversion into a new life of Christian godliness. Although the preachers emphasized that religious experience had to be personal and emotional rather than mere avowal of correct belief and deference to church authority, they nevertheless firmly maintained that salvation was a gift preordained by God, not a matter of individual choice. While seeming to adhere to a more traditional view of man's sinfulness and God's omnipotence, the revivalists simultaneously presented a challenge to existing authority that was radical and, in the eyes of some, subversive. For the revivalist preachers appealed directly to individuals, often bypassing formal institutions and creeds. Indeed, some of the best-known preachers of the Awakening were itinerants who had no church of their own, such as James Davenport, Gilbert and William Tennent, and, not least, George Whitefield, John Wesley's assistant in the English Methodist movement, who came to preach in America in 1739.

The upshot of this apparent rebirth of religious zeal on the part of individuals, both within and outside existing congregations, was that the new converts formed breakaway groups such as the New Light Congregationalists or the New Side Presbyterians, or else they left altogether and joined more sympathetic sects already in existence like the Baptists. This resulted, many historians have claimed, in the further diversification and decentralization of organized religion in the colonies. It may also have contributed to a greater degree of toleration and an increasing demand for freedom of religion and conscience. Ironically, this seeming democratization of religion was brought about by men preaching a doctrine that placed human goodness and free will at a discount.

Historians have approached the revivals of the mid-eighteenth century from several angles. Some have concentrated their attention on the ideas involved, seeing the episode's significance in the theology and religious thought that it introduced. More recently, others have examined the social and institutional context within which it occurred, drawing attention to the structural and governmental features of the towns where revivals took place as well as to the nature of church governance and finance and the authority of the ministers.

The two selections that follow adopt yet another perspective, namely a focus on the scope and impact of the revivals. Were the revivals so numerous and extensive and their consequences so far-reaching that the episode can appropriately be called "the Great Awakening"? Richard Bushman of the University of Delaware describes it this way; he sees the Awakening as a critical event in colonial history, one that gave rise to social and intellectual developments beyond even those that were religious in thrust. These, in turn, had a shaping influence on American thought and behavior on the eve of the break with England in the 1760s. Although this estimate of the Great Awakening's impact has often been endorsed, it has also been questioned as being exaggerated. Jon Butler, now of Yale University, takes an even more radical stance on this issue. He argues that not only has the significance of the event been blown out of proportion but its content and scope also. Maybe it was a religious awakening of some kind, he suggests, but "the Great Awakening" it certainly was not.

QUESTIONS TO CONSIDER

1. Why, according to Bushman, did the Great Awakening occur and what was its significance?

2. Butler thinks that the revivals of the 1740s have been accorded far greater significance than they warrant. On what grounds does he argue this case?

3. How do you account for such a great divergence of interpretation as is evident in these two essays on the Great Awakening?

The Great Awakening in Connecticut

Richard L. Bushman

In 1721 an extraordinary number of conversions occurred in Windsor, Windham, and two parishes in Norwich. For the first time a rash of revivals occurred instead of individual instances spotted across the face of the colony at wide intervals in time. Another series, beginning in Northampton in 1735, followed the same pattern on a much larger scale. Religious excitment moved down the Connecticut Valley, eastward from the river into the backcountry, and in both directions along the coast.

The conversion spirit spread rapidly because religious tension was high. [Jonathan] Edwards said that news of the 1735 revival struck "like a flash of lightning, upon the hearts" of the people. Throughout the decade ministers often had to comfort *"Souls in Distress under Inward Troubles."* [Thomas] Clap found this pastoral work the most difficult of his duties: "Persons are oftentimes under great Trouble and Distress of Mind," he wrote in 1732, "and sometimes brought almost to Despair." A colleague in 1737 offered suggestions on the best method of leading persons under concern "thro' the Work of Humilia-

tion . . . unto Christ." The tide of conversions was already rising in 1740 when [George] Whitefield visited New England.

The need for an Awakening to heal society as well as to save men's souls was widely acknowledged. For eighty years the clergy had deplored the declension of piety. As vice, injustice, pride, contempt for authority, and contention in church and town became more prevalent, law after law was added to the books to restrain corruption but without appreciable effect. "There have been many Enquiries after the *Cause of our Ill State,*" lamented the election sermon of 1734, "and after proper *Means* and *Methods* of Cure: Yea, and many *Attempts,* but alas, to how little purpose!" Ministers pleaded with their congregations *"to awake out of Sleep."* Privately they sought ways "to revive a Concern about religion." Congregations fasted and prayed to humble themselves "before God Under the sense of Leaness and bareness . . . and to Implore the divine Graces to be poured out." After the Windham revival in 1721, the pastor exclaimed, "Oh! that the same Good *Spirit from on High* were poured out upon the rest of the Country." Hearing of Whitefield's success in the middle and southern colonies, several leading New England ministers invited him to visit and preach, and Governor Talcott gratefully welcomed him to Connecticut in 1740.

For six weeks in September and October

The fervor of the Great Awakening was intensified by the eloquence of touring preachers such as George Whitefield, who enthralled his audiences.

Whitefield toured New England, releasing a flood of religious emotions wherever he went. Along his route from Boston to Northampton, down the Connecticut Valley, and westward along the Sound hundreds were converted, and the itinerants Gilbert Tennent of New Jersey and James Davenport of Long Island continued the work through 1741 and 1742. Local ministers, adopting Whitefield's style of preaching, started revivals in their own congregations and aided neighboring pastors in theirs. The increase of admissions to full communion is a measure of the volume of religious experience.

The revivals occurred throughout the colony. Even though some areas, such as the first parish in Fairfield, did not respond, religious activity flourished all around them. Coast and inland towns, new and old towns, towns in the east and in the west participated in the Awakening. Although it was probably more intense in the east than in the west and on the coast and large rivers than inland, no area was immune to the contagion.

The Awakening affected people of all classes. One clergyman reported that men of "all orders and degrees, or all ages and characters" were converted. Edwards marveled that "some that are wealthy, and of a fashionable, gay education; some great beaus and fine ladies" cast off their vanities and humbled themselves. In town after town leading citizens participated along with more common people. A comparison of the taxes of persons admitted to communion in two Norwich parishes from 1740 to 1743 with the taxes of the town as a whole shows that economically the new converts represented an almost exact cross-section of the population.

The revivals Whitefield precipitated seemed to fulfill all the hopes placed in him. Vicious persons repented of their sins, inveterate absentees from worship returned, love for the minister waxed strong, contention in the town died away, and interest in worldly pursuits shifted to the scriptures and the state of one's soul. People could not get enough preaching: meetings were added to the regular schedule, and worshippers met privately to discuss religion. When the Hartford County Association in June 1741 urged ministers to hold extra meetings, preaching alternately for each other if necessary, it declared that the "awakening and Religious Concern, if duly cultivated and directed may have a very happy Influence to promote Religion and the Saving Conversion of Souls."

A few ministers were dubious from the start, however, and their doubts steadily darkened into dislike. The news of enthusiasm on Long Island made Daniel Wadsworth, pastor of the first church in Hartford, uncomfortable even before Whitefield arrived. Upon seeing him in October 1740, Wadsworth was uncertain "what to think of the man and his

Itinerant preachings," and by the following spring "irregularities and disorders" in the town worried him. In August 1741 the Hartford Association declared against itinerants and their unjust censures of other ministers. The clergy agreed that no weight was to be given to "those screachings, cryings out, faintings and convulsions, which, sometimes attend the terrifying Language of some preachers," nor to the "Visions or visional discoveries by some of Late pretended to." The following month, after reports of Davenport's conduct had reached Hartford, Wadsworth concluded that "the great awakening etc. seemes to be degenerating into Strife and faction." Itinerants had turned people "to disputes, debates and quarrels." "Steady christians and the most Judicious among ministers and people," he observed at the end of September 1741, "generally dislike these new things set afoot by these Itinerant preachers." By the end of 1741 open opposition appeared to what had at first been considered to be a work of grace.

At the request of several ministers, the Assembly in October 1741 underwrote the expenses of a general convention of ministers to stop the "unhappy misunderstandings and divisions" in the colony and to bring about "peace, love and charity." Probably in response to the resolves of the clergy, the Assembly enacted a law in the spring of 1742 forbidding itinerants. Ministers were to obtain permission from the congregation and the pastor of a parish before preaching there. If a complaint was lodged against a pastor for preaching outside of his parish, the magistrates were not to enforce collection of his salary, and unordained persons and ministers without congregations or from other colonies were required to obtain permission before preaching. Realizing that one consociation might be more favorable to revival preachers or contentious individuals than another, the Assembly forbade any to advise or to license candidates to preach in the jurisdiction of another. Thus this act outlawed itineracy, the primary method of spreading the revival,

and thereby officially denounced the Awakening. When Whitefield next visited Connecticut in 1744, most pulpits were closed to him.

Conversions waned after 1743. Only sporadic and isolated revivals occurred in the next fifty years, and none was comparable in size to the Great Awakening. But the impact of the experience was felt long afterwards. The converted were new men, with new attitudes toward themselves, their religion, their neighbors, and their rulers in church and state. A psychological earthquake had reshaped the human landscape.

What had happened to prepare so large a portion of the population for this momentous change? What power was there in the words of a sermon to plunge a person into the blackest despair and then bring him out into light and joy, a new man? The answer lay in the revivalist's message. He told his listeners that they were enemies of God and certain to be damned. When sufficiently crushed by their sinfulness, they learned that good works would never save them but that God's free grace would. This idea lifted men from their misery and restored them to confidence in God's love. Men who had come to believe that they were damnably guilty were ready to rely on unconditional grace.

The peculiarities of the Puritan personality partly account for the listeners' conviction that they were worthy only of damnation and hence wholly dependent on God's favor. Hypersensitive to overbearing authority and always afraid of its destructive power, Puritans instinctively resisted whenever it threatened—but not without guilt. Since they could not avoid conflicts, surrounded as they were by rulers and laws, they lived in the consciousness of multiple offenses. They did not separate earthly clashes with authority from sins against God, for they believed the rulers and laws derived their power from the heavens. With life so structured, deep feelings of guilt inevitably grew.

These tensions had existed long before 1740, but despite pleas from the clergy, conversions had been few. Not until 1721 were any appreciable number of men sufficiently overpowered by their own sinfulness to rely wholly on God's grace and be converted. Two conditions prepared men for conversion: an increased desire for material wealth that ministers called worldly pride or covetousness, and the growing frequency of clashes with authority entailed in the pursuit of wealth. Both were the results of economic expansion, and both were, in the Puritan mind, offenses against God.

The Puritans' feelings about wealth were ambiguous. Even the most pious associated it with a secure place in the community and divine approval, and everyone accorded great respect to rich men, numbering them among the rulers of society. Prosperity was a sign of good character: all were expected to practice industry and thrift, the virtues that brought the rewards of wealth. To some extent worldly success was a token of God's favor: none felt constrained to stint their efforts to prosper in their callings.

Yet the dangers of riches also were well known. The rich were prone to *"fall into Temptation,"* Cotton Mather warned, and be *"drowned in Perdition."* "There is a venom in *Riches,"* he said, "disposing our depraved Hearts, to cast off their *Dependence on God."* It was a maxim of the Jeremiads that "where a Selfish, Covetous spirit and Love of this world prevails, there the Love of God decayeth." When Connecticut's first published poet, Roger Wolcott, occupied himself with the theme of the divine wrath visited on seekers of earthly honor and wealth, he explained that he might have chosen the path of pride himself, "but that I see Hells flashes folding through Eternities." In this world money answered everything but a guilty conscience.

The contradiction in the prevailing attitudes toward wealth perplexed both the ministers and the people. Pastors complained that men excused avarice as justifiable enterprise. "They will plead in defense of a Worldly Covetous spirit, under the colour or specious pretence of Prudence, Diligence, Frugality, Necessity." Cotton Mather lamented that even the farmer was grasped with worldliness, yet he turned away rebukes with the assertion that he was merely pursuing his calling as a husbandman. The people could not distinguish respectable industry from covetousness: their ambitions drove them on year after year, while self-doubts were never far below the surface. Robert Keayne, the wealthy Boston merchant of the early period, built a fine fortune, but at great cost. When censured by the clergy for acting against the public good, he was crushed and, in a document written to clear himself of guilt, poured out the tensions he had long felt.

Throughout the seventeenth century a few Puritans experienced Keayne's miseries, but the temptations of worldly pride were too remote to hurt the consciences of most. The opportunities for gain were largely inaccessible to ordinary men until after 1690, when economic expansion opened new prospects to many more farmers and merchants. Common men could take up a small trade or invest in a ship sailing to the West Indies, and land purchased in a new plantation doubled in value within a few years. The expansive economy of the early eighteenth century unleashed ambitions restrained by the absence of opportunity. Everyone hoped to prosper; the demand for land banks and the 300-percent increase in per capita indebtedness were measures of the eagerness for wealth. An indentured farmhand in the 1740s complained that his master never spoke about religion: "His whole attention was taken up on the pursuits of the good things of this world; wealth was his supreme object. I am afraid gold was his God."

In the midst of this economic growth, the ministers faithfully excoriated the spreading worldliness. It was obvious, one minister wrote, "that the Heart of a People is gone off from God and gone after the Creature; that they are much more concerned about getting Land and Money and Stock, then they be about getting Religion revived." "The Concern is not as heretofore to accommodate themselves as to the Worship of God," it was said in 1730, "but Where they can have most Land, and be under best advantages to get Money." These accusations were put aside with the usual rationalizations, but so long as the ministers reminded men that riches cankered their souls, a grave uncertainty haunted everyone who pursued wealth.

The desire to prosper also precipitated clashes with law and authority, adding to accumulating guilt. With increasing frequency after 1690 people fought their rulers or balked at the laws, usually as a consequence of their ambition. Such friction wore away confidence as it convinced men inwardly of their own culpability.

Under more peaceful circumstances law and authority protected the Puritan from the asperities of his own doctrines. Taken seriously, Puritan theology kept men in unbearable suspense about their standing with God: He chose whom He would to be saved, and the rest were cast into the fires of hell. But the founding fathers had qualified this pure conception of divine sovereignty by stressing the authority vested in the social order. Since civil and ecclesiastical rulers were commissioned by God and the laws of society were an expression of His will, obedience to Connecticut's government was in effect obedience to divine government, and the good will of the rulers was an omen of God's good will. So long as man complied with the law and submitted to authority, he was safe from divine punishment.

After 1690, in their ambition to prosper, people disregarded the demands of social order. Nonproprietors contested the control of town lands with proprietors, and outlivers struggled with the leaders in the town center to obtain an independent parish. In the civil government settlers fought for a clear title to their lands and new traders for currency. Church members resisted the enlargement of the minister's power or demanded greater piety in his preaching. All these controversies pitted common men against rulers and the laws.

Under these circumstances the social order became a menace to peace of mind rather than a shield against divine wrath. Just as conformity gave an inward assurance of moral worth, so resistance, even in spirit, was blameworthy. Dissenters, in politics or economics as well as religion, could not oppose the community fathers whom God had set to rule without feeling guilty. Even when a move to the outlands or complaints about a minister's arrogance were well justified, the participants in the action feared that they sinned in resisting.

Few men in 1740 were outright rebels, for strong loyalties still bound almost all to their communities. By comparison with their forebears of 1690, however, this later generation was estranged. It could not comfort itself in the recollection of a life of conformity to the divinely sanctioned order. In part it was emboldened by the wealth it had sought and often gained, but that provided an unsteady support when the pursuit of riches was so often condemned. However hardened the contentious appeared, guilt generated by an undue love of wealth and by resistance to the social order had hollowed out their lives.

East of the Connecticut River, in the most rapidly expanding section of the colony, turmoil was greatest. Extravagant growth plunged the towns into strife over land titles, currency, and religion. The party battles loosened the social structure and alienated men from their social and religious leaders. Economic opportunity also aroused the hunger for land and commercial success. Here the revival was noticeably most intense. "Whatever be the reason," Ezra Stiles commented later, "the eastern part of Connecticut . . . are of a very mixt and uncertain character as to religion. Exhorters, Itinerants, Separate Meetings rose in that part." Around three-quarters of the separations between 1740 and 1755 occurred east of the Connecticut River. The greatest number in any town—four—were in Norwich, the commercial center of the east. Nearby towns—New London, Groton, Stonington, Lyme, Windham, and Preston—had similarly prospered, and a third of the separations in the colony took place in these towns and Norwich. These departures, roughly measuring the fervor of the Awakening, were the outcome of the personal instability eastern men felt after a half-century of extraordinary expansion.

Before Whitefield arrived, ministers sensed the shaky state of their parishioners' confidence. One pastor noted the grave uncertainty of people under spiritual concern: "They want to know they shall be sure they believe, that they love God, that they are in the right way, are sincere and the like." As the ministers recognized, an outward show usually covered somber doubts: reprobates disguised or fled from their real condition while inwardly they suffered from a consciousness of guilt.

Whitefield broke through this facade. Though he stood apart from the established clergy, he was accepted by them. He did not represent the repressive ministerial rule, which entered so largely into the conflicts of the period, but nevertheless came clothed with acknowledged authority. The revivals he started in the middle colonies also imbued him with a reputation of extraordinary power. "Hearing how god was with him every where as he came along," one awakened person later reported, "it solumnized my mind and put me in a trembling fear before he began to preach for he looked as if he was Cloathed with authority from the great god." Besides, he was an impassioned and fluent preacher.

Whitefield moved his hearers because excessive worldliness and resistance to the divinely sanctioned social order had already undermined their confidence. He told men what they already knew subconsciously: that they had broken the law, that impulses beyond their control drove them to resist divine authority, and that outward observance did not signify loving and willing submission. Confronted with truth, his listeners admitted that they were "vile, unworthy, loathsom" wretches. "Hearing him preach," a converted man said, "gave me a heart wound. By gods blessing my old foundation was broken up and i saw that my righteousness would not save me."

This confrontation of guilt, the first part of conversion, drove men to despair, but the revivalists did not leave their hearers there to suffer. By publicly identifying the sources of guilt and condemning them, the preachers also helped to heal the wounds they first inflicted. Converts were persuaded that by acknowledging and repudiating their old sins, they were no longer culpable. The reborn man was as joyful and loving when the process was completed as he was miserable at its start.

Converts were told, for instance, that wealth held no attractions for the saintly. The business of Christ's disciples, one preacher taught, "is not to hunt for Riches, and Honours, and Pleasures in this World, but to despise them, and deny themselves, and be ready to part with even all the lawful Pleasures and Comforts of the World at any Time." In a dramatic gesture expressing a deep impulse, Davenport had his followers gather the symbols of worldliness—wigs, cloaks, hoods, gowns, rings, necklaces—into a heap and burn them.

Converts responded eagerly, casting off with great relief their guilt-producing ambition. The pious David Brainerd spontaneously broke into poetry:

Farewell, vain world; my soul can bid
  Adieu:
My Saviour's taught me to abandon you.

After Isaac Backus was converted, he felt that he "should not be troubled any more with covetousness. The earth and all that is therein appeared to be vanity." His mother, also a convert, felt ready to "give up my name, estate, family, life and breath, freely to God." She would not relinquish her peace of soul "no, not to be in the most prosperous condition in temporal things that ever I was in." For many the choice was to enjoy peace of soul or prosperity. The pursuit of wealth and an easy conscience were incompatible. Jonathan Edwards noted a temptation among converts to go to extremes and "to neglect worldly affairs too much." They were unwilling to jeopardize their newfound peace by returning to worldliness.

The revivalists undermined the social order, the other main source of guilt, not by repudiating law and authority, but by denying them sanctifying power. Estrangement from rulers and the traditional patterns of life was demoralizing as long as the social order was considered divine, but Awakening preachers repeatedly denied that salvation came by following the law. No amount of covenant owning, Sabbath observance, moral rectitude, or obedience to rulers redeemed the soul. Praying, Bible study, and attendance at worship might result solely from worldly motives, to avoid disgrace or to pacify a guilty conscience. "Civility and external Acts belonging to Morality," one revivalist taught, "are no Part of the Essence of the Religion of Christ." Without grace, "tho men are adorn'd with many amiable qualities, and lead sober, regular, and to all appearance religious lives, yet they remain under the condemning sentence of the Law, and perish at last in a state of unsanctified nature." Reborn men were expected to practice moral virtues, but their salvation was not at stake. Obedience brought no assurance of grace, and disobedience did not entail damnation. Though still driven to resist rulers or to depart from the approved pattern of community life, believers in the revival message felt little guilt.

In this fashion the Awakening cleared the air of tensions. Men admitted that they had lusted after wealth, condemned themselves for it, and afterwards walked with lighter hearts. They ended the long struggle with the social order by denying its power to save and hence to condemn. After a century of Puritan rule, law and authority were burdens too heavy to

bear. All the anxiety they evoked was released when men grasped the idea that salvation came not by obedience to law.

In the converts' minds the escape from guilt was possible because of God's grace. The idea that the law could not condemn if God justified contained the deepest meaning of the Awakening. The rules and rulers, who governed both externally and in the conscience, had judged men and found them wanting until God out of His good grace suspended the sentence of damnation. The authority of Christ nullified earthly authority. Edwards said that converted men exulted that "God is self-sufficient, and infinitely above all dependence, and reigns over all." In the inward struggle with guilt, God's infinite power overruled the older authority that had stood over every Puritan conscience, judging and condemning.

In that moment of grace the Awakening worked its revolution. Henceforth a personal relation with God governed reborn men who were empowered by faith to obey the God they knew personally above the divine will manifest in earthly law and authority. It was characteristic of the converted to "renounce all confidence in everything but Christ, and build all their hopes of happiness upon this unalterable Rock of Ages." "I seemed to depend wholly on my dear Lord," Brainerd reported following his conversion. "God was so precious to my soul that the world with all its enjoyments was infinitely vile. I had no more value for the favor of men than for pebbles. The Lord was my ALL." Though the old authority was still a substantial force in every life, it did not structure the identity of converts as much as their own bright picture of God.

Under the government of this personal, internal authority, converts experienced a peace and joy unknown under earthly fathers and their old conscience. God's grace dissolved uncertainty and fear. The convert testified to the "sweet solace, rest and joy of soul," the image of God bestowed. "The thought of having so great, so glorious, and excellent a Being for his Father, his Friend, and his Home, sets his heart at Ease from all his anxious Fears and Distresses." The power to replace oppressive authority figures with faith in a loving God was the ultimate reason for the revivalists' success.

Thus, the men affected by the Awakening possessed a new character, cleansed of guilt and joyful in the awareness of divine favor. Unfortunately for the social order, however, their personal redemption did not save society. In making peace with themselves, converts inwardly revolted against the old law and authority, and, as time was to show, they would eventually refuse to submit to a social order alien to their new identity. Conservative suspicions of the revival were confirmed when reborn men set out to create a new society compatible with the vision opened in the Great Awakening.

The Great Awakening as Interpretative Fiction

Jon Butler

In the last half-century, the Great Awakening has assumed a major role in explaining the political and social evolution of prerevolutionary American society. Historians have argued, variously, that the Awakening severed intellectual and philosophical connections between America and Europe (Perry Miller), that it was a major vehicle of early lower-class protest (John C. Miller, Rhys Isaac, and Gary B. Nash), that it was a means by which New England Puritans became Yankees (Richard L. Bushman), that it was the first "intercolonial movement" to stir "the people of several colonies on a matter of common emotional concern" (Richard Hofstadter following William Warren Sweet), or that it involved "a rebirth of the localistic impulse" (Kenneth Lockridge). . . .

These claims for the significance of the Great Awakening come from more than specialists in the colonial period. They are a ubiquitous feature of American history survey texts, where the increased emphasis on social history has made these claims espe-cially useful in interpreting early American society to twentieth-century students. Virtually all texts treat the Great Awakening as a major watershed in the maturation of prerevolutionary American society. *The Great Republic* terms the Awakening "the greatest event in the history of religion in eighteenth-century America." *The National Experience* argues that the Awakening brought "religious experiences to thousands of people in every rank of society" and in every region. *The Essentials of American History* stresses how the Awakening "aroused a spirit of humanitarianism," "encouraged the notion of equal rights," and "stimulated feelings of democracy" even if its gains in church membership proved episodic. These texts and others describe the weakened position of the clergy produced by the Awakening as symptomatic of growing disrespect for all forms of authority in the colonies and as an important catalyst, even cause, of the American Revolution. The effect of these claims is astonishing. Buttressed by the standard lecture on the Awakening tucked into most survey courses, American undergraduates have been well trained to remember the Great Awakening because their instructors and texts have invested it with such significance.

Does the Great Awakening warrant such en-

Butler, Jon, "Enthusiasm Described and Decried: The Great Awakening as Interpretative Fiction," *Journal of American History,* 69 (Sept. 1982), 305–325. Copyright © 1982 Organization of American Historians. Reprinted by permission.

thusiasm? Its puzzling historiography suggests one caution. The Awakening has received surprisingly little systematic study and lacks even one comprehensive general history. The two studies . . . that might qualify as general histories actually are deeply centered in New England. They venture into the middle and southern colonies only occasionally and concentrate on intellectual themes to the exclusion of social history. . . . The result is that the general character of the Great Awakening lacks sustained, comprehensive study even while it benefits from thorough local examinations. The relationship between the Revolution and the Awakening is described in an equally peculiar manner. Alan Heimert's seminal 1966 study, *Religion and the American Mind from the Great Awakening to the Revolution,* despite fair and unfair criticism, has become that kind of influential work whose awesome reputation apparently discourages further pursuit of its subject. Instead, historians frequently allude to the positive relationship between the Awakening and the Revolution without probing the matter in a fresh, systematic way.

The gap between the enthusiasm of historians for the social and political significance of the Great Awakening and its slim, peculiar historiography raises two important issues. First, contemporaries never homogenized the eighteenth-century colonial religious revivals by labeling them "the Great Awakening." Although such words appear in Edwards's *Faithful Narrative of the Surprising Work of God,* Edwards used them alternately with other phrases, such as "general awakening," "great alteration," and "flourishing of religion," only to describe the Northampton revivals of 1734–35. He never capitalized them or gave them other special emphasis and never used the phrase "the Great Awakening" to evaluate all the prerevolutionary revivals. Rather, the first person to do so was the nineteenth-century historian and antiquarian Joseph Tracy, who used Edwards's otherwise unexceptional words as the title of his

famous 1842 book, *The Great Awakening.* Tellingly, however, Tracy's creation did not find immediate favor among American historians. Charles Hodge discussed the Presbyterian revivals in his *Constitutional History of the Presbyterian Church* without describing them as part of a "Great Awakening," while the influential Robert Baird refused even to treat the eighteenth-century revivals as discrete and important events, much less label them "the Great Awakening." Baird all but ignored these revivals in the chronological segments of his *Religion in America* and mentioned them elsewhere only by way of explaining the intellectual origins of the Unitarian movement, whose early leaders opposed revivals. Thus, not until the last half of the nineteenth century did "the Great Awakening" become a familiar feature of the American historical landscape.

Second, this particular label ought to be viewed with suspicion, not because a historian created it—historians legitimately make sense of the minutiae of the past by utilizing such devices—but because the label itself does serious injustice to the minutiae it orders. The label "the Great Awakening" distorts the extent, nature, and cohesion of the revivals that did exist in the eighteenth-century colonies; encourages unwarranted claims for their effects on colonial society; and exaggerates their influence on the coming and character of the American Revolution. If "the Great Awakening" is not quite an American Donation of Constantine, its appeal to historians seeking to explain the shaping and character of prerevolutionary American society gives it a political and intellectual power whose very subtlety requires a close inspection of its claims to truth.

How do historians describe "the Great Awakening"? Three points seem especially common. First, all but a few describe it as a Calvinist religious revival in which converts acknowledged their sinfulness without expecting salvation. These colonial converts thereby distinguished themselves from Englishmen caught up in contemporary Methodist revivals and from Americans involved in the so-called Second Great Awakening of the early national period, both of which imbibed Arminian principles that allowed humans to believe they might effect their own salvation in ways that John Calvin discounted.

*   *   *

"The Great Awakening" also is difficult to date. Seldom has an "event" of such magnitude had such amorphous beginnings and endings. In New England, historians agree, the revivals flourished principally between 1740 and 1743 and had largely ended by 1745, although a few scattered outbreaks of revivalism occurred there in the next decades. Establishing the beginning of the revivals has proved more difficult, however. Most historians settle for the year 1740 because it marks British iterant George Whitefield's first appearance in New England. But everyone acknowledges that earlier revivals underwrote Whitefield's enthusiastic reception there and involved remarkable numbers of colonists. Edwards counted thirty-two towns caught up in revivals in 1734–35 and noted that his own grandfather, Stoddard, had conducted no less than five "harvests" in Northampton before that, the earliest in the 1690s. Yet revivals in Virginia, the site of the most sustained such events in the southern colonies, did not emerge in significant numbers until the 1750s and did not peak until the 1760s. At the same time, they also continued into the revolutionary and early national periods in ways that make them difficult to separate from their predecessors.

Yet even if one were to argue that "the Great Awakening" persisted through most of the eighteenth century, it is obvious that revivals "swept" only some of the mainland colonies. They occurred in Massachusetts, Connecticut, Rhode Island, Pennsylvania, New Jersey, and Virginia with some frequency at least at some points between 1740 and 1770. But New Hampshire, Maryland, and Georgia witnessed few revivals in the same years, and revivals were only occasionally important in New York, Delaware, North Carolina, and South Carolina. The revivals also touched only certain segments of the population in the colonies where they occurred. The best example of the phenomenon is Pennsylvania. The revivals there had a sustained effect among English settlers only in Presbyterian churches where many of the laity and clergy also opposed them. The Baptists, who were so important to the New England revivals, paid little attention to them until the 1760s, and the colony's taciturn Quakers watched them in perplexed silence. Not even Germans imbibed them universally. At the same time that Benjamin Franklin was emptying his pockets in response to the preaching of Whitefield in Philadelphia—or at least claiming to do so—the residents of Germantown were steadily leaving their churches. . . .

Whitefield's revivals also exchanged notoriety for substance. Colonists responded to him as a charismatic performer, and he actually fell victim to the Billy Graham syndrome of modern times: his visits, however exciting, produced few permanent changes in local religious patterns. For example, his appearances in Charleston led to his well-known confrontation with Anglican Commissary Alexander Garden and to the suicide two years later of a distraught follower named Anne LeBrasseur. Yet they produced no new congregations in Charleston and had no documented effect on the general patterns of religious adherence elsewhere in the colony. The same was true in Philadelphia and New York City, despite the fact that Whitefield preached to enormous crowds in both places. Only Bostonians responded differently. Supporters organized in the late 1740s a new "awakened" congregation that reputedly met with considerable initial success, and opponents adopted a defensive posture exemplified in the writings of Charles Chauncy that profoundly affected New England intellectual life for two decades.

Historians also exaggerate the cohesion of

leadership in the revivals. They have accomplished this, in part, by overstressing the importance of Whitefield and Edwards. Whitefield's early charismatic influence later faded so that his appearances in the 1750s and 1760s had less impact even among evangelicals than they had in the 1740s. In addition, Whitefield's "leadership" was ethereal, at best, even before 1750. His principal early importance was to serve as a personal model of evangelical enterprise for ministers wishing to promote their own revivals of religion. Because he did little to organize and coordinate integrated colonial revivals, he also failed to exercise significant authority over the ministers he inspired.

The case against Edwards' leadership of the revivals is even clearer. Edwards defended the New England revivals from attack. But, like Whitefield, he never organized and coordinated revivals throughout the colonies or

even throughout New England. Since most of his major works were not printed in his lifetime, even his intellectual leadership in American theology occurred in the century after his death. Whitefield's lack of knowledge about Edwards on his first tour of America in 1739–40 is especially telling on this point. Edwards' name does not appear in Whitefield's journal prior to the latter's visit to Northampton in 1740, and Whitefield did not make the visit until Edwards had invited him to do so. Whitefield certainly knew of Edwards and the 1734–35 Northampton revival but associated the town mainly with the pastorate of Edwards' grandfather Stoddard. As Whitefield described the visit in his journal: "After a little refreshment, we crossed the ferry to Northampton, where no less than three hundred souls were saved about five years ago. Their pastor's name is Edwards, successor and grandson to the great

Revivals of religion in the 1740s stimulated the formation of more than two hundred new congregations.

Stoddard, whose memory will be always precious to my soul, and whose books entitled 'A Guide to Christ,' and 'Safety of Appearing in Christ's Righteousness,' I would recommend to all."

What were the effects of the prerevolutionary revivals of religion? The claims for their religious and secular impact need pruning too. One area of concern involves the relationship between the revivals and the rise of the Dissenting denominations in the colonies. Denomination building was intimately linked to the revivals in New England. There, as C. C. Goen has demonstrated, the revivals of the 1740s stimulated formation of over two hundred new congregations and several new denominations. This was accomplished mainly through a negative process called "Separatism," which split existing Congregationalist and Baptist churches along prorevival and antirevival lines. But Separatism was of no special consequence in increasing the number of Dissenters farther south. Presbyterians, Baptists, and, later, Methodists gained strength from former Anglicans who left their state-supported churches, but they won far more recruits among colonists who claimed no previous congregational membership.

Still, two points are important in assessing the importance of revivals to the expansion of the Dissenting denominations in the colonies. First, revivalism never was the key to the expansion of the colonial churches. Presbyterianism expanded as rapidly in the middle colonies between 1710 and 1740 as between 1740 and 1770. Revivalism scarcely produced the remarkable growth that the Church of England experienced in the eighteenth century unless, of course, it won the favor of colonists who opposed revivals as fiercely as did its leaders. . . .

Second, the expansion of the leading evangelical denominations, Presbyterians and Baptists, can be traced to many causes, not just revivalism or "the Great Awakening." The growth of the colonial population from fewer than three hundred thousand in 1700 to over two million in 1770 made the expansion of even the most modestly active denominations highly likely. This was especially true because so many new colonists did not settle in established communities but in new communities that lacked religious institutions. As Timothy L. Smith has written of seventeenth-century settlements, the new eighteenth-century settlements welcomed congregations as much for the social functions they performed as for their religious functions. Some of the denominations reaped the legacy of Old World religious ties among new colonists, and others benefited from local anti-Anglican sentiment, especially in the Virginia and Carolina backcountry. As a result, evangelical organizers formed many congregations in the middle and southern colonies without resorting to revivals at all. The first Presbyterian congregation in Hanover County, Virginia, organized by Samuel Blair and William Tennent, Jr., in 1746, rested on an indigenous lay critique of Anglican theology that had turned residents to the works of Martin Luther, and after the campaign by Blair and Tennet, the congregation allied itself with the Presbyterian denomination rather than with simple revivalism.

The revivals democratized relations between ministers and the laity only in minimal ways. A significant number of New England ministers changed their preaching styles as a result of the 1740 revivals. Heimert quotes Isaac Backus on the willingness of evangelicals to use sermons to " 'insinuate themselves into the affections' of the people" and notes how opponents of the revivals like Chauncey nonetheless struggled to incorporate emotion and "sentiment" into their sermons after 1740. Yet revivalists and evangelicals continued to draw sharp distinctions between rights of ministers and the duties of the laity. Edwards did so in a careful, sophisticated way in *Some Thoughts concerning the Present Revival of Religion in New England.* Although he noted that "disputing, jangling, and contention" surrounded "lay exhorting," he agreed that "some exhorting is a Christian duty." But he quickly moved to a strong defense of ministerial prerogatives, which he introduced with the proposition that "the Common people in exhorting one another ought not to clothe themselves with the like authority, with that which is proper for ministers." Gilbert Tennent was less cautious. In his 1740 sermon *The Danger of an Unconverted Ministry,* he bitterly attacked "Pharisee-shepherds" and "Pharisee-teachers" whose preaching was frequently as "unedifying" as their personal lives. But Gilbert Tennent never attacked the ministry itself. Rather, he argued, for the necessity of a *converted* ministry precisely because he believed that only preaching brought men and women to Christ and that only ordained ministers could preach. Thus, in both 1742 and 1757, he thundered against lay preachers. They were "of dreadful consequence to the Church's peace and soundness in principle. . . . [F]or Ignorant Young Converts to take upon them authoritatively to Instruct and Exhort publickly tends to introduce the greatest Errors and the greatest anarchy and confusion."

*   *   *

Did itinerants challenge this ministerial hegemony?

Actually, itinerancy produced few changes in colonial American society and religion and is frequently misunderstood. Although some itinerants lacked institutionally based formal educations, none are known to have been illiterate. The most famous itinerant of the century, Whitefield, took an Oxford degree in 1736, and the most infamous, Davenport, stood at the top of his class at Yale in 1732. Itinerants usually bypassed the local church only when its minister opposed them; when the minister was hospitable, the itinerants preached in the church building. One reason itinerants eschewed the coercive instruments of the state was that they never possessed them before the Revolution.

But after the Revolution the denominations they represented sought and received special favors from the new state governments, especially concerning incorporation, and won the passage of coercive legislation regarding mortality and outlawing blasphemy. Finally, itinerants seldom ventured into the colonial countryside "clothed only with spiritual authority." Instead, itinerants acknowledged the continuing importance of deference and hierarchy in colonial society by stressing denominational approbation for their work. Virtually all of them wore the protective shield of ordination—the major exceptions are a few laymen who itinerated in New England in the early 1740s and about whom virtually nothing is known—and nearly all of them could point to denominational sponsorship. Even Virginia's aggressive Samuel Davies defended himself to the Bishop of London, Gov. William Gooch, and the sometimes suspicious backcountry settlers to whom he preached by pointing to his ordination and sponsorship by the Presbytery of New Castle. Only Davenport ventured into the countryside with little more than the spirit (and his Yale degree) to protect him. But only Davenport was judged by a court to have been mentally unstable.

In this context, it is not surprising that the eighteenth-century revivals of religion failed to bring significant new power—democracy—to the laity in the congregations. Although Gilbert Tennent argued that the laity had an obligation to abandon unconverted, unedifying ministers in favor of converted ones, it is not possible to demonstrate that the revivals increased the traditional powers that laymen previously possessed or brought them new ones. Congregations throughout the colonies had long exercised considerable power over their ministers through their effective control of church spending and fund raising as well as through the laity's ability simply to stop attending church services at all. As examples, witness alone the well-known seventeenth-century disputes between ministers and their listeners in

Sudbury and Salem Village in Massachusetts and the complaints against ministers brought by the laity to the Presbytery of Philadelphia between 1706 and 1740. Yet, although the revivals should have increased this lay willingness to complain about ministerial failings, no historian ever has demonstrated systematically that this ever happened.

Nor did the revivals change the structure of authority within the denominations. New England Congregationalists retained the right of individual congregations to fire ministers, as when Northampton dismissed Edwards in 1750. But in both the seventeenth and eighteenth centuries, these congregations seldom acted alone. Instead, they nearly always consulted extensively with committees of ordained ministers when firing as well as when hiring ministers. In the middle colonies, however, neither the prorevival Synod of New York nor the antirevival Synod of Philadelphia tolerated such independence in congregations whether in theory or in practice. In both synods, unhappy congregations had to convince special committees appointed by the synods and composed exclusively of ministers that the performance of a fellow cleric was sufficiently dismal to warrant his dismissal. Congregations that acted independently in such matters quickly found themselves censured, and they usually lost the aid of both synods in finding and installing new ministers.

Did the revivals stir lower-class discontent, increase participation in politics, and promote democracy in society generally if not in the congregations? Even in New England the answer is, at best, equivocal. Historians have laid to rest John C. Miller's powerfully stated argument of the 1930s that the revivals were, in good part, lower-class protests against dominant town elites. The revivals indeed complicated local politics because they introduced new sources of potential and real conflict into the towns. New England towns accustomed to containing tensions inside a single congregation before 1730 sometimes had to deal with

tensions within and between as many as three or four congregations after 1730. Of course, not all of these religious groups were produced by the revivals, and . . . some towns never tolerated the new dissidents and used the "warning out" system to eject them. Stil, even where it existed, tumult should not be confused with democracy. Social class, education, and wealth remained as important after 1730 in choosing town and church officers as they had been before 1730. . . .

Recently, however, the specter of lower-class political agitation rampaging through other colonies disguised as revivals of religion has been raised in Nash's massive study of the northern colonial port cities and in Isaac's work on prerevolutionary Virginia. But in direct if quite different ways, both historians demonstrate the numerous difficulties of linking lower-class protest and political radicalism with "the Great Awakening." Nash notes that the link between lower-class political protest and revivalism was strongest in Boston. There, a popular party closely associated with the revivals attacked the city's propertied elite through the election process while the revivals prospered in the early 1740s. But the unfortunate lack of even a single tax list for the period and the lack of records from either the political dissidents or the revival congregations make it impossible to describe the social composition of either group with precision, much less establish firm patterns of interrelatedness. As a result, historians are forced to accept the nightmares of the antirevivalist Chauncy and the fulminations of the *Boston Evening Post* as accurate descriptions of all the agitators' religious and political principles. . . .

Isaac's recent work on Virginia demonstrates that the Baptist revival movement there in the 1760s and 1770s shattered the old Anglican-aristocratic alliance so thoroughly that its political importance hardly can be questioned. But two points are especially significant in assessing the relationship of Isaac's work to the problem of "the Great Awakening." First, Isaac nowhere argues that the Virginia revivals demonstrate either the power or even the existence of a broadly based revival movement in the prerevolutionary colonies. Indeed, as he describes the process, Virginia's Baptists succeeded out of a nearly unique ability to confront a political and religious aristocracy that also was virtually unique in the colonies. Second, we do not yet know how democratic and egalitarian these Baptists were within their own ranks. For example, we do not know if poor, uneducated Baptists became elders and preachers as frequently as did richer, better-educated Baptists. Nor do we know how judiciously Baptists governed non-Baptists in the southside and backcountry counties where they were strong but where many settlers eschewed any denominational affiliation.

*   *   *

What, then, of the relationship between the revivals and the American Revolution? Obviously, the revivals provided little focus for intercolonial unity in the way some historians have described. They appeared too erratically in too few colonies under too many different auspices to make such generalizations appropriate. The eighteenth-century colonial wars are more appropriate candidates for the honor. They raised significant legislative opposition to the crown in many colonies and cost many colonists their lives, especially in the last and most "successful" contest, the French and Indian War. Nor is it possible to demonstrate that specific congregations and denominations associated with the revivals originated anti-British protest that became uniquely important to the Revolution. . . . The connection is equally difficult to make with denominations. Connecticut New Lights and Pennsylvania Presbyterians played important roles in the colonial protests, but their activity does not, in itself, link revivals to the Revolution in any important way. First, the revivals in both places occurred a quarter of a century

before the Revolution began. Second, neither group expanded in the 1740s or sustained its membership later exclusively because of the revivals. Third, the British probably angered laymen of both groups because the latter were important politicians rather than because they were New Lights and Presbyterians. Or, put another way, they were political leaders who happened to be New Lights and Presbyterians rather than Presbyterians and New Lights who happened to be politicians.

*   *   *

What, then, ought we to say about the revivals of religion in prerevolutionary America? The most important suggestion is the most drastic. Historians should abandon the term "the Great Awakening" because it distorts the character of eighteenth-century American religious life and misinterprets its relationship to prerevolutionary American society and politics. In religion it is a deus ex machina that falsely homogenizes the heterogeneous; in politics it falsely unites the colonies in slick preparation for the Revolution. Instead, a four-part model of the eighteenth-century colonial revivals will highlight their common features, underscore important differences, and help us assess their real significance.

First, with one exception, the prerevolutionary revivals should be understood primarily as regional events that occurred in only half the colonies. Revivals occurred intermittently in New England between 1690 and 1745 but became especially common between 1735 and 1745. They were uniformly Calvinist and produced more significant local political ramifications—even if they did not democratize New England—than other colonial revivals except those in Virginia. Revivals in the middle colonies occurred primarily between 1740 and 1760. They had remarkably eclectic theological origins, bypassed large numbers of settlers, were especially weak in New York, and produced few demonstrable political and social changes. Revivals in the southern colonies did not occur in significant numbers until the 1750s, when they were limited largely to Virginia, missed Maryland almost entirely, and did not occur with any regularity in the Carolinas until well after 1760. Virginia's Baptist revivalists stimulated major political and social changes in the colony, but the secular importance of the other revivals has been exaggerated. A fourth set of revivals, and the exception to the regional pattern outlined here, accompanied the preaching tours of the Anglican itinerant Whitefield. These tours frequently intersected with the regional revivals in progress at different times in New England, the middle colonies, and some parts of the southern colonies, but even then the fit was imperfect. Whitefield's tours produced some changes in ministerial speaking styles but few permanent alterations in institutional patterns of religion, although his personal charisma supported no less than seven tours of the colonies between 1740 and his death in Newburyport, Massachusetts, in 1770.

Second, the prerevolutionary revivals occurred in the colonial backwaters of western society where they were part of a long-term pattern of erratic movements for spiritual renewal and revival that had long characterized western Christianity and Protestantism since its birth two centuries earlier. Thus, their theological origins were international and diverse rather than narrowly Calvinist and uniquely American. Calvinism was important in some revivals, but Arminianism and Pietism supported others. This theological heterogeneity also makes it impossible to isolate a single overwhelmingly important cause of the revivals. Instead, they appear to have arisen when three circumstances were present—internal demands for renewal in different international Christian communities, charismatic preachers, and special, often unique, local circumstances that made communities receptive to elevated religious rhetoric.

Third, the revivals had modest effects on colonial religion. This is not to say that they were "conservative" because they did not always uphold the traditional religious order. But they were never radical, whatever their critics claimed. For example, the revivals reinforced ministerial rather than lay authority even as they altered some clergymen's perceptions of their tasks and methods. They also stimulated the demand for organization, order, and authority in the evangelical denominations. Presbyterian "New Lights" repudiated the conservative Synod of Philadelphia because its discipline was too weak, not too strong, and demanded tougher standards for ordination and subsequent service. After 1760, when Presbyterians and Baptists utilized revivalism as part of their campaigns for denominational expansion, they only increased their stress on central denominational organization and authority.

Indeed, the best test of the benign character of the revivals is to take up the challenge of contemporaries who linked them to outbreaks of "enthusiasm" in Europe. In making these charges, the two leading antirevivalists in the colonies, Garden of Charleston and Chauncy of Boston, specifically compared the colonial revivals with those of the infamous "French Prophets" of London, exiled Huguenots who were active in the city between 1706 and about 1730. The French Prophets predicted the downfall of English politicians, raised followers from the dead, and used women extensively as leaders to prophesy and preach. By comparison, the American revivalists were indeed "conservative." They prophesied only about the millennium, not about local politicans, and described only the necessity, not the certainty, of Salvation. What is most important is that they eschewed radical change in the position of women in the churches. True, women experienced dramatic conversions, some of the earliest being described vividly by Edwards. But, they preached only irregularly, rarely prophesied, and certainly never led congregations, denominations, or sects in a way that could remotely approach their status among the French Prophets.

Fourth, the link between the revivals and the American Revolution is virtually nonexistent. The relationship between prerevolutionary political change and the revivals is weak everywhere except in Virginia, where the Baptist revivals indeed shattered the exclusive, century-old Anglican hold on organized religious activity and politics in the colony. But, their importance to the Revolution is weakened by the fact that so many members of Virginia's Anglican aristocracy also led the Revolution. In other colonies the revivals furnished little revolutionary rhetoric, including even millennialist thought, that was not available from other sources and provided no unique organizational mechanisms for anti-British protest activity. They may have been of some importance in helping colonists make moral judgments about eighteenth-century English politics, though colonists unconnected to the revivals made these judgments as well.

In the main, then, the revivals of religion in eighteenth-century America emerge as nearly perfect mirrors of a regionalized, provincial society. They arose erratically in different times and places across a century from the 1690s down to the time of the Revolution. Calvinism underlay some of them, Pietism and Arminianism others. Their leadership was local and, at best, regional, and they helped reinforce—but were not the key to—the proliferation and expansion of still-regional Protestant denominations in the colonies. As such, they created no intercolonial religious institutions and fostered no significant experiential unity in the colonies. Their social and political effects were minimal and usually local, although they could traumatize communities in which they upset, if only temporarily, familiar patterns of worship and social behavior. But the congregations they occasionally produced usually blended into the traditional social system, and the revivals abated without shattering its structure. Thus, the revivals of religion in prerevolutionary America seldom became proto-revolutionary, and they failed to change the timing, causes, or effects of the Revolution in any significant way.

Of course, it is awkward to write about the eighteenth-century revivals of religion in America as erratic, heterogeneous, and politically benign. All of us have walked too long in the company of Tracy's "Great Awakening" to make our journey into the colonial past without it anything but frightening. But as Chauncy wrote of the Whitefield revivals, perhaps now it is time for historians "to see that Things have been carried too far, and that the Hazard is great . . . lest we should be over-run with *Enthusiasm*."

Part Five

The Origins and Nature of the American Revolution

Wars present historians with some of the most difficult problems to solve, because they are invariably embarked upon by the protaganists as a last resort after a long-term relationship or an extended process of negotiation has collapsed. As a result, any explanation of why military conflicts occurred requires historians to examine a pattern of events whose nature is complex and whose meaning can only be discovered by going far back in time.

The American war for independence from the British presents further complications because for Americans it is an episode in their history that is pervaded with patriotic sentiment and national self-justification. The historian has, therefore, to probe beyond these strong feelings in order to discover the actual events and their causes, rather than to accept what people *want* to think occurred.

Although historians have, for the most part, avoided taking sides, their writings on the subject have fallen into broad categories that correspond to the perspectives of the two combatants. The first approach is America-centered, whereas the second takes a broader, transatlantic view. The latter vantage point, labeled the "Imperial" interpretation, does not necessarily espouse the British position; rather, it attempts to understand the conflict as emerging from a breakdown in the relationship between Britain and its North American colonies. Invariably, it considers the problems of the 1760s and 1770s as part of a larger difficulty Britain was experiencing in the administration of its far-flung overseas possessions, which included Canada, India, and the West Indies, as well as several other outposts. Misunderstandings, conflicting interests and priorities, and simple mismanagement are cited as causal factors leading to the rupture with the North American colonies.

By contrast, historians who adopt an America-centered approach focus on how American colonists perceived the relationship with Britain, and particularly emphasize the changes in the colonists' attitudes toward Britain. After fighting with their British fellow-countrymen in a war against the French in the early 1760s, the colonists found themselves, just a decade later, vowing resistance to British rule and then actively seeking independence. During this process, there emerged among the colonists an awareness that they had a separate identity as Americans, with different interests and a different destiny. Because this change in the colonists' self-perception is thought to be critical in bringing about the separation, some historians conclude that this is the ultimate explanation of the war in America. This approach has been called the Whig interpretation because of its emphasis on the course pursued by the rebels who referred to themselves as Whigs, in contrast to the Tories, as the loyalists were called.

Within this America-centered perspective, there is another variant, often described as the Progressive school, because historians living in the early twentieth-century Progressive Era were those who first introduced it. Rather than concentrate on the dispute with Britain, these historians draw attention to differences of opinion within the colonies, not just between Whigs and Tories, but between the political and economic elite in America and those elements in the society that for various reasons disputed their authority and power. In other words, American society was experiencing internal conflict, despite its leaders' attempt to establish a united front against the threat from Britain.

These challenges to the hegemony of the elite arose from common people living and working in the cities as well as from settlers in the backcountry of many of the colonies who resented the dominance of the coastal areas. As Carl Becker, one of the Progressive historians, aptly describes the situation, there was not only a struggle with the British over "home rule," but simultaneously a dispute over "who should rule at home." Although historians with this point of view do not offer a distinctive explanation of why the colonists broke with Britain, they do suggest that the conflict had another dimension. In a sense, it had a second front. Rather than being merely a war for independence, the American Revolution contained within it an internal social conflict with revolutionary implications.

The selections for this topic represent these three divergent viewpoints. To challenge the reader, they are presented in the order that they were published and not in accord with the sequence outlined above. Bernard Bailyn's book on the coming of the Revolution, called *The Ideological Origins of the American Revolution* (1967), has been perhaps the most influential work on the subject in the past generation. In this book, Professor Bailyn of Harvard University analyzes the pamphlets and propaganda issued by the intellectual spokesmen of the American cause. This selection is abridged from one of the chapters entitled "The Logic of Rebellion." Gary Nash of the University of California at Los Angeles published an important study of the major American seaboard cities during the Revolutionary era, called *The Urban Crucible: Social Change, Political Consciousness, and the Origins of the American Revolution* (1979). The article that is presented here is a piece he wrote while working on the book, and it is a preview of some of the themes pursued in it. Lastly, there is the article by Jack Greene of Johns Hopkins University, who is also a major historian of the American Revolution. His piece examines the dramatic shift in Anglo-American relations in the wake of the Seven Years' War, also known as the French and Indian War.

QUESTIONS TO CONSIDER

1. Why, in Bailyn's view, did the American colonists rebel?

2. In what ways does Nash's approach to and understanding of the coming of the American Revolution differ from Bailyn's?

3. Obviously Greene is not suggesting that the Seven Years' War caused the American Revolution. But what exactly is its role, as he sees it, in bringing on the dispute with Britain?

The Seven Years' War and the American Revolution

Jack P. Greene

I

That there was a causal connection between the Seven Years' War and the American Revolution has been so widely assumed as to become a scholarly orthodoxy. The close temporal relationship between the formal conclusion of the war in 1763 and the Stamp Act crisis in 1764–66, the first dramatic episode in the chain of events that would, a decade later, lead to separation, immediately raises the question of whether either the *experience* or the *outcome* of the war affected the events of the mid-1760s and beyond. For purposes of analysis, this question must be broken down into two parts. First, in what ways did the war contribute to those metropolitan actions that touched off the conflict? Second, how did the war affect the colonial response to those actions? Much scholarly energy has been devoted to both of these questions, albeit much of that energy has been animated by a desire to fix responsibility for inaugurating the dispute on one side of the Atlantic or the other. But no one has yet produced the comprehensive, systematic, and unpassionate analysis necessary

to enable us to specify fully and persuasively the precise causal relationship between the Seven Years' War and the American Revolution. What follows is a brief and preliminary effort toward that objective.

II

Perhaps the single most important result of the war in terms of the metropolitan-colonial relationship was the vivid enhancement of awareness on both sides of the Atlantic of the crucial significance of the colonies to Britain both economically and strategically. Such an awareness was scarcely new and had indeed been powerfully manifest in the heightened concern with the colonies exhibited by metropolitan officials after 1748. But the decision to undertake a major national effort to protect British interests in America and the long and expensive war that followed inevitably contributed to intensify both metropolitan and colonial sensitivities to the importance of America for Britain. Thereafter, no one who was 'the least acquainted' with either the colonies 'or the concerns of the nation in them' could possibly doubt that they 'must absolutely be of the utmost conciquence to the defence, wellfare & happiness of These Kindoms'. 'To be convinced of their importance at first sight', one had only to look at the 'sum total of the yearly produce of our

Reprinted by permission from the January 1980 issue of *Journal of Imperial & Commonwealth History* published by Frank Cass and Company Limited, 11 Gainsborough Road, London E11, England. Copyright © 1980 Frank Cass & Co. Ltd.

plantations'. The sum, 'upon a moderate computation', amounted to between five and six million pounds sterling per annum, in addition to which the colonists employed between forty and fifty thousand seamen and nearly two thousand ships each year. To be sure, the colonial trade amounted to no more than '*one third* Part' of Britain's foreign commerce, but the mere fact that all other branches of foreign trade could be obstructed while the colonial trade 'must still continue soley our Own' made it 'of greater advantage to us than all other Foreign Trades we are in possession of.'

The truth of this proposition seemed to be evident in both the growing wealth and international status of Britain and the obvious envy of its colonial possessions by its European rivals. 'Every body knows', said the New York lawyer William Smith, Jr., after the war, that the population, wealth, and power of Britain had been 'vastly inhanced since the Discovery of the New World'. Simple comparisons 'of the number and force of our present fleets, with our fleet in Queen Elizabeth's time before we had colonies', of 'the antient with the present state of our towns and ports on our western coast, Manchester, Liverpool, Kendal, Lancaster, Glasgow, and the countries round them, that trade with and manufacture for our colonies, not to mention Leeds, Halifax, Sheffield and Birmingham', or of the difference 'in the numbers of people, buildings, rents and the value of land' within living memory, wrote Benjamin Franklin, were sufficient to indicate that to a very significant degree it had been the colonies that had made 'this nation both prosperous at home, and considerable abroad'. To what else other than its colonies could be attributed Britain's extraordinary rise from 'the third or fourth Place in the Scale of *European* Powers' to 'a Level with the most Mighty in Europe'? What else would Britain's 'most daingerous Rivalls in Trade, and most implacable Enemies the French' make 'every effort in their power to wrest this inestimable Fountain of wealth & strength out of our hands'?

More and more during the war, commentators asserted that the American colonies had obviously 'become a great source of that wealth, by which this nation maintains itself, and is respected by others'. If they were indeed 'the great support, not only of the trade and commerce, but even of the safety and defence of Britain itself', then it followed that without them 'the people in Britain would make but a poor figure, if they could even subsist as an independent nation'. 'Every body is agreed', said one observer, that 'our existence as a . . . commercial and independent Nation' as well as 'a free and happy people' depended upon America: 'by trade we do, and must, if at all, subsist; without it we can have no wealth; and without wealth we can have no power; as without power we can have no liberty'. The chain of logic was inexorable: trade was the very essence of both British greatness and British liberty, and the great extent to which that trade depended upon 'our dominions in *America*' necessarily meant that for Britain America was 'an object of such magnitude as' could never 'be forgot[ten] or neglected'.

If the war stimulated the emergence of a heightened realisation of the 'Infinite Advantage our American Collonys are of to these Kingdoms', it also focused attention more directly than ever before upon a welter of problems that seemed to point to both the structural weakness of the empire and the fragility of metropolitan authority in the colonies. As Josiah Tucker had predicted at the very beginning of hostilities, the war turned out to be a rich 'Harvest for Complaints'. Foremost among the problems revealed by the war was the difficulty of mobilising the military potential of the colonies. At best, the system of royal requisitions to individual colonies that was used throughout the war to supplement the men and supplies sent from Britain in ever larger numbers beginning in 1756 seemed to yield but spotty returns. Many colonies voted less than requested or encumbered appropriations with annoying restrictions, while a few failed to give any assistance at all and even refused quarters to metropolitan troops. To British commanders in the colonies, such behaviour was extraordinarily vexatious, and in their strident reports to London authorities they made few distinctions between those colonies that had and those that had not cooperated with them. 'The delays we meet with, in carrying on the Service, from *every* parts of this Country, are immense', the Commander-in-Chief, Lord Loudoun, complained to his superior, Cumberland, in August 1756. 'In Place of Aid to the Service every impediment, that it is possible to invent', he wrote to Halifax, head of the Board of Trade, a few months later, 'is thrown in the Way'. Colonial legislators 'assumed to themselves, what they call Rights and Priviledges, totally unknown in the Mother Country . . . for no purpose', it seemed to Loudoun, 'but to screen them, from giving any Aid, of any sort, for carrying on, the Service, and refusing us Quarters'. Reports of such self-interested behaviour reached London with sufficient frequency as to become commonplace even outside official government circles.

The great extent to which colonial legislators had already managed to undermine metropolitan authority by their assumption of such extravagant rights and privileges was a second and, from a long-range point of view, potentially even more worrying problem underscored for London authorities by the experience of the war. It was a rare governor who, like Charles Pinfold of Barbados, could at any time during the war write home that 'Every thing proposed to me in England has been carried into Execution and with an Unanimity that exceeded the Example of former times'. Indeed, the common report was precisely the opposite. 'At present I have His Majesties Commission and Instructions for my Government, and direction, in all public Concerns', lamented Benning Wentworth from New Hampshire, 'but from the incroachments Made by the Assembly, both are in a manner Rendered useless'. 'Such is the defective State of the Govern-

ments', echoed Thomas Pownall of Massachusetts, 'that there can not on the Continent be produced an instance of the Governors being able to carry his Majesty's Instructions into Execution where the People have disputed them'. Even in the new and more closely supervised colonies of Georgia and Nova Scotia, the legislatures were 'industriously attempting to usurp the same power[s]' as those already exercised with such 'great Licence' by their counterparts in the older colonies. Everywhere in the colonies, the '*leading* People' appeared to raise disputes with metropolitan representatives merely 'to have a merit with the others, by defending their Liberties, as they call them'. So long had the colonists thus been 'suffered to riot in privileges' that royal governors had become little more than '*Cyphers*', 'Pompous Titled Nothing[s]' of very little use "to those who employ[ed]" them, while metropolitan authority had obviously been by far 'already too much weakened'.

The same conclusion could be drawn from mounting evidence of colonial disregard for metropolitan economic regulations. For several decades prior to the war, complaints had filtered into London of a growing 'illicit trade which all the colonies have run more or less into.' In New York and New England and particularly in Rhode Island, it was charged, there was 'scarce a man in all that country who' was 'not concerned in the smuggling trade' in Dutch, French, and French Caribbean goods, a trade, moreover, that had long since been 'sanctified with the name of *naturalising* foreign goods'. What had seemed so patently 'destructive of the national interests' of Britain in peacetime came to appear totally pernicious—and self-serving—during the war, which brought a marked increase in reports of colonial violations of the navigation acts. Military and naval commanders, royal governors, metropolitan customs officials: all described a brisk trade throughout the war not only with the neutral Dutch but with the enemy French in the West Indies, either indirectly by way of neutral ports or directly under the guise of flags of truce to exchange prisoners of war. The result was that the French islands were 'provided with a Sufficient Stock of provisions' and everything else they needed 'in spite of all the Regulations'. Metropolitan efforts to curtail this trade were largely ineffective, and at the end of the war, one customs official estimated that smuggled molasses from the French West Indies into the northern colonies had increased 500 percent during the war, while another observer asserted that nearly 90 percent of the tea consumed in the colonies was being smuggled from the Netherlands. In the face of such reports few in Britain could any longer doubt by 1763 that 'a spirit of Illicit trade' prevailed 'more or less throughout the Continent[al]' colonies, in America and that there was 'almost a universal desire in the People [there] to carry on a trade with foreigners not only in America but in Europe'.

But these were only the most flagrant examples by which the colonists acted 'wholly in conformity to their own selfish or rapacious views', and obstinately refused to do what was 'necessary for the good of the whole' during the war. Unscrupulous traders and land developers cheated Indians in utter disregard for either fairness or the safety of the older settlements and thus created a highly unfavourable disposition among the Indians to the 'British Interest'. Colonial assemblies used metropolitan needs for military assistance to extract still further privileges from Crown officials and, in many cases, financed their war contributions by issuing massive amounts of paper currency, at least some of which was so inadequately secured as to depreciate rapidly and thereby to exacerbate fears among metropolitan mercantile interests that the colonists would seek to pay their debts in depreciated currency. In one area after another during the war, the colonists thus behaved in ways that seemed to make it perfectly obvious that they had but slight regard for either the interests or the authority of the metropolis.

At least since the beginning of the century, metropolitan officials and traders had exhibited what seemed to Americans an 'unnatural Suspicion' that the colonies would 'one Time or other' rebel and throw 'off their dependence on Britain'. Increasingly evident in the decade just prior to the war, such fears, Americans insisted, were both 'groundless and chimerical'. But colonial behaviour during the war with its many manifestations of a 'general disposition to independence' only seemed to belie their protestations and to provide growing evidence that they would seek 'a Dissolution' of the empire at the earliest opportunity. Not just the experience but the result of the war operated to heighten metropolitan fears of colonial independence. For it had been frequently argued by students of colonial affairs both before and during the war that only 'their apprehensions of the French' and their dependence upon Britain for protection kept the colonists 'in awe' and prevented their 'connection . . . with their mother country from being quite broken off'. To 'drive the French out of all N. America', Josiah Tucker had declared in 1755, 'would be the most fatal Step We could take'. By eliminating the one certain 'guarantee for the[ir] good behavior' towards and 'dependence on their mother country', such a move, it was widely suggested, would both further 'their love of independence' and place 'them [entirely] above controul' by Britain, which they would subsequently ignore, rival, and perhaps even destroy.

*　　*　　*

By the concluding years of the war, the question was no longer whether imperial administration would be reformed at the conclusion of the war but how. Many advocates of reform counselled a mild approach. Arguing that measures specifically calculated to 'cement friendships on both sides' would 'be of more lasting benefit to both countries, than all the armies that Britain can send thither', they contended that the most effective way to secure the dependence of the colonies was 'by promoting . . . their welfare, . . . instead of checking their growth, or laying them under any other inconvenience', and warned against all 'violent innovations'. But the tide of metropolitan sentiment was running powerfully in a contrary direction. There was no desire either to oppress or stifle the colonies. 'The increase in our Colonies', said Secretary of the Treasury Charles Jenkinson in early 1765, 'is certainly what we wish', and most people seem to have recognised with Thomas Whateley that the 'Mother Country would suffer, if she tyrannized over her Colonies'. Yet, it was widely agreed, as [the Marquis of] Bute [the chief personal adviser to the King] reportedly observed immediately after the Treaty of Paris in 1763, both that it was essential 'to bring our Old Colonies into order' and that the best way to accomplish that end was through the imposition of stricter controls. Thenceforth, in Jenkinson's words, the colonies were to be administered 'in such a manner as will keep them useful to the Mother Country'.

Thus, as Bernhard Knollenberg has shown, virtually every metropolitan measure undertaken in reference to the colonies not simply from 1763 but from the defeat of the French in Canada in 1759 was calculated to restrict their scope for economic and political activity. In even more detail, Thomas C. Barrow has demonstrated to what a great extent the new trade regulations of 1763–64, including the use of the navy and royal vice-admiralty courts as agencies of enforcement, an increase in the size of the customs establishment, and the introduction of a residence requirement for customs officials were designed not only to produce a revenue but to destroy 'the long-continued commercial independence of the American colonies' by eliminating all except certain specifically permitted commerce between them and Europe and making it more expensive to trade with foreign islands in the Caribbean. Similarly, the decision to exercise

caution in the authorisation of settlement to the west of the Appalachians was intended not simply to prevent clashes between Europeans and Indians or to establish a foundation for better relations with the Indians but also, as former Georgia governor Henry Ellis remarked, to prevent settlers from 'planting themselves in the Heart of America, out of the reach of Government, and where, from the great Difficulty of procuring European Commodities, they would be compelled to commence Manufacturs to the infinite prejudice of Britain', a possibility that had worried observers since before the war.

In the civil sphere, metropolitan officials were less systematic and more tentative. They revealed no disposition to try to do away with representative institutions in the colonies. They were willing to entertain a variety of proposals for the extensive 'amendment of Government' in the colonies by act of Parliament, including the establishment of a single governor general for the colonies together with an annual congress of deputies from each colony, the resumption by the Crown of the charters of Connecticut and Rhode Island, and the creation of a permanent revenue to put royal governors 'upon a more respectable and independent Footing'. But, although the Board of Trade favoured the last two of these proposals, metropolitan officials did not immediately act upon any of them. Perhaps because of the complexity of the problem, they eschewed, for the time being at least, any effort to undertake the comprehensive alteration of the colonial constitutions recommended by many. But in dealing with the separate colonies after 1759, they rarely failed to act upon the conclusions, first reached by the Board of Trade between 1748 and 1756 and further reinforced by the experience of the war, that the colonies were 'not sufficiently obedient' and, as Granville told Franklin in 1759, had 'too many and too great Privileges; and that it' was 'not only the Interest of the Crown but of the Nation to reduce them'. To that end, metropolitan officials sought to correct as many as possible of the 'many Errors and unconstitutional Regulations & practices' that had 'taken place and prevailed' in all the old colonies by 'Clipping the Wings of the Assemblies in their Claims of all the Privileges of a House of Commons' and holding them to an 'absolute Subjection to Orders sent from' London 'in the Shape of Instructions', objectives they sought to accomplish primarily by strictly requiring suspending clauses in all colonial legislation of unusual character and disallowing all laws that appeared in any way to be 'injurious to the preogative', detrimental to metropolitan authority, or conducive to the establishment in the colonies of 'a greater measure of Liberty than is enjoyed by the People of England'.

If the Seven Years' War intensified metropolitan appreciation of both the value of the colonies and the weakness of metropolitan authority over them, it also contributed to three structural changes that would have an important bearing upon metropolitan calculations concerning the colonies after the war. First, the war brought Parliament more directly and intimately into contact with the colonies than at any time since the late seventeenth century. The huge expenditures required for American defence as well as the smaller annual appropriations for the new royal colonies of Georgia and Nova Scotia helped to fix Parliamentary attention upon the colonies more fully than ever before and contributed to an increasingly widely held assumption that Parliament should be directly involved in reconstructing the imperial system after the war. Such an assumption was scarcely novel insofar as it applied to the commercial relationship between Britain and the colonies: since the 1960s Parliament had taken responsibility for regulating trade and other aspects of the economic life of the colonies. Prior to the war, however, administration had involved Parliament in the internal affairs of the colonies only in very exceptional circumstances. Yet, with their growing frustration over their inability to enforce colonial compliance with their directives during their reform attempts between 1748 and 1757 metropolitan authorities had been more and more driven to threaten Parliamentary intervention to force the colonies into line. . . .

During the war, moreover, a chorus of proposals from both inside and outside the government called for 'the legislative power of Great Britain to make a strict and speedy inquiry . . . to remedy disorders . . . and to put the government and trade of all our colonies into' a 'good and sound . . . state'. Not just the commerce but the internal civil affairs, it came to be very widely assumed, required Parliamentary attention. 'Nothing', declared Thomas Pownall, could 'restore the Authority of the Crown & settle the Rights of the People according to the true Spirit of the British Constitution but an Act of Parliament' because, William Knox added in spelling out the lessons of the war and immediately pre-war period, 'no other Authority than that of the British Parliament will be regarded by the Colonys, or be able to awe them into acquiescence.' Such sentiments revealed a well-developed conviction that in 'the perpetual struggle in every Colony between Privilege and Prerogative' the metropolitan government would thenceforth no longer hesitate to turn to Parliament to achieve what it would be unable to accomplish through executive action alone. As Isaac Norris, speaker of the Pennsylvania Assembly appreciated in trying to understand the new Grenville measures of 1764–65, the idea of resorting to the 'Power of Parliament to make general Colony Laws' and otherwise intervene in the internal affairs of the colonies was 'no new Scheme'. It had been often suggested during the decade prior to the war. But as Norris understood, it was 'the War in America' that had 'brought it to the Issue we now see and are like to feel both now and hereafter'.

Though some thought that the colonists would not resist any Parliamentary effort to 'new model the Government' and trade of the colonies, metropolitan officials were not blind to the possibility that even the august authority of Parliament might be contested in America. 'From their partial Interests and Connection', the colonists could in fact be expected to 'give all the Opposition on their power to . . . any . . . matter . . . for the General Good'. During the war, metropolitan civil and military representatives had taken note of the 'slight [regard] people of this Country affect to Treat Acts of Parliament with', and Lord Loudoun had reported that it was 'very common' for colonists to say, defiantly, that 'they would be glad to see any Man durst Offer to put an English Act of Parliament in Force in this Country'. But a second structural change brought about by the war gave London authorities confidence that any opposition to Parliamentary measures could be easily overcome. The idea of using royal troops in a coercive way against the colonies had been considered during the late 1740s and early 1750s, but no significant body of troops was readily available. Only with the rapid buildup of an American army beginning in 1756 did the metropolis have, for the first time in the history of the North American empire, significant coercive resources in the colonies. During the war, several governors, including Robert Hunter Morris of Pennsylvania, had argued that it was 'next to impossible without a standing force to carry the Laws [of Parliament] into Execution' and, like Thomas Pownall and Henry Ellis of Georgia, he had urged the necessity of using the military to reinforce civil authority. 'A military force is certainly necessary to render Government respectable, & the Laws efficacious', wrote Ellis in June 1757, '& perhaps not more so in any country upon earth than this, which abounds with ungovernable and refractory people'. Pownall agreed: 'tis necessary', he wrote to Halifax less than a month later, 'that the Military should carry into effect those matters which the Civil thro it's weakness cannot'. Others wrote in a similar vein. Thus, in urging the quick adoption of a plan to reduce the colonies to a 'state of subordination and improvement' near the end of the war, customs comptroller Nathaniel Ware warned that 'if an effectual reformation be not introduced before those troops are withdrawn which could have been thrown in [to the colonies] upon no less occasion [than the war] without giving a general alarm, one may venture to pronounce it impossible afterwards'. With the colonies 'now surrounded by an army, a navy, and . . . hostile tribes of Indians', Maurice Morgann, adviser to Shelburne, agreed, there would be no better 'time (not to oppress or injure them in any shape) but to exact a due deference to the just and equitable demands of a British Parliament'.

The decision to keep a large contingent of troops in America following the war was almost certainly not the result of the sort of calculated deception suggested by Captain Walter Rutherford, a British officer in the colonies, who proposed in 1759 that troops be retained in the colonies 'apparently for their defence, but also to keep them in proper subjection to the Mother Country'. But neither, as some later historians have contended, were security of the new conquests against their former possessors nor the desirability of distributing troops 'amongst the several Members' of the 'Empire, in proportion to their ability to support them' the only considerations behind this decision. As William Knox explained in a long memorandum in 1763, 'one great purpose of stationing a large Body of Troops in America' was 'to secure the Dependence of the Colonys on Great Britain' by, another observer remarked, 'guarding against any Disobedience or Disaffection amongst the Inhabitants, . . . who already begin to entertain some extravagent Opinions, concerning their Relations and Dependence on their Mother Country'. With such a large military force in the colonies—7500 troops in all—metropolitan officials at the end of the Seven Years' War could now proceed with the business of imperial reconstruction with reasonable confidence that they had the resources near at hand to suppress any potential colonial opposition.

But there seemed to be little reason to fear extended colonial resistance. For, people in Britain believed, the war had shown Americans to have little stomach for a fight. Not only had they proved to be "execrable Troops', they had also shown themselves unwilling to stand up to military power. As Loudoun concluded from his successful use of the threat of force to overcome colonial opposition to providing quarters for troops in 1756–57, the colonists 'wou'd invade every Right of the Crown, if permitted, but . . . if the Servants of the Crown wou'd do their Duty, and stood firm, they wou'd always Submit'. Even if they were braver than they appeared during the war, however, the 'mutual jealousies amongst the several Colonies would always', Lord Morton observed, prevent a united resistance and thus 'keep them in a state of dependence'. With fourteen separate colonies in the continent in 1763, all with 'different forms of government, different laws, different interests, and some of them different religious persuasions and different manners', it was no wonder that they were 'all jealous of each other. Indeed, as Benjamin Franklin reported, their 'jealousy of each other was so great that' they would never be 'able to effect . . . an union among themselves' and there was therefore absolutely no possibility that they could ever become '*dangerous*' to Britain.

But perhaps the most important structural change produced by the war was not the increasing involvement of Parliament in American affairs or even the introduction of an army into the colonies but the elimination of France and Spain from eastern North America. Following contemporaries, historians have emphasised the importance of this development as a precondition for colonial resistance after 1763. Of far greater importance, in all probability, was its effect upon the mentality of those in power in the metropolis. For the destruction of French power not only made the colonies less dependent upon Britain for protection; it also left Britain with a much freer hand to proceed with its programme of colonial reform by

removing the necessity that had operated so strongly during the first half of the war for conciliatory behaviour towards the colonies to encourage them to cooperate against a common enemy. Colonial leaders appreciated this point quite fully in the wake of the Grenville programme. Many people found an anonymous Frenchman visiting the colonies in 1765, were saying that if the 'french . . . were [still] in Canada the British parlem't would as soon be D[ea]d as to offer to do what they do now'. John Dickinson agreed. The colonists, he declared in 1765, 'never would have been treated as they are if Canada still continued in the hands of the French'.

If the structural changes produced by the war—the instrusion of Parliament into colonial matters, the presence of a metropolitan army, and the removal of international pressures for conciliating the colonies—provided metropolitan officials with favourable conditions for undertaking a sweeping reformation of the imperial system, while their heightened awareness of both the value of the colonies and the fragility of their authority over them served as a motive, they were pushed even more strongly in this direction by their own interpretation of the purposes of the war and the relative contributions of Britain and the colonies. For the belief was widespread in London that the war had been undertaken not on behalf of any specifically metropolitan objectives but for the protection of the colonies. As Shelburne put it in a speech in the House of Lords in December 1766, the 'security of the British Colonies in N. America was the *first* cause of the War'. Britain's generosity, in fact, seemed to contrast sharply with the colonies' parsimony. Britain, wrote Thomas Whateley, had certainly 'engaged in the Defence of her most distant Dominions, with more alacrity than the Provinces themselves that were immediately attacked', while the colonists had repeatedly refused 'to sacrific their own partial Advantages to the general good' and brazenly taken 'advantage of their Countrys distresses' to cram 'their modes down the throat[s] of the Governor[s]' in shortsighted and selfish disputes over privileges. In return for such generous treatment, metropolitan leaders expected the colonists to show both a deep appreciation and a strong sense of the great 'obligation they owe[d] her'. Instead, they received nothing but ingratitude, the sting of which was made all the more painful by the fact that Britain had accumulated a huge debt of between £100,000,000 and £150,000,000 and a high annual rate of taxation as a result of the war and had even reimbursed the colonies for their own military appropriations by nearly £1,100,000. Nor was such recompense made any less galling by the colonists' vaunted prosperity. While the parent society wallowed in debt and groaned under high taxes, its 'vigorous Offspring' in America seemed to be enjoying low taxes and a flourishing economy that enabled them to riot in opulence and luxury.

III

The colonial response to the war could scarcely have been more different. Scholars have traditionally emphasised the extent to which the war contributed to colonial discontent with British rule. . . . Some of their discontent derived from Crown attempts to centralise Indian administration and still more from the overt condescension of British regulars towards American provincials and a discriminatory military structure that assigned American officers and soldiers to subordinate roles. Most, however, arose from the insistence by British military commanders that mil-

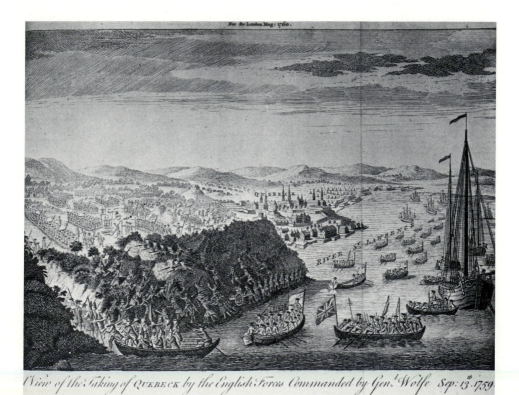

View of the Taking of QUEBECK by the English Forces Commanded by Gen.ˡ Wolfe Sep: 13ᵗʰ 1759.

Britain's conquest of Canada in 1759 with the cooperation of the colonists on an unprecedented scale raised American self-esteem and pride.

itary necessity overrode all other considerations. 'Granted sweeping powers by the Crown', they 'imposed embargoes on shipping, ordered press gangs into the street and countryside to seize men and property, forced citizens to quarter soldiers in their homes, and insisted that the authority of colonial political agencies was subordinate to their own military power'.

Well before the war, of course, the colonists had learned to be wary of metropolitan power and intentions. 'From some hard usage, received in former times', principally from 'the governors and other officers sent among them', they had long 'entertained an opinion that *Britain* was resolved to keep them low, and [was] regardless of their welfare', and their rejection of the Albany Plan of Union in 1754 on the eve of the war can be interpreted at least in part as an expression of this wariness. . . . Against the background of the new aggressiveness toward the colonies exhibited by London authorities during the decade preceding the war, moreover, metropolitan behaviour during the war appeared even more ominous, and some colonists, like William Smith, Jr., worried that the 'long hand of the Prerogative' would 'be stretched over to us, more than ever, upon the conclusion of the next general peace'. Nor did the colonists respond entirely favourably to the rising chorus of suggestions both immediately before and throughout the war for Parliamentary intervention in the internal affairs of the colonies, and at least one colonial leader, Stephen Hopkins, the elected governor of Rhode Island, reportedly declared in 1757 'that the King & Parliament had no more Right to make Laws for us than the Mohawks' and that whatever might be said 'concerning the Arbitrary Despotic Government of the Kingdom of France, yet nothing could be more tyrannical, than our being Obliged by Acts of Parliament To which we were not parties to the making; and in which we were not Represented'.

Similarly, . . . the many restrictive policies implemented by the metropolis during the later stages of the war following the conquest of Canada in 1759 elicited considerable colonial discontent. Colonial legislators resented the demonstrable increase in metropolitan limitations upon the supervision of their law-making powers. By effectively 'strip[ping] us of all the Rights and Privileges of British Subjects', complained Colonel Richard Bland, the Virginia lawyer and antiquarian, such limitations threatened to undermine the customary constitutions of the colonies and 'to put us under' a 'despotic Power' of the sort usually associated with 'a French or Turkish Government'. At least in the northern colonies, colonial merchants were equally unhappy with metropolitan efforts to enforce the trade laws more systematically and especially with their attempts to suppress colonial trade with enemy islands. Far from being 'pernicious and prejudicial' to either Britain or the war effort, such trade, they argued, was 'of the greatest benefit to the kingdom, and the mein sourse from whence we have been enabled to support the extraordinary demands for cash, that have been made upon us in order to enable his majesty to 'carry on the present just and necessary, but most expensive war.' Even to interfere with, much less to suppress, a trade that was ultimately responsible for bringing the British nation annual profits of over 600 per cent and cash in the amount of £1,500,000 seemed to colonial traders incomprehensible. Because there had never been a total prohibition of trade between the home islands and France at any time during the war, moreover, it also seemed to be patently discriminatory against colonial merchants, who professed to find it explicable only in terms of the 'undue influence of the [British] *West-Indians*' and metropolitan partiality for their interests over that of the continental colonists. In addition, some colonists were sceptical about metropolitan intentions to keep a standing army in the colonies after the war. They wondered with Cortlandt Skinner of New Jersey why, 'when a few independent Companies' had been 'sufficient for the continent' for over a century when the French were in possession of Canada, Britain suddenly required a permanent garrison of 'so many regiments when every [European] enemy is removed at least a thousand miles from our borders' and worried that the army was really intended 'to check us'.

In the final analysis, however, the anxieties with which the colonists emerged from the war appear far less important than the high levels of expectations. For on balance the war seems to have been for the colonists a highly positive experience. For one thing, the war had brought large sums of specie into the colonies through military and naval spending and successful privateering and had been highhly profitable for many people, especially in the northern colonies where most of the troops were stationed. But the psychological benefits the colonists derived from the war would seem to have been far more significant than these material ones. That so much of the war had been fought on colonial soil and that the metropolitan government had made such an enormous effort and gone to such a great expense to defend them were extraordinarily reinforcive of colonial self-esteem and gave rise to an expanded sense of colonial self-importance. Moreover, the colonists took great pride in the fact that they had themselves made an important contribution to the war. Historians have often taken at face value contemporary metropolitan opinion that, with a few notable exceptions, the colonies had not exerted themselves in voting men and money for the war, and that the requisition system through which the administration had sought to mobilise colonial contributions to the war was, in the judgment of George Louis Beer, 'largely a failure'. Yet, as John M. Murrin has recently pointed out, the subsidy policy adopted by the metropolitan government beginning in 1756 by which it reimbursed the colonies with specie voted by Parliament according to the amounts they actually expended for the war worked with 'reasonable efficiency'. 'By offer-ing valuable rewards to specie-poor colonies, it actually stimulated competition among them in support of imperial goals', he argues: 'At an annual expense to Britain of £200,000 (later reduced to £133,000), the colonies raised about twenty thousand provincials per year through 1762, paying about half the cost themselves'.

The following table not only reinforces Murrin's point but shows that the colonial contribution to the war was both more evenly distributed and far more substantial than historians have appreciated. Massachusetts and Virginia, the two colonies that subsequently took the lead in the resistance movement after 1763, were together responsible for half of total net expenditures, but Pennsylvania, New Jersey, New York, Connecticut, and, in terms of taxes per adult white male, even South Carolina all expended respectable sums. Besides the new colony of Georgia, only New Hampshire, North Carolina, Maryland and, to a lesser extent, Rhode Island did not vote substantial amounts and thereby place their inhabitants under significantly higher tax burdens than they had been used to before the war.

For the colonists, the knowledge that they had, for the first time in their histories, made such an important contribution to such a great and glorious national cause increased the immediacy and strength of their ties with Britain and produced a surge of British patriotism. They had long had, in Thomas Pownall's words, a 'natural, almost mechanical affection to Great Britain', an affection that was deeply rooted in ties of blood and interest, satisfaction with their existing prosperous condition, and pride in being linked to a great metropolitan tradition that, they believed, guaranteed them the same 'privileges and equal protection', the same 'liberty and free constitution of government', that were the joyous boast of Britons everywhere and the jealous envy of the rest of the civilised world. The extraordinary British achievements in the Seven Years' War could only intensify this deep affection for and pride in being British, which came pouring out during the later stages of the war in a veritable orgy of celebrations, first, of the great British victories in Canada, the West Indies, and Europe; then of the accession of a vigorous, young, British-born king, George III, in 1760; and, finally, of the glorious Treaty of Paris in 1763, a treaty that made the British Empire the most extensive and powerful in the Western world since Rome. British national feeling among the colonists had probably never been stronger than it was in the early 1760s.

The feeling of having been a partner in such a splendid 'national' undertaking, even if only a junior partner, not only intensified the pride of the colonists in their attachment to Britain, it also heightened their expectations for a larger—and more equivalent—role within the Empire, a role that would finally raise them out of a dependent status to one in which they were more nearly on a par with Britons at home. It also stimulated visions of future grandeur—within the British Empire. 'Now commences the Aera of our quiet Enjoyment of those Liberties, which our Fathers purchased with the Toil of their whole Lives, their Treasure, their Blood', ecstatically declared Reverend Thomas Barnard of Salem, Massachusetts, in one of many similar sermons celebrating the conclusion of the Seven Years' War: 'Safe from the Enemy of the Wilder-

Colonial Contributions to the Seven Years' War

A. Expenditures

Colony	Expenditures	% Total	Reimbursed by Parliament	% Reimbursed	Net Expenditures	% Total
	£		£		£	
Massachusetts	818,000	31.8	351,994	43.0	466,006	31.1
Virginia	385,319	15.0	99,177	25.7	286,142	19.1
Pennsylvania	313,043	12.2	75,311	24.1	237,732	15.9
New Jersey	204,411	8.0	51,321	25.1	153,090	10.2
New York	291,156	11.3	139,468	47.9	151,688	10.1
South Carolina	90,656	3.5	10,226	11.3	80,430	5.4
Maryland	39,000	1.5	0	0.0	39,000	2.6
Rhode Island	80,981	3.2	51,480	63.6	29,501	1.9
Connecticut	259,875	10.1	231,752	89.2	28,123	1.9
North Carolina	30,776	1.2	11,010	35.8	19,766	1.3
New Hampshire	53,211	2.1	47,030	88.4	6181	0.4
Georgia	1820	0.1	0	0.0	1820	0.1
Totals	2,568,248	100.0	1,068,769	41.6	1,499,479	100.0

B. Tax Per Adult White Male

Colony	Tax	Colony	Tax	Colony	Tax
	£		£		£
South Carolina	10.94	Virginia	7.20	North Carolina	1.28
Massachusetts	10.70	Pennsylvania	6.62	Georgia	1.51
New Jersey	8.77	Rhode Island	3.51	Connecticut	1.01
New York	7.52	Maryland	1.91	New Hampshire	0.84

ness, safe from the griping Hand of arbitrary Sway and cruel Superstition; here shall be the late founded Seat of Peace and Freedom. Here shall our indulgent Mother, who has most generously rescued and protected us, be served and honoured by growing Numbers, with all Duty, Love and Gratitude, till Time shall be no more'. The expulsion of the French had at once both rendered the colonies safe and opened up half a continent for their continued expansion. Now that this vast and rich area had finally been 'secured to the British Government', the colonists confidently expected that as a matter of course liberty would 'be granted to his Majestys Subjects in' the 'Colonies to Settle the Lands on Ohio' and elsewhere in the West. Once these lands had been settled, prospects for Britain, and America, colonists predicted with assurance, would be almost without limits. 'The State, Nature, Climate, and prodigious Extent of the American Continent' obviously provided 'high Prospects in favor of the Power, to which it belongs'. With all of eastern North America for its granary, Britain could become one extended town of manufacturers, and this powerful Anglo-American partnership would enable the British Empire to 'maintain and exalt her Supremacy, until Heaven blots out all the Empires of the World.' Given their crucial role in these developments, the colonists had no doubt, as an anonymous pamphleteer had phrased it early in the war, that they would 'not be thought presumptuous, if they consider[ed] themselves upon an equal footing with' Englishmen at home or be 'treated the worse, because they will be *Englishmen*'. Conscious of the strenuous and critical character of their exertions during the war, they now thought that they had every 'reason to expect that *their* interest should be considered and attended to, that *their* rights . . . should be preserved to them'. 'Glowing with every sentiment of duty and affection towards their mother country', they looked forward at war's end to 'some mark of tenderness in return. As soon as the metropolitan government recognised their

great 'services and suffereings' during the war, they felt sure, it would be compelled even 'to enlarge' their Priviledges'.

IV

The experience of the Seven Years' War thus sent the postwar expectations of men on opposite sides of the Atlantic veering off in opposite directions. More aware than ever of the value of the colonies, increasingly anxious about the fragility of metropolitan authority over them, and appalled by their truculent and self-serving behaviour during the war, the metropolitan government was determined to bring them under tighter regulations at the end of the war and willing to use the authority of Parliament to do so. By contrast, the colonists, basking in a warm afterglow of British patriotism, minimised evidence accumulated before and during the war that metropolitans had other, less exalted plans for them, and looked forward expansively to a more equal and secure future in the Empire. At the same time, the removal of the Franco-Spanish menace from the eastern half of North America had both made the colonists somewhat less dependent upon Britain for protection and left subsequent British governments much freer to go ahead with a broad programme of reform, while the presence of a large number of royal troops in the colonies gave them confidence that they could suppress potential colonial resistance and seemed to make the caution and conciliation they had traditionally observed towards the colonies less necessary. In combination, these psychological consequences and structural changes produced by the war made the relationship between Britain and the colonies far more volatile than it had ever been before.

Given this situation, it was highly predictable that British officials in the 1760s would take some action, probably by bringing Parliamentary authority to bear upon the colonials in new, unaccustomed, and hence, for the colonists, illegitimate ways and that such action, so completely at variance with the colonists' hopes and expectations, would be interpreted by the colonists as both a betrayal and a violation of the customary relationship between them and Great Britain. For the colonists, it was not only the new taxes and restrictive measures in themselves that so deeply offended them in the mid-1760s but the injustice, ingratitude, and reproach those measures seemed to imply. When they discovered through these measures that their obedience during the war would be rewarded not by the extension but the 'loss of their freedom', that, as the Massachusetts lawyer Oxenbridge Thacher exclaimed, they had been 'lavish of their blood and treasure in the late war only to bind the shackles of slavery on themselves and their children' and that Britain intended to treat all the colonies, regardless of whether they had contributed heavily to the war or not, without distinction, with 'the rude hand of a ravisher', they felt a deep sense of disappointment, even betrayal, as if, in the words of Richard Henry Lee, they had "hitherto been suffered to drink from the cup of Liberty' only that they might 'be more sensibly punished by its being withdrawn, and the bitter dregs of Servility forced on us in its place'. Perhaps more than any other single factor, the sense of betrayal, the deep bitterness arising out of the profound disjunction between how, on the basis of their performance during the Seven Years' War, they thought they deserved to be dealt with by the metropolis and the treatment actually accorded them, supplied the energy behind their intense reaction to the Grenville programme in 1765–66. For metropolitans, on the other hand, the colonists' powerful resistance to the Grenville measures only operated to confirm ancient fears that the allegiance of these valuable colonies to Britain was highly tenuous, that their authority in the colonies was dangerously weak, and that the ungrateful colonists were bent upon escaping from their control and establishing their independence.

By contributing so heavily to the creation of the intellectual and psychological climate and a structural situation that produced these actions and reactions, the Seven Years' War thus had a profound, if complex, bearing upon the emerging confrontation between Britain and its North American colonies and served as an important component in the causal pattern of the American Revolution.

The Logic of Rebellion

Bernard Bailyn

The colonists believed they saw emerging from the welter of events during the decade after the Stamp Act a pattern whose meaning was unmistakable. They saw in the measures taken by the British government and in the actions of officials in the colonies something for which their peculiar inheritance of thought had prepared them only too well, something they had long conceived to be a possibility in view of the known tendencies of history and of the present state of affairs in England. They saw about them, with increasing clarity, not merely mistaken, or even evil, policies violating the principles upon which freedom rested, but what appeared to be evidence of nothing less than a deliberate assault launched surreptitiously by plotters against liberty both in England and in America. The danger to America, it was believed, was in fact only the small, immediately visible part of the greater whole whose ultimate manifestation would be the destruction of the English constitution, with all the rights and privileges embedded in it.

This belief transformed the meaning of the colonists' struggle, and it added an inner accelerator to the movement of opposition. For, once assumed, it could not be easily dispelled: Denial only confirmed it, since what conspirators profess is not what they believe; the ostensible is not the real; and the real is deliberately malign.

It was this—the overwhelming evidence, as they saw it, that they were faced with conspirators against liberty determined at all costs to gain ends which their words dissembled—that was signaled to the colonists after 1763, and it was this above all else that in the end propelled them into Revolution.

Suspicion that the ever-present, latent danger of an active conspiracy of power against liberty was becoming manifest within the British Empire, assuming specific form and developing in coordinated phases, rose in the consciousness of a large segment of the American population before any of the famous political events of the struggle with England took place. No adherent of a nonconformist church or sect in the eighteenth century was free from suspicion that the Church of England, an arm of the English state, was working to bring all subjects of the crown into the community of the Church; and since toleration was official and nonconformist influence in English politics formidable, it was doing so by stealth, disguising its efforts, turning to improper uses devices that had been created for benign purposes. In particular, the Society for the Propagation of the Gospel in Foreign Parts, an arm of the Church created in 1701 to aid in bringing the Gospel to the pagan Indians, was said by 1763 to have "long had a formal design to root out Presbyterianism, etc., and to establishing both episcopacy and bishops. . ."

Excerpted by permission of the author and the publishers from pages 94–107, 111–114, 117–125, 138–142 of *The Ideological Origins of the American Revolution* by Bernard Bailyn, Cambridge, Massachusetts: The Belknap Press of Harvard University Press. Copyright © 1967 by the President and Fellows of Harvard College.

Fear of an ecclesiastical conspiracy against American liberties, latent among nonconformists through all of colonial history, thus erupted into public controversy at the very same time that the first impact of new British policies in civil affairs was being felt. And though it was, in an obvious sense, a limited fear (for large parts of the population identified themselves with the Anglican Church and were not easily convinced that liberty was being threatened by a plot of Churchmen) it nevertheless had a profound indirect effect everywhere, for it drew into public discussion—evoked in specific form—the general conviction of 18th-century Englishmen that the conjoining of "temporal and spiritual tyranny" was, in John Adams' words, an event totally "calamitous to human liberty" yet an event that in the mere nature of things perpetually threatened. For, as David Hume had explained, "in all ages of the world priests have been enemies to liberty . . . Liberty of thinking and of expressing our thoughts is always fatal to priestly power . . . and, by an infallible connection which prevails among all kinds of liberty, this privilege can never be enjoyed . . . but in a free government. Hence . . . all princes that have aimed at despotic power have known of what importance it was to gain the established clergy; as the clergy, on their part, have shown a great facility in entering into the views of such princes." Fear of the imposition of an Anglican episcopate thus brought into focus a cluster of ideas, attitudes, and responses alive with century-old Popish-Stuart-Jacobite associations that would enter directly into the Revolutionary controversy in such writings as John Adams' *Dissertation on the Canon and Feudal Law* (1765) and Samuel Adams' "A Puritan" pieces published in the *Boston Gazette* in 1768. And more than that, it stimulated among highly articulate leaders of public opinion, who would soon be called upon to interpret the tendency of civil affairs, a general sense that they lived in a conspiratorial world in which what the highest officials professed was not what they in fact intended, and that their words masked a malevolent design.

Reinforcement for this belief came quickly. Even for whose who had in no way been concerned with the threat of an episcopal establishment, the passage of the Stamp Act was not merely an impolite and unjust law that threatened the priceless right of the individual to retain possession of his property until he or his chosen representative voluntarily gave it up to another; it was to many, also, a danger signal indicating that a more general threat existed. For though it could be argued, and in a sense proved by the swift repeal of the

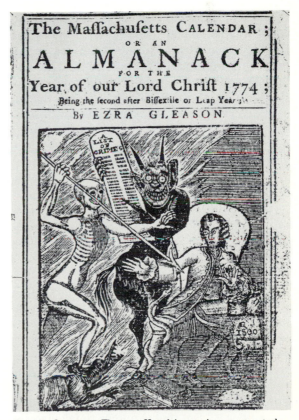

British Governor Thomas Hutchinson is represented on the cover of The Massachusetts Almanack *as being in league with the devil. Popular leaders in the Bay Colony, such as John Adams and Josiah Quincy, attributed the basest of motives to Hutchinson's machinations.*

act, that nothing more was involved than ignorance or confusion on the part of people in
power who really knew better and who, once
warned by the reaction of the colonists, would
not repeat the mistake—though this could be,
and by many was, concluded, there nevertheless appeared to be good reason to suspect that
more was involved. For from whom had the
false information and evil advice come that had
so misled the English government? From officials in the colonies, said John Adams, said
Oxenbridge Thacher, James Otis, and Stephen
Hopkins—from officials bent on overthrowing
the constituted forms of government in order to satisfy their own lust for power, and
not likely to relent in their passion. Some of
these local plotters were easily identified. To
John Adams, Josiah Quincy, and others the
key figure in Massachusetts from the beginning to the end was Thomas Hutchinson who
by "serpentine wiles" was befuddling and vic-
timizing the weak, the avaricious, and the incautious in order to increase his notorious engrossment of public office. In Rhode Island it
was, to James Otis, that "little, dirty, drinking,
drabbing, contaminated knot of thieves, beggars, and transports . . . made up of Turks,
Jews, and other infidels, with a few renegado
Christians and Catholics" —the Newport junto,
led by Martin Howard, Jr., which had already
been accused by Stephen Hopkins and others
in Providence of "conspiring against the liberties of the colony."

But even if local leaders associated with
power elements in England had not been so
suspect, there were grounds for seeing more
behind the Stamp Act than its ostensible purpose. The official aim of the act was, of course,
to bring in revenue to the English treasury. But
the sums involved were in fact quite small, and
"some persons . . . may be inclined to acquiesce under it." But that would be to fall directly
into the trap, for the smaller the taxes, John
Dickinson wrote in the most influential pamphlet published in America before 1776, the
more dangerous they were, since they would

the more easily be found acceptable by the
incautious, with the result that a precedent
would be established for making still greater
inroads on liberty and property.

> Nothing is wanted at home but a PRECEDENT,
> the force of which shall be established by the
> tacit submission of the colonies. . . . If the Par-
> liament succeeds in this attempt, other statutes
> will impose other duties . . . and thus the Parlia-
> ment will levy upon us such sums of money as
> they choose to take, *without any other* LIMITA-
> TION *than their* PLEASURE.

Others saw more drastic hidden meanings
and implications in the passage of the Stamp
Act. "If the real and only motive of the minister was to raise money from the colonies,"
Joseph Warren wrote in 1766, "that method
should undoubtedly have been adopted which
was least grievous to the people." Choice of so
blatantly obnoxious a measure as the Stamp
Act, consequently, "has induced some to imagine that the minister designed by this act to
force the colonies into a rebellion, and from
thence to take occasion to treat them with
severity, and, by military power, to reduce them
to servitude." Such a supposition was perhaps
excessive: "charity forbids us to conclude [the
ministry] guilty of so black a villainy. But . . . it
is known that tyrannical ministers have, at
some time, embraced even this hellish measure to accomplish their cursed designs," and
speculation based on "admitting this to have
been his aim" seemed well worth pursuing. To
John Adams it seemed "very manifest" that the
ultimate design behind the Stamp Act was an
effort to forge the fatal link between ecclesiastical and civil despotism, the first by strip-
ping the colonists "in a great measure of the
means of knowledge, by loading the press, the
colleges, and even an almanac and a newspaper with restraints and duties," the second, by
recreating the inequalities and dependencies
of feudalism "by taking from the poorer sort
of people all their little subsistence, and conferring it on a set of stamp officers, distrib-

utors, and their deputies." This last point was the most obvious: "[A]s the influence of money and places generally procures to the minister a majority in Parliament," Arthur Lee wrote, so an income from unchecked taxation would lead to a total corruption of free government in America, with the result that the colonies would "experience the fate of the *Roman* people in the deplorable times of their slavery."

But by then, in 1768, more explicit evidence of a wide-ranging plot was accumulating rapidly. Not only had the Townshend Duties, another revenue act, been passed by Parliament despite all the violence of the colonists' reaction to the Stamp Act, but it was a measure that enhanced the influence of the customs administration, which for other reasons had already come under suspicion. There had been, it was realized by the late 1760s a sudden expansion in the number of "posts in the [colonial] 'government' . . . worth the attention of persons of influence in Great Britain" —posts, Franklin explained, like the governorships, filled by persons who were

> generally strangers to the provinces they are sent to govern, have no estate, natural connection, or relation there to give them an affection for the country . . . they come only to make money as fast as they can; are sometimes men of vicious characters and broken fortunes, sent by a minister merely to get them out of the way.

By the late 1760s, in the perspective of recent events, one could see that the invasion of customs officers "born with long claws like eagles," had begun as far back as the last years of the Seven Years' War and was now being reinforced by the new tax measures. The wartime Orders in Council demanding stricter enforcement of the Navigation Laws; the Sugar Act of 1764, which had multiplied the customs personnel; and the American Board of Customs Commissioners created in 1767 with "power," Americans said, "to constitute as many under officers as they please"—all these devel-

opments could be seen to have provided for an "almost incredible number of inferior officers," most of whom the colonists believed to be "wretches . . . of such infamous characters that the merchants cannot possibly think their interest safe under their care." More important by far, however, was their influence on government.

For there was an obvious political and constitutional danger in having such "a set of *idle drones,*" such "lazy, proud, worthless *pensioners* and *placemen,*" in one's midst. It was nothing less than "a general maxim," James Wilson wrote,

> that the crown will take advantage of every opportunity of extending its prerogative in opposition to the privileges of the people, [and] that it is the interest of those who have *pensions* or *offices at will* from the crown to concur in all its measures.

These "baneful harpies" were instruments of power, of prerogative. They would upset the balance of the constitution by extending "*ministerial influence* as much beyond its former bounds as the late war did the British dominions." Parasitic officeholders, thoroughly corrupted by their obligations to those who had appointed them, would strive to "*distinguish themselves* by their sordid zeal in defending and promoting measures which *they know beyond all question to be destructive* to the *just rights* and *true interests* of their country." Seeking to "*serve the ambitious purposes of great men at* home," these "*base-spirited wretches*" would urge—were already urging—as they logically had to, the specious attractions of "SUBMISSIVE behavior." They were arguing with a plausible affectation of *wisdom* and *concern* how *prudent* it is to please the *powerful*—how *dangerous* to provoke them—and then comes in the perpetual incantation that freezes up every generous purpose of the soul in cold, inactive expectation—"that if there is any request to be made, compliance will obtain a favorable attention."

In the end, this extension of executive patronage, based on a limitless support of government through colonial taxation, would make the whole of government "merely a ministerial engine"; by throwing off the balance of its parts, it would destroy the protective machinery of the constitution.

But even this did not exhaust the evidence that a design against liberty was unfolding. During the same years the independence of the judiciary, so crucial a part of the constitution, was suddenly seen to be under heavy attack, and by the mid-1760s to have succumbed in many places.

This too was not a new problem. The status of the colonial judiciary had been a controversial question throughout the century. The Parliamentary statute of 1701 which guaranteed judges in England life tenure in their posts had been denied to the colonies, in part because properly trained lawyers were scarce in the colonies, especially in the early years, and appointments for life would prevent the replacement of ill qualified judges by their betters, when they appeared; and in part because, judicial salaries being provided for by temporary legislative appropriations, the removal of all executive control from the judiciary, it was feared, would result in the hopeless subordination of the courts to popular influences. The status of the judiciary in the 18th century was therefore left open to political maneuvering in which, more often than not, the home government managed to carry its point and to make the tenure of judges as temporary as their salaries. Then suddenly, in the early 1760s, the whole issue exploded. In 1759 the Pennsylvania Assembly declared that the judges of that province would thereafter hold their offices by the same permanence of tenure that had been guaranteed English judges after the Glorious Revolution. But the law was disallowed forthwith by the crown. Opposition newspapers boiled with resentment; angry speeches were made in the Assembly; and a pamphlet appeared explaining in the fullest detail the bearing of judicial independence on constitutional freedom.

In New York the issue was even more inflamed and had wider repercussions. There, the judges of the Supreme Court, by a political maneuver of 1750, had managed to secure their appointments for life. But this tenure was interrupted by the death of George II in 1760, which required the reissuance of all crown commissions. An unpopular and politically weak lieutenant governor, determined to prevent his enemies from controlling the courts, refused to recommission the judges on life tenure. The result was a ferocious battle in which the opposition asserted New York's "*undoubted right* of having the judges of our courts on a constitutional basis," and demanded the "liberties and privileges" of Englishmen in this connection as in all others. But they were defeated, though not by the governor. In December 1761 orders were sent out from the King in Council to all the colonies, permanently forbidding the issuance of judges' commissions anywhere on any tenure but that of "the pleasure of the crown."

All the colonies were affected. In some, like New Jersey, where the governor's incautious violation of the new royal order led to his removal from office, or like North Carolina, where opposition forces refused to concede and managed to keep up the fight for permanent judicial tenure throughout the entire period from 1760 to 1776, the issue was directly joined. In others, as in Massachusetts, where specific Supreme Court appointments were vehemently opposed by anti-administration interests, the force of the policy was indirect. But everywhere there was bitterness at the decree and fear of its implications, for everywhere it was known that judicial tenure "at the will of the crown" was "dangerous to the liberty and property of the subject," and that if the bench were occupied by "men who depended upon the smiles of the crown for their daily bread," the possibility of having an independent judiciary as an effective check upon executive power would be wholly lost.

*   *   *

John Wilkes' career was crucial to the colonists' understanding of what was happening to them; his fate, the colonists came to believe, was intimately involved with their own. Not only was he associated in their minds with general opposition to the government that passed the Stamp Act and the Townshend Duties, that was flooding the colonies with parasitic placemen, and that appeared to be making inroads into the constitution by weakening the judiciary and bestowing monopolies of public offices on pliant puppets—not only was he believed to be a national leader of opposition to such a government, but he had entered the public arena first as a victim and then as the successful antagonist of general warrants, which, in the form of writs of assistance, the colonists too had fought in heroic episodes known throughout the land. He had, moreover, defended the sanctity of private property against confiscation by the government. His cause was their cause. His *Number 45 North Briton* was as celebrated in the colonies as it was in England, and more generally approved of; its symbolism became part of the iconography of liberty in the colonies. His return from exile in 1768 and subsequent election to Parliament were major events to Americans. Toasts were offered to him throughout the colonies, and substantial contributions to his cause as well as adulatory letters were sent by Sons of Liberty in Virginia, Maryland, and South Carolina. A stalwart, independent opponent of encroaching government power and a believer in the true principles of the constitution, he was expected to do much in Parliament for the good of all: so the Bostonians wrote him in June 1768 "your perseverance in the *good old cause* may still prevent the great system

from dashing to pieces. 'Tis from your endeavors we hope for a royal 'Pascite, ut ante, boves,' and from our attachment to 'peace and good order' we wait for a constitutional redress: being determined that the King of Great Britain shall have subjects but not slaves in these remote parts of his dominions."

By February 1769 it was well known that *"the fate of Wilkes and America must stand or fall together."* The news, therefore, that by the maneuvers of the court party Wilkes had been denied the seat in Parliament to which he had been duly elected came as a profound shock to Americans. It shattered the hopes of many that the evils they saw around them had been the result not of design but of inadvertence, and it portended darker days ahead. When again, and then for a second, a third, and a fourth time Wilkes was reelected to Parliament and still denied his seat, Americans could only watch with horror and agree with him that the rights of the Commons, like those of the colonial Houses, were being denied by a power-hungry government that assumed to itself the privilege of deciding who should speak for the people in their own branch of the legislature. Power had reached directly and brutally into the main agency of liberty. Surely Wilkes was right: the constitution was being deliberately, not inadvertently, torn up by its roots.

Meanwhile an event even more sinister in its implications had taken place in the colonies themselves. On October 1, 1768, two regiments of regular infantry, with artillery, disembarked in Boston. For many months the harassed Governor Bernard had sought some legal means or excuse for summoning military help in his vain efforts to maintain if not an effective administration then at least order in the face of Stamp Act riots, circular letters, tumultuous town meetings, and assaults on customs officials. But the arrival of troops in Boston increased rather than decreased his troubles. For to a populace steeped in the literature of eighteenth-century English politics the presence of troops in a peaceful town had such portentous meaning that resistance instantly stiff-ened. It was not so much the physical threat of the troops that affected the attitudes of the Bostonians; it was the bearing their arrival had on the likely tendency of events. Viewed in the perspective of Trenchard's famous tracts on standing armies and of the vast derivative liter-ature on the subject that flowed from the En-glish debates of the 1690s, these were not sim-ply soldiers assembled for police duties; they were precisely what history had proved over and over again to be prime movers of the process by which unwary nations lose "that precious jewel *liberty.*" The mere rumor of possible troop arrivals had evoked the age-old apprehension. "The raising or keeping a stand-ing army within the kingdom in time of peace, unless it be with the consent of Parliament, is against the law," the alarmed Boston Town Meeting had resolved. It is, they said,

> the indefeasible right of [British] subjects to be *consulted* and to give their *free consent in person* or by representatives of their own free election to the raising and keeping a stand-ing army among them; and the inhabitants of this town, being free subjects, have the same right derived from nature and confirmed by the British constitution as well as the said royal charter; and therefore the raising or keeping a standing army without their consent in person or by representatives of their own free election would be an infringement of their natural, con-stitutional, and charter rights; and the employ-ing such army for the enforcing of laws made without the consent of the people, in person or by their representatives, would be a grievance.

But the troops arrived, four regiments in all: in bold, stark actuality a standing army—just such a standing army as had snuffed out free-dom in Denmark, classically, and elsewhere throughout the world. True, British regulars had been introduced into the colonies on a permanent basis at the end of the Seven Years' War; that in itself had been disquieting. But it had then been argued that troops were needed to police the newly acquired territories, and that they were not in any case to be regu-

larly garrisoned in peaceful, populous towns. No such defense could be made of the troops sent to Boston in 1768. No simple, ingenuous explanation would suffice. The true motive was only too apparent for those with eyes to see. One of the classic stages in the process of de-stroying free constitutions of government had been reached.

To those most sensitive to the ideological currents of the day, the danger could scarcely have been greater. "To have a standing army!" Andrew Eliot wrote from Boston to Thomas Hollis in September 1768, "Good God! What can be worse to a people who have tasted the sweets of liberty! Things are come to an unhappy crisis; there will never be that har-mony between Great Britain and her colonies that there hath been; all confidence is at an end; and the moment there is any blood shed all affection will cease." He was convinced, he wrote, that if the English government "had not had their hands full at home they would have crushed the colonies." As it was, En-gland's most recent actions tended only "to hasten that independency which at present the warmest among us deprecate." "I fear for the nation," he concluded, and his fears were shared not only by all liberty-minded Bosto-nians but also, through the stimulation of the "Journal of the Times," a day-by-day account of Boston "under military rule" that was, in effect, syndicated throughout the colonies, it was shared by politically and ideologically sen-sitive Americans everywhere. Time did not ease these anxieties; it merely complicated them. Fear and hatred became edged with contempt. "Our people begin to despise a military force," Eliot observed a year after the troops had first appeared; they coolly woo away the sol-diers and drag offending officers before the courts—which, he grimly added, continue to function "notwithstanding all their efforts."

*   *   *

Unconstitutional taxing, the invasion of placemen, the weakening of the judiciary, plural officeholding, Wilkes, standing armies—these were major evidences of a deliberate assault of power upon liberty. Lesser testimonies were also accumulating at the same time: small episodes in themselves, they took on a large significance in the context in which they were received. Writs of assistance in support of customs officials were working their expected evil: "our houses, and even our bedchambers, are exposed to be ransacked, our boxes, trunks, and chests broke open, ravaged and plundered by wretches whom no prudent man would venture to employ even as menial servants." Legally convened legislatures had been "adjourned . . . to a place highly inconvenient to the members and greatly disadvantageous to the interest of the province"; they had been prorogued and dissolved at executive whim. Even the boundaries of colonies had been tampered with, whereby *"rights of soil"* had been eliminated at a stroke. When in 1772 the Boston Town Meeting met to draw up a full catalogue of the "infringements and violations" of the "rights of the colonists, and of this province in particular, as men, as Christians, and as subjects," it approved a list of twelve items, which took seventeen pamphlet pages to describe.

But then, for a two-year period, there was a détente of sorts created by the repeal of the Townshend Duties, the withdrawal of troops from Boston, and the failure of other provocative measures to be taken. It ended abruptly, however, in the fall and winter of 1773, when, with a rush, the tendencies earlier noted were brought to fulfillment. In the space of a few weeks, all the dark, twisted roots of malevolence were finally revealed, plainly, for all to see.

The turning point was the passage of the Tea Act and the resulting Tea Party in Boston in December 1773. Faced with this defiant resistance to intimidation, the powers at work in England, it was believed, gave up all pretense of legality—"threw off the mask," John Adams said in a phrase that for a century had been used to describe just such climactic disclosures—and moved swiftly to complete their design. In a period of two months in the spring of 1774 Parliament took its revenge in a series of coercive actions no liberty-loving people could tolerate: the Boston Port Act, intended, it was believed, to snuff out the economic life of the Massachusetts metropolis; the Administration of Justice Act, aimed at crippling judicial processes once and for all by permitting trials to be held in England for offenses committed in Massachusetts; the Massachusetts Government Act, which stripped from the People of Massachusetts the protection of the British constitution by giving over all the "democratic" elements of the province's government—even popularly elected juries and town meetings—into the hands of the executive power; the Quebec Act, which, while not devised as a part of the coercive program, fitted it nicely, in the eyes of the colonists, by extending the boundaries of a "papist" province, and one governed wholly by prerogative, south into territory claimed by Virginia, Connecticut, and Massachusetts; finally, the Quartering Act, which permitted the seizure of unoccupied buildings for the use of troops on orders of the governors alone even in situations, such as Boston's, where barracks were available in the vicinity.

Once these coercive acts were passed, there could be little doubt that "the system of slavery fabricated against America . . . is the offspring of mature deliberation." To the leaders of the Revolutionary movement there was, beyond question, "a settled, fixed plan for *enslaving* the colonies, or bringing them under arbitrary government, and indeed the nation too." By 1774 the idea "that the British government—the *King, Lords,* and *Commons*—have laid a regular plan to enslave America, and that they are now deliberately putting it in execution" had been asserted, Samuel Seabury wrote wearily but accurately, "over, and over, and over again." The less inhibited of the colonial orators were quick to point out that "the MONSTER of a standing ARMY" had sprung directly from "a PLAN . . . *systematically* laid, and pursued by the British *ministry,* near twelve years, for enslaving America"; the Boston Massacre, it was claimed, had been "planned by Hillborough and a knot of treacherous knaves in Boston." Careful analysts like Jefferson agreed on the major point; in one of the most closely reasoned of the pamphlets of 1774 the Virginian stated unambiguously that though "single acts of tyranny may be ascribed to the accidental opinion of a day . . . a series of oppressions, begun at a distinguished period and pursued unalterably through every change of ministers, too plainly prove a deliberate and systematical plan of reducing us to slavery." So too the fastidious and scholarly John Dickinson, though in 1774 he still clung to the hope that inadvertence, at least on the part of the King, was involved, believed that "a plan had been deliberately framed and pertinaciously adhered to, unchanged even by frequent changes of ministers, unchecked by any intervening gleam of humanity, to sacrifice to a passion for arbitrary dominion the universal property, liberty, safety, honor, happiness, and prosperity of us unoffending yet devoted Americans." So too Washington, collaborating with George Mason in writing the Fairfax Resolves of 1774, agreed that the trouble had arisen from a "regular, systematic plan" of oppression, the English government "endeavoring by every piece of art and despotism to fix the shackles of slavery upon us"; he was convinced "beyond the smallest doubt," he wrote privately, "that these measures are the result of deliberation . . . I am as fully convinced as I am of my own existence that there has been a regular, systematic plan formed to enforce them." The more sensitive observers were to ideological issues—the more practiced in theoretical discourse—the more likely they were to find irrefutable evidence of what Richard Henry Lee called "designs for destroying our constitutional liberties." In 1766 Andrew Eliot had been unsure; the Stamp Act, he wrote, had been "calculated (I do not say designed) to enslave the colonies." By 1768 things had wors-

ened, and the distinction between "calculation" and "design" disappeared from his correspondence. "We have everything to fear and scarce any room to hope," he then wrote to Hollis; "I am sure this will put you in mind of 1641." He was convinced that the English government "had a design to new-model our constitution, at least in this province," and they would already have succeeded had they not been so occupied with other business at home. His friends in Boston concurred, and, beginning in 1770 wrote out in a series of town resolutions, instructions to representatives, and House declarations their conviction that

> a deep-laid and desperate plan of imperial despotism has been laid, and partly executed, for the extinction of all civil liberty . . . The august and once revered fortress of English freedom—the admirable work of ages—the BRITISH CONSTITUTION seems fast tottering into fatal and inevitable ruin. . . .

But who, specifically, were these enemies, and what were their goals? Josiah Quincy, at the center of affairs in London in the winter of 1774–75, was convinced "that all the measures against America were planned and pushed on by Bernard and Hutchinson." But most observers believed that local plotters like Hutchinson were only "creatures" of greater figures in England coordinating and impelling forward the whole effort. There were a number of specific identifications of these master influences. One of the most common was the claim that at the root of the evil stood the venerable John Stuart, Lord Bute, whose apparent absence from politics since 1763 could be seen as one of his more successful dissimulations: "[H]e has been aiming for years . . . to destroy the ancient right of the subjects," and now was finally taking steps to "overthrow both . . . King and state; to bring on a revolution, and to place another whom he [is] more nearly allied to upon the throne." Believing the people to "have too much liberty," he intended to reduce them to the "spiritless

SLAVES" they had been "in the reign of the *Stuarts.*" So it had seemed to Arthur Lee, who had written from London at the beginning of the period that "Lord Bute, though seemingly retired from the affairs of court, too plainly influences all the operations of government"; the hard facts, he said, lead one to condemn "the unprincipled ambition and partiality of the Scots lord as having produced all the mischiefs of the present period." Eliot too feared "this mysterious THANE," declaring in 1769 that "he has too much influence in the public measures." Five years later John Dickinson still lumped together "the Butes, Mansfields, Norths, Bernards, and Hutchinsons" as the people "whose falsehoods and misrepresentations have enflamed the people," and as late as 1775 an informed American could write confidently from London that "this plan you may be assured was devised by Lords North, Bute, and Jenkinson only." A more general version of this view was that a Stuart-Tory party, the "corrupt, Frenchified party in the nation," as it was described in 1766—"evil-minded individuals," Jonathan Mayhew believed, "not improbably in the interests of the houses of Bourbon and the Pretender"—was at work seeking to reverse the consequences of the Glorious Revolution. It was a similar notion that in all probability accounts for the republication of Rapin's *Dissertation on . . . the Whigs and Tories* in Boston in 1773; and it was this notion that furnished Jefferson with his ultimate understanding of the "system" that sought to destroy liberty in America. Still another explanation, drawing no less directly on fears that had lain at the root of opposition ideology in England since the turn of the century, emphasized the greed of a "monied interest" created by the crown's financial necessities and the power of a newly risen, arrogant, and irresponsible capitalist group, that battened on wars and stock manipulation. The creation of this group was accompanied "by levying of taxes, by a host of tax gatherers, and a long train of dependents of the crown. The practice grew into

system, till at length the crown found means to break down those barriers which the constitution had assigned to each branch of the legislature, and effectually destroyed the independence of both Lords and Commons."

The most common explanation, however— an explanation that rose from the deepest sources of British political culture, that was a part of the very structure of British political thought—located "the spring and cause of all the distresses and complaints of the people in England or in America" in "a kind of fourth power that the constitution knows nothing of, or has not provided against." This "overruling arbitrary power, which absolutely controls the King, Lords, and Commons," was composed, it was said, of the "ministers and favorites" of the King, who, in defiance of God and man alike, "extend their usurped authority infinitely too far," and, throwing off the balance of the constitution, make their "despotic will" the authority of the nation.

> For their power and interest is so great that they can and do procure whatever laws they please, having (by power, interest, and the application of the people's money to *placemen* and *pensioners*) the whole legislative authority at their command. So that it is plain (not to say a word of a particular reigning arbitrary *Stuarchal* power among them) that the rights of the people are ruined and destroyed by ministerial *tyrannical* authority, and thereby . . . become a kind of slaves to the ministers of state.

This "junto of courtiers and state-jobbers," these "court-locusts," whispering in the royal ear, "instill in the King's mind a divine right of authority to command his subjects" at the same time as they advance their "detestable scheme" by misinforming and misleading the people. . . .

The fact that the ministerial conspiracy against liberty had risen from corruption was of the utmost importance to the colonists. It gave a radical new meaning to their claims: it transformed them from constitutional arguments to expressions of a world regenerative creed. For they had long known—it had been known everywhere in the English-speaking world in the 18th century—that England was one of the last refuges of the ancient gothic constitution that had once flourished everywhere in the civilized world. And now, in the outpourings of colonial protest, it was again repeated, but with new point and urgency, that by far "the greatest part of the human race" already lies in "total subjection to their rulers." Throughout the whole continent of Asia people are reduced "to such a degree of abusement and degradation"

> that the very idea of liberty is unknown among them. In *Africa,* scarce any human beings are to be found but barbarians, tyrants, and slaves: all equally remote from the true dignity of human nature and from a well-regulated state of society. Nor is *Europe* free from the curse. Most of her nations are forced to drink deep of the bitter cup. And in those in which freedom seem to have been established, the vital flame is going out. Two kingdoms, those of *Sweden* and *Poland,* have been betrayed and enslaved in the course of one year. The free towns of *Germany* can remain free no longer than their potent neighbors shall please to let them. *Holland* has got the forms if she has lost the spirit of a free country. *Switzerland* alone is in the full and safe possession of her freedom.

And if now, in this deepening gloom, the light of liberty went out in Britain too—in Britain, where next to "self-preservation, political liberty is the main aim and end of her constitution"—if, as events clearly portended and as "senators and historians are repeatedly predicting . . . continued corruption and standing armies will prove mortal distempers in her constitution"—what then? What refuge will liberty find?

"To our own country," it was answered, "must we look for the biggest part of that liberty and freedom that yet remains, or is to be expected, among mankind. . . . For while the greatest part of the nations of the earth are held together under the yoke of universal slavery, the North American provinces yet remain *the country of free men:* the *asylum,* and the last, to which such may yet flee from the common deluge." More than that: "[O]ur native country . . . bids the fairest of any to promote *the perfection and happiness of mankind.*" No one, of course, can predict "the state of mankind in future ages." But insofar as one can judge the ultimate "designs of providence by the number and power of the causes that are already at work, we shall be led to think that the perfection and happiness of mankind is to be carried further in America than it has ever yet been in any place." Consider the growth the colonies had enjoyed in so short a time—growth in all ways, but especially in population: a great natural increase it had been, supplemented by multitudes from Europe, "tired out with the miseries they are doomed to at home," migrating to America "as the only country in which they can find food, raiment, and rest." Consider also the physical vigor of the people. But above all consider the moral health of the people and of the body politic.

> The fatal arts of luxury and corruption are but comparatively beginning among us. . . . Nor is corruption yet established as the common principle in public affairs. Our representatives are not chosen by bribing, corrupting, or buying the votes of the electors. Nor does it take one half of the revenue of a province to manage her house of commons. . . . We have been free also from the burden and danger of standing armies . . . Our defense has been our *militia* . . . the general operation of things among ourselves indicate strong tendencies towards a state of greater perfection and happiness than mankind has yet seen.

No one, therefore, can conceive of the cause of America as "the cause of a mob, of a party, or a faction." The cause of America "is the cause of *self-defense,* of *public faith,* and of the *liberties of mankind.* . . . 'In our destruction, liberty itself expires, and human nature will despair of evermore regaining its first and original dignity.' "

This theme, elaborately orchestrated by the

colonial writers, marked the fulfillment of the ancient idea, deeply embedded in the colonists' awareness, that America had from the start been destined to play a special role in history. The controversy with England, from its beginning in the early 1760s, had lent support to that belief, so long nourished by so many different sources: the covenant theories of the Puritans, certain strands of Enlightenment thought, the arguments of the English radicals, the condition of life in the colonies, even the conquest of Canada. It had been the Stamp Act that had led John Adams to see in the original settlement of the colonies "the opening of a grand scene and design in providence for the illumination of the ignorant and the emancipation of the slavish part of mankind all over the earth." And Jonathan Meyhew, celebrating the conclusion of the same episode, had envisioned future streams of refugees escaping from a Europe sunk in "luxury, debauchery, venality, intestine quarrels, or other vices." It was even possible, Mayhew had added, "who knows?" that "our liberties being thus established, . . . on some future occasion . . . we or our posterity may even have the great felicity and honor to . . . keep Britain herself from ruin."

Now, in 1774, the "future occasion" was believed to be at hand. After the passage of the Coercive Acts it could be said that "all the spirit of patriotism or of liberty now left in England" was no more than "the last snuff of an expiring lamp," while "the same sacred flame . . . which once showed forth such wonders in Greece and in Rome . . . burns brightly and strongly in America." Who ought then to suppress as "whimsical and enthusiastical" the belief that the colonies were to become "the foundation of a great and mighty empire, the largest the world ever saw to be founded on such principles of liberty and freedom, both civil and religious . . . [and] which shall be the principal seat of that glorious kingdom which Christ shall erect upon earth in the latter days"? America "ere long will build an empire upon the ruins of Great Britain; will adopt its constitution purged of its impurities, and from an experience of its defects will guard against those evils which have wasted its vigor and brought it to an ultimately end." The hand of God was "in America now giving a new epoch to the history of the world."

In the invigorating atmosphere of such thoughts, the final conclusion of the colonists' logic could be drawn not with regret but with joy. For while everyone knew that when tyranny is abroad "submission is a crime"; while they readily acknowledged that "no obedience is due to arbitrary, unconstitutional edicts calculated to enslave a free people"; and while they knew that the invasion of the liberties of the people "constitutes a state of war with the people" who may properly use "all the power which God has given them" to protect themselves—nevertheless they hesitated to come to a final separation even after Lexington and Bunker Hill. They hesitated, moving slowly and reluctantly, protesting "before God and the world that the utmost of [our] wish is that things may return to their old channel." They hesitated because their *sentiments of duty and affection* were sincere; they hesitated because their respect for constituted authority was great; and they hesitated too because their future as an independent people was a matter of doubt, full of the fear of the unknown. . . .

The Growth of Prerevolutionary Urban Radicalism

Gary B. Nash

Recent studies of the American Revolution have relied heavily on the role of ideas to explain the advent of the American rebellion against England. The gist of the ideological interpretation of the Revolution is that colonists, inheriting a tradition of protest against arbitrary rule, became convinced in the years after 1763 that the English government meant to impose in America "not merely misgovernment and not merely insensitivity to the reality of life in the British overseas provinces but a deliberate design to destroy the constitutional safeguards of liberty, which only concerted resistance—violent resistance if necessary—could effectively oppose." It was this conspiracy against liberty that "above all else . . . propelled [the colonists] into Revolution."

An important corollary to this argument, which stresses the colonial defense of constitutional rights and liberties, is the notion that the material conditions of life in America were so generally favorable that social and economic factors deserve little consideration as a part of the impetus to revolution. "The outbreak of the Revolution," writes Bernard Bailyn, a leading proponent of the ideological school, "was not

the result of social discontent, or of economic disturbances, or of rising misery, or of those mysterious social strains that seem to beguile the imaginations of historians straining to find pecular predispositions to upheaval." Nor, asserts Bailyn, was there a "transformation of mob behavior or of the lives of the 'inarticulate' in the pre-Revolutionary years that accounts for the disruption of Anglo-American politics." Another historian, whose focus is economic change and not ideas, writes that "whatever it might have been, the American Revolution was not a rising of impoverished masses—or merchants—in search of their share of the wealth. The 'predicament of poverty,' in Hannah Arendt's phrase, was absent from the American scene"—so much so that even though the "secular trend in the concentration of wealth created an increasing gulf between the rich and the poor over the years separating 1607 and 1775, the fact remains that not only were the rich getting richer but the poor were also, albeit at a slower rate."

One of the purposes of this essay is to challenge these widely accepted notions that the "predicament of poverty" was unknown in colonial America, that the conditions of everyday life among "the inarticulate" had not changed in ways that led to toward a revolutionary predisposition, and that "social discontent," "economic disturbances," and "social strains" can generally be ignored in searching for the roots of the Revolution. I do not suggest that we replace an ideological construction with a mechanistic economic interpretation, but argue that a popular ideology, affected by rapidly changing economic conditions in American cities, dynamically interacted with the more abstract Whig ideology borrowed from England. These two ideologies had their primary appeal within different parts of the social structure, were derived from different sensibilities concerning social equity, and thus had somewhat different goals. The Whig ideology, about which we know a great deal through recent studies, was drawn from English sources, had its main appeal within upper levels of colonial society, was limited to a defense of constitutional rights and political liberties, and had little to say about changing social and economic conditions in America or the need for change in the future. The popular ideology, about which we know very little, also had deep roots in English culture, but it resonated most strongly within the middle and lower strata of society and went far beyond constitutional rights to a discussion of the proper distribution of wealth and power in the social system. It was this popular ideology that undergirded the politicization of the artisan and laboring classes in the cities and justified the dynamic role they assumed in the urban political process in the closing decades of the colonial period.

It is toward understanding this popular ideology and its role in the upsurge of revolutionary sentiment and action in the 1760s that this essay is devoted. Our focus will be on the three largest colonial cities—Boston, New York, and Philadelphia. Other areas, including the older, settled farming regions and backcountry, were also vitally important to the upwelling of revolutionary feeling in the fifteen years before 1776 and in the struggle that followed. But the northern cities were the first areas of revolutionary ferment, the communication centers where newspapers and pamphlets spread the revolutionary message, and the arenas of change in British North America where most of the trends overtaking colonial society in the eighteenth century were first and most intensely felt.

To understand how this popular ideology swelled into revolutionary commitment within the middle and lower ranks of colonial society, we must first comprehend how the material conditions of life were changing for city dwellers during the colonial period and how

The Pennsylvania Journal's protest against the Stamp Act depicts the stamp as a skull and crossbones. Newspapers and pamphlets in major cities generated a surge of protest.

people at different levels of society were affected by these alterations. We cannot fathom this process by consulting the writings of merchants, lawyers, and upper-class politicians, because their business and political correspondence and the tracts they wrote tell us almost nothing about those below them in the social hierarchy. But buried in more obscure documents are glimpses of the lives of both ordinary and important people—shoemakers and tailors as well as lawyers and merchants. The story of changing conditions and how life in New York, Philadelphia, and Boston was experienced can be discerned, not with perfect clarity but in general form, from tax, poor relief, and probate records.

I

The most generally recognized alteration in eighteenth-century urban social structures is the long-range trend toward a less even distribution of wealth. Tax lists for Boston, Philadelphia, and New York, ranging over nearly a century prior to the Revolution, make this clear. By the early 1770s the top 5 percent of Boston's taxpayers controlled 49 percent of the taxable assets of the community, whereas they had held only 30 percent in 1687. In Philadelphia the top twentieth increased its share of wealth from 33 to 55 percent between 1693 and 1774. Those in the lower half of society, who in Boston in 1687 had commanded 9 percent of the taxable wealth, were left collectively with a mere 5 percent in 1771. In Philadelphia, those in the lower half of the wealth spectrum saw their share of wealth drop from 10.1 to 3.3 percent in the same period. It is now evident that the concentration of wealth had proceeded very far in the eighteenth-century cities.

Though city dwellers from the middle and lower ranks could not measure this redistribution of economic resources with statistical precision, they could readily discern the general trend. No one could doubt that upper-class merchants were amassing fortunes when four-wheeled coaches, manned by liveried Negro slaves, appeared in Boston's crooked streets, or when urban mansions, lavishly furnished in imitation of the English aristocracy, rose in Philadelphia and New York. Colonial probate records reveal that personal estates of £5000 sterling were rare in the northern cities before 1730, but by 1750 the wealthiest town dwellers were frequently leaving assets of £20,000 sterling, exclusive of real estate, and sometimes fortunes of more than £50,000 sterling—equivalent in purchasing power to about 2.5 million dollars today. Wealth of this magnitude was not disguised in cities with populations ranging from about 16,000 in Boston to about 25,000 in New York and Philadelphia and with geographical expanses half as large as public university campuses today.

While urban growth produced a genuinely wealthy upper class, it simultaneously created a large class of impoverished city dwellers. All of the cities built almshouses in the 1730s in order to house under one roof as many of the growing number of poor as possible. This was the beginning of a long trend toward substituting confinement in workhouses and almshouses for the older familial system of direct payments to the poor at home. The new system was designed to reduce the cost of caring for a growing number of marginal persons—people who, after the 1730s, were no longer simply the aged, widowed, crippled, incurably ill, or orphaned members of society, but also the seasonally unemployed, war veterans, new immigrants, and migrants from inland areas seeking employment in the cities. These persons, whose numbers grew impressively in the 1750s and 1760s, were now expected to contribute to their own support through cloth weaving, shoemaking, and oakum picking in city workhouses.

Beginning in Boston in the 1740s and in New York and Philadelphia somewhat later poverty scarred the lives of a growing part of the urban populations. Among its causes were periodic unemployment, rising prices that outstripped wage increases, and war taxes, which fell with unusual severity on the lower classes. In Boston, where the Overseers of the Poor had expended only £25–35 sterling per thousand inhabitants in the 1720s and 1730s, per capita expenditures for the poor more than doubled in the 1740s and 1750s, and then doubled again in the last fifteen years of the colonial period. Poor relief rose similarly in Philadelphia and New York after 1750.

In the third quarter of the eighteenth century poverty struck even harder at Boston's population and then blighted the lives of the New York and Philadelphia laboring classes to a degree unparalleled in the first half of the century. In New York, the wartime boom of 1755–1760 was followed by postwar depression. High rents and unemployment brought hundreds of families to the edge of indigency. The incidence of poverty jumped more than fourfold between 1750 and 1775. By 1772 a total of 425 persons jostled for space in the city's almshouse, which had been built to accommodate about 100 indigents. In Philadelphia, in the decade before the Revolution, more than 900 persons each year were admitted to the city's institutions for the impoverished—the almshouse, workhouse, and Hospital for the Sick Poor. The data on poor relief leave little room for doubt that the third quarter of the eighteenth century was an era of severe economic and social dislocation in the cities, and that by the end of the colonial period a large number of urban dwellers were without property, without opportunity, and, except for public aid, without the means of obtaining the necessities of life.

The economic changes that redistributed wealth, filled the almshouses to overflowing, and drove up poor rates, also hit hard at the lower part of the middle class in the generation before the Revolution. These people—master artisans rather than laborers, skilled shipwrights rather than merchant seamen, shop-keepers rather than peddlers—were financially humbled in substantial numbers in Boston beginning in the 1740s and in Philadelphia and New York a dozen years later.

In Boston, this crumbling of middle-class economic security can be traced in individual cases through the probate records and in aggregate form in the declining number of "taxables." In that city, where the population remained nearly statis, at about 15,500 from 1735 to the Revolution, the number of "rateable polls" declined from a high of more than 3600 in 1735, when the city's economy was at its peak, to a low of about 2500 around mid-century. By 1771, Boston's taxables still numbered less than 2600. This decline of more than a thousand taxable adults was not caused by loss of population but by the sagging fortunes of more than 1000 householders—almost one third of the city's taxpaying population. Boston's selectmen made this clear in 1757 when they pointed out that "besides a great Number of Poor . . . who are either wholly or in part maintained by the Town, & so are exempt from being Taxed, there are many who are Rateable according to Law . . . who are yet in such poor Circumstances that Considering how little business there is to be done in Boston they can scarcely procure from day to day daily Bread for themselves & Families."

In Philadelphia, the decay of a substantial part of the "middling sort" similarly altered the urban scene, though the trend began later and did not proceed as far as in Boston. City tax collectors reported the names of each taxable inhabitant from whom they were unable to extract a tax, and the survival of their records allows for some precision in tracing this phenomenon. Taxpayers dropped from the rolls because of poverty represented less than 3 percent of the taxables in the period before 1740, but they increased to about 6 to 7 percent in the two decades beginning in 1740, and then to one in every ten taxpayers in the fifteen years before the Revolution.

The probate records of Boston and Philadelphia tell a similar tale of economic insecurity hovering over the middle ranges of urban society. Among these people in Boston, median wealth at death dropped sharply between 1685 and 1735 and then made a partial but uneven recovery as the Revolution approached. The average carpenter, baker, shopkeeper, shipwright, or tavernkeeper dying in Boston between 1735 and 1765 had less to show for a lifetime's work than his counterpart of a half century before. In Philadelphia, those in the lower ranges of the middle class also saw the value of their assets, accumulated over a lifetime's labor, slowly decline during the first half of the eighteenth century, though not so severely as in Boston. The startling conclusion that must be drawn from a study of nearly 4500 Boston and Philadelphia inventories of estates at probate is that population growth and economic development in the colonial cities did not raise the standard of living and broaden opportunities for the vast majority of people, but instead conferred benefits primarily upon those at the top of the social pyramid. The long-range effect of growth was to erode the personal assets held at death by those in the lower 75 percent of Boston society and the lower 60 percent of Philadelphia society. Though many city dwellers had made spectacular individual ascents from the bottom, in the manner of Benjamin Franklin of Philadelphia or Isaac Sears of New York, the statistical chances of success for those beginning beneath the upper class were considerably less after the first quarter of the eighteenth century than before. The dominating fact of late colonial life for many middle-class as well as most lower-class city folk was not economic achievement but economic frustration.

II

Understanding that the cities were becoming centers of frustrated ambition, propertylessness, genuine distress for those in the lower strata, and stagnating fortunes for many in the middle class makes comprehensible much of the violence, protest, and impassioned rhetoric that occurred in the half-generation before the colonial challenge to British regulations began in 1764. Upper-class colonists typically condemned these verbal attacks and civil disorders as the work of the "rabble," the "mob," the "canaille," or individuals "of turbulent disposition." These labels were used to discredit crowd activity, and historians have only recently recognized that the "rabble" often included a broad range of city dwellers, from slaves and servants through laborers and seamen to artisans and shopkeepers—all of whom were directly or indirectly expressing grievances. Cutting across class lines and often unified by economic conditions that struck at the welfare of both the lower and middle classes, these crowds began to play a large role in a political process that grew more heated as the colonial period came to an end. This developing consciousness and political sophistication of ordinary city dwellers came rapidly to fruition in the early 1760s and thereafter played a major role in the advent of the Revolution.

*   *   *

III

The crescendo of urban protest and extralegal activity in the prerevolutionary decades cannot be separated from the condition of people's lives. Of course those who authored attacks on the growing concentration of wealth and power were rarely artisans or laborers; usually they were men who occupied the middle or upper echelons of society, and sometimes they were men who sought their own gain—installment in office, or the defeat of a competitor for government favors. But whatever their motives, their sharp criticisms of the changes in urban society were widely shared among humbler townspeople. It is impossible to say how much they shaped rather than reflected the views of those in the lower half of the social structure—urban dwellers whose opportunities and daily existence had been most adversely affected by the structural changes overtaking the colonial cities. But the willingness of broad segments of urban society to participate in attacks on narrowly concentrated wealth and power—both at the polls where the poor and propertyless were excluded, and in the streets where everyone, including women, apprentices, indentured servants, and slaves, could engage in action—should remind us that a rising tide of class antagonism and political consciousness, paralleling important economic changes, was a distinguishing feature of the cities at the end of the colonial period.

It is this organic link between the circumstances of people's lives and their political thought and action that has been overlooked by historians who concentrate on Whig ideology, which had its strongest appeal among the educated and well-to-do. The link had always been there, as detailed research into particular communities is beginning to show. But it became transparently clear in the late colonial period, even before England began demanding greater obedience and greater sacrifices in the colonies for the cause of the British Empire. The connection can be seen in New York in the 1760s, where the pleas of the impoverished against mercenary landlords were directly expressed in 1762, and where five years later the papers were pointing out that while the poor had vastly increased in recent years and while many families were selling their furniture at vendue to pay their rent, carriage owners in the city had grown from five to seventy. The link can also be seen in Philadelphia, where growing restlessness at unemployment, bulging almshouses, rising poor taxes, and soaring prices for food and firewood helped to politicize the electorate and drew unprecedented numbers of people to the polls in the last decade of the colonial period.

However, it was in Boston, where poverty had struck first, cut deepest, and lasted longest, that the connection between changing urban conditions and rising political radicalism is most obvious. That it preceded the post-1763 imperial debate, rather than flowing from it, becomes apparent in a close examination of politics in that city between 1760 and 1765.

The political factionalism of these years has usually been seen as a product of the accession of Francis Bernard to the governorship in 1760 and the subsequent appointment of Thomas Hutchinson to the chief justiceship of the colony over the claims of James Otis, Sr., who thought he had been promised the position. Hutchinson, already installed as lieutenant-governor, judge of probate, president of the provincial council, and captain of Castle William, now held high office in all three branches of government—executive, judicial, and legislative. The issues, as historians have portrayed them, were plural officeholding, prosecution of the colony's illegal traders under writs of assistance, and, ultimately, the right of England to fasten new imperial regulations on the colony. But running beneath the surface of these arguments, and almost entirely overlooked by historians, were issues that had far greater relevance to Boston's commonality.

For ordinary Bostonians, Thomas Hutchinson had long been regarded as a man who claimed to serve the community at large but devised policies which invariably benefitted the rich and hurt the poor. As far back as 1738, Hutchinson had disregarded instructions from the town meeting and pressed the General Court to pass deflationary measures that hurt the pocketbooks of common people, particularly those in debt. Hutchinson continued his hard money campaign in the 1740s. During the 1747 impressment riot, when an angry crowd took control of Boston and demanded the release of some fifty of the town's citizens seized for service in His Majesty's ships, Hutchinson lined up behind the governor in defense of law and order. Alongside other merchants who were chalking up handsome profits on war contracts issued by Governor William Shirley, Hutchinson now stood at the governor's side as his house was surrounded by a jeering, hostile crowd that battered the sheriff and then "swabb'd in the gutter" and locked in the town stocks a deputy sheriff who attempted to disperse them. Hutchinson and his future brother-in-law, Andrew Oliver, joined two other merchants in drafting a report condemning the impressment proceedings as a "Riotous Tumultuous Assembly" of "Foreign Seamen, Servants, Negroes, and Other Persons of Mean and Vile Condition."

One year later, Hutchinson became the designer and chief promoter of a plan for drastically devaluing Massachusetts currency. Enacted into law after bitter debate, the hard money plan was widely seen as a cause of the trade paralysis and economic recession that struck Boston in the early 1750s. Hutchinson's conservative fiscal measure was roundly attacked in the Boston press and specifically criticized for discriminating against the poor. Four months after the Hutchinson plan became law, Boston's voters turned him out of the House. Shortly thereafter, when his home mysteriously caught fire, a crowd gathered in the street, cursing Hutchinson and crying, "Let it burn!" A rump town meeting sardonically elected Hutchinson tax collector, a job which would take him out of his mansion and into the streets where he might personally see how laboring-class Bostonians were faring during hard times.

The animosity against Hutchinson continued during the next decade, because he aligned himself with a series of unpopular issues—the excise tax of 1754, the Albany Plan of the same year, and another devaluation scheme in 1761. More than anyone in Boston in the second third of the eighteenth century, Thomas Hutchinson stood in the common people's view as the archetype of the cold, grasping, ambitious, aristocratic merchant-politician who had lost touch with his humbler neighbors and cared little whether they prospered or failed.

Fanning the flames of rancor toward Hutchinson in the early 1760s was his lead-ership of a small group of conservative merchants and lawyers, known in the popular press as the "Junto." These men were known not only for fiscal conservatism but for their efforts to dismantle the town meeting system of government in Boston in order to enlarge their power while curbing that of the middle and lower classes. Most of them were friends of the new governor, Francis Bernard, enjoyed appointments in the provincial government, belonged to the Anglican church, and were related by blood or marriage. Among them were Hutchinson, Andrew and Peter Oliver, Eliakim Hutchinson, Charles Apthorp, Robert Auchmuty, Samuel Waterhouse, Charles Paxton, Thomas Flucker, John Erving, Jr., Edmund Trowbridge, and Chambers Russell.

The move to overthrow the town meeting in 1760 had deep roots. In 1715 and again the early 1730s conservative merchants had argued that Boston should substitute a borough government for the town meeting. Under municipal incorporation, a system of town government widely used in England as well as in Philadelphia, appointed alderman would serve life terms and would elect the mayor. Under such a plan most municipal officers would be appointed rather than elected. The proposal was designed to limit popular participation in government and transfer control of the city to the elite, whose members argued that they would institute greater order and efficiency.

Both earlier attempts to scrap the town meeting had been staunchly attacked by pamphleteers, who warned that such "reforms" would give exorbitant power to men whose wealth and elevated social status were frail guarantees that they would act in the public interest. The gulf between the rulers and the ruled, between the rich and poor, would only increase, they prophesied, and the people would pay a fearful price for abdicating their political rights. Those who favored incorporation, argued a pamphleteer in 1715, despised "Mobb Town Meetings," where the rich, if they wished to participate, had to mingle with less elevated townspeople. They wished to substitute the rule of the few so that "the Great Men will no more have the Dissatisfaction of seeing their Poorer Neighbours stand up for equal Privilege with them." But neither in 1715 nor in the early 1730s could the elite push through their reorganization of town government.

The town meeting continued to rankle those who regarded laboring people as congenitally turbulent, incapable of understanding economic issues, and moved too much by passion and too little by reason to make wise political choices. Governor Shirley expressed this view most cogently after the demonstration against British impressment of Boston citizens in 1747: "What I think may be esteemed the principal cause of the Mobbish turn in this Town is its Constitution; by which the Management of it is devolv'd upon the populace assembled in their Town Meetings . . . where the meanest Inhabitants . . . by their constant Attendance there generally are the majority and outvote the Gentlemen, Merchants, Substantial Traders and all the better part of the Inhabitants; to whom it is irksome to attend." When so many workingmen, merchant seamen, and "low sort of people" could participate in town meetings, the governor lamented, what could be expected but "a factious and Mobbish Spirit" that kept educated and respectable people away?

In 1760, five months before Hutchinson's appointment as chief justice, the conservative "Junto" made another attempt to gain control of the town government. Realizing that common Bostonians could not be gulled into surrendering their political rights, the "Junto" plotted a strategy for swinging the May elections in Boston and sending to the General Court four representatives who would convince the House to pass a law for incorporating Boston. A "Combination of Twelve Strangers," who called themselves "The New and Grand Corcas," warned the populist *Boston Gazette,* were designing to "overthrow the ancient Constitution of our Town-Meeting, as being pop-

ular and mobbish; and to form a Committee to transact the whole Affairs of the Town for the future." In order to control the elections, the article continued, the "Junto" would attempt to keep "tradesmen, and those whom in Contempt they usually term the Low lived People," from voting. They would challenge their eligibility at the polls, attempt to buy their votes, and threaten them with arrest and loss of their jobs. As Samuel Adams later remarked, it was obvious that Hutchinson was bent on destroying the "Democratic part" of government. On the eve of the election, the "Committee of Tradesmen," working with the "old and true Corcas," used the press to urge Boston's working people to stand up to these threats. The articans should "put on their Sabbath Cloathes . . . wash their Hands and faces that they may appear neat and cleanly," spurn the vote-buying tactics of the "Junto," and elect men who represented their interests.

A record number of voters turned out on 13 May 1760, as both factions courted the electorate. The result was indecisive. Royall Tyler, vociferously opposed by the Anglican "Junto," was reelected. But Benjamin Prat and John Tyng, who during the preceding year had taken an unpopular stand on sending the province ship to England, lost their seats to two moderates, Samuel Welles and John Phillips, who were supported by the Hutchinsonians. The conservatives had succeeded to this extent in creating a "popular" issue and using it to rally the electorate against two of the Caucus' candidates. It was enough to hearten the Hutchinsonians, who now had reason to anticipate other electoral successes, and to galvanize the anti-Hutchinsonians into redoubling their efforts among Boston's electorate.

In the period immediately after the 1760 election, James Otis made his meteoric rise in the "popular" party in Boston, leading the fight to curb the growing power of the Hutchinsonian circle. The Otis-Hutchinson struggle his usually been interpreted as a fight over the regulation of trade and oligarchic officeholding, or, more recently, as the culmination of a long-standing interfamily competition. In both interpretations Otis appears as a sulphurous orator and writer (either brilliant or mad according to one's views), who molded laboring-class opinion, called the "mob" into action, and shaped its behavior. To a large extent, however, Otis was only reflecting the perceptions and interests of common Bostonians in his abusive attacks on the lieutenant governor and his allies. For two years after the 1760 elections, which were dangerously indecisive from the viewpoint of the "popular" party, Otis filled the *Gazette* with vitriolic assaults on the Hutchinson clique, each fully answered in the conservative *Evening-Post*. Woven into Otis' offensive was the theme of resentment against wealth, narrowly concentrated political power, and arbitrary political actions that adversely affected Boston's ordinary people. But rather than seeing this campaign solely as an attempt to mobilize the artisans and laborers, we should also understand it as a reflection of opinion already formed within these groups. For years Boston's common people had shown their readiness to act against such oppression—in preventing the exportation of grain, in destroying the public market, and in harassing arbitrary officeholders. Otis, keenly aware of the declining fortunes and the resentment of ordinary townspeople, was mirroring as well as molding popular opinion.

In 1763 the Hutchinson circle made another attempt to strike at the town meeting system of politics, which was closely interwoven with the Boston Caucus. Election messages in the *Evening-Post* urged the electorate to "keep the Public Good only in View" while burying "in everlasting Oblivion" old prejudices and animosities. But this much said, the paper ran a scathing "expose" of the Caucus, which read like the confessions of an ex-Communist. Allegedly written by a former member of the Caucus, it explained how Caucus leaders conducted all political affairs behind closed doors and in smoke-filled rooms. Then, "for form

sake," the leaders "prepared a number of warm disputes . . . to entertain the lower sort; who are in an ecstasy to find the old Roman Patriots still surviving." All townspeople were invited to speak at these open meetings, it was claimed, but to oppose Caucus leaders was to earn their "eternal animosity" and end forever any chance of obtaining town office. Democracy, as practiced by the Caucus, was nothing but sham, mocked the *Evening-Post* writer.

The attempt to "expose" the Caucus as a dictatorial clique, with little genuine interest in the laboring classes, failed miserably. The Caucus responded by organizing its most successful roundup of voters in Boston's colonial history. On election day, 1089 voters went to the poll, a number never to be exceeded even in the tumultuous years of the following decade. They drubbed the candidates favored by the Hutchinsonians. James Otis, the leading anti-Hutchinsonian, got the largest number of votes and was installed as moderator of the town meeting—a token of the confidence in which he was held for his open-handed attacks on Hutchinson.

The bitter Otis-Hutchinson fight of the early 1760s, carried on *before* English imperial policy became an issue in Massachusetts, revolved around a number of specific issues, including the replacement of William Bollan as provincial agent, the establishment of an Anglican mission in the shadow of Harvard College, the multiple offices held by Hutchinson and his relatives, the writs of assistance, and other problems. But more fundamentally, the struggle matched two incompatible conceptions of government and society. Developed during the controversies of preceding decades, these conceptions were spelled out in an outpouring of political rhetoric in the early 1760s and in the crystallization of two distinct factions.

James Otis, Samuel Adams, Royall Tyler, Oxenbridge Thacher, and a host of other Bostonians, linked to the artisans and laborers through a network of neighborhood taverns, fire companies, and the Caucus, espoused a vision of politics that gave credence to laboring-class views and regarded as entirely legitimate the participation of artisans and even laborers in the political process. This was not a new conception of the rightful political economy, but a very old one. The leaders of this movement were merely following in the footsteps of earlier popular leaders—from John Noyes to Elisha Cooke to James Allen. The town meeting, open to almost all property owners in the city and responsive to the propertyless as well, was the foundation of this system. By no means narrowly based, the "popular" party included many of the city's merchants, shopkeepers, lawyers, doctors, clergymen, and other well-to-do men. They provided leadership and filled the most important elective offices—overseers of the poor, tax assessors, town selectmen, and delegates to the House of Representatives. Lesser people filled minor offices and voiced their opinions at the town meetings where they were numerically dominant.

For the conservative merchants and lawyers, led and personified by Thomas Hutchinson, the old system spelled only chaos. "Reform" for these men meant paring back the responsibilities of the town meeting, substituting appointive for elective officeholders, restricting the freedom of the press, and breaking down the virulent anti-Anglican prejudice that still characterized the popular party. Like their opponents, members of the "prerogative" party had suffered as Boston's economy stagnated after 1740. But they saw the best hope for reviving the economy in handing over the management of town government to the wealthy and well-born exclusively. To see Otis address the crowd and to witness "the Rage of Patriotism . . . spread so violently . . . thro' town and country, that there is scarce a cobler or porter but has turn'd mountebank in politicks and erected his stage near the printing-press" was their vision of hell.

Between 1761 and 1764 proponents of the "popular" and "prerogative" conceptions of pol-

itics engaged in a furious battle of billingsgate that filled the columns of the *Gazette* and *Evening-Post*. It is easy to be diverted by the extreme forms which the scurrility took. Charges of "Racoon," "stinking Skunk," "Pimp," "wild beast," "drunkard," and dozens of other choice titles were traded back and forth in verbal civil war. But more important than this stream of epithets was the deep-seated, class-tinged animosity . . . the polemical pieces exposed: hatred and suspicion of laboring people on the part of the Hutchinsonians; suspicion and hatred of the wealthy Anglican prerogative elite held by the common people.

Thus, Thomas Pownall, the popular governor from 1757 to 1760, was satirized by a conservative for confusing class lines by going aboard ships in Boston harbor to talk with "common people about ship-affairs" and mingling in the streets with the "dirtiest, most luberly, mutinous, and despised part of the people." The anti-Hutchinsonians, on the other hand, urged Bostonians to oppose "The Leviathan in power [Hutchinson], or those other overgrown Animals, whose influence and importance is only in exact mathematical proportion to the weight of their purses." The Caucus, decried a Hutchinsonian, talked incessantly about the right "for every dabbler in politicks to say and print whatever his shallow understanding, or vicious passions may suggest, against the wisest and best men—a liberty for fools and madmen to spit and throw firebrands at those of the most respectable and most amiable character." In retort, Otis, speaking as a mechanic, poured out his resentment: "I am forced to get my living by the labour of my hand; and the sweat of my brow, as most of you are and obliged to go thro' good report and evil report, for bitter bread, earned under the frowns of some who have no natural or divine right to be above me, and entirely owe their grandeur and honor to grinding the faces of the poor, and other acts of ill gotten gain and power." In reply, the conservatives charged anarchy: "The day is hastening, when some who are now, or, have lately been the darling idols of a dirty very dirty witless rabble commonly called the little vulgar, are to sink and go down with deserved infamy, to all posterity." This was doubtful, retorted a writer in the *Gazette:* the problem was that the rich were obsessed with money and "couldn't have the idea of riches without that of poverty. They must see others poor in order to form a notion of their own happiness." Thus, in what was once a flourishing town, "a few persons in power" attempted to monopolize politics, and promoted projects "for keeping the people poor in order to make them humble. . . ."

Reciprocal animosity and mistrust, suffusing the newspapers and pamphlets of the late colonial period, reveal the deeply rooted social tensions that Bostonians would carry into the revolutionary era. These tensions shaped the ways in which different social groups began to think about *internal* political goals once the conflict against *external* authority began. In the end, the Hutchinson faction, looking not to the future but staring into the distant past, faced an impossible task—to convince a broad electorate that the very men who had accumulated fortunes in an era when most had suffered were alone qualified to govern in the interest of the whole community. Lower- and middle-class Bostonians had heard fiscal conservatives and political elitists pronounce the same platitudes for half a century. Even now, a generation before James Madison formally enunciated an interest-group theory of politics, they understood that each group had its particular interst to promote and that aristocratic politicians who claimed to work for the commonweal were not be trusted. Such men employed the catchwords of the traditional system of politics—"public good," "community," "harmony," and "public virtue"—to cloak their own ambitions for aggrandizing wealth and power. The growing inequalities of wealth in Boston, which could be readily seen in the overcrowded almshouse and flocks of outreliefers in contrast to the urban splendor of

men like Hutchinson and Oliver, were proof enough of that.

IV

Only by understanding the long animosity that the common people of Boston held for Thomas Hutchinson and his clique can sense be made of the extraordinary response to the Stamp Act in Boston in August 1765—the systematic destruction of the houses of Hutchinson and other wealthy and conservative Boston officials—and of the course of revolutionary politics in the city in the years that followed. It is possible, of course, to revert to the explanation of Peter Oliver, who, at the time, argued that "the People in general . . . were like the Mobility of all Countries, perfect Machines, wound up by any Hand who might first take the winch." In this view, the crowd was led by the nose by middle- and upper-class manipulators such as Otis and Samuel Adams, and used to further their own political ambitions. In this Newtonian formulation, the crowd could never be self-activating, for thought and planned action could have their source only in the minds of educated persons.

Such explanations, however, bear no relationship to the social realities in Boston at the time or to the long history of popular protest in the city. Again and again in the eighteenth century the Boston crowd had considered its interest, determined its enemies, and moved in a coordinated and discriminating way to gain its ends through street action. It was frequently supported in this by men higher up on the social scale—men who shielded the crowd leaders from subsequent attempts to the authorities to punish them. Thus, several socioeconomic groups, with interests that often coincided but sometimes diverged, found it profitable to coordinate their actions.

The attacks on Andrew Oliver's house on the evening of 14 August 1765, and on Hutchinson's house twelve days later, were entirely consistent with this pattern of politics. On the evening of 14 August, the crowd, led by the shoemaker Ebenezer MacIntosh, culminated a day of protest against the Stamp Act by reducing Oliver's mansion to a shambles. Accompanied by the sheriff, Hutchinson attempted to stop the property destruction. For his trouble, he was driven off with a hailstorm of stones. Less than two weeks later it was Hutchinson's turn. Forcing him and his family to flee, the crowd smashed in the doors with axes, reduced the furniture to splinters, stripped the walls bare, chopped through inner partitions until the house was a hollow shell, destroyed the formal gardens behind the house, drank the contents of the wine cellar, and carried off every moveable object of value except some of Hutchinson's books and papers, which were left to scatter in the wind. Not a person in Boston, neither private citizen nor officer of the law, attempted to stop the crowd. Its members worked through the night with almost military precision to raze the building, spending three hours alone "at the cupola before they could get it down," according to Governor Bernard.

Historians agree that in destroying the Boston mansions of Oliver and Hutchinson, the crowd was demonstrating against the Stamp Act. Oliver had been appointed Stamp Collector, and Hutchinson, though he publicly expressed his view that the act was unwise, had vowed to use his authority as lieutenant-governor to see it executed. But in conducting probably the most ferocious attack on private property in the history of the English colonies, the crowd was demonstrating against far more than Parliamentary policy. Stamp collectors were intimidated and handled roughly in many other cities. But nowhere else did the crowd choose to destroy property on such a grand scale and with such exacting thoroughness. The full meaning of these attacks can be extracted only by understanding the long-standing animus against the Oliver-Hutchinson circle. Beyond intimi-

dating British officialdom, the crowd was giving vent to years of hostility at the accumulation of wealth and power by the aristocratic, Hutchinson-led prerogative faction. Behind every swing of the ax and every hurled stone, behind every shattered plate and splintered mahogany chair lay the fury of a Bostonian who had read or heard the repeated references to the people as "rabble," and who had suffered economic hardship while others grew rich. The handsome furnishings in the houses of Hutchinson, Oliver, and others that fell before the "Rage-intoxicated rabble," as one young upper-class lawyer put it, provided psychological recompense for those Bostonians who had lost faith that opportunity or equitable relationships any longer prevailed in their city.

The political consciousness of the crowd and its use of the Stamp Act protests as an opportunity for an attack on wealth itself were remarked upon again and again in the aftermath of the August crowd actions. Fifteen houses were targeted for destruction on the night of 27 August, according to Governor Bernard, in what he thought had become "a War of Plunder, of general levelling and taking away the Distinction of rich and poor." "Everything that for years past, had been the cause of any unpopular discontent was revived," he explained; "and private resentments against persons in office worked themselves in and endeavoured to exert themselves under the mask of the public cause." On the same say, the governor warned that unless "persons of property and consideration did not unite in support of government" —by which he meant that a way must be found to employ the militia or some kind of *posse comitatus* to control crowd actions—"anarchy and confusion" would continue in "an insurrection of the poor against the rich, those that want the necessities of life against those that have them." On 10 September, two weeks after the destruction of Hutchinson's house, another Boston merchant wrote that "the rich men in the town" were seized with apprehension and "were moveing their cash & valuable furniture,&c" to the homes of poorer friends who were above suspicion.

Seen in the context of three generations of social and economic change in Boston, and set against the drive for power of the Hutchinson-Oliver faction in Massachusetts, the Stamp Act riots provide a revealing example of the "moral economy of the crowd" in the early stages of the revolutionary movement. Members of the Boston "mob" needed no upper-class leaders to tell them about the economic stagnation of the late colonial period that had been affecting their lives and the structure of opportunity in the town. Nor did they need to destroy the homes of Oliver and Hutchinson in order to obtain the promise of these officeholders to hold the Stamp Act in abeyance. Instead, the crowd paid off some old debts and served notice on those whom it regarded as enemies of its interests. It was the culminating event of an era of protest against wealth and oligarchic power that had been growing in all the cities. In addition, it demonstrated the fragility of the union between protesting city dwellers of the laboring classes and their more bourgeois partners, for in the uninhibited August attacks on property, the Boston crowd went much farther than Caucus leaders such as James Otis and Samuel Adams had reckoned or wished to countenance.

V

In the other cities the growing resentment of wealth, the rejection of an elitist conception of politics, and the articulation of artisan- and laboring-class interests also gained momentum after 1765. These were vital developments in the revolutionary period. Indeed, it was the extraordinary new vigor of urban laboring people in defining and pursuing their goals that raised the frightening spectre of a radicalized form of politics and a radically changed society in the minds of many upper-class city dwellers, who later abandoned the resistance

movement against England that they had initially supported and led.

That no full-fledged proletarian radical ideology emerged in the decade before the Revolution should not surprise us, for this was a preindustrial society in which no proletariat yet existed. Instead, we can best understand the long movement of protest against concentrated wealth and power, building powerfully as social and economic conditions changed in the cities, as a reflection of the disillusionment of laborers, artisans, and many middle-class city dwellers against a system that no longer delivered equitable rewards to the industrious. "Is it equitable that 99, rather 999, should suffer for the Extravagance or Grandeur of one," asked a New Yorker in 1765, "especially when it is considered that Men frequently owe their Wealth to the impoverishment of their Neighbors?" Such thoughts, cutting across class lines, were gaining force among large parts of the urban population in the late colonial period. They were directed squarely at outmoded notions that only the idle and profligate could fail in America and that only the educated and wealthy were entitled to manage political affairs.

But the absence of clearly identifiable class consciousness and of organized proletarian radicalism does not mean that a radical ideology, nurtured within the matrix of preindustrial values and modes of thought, failed to emerge during the Revolution. Though this chapter in the history of the Revolution is largely unwritten, current scholarship is making it clear that the radicalization of thought in the cities, set in motion by economic and social change, advanced very rapidly once the barriers of traditional thought were broken down. A storm of demands, often accompanied by crowd action to ensure their implementation, rose from the urban "tradesmen" and "mechanicks": for the end of closed assembly debates and the erection of public galleries in the legislative houses; for published roll-call votes that would indicate how faithfully elected legislators followed the wishes of their constituents; for open-air meetings where laboring men could help devise and implement public policy; for more equitable laying of taxes; for price controls instituted by and for the laboring classes to shield them from avaricious men of wealth; and for the election of mechanics and other ordinary people at all levels of government.

How rapidly politics and political ideology could be transformed, as colonists debated the issue of rebellion, is well illustrated by the case of Philadelphia. In one brief decade preceding the Revolution the artisanry and laboring poor of the city moved from a position of clear political inferiority to a position of political control. They took over the political machinery of the city, pushed through the most radical state constitution of the period, and articulated concepts of society and political economy that would have stunned their predecessors. By mid-1776, laborers, artisans, and small tradesmen, employing extralegal measures when electoral politics failed, were in clear command in Philadelphia. Working with middle-class leaders such as James Cannon, Timothy Matlack, Thomas Young, and Thomas Paine, they launched a full-scale attack on wealth and even on the right to acquire unlimited private property. By the summer of 1776 the militant Privates Committee, which probably represented the poorest workers, became the foremost carrier of radical ideology in Pennsylvania. It urged the voters, in electing delegates for the constitutional convention, to shun "great and overgrown rich men [who] will be improper to be trusted, [for] they will be too apt to be framing distinctions in society, because they will reap the benefits of all such distinctions." Going even further, they

drew up a bill of rights for consideration by the convention, which included the proposition that "an enormous proportion of property vested in a few individuals is dangerous to the rights, and destructive of the common happiness, of mankind; and therefore every free state hath a right by its laws to discourage the possession of such property." For four years, in an extremely fluid political scene, a radicalized artisanry shaped—and sometimes dominated—city and state politics, while setting forth the most fully articulated ideology of reform yet heard in America.

These calls for reform varied from city to city, depending on differing conditions, past politics, and the qualities of particular leaders. Not all the reforms were implemented, especially those that went to the heart of the structural problems in the economy, Pennsylvania, for example, did not adopt the radical limitation on property holding. But that we know from hindsight that the most radical challenges to the existing system were thwarted, or enjoyed only a short period of success, does not mean that they are not a vital part of the revolutionary story. At the time, the disaffected in the cities were questioning some of the most fundamental tenets of colonial thought. Ordinary people, in bold opposition to their superiors, to whom custom required that they defer, were creating power and suggesting solutions to problems affecting their daily lives. As other essays in this book explain, how far these calls for radical reform extended and the success they achieved are matters that historians have begun to investigate only lately. But this much is clear: even though many reforms were defeated or instituted briefly and then abandoned, political thought and behavior would never again be the same in America.

Part Six

The Federal Constitution and Its Political Significance

For two years, from 1787 to 1789, the new nation was preoccupied by a vigorous and critical debate over whether to adopt the constitution proposed by the convention at Philadelphia. The outcome was not at all certain, and it took much convincing in the form of lengthy explanations such as the *Federalist Papers* as well as significant concessions such as the granting of ten initial amendments known as the Bill of Rights, to get enough state conventions to ratify.

Yet once ratification was secured, the country's new fundamental law was accepted with great enthusiasm and quickly became regarded as a document akin to Holy Writ. Moreover, unlike the constitutions of the states, which would subsequently be rewritten and amended many times, the Federal Constitution has never been thoroughly revised and only occasionally amended. This rapid change of attitude and the ensuing veneration of the Constitution have long puzzled historians. The two selections that follow offer explanations for this startling reversal, but they are very different from each other.

John Murrin of Princeton University has been the proponent of a rather unorthodox view about American society in the Revolutionary era. He claims that the American colonies were still quite British in attitude and custom when they decided to break with Britain in the 1770s. Lacking a well-developed sense of distinctiveness and without much cohesion among themselves, the newly independent United States possessed few of the attributes of nationhood. Because of this vacuum, the Constitution was seen as a rallying point, both institutional and symbolic, that could supply what was dangerously lacking.

The view of Lance Banning of the University of Kentucky is quite different. He claims that, despite the conflicting positions that arose and were so rampant in the debate over ratification, there was nevertheless an underlying unity within the American population and its political leaders. This cohesion was based, not on common institutions, but on a widely shared conception, or philosophy, concerning the nature of government. This view about what kind of government should prevail in the new nation had emerged in the years before Independence. Then, later, in the deliberations over the Articles of Confederation and the Federal Constitution, it had supplied the ideological framework that had shaped the debate. Thus, although there were differences over the specifics and the mechanics, there was agreement on the general principles.

Before turning the reader loose on Professor Banning's article, some elucidation of what this political theory was all about would probably be helpful. The ideology that Professor Banning is referring to is called *republicanism,* and it connotes a set of ideas that meant more than simply a form of government without a king, a system that people at the time called a republic as opposed to a monarchy. Until recently, historians and political scientists, indeed Americans in general, had thought that the political philosophy that was the driving force in the American Revolution, and then was the guiding principle of the new nation, was something rather different. Often called Lockeanism, it was derived from the views of John Locke, the seventeenth-century British philosopher, who argued that man was motivated basically by self-interest and that therefore government had to acknowledge this reality and adjudicate the competition between individuals and interests in society. It followed that those governments would be most successful that allowed these competing elements free play and did not try to impose on them some notion of common good or communal purpose.

The discovery that this may well not have been the prevailing ideology has caused great excitement among historians and has led to some rather dramatic, and of course controversial, reinterpretations. It is as if the American Revolution as well as the course of early United States history have been seen in a quite different light. And the republicanism that has caused all this stir is thought to have emphasized values and priorities that are considerably unlike those in Lockean orthodoxy. Rather than the individualism, self-interest, and material acquisitiveness of the Lockean paradigm, republicanism stresses the importance to a well-governed polity of a citizenry that is virtuous and is committed to the attainment of social harmony and the realization of the common good. Lacking the coercive power of a king to hold it together, a republic relies upon the support and cooperation of its citizens. The latter have to be devoted to the republic's well-being and alert to the inevitable attempts by designing, self-interested men who will try to acquire and monopolize power, thereby undermining and eventually destroying the republic. In other words, this civic pride and responsibility, or virtue, was an essential quality for the citizens of a republic, for it was virtue alone that could ensure the survival of a republic like the United States.

This ideology of classical republicanism, which was derived from a particular line of thought originating in mid-eighteenth century England, is what many, though not all, historians now believe was the dominant element in the political thought of Americans of the Revolutionary and Early National periods. And it is this set of ideas that Professor Banning suggests provided the context for the debate over the Constitution. If he is right, then it follows that, with the ideological framework already accepted, concurrence on the document was not difficult to obtain, once the details were settled.

QUESTIONS TO CONSIDER

1. Do you think America was as British in the late eighteenth century as Murrin claims?

2. What role did the republican ideology that Banning sees as so significant play in producing the fulsome support of the Constitution in the 1790s?

3. Which of these two explanations do you find more plausible? Perhaps you are convinced by neither of them.

Republican Ideology and the Triumph of the Constitution, 1789 to 1793

Lance Banning

In 1787 the men who signed the Constitution went home from Philadelphia determined to seek an unconditional victory for their new plan of government for the United States. To Federalists the alternative was clear: the people must accept the new plan of government or face the certain prospect of political debility and social collapse. Antifederalist convictions were equally strong. For opponents of the Constitution no threat was so outrageous, no evil so chimerical, that they could not see it lurking in the Federalist plan. If we are to listen to the participants, the struggle over the Constitution was a dispute between contending social interests over a question no less vital than the future of republican government in America and the world.

Yet no anticonstitutional party emerged in the new United States. As early as the spring of 1791 the Constitution was accepted on all sides as the starting point for further debates. Within four years of ratification, the Republican opponents of the new administration—a party that probably included a majority of the old Antifederalists—insisted they stood together to defend the Constitution against a threat that originated within the government itself. [I]nterest in fundamental amendments persisted for years, but determined opposition to the new plan of government disappeared almost as quickly as it arose.

Too little thought has been given to this remarkable turn of events, and its most peculiar feature remains to be explained. Revolutionary France tried six constitutions in fifteen years. Most of a century of civil strife lay behind the constitutional consensus of 18th-century England. The quick apotheosis of the American Constitution was a phenomenon without parallel in the western world. Nowhere has fundamental constitutional change been accepted with so much ease. Nowhere have so many fierce opponents of a constitutional revision been so quickly transformed into an opposition that claimed to be more loyal than the government itself. Why was America unique?

As long ago as 1835 Alexis de Tocqueville observed that America had no democratic revolution in the European sense, and therefore had no dispossessed estates to linger in inveterate enmity to the new order of affairs. Counterrevolution lacked a social base. Accordingly,

"Republican Ideology and the Triumph of the Constitution, 1789-1793" by Lance Banning, *The William and Mary Quarterly*, Vol. 31, April 1974. Reprinted by permission of the author.

a thorough explanation of the weakness of anticonstitutional tendencies in the new United States might recognize that a society without social orders may well have been a precondition for constitutional consensus. Of course, that did not make it certain that consensus would quickly appear. It does not explain the peculiar inclination of so many opponents of constitutional revision to turn so abruptly to a fundamentalist defense of the plan.

Other traditional explanations ultimately come to ground on similar shoals. To account for the rapid collapse of opposition to the Constitution historians have emphasized the swift adoption of the Bill of Rights, the weakness of Antifederalist organization, the prosperity of the 1790s, and the people's trust in a venerated head of state. All these, surely, we conditions for success. Without them the Constitution might have failed. By themselves, however, they do not explain the startling kind of triumph that occurred.

The Bill of Rights may have satisfied Antifederalist demands for additional protection for valued civil liberties, but, as we shall see, it did not attempt to answer strong objections to the governmental structure of the federal plan. The venerated George Washington was at the head of the new government, but it was not entirely obvious in these early years that the President, rather than his cabinet members, would control the executive's course. Prosperity did provide a beneficent climate for the new Constitution, yet we may legitimately wonder whether the effects of good times were felt strongly or swiftly enough to account for what had happened by 1791. Finally, the organizational weakness of Antifederalism cannot explain why, intellectually, the Antifederalists had no heirs. No list of conditions that favored the new government can help us more than marginally if we want to see why the opposition of the 1790s rejected Antifederalist criticisms, becoming constitutional literalists instead. To understand this we need new insight into what was happening within men's minds. What kind of mental process could produce a transformation so rapid and complete?

Part of the answer—part of it only—can be found in the nature of the ratification dispute. Americans of the Revolutionary generation shared a powerful determination to make republicanism work. The intense convictions that caused men to quarrel mightily over the proper nature of the new Constitution were coupled with a willingness on the part of nearly everyone, once the people had delivered their decision, to support a settlement that no one thought ideal. Most men entered upon the experiment with considerable suspicion but in remarkably good faith.

Acquiescence in the people's decision may also have been eased for the Antifederalists because their objections to the Constitution had never reached as far as the basic principles of governmental structure around which the Convention had ordered its plan. There is a sense in which the ratification contest was a fight within the camp. The dispute developed within a strong consensus which restrained disagreement within relatively narrow bounds. Few Antifederalists denied that a proper constitution should provide for a bicameral legislature within a system of balanced powers. Both sides were liberal, both republican; they agreed that the genius of the people was democratic, and they were equally committed by a shared majoritarian philosophy to abide by the verdict of the nation. For the first time in history an entire people had ratified an organic law.

Still, we must not minimize the conflict. Consensus is always more apparent in hindsight than in the midst of dispute, and even a large degree of underlying consensus leaves abundant room for serious differences of view. The quarrel over the Constitution was altogether real, a bitter disagreement of great ideological depth. Indeed, the more closely we examine the substance of Antifederalist objections to the Constitution, the more we are likely to compound our puzzlement over the ready acceptance of the fundamental law. Most

Antifederalists denied that America could support a republican government of national extent. Many of them wondered whether the new Constitution was genuinely republican at all. All of them doubted that the proposed plan of government promised sufficient safeguards for the republican liberty that everyone professed to desire. Elbridge Gerry called the Constitution a "many headed monster; of such motley mixture, that its enemies cannot trace a feature of Democratick or Republican extract; nor have its friends the courage to denominate [it] a Monarchy, an Aristocracy, or an Oligarchy." Speaking for many of his fellows, George Mason predicted that "this government will commence in a moderate aristocracy; it is at present impossible to foresee whether it will, in its operation, produce a monarchy or a corrupt oppressive aristocracy; it will most prob-

ably vibrate some years between the two, and then terminate in one or the other."

Inevitably the Antifederalists questioned the motives of those who had devised such a plan. The era of the American Revolution was a period of political paranoia. Social and political events were seldom conceived to have causes apart from conscious purpose, and the purposes of any group organized to have an impact on government were automatically thought of as malignant. Visions of conspiracy were endemic in these years, and Federalist conduct encouraged their play. The delegates to the Constitutional Convention debated in strict secrecy, exceeded the authority granted them by the Congress and their states, and produced a document shocking in the degree of change it proposed. Then, in support of a plan of government suspiciously similar to the old

George Washington addressing the Constitutional Convention. The Convention was perceived by Antifederalists as an attempt to introduce aristocracy and despotism into the United States.

British form, they went to the people with an unshakable opposition to prior amendments or a second convention, an unseemly haste in pushing the ratification process, and tactics of questionable legality in some of the states. When these actions were added to the undisguised antipopular feelings of some of the Federalist leaders, their opponents had all the reason they required to suspect that the self-styled "better sort" had launched an aristocratic conspiracy against American liberty. Antifederalists generally viewed the Constitution as the first step in a plot to revive the tyranny of mixed monarchy or to introduce into the United States the horrors of aristocracy and despotism.

These anxieties persisted after ratification was complete, and there is no reason to doubt that they were honestly felt. During the first year of the new government, Antifederalist fears of hereditary rule provoked sharp conflicts over protocol between the branches of the new government, the character of presidential receptions, and a title for the head of state. Moreover, it was nothing other than "monarchy," "aristocracy," and imitation of Great Britain that the developing "Republican interest" soon claimed to detect in the Federalist administration of affairs.

We return to our original problem. If Antifederalists genuinely believed that the Constitution would endanger republican government in the United States, how could they so easily accede to it? Given the nature of the Antifederalist critique, why was it that so few Republicans attributed the advance of "monarchy" and "aristocracy" to the constitutional settlement itself? How did it come to pass that, almost from the beginning of the new government, opponents of the administration chose to rest their objections on the strict words of this frail Constitution, insisting on a literal interpretation of a document that many of them had vilified on fundamental grounds?

Historians have recently given us a likely place to look for the missing element in our explanations. In the past few years, preeminently through the efforts of Bernard Bailyn and Gordon S. Wood, we have learned much about the impact on Revolutionary America of certain aspects of 18th-century English political thought. Colonial Americans had participated fully in the admiration for Britain's balanced constitution, and they had been particularly attracted to the opposition strands in British thought, whose critique of governmental techniques and social trends identified the development of ministerial government, parliamentary influence, and English public finance with a degeneration of the ancient constitution into a tyranny in disguise. Colonial advocates used the ideas of British oppositionists to legitimize the Revolution. The theories of classical republicans and 18th-century critics of ministerial rule helped define an American character and contributed fundamentally to American constitutional thought.

Recently, a growing number of historians have shown that recognition of the persistent influence of inherited English thought can also contribute significantly to our understanding of politics in the new republic. But there is still much more to learn through careful exploration of this universe of thought, for only its general contours have been traced. What is needed is close examination of the specific structure of inherited ideas, as well as fuller study of their influence. Among other things, such as examination can show that, intellectually, the Republicans of the 1790s were the "country" party of the United States. Their quarrel with Federalism was much more systematically ideological than has been seen. It rested on a complete and consistent Americanization of English opposition thought. Recognizing this, we may be able to obtain new insight into the triumph of the Constitution.

In *The Creation of the American Republic* Wood argues that acceptance of the Constitution marked the end of classical politics in the United States. This is only true in a limited sense. The Federalists' great achievement, as Wood explains, was to separate the idea of a balance of governmental functions from the idea of a balance of social estates, with which it had long been joined. America's revolutionary concept of popular sovereignty made it possible to imagine a constitutional structure in which the people would be represented in all of the branches of the government, yet present in none. This concept of a balanced government that would rest in all its parts on the undifferentiated body of the people was an innovation of fundamental significance, the foundation for a new kind of state. Still, the idea of a balance of social estates, which Federalists rejected, was only part of a larger universe of classical republican thought. Its passing did not invalidate the larger structure of inherited ideas in terms of which Anglo-Americans had long perceived and formulated their social and political concerns.

Ratification of the Constitution assured the gradual rejection of the ancient habit of thinking in terms of a governmental balance of social estates, although it was years before most men would rid themselves entirely of a residual tendency to associate the branches of the new government with democracy, aristocracy, and monarchy. But this rejection did not entail repudiation of other classical concerns. Most of the inherited structure of 18th-century political thought persisted in America for years after 1789. And this persistence was not a matter of a shadowy half-life of fragmentary ideas. A structured universe of classical thought continued to serve as the intellectual medium through which Americans perceived the political world, and an inherited political language was the primary vehicle for the expression of their hopes and discontents. For every literate American the traditional constructs entailed particular concerns. A detailed knowledge of this inherited structure of thought is necessary if we are to understand the limits within which Americans went about the creation of a new kind of state and the ways in which they debated its virtues and defects.

From its inception in ancient times, through Niccolo Machiavelli, to its proponents in times of civil unrest in England, the theory of balanced government had been a response to the problem of constitutional instability. Among the many strengths of balanced government none was more important than the protection it was thought to offer against the tendency of any simpler constitution to degenerate into a form of government that would prove oppressive to a segment of the people, driving them to revolt. Proponents of balanced government began with the assumption that, whenever they are able, men will pursue their individual interests at the expense of other members of the state. A simple democracy might originate, for example, in a universal determination to seek the public good. Eventually, however, human nature would have its way and the selfish interests of a majority would lead them to oppress the rest, who would then rise against the government and found an aristocratic state. Degeneration would follow every revolution in an endless cycle of political instability as long as private interest went unchecked. Only a balanced constitution offered a release. With its devices for pitting power against power and interest against interest in such a way that each group in a society would be guarded against the rapacity of the rest, a balanced government might offer a period of constitutional peace.

Of course, none of the proponents of a balanced constitution believed that the mere inauguration of a balance could change the basic characteristics of man. The concern with selfish interest and the clash of contending groups—the concern which gave rise to the theory of balanced government in the first place—demanded from its proponents unremitting attention to the stability of the state. While theorists hoped that each part of a balanced government would exert its power to protect the balance, they also expected each to attempt to expand its power at the expense of the others. Success by any part of the government in its attempts to encroach on the proper province of another meant constitutional degeneration, since the government would increasingly approximate one or another of the simpler forms. Constitutional degeneration was the technical definition of "corruption," a word that conveyed an image of progressive, organic decay. Corruption was a growing cancer which meant the inevitable destruction of the liberty and property of some social group and the ultimate dissolution of the state. Corruption was the normal direction of constitutional change.

Virtually all of this traditional reasoning applied to the Constitution of the United States. Men were still selfish, power still ambitious, tyranny still a consequence of the accumulation of governmental powers in a single set of hands. The assumption of human selfishness, the very principle which required a government of divided powers, induced in America, as it had in 18th-century England, an expectation that the delicate balance of the Constitution would be subject to decay. Each part of the government could be expected to encroach on the spheres of the others in an attempt to seize all power for itself. In the first years of the new government a shared anticipation of constitutional decay helps account for the intensity of partisan feeling on both sides of disputes, enabling us to understand the exaggerated sense of danger that was prevalent on both sides. Fear of constitutional degeneration is an indispensable explanation for the rise of party conflict.

After years of constitutional experimentation and more than half a century of repeated analysis of the course and nature of governmental decay, Americans of 1787 had a rather clear idea of the kind of constitution they desired. It would be a balanced constitution freed from all connection with nobles, kings, and priests, and guarded with all of modern ingenuity against the openings for corruption that had ruined the British state. This was the kind of constitution the Federalists hoped they had achieved—a genuinely republican constitution

which checked each part of government with the countervailing power of other parts and left no room for the rotten boroughs, parliamentary placemen, and irresponsible ministers that had destroyed constitutional liberty in England.

Antifederalists obviously disagreed. Confronted with the Constitution, many of them concluded that the small lower house—a part of government still closely associated with democracy in many minds—could never adequately represent the people. Worse, it seemed entirely likely that the more aristocratic and monarchical branches of the proposed government would combine to overbear the assembly and reduce it to a sham. Federalists might take a democratic pride in a House of Representatives elected on as popular a basis as any branch of government in the states and resting on electorates so large as to defeat any scheme for bribery in elections. Antifederalists saw in the small number of representatives a fertile field for bribery and executive influence and only the "shadow" of democratic representation. To them the balance of the Constitution was tilted from the start, and the cooperation of president and Senate required by numerous violations of a proper separation of powers assured the eventual destruction of its democratic elements. Fear of constitutional degeneration helps explain the most incredible Antifederalist prophecies of doom.

Fear of degeneration, however, was not a monopoly of a single side. When the new government was established in 1789, articulate Americans commonly anticipated constitutional decay. Many Federalists, for example, were preoccupied with an ancient set of constitutional fears. From Aristotle forward, proponents of a balanced constitution had predicted that balanced governments would degenerate in the direction of whichever element of government was strongest in the mixture. Thus, democratic commonwealths would tend to become simple democracies, while aristocratic commonwealths would tend toward simple aristocracy. Throughout the Confederation period American nationalists had been preoccupied with an excess of democracy in the states. Many of them doubted that the Constitution would suffice to end this threat. After 1789, the nationalists who remained Federalists continued to believe that the people's traditional localism and faith in a lower house were still the predominant dangers to a balanced state. The people's proclivities might lead them to confer increasing power on the most democratic branch of the federal government or to reverse the flow of power from the nation to the states. In either case the original equilibrium of the Constitution could not survive.

Other Americans—Federalists and Antifederalists alike—were impelled by a different, although equally traditional, set of concerns. Suspecting that the framers had checked democracy as much as or even more than was to be desired and distrusting the dangerous ambition which traditionally followed power, they expected threats to the stability of the Constitution to proceed from its executive part. Political centralization and executive aggrandizement, the old foes of Revolutionary experience, were thought likely to pose the greatest danger to the infant state.

For both these groups in the context of American constitutionalism in 1789 the natural response was a posture of defense. Traditional ways of thinking prepared them poorly for any other poise. These men had grown up English. For them the major historical precedent for continuing opposition to a constitutional settlement was still the Tory resistance to the decisions of 1689. Americans were a nation of Whigs. They thought of Tories as proponents of unrestrained executive power, and they had been reared in a historical tradition which saw the Glorious Revolution as a saving restoration of ancient constitutional law, a standard of governmental perfection against which one could measure contemporary decline. According to their histories of England and of Rome, constitutional change, like wa-

ter, always flowed downhill. Against the great Whig theme of constitutions in decay, only one small school of "Tory" writers supported a belief in the possibility of progressive constitutional improvement. Beset by Bolingbroke and other critics, who used Whig history to condemn the ministry of Walpole as the culmination of a steady process of decay, defenders of Sir Robert argued that the growth of ministerial influence was necessary to adjust the ancient constitution to the increasing dominance of the Commons. Valuable as history, this was also special pleading on behalf of the arch-villain of America's favorite Old Whigs. It was a "court" tradition, foreign to a people long since committed to "country" ideas. A settled determination to overthrow a constitution or a persistent effort at progressive constitutional change was neither of them native to the American grain.

This is not to say that persistent discontent was unimaginable or that Americans could not conceive of constitutional change. The new plan of government was itself a constitutional revision. Most of its framers originally expected that time would reveal some defects, and they made deliberate provision for amendments. Almost immediately, the nation added ten amendments of a libertarian sort. Few men were entirely happy with the Constitution, and there were always some who wanted major change. Significantly, however, generations passed without structural alterations. Once ratification was completed, most of the political nation found itself on different mental terrain. Demands for alteration now ran precisely counter to the natural paths. A greater intellectual inheritance now warned against attempts at change.

To most of the Revolutionary generation, almost by definition a constitution was something to protect, a fragile structure raised from chaos in liberty's defense. The people had been consulted. Whiggish theory taught that the majority must rule. The classical republican foundations of American constitutional thought taught that a constitution, once established, changed only for the worse. To this axiom all the best authorities in political science, from Aristotle to Jean Louis De Lolme, united in assent, and all the Whig historians agreed. The recognized task of friends of liberty was neither counterrevolution nor reform. It was to guard against social and political degeneration and to force a frequent recurrence to the original principles of a free and balanced constitution.

A powerful inclination to insist on the original terms of the Constitution thus greeted the new government from its start, an inclination that seems inevitable when we have grasped the context of Anglo-American thought. In this sense, if not in others, ratification immediately altered the framework for debate. In Congress in 1789, as James Madison and his supporters sought to complete the strong central government outlined in the Convention's plan, it was members of an Antifederalist persuasion—Gerry, Richard Jackson, and John Page—who insisted on the strict words of the Constitution and cried alarm at every indication of the slightest departure therefrom. Those most suspicious of the new plan of government instinctively fought to make sure that "corruption" would never find a start. This reflexive literalism does not in itself explain the apotheosis of the Constitution, but it is essential to the explanation.

No man's thought is altogether free. Men are born into an intellectual universe where some ideas are native and others are difficult to conceive. Sometimes this intellectual universe is so well structured and has so strong a hold that it can virtually determine not only the ways in which a society will express its hopes and discontents but also the central problems with which it will be concerned. In 1789 Americans lived in such a world. The heritage of classical republicanism and English opposition thought, shaped and hardened in the furnace of a great Revolution, left few men free. This universe contained no familiar ways of thinking about gradual constitutional improvement or persistent opposition to a fundamental law. It demanded a concern with preservation and assured the presence of an inclination to insist on strict adherence to original terms. A leaning toward constitutional literalism, a tendency engendered by some of the strongest currents in Anglo-American thought and powerfully reinforced by Antifederalist prophecies of constitutional decay, prepared the way for constitutional apotheosis. It also does much to explain the appearance of an opposition party that would quickly elevate the Constitution as the palladium of American liberty.

Americans of the Revolutionary generation were a nation of political physicians, expert diagnosticians of the subtlest symptoms of constitutional decay. They knew that constitutional degeneration could assume many forms, and they watched in fearful expectation for any of its signs. They knew, for example, that it might appear in the guise of a change in the moral habits of the people. Wood has shown that during the middle years of the 1780s it was the detection of a growth of popular licentiousness that led many nationalists to decide on the necessity of constitutional change. In the 1790s men of both political parties continued to watch for symptoms of this sort of decline. Similarly, as we have seen, both parties understood that constitutional degeneration could begin with a tendency by any part of government to encroach on the sphere of another. The battles in Congress in 1789 can be interpreted as products of this fear, and it seems to have been a similar concern with encroachment that started Republican leaders on the way to opposition.

In 1789, when he agreed to serve in Washington's cabinet, Thomas Jefferson declared himself more nearly a Federalist than not. No one, of course, had had a more important part in the creation of a vigorous central government than Jefferson's friend, Madison. During the first year of the new government, while Jefferson made his way back from France, Madison acted as congressional leader of the forces who meant to assure a strong and independent executive power. He parted with the administration only on the questions of discrimination and national assumption of the debt, policies that Virginians considered sectionally unjust. On these issues, however, both Madison and Jefferson were willing to compromise for the sake of federal union. The two Virginians did not move firmly into a more general opposition until they were confronted with Alexander Hamilton's proposal for a national bank. Then, already troubled by what seemed to them a growing sectional bias in the laws, they saw in the broad construction of federal powers that Hamilton advanced in support of the Bank a powerful blow at the barriers against an indefinite expansion of federal authority and, with it, the enhancement of the dangerous power of a northern majority. In response they demanded a narrow interpretation of constitutional limitations on federal authority.

Significantly, it was not the Bank itself so much as the constitutional interpretation advanced in its defense that was the original focus of the Virginians' concern. Their fears were unashamedly sectional, but they were also something more than that. From the beginning, more was implicit in Jeffersonian strict constructionism than the particularistic defense of local interests usually associated with a doctrine of states' rights. The balance of constitutional powers between the nation and the states, like the balance within the federal government between executive and legislative branches, was part of the equilibrium on which liberty and stability were thought to depend. Deviation from this equilibrium—change in any form—was constitutional corruption, a danger to the foundations of the state. For Madison, accordingly, defense of the residual powers of the people and the states was no less a duty than his earlier defense of executive independence against the threat of encroachment by the legislative branch. Hamilton's broad construction of federal powers endangered not just southern interests but the

fragile balance that assured a republican state. It was one of several signals that touched an alarm.

Already the character of the Virginians' opposition had begun to change. At first, Jefferson and Madison feared a sectional injustice, and they concentrated their objections on specific policies and on the danger of deviation from the original balance between the nation and the states. Meanwhile, a growing number of newspaper writers and congressional critics were beginning to sense in Federalist policy a subtler and more general kind of threat. A common train of worries seems to have occurred independently to men in various stations in different parts of the country, old Federalists and Antifederalists alike. It made little difference where they had stood in 1789. All were gradually attracted to an interpretation of events and definition of concerns that reflected the inherited ideology. In this process of definition, self-justification, and appeals for popular support, a true political party began to form.

Over the course of the 18th century generations of English oppositionists had analyzed a special kind of constitutional corruption until all but the most illiterate could mark its every stage. The basic mechanism of this corruption was the subversion of legislative independence—and therefore balanced government—by an ambitious executive through the calculating use of offices, pensions, and titles to suborn the members of the legislature. The usual accompaniments of executive influence were standing armies, rising taxes, chartered corporations, and an enormous public debt.

No technique of constitutional subversion was more insidious than "governing by debt." Since the early 18th century a great public debt, with a chartered bank and other privileged corporations, had been identified by English opposition writers as a mechanism designed to extend the influence of a scheming ministry from Parliament into the country at large. Like parliamentary placemen, members of privileged corporations and holders of the debt depended for their livelihoods on the continuing favor of the government. These "paper men" were not independent citizens, who could be trusted with the liberty of others, but creatures of the executive will. Preying on the public treasury in exchange for their support of the ministry, they drained a nation of its wealth. Parading their dishonesty, their subservience, and their unearned riches, these servants of corruption made a mockery of decency and honest work. The power of their riches and the influence of their licentious example undermined the virtuous habits of an entire commonwealth, whose people were thus impoverished and made fit subjects for despotism. With its servants in the legislature and its "paper men" outside, an ambitious ministry could both establish and mask its tyranny.

Reared on a diet of opposition writings, many Americans of 1789 anticipated certain specific measures in any conspiratorial plot to subvert republican government, certain typical stages in any process of constitutional decay. When the new Constitution was established, in the midst of many warnings of a plot, Americans of both Federalist and Anti-federalist persuasion watched every step with conscientious suspicion, fearing executive influence, distrusting a regular army, uncertain how to handle the public debt. These fears were explosives to which Hamilton gradually laid a fuse. Recreating the essentials of English governmental finance, he struck men's sensitivities in their sorest point. Step by step he presented them with a threat they had to recognize, a danger that ultimately justified their anxieties. Uneasiness with the tone and tendency of the Federalists' social style and concern for sectional interests came together with a fear of executive influence on the legislature and a sense of danger to the moral foundations of republican life to suggest a consistent interpretation of administration policy and a frightening analysis of the course of the infant state.

By the end of 1792 the administration confronted a determined opposition that challenged its policies on fundamental grounds. As the full range of Hamilton's economic policy gradually became clear, Jefferson and Madison and a growing number of other critics in Congress and the press could scarcely avoid a conspiratorial conclusion. United with suspicions of a conspiracy to restore mixed monarchy to the United States, the old English criticism of government by money and executive attempts to undermine the constitution again became the core of a consistent ideology of opposition to the men in power. In a process too complicated to summarize in detail, the English opposition theory which had provoked so many worries provided a model for an American version of "country" ideology.

Reviving the old ideas, opponents charged that Hamilton was another Walpole, a "prime minister" whose economic program created in Congress and in the country a "phalanx" of stockholders and bank directors who were committed by their economic interests to follow his every command. Stockholders and bank directors in Congress were servants of the executive branch, whose presence in the legislature destroyed its independence, endangered balanced government, and subverted the popular will. In the country at large, hordes of avaricious speculators and "paper creatures" of the executive fattened on public spoils, mocking virtuous habits and forming the dissolute and privileged core for a new aristocracy. With the aid of these creatures Hamilton was directing an elaborate and effectual conspiracy to create a government of the British sort. The goal of this Federalist conspiracy could be summarized in a word. That word was "liberticide."

Careful study of the public writings of the 1790s—pamphlets, broadsides, and newspaper articles—will demonstrate that condemnation of a carefully contrived conspiracy to destroy republican government was the central accusation in the Republican indictment of Federalism. The evidence suggests that party leaders believed in the actuality of this conspiracy and that they used this conviction to define their character to themselves as well as to appeal successfully for popular support. As earlier in England, the criticism of executive influence on the legislature became the center of a systematic argument that, in widening circles, could ultimately encompass all manner of social and political discontents. In time, some Republicans would accuse the administration of deliberately losing an Indian war or even of provoking the Whiskey Rebellion in order to provide itself with an excuse for maintaining a dangerous standing army. Charges such as these were credible to men who were convinced of the reality of a liberticide plot, although most Republicans never went this far.

Throughout the 1790s opposition to a supposed Federalist conspiracy provided the most important justification for Republican conduct and the general framework for fundamental criticism of specific Federalist plans. It gave rise to the Republican party in the first place. It prepared the party to interpret the administration's foreign policy as an attempt to ally the country with Britain and the forces of international despotism against liberty and the French. Finally, it required the party to see in the crisis legislation of 1798 the predictable culmination of a liberticide design. For a party which opposed the Federalist administrations on such grounds as these, constitutional literalism was more than a pose, more than a temporary tactic in the warfare of sectional and economic interests. Defense of a republican constitution was the reason for its being. . . .

To Republican minds, a broad interpretation of constitutional powers was one of several means by which the Federalists planned to subvert republican government in the United States. Insistence on a strict interpretation of executive authority and attacks on executive attempts to undermine the independence of the legislative branch were two of several methods of defense. Another way to maintain the original equilibrium of the Constitution was to insist on the preservation of the residual rights of the people and the states.

Particularly in the years when they could

not break the Federalists' grip on the national government, the Republicans were determined to prevent federal encroachment on the remaining bastions of liberty in the states. During the crisis of 1798 Jefferson and other Republicans even considered state nullification of federal laws. This does not mean that they were primarily proponents of local rights—a traditional interpretation that creates more problems than it solves. The Virginia and Kentucky Resolutions of 1798 were episodes in a broader defense of civil liberties and of republican government itself. For most Republicans of the 1790s, the federal system was one of many protections for liberty in a time of dreadful peril. States' rights would naturally seem less crucial when the peril had been brought to an end.

Meanwhile, states' rights and strict construction were necessary parts of a systematic defense of republican liberty against a conspiratorial threat. Near the end of his long life Jefferson remembered the struggle of the 1790s in a way that made this plain. "The contests of that day," as he recalled them, "were contests of principle, between the advocates of republican and those of kingly government." A faction of American monarchists, active since Revolutionary days, had seized the powers of government during the administrations of Washington and John Adams. They had systematically sought to replace the republican government with a constitution modeled on the British form. The object of their Republican opponents had been "to preserve the legislature pure and independent of the Executive, to restrain the administration to republican forms and principles, and not permit the constitution to be construed into a monarchy, and to be warped in practice into all the principles and pollutions of their favorite English model."

*   *   *

But opposition to the progress of social and political corruption traditionally required an ancient constitution against which it could measure the degeneration of the present day. A critique of constitutional corruption needed an accepted constitution that could be seen to undergo a process of decay. Lacking an ancient constitution, the Republicans instinctively settled for the next best thing. Symbolically speaking, they made the Constitution old. Paradoxically, then, it was the appearance of a deeply felt opposition to the policies of our first administration that assured the quick acceptance of the Constitution that had been committed to its care. More than the government itself, the opposition had to have an unchallengeable constitution on which it could rely.

The world of classical constitutionalism—a world which Americans found inescapable in 1789–was a world with little precedent for continuing resistance to a constitutional settlement. It was a world that hobbled anticonstitutional feelings and predisposed men to defend a fundamental law. It drove men to oppose an energetic government at a time when the American union was still insecure, but it compelled them to challenge the administration, not the government itself. It forced the Republican party to defend a sacred constitution against an executive threat. This world of classical politics assured the quick apotheosis of the Constitution of the United States.

A Roof without Walls

The Dilemma of
American National Identity

John M. Murrin

The United States Constitution, as we have come to realize, provided an innovative answer to the legal problem of sovereignty within a federal system. This difficulty had destroyed the British Empire by 1776, and by 1787 it seemed likely to reduce the Congress of the United States to impotence. The Federalists solved this dilemma by applying on a continental scale the new principles of revolutionary constitutionalism that the states had explored and developed between 1776 and 1780, the year in which the Massachusetts Constitution completed the model. To be fully legitimate, a constitution had to be drafted by a special convention and ratified by the people. By so institutionalizing the premise that the people alone are sovereign, and not government at any level, Americans made it possible for a sovereign citizenry to delegate some powers to the states, others to the central government. We still live happily, more or less, with the benefits of this discovery.

But the Constitution was also a more tentative answer to a broader cultural problem. It established what Francis Hopkinson called a "new roof" over an American union of extremely diverse states. Opponents of the Constitution often warned that "the several parts of the roof were so framed as to mutually strengthen and support each other," he contemptuously declared, "and therefore, there was great reason to fear that the whole might stand independent of the walls." With heavy logic, he refuted this possibility.

Hopkinson had the right image but the wrong alignment. The Federalists, not their opponents, were building a roof without walls.

I

The American Revolution was not the logical culmination of a broadening and deepening sense of separate national identity emerging among the settlers of North America. The sprawling American continents had taken a remarkably homogeneous people, the Indians, and divided them into hundreds of distinct so-

"A Roof without Walls: The Dilemma of American National Identity" by John M. Murrin from *Beyond Confederation: Origins of the Constitution and American National Identity,* edited by Richard Beeman, Edward C. Carter, and Stephen Botein. Copyright © 1987 The University of North Carolina Press. Published for the Institute of Early American History and Culture, Williamsburg. Reprinted by permission.

cieties over thousands of years. America was quite capable of doing the same to Europeans. The seventeenth century created, within English America alone, not one new civilization on this side of the Atlantic, but many distinct colonies that differed as dramatically from one another as any of them from England. Even the Revolution would establish, not one new nation, but two distinct polities: the United States and Canada. A century later the Civil War nearly added a third. The Latin America wars for independence produced twenty-two nations from a few vice-royalties.

For the English, the Atlantic functioned much as a prism in the seventeenth century, separating the stream of immigrants into a broad spectrum of settlements from the Caribbean to New England. Most colonies shared many important traits with immediate neighbors (Massachusetts with Connecticut, Maryland with Virginia, St. Kitts with Barbados), but differences became cumulative as one advanced farther along the spectrum. At the extremes—Barbados and Massachusetts, for instance—the colonies had almost nothing in common.

Historical demography suggests the larger pattern. For complex reasons that included climate and settler motivation, the farther north one went, the greater that life expectancy generally became, the higher the percentage of women in the colony, and the sooner population growth by natural increase set in. The extent of population mixture also followed the spectrum. New Englanders really were English. The Middle Atlantic colonies threw together most of the peoples of northwestern Europe. The Chesapeake added a significant African population, which would expand dramatically from the 1690s on. Africans eventually outnumbered Europeans by two to one in South Carolina and by much greater ratios in the islands. Climate and demography also affected local economies. Apart from the fur trade, few settlers north of Maryland engaged in economic activities strange to Europeans.

As rapidly as possible, they even converted to European crops (without abandoning maize), grown mostly through family labor. But the staple colonies specialized in the growth and export through unfree labor of non-European crops, especially tobacco and sugar. The West Indies did not even try to raise enough food to feed the settlers and their servants and slaves.

Government and religion also followed the spectrum. At the province level, New England gloried in its corporate autonomy, which Rhode Island and Connecticut would retain until the Revolution. Royal government, by contrast, really defined itself in the Caribbean during the Restoration era. On the mainland south of New England, most settlers lived under proprietary governments that eventually became royal, but Virginia had been royal since 1624, and Maryland and Pennsylvania regained their proprietary forms after losing them for a time following the Glorious Revolution. In local government, the New England town—a variation of the traditional English village—spread no farther south than East Jersey. English counties, not villages, became the dominant form of local organization from West Jersey through North Carolina, and parishes prevailed in South Carolina and the islands. In general, the farther north one traveled, the higher became the percentage of local resources that settlers were willing to spend on religion. Formally, the Old World established church, the Church of England, became the New World establishment everywhere from Maryland south by 1710. In the Middle Atlantic region, dissent and establishment fought to a standstill, with toleration the big winner. In New England except for Rhode Island, Old World dissent became New World establishment.

Some uniformities different from England's did emerge to bridge these cultural chasms. Except in the smaller islands, all of the colonies enjoyed a more widespread distribution and ownership of land. No colony successfully reproduced a hereditary aristocracy. Indeed, younger sons enjoyed liberties in North America hard to match in any European society. Similarly, England's complex legal system was everywhere simplified and streamlined. And except in Quaker communities, the settlers also adopted a ferocious style of waging war. For Europe's more limited struggles among trained armies, they substituted people's wars of total subjection and even annihilation. Their methods were deliberately terroristic. They, not the Indians, began the systematic slaughter of women and children, often as targets of choice. Finally, the English language became more uniform in America than in England simply because no colony was able to replicate the mother country's rich variety of local dialects.

Nevertheless, the overall differences stand out more starkly than the similarities. The spectrum of seventeenth-century settlement produced, not one, but many Americas, and the passage of time threatened to drive them farther apart, not closer together. Most of what they retained in common—language, Protestantism, acquisitiveness, basic political institutions—derived from their shared English heritage, however institutionally skewed, and not from their novel encounters with the continent of North America.

II

Between the Glorious Revolution of 1688–89 and the Peace of Paris of 1763, the colonies grew more alike in several respects. As new generations adjusted to climate, life expectancy improved south of Pennsylvania, population became self-sustaining, and family patterns grew more conventional. Warfare retained its original brutality in conflicts with Indians, but it too Europeanized as the primary enemy became the settlers and soldiers of other European empires. The widespread imposition of royal government through the 1720s gave public life structural similarities it had lacked in the seventeenth century.

As these examples suggest, British North America in fundamental ways became more European, more English, in the eighteenth century. The growth of cities, the spread of printing and newspapers, the rise of the professions, and the emulation of British political culture all encouraged this trend. But the colonies did not all change in the same way. New England anglicized at the core. On the fringes of the social order, it retained much of its original uniqueness, such as the Puritan Sabbath and annual election sermons. The southern colonies anglicized on the fringes while remaining unique at the core, which now more than ever was characterized by plantations and slave labor. A planter's economic base had no English counterpart, but his daily behavior closely imitated gentry standards. In the Middle Atlantic region, where emulation of England always had ethnic and class overtones, the pattern was less clear.

A few examples will have to suffice in illustrating this process. New England increasingly replicated basic European institutions. Southern provinces, by contrast, imported much of what they needed and did not acquire the same capacity to produce their own. Thus, for instance, every college but one was north of Maryland in 1775. New England trained virtually all of its own clergy, lawyers, and physicians. By contrast, no native-born South Carolinian (and only a few dozen Virginians out of the several hundred men who took parishes in the colony) became Anglican clergymen. All of South Carolina's bar and much of Virginia's was trained in England. Similarly, New Englanders wrote their own poetry, much of it bad, while Maryland imported poets, a few of them quite good (such as Richard Lewis).

Perhaps the change was most conspicuous in public life. In the seventeenth century many colony founders had tried quite consciously to depart from and improve upon English norms. They attempted to build a city upon a hill in Puritan Massachusetts, a viable autocracy in ducal New York, a holy experiment of brotherly love in Quaker Pennsylvania, a rejuvenated feudal order in Maryland, and an aristocratic utopia in Carolina. But from about the second quarter of the eighteenth century, colonial spokesmen expressed ever-increasing admiration for the existing British constitution as the human wonder of the age. Improvement upon it seemed scarcely imaginable. North American settlers read British political writers, absorbed their view of the world, and tried to shape their provincial governments into smaller but convincing replicas of the metropolitan example.

One conspicuous consequence was imperial patriotism. The generation in power from 1739 to 1763 fought two global wars and helped to win the greatest overseas victories that Britain had ever seized. Despite frequent disputes in many colonies, royal government achieved greater practical success in America than at any other time in its history to 1776. Colonial expressions of loyalty to Britain became far more frequent, emotional, intense, and eloquent than in earlier years. To the extent that the settlers were self-conscious nationalists, they saw themselves as part of an expanding *British* nation and empire. Loyalty to colony meant loyalty to Britain. The two were expected to reinforce one another.

Occasionally a new vision of a glorious future for the American continent would appear in this rhetoric, but almost without exception these writers confined their exuberance to an Anglo-American context. North America would thrive *with* Britain, Nathaniel Ames' almanacs excitedly told New Englanders. Because population grew faster in America than in Europe, mused Benjamin Franklin, the colonies would one day surpass the mother country and perhaps crown and Parliament would cross the ocean to these shores.

In other words, political loyalties to an entity called America scarcely yet existed and could not match the intensity with which settlers revered either their smaller provinces or the larger empire. Despite the frequent worries voice in the British press or expressed by British placemen in America, native-born

North Americans showed no interest in political union, much less independence. Every colony involved rejected the Albany Plan of Union of 1754 regardless of the manifest military peril from New France.

This reality was far from obvious to the British. They, not the settlers, imagined the possibility of an independent America. Imposing new patterns of uniformity on colonies that they had to govern routinely, few London officials grasped the extent or significance of local differences 3000 miles away. The British worried about the whole because they did not understand the parts, and they reified their concerns into a totality they called America. Debate over the Canada cession focused these anxieties more sharply than ever before and also revealed that British writers almost took it for granted that one day the American colonies would demand and get their independence. Wise policy required that Britain avert this result for as long as possible.

In a word, America was Britain's idea. Maybe it was even Britain's dream, but if so, it soon became her nightmare. Every countermeasure taken to avert the horror seemed only to bring it closer. Nothing is more ironic in the entire span of early American history than the way in which Britain finally persuaded her North American settlers to embrace a national destiny that virtually none of them desired before the crisis of 1764–76.

There was, in short, nothing inevitable about the creation and triumph of the United States. Rather, the American nation was a by-product that at first nobody wanted. The British believed that they were doing everything they could to avoid such a thing. The settlers until almost the last moment denied that they had anything of the kind in mind. Only British oppression, they insisted, could drive them from the empire.

At one level the Revolution was thus the culminating moment in the process of anglicization. The colonists resisted British policy, they explained with increasing irritation and anger, because London would not let them live *as Englishmen*. They demanded only the common rights of Englishmen, such as no taxation without representation and trial by jury, and not unique privileges for Americans. (At the same time, they did believe that the availability of land in North America gave them unique benefits unavailable to fellow subjects at home.) Britain demanded that North Americans assume their fair share of common imperial obligations and embarked on a reform program after 1763 that was designed to centralize and rationalize the empire. Beginning with the Stamp Act crisis of 1764–66, London thus polarized the needs of the whole and the rights of the parts. She was never able to put them together again.

Precisely because public life in America was so thoroughly British, the colonists resisted Britain with all the available weapons of eighteenth-century politics—ideology, law, petitions, assembly resolves, grassroots political organizations, disciplined crowd violence. Until 1774, when the Continental Congress finally provided an American institutional focus for general resistance, patriot leaders looked to the radical opposition movement in London as the logical center of their own. Not surprisingly, until the Congress met, more of its members had visited London than Philadelphia. The Revolution, in short, was a crisis of political *integration* and centralization that Britain could not master. Britain could not control politically the forces that were drawing the parts of the empire closer together. That failure left patriots on this side of the ocean alone with America. They had shown that they would fight and even confederate to protect the rights of the parts. They had yet to discover whether they could create enough sense of common identity to provide for the needs of the whole. The challenge was exhilarating—and terrifying.

III

Perhaps we can now appreciate the dilemma of American national identity. To the extent that North Americans were more alike by 1760 than they had been in 1690 or 1660, Britain had been the major focus of unity and the engine of change. To repudiate Britain meant jeopardizing what the settlers had in common while stressing what made them different from one another. Older patriots quickly sensed the danger. If goaded into the attempt, the colonies would indeed be able to win their independence, John Dickinson assured William Pitt in 1765. "But what, sir, must be the Consequences of that Success? A Multitude of Commonwealth, Crimes, and Calamities, of mutual Jealousies, Hatreds, Wars and Devastations; till at last the exhausted Provinces shall sink into Slavery under the yoke of some fortunate Conqueror." Younger patriots were more confident about America. They welcomed the chance to become fabled heroes in their ironic quest to prove that the British had been right about America all along and that their own doubts and hesitations were unworthy of their lofty cause. At his Yale commencement of 1770, John Trumbull predicted the eventual supremacy of America in the arts and sciences, called the colonies a nation, and exulted in the deluge of blood that would accompany this transition to greatness.

> See where her Heroes mark their glorious
> way,
> Arm'd for the fight and blazing on the day
> Blood stains their steps; and o'er the con-
> quering plain,
> 'Mid fighting thousands and 'mid thou-
> sands slain,
> Their eager swords promiscuous carnage
> blend,
> And ghastly deaths their raging course
> attend.
> Her mighty pow'r the subject world shall
> see;
> For laurel'd Conquest waits her high de-
> cree.

The colonists would inherit from Britain, not just their own continent, but the world. America's fleets would "Bid ev'ry realm, that hears the trump of fame,/Quake at the distant terror of her name." Trumbull hardly needed to announce the moral, but he did anyway. Although the process would take some centuries to complete, America's triumphs would hide "in brightness of superior day / The fainting gleam of Britain's setting ray."

This bloodcurdling rhetoric probably concealed real anxieties. Any task that sanguinary —that worthy of heroes—was quite daunting. Not only would an American national identity have to be forged in a brutal war with the world's mightiest maritime power, but the settlers would have to do so without the usual requisites of nationhood. Sir Lewis Namier has contrasted two basic types of European nationalism from the eighteenth century to the present. Both reduce to a question of human loyalties. To what social collectivity do people choose or wish to be loyal? One pattern was traditional and, at root, institutional. England was a nation because it possessed reasonably well-defined boundaries and a continuity of monarchical rule for about 900 years. The crown had created Parliament, which became both a reinforcing and a competing focus for loyalties as the two, together with their public, defined England's distinct political culture in the seventeenth century. Switzerland provided Namier with another example. This mountainous republic forged a common institutional identity among its several cantons despite their division into three languages and two major religions.

The other model, just beginning to find important spokesmen in late-eighteenth-century Germany, was linguistic nationalism. Among a people who shared no common institutional links, language seemed an obvious focus for loyalty. Even though the boundaries between competing languages were by no means clear-cut, this type of nationalism would come to dominate Central and Eastern Europe in the nineteenth and twentieth centuries. Whereas institutional nationalism had the potential to absorb waves of reform without internal upheaval, linguistic nationalism recognized no obvious geographical boundaries and had to replace existing political institutions with new ones to achieve full expression. Although it began with warm sentiments of benign humanitarianism, it was far more likely to become militaristic and destructive, and by the twentieth century it could be deflected into overt racism whenever it seemed necessary to distinguish true Germans, for example, from outsiders who had merely mastered the languages over several generations.

The most fascinating and troubling feature about the American case is that neither model could work here. The American continent could boast no common historic institutions other than crown and Parliament. It had acquired no shared history outside its British context. Likewise, the American settlers possessed only one language in common: English. In both cases, the logic of national identity pointed back to Britain, to counterrevolution, to a repudiation of the bizarre events of 1776. From this perspective, the loyalists were the true nationalists. Many older patriots implicitly agreed, at least to the extent that they too equated nationhood with the institutionalization of centralized power. To them centralization meant a severe challenge to liberty, a threat to the Revolution itself. Yet all patriots understood that, unless they could unite and fight together effectively, they would lose the war. Their early answer to this dilemma was virtue. Americans had it; the British had lost it. Virtue, or patriotism, would inspire the settlers to sacrifice their private interests, even their lives, for the general welfare.

As the struggle progressed into a seemingly endless war and the North Americans (often for the first time) came into intimate contact with each other, this conviction wore thin. The shock of recognition was uncomfortable and disturbing, for it was just as likely to expose differences as similarities. It revealed, in effect, the underlying spectrum of settlement. Too often the Americans discovered that they really did not like each other very much, but that they needed common trust to survive. Mutual suspicion and fascination jostled for preeminence in the hearts of patriots. The language of virtue may have intensified the sense of hostility, for it became all too easy to explain any annoying cultural differences as someone else's lack of virtue and commitment. The terms of opprobrium that Americans hurled at each other may even have contained more venom than did the anti-British polemics of the period, many of which reflected the anguish of an ancient and real affection now inexplicably betrayed.

The most conspicuous fault line divided New Englanders from everyone else, although other antagonisms surfaced as well. Yankees could not conceal their sense of moral superiority, which often seemed rankly hypocritical to observers from other regions. "We Pennsylvanians act as if we believe that God made of one blood all families of the earth," complained William Maclay; "but the Eastern people seem to think that he made none but New England folks." One New York merchant, Gerard G. Beekman, thought that nearly everyone in Connecticut "has proved to be d—d ungreatfull cheating fellows." Thirteen years later he was still denouncing "the best of them out of that damd Cuntry" for defaulting on their debts. Lewis Morris, Jr., could not even keep a similar sense of disgust out of his last will and testament in 1762. He ordered that his son Gouverneur Morris (the later patriot) receive

> the best Education that is to be had in Europe or America but my Express Will and Directions are that he be never sent for that purpose to the Colony of Connecticut least he should imbibe in his youth that low Craft and cunning so Incident to the People of that Country, which is so interwoven in their constitutions that all their art cannot disguise it from the World tho' many of them under the sanctified Garb of Religion have Endeavored to Impose themselves on the World for honest Men.

When John Adams passed through New York City in 1774, he heard Yankees castigated as "Goths and Vandalls," infamous for their "Levelling Spirit." He retaliated in the privacy of his diary by speculating on the shocking lack of gentility and good breeding among the New York elite. To Abigail Adams, Virginia riflemen seemed every bit as loathsome and barbaric as British propaganda claimed.

Sometimes regional hatreds became severe enough to reduce the northern department of the Continental army to near impotence. Yankees showed such complete distrust of New York's General Philip Schuyler that he virtually lost the ability to command. Soldiers from other parts of America, reported Captain Alexander Graydon of Pennsylvania, retaliated in kind. They regarded the eastern men as "contemptible in the extreme," in part because their officers were too egalitarian. In 1776 a court-martial acquitted a Maryland officer accused of showing disrespect to a New England general. "In so contemptible a light were the New England men regarded," explained Graydon, who sat on the court, "that it was scarcely held possible to conceive a case, which could be construed into a reprehensible disrespect of them."

IV

American national identity was, in short, an unexpected, impromptu, artificial, and therefore extremely fragile creation of the Revolution. Its social roots were much weaker than those that brought forth the Confederate States of America in 1861, and yet the Confederacy was successfully crushed by military force.

At first Congress tried to govern through consensus and unanimity. That effort always created strain, and it finally broke down in 1777–78. Thereafter no one could be certain whether the American union could long outlast the war. In June 1783 a mutiny in the Pennsylvania line drove Congress from

Philadelphia. The angry delegates gathered in the small crossroads village of Princeton, New Jersey, where they spent an anxious four months in uncomfortable surroundings. They found that they had to contemplate the fate of the Union. Could the United States survive with Congress on the move and its executive departments somewhere else? Charles Thomson, secretary to Congress since 1774, doubted that the Union could endure without British military pressure to hold the several parts together. This worry obsessed him for months. By 1786 New England delegates were talking openly of disunion and partial confederacies, and this idea finally appeared in the newspapers in early 1787.

Instead, a convention of distinguished delegates met in Philadelphia that summer. It drafted a Constitution radically different from the Articles of Confederation. By mid-1788 enough states ratified the plan to launch the new government in April 1789. This victory followed a titanic struggle in which the Constitution had almost been defeated by popularly chosen conventions in nearly every large state. Among the small states, New Hampshire and Rhode Island also seemed generally hostile.

Ratification marked a victory for American nationalism, as folklore has always told us, but it also perpetuated political conflict, which continued without pause into the new era. Most patriots equated union with harmony and were quite upset by the turmoil of the 1790s. The only union they could maintain was accompanied by intense political strife, a pattern of contention that did, however, observe certain boundaries. It had limits.

The actions of the Washington administra-

The federal edifice represented in this 1788 cartoon would be in place when eleven of the thirteen states ratified the Constitution.

tion in its first few years seemed to vindicate the gloomiest predictions of the Antifederalists, but these proud patriots did not respond by denouncing the Constitution. Instead, they began the process of deifying it. They converted it into an absolute standard and denounced their opponents for every deviation from its sublime mandates. In effect they returned to their anchorage in British political culture to find a harbor in which their ship might float. They converted the Constitution into a modern and revolutionary counterpart for Britain's ancient constitution. To keep the central government going at all, they embraced the venerable antagonism between court and country, corruption and virtue, ministerial ambition and legislative integrity. The Federalists claimed only to be implementing the government created by the Constitution. Their Jeffersonian opponents insisted that they, in turn, were merely calling the government to proper constitutional account. But they both accepted the Constitution as their standard, a process that kept the system going and converted its architects into something like popular demigods within a generation.

The lesson taught by the first American party system was curious in the extreme. Americans would accept a central government only if it seldom acted like one. The British Empire had crumbled while trying to subordinate the rights of the parts to the needs of the whole. The Continental Congress had brought American union to the edge of disintegration by protecting the rights of the parts at the expense of common needs. The Constitution seemed to provide an exit from this dilemma, a way of instilling energy in government while showing genuine respect for revolutionary principles. But it did not work quite that way. Vigorous policies by the central government always threatened to expose the underlying differences that could still tear America apart. The spectrum of settlement had been muted, warped, and overlaid with new hues, but it was still there. Thus, although everyone

soon agreed that the new government was a structural improvement on the Articles, it exercised very few substantive powers in practice that people had not been happy to allocate to the old Congress. In a word, the Constitution became a substitute for any deeper kind of national identity. American nationalism is distinct because, for nearly its first century, it was narrowly and peculiarly constitutional. People knew that without the Constitution there would be no America.

In the architecture of nationhood, the United States had achieved something quite remarkable. Francis Hopkinson to the contrary, Americans had erected their constitutional roof before they put up the national walls. Hovering there over a divided people, it aroused wonder and awe, even ecstasy. Early historians rewrote the past to make the Constitution the culminating event of their story. Some of the Republic's most brilliant legal minds wrote interminable multivolume commentaries on its manifold virtues and unmatched wisdom. Orators plundered the language in search of fitting praise. Someone may even have put the document to music. This spirit of amazement, this frenzy of self-congratulation, owed its intensity to the terrible fear that the roof could come crashing down at almost any time. Indeed, the national walls have taken much longer to build.

The very different Americas of the seventeenth century had survived into the nineteenth after repudiating the Britain from whom they had acquired their most conspicuous common features in the eighteenth. While the Republic's self-announced progenitors, New England and Virginia, fought out their differences into the Civil War, the middle states quietly eloped with the nation, giving her their most distinctive features: acceptance of pluralism, frank pursuit of self-interest, and legitimation of competing factions.

The Constitution alone could not do the job, but the job could not be done at all without it. The Constitution was to the nation a more successful version of what the Halfway Covenant had once been to the Puritans, a way of buying time. Under the shade of this lofty frame of government, the shared sacrifices of the Revolutionary War could become interstate and intergenerational memories that bound people together in new ways. Ordinary citizens could create interregional economic links that simply were not there as late as 1790, until a national economy could finally supplant the old imperial one. Like the Halfway Covenant, the Constitution was an ingenious contrivance that enabled a precarious experiment to continue for another generation or two with the hope that the salvation unobtainable in the present might bless the land in better times.

Part Seven

Political Parties in the Age of Jackson

The political leaders of the Revolutionary generation did not like, indeed they feared, political parties. In the system of government that they created in the U.S. Constitution, they made no provision for parties and did not even mention them as possible features of the political world they envisioned. To them, parties were invidious; they prevented men from thinking and acting independently in matters of public interest, and they tended to foment divisions that were dangerous to national unity. But, in the 1820s, with the introduction of virtually universal male suffrage and the appearance of a well-organized party around the candidacy of Andrew Jackson, the Founders' fears seemed to have been realized. Why this change occurred is a difficult question to answer, but the reality was that party politics had arrived and was to become an accepted feature of the nation's public life.

During the Jacksonian era, many contemporaries still viewed parties with disfavor, but they especially did not like the practices and characteristics that these particular parties began to adopt. Their methods of electioneering were often regarded as demeaning as was their reluctance to elevate the tone of political discourse by addressing issues and matters of grand policy. In addition, their emergence gave rise to a class of men whose lives and careers were dedicated to getting their candidates elected and keeping them in office, thereby ensuring themselves continued employment. Thus, parties were seen as vote-getting machines, rather than media for the articulation of political issues.

Nevertheless, there were others who pointed out that the parties were successful at mobilizing and involving an electorate that had become extremely numerous and diverse. Mass participation and high voter turnout were in fact characteristics of this new system. Furthermore, the parties were not simply Tweedledum and Tweedledee. Although they may have muted or downplayed sharply contrasting positions on public issues, the parties' respective identities were quite distinctive, and these in turn were articulated by the leaders and perceived by the voters.

Like the actual inhabitants of the political world of the early Democrats and Whigs, historians have reacted to these two new parties in ways that are either disparaging or else apologetic. The selections on this topic reflect these divergent evaluations. Edward Pessen of the City University of New York has been a persistent critic of the claims made on behalf of Andrew Jackson and the party he headed as well as of the Age of Jackson, which Old Hickory symbolized. The piece by Professor Pessen is taken from his *Jacksonian America: Society, Personality, and Politics* (1969), which demythologized the Age of the Common Man and exposed its shortcomings and hypocrisies, warts and all. The other selection is by Daniel Walker Howe of the University of California at Los Angeles, and it is extracted from his book, *The Political Culture of the American Whigs* (1979). His focus is, of course, on the political opponents of the Jackson Democrats. But that is not the only difference, since he discovers a quite distinctive set of social values and approaches to politics that distinguished the Whigs from their rivals. These were not differences that could be spelled out on an issue-by-issue basis. Rather, they constituted a set of assumptions about the relationship between government and society as well as between government and the economy that would be applied on specific policy questions. It could be argued that this kind of divergence is actually more basic, even more principled, than one over specific issues and policies.

In passing, it is worth noting that there lies behind this disagreement over the nature of the first political parties in American history an enduring concern among historians as well as political observers in general about the quality of American public life. It is often lamented that politics in the United States is bland and devoid of issues. Instead of representing clear-cut and programmatic alternatives, as is sometimes true elsewhere, American parties tend to emphasize personality and style and to downplay differences and content. The result is that elections often represent, not a distinct choice, but a preference between barely distinguishable options. On the other hand, a persuasive case can also be made in defense of the parties and the political system in America. But, for our purposes, the point is that party politics in the United States originated in the Jacksonian era. Consequently, the perennial debate about the quality of American politics is projected back to the point at which this controversial and much-criticized practice was launched and shaped.

QUESTIONS TO CONSIDER

1. Why does Pessen deplore the kind of political behavior he describes? Do you agree with his evaluation of it?

2. What, in Howe's view, was the Whig approach to politics?

3. How is it possible for Pessen and Howe to come to such divergent positions on the nature and caliber of party politics in the Jacksonian era?

The Rise of Major Parties: Democrats and Whigs

Edward Pessen

Great national parties reemerged during the era of Andrew Jackson. If, as Edmund Burke had said, a political party is "a body of men united for promoting by their joint endeavor the national interest upon some particular principle in which they are all agreed," the Democratic and Whig organizations would hardly qualify. Only the parties of principle such as the Liberty or antislavery party, the Working Men, the nativist groups that organized under a variety of names, and the Antimasonic party—at least at the beginning of its career—met the Burkean standard. But of course party is as party does. In the late 1820s the United States gave birth to a new kind of political party not dreamed of in the political theory of earlier thinkers. It was capable of appealing to all manner of men, standing for diverse things to its different constituencies and organized and led by men united above all in behalf of no loftier principle than winning office for themselves. The modern American major party was thus born during the period.

At the beginning of the era there were no distinct national parties—or there was only one party. The political effect was the same in either case. The disappearance of the Feder-alists left the field to the Jeffersonian party as was illustrated by the near unanimous election of Monroe in 1820. The claim was put forward once more, as it had been in the early days of the first Washington Administration, that "party division was bad and that a one-party system best served the national interest." Of course what was the orthodox party in 1820 had been the heterodox thirty years earlier. Thus the contest of 1824 was ostensibly among good Republicans all. Jackson supporters were unabashed at the repudiation of the Hero by Jefferson. For that matter, all of William H. Crawford's opponents repudiated what until that point had been considered a major principle of pure Republicanism: the support of the presidential candidate nominated by the party's congressional caucus. Van Buren had referred to the caucus as the mainstay of the Republican faith. But the ambitious candidates would not permit abstract traditions to frustrate their drive for high office, insisting all the while on their devotion to Jeffersonian ideals. The electorate in effect sustained their claims. The bitter contest of 1828 was between Jacksonians who referred to themselves either as Republicans or Democrats and the followers of John Quincy Adams and Clay—Republicans or National Republicans.

For all the continued insistence by both sides on their good Republicanism, the fact is that midway through the Adams Administration a new political party was formed—by its opponents. Masterfully organized in Congress by Van Buren, and throughout the country by friends of Old Hickory, the new party reiterated its devotion to the principles of the Sage of Monticello, but its practice effectively separated out supporters of Andrew Jackson from his critics. At its birth it was the Jackson party and so it remained until the Hero's death, its leaders consulting and paying attention to his wishes after his departure from the White House, as they had followed them during his residence there.

Jackson's opponents responded to the formation of a national Democratic party by creating a National Republican party. This group attempted to imitate the skillful organization, the committee network, and the hard-hitting party press of the Democrats, but it succeeded only in part. Although strong elsewhere in the country it failed altogether to build a base in the South. It did not last very long beyond the decisive electoral defeat it suffered in 1832. In 1834, however, a formidable major rival to the Jacksonian Democracy emerged in the form of the Whig party. This new party was strong in all sections. Led by Henry Clay, it was able to mount powerful political campaigns on the national and state levels all during the 1830s and 1840s, while the Whig share of the nation's electorate roughly equaled that of their Jacksonian opponents. The belief was widely held then as later that the constituencies of the two parties were as different in wealth and social status as the parties were believed to be unlike in philosophy and program. In any case, the nation once again as in the days of the Washington Administrations had two great political organizations competing for control of government.

There was not then nor is there now agreement as to the reasons for the reemergence of a two-party system. Jackson's congressional partisans naturally enough liked to emphasize their dedication to democratic beliefs that were ostensibly jeopardized by the Adams administration. On the state level the factions that jumped on Old Hickory's bandwagon had as little difficulty in justifying their affiliation on the high ground of political principle. But that the early organizers of the Democracy found it politic to explain the origins of their party in lofty terms is no indication that their argument was anything more than self-serving propaganda. In view of the mystery surrounding Jackson's own opinions, the fact that some of his supporters had seemed to shop around for a candidate—any candidate—who seemed capable of winning in 1828, and the total disregard for ideological matters shown by the Tennessee realists who launched Jackson's national campaign, it is hard to credit the theory that the national Democratic party was called into being in order to achieve the political convictions of its founders. The champions of Andrew Jackson seemed to be inspired mainly by the dream of electoral success for their candidate and the political rewards that would be earned accordingly by his loyal supporters.

The emergence of a national organization dedicated to the election of Andrew Jackson as President profoundly affected state politics. On the state level there had never been an era of good feelings. Bitter wrangling among opposing political factions was as much the rule during the reign of Monroe as it had been in the days of John Adams. Opposing state leaders were not averse to labeling their own cliques "Republican" or "Jeffersonian" or even "Democratic." State politics had been characteristically a sordid business, preoccupied with the pursuit of office by any means, nepotism, and partisan legislation. Parties there were but, as in New York State, they "continued more from memory and habit than from calculated differences of interest." A Martin Van Buren or a De Witt Clinton in New York, a William Blount in Tennessee, or an Isaac Hill in New Hampshire was followed not for what he believed in but for what he could deliver. These men and others like them transferred their affections to Andrew Jackson for similarly amoral reasons.

A kind of coattails politics became the rule,

state friends of Jackson obviously hoping to become the local beneficiaries of a national landslide for the Hero. Some clusters of office seekers insisted they were truer Jacksonians than others. Where rival Jacksonian factions arose, as in North Carolina, the split was caused not by ideological differences but by competition for office. Radicals and conservatives were present in both groups. Pennsylvania's Democrats were badly split—as they had been before they became Jacksonians—and for reasons that continued to have nothing to do with political or social philosophy. In New York, on the other hand, what became the Democratic party was a monolith that brooked no opposition. This of course was the Regency, created in the early 1820s to gain and hold political power for Martin Van Buren and his friends. Andrew Jackson's great lure to this pragmatic machine had little to do with political principles. In the Empire State, in fact, the general's new supporters commented that they did not quite know where their candidate stood on the important issues of the day. Political profit seemed to be the explanation of their attachment to the Hero. Jackson's early popularity in Missouri derived from his heroic military reputation, not his beliefs. His party won overwhelming political victories in that state throughout the era by attracting the votes of thousands of Missourians who were in fact opposed to its well-known national "principles." For Maryland, Mark Haller has noted that the Jackson party developed primarily as a coalition of dissident politicians, "composed of former Federalist leaders, personal friends of John C. Calhoun, Republican followers of William H. Crawford, and ambitious younger politicians. Jackson leaders in Maryland, as they were painfully aware, had no distinctive economic issues or legislative program to rally their supporters. . . . They were, in short, united chiefly in a desire to secure the victory of Old Hickory and of his loyal followers in Maryland."

If the Jackson party organizers were essen-

tially astute realists rather than democratic or radical firebrands, they were not totally lacking in political convictions. Certainly the Democracy was very much concerned if not preoccupied with defending slavery from political attack. The Virginia-New York alliance that was the bedrock of the Jackson party rested on the Southerners' dedication to preserving the "peculiar institution" and Van Buren's sympathy for their position. It was no accident that the national leader of the party was Andrew Jackson, slaveowner and friend to slavery, rather than John Quincy Adams, its enemy. Northern democrats tended to be more proslavery than their political opponents in that section. Free Negroes knew this and voted—where they could vote—accordingly. The English visitor Edward Abdy "never knew a man of color that was not an anti-Jackson man." Although Democratic ardor for slavery indicates that the new party was not entirely a creature of expediency, it hardly constitutes support for the old theory first popularized by Jacksonians themselves that theirs was the party of the common man. The principle of laissez-faire discernible in the stance of some Jacksonian congressional leaders at the party's inception is similarly hard to equate with an ideological interpretation of the party's origins.

Convictions of any sort had little to do with it. The Democratic party was conceived in lust for political office by men who had in common mainly their desire to replace John Quincy Adams with Andrew Jackson. At its birth it was a heterogeneous catchall whose great national leader had taken pains to avoid committing himself on the important issues.

The short-lived National Republican party seemed much more concerned with principles than were their Democratic opponents. Although it too was a broad coalition, it was not all things to all men. Its national leaders, John Quincy Adams, Henry Clay, and Daniel Webster, favored a degree of federal involvement in the economy that was frightening to many Jacksonians. Since Andrew Jackson's popularity was so manifest in the years after his first election to the presidency, it might seem that the failure to jump on his bandwagon attested to his opponents' convictions. For all their diversity the National Republicans appeared to share certain political beliefs, which they took seriously enough to jeopardize their own chances, particularly on the state and local level.

To a *national* figure such as Clay, the American System was an astute concept in the sense that it had the effect of exalting his ambition and personal hostility to Jackson into a position seemingly grounded in principle. But the local personages who courted election defeat by supporting internal improvements, a high tariff, or the second BUS, obviously found these issues important in their own right. Support of internal improvements, however, hardly betokened doctrinaire zeal in behalf of an abstract political theory. The farmers, millers, and speculators who favored canal expansion by whatever means did so because it enhanced their real interests or because they thought it did. Jackson's inconsistency on the issue was matched by that of his local followers: Jacksonians were by no means inveterate enemies of improvements. Nor were the early National Republican supporters of federally financed transportation projects the stuff of martyrs. Ordinarily, if such sentiments were strong in a given locality, it was likely too that they

BORN TO COMMAND.

OF VETO MEMORY.

HAD I BEEN CONSULTED.

KING ANDREW THE FIRST.

The Whig party was unified in its opposition to the politics of Andrew Jackson, or "King Andrew," as its members called him.

were popular at the polls. No more than the Democrats was the National Republican party a manifestation of a consistent political theory firmly subscribed to.

The great political organization that fought against the Democrats for most of the period and which, like the Jacksonians, proved capable of attracting massive support in all sections of the country was the Whig party. There is no agreement as to how the party came to be named. Clay used the term Whig in a Senate speech on March 14, 1834, attacking the removal of the deposits. Two years earlier nullifiers in South Carolina and Georgia had applied it to their cause. The eminent New York merchant, Philip Hone, and James W. Webb, publisher of the New York *Courier,* each claimed the honor of having been the first to conceive the name for the new anti-Jackson party. Actually, the term "Whig" had been used in American politics since the days of the Revolution. If there is some doubt as to how the Whig party came to be named, there is little or none as to what accounted for its appearance. What called the Whig party into being was not a classical principle of politics or society. At its birth its discordant elements were united by one thing above all: their opposition to the political behavior of Andrew Jackson. "King Andrew" they thereafter called him. Their choice of name explained what the creators of the new party thought they were about.

According to John Quincy Adams the Whigs at birth were a heterogeneous coalition of five distinct groups, united only by their opposition to the election of Jackson's heir apparent, Martin Van Buren. These were "part of the southern democracy: deserters from Jacksonism in two divisions [Calhoun nullifiers and Hugh White Tennesseans]; Clay Democrats; the 'Webster federalists'; Antimasons; and a disgruntled segment of the Pennsylvania Democrats." "It is needless to say of these parties," he wrote to A. H. Everett, "there are not two that would hold any great political principles in common. Most of them call

themselves Whigs, only for the sake of calling their adversaries Tories." Even the early 20th-century historians of Whiggery who, in the fashion of their time, interpreted the party as the ideological opposite of the Democrats, conceded that at its birth the Whig party lacked a distinct ideological identity. Its leaders "often had entirely opposite opinions and sentiments upon every important question . . . preceding the formation of the Whig coalition." They could agree only on a name and on what they opposed.

The new crystallization of anti-Jacksonian political sentiments sharply affected state politics. Whig parties came into being in the states or, to put it another way, the Whig label was, after 1834, affixed to state coalitions at least as diverse and as unconcerned with agreement on a "particular principle" of politics as were their Congressional counterparts. In Tennessee, for example, the impetus for creating the new party was said to have come from a number of men grown disenchanted with Andrew Jackson and in every case for personal reasons rather than principle: Colonel John Williams who resented his defeat by Jackson in the Senatorial contest of 1823; Jesse Benton, who never forgot nor forgave his humiliation by Jackson in their brawl twenty years earlier; James Jackson, aggrieved at being left out on a limb by the Chickasaw land deal in 1828; Andrew Erwin, the father-in-law of the young man Jackson killed in a gambling quarrel; and Newton Cannon, who had incurred Jackson's wrath for once voting, as a juror, for the acquittal of one of Jackson's enemies. Out of such a mixture of hatreds, ambitions, jealousy, and a "modicum of principles," the Whig party took shape in the spring of 1834.

In a state such as Missouri, in which political opposition to Jackson was utterly unrewarding politically, a formal Whig party emerged only after The Hero vacated the White House. The new party's relatively few stalwarts seemed readily identifiable as former National Republicans pure and simple. Local issues could also account for Whig organization. Thus citizens in a number of Michigan cities were evidently moved to create a formal party structure by their fear of the alleged corruption that would follow an extension of the suffrage to foreign Catholics. The new Whig party in the states of New York and Pennsylvania had little to do with one another but they had much in common, particularly in the goals they pursued. According to [Glyndon] Van Deusen, New York's original Whigs were a strange amalgam, consisting of "states' righters and nationalists, Masons and Antimasons, pro- and anti-Clay men, pro- and anti-Bank men, merchants and manufacturers, farmers and laborers" —united in opposition to Jackson, Van Buren, and the Regency. So heterogeneous a coalition could easily fall into disarray. Later Greeley would rail against the "dirty, disgraceful, miserable . . . fraction" that alone prevented sweeping Whig successes in New York. Opposed to the Regency largely out of expediency, New York's Whigs had as "their immediate and chief objective . . . control of the state." The motley groups which created Pennsylvania's Whig party had similarly realistic ambitions, but found at first they "could not advance a concrete program because this would cause the coalition to dissolve."

For all their realism, however, the Whigs no less than their opponents did believe in certain principles. Opposition to Andrew Jackson was an expression, albeit an indistinct one, of political beliefs of sorts. The Whig charge of executive tyranny, if taken at face value, was made by men who believed in the Lockean and Jeffersonian concept of legislative dominance. Some skeptics have wondered whether Whigs would have been so opposed to a strong President had his name been Clay rather than Jackson. There is little reason to believe that any man but Jackson would have been capable of the enormities both of style and substance that he, in fact, committed as the nation's Chief Executive. Whig theories of the Executive were consistent and probably sincere expressions of constitutional convictions. It was not Andrew

Jackson's person that most Whigs objected to, but his official acts. Thomas Hart Benton, who had as much reason as his brother to hate Old Hickory, did not become a Whig, after all. He belonged to that legion of men who had no fault to find with arbitrary means used to accomplish ends with which they were in sympathy.

Whig objections were not to mannerisms but to concrete policies. The precipitating issue that impelled the Administration's diverse opponents to coalesce was the removal both of the deposits as well as of the Secretaries of the Treasury who would not go along with it. No doubt some Whigs found this issue a convenient pretext essentially which might help them win office. The banking issue, for all the flaming rhetoric used to describe it, was not an ideological issue in the common meaning of the term. Rich men were on both sides of the issue and for good reason. If poor men were largely on one side of it, it was not because they should have been but rather, as Thurlow Weed had pointed out in 1832, because the demagogic phrases in Kendall's veto message had captured their imagination. Jacksonian leaders in a number of states had believed Biddle's Bank an excellent institution but not so excellent as to lead them to jeopardize their personal political careers by supporting it, after 1832. The views of the first Whig leaders were thus not fundamentally unlike those of their Democratic opponents in the sense that Jacobin principles differed from Monarchist, or English Tory from English Whig. But if the differences between the American major parties were more over means than ends, they were real differences nonetheless.

While the new parties seem to have sprung into existence for reasons having little to do with classic principles or convictions, their subsequent behavior has been widely interpreted as proof of their fundamentally dissimilar character. Of course the parties were different—in program, style, propaganda, and in the kinds of support they attracted. But the question is: were they opposed in the sense that Arthur Schlesinger, Jr., suggested? Was one the party of the people, devoted to a truly radical program, followed by a motley mass of have-nots and underprivileged? Was the other a party of wealth, committed to a conservative program that was justifiably supported by the established orders?

That the era's leading political figures were cut from the same cloth, regardless of party affiliation, suggests the similarity of the political organizations they led. But to *suggest* is not to *establish*. Parties led by similar types can themselves be unlike. A comparison of the Whigs and Democrats, if it is to be fruitful, must be based on their actual performance. Fortunately the historical record has been examined intensively in recent years, resulting in scores of rewarding studies of Jacksonian politics, particularly on the state and local level, that make possible a modern synthesis. It is not to give the story away to note at this point that the recent work deals in nuances, in shades other than black and white. The truths concerning Jacksonian parties are more subtle than the contemporary partisan rhetoric or, for that matter, the scholarly controversy of a few decades ago, might suggest.

Many contemporaries seemed convinced that party clashes in this country were similar to the conflicts that divided men on the Continent and in Great Britain. Writings of the Democrats and the Whigs, Emerson said "one has the best cause, and the other contains the best men." According to him, the former party stood for reform, democracy, and "facilitating in every manner the access of the young and the poor to sources of wealth and power," while the Whigs, for all the moral superiority of their members, were "timid and merely defensive of property." Emerson was one of that sizable group of contemporaries who believed not only that the major parties were different but that the differences concerned precisely the bedrock issues that classically separated men

into opposing parties. In Virginia the story was told that John Syme, asked if a Democrat could be a gentleman, "was wont to tap his snuff box significantly, and reply, 'Well, he is apt not to be; but if he is, he is in damned bad company.' "

The painters, sculptors, poets, essayists, and novelists proudly claimed by the Democracy, particularly in Massachusetts, did in fact identify themselves with the Jackson party in inordinate numbers. In Harriet Martineau's phrase, "the men of genius were with the Democracy." Of course men of genius were not necessarily gifted in political analysis. George Bancroft's romantic notion that the popular judgment is never wrong in artistic matters raises questions about his own political acuity. Then as later, creative men innocent of the ways of politics could hold to views that grossly oversimplified the political warfare of their time. Some writers may have been Democrats because of the jobs offered them. Whatever the reasons, the fact remains that many creative figures subscribed to the Emersonian thesis that the one party was more democratic and radical than the other.

Since a popular belief is itself an important historical fact, regardless of its wisdom or accuracy, contemporary conceptions—or misconceptions—about the nature of Jacksonian Democracy cannot be entirely discounted. Yet it is significant that much of the contemporary comment stressing the alleged gulf separating the parties came from interested or partisan rather than disinterested sources. As early as 1828, on the occasion of Jackson's visit to New York City, the editor of the *American* referred contemptuously to the crowd that surrounded the Hero as a mob made up of mechanics rather than the city's "most respected inhabitants." During the bank war, a Boston journal charged that the "spirit of Jacobinism" was "the same that pervaded in France during the worst period of the Revolution." Florida's Whigs joined Webster in excoriating Democratic Jacobinism, leveling, and revolutionary agrarianism. Traveling in New York during the years of the Van Buren Administration, John S. Buckingham heard the Democrats denounced as "atheists, infidels, agrarians, incendiaries, men who were without religion and honesty, who desire to pull down all that is venerable in the institutions of the country, to seize the property of the rich, and divide it among the poor," among other things. It was precisely such Whig charges that helped produce Van Buren's victory, for as William H. Seward wrote Thurlow Weed, just prior to the 1836 election, "[T]he people are for him. Not so much for him as for the principle they suppose he represents. . . . It is with them the poor against the rich." In view of his own party's insistent repetition of this theme, Seward thought it only natural that common men would identify with the Democrats.

The Democrats gloried in the charge—to the extent that it was politically useful. Revolutionary agrarians, they assured the nation, they were not. But as true champions of the lowly was it not to be expected that they would be outrageously abused by the sycophants of aristocracy? The Regency leader, Michael Hoffman, saw the early party battles in terms of "the aristocracy and the democracy arrayed against each other." In the aftermath of the bank war, a New England Democratic organ found it fitting that "farmers, mechanics, laboring men . . . the true bone and sinew—the virtue, honesty and patriotism of the country," were aligned with the party of Jackson. The years of the bank struggle were particularly productive of this kind of discussion. Radical editors who now found themselves in harmony with the Democracy they heretofore had criticized, contributed their flair for polemics to the cause. George Henry Evans' labor journal, *The Man,* ran jingles explaining that aristocrats and "such as Hartford Feds oppose the poor and Jackson," while its columns charged that if the "Troy Whigs had their way, the poor would be placed in a complete state of vassalage." Tory Whigs! They also hinted at Whig management of the burning down of the Ursuline Convent.

Sometimes fiery Democratic language camouflaged most moderate Democratic thought, as in the case of a Boston *Post* election year editorial urging keener community appreciation of the working classes. Success and esteem, according to the Democratic editor, were to be won by mechanics through "industry, temperance and frugality"—precisely the roads to lower class upward movement that were traditionally urged by the most timid defenders of the status quo. Of course if party propaganda was read and heard, it is likely that it was neither listened to with great care nor read with an eye for nuance. On the other hand, it does seem clear that many voters did not discount altogether the mutual recriminations showered down by the great parties on one another. Whig leaders obviously thought it good politics to brand the Jacksonians revolutionist, while Democrats hoped to profit in turn from labeling their enemies aristocrat. Observing that the poor outnumbered the rich, Seward had misgivings about the astuteness of his party's diatribes. National election results for the era confirm his widsom. Politically astute or no, the Whig "interpretations" and the Democratic responses to them, were also to foster oversimplified notions about the major parties, leaving the impression in the minds of later generations that the great parties of the age of Jackson were, as their zealous protagonists described them, representatives of conflicting interests in American society.

A surprising number of contemporaries, however, thought otherwise. Some of them were themselves Jacksonians. The eminent anti-Bank radical, Robert Rantoul, in the midst of the controversy over the second BUS, confided to his memories his belief that "our party contests have not that intrinsic importance with which the lively fancies of the heated partisans often invest them; . . . they are often in a great degree struggles for office. . . ." Even the editors of the *Democratic Review,* the Jackson party organ, conceded that "the violence of the party warfare in which we are perpetually engaged" obscured the basic agreements and the common "democratic sentiment and spirit" of members of both parties. To Francis Baylies, a former Massachusetts Federalist visiting New York in the mid-1830s, "with the Whigs and Van Burenites it is a contest of office and nothing else," between these two "miserable" parties. Franklin E. Plummer, champion of Mississippi's lower classes, in 1834 denounced the Democratic party of his state as no better than the Whigs and, like them, "lacking any real concern for the interests of the major class," the workers. At the time he spoke he continued to support the Bank Veto. Plummer's views were similar to those expressed by labor leaders throughout the country, before and after the Bank War.

The accusation made first in Philadelphia in 1828 by the *Mechanic's Free Press,* that the Democrats were more dangerous to the working classes because more deceitful than their opponents, was repeated regularly in the labor press during the following decade. Such leaders as John Commerford of the New York Trades' Union counseled labor that the major parties were frauds: "Stand aloof, remember we have no alliance with either of the humbugs," he advised. The Pennsylvania labor veteran, John Ferral, hoped that workers would not permit themselves to be duped by the shrewd politicians in control of both parties. Lesser known labor correspondents warned that "designing demagogues [had] . . . set themselves up as political reformers under the name of Democrats . . . and Whigs, and a catalogue of names used as baits" to lure mechanics "into the nets of political fishers of all parties." To the prolabor dissidents who broke with the New York Democracy in 1836, "the leaders of the two great political parties under which the people have arrayed themselves are selfish and unprincipled; the objects of both are power, honors, and emolument." Nor were these criticisms atypical. They were representative of a persistent denunciation by Working Men's party and trade union leaders alike of

the major parties as of the political system the latter ostensibly dominated in the interests of the wealthy classes.

Less embattled figures also that political hyperbole only masked the basic similarities of the major parties. Tocqueville had concluded that America lacked great parties in the absence of great issues; "and if her happiness is therefore considerably increased, her morality has suffered." No party seemed "to contest the present . . . course of society," while all the shouting was over differences and issues so slight as "to be incomprehensible or puerile." He was no doubt influenced by what John Latrobe and Jared Sparks had told him. Latrobe had said, "realistically speaking, there are no parties in the United States: everything is reduced to a question of men; there are those who have the power and those who want to have it, the people in and [the people] out." According to Sparks, "there were no political parties properly so called: only local interests and personal rivalries." For all the clamor, "their differencees were those of personal preference, rather than of principle." Several years later, when party bitterness was at its height, Francis Lieber observed that "however great the excitement may appear, on paper or in words, the people know very well that their lives and property are not in jeopardy; that whatever party may come in or go out, the broad principles of the whole system will be acted upon, the general laws will be preserved." Harriet Martineau found it "remarkable how nearly [the] . . . positive statements of political doctrine [of Whigs and Democrats] agree, while they differ in almost every possible application of their common principles."

Many influential persons thus saw through —or thought they saw through—the sham nature of the era's party battles. Their voices, however, were muted if not drowned out by the sounds of partisan political trumpeting. The fact remains that if contemporary opinion was not equally divided between those who took party rhetoric seriously and those who did not, a significant number of respected persons dissented from the Emersonian view of the parties.

The school of thought that finds the Whigs and the Jacksonian Democrats dissimilar makes much of the allegedly contrasting philosophies and beliefs of the parties. This is both understandable and sensible. What the parties and their spokesmen said obviously throws some light on the character of the parties. The question is: how much light? In answering this question, at one extreme stand historians who appear to take party statements at face value. At the other stand those who would discount them entirely.

The search for the parties' true beliefs is a most difficult one. There is the insoluble problem of determining the weight to be affixed formal party pronunciamentos on the one hand and the more informal remarks by individuals on the other. The two are very different kinds of statement. How seriously can one take policy statements which were admittedly not binding either on the men who made them or on those to whom they were addressed? What is "party thought" when party leaders think contradictory thoughts about a given problem? How distinguish between a demagogic comment, motivated only by a desire to sway voters, and a sincere revelation of a true conviction? These are some of the problems that attend a discussion of party philosophy and principles.

In the case of parties as dedicated to winning office as were the Jacksonian Democrats and the Whigs, it is hard to take their platforms seriously as expressions of true belief. For that matter, national platforms were avoided until 1840 when the beleaguered Democracy tried to explain away its role in causing the depression. The Whigs waited until 1844, in that year building a platform for Henry Clay that alas proved a mite too broad and not sufficiently solid. It had more to do with gathering votes than anything else. No doubt many Democrats sincerely wanted to put down the second Bank of the United States. But their willingness to replace

it by dozens of other banks as repository for federal funds is hardly convincing evidence of the anticapitalistic animus attributed to them by some scholars. The age of popular suffrage called forth demagogic party pronouncements in behalf of socially mild programs. That one party, the Whigs, typically eschewed such propaganda, while the other, the Democrats, relied on it enthusiastically, reveals a difference in tactics as in the public image sought, rather than in fundamental beliefs.

The belief in Jacksonian radicalism nevertheless persists. Glyndon G. Van Deusen, the outstanding modern authority on the era, while denying that the Democracy was "in any real sense a party that actually arrayed or sought to array the masses against the classes," judges that it moved in that direction. Like many other historians he detects a transition that significantly altered this one-time opportunistic coalition: "[S]ix years after Jackson had entered the Executive Mansion, the party could still be described as moving slowly and spasmodically to the left." Obviously, the definition assigned the term "left" determines the validity of this view. Right-wing usage has tried to make the term as inclusive as possible, the better to stigmatize liberals in a society suspicious of the term. As used by social scientists, however, the left has traditionally stood for a radical position calling for drastic modification if not abolition of a system of private property, far-reaching social reforms, and the subordination of liberty to equality if necessary to accomplish its goals. While parties of the left have made much of expanding the suffrage, like the English Chartists they applauded the reform as the necessary precondition for rearranging society in the interests of have-nots. When the term is thus defined, no significant leftward movement can be detected in the Democratic party's behavior either in the later years of the Jackson or in the Van Buren Administrations.

The one Locofoco doctrine that the party took over was neither left nor right: it was a currency policy capable of earning support from conservatives and bankers for the good reason that it had no appreciable effect on property. The party's antitariff views were not beloved of manufacturers, but they were hardly a radical, proconsumer position, supported as they were by wealthy merchants and planters, and—as modern economic historians have noted—lacking as they were in great significance for the economy. Cheap public land did mean a reduced starting price at public auction, yet it did not seriously interfere with speculation. Many Democrats favored revision of "aristocratic" corporation laws that in effect gave monopolies to the privileged recipients of special charters. Democratic opposition to freer incorporation laws could also be made to appear downright anticapitalistic. In New York it was a tactic used in an attempt to maintain the privileges of Democratic bankers—prior beneficiaries of the special acts of incorporation passed by Regency-dominated state legislatures. If these mixed Democratic attitudes do not cancel each other out, certainly they raise doubts as to the actual crucial nature of the issue, for all the marvelous rhetoric used in public discussion of it. Even the famous rulings of the Taney Court, most of whose members had like Taney himself been appointed by Old Hickory, are not quite the egalitarian decrees some exaggerated comments make them out to be.

Roger B. Taney of Maryland was a former Federalist of conservative monetary and social beliefs. He had endeared himself to Jackson by the unswerving support he gave to the Hero's war on the second Bank of the United States and by what even Taney's sympathetic chief biographer regarded as his "sycophantic" behavior in the controversy that arose within the Administration over the removal of the deposits. Taney won Jackson's heart when he agreed to replace as Secretary of the Treasury the recalcitrant William J. Duane, who was unwilling to order the removal of the deposits and who was summarily dismissed for his obstinacy. Duane himself had replaced Louis McLane, whose "promotion" to the State Department had evidently been planned prior to and per-

haps in anticipation of McLane's refusal to remove the deposits. Taney's great claim to fame, of course, was his decision in the Dred Scott case. That ruling was not inconsistent with the principles underlying his and his court's important decisions during the Jacksonian era. . . .

The decision that is chiefly responsible for the radical reputation of the early Taney Court is the one Taney delivered in 1837 in the case of the *Charles River Bridge Company* v. *Warren Bridge Company*. In this undeniably liberal and liberating ruling, Taney brushed aside the theory that a toll bridge company had an implied right not to have competition in the form of a free bridge built over the same river. "In a country like ours," he argued, "free, active, and enterprising, continually advancing in numbers of wealth, new channels of communication are daily found necessary both for travel and trade; and are essential to the comfort, convenience, and prosperity of the people." The advocates of the entrepreneurial theory of Jacksonian Democracy have no stronger documentation than the Charles River decision, for in it the Jacksonian Court ruled not against private property or capitalism, but in favor of an expanding capitalistic society and the free competition necessary to assure it. There was nothing radical in this decision except some of its language. In implying that no interest was equal in weight to the community's, the Court suggested to some overwrought people that it was prepared to impair contracts or acquiesce in attacks on property. Such newspapers as the Boston *Daily Advertiser* and the New York *Commercial Advertiser* lamented the alleged "subversion of the principles of law and property" and the threat to corporate investments inherent in the decision. Two years later, when in *Bank of Augusta* v. *Earle,* Taney once again stated his opposition to an implied right—this time however against the State of Georgia—arguing that although a corporation was not a citizen and could not emigrate to where it was not wanted, "the principle of comity . . . in the absence of a clear prohibition [by the state, means] the right to do business ought to be assumed," he was now attacked by many Democrats for his "surrender" and "betrayal." It is difficult to disagree with the judgment that Whig unhappiness and near hysteria in the one case, like the Democratic reaction in the other, were due to misinterpretation of their significance.

If "Jacksonian thought" or "Democratic thought" is what representative Jacksonian leaders believed about social and economic issues, a most discordant blending it would be, albeit one whose essential conservatism would shine through. Its heterogeneity mirrored the diversity of the party's following. There were Democrats and Democrats. Such amoralists as Henshaw, Samuel Swartwout, Samuel Gwin, and Robert J. Walker were most unlike Marcus Morton, William Leggett, and Richard M. Johnson. Further clouding the issue was the tendency of Jacksonian publicists to frame public statements in a language that was more useful in giving an impression of Democratic egalitarianism than in clarifying their beliefs. Particularly misleading has been the readiness of some scholars to treat the writings and speeches of men of unusual articulateness and even more atypical radicalism as though they were *representative* of Jacksonian thinking. Historians who are convinced that the Jacksonian coalition was dedicated to drastic alteration of American capitalistic society will understandably search for the intellectual foundations of this radical movement and find them in the work of noted dissenters. The prosaic actual achievements of the Democratic party, nationally and within the states, however, best explain why collections of such writings constitute Jacksonian thought only in the sense that the ideas contained within them were expressed while Andrew Jackson was alive.

Democratic policies which contradicted Democratic pronouncements do not inspire respect for the latter as serious statements of intentions. At the same time that Democratic leaders took up the cry against monopolies,

Democratic legislatures approved monopolistic charters "as if propelled by steam power," according to the Regency leader, Azariah Flagg, conferring them naturally enough on deserving Democratic entrepreneurs. "Untrue to their own principles!" charged the Locofocos. New Jersey Democrats were perfectly capable of attacking monopoly in general while bending all their energies in the state legislature to assure a continued monopoly over the route from New York to Philadelphia for the Camden and Amboy Railroad they controlled. Developing an interesting division of labor, "in national contests the party adopted an anti-monopoly ideology . . . but in the state the party balked at carrying through an anti-monopoly campaign because of the close connection between many of the party leaders and New Jersey corporations." Their antimonopoly slogans were meaningless in the judgment of their leading student.

Florida's Democrats espoused a philosophy more democratic and radical than that of their opponents, favoring expansion both of the suffrage as of business opportunities. However, a gap of varying proportions between the party's philosophy and its pronouncements, on the one hand, and the party's practices and its activities on the other," has been discerned. Specifically, Jacksonians in Florida talked up popular sovereignty while they opposed the wishes of their own electorate on the statehood issue. They talked of aid to debtors but passed legislation that helped planters. For all their talk of the common man, labor turned to the Whigs in view of Democratic inaction. In a sense, of course, Democratic negativism was a rare example of the concord of their theory and practice. President Van Buren's first message to Congress reminded the people that "all communities . . . are apt to look to government for too much. . . . But this ought not to be," he admonished. His philosophy was one that actual Democratic policy closely followed.

It is hard to pin down a formal Whig program. In its first presidential campaign, in 1836, the party ran a number of favorite sons, who jointly subscribed only to the hope that they could beat Van Buren by forcing the contest into the House. In 1840 General Harrison kept mum, slogan makers extolled log cabins and hard cider, Whig leaders concentrated on the Van Buren depression. And the following campaign was marked by Clay's unsuccessful attempt to avoid committing himself and his party to controversial policies. For most of the period formal statements were forthcoming from state or local groups rather than national. And as in the case of the declaration of Whig principles supported by a Massachusetts meeting in 1840, they were uninformative documents: They show that the Whigs wished to be considered more sensible than their "agrarian" opponents, whose penchant for revolution ostensibly jeopardized all hard-earned wealth. A resolution passed by a meeting of Philadelphia Whigs, affirming the interdependence of classes, or an editorial in the *National Intelligencer,* were not binding, not indicative of anyone's viewpoint but the particular individual or group responsible for it, even in the latter sense requiring some discounting of its language.

Given the paucity, the hyperbole, and the small force of so-called party statements, historians of Whig thought have sensibly paid little attention to them, focusing instead on the utterances of Clay, Webster, Weed, Hone, Greeley, White, Mangum, Crittenden, Bell, dozens of little-known publishers and the better known Gales and Seaton, and sundry other individual Whigs. "Whig thought" turns out not to be the party's formal beliefs but a kind of blending of the thinking of diverse individuals. Obvious problems arise. For example, were Calhoun's ideas Whig ideas for the less than five years that he aligned himself with the party? What does give validity to the exercise of the scholars, however, is the fair degree of consistency and agreement on social, economic, and political beliefs among the men who called themselves Whig.

In our era of striking revisions and reinter-pretations of history, older versions of Whig thought have been modified to an amazingly small extent by new. American historians in the early 20th century were drawn toward a New History whose scope was broad, whose spirit was critical, and whose goals were humane and democratic. Brave new historical thought *circa* 1915 was excited at its discovery that American history, like European, was racked by social and class conflict, and that powerful economic interests here as elsewhere sought to control politics to their own advantage. Working in this intellectual atmosphere, such scholars of Jacksonian politics as Dixon Ryan Fox, Arthur C. Cole, E. Malcolm Carroll and their students concluded not only that bitter social and economic conflict marked the Jacksonian era, but that the great opposing interests were represented politically by the two major parties. In this view the Whigs were the party of property. Their beliefs and philosophy were profoundly conservative. They viewed with alarm all evidences of social disorder. They liked to think that the interests of all social classes were similar. Interestingly, a modern study of Whig thought that is out of sympathy with the assumptions that governed the work of earlier students, revises only slightly their views of Whig conservatism. It is evidently impossible to make radicals out of the party of Clay and Webster. The Whig, Edward Everett, *was* opposed to labor parties. The Whig editors of the Boston *Courier, were* convinced that men of affairs should run society.

In contrast to the historians of Charles Beard's day, a recent reappraisal of Whig theory stresses the similarity of aims of the major parties. According to Glyndon Van Deusen, Whigs "sought the prosperity of the people as a whole, and both parties oriented, just as the two major parties do today, around a middle-class norm." Their divergences "were more over means than ultimate ends." At his hands the Whigs emerge not so much as the party of conservatism as the party of energy, optimism, nationalism, constructiveness, and humanitarianism, ready to use government to build roads, canals, schools, and promote the welfare of the poor and the indigent. He is by no means the only historian who finds that both in theory and practice the Whigs approached the spirit of the New Deal more closely than did the Jacksonian Democrats.

Some earlier judgments were harsher than the facts warranted. Aware that new immigrants tended to become Democrats, Whigs in a number of states did cooperate with nativists. Yet such leaders as Seward, Weed, and Greeley wished foreigners to be received on an equal footing with old settlers, their concern springing "from an honorable and sympathetic spirit." Many Missouri Whigs frowned at the policy of some "pragmatists" in their party to harmonize their efforts with nativists, a cooperation that hurt the Whigs at the polls. For that matter Whigs had more humane views than their major opponents with regard to most issues involving race. They championed the rights of Indians, urging that treaty guarantees of these rights be upheld. In the North their attitude toward free Negroes was more liberal than that of Democrats. Many southern Whigs either opposed the gag resolution or actually supported old Adams' fight against it. Surely it is no accident that of sixty New England abolitionists examined by David Donald—"not merely the leaders but their followers as well"—all but one were members of the Whig party. An admirable attitude on racial matters is neither conservative nor radical, but that fact detracts not at all from the significance of the attitude. There are other ways of classifying beliefs, after all, than in the terms used by economic determinists.

Southern Whigs in the early 1840s by and large stood for "honest banking and sound finance." In Georgia and Mississippi they opposed "the flood of relief measures" that came before the legislatures and rejected repudiation. In Kentucky and Louisiana, Whig governors refused to call special sessions to consider such legislation, emphasizing instead the responsibility of national government. If such Whig practice was timid, it was certainly in accord with the ideas of that monetary conservative, Andrew Jackson. Conservative banking practice of course has no connection with conservative social philosophy: many speculative Jacksonian practitioners of wildcat banking were firm supporters of a class society.

If beliefs are displayed in actions, Whigs were occasionally radical. It was Thaddeus Stevens who led the fight for free unstigmatized public schools in Pennsylvania. In New York state in 1839 it was a Whig governor who cleared the jails of antirenters, while "Whig legislators did not as a group oppose the measures by which the ancient privileges of the great landlords were diminished one by one." A realistic critic noted that Whigs "were as willing to attract five thousand voters as were the Democrats." The trouble with so hard-boiled an interpretation is not only that it is hard to prove but that it seems to leave out altogether the possibility that some element of conviction may be present in political behavior. The Whig farmers who sacked the office of the Mayville land agent, give every evidence of having been quite sincere. The anti-Jacksonian mayor of Boston in 1832 showed a greater sensitivity to the needs of commoners than had his Jacksonian opponent.

Too much should not be made of the philosophy of a party whose own leaders said, as did Thurlow Weed in 1839, that anyone who believed that the Democrats should be driven from office because they were responsible for hard times "is a Whig no matter by what name he has been called or is called." Earlier studies of "Whig theory" were usually undertaken by men convinced that the parties were fundamentally different and that their words were to be taken seriously. The present era's greater skepticism toward political mouthings may not merely be a reflection of a changed political atmosphere but simply a truer appraisal. To a generation that better than any other seems to understand the *complexity* of truth, party statements can neither be taken at face value nor dismissed out of hand. So-called Whig theory was not really that. It was the oftentimes contradictory notions of diverse men, many of whom were well explained in Weed's simple, almost cynical, definition of a Whig. In common with the other major party, Whigs accepted the fundamental institutions of their society. In contrast to the Democrats they were sensitive to the plight of the dark-skinned. While they favored economic and political policies that differentiated them from their opponents, neither the Whig nor the Jacksonian measures represented the kind of social cleavage suggested in the more overwrought oratory of the times.

The Whigs and Their Age

Daniel Walker Howe

"Of all the parties that have existed in the United States, the famous Whig party was the most feeble in ideas." So wrote Henry Adams in 1879, and his dismissive assessment proved to be remarkably durable. The judgment seems to have originated with antislavery ex-Whigs like George W. Julian and Joshua R. Giddings. It expressed the bitterness of disillusionment; these men had invested much of themselves in the party but had been unable, in the end, to carry its leadership with them on the slavery question. Because the Whig party had failed them on a matter of principle, they charged it with having had no principles. During the 20th century, this view of the Whigs persisted. "While the shifting of parties on alleged principles is a common phenomenon of politics, yet possibly no party was ever so thoroughly committed to it as was the Whig," declared Henry Mueller in 1922. The opinion that the Whigs were unprincipled opportunists has been widely shared by the two most prominent schools of American historiography: the progressive historians, who have accused the Whigs of insincerity, and the consensus historians, who have insisted on the nonideological nature of all American politics. To look at the writings of the Whigs themselves, however, is to find a different statement of the case. They claimed that the two major parties of their day embodied "two great conflicting ideas, which go to the root" of American life, and they repeatedly formulated cohesive presentations of their own philosophy.

The Whigs and the Democrats were the two major rivals of what historians term the second American party system. The Federalists and Jeffersonian Republicans composed the first, the Republicans and Democrats, the third and present system. There were political factions of various kinds in colonial America as well; but since they were local and usually informal in organization, they are not counted in enumerating the nationwide systems. The second party system took shape out of the factionalism of the late 1820s and early 1830s. It lasted until the mid-1850s, when the Whig party disintegrated and the modern Republican party was born.

There are, of course, reasons why the Whigs have been less well remembered than the Democrats. The most important is that the Whigs were less successful in competing for national office, and in history, as in life, nothing succeeds like success. Another is that the Democratic party still survives as an institution (it is the oldest political party in the world), while the Whig party does not. The Whigs were also the victims of sheer bad luck. American history is usually written from the vantage point of the White House; but the two presidents whom the Whigs elected, William Henry Harrison in 1840 and Zachary Taylor in

1848, both died in office after serving, respectively, only one month and sixteen months. The great Whig senators, Daniel Webster and Henry Clay, of course have permanent places in the American memory, but no purely congressional leader has ever been able to capture the public imagination as successfully as have our most dynamic chief executives.

Nevertheless, the Whigs should not be ignored by anyone seeking to understand America and its past. In fact, the Whig party was more powerful than a quick look at the presidential elections of the period would indicate. (The Democrats won five to the Whigs' two.) The actual strength of the two major parties in the days of the Whigs and Jacksonians was almost equal. In most parts of the country only a few percentage points separated winners from losers at the polls. Indeed, the fairly even distribution of partisan strength is one of the distinctive characteristics of the second American party system. In the time of the first and third party systems there have been cities, states, and whole regions that have been virtually one-party monopolies; under the second system it was rare for either party to enjoy such overwhelming dominance over an extensive area. The relative weakness of the Whig party in presidential politics gives little sign of its strength in congressional, state, and local politics.

As one of the two major parties in a constitutional democracy, the Whigs counted approximately half the voting population as at least occasional supporters. So large a constituency was naturally very heterogeneous. There were Whigs in all occupational groups, economic classes, social strata, geographic regions, and religious denominations. Despite this diversity, one can hazard some generalizations about the kinds of people who became Whigs, just as political scientists today (aided by far more complete data) can distinguish Republicans from Democrats in the population. Business and professional men tended to be Whigs. Industrial workers did not necessarily

vote against their employers; frequently, wage earners and others who felt they had a stake in the growth of manufacturing were also Whigs. With regard to people engaged in agriculture it is harder to judge, but there is reason to believe that farmers who produced for a commercial market were more likely to be Whigs than were those engaged in self-sustaining, or subsistence, agriculture. The Whig party was especially strong in southern New England and in parts of the country (such as eastern Tennessee) that hoped for government-aided economic-development projects—"internal improvements," as they were then called. People of New England extraction and members of the sects of New England Protestantism (Congregationalists, Unitarians, "New School" Presbyterians) also seem to have voted Whig in disproportionate numbers. Statistical evidence is spotty, but observers at the time usually assumed that people with greater income, education, and respectability were more likely to be Whig. "The active, enterprizing, intelligent, well-meaning & wealthy part of the people," Ralph Waldo Emerson called them. Yet those at the very bottom of the social ladder also generally supported the Whigs: the blacks, insofar as they were permitted political participation, found the Whigs decidedly the lesser of white evils.

The lifetime of the Whig party (roughly, 1834–54) was an era of intense political excitement. The nation faced momentous choices regarding war and peace, imperialism, ethnic diversity, the educational system (or lack thereof), and the expropriation of the American Indians. The very nature of the federal Constitution and the supremacy of the national government lay open to question; many state constitutions were also being written or rewritten and their legislatures reapportioned. At these constitutional conventions and on other occasions, fundamental issues of political obligation were raised. Over economic matters, politicians diverged sharply, debating the financial structure of the country and the money people handled every day; the sources of federal revenue and the possibility of sharing it with the states; government aid to business and business aid to government; the right of individuals, corporations, and governments to go bankrupt; and the right of labor—and of capital—to organize. Slavery and race relations constituted the prime moral issue of the day, but there were many others, among them the punishment of criminals, relationships between the sexes, federal funding for insane asylums, and laws regulating or prohibiting alcohol, which many people were coming to regard for the first time as a dangerous drug. All this took place in an atmosphere of violence, both individual and collective. Dueling, lynching, rioting, slave insurrections and plots, rebellions in Rhode Island and New York, warfare in Florida, Texas, and Mexico and along the frontier—these too became political issues.

"The spirit of the age," Frances Wright observed, was "to be a little fanatical." She spoke truly (if half in jest), for the questions being argued were important ones and they stirred deep passions. Mass politics was new, political parties were new, and the electorate was not yet jaded. The base of political participation, as measured by the voting qualifications, was wider in Jacksonian America (notwithstanding the exclusion of women and most nonwhites) than in any previous time or contemporary other place. What is more, this potential for widespread participation was realized, for the percentage of white men going to the polls soared from 27 in 1824 to 78 in 1840. Because the two major parties were fairly evenly matched, competition between them was keen. Elections were frequent because there were many annual and biennial terms of office, and the voting days in different states were staggered throughout the year. Results of national elections trickled in slowly for weeks. United States senators were chosen by state legislatures that sometimes spent months reaching a decision. Thus, political agitation was more or less constant.

The parties' energetic campaigning produced not only high voter participation but also a high degree of party regularity. Neither the participation nor the regularity has been equaled in America since. Straight party voting was facilitated by ballots printed by the parties themselves, often listing only their own candidates; to vote for someone else, it was then necessary literally to "scratch the ticket" and write in a different name. But high voter participation and polarization between the parties also reflected diverging programs on matters of deep concern. When the second American party system emerged from a confusion of personal and factional rivalries within the Jeffersonian Republican party in the 1820s, voters sorted themselves out into two parties with recognizably differing approaches to government: the Democrats and the Whigs.

Party politics was our first national sport, and the public played and watched the great game with enthusiasm. Torchlight parades, electioneering songs and slogans, debates, and speeches were popular entertainment. But there was a serious side to all this "politicking" that is sometimes overlooked. If the press was intensely partisan (on both sides) and many voters were fervently committed, it was not simply out of longing for diversion. The fact is that the politicians were talking about important matters. The politics of the 1830s and the 1840s centered on issues to a far greater extent than did the politics of, say, the post-Reconstruction era.

Some historians have felt that the intensive political campaigning and frequent elections of the mid-nineteenth century "exaggerated" the amount of social conflict that actually existed. It is certainly true that party feeling ran high. In 1835 an attempt was made on the life of Andrew Jackson by a man now thought to have been insane. The President suspected that his political opposition was behind the attack. And a young Whig politician, who was really a very decent person, commented that, although it was good that Jackson had survived, it was appropriate that "the chief who violated the Constitution, proscribed public virtue, and introduced high-handed corruption into public affairs and debauchery into private circles" (a reference to the wife of Secretary of War Eaton) should have been the object of the first assassination attempt on an American President. Typically, however, Whig-Jacksonian political conflicts expressed broad social divisions rather than incidents involving pathological individuals or imaginary dangers. What is more, even technical issues like the tariff were often debated with considerable sophistication and accurate perception of where one's interests lay. On balance, the intense involvement of multitudes in politics probably manifested "the worth, not the evils," of democracy.

In recent years an impressive body of scholarship has demonstrated the importance of the differences between the Democratic and Whig parties. Detailed analyses of voting patterns in Congress and the state legislatures have revealed both the sharpness of partisanship and its substance. Investigators who have looked at individual states have been finding that the voters as well as the politicians were concerned about issues and were purposeful in making political choices. As a result, political historians are now more willing to acknowledge that Whiggery had a coherence and a program.

The chief reason for remembering the Whig party today is that it advanced a particular program of national development. The Whig economic platform called for purposeful intervention by the federal government in the form of tariffs to protect domestic industry, subsidies for internal improvements, and a national bank to regulate the currency and make tax revenues available for private investment. Taken together, the various facets of this program disclose a vision of America as an economically diversified country in which commerce and industry would take their place alongside agriculture. Practically all Americans expected and wanted their nation to grow and prosper, but they disagreed as to how progress might

best be achieved. The Democrats inclined toward free trade and laissez-faire; when government action was required, they preferred to leave it to the states and local communities. The Whigs were more concerned with providing centralized direction to social policy.

Yet the meaning of Whig ideas and how they differed from those of the Democrats have frequently been masked from later observers. The conventions of heroic oratory, moral philosophy, and "country-party" fear of conspiracy, when not recognized as such, can make Whig statements seem platitudinous, obfuscating, or hysterical. Moreover, Democrats and Whigs could arrive at similar policy conclusions from entirely different premises; their common support for public education, general laws of incorporation, and the introduction of bankruptcy proceedings are examples of a consensus on means obscuring differences with respect to ends. Sometimes party issues had more intellectual significance than is immediately apparent; the award of legislative printing contracts, for example, not only bestowed material favors on one's friends but influenced how fully and accurately one's speeches would be reported. Records printed by enemies had a way of being unsympathetic abridgments of remarks. Even issues that seem like mere gossip today, such as the accusation of adultery against President Jackson and his wife Rachel, can reveal something about the attitudes of a party's constituency. This issue, like the charges against Secretary Eaton and Peggy O'Neale, cast the Whigs in their accustomed role as defenders of middle-class morality.

The most important single issue dividing the parties, and the source of the most acute disappointment to the Whigs after President Harrison had been succeeded by Tyler, concerned the banking system. Jackson's veto of the recharter of the Second Bank of the United States in 1832 became the point of departure for a generation of political partisanship. The banking-currency issue (that is, the right

Silencing Jackson, Henry Clay is shown stitching the President's lips during the battle over the Bank of the U.S. The Senate had censured Jackson and he wrathfully replied. Then Clay refused to let Jackson's retort be officially recorded in the Senate.

of banks to issue their own paper money) mattered at the state as well as the federal level. Many states redrafted their constitutions during the Jacksonian period and had to decide whether they would authorize state banking monopolies (usually mixed public-private corporations), specially chartered banks, "free banking," or no banks of issue at all. As time went by, the parties tended to polarize with respect not only to rechartering a national bank but to the function of banking in general. The Democrats gradually became more committed to "hard money" (specie or government-issued currency), while the Whigs became defenders of "the credit system" (in which banks were the issuers of currency).

Besides their alternative economic programs, the parties also possessed different eth-nic constituences. The Whigs were predominantly the party of Yankee Protestants and British-American immigrants. The Democrats were stronger among folk of Dutch and German descent and among Catholics. These ethnic identities coexisted with the parties' economic identities in ways historians have not altogether sorted out, but it would be a mistake to assume that the ethnic and economic interpretations of the second party system are mutually exclusive. Very likely the affluent were attracted to Whiggery by the party's economic program, poor men more often by its ethnic identification. In many situations, of course, the ethnic and economic appeals would have reinforced each other. The parties' ethnic appeals were no less real than their economic ones; the act of voting can express "a blend ones; the act of voting can express "a blend of ethnic, class, or status resentments in quite rational fashion, given available perceptions of 'friends' and 'enemies.'"

An ethnic partisanship that was quite rational is evident in the support that black voters gave to the Whig party in reaction to the strident white supremacy that was the stock-in-trade of so many Democratic spokesmen. Only four states in the far Northeast allowed black men to vote on the same basis as white men; elsewhere blacks either had to meet higher qualifications than whites or were disfranchised altogether. In New York state, some 3000 black men could meet the $250 property test imposed on them to vote; had they been exempted from it, as white men were, there would have been 10,000 black voters, and Henry Clay would have been elected President in 1844. Black suffrage was a partisan issue that the Democrats strenuously opposed and the Whigs, somewhat less strenuously, supported. The Democrats succeeded in disfranchising blacks altogether in New Jersey, Connecticut, and Pennsylvania during the Jacksonian period; only in Rhode Island did the blacks gain suffrage through the Whigs. Eventually, blacks became disillusioned with the slender returns Whiggery won for them; when the Whig party was disintegrating, they were among those who were drifting away from it.

Much scholarship during the past two decades has demonstrated the usefulness of treating political parties as "reference groups" possessing distinctive "value systems." Not the least of the advantages of reference-group theory is its applicability to both economic-class and ethnoreligious segments of the population, offering the hope of transcending the debate over which of these factors separated Democrats from Whigs. Whigs thought of themselves as the "sober, industrious, thriving people"—a self-image that included moral as well as economic virtues. The party battles of the Whig-Jacksonian era can be seen as conflicts over values that included but went beyond politics, strictly defined. Whiggery was as much a cultural or moral posture as an economic or political program.

The value context of Whiggery was established by the Second Great Awakening, a series of religious revivals that reached its highest peaks of fervor during the lifetime of the Whig party. The Awakening has been well described as "a comprehensive program designed to Christianize every aspect of American life." Leaders of the Awakening like Charles G. Finney considered politics "an indispensable part of religion." For their part, Whig political leaders like Henry Clay and Daniel Webster cultivated good public and private relations with clerical opinion-shapers. Clay, for example, introduced a congressional resolution for a day of national "humiliation and prayer" in response to a cholera epidemic (Jacksonians blocked it as violating the separation of church and state). Webster unsuccessfully contested the will of Stephen Girard, a wealthy Philadelphian who had left a bequest for an orphanage in which no clergyman could set foot. If the Church of England was the Tory party at prayer, the Whig party in the United States was in many ways the evangelical united front at the polling place.

An important feature of the Whig program was its coherence. Whig positions on banking, the tariff, internal improvements, the sale of public lands, and the distribution of federal revenue to the states were interlocking facets of one economic program. But the broader consistency of Whiggery went beyond the specific provisions of Henry Clay's "American System." The moral issues the party espoused sometimes had direct relevance to its economic program. For example, the repudiation of bonds by several Democratic state legislatures after the Panic of 1839 was generally denounced by Whigs throughout the country as defaulting upon a moral obligation as well as hindering economic development. At other times the relationship was indirect; Whig moral opposition to the dispossession of the Ameri-

Whig land policy. Often, of course, the conomic issues themselves were argued in moral and broadly symbolic terms. The banking-currency debate has recently been interpreted as a conflict between two political cultures in the western states.

In their own eyes, the Whigs had a more coherent, rational, and constructive program than their antagonists, whom they accused of relying on patronage, passion, and sheer negativism. They may not have been wrong to think this. Despite the frequent assertions by historians that the Whig party was held together merely by desire for office, there is reason to believe that it was, if anything, more issue-oriented or program-oriented, and less concerned with office as such, than the Democrats. That Whiggery was more constructive, in a literal sense, than Democracy is clear. Each of the two times the Whigs elected a President, he called a special session of Congress to act on a legislative program. The antebellum Democratic Presidents, by contrast, are known for their vetoes: Jackson's of the Bank and the Maysville Road, Polk's of river and harbor improvements, Pierce's of aid to insane asylums, Buchanan's of a homestead act. When Martin Van Buren complained, during the Panic of 1837, that people "looked to the government for too much," Henry Clay retorted that the people were "entitled to the protecting care of a paternal government." And a less directly interested contemporary confided these observations to his journal: "Since I have been in N.Y. I have grown less diffident of my political opinions. I supposed once the Democracy might be right. I see that they are aimless. Whigs have the best men, Democrats the best cause. But the last are destructive, not constructive. What hope, what end have they?"

Historians have generally treated aspects of the Whig program in the course of trying to define Jacksonian Democracy. Arthur M. Schlesinger, Jr.'s, seminal description of "the Age of Jackson" includes an excellent chapter on the Whigs, though it concludes that "The widening chasm between private belief and public profession took all seriousness out of Whiggery as a social philosophy." Marvin Meyers' fascinating study of "the Jacksonian persuasion" proposes that the Whigs appealed to Americans' hopes; the Democrats, to Americans' fears. This distinction works well for economic policy, though in other realms the Whigs, too, had their apprehensions. On cultural and moral issues, such as immigration, temperance, or slavery, it was more often the Whigs who were anxious and the Democrats who were optimistic or complacent.

One of the most useful characterizations of Whig policy that has been offered is that it supported "the positive liberal state." This ideal implied the belief that the state should actively seek "to promote the general welfare, raise the level of opportunity for all men, and aid all individuals to develop their full potentialities." The Democrats, by contrast, believed in a "negative liberal state," which left men free to pursue their own definition of happiness. A great advantage of this distinction between the parties is that it implies a connection between the economic and moral aspects of Whiggery. In both cases, the Whigs believed in asserting active control. They wanted "improvements" both economic and moral, and they did not believe in leaving others alone.

For all its helpfulness, however, there is danger in calling the Whigs champions of "the positive liberal state." It makes them sound too much like twentieth-century liberals. Actually, the differences between the Whigs and twentieth-century liberals are more important than the similarities. Whig policies did not have the object of redistributing wealth or diminishing the influence of the privileged. Furthermore, the Whigs distrusted executives in both state and federal government (they had been traumatized by the conduct of Jackson), whereas twentieth-century liberals have endorsed strong executives more often than not. For all their innovations in economic policy, the Whigs usually thought of themselves as conservatives, as custodians of an identifiable political and cultural heritage. Most deeply separating the Whigs from twentieth-century liberals were their moral absolutism, their paternalism, and their concern with imposing discipline.

The terms "positive liberal" and "negative liberal" have another disadvantage: they suggest that the Whigs and Democrats differed only as to means, that they were agreed upon ends. But the specific disagreements over policy between the parties were rooted in the larger differences between them regarding the nature and destiny of American society. Whigs and Democrats presented the electorate with rival images of national purpose. To put things very broadly, the Whigs proposed a society that would be economically diverse but culturally uniform; the Democrats preferred the economic uniformity of a society of small farmers and artisans but were more tolerant of cultural and moral diversity.

One historian has proposed that the Democrats were primarily interested in the quantitative expansion of American society through *space,* whereas the Whigs were concerned with its qualitative development through *time.* This is a perceptive distinction. For the Democrats, "manifest destiny" was the logical consequence of their preoccupation with a uniform agricultural empire. For the Whigs, on the other hand, "internal improvement," or economic (and moral) development, was more important than external expansion. As Horace Greeley noted in 1851:

> Opposed to the instinct of boundless acquisition stands that of Internal Improvement. A nation cannot simultaneously devote its energies to the absorption of others' territories and the improvement of its own. In a state of war, not law only is silent, but the pioneer's axe, the canal-digger's mattock, and the housebuilder's trowel also.

Though the Whigs were a diverse lot, the number of thematic reverberations in their political and social expression is remarkable. Three in particular seem to stand out. First, because of their commitment to "improvement," Whigs were much more concerned than Democrats with providing conscious direction to the forces of change. For them, real progress was not likely to occur automatically; it required careful, purposeful planning. Social progress took place much as the education of the individual did, through careful cultivation of that which was valued and rigorous suppression of that which was not. Second, while Jacksonian rhetoric emphasized "equality" (restricted in practice to equality of opportunity for white males), Whig rhetoric emphasized "morality"—or "duties" rather than "rights." Whig morality was corporate as well as individual; the community, like its members, was expected to set an example of virtue and to enforce it when possible. A third recurring theme in Whig rhetoric was the organic unity of society. Whereas the Jacksonians often spoke of the conflicting interests of "producers" and "nonproducers," the "house of have" and the "house of want," the Whigs were usually concerned with muting social conflict. In their determined assertion of the interdependence of different classes, regions, and interest groups, one recognizes the same analogy between the individual and society that also characterized the other two main principles of Whig social thought.

In the long run, the Whigs' contribution to American society proved at least as great as that of their Democratic contemporaries. The economic and technological changes going on in the nineteenth century ultimately produced an economy more like that envisioned by the Whigs than like the arcadia the Jeffersonians and Jacksonians idealized. Most of the Whigs' economic platform was enacted by their successors: the Republican party firmly established a protective tariff and subsidized business enterprise, and the Democrats under Wilson finally organized a nationwide banking system, though it operated on different principles from those the Whigs had envisioned. The political evolution of the country has consistently increased the power of the federal government; "states' rights" retains less power as a political rallying cry than ever. Some of the social reforms the Whigs supported have passed into history so completely that by now we are more conscious of their shortcomings than of their achievements (free public education, for example). Other Whig objectives were never attained (such as respect for the rights of the Indians) or proved disastrous when finally implemented (like prohibition of liquor). As for the Jacksonians, the individualism and egalitarianism they preached have firmly taken root in the American character; the imposition of that cultural uniformity sought by the Whigs has long since become a lost cause. But as long as there are still people who strive to awaken a sense of public responsibility in politics and the arts, the spirit of the Whig reformers will not be altogether dead. Since America has become diversified both economically and culturally, perhaps one could say that the Whigs and Jacksonians have each had half their vision fulfilled.

Part Eight

A Ferment of Reform, 1830–1860

n the second quarter of the nineteenth century, America witnessed a remarkable outburst of reform activity. During the 1830s and 1840s a multitude of individuals got involved in movements to reform some aspect or other of the society. They formed countless societies and associations for the elimination of abuses and for the betterment of individuals. There were temperance advocates, pacifists, abolitionists; reformers addressing the problems of the indigent, the disabled, and the criminal and delinquent; proponents of improved health and of public schools; women demanding better treatment from their husbands and from society at large. And there were even some who withdrew and formed utopian communities as examples of what a thoroughly reformed society might be like. Among the reformers themselves were some of the most colorful figures in American history, such people as William Lloyd Garrison, the unconventional and uncompromising abolitionist, and Sylvester Graham, the eccentric health reformer and creator of the Graham cracker.

This ferment of reform was a dominant feature in American society and thought from the Jacksonian era when it began until the Civil War, when its energy and concerns were redirected into other preoccupations. So numerous and diverse were the reforms, however, that merely describing them and their activities may seem to be all that the historian can manage to do. But, of course, that is far from satisfactory and, besides, the task of the historian is to explain, not just describe. So the question that immediately arises is why this remarkable phenomenon occurred. After all, the new nation was in its infancy, so it is hard to imagine that so much had gone wrong in such a short period of time that reform was imperative. A second query arising from the first is that the simultaneous emergence of all these different reforms suggests that they possessed something in common, that there was a perspective on American society that they all shared. Furthermore, since most of these reforms were to reappear in American history—temperance, prison reform, pacifism, for example, though not abolition—was there a quality about these reforms in the 1830s and 1840s that was not present later? In other words, what was the essence of reform in this particular period?

In trying to answer these questions, historians have basically taken two approaches. The first is to see reform as a response to the dramatic changes in the nation's economy and social institutions during the Age of Jackson. This was, after all, the beginning phase in the country's industrialization, and people were moving from the countryside to the mills and factories in the growing towns. As a result, patterns of work were being transformed, and customary social functions and roles were being disrupted. To address these new problems and unfamiliar situations, so it is argued, the reformers and their associations came into existence.

The second approach concentrates on the reformers themselves and tries to discover what their views and intentions were. If the problems they dealt with were, as was just suggested, unfamiliar and the result of unanticipated changes, the reformers' concern conceivably might be to restore values that were disappearing or to ensure that they themselves as a social group were able to control and direct these new forces in society. Indeed, historians have suggested both views. In either case, the reformers would be responding in a nostalgic and conservative way to these unwelcome innovations. Although some reformers may have been averse to these changes and wanted to look back rather than forward, the great majority did not. Instead, they seem to have regarded the era with great optimism and anticipation, convinced that this was a moment of unparalleled opportunity in which individuals could be emancipated from old restraints and thereby enabled to realize their full potential. Often involved in the religious revivals of the Second Great Awakening that swept the northern states in the 1820s and influenced by the ideas of the European romantics and their American equivalents like Emerson and Thoreau, the reformers were imbued with a strong belief in the essential goodness, even perfectability, of man. And this conviction propelled them, with a sense of urgency and a zeal that was relentless, into reform work aimed at creating a society of autonomous, fully realized individuals.

The articles selected for this topic are representative of these two approaches. One sees reform arising from, and operating within, a social matrix, whereas the other examines the reformers' own writings to discover what they were trying to do. The titles of both of them seem to suggest analogies with the women's liberation and sexual liberation that were features of the 1960s and 1970s. But the reader will soon see that there are actually few parallels. Although the 1960s were an era of reform, its spirit was quite different from that of the mid-nineteenth century.

Ronald Walters of Johns Hopkins University examines the thought of the reformers. Noticing a curious preoccupation in abolitionist writings with the temptations toward sexual indulgence and the exercise of arbitrary power that slave owning presented to the masters, Professor Walters discovers that a similar concern about the dangers of uncontrolled desire and will permeated the thought of other reformers. Whereas the individualism of the 1960s stressed "doing your own thing" and "letting it all hang out," the individualism of the 1830s reformers assumed that a person could only be autonomous and self-realized through self-control, especially control of physical needs and desires. Thus, to the optimistic reformers of the earlier era, self-restraint, not uninhibitedness, was the hallmark of the free individual.

The approach of Carroll Smith-Rosenberg is rather different. In her focus on the social origins and implications of reform, Professor Smith-Rosenberg of the University of Pennsylvania unearths an overlooked facet of reform in the Jacksonian era. This was the movement for moral reform, namely the ending of prostitution and of the double standard in sexual morality. The reformers concerned were exclusively women who were respectable and well-to-do, and their involvement in this kind of activity was in response to social changes that they thought threatened the family. Ironically, their leaving the home to engage in activities with other women produced, in turn, related changes in familial relations and in their own role as women and wives.

QUESTIONS TO CONSIDER

1. Why, in Walters' view, were reformers of this era so concerned about self-control?

2. What are the social stress and the changing sex roles that Smith-Rosenberg mentions at the beginning of her article, and how do they relate to reform?

3. Account for the differences in subject matter and approach between Walters and Smith-Rosenberg.

The Erotic South: Civilization and Sexuality in American Abolitionism

Ronald G. Walters

American antislavery sentiment took a very different turn after 1831. Whereas early abolitionism accepted a gradual end to slavery, after 1831 immediate emancipation became the goal, and abolitionism became a passion driving men and women into lifelong reform careers. Yet slavery was not new in 1831—it had been present for nearly two centuries. And slavery did not suddenly become evil in 1831; by abolitionist logic it had been sinful all along. Still, a number of northern whites who had little direct contact with the institution joined blacks in becoming acutely aware of it, so much so that they felt compelled to seek its instant destruction. There is a mystery here, a need to account for the rise of a particular kind of antislavery sentiment at a particular moment in time. The problem, however, is not fully to be resolved by a search for direct "causes" of post-1830 abolitionism. There is the related, perhaps prior, task of charting antislavery's form, a need to determine why it seized upon certain issues while ignoring others, why its images were so compelling to whites who might well have ignored slavery, and why those who accepted abolitionism's call

also drifted into a striking and novel variety of other reforms.

Historians attempting to assess the antislavery impulse have sometimes seized upon the doctrine of "disinterested benevolence," a product of 1820s revivalism and an encouragement for anxious moralists to engage in good works as proof of salvation. Yet such benevolence was anything but emotionally disinterested, as at least one person possessed by it realized. Jane Swisshelm, herself a prominent abolitionist and feminist, cited the zealous commitment of William Lloyd Garrison, pioneer of post-1830 abolitionism. "It is necessary to his existence that he should work," she wrote, "—work for the slave; and in his work he gratifies all the strongest instincts of his nature, more completely than even the grossest sensualist can gratify *his,* by unlimited indulgence." Jane Swisshelm revealed more than she imagined by setting up an antithesis between William Lloyd Garrison and the "sensualist." Antislavery was not simply a result of sexual fears or sexual repression (these, like slavery, existed well before 1831): but antislavery after 1831 gained direction and force from changing, culturally determined attitudes about sex, attitudes which merged with other assumptions to make conditions in the South appear uncomfortably applicable to the North, attitudes which both shaped perception of the problem and guided reformers to a new set of answers in the half-century after 1830, ultimately helping bridge the distance between immediate emancipation and a postwar world in which fit and unfit were presumed to struggle for survival.

Charles K. Whipple described slavery as "absolute, irresponsible power on one side, and entire subjection on the other." Like virtually all abolitionists he grounded his objections to the institution on this relationship of utter submission and total dominance between bondsman and master. There were, of course, other kinds of emphasis possible. Earlier humanitarian reform stressed slavery's suffering and cruelty but, no matter how useful examples of these might be in stirring sentiment, most post-1830 abolitionists finally denied that ill-treatment was what made bondage so terrible. Theodore Dwight Weld, after combing southern newspapers and exhausting eyewitnesses for horror stories about slavery, asserted that atrocities were not the institution's most basic feature. The "combined experience of the human race," he thought, proved that such "cruelty is the spontaneous and uniform product of arbitrary power. . . ." Abuse was only an effect of submission and dominance. Even those who began by looking at slavery in still another way, in terms of "the chattel principle," came around (like Weld) to a definition which was neither economic nor institutional nor based on specific treatment. "Slavery is the act of one holding another as property," a correspondent to the *Philanthropist* declared, adding "or one man being wholly subject to the will of others." In his mind slavery (as a property relationship) resolved itself into a matter of power just as surely as it did for Whipple or Weld.

Slaveholders were not reluctant heirs to their authority, as it appeared to abolitionists: so driving was the urge to dominate that it outdistanced all other possible motives, including greed. Garrison thought "the masterpassion in the bosom of the slaveholder is not the love of gain, but the possession of absolute power, unlimited sovereignty." Nevertheless, abolitionists maintained that slaveholders were not peculiar in their failings but rather that they demonstrated what all people should beware of. C. K. Whipple and Theodore Dwight Weld, after detailing in their different ways slavery's devastating effects, each reminded readers that the danger was not confined to white Southerners. "No human being is fit to be trusted with absolute, irresponsible power," claimed Whipple. "If the best portion of our community were selected to hold and use such authority [as masters possess], they would very soon be corrupted." "Arbitrary power is to the mind what alochol is to the body: it intoxicates," Weld believed. "It is perhaps the strongest human passion; and the more absolute the power, the stronger the desire for it; and the more it is desired, the more its exercise is enjoyed. . . . The fact that a person intensely desires power over others, *without restraint,* shows the absolute necessity of restraint." Man might have an innate moral sense, he might at times be molded by his race or environment, but abolitionists were at bottom certain that man also had a deeply implanted drive to tyrannize over others—a drive which required constant vigilance and suppression.

If the slaveholder was not unique in lusting after power, then neither was slavery the only example of coercion and "arbitrary power" disturbing to abolitionists. Few were so extreme as Abby Kelley Foster, who took her nonresistant principles to the point where, an amazed visitor reported, she was "very conscientious not to use the least wordly authority over her child." Other abolitionists, even those less dogmatic (or foolhardy) than Mrs. Foster, were outraged by the tyranny of preacher, politician, corrupt public opinion and institutions. Slavery might be a special case because of its magnitude and because it followed racial lines, but the principle could appear elsewhere. Long before antislavery politicians attempted to persuade white Northerners that the Slave Power endangered their own liberties, not merely the slave's, abolitionists warned that arbitrary authority did not stop with master and chattel. "Who is safe?" asked Henry B. Stanton in 1836. "Can you confine the operations of this principle to the black man?" Suppression of civil liberties and stories of whites sold into slavery were only exaggerated reminders that you, in fact, could not do so.

Slavery, then, stood as the virtual distillation of malevolence lurking in the breast of man. The institution, Lydia Maria Child decided, "concentrated the strongest evils of human nature—vanity, pride, love of power, licentiousness, and indolence" —all stemming from man's unrestrained will to dominate. Yet Americans of an earlier generation had also been suspicious of man's ability to wield authority. Such hostility appeared blatantly at the time of the American Revolution, and it had even then been applied to slavery. John Woolman, almost a lifetime before Garrison's career began, argued against the institution because "so long as men are biassed by narrow self-love, so long an absolute power over other men is unfit for them." John Adams, in 1765, could write of "the love of power, which had been so often the cause of slavery." But, deep as fear of power had been among the Revolutionary generation, it took on new life after 1830: in addition to bearing an invigorated affinity to a romantic age's "individualism," it regained vitality among antebellum whites who seemed to be losing control over their own destinies, as middle-class moralists well might be in an industrializing nation where the political system was passing into the hands of strange and uncouth men. Also, the concept of "power" was coming by the 1830s to fit into a new web of associations which ensnared some of the deepest and most mysterious forces abolitionists believed to be in all men. These included the deepest, most mysterious, most fearful force of all: human sexuality. For abolitionists the distance was not great from lust for power to mere lust.

Abolitionists did not dwell "excessively" on sexual misconduct in the South—their writings have little merit as pornography. Furthermore, for centuries whites had imagined (and cultivated) erotic potential in interracial contact. Nevertheless, this potential could be organized into more than one pattern of perception and antislavery propaganda directly reversed a prevalent assumption by presenting white men, not black men, as sexual aggressors. Early in his career Garrison set the tone. He was accosted by a slaveholder who posed American racism's classic question: "How should you like to have a black man marry your daughter?" Garrison replied that "slaveholders generally should be the last persons to affect fastidiousness on that point; for they seem to be enamoured with amalgamation." The retort was unanswerable and survived down to the Civil War. It was, in part, simply fine strategy, pointing both to an obvious hypocrisy and a very real consequence of slavery.

*   *   *

"Illicit intercourse" was embedded in the very conditions of southern life, abolitionists believed. For the master "the temptation is always at hand—the legal authority absolute—the actual power complete—the vice a profitable one" if it produced slaves for market"—and the custom so universal as to bring no disgrace. . . ." In addition, the planter, who had others to work for him, could be indolent and this had a "very debasing" effect on "less intellectual minds." Consequently such men "are driven by it to seek occupation in the lowest pleasures." John Rankin felt that "we may always expect to find the most confirmed habits of vice where idleness prevails." Also, there was scandalous nudity among slaves. One author, using the apt pseudonym, "Puritan," was appalled that "not only in taverns, but in boarding houses, and, the dwellings of individuals, boys and girls verging on maturity altogether unclothed, wait upon ladies and

ISAAC and ROSA, Emancipated Slave Children,
From the Free Schools of Louisiana.
Photographed by KIMBALL, 477 Broadway, N.Y.
Entered according to Act of Congress, in the year 1863 by GEO. H.
HANKS, in the Clark's Office of the U. s. for the Sou. Dist. of N.Y

Abolitionists believed that "illicit intercourse" between master and slaves was inherent in the culture of the South.

gentlemen, without exciting even the suffusion of a blush on the face of young females, who thus gradually become habituated to scenes of which delicate and refined northern women cannot adequately conceive." As if that were not enough, free and easy association between slave children and white children on the plantation spread the depravity of the back cabins (where there was no incentive to virtue) to the big house once again. "Between the female slaves and the misses there is an unrestrained communication," southern-born James A. Thome explained to the American Anti-Slavery Society. "As they come in contact through the day, the courtesan feats of the over night are whispered into the ear of the unsuspecting [white] girl and posion [SIC] her youthful mind."

In its libidinousness the South could only be compared to other examples of utter depravity and dissolution. Thome informed an audience of attentive young ladies that "THE SOUTHERN STATES ARE ONE GREAT SODOM" and his account was seconded by another abolitionist who had lived in Virginia and Maryland. "The sixteen slave States constitute one vast brothel," the *Liberator* declared in 1858. Twenty years earlier the *Pennsylvania Freeman* spoke of the "great moral lazarhous of Southern slavery...." Thomas Wentworth Higginson decided that, compared to the South, "a Turkish harem is a cradle of virgin purity." Henry C. Wright preferred comparison with New York's notorious Five Points district, much to its advantage, of course. Like Sodom, brothels or a harem, the South appeared to be a place in which men could indulge their erotic impulses with impunity.

Yet, in the nature of things, there must be retribution. It could be physiological since— the 19th century assumed—sexual excesses ultimately destroyed body and mind. Planters, according to Mrs. Louisa Barker, exemplified the "wreck of early manhood always resulting from self-indulgence." They were "born with feeble minds and bodies, with just force enough to transmit the family name, and produce in feebler characters a second edition of the father's life." Mrs. Barker's comments were consistent with the way other abolitionists viewed the South and with the way her times viewed sex, but they were almost unique in antislavery literature—although the character of the languid but erratic planter was not....

The issue of miscegenation forever dogged the antislavery movement, and by stressing southern licentiousness abolitionists could turn on their accusers. They could speak of the slave system's "dreadful amalgamating abominations" and argue that such would "experience, in all probability, a tenfold diminution" with emancipation. They could go as far as Elijah Lovejoy and claim "one reason why abolitionists urge the abolition of slavery is, that they fully believe it will put a stop, in a great and almost entire measure, to that wretched, and shameful, and polluted intercourse between the whites and the blacks, now so common, it may be said so universal, in the slave states." Yet propaganda advantages—if they were the only consideration—would have been greater had abolitionists not also insisted, as they did at times, that "the right to choose a partner for life is so exclusive and sacred, that it is never interfered with, except by the worst of tyrants." Garrison, with his usual tactless boldness, even asserted perfect racial equality and concluded that "inter-marriage is neither unnatural nor repugnant to nature, but obviously proper and salutary, it being designed to unite people of different tribes and nations, and to break down those petty distinctions which are the effect of climate or locality of situation. . . ." Such frontal assaults on antimiscegenation sentiment, if nothing else, show that sexual attitudes were not something merely to be played upon for achievement of social power.

Instead, what abolitionists wrote about southern sexuality must be put in relation to 19th-century assumptions and to conditions in the North which gave urgency to concern for licentiousness, as well as in relation to other reform interests displayed by those involved in the antislavery crusade.

It was possible for abolitionists to perceive the South as a society given over to lust not simply because miscegenation and unhallowed sex occurred under slavery. After all, erotic activity between master class and bondsmen did not originate in 1831 (nor did disgust with southern morals—New England Federalists a generation before had that in abundance). And miscegenation may well have been decreasing at the very time it became a staple of antislavery propaganda. Nevertheless, antebellum

northern sensibility was sharpened by presuming an interchangeability between power and sexuality, by believing that man's nature, if unchained, exhibited fearsome and diverse urges to dominate and possess. Sexuality therefore seemed to exist in the master-slave relationship itself (or, rather, in man himself) not just in the South, which was only an archetype. One abolitionist noted that "Clerical Slave-Holding in Connecticut" some years before had resulted in a "constant illicit intercourse" between ministers and their female slaves. In other words, it could happen anywhere—even with clergymen and even in Connecticut.

Portions of the abolitionist's view possess an eternal validity: some human beings have always turned tyranny into erotic pleasure. But belief that submission and dominance lead to sexual license had much wider currency in 19th-century America than in previous centuries or in our own day. Victorian pornography, for instance, exploited situations of power and powerlessness more than the contemporary variety does (despite some lurid exceptions) and probably more than ancient bawdy literature generally did. In one 19th-century classic the action took place in a harem where "The Lustful Turk," a darkly sensual being, literally reduced women (even good English women!) to sexual slaves. His power was both political and erotic, and his desires were as unchecked as they were varied. This was strikingly similar to antislavery images of the South and the slaveholder, a similarity increased when one of the lustful Turk's victims made a speech in which she attacked slavery as "the most powerful agent in the degradation of mankind," a charming bit of abolitionism amidst depravity. In more respectable Victorian circles it was thought that servants, another class of underling, were both sexually corrupted and agents of corruption, a matter which later attracted the attention of Sigmund Freud.

A similar sense that subordination engendered debauchery shaped contemporary anti-

Catholic diatribes. George Bourne, an early and important abolitionist, doubled as a Catholic baiter and found his careers easily reconciled. He pictured the South as an erotic society where whites "have been indulged in all the vicious gratifications which lawless power and unrestrained lust, can amalgamate. . . ." Much the same, he believed, prevailed in that other closed society, the convent. There (in Bourne's imagination) the priest's absolute power and unchecked erotic energy replaced the planter's, and the seduction and seductiveness of nuns replaced female slaves.

Enough southern sensuality existed to fuel the minds of men like Bourne and of abolitionists less determined than he to ferret out licentiousness. But in antislavery propaganda southern sensuality, as much as anything, illustrated a general and not very lovely principle abolitionists held to be true about man and what possession of power did to him. "We know what human nature is: what are its weaknesses, what its passions," the *Philanthropist* asserted confidently, as it remarked upon the plantation's potential for depravity. Plantations, like a moralist's equivalent for the settings of pornographic novels, were simply places where the repressed could come out of hiding. Abolitionists saw both what was actually there—erotic encounters did occur—and what associations of power with sex prepared them to see.

The abolitionist critique's intensity was not just a matter of these associations, nor was it just recognition that sexuality could flourish under slavery. After all, neither possession of power nor of sexual opportunity is innately fearsome; it may be more natural to relish both. The existence of southern licentiousness and arbitrary will, however, helped abolitionists define the South, slaveholders, and slavery in such a way that they became symbols of negation, opposites against which to measure what was good and progressive. And that measurement necessarily reflected a number of firmly held judgments about what man and society should be.

In 1839, unconsciously forecasting the insight of a later and more famous Victorian moralist, Theodore Dwight Weld wrote that "Restraints are the web of civilized society, warp and woof." James G. Birney, musing to his diary in 1850, decided: "The reason that savage & barbarous nations remain so—& unrighteous men, too—is that they manage their affairs by passion—not by reason. Just in proportion as reason prevails, it will control & restrain passion, & just in proportion as it prevails, & passion diminishes nations emerge from ignorance & darkness & become civilized." Here was a feeling that civilization, if not its discontents, depended on curbing what another abolitionist called "the fatal anarchy of the lowest passions."

Of course these passions were not exclusively sexual. Birney would not have argued that "salvage & barbarous nations" governed themselves by erotic means. But sex was clearly among the most formidable components of the "animal nature," which was to be subdued before humans or their society could be counted as civilized. Theodore Parker decided when a man "is cultivated and refined, the sentiment [of love] is more than the appetite [of sex]; the animal appetite remains but it does not bear so large a ratio to the whole consciousness of the man as before. . . ." The proper gentleman, like the proper lady, triumphed over sensuality. Sarah Grimké, emerging from a different tradition of gentility than Parker's, agreed with his estimate. It was impossible for men and women to enjoy the relationship God intended until "our intercourse is purified by the forgetfulness of sex. . . ." This resonated, almost as a linguistic pun, with an older, basically biblical, tradition which held (as restated by Beriah Green) that "All visible slavery is merely a picture of the invisible sway of the passions." In the minds of Christians slavery had always borne with it imputations of sin and human willfulness, but it took the 19th century, and a millennialistic nation, to transfer these ancient associations from slave to master and to impose upon them a drive for "civilization" and for (what was virtually the same thing) control, particularly control of the inner and lusty man.

Slavery was a guidepost, marking the outer limits of disorder and debauchery; but abolitionist perceptions of human failings neither began nor ended with the South's peculiar institution—reformers defined their own moral responsibilities in much the same terms they applied to slaveholders and other sinners. "And how is slavery to be abolished by those who are slaves themselves to their own appetites and passions?" Beriah Green asked. The *Emancipator* noted "the common acceptance of things" in which "men deem themselves the most happy when they can the most easily set aside known prohibitions and indulge in certain propensities." It contrasted this with the "early propagators of the religion of the cross" who had "no animal passions to gratify" as they were led to martyrdom. The lesson was unmistakable: a man who would do good must first conquer himself.

The courtship of Theodore Dwight Weld and Angelina Grimké, a veritable orgy of restraint, revealed that reformers were willing to practice what they preached. Weld regarded his emotions for Miss Grimké as a challenge to be overcome. "It will be a relief to you," he triumphantly assured Angelina in March 1838, "to know that I have acquired *perfect self-control,* so far as any *expression* or *appearance* of deep feeling is visible to others." Angelina earlier chided him for carrying things too far. "Why this waste of moral strength?" she asked. But she likewise thought of civilization as a repression of mankind's deeper and more mysterious forces. She responded ecstatically upon finding how elevated Weld's views of courtship were—how similar to her own, how unsensual. ". . . I have been tempted to think marriage was *sinful,* because of what appeared to me almost invariably to prompt and lead to it," she wrote. "Instead of the higher, nobler sentiments being first aroused, and leading on the lower passions *captive* to their will, the *latter* seemed to be *lords* over the *former.* Well I am convinced that men in general, the vast majority, believe most seriously that women were made to gratify their animal appetites, *expressly* to minister to *their* pleasure. . . ." The couple's control extended beyond the awkwardness of courtship. A few years after their marriage James G. Birney visited them, remarking to his diary, with a touch of envy, "Their self-denial—their firmness in principles puts me to shame." The Welds, their passions correctly ordered, settled into a long and gently loving life together.

Abolitionists not only controlled their own passional natures, and sought to control the South's, they also detected more general threats which (again) they frequently put in terms of rampant sexuality. "There is not a nation nor a tribe of men on earth so steeped in sexual pollution as this," Henry C. Wright thought. Thomas Wentworth Higginson saw the mass of men "deep in sensual vileness," while William Lloyd Garrison attacked a colonizationist not simply for his views on slavery but also for refusing to believe that "licentiousness pervades the whole land." William Goodell credited the South with an especial licentiousness, but the baneful influence did not stop there; instead it "pollutes the atmosphere of our splendid cities, and infects the whole land with the leprosy of Sodom." Less metaphorical, Stephen Pearl Andrews flatly stated that "Prostitution, in Marriage and out of it, and solitary vice, characterize Society as it is." The South might lead in debauchery, but the sin itself jeopardized the North as well.

Once problems were defined in such a way—as loss of moral control and consequent growth of licentiousness—then perception and real conditions fit neatly together. Southern sensuality forecast growing northern sensuality, and southern "barbarism," in turn, confirmed abolitionists in their fears about what unbridled human nature could produce anywhere. Even the South's economic state provided proof, for, despite grumblings, abolitionists at heart conceived of Northern industrial growth as a sign of advancing civilization. Moral guidance might well be imperative, but economic diversification itself was good, and it was not going on below the Mason-Dixon line—time and again antislavery propaganda pictured the South as an economically backward region, building neither factories nor railroads, seldom even paying its debts. Progress, in fact, could not long continue in a region where man lost control of himself. Only with destruction of the master's arbitrary power and restoration of moral restraint on all Southerners could the South develop spiritually and economically; only with strengthened restraint could the North continue to develop. Here abolitionism drew directly upon change in northern society, taking it to be both a cause for anxiety and, more important, a means of weighing the South's lack of progress, its failure to share the benefits of 19th-century civilization.

There were, however, more indirect consequences to industrialization than obvious economic development, and these would likewise conspire to reinforce abolitionist images of southern depravity and, further, to imply specific cures for general social evils. At first glance some of these consequences seem quite far removed from slavery since they touched society's most pervasive institution—the family. Although the interrelation between family change and economic change is still something of a puzzle, family patterns in America clearly underwent alteration from 1800 onward. The birth rate dropped steadily but appreciably throughout the 19th century (particularly in the Northeast where both industrialization and reform impulses found the atmosphere most congenial). And the home appears to have been declining in economic functions: fewer goods were made in it as a wider variety of products were factory produced and store bought; men increasingly commuted to work; and middle-class women

seemed to be losing their most apparent economic roles—no longer contributing to a family enterprise, purchasing products rather than making them, and even having immigrant servants available to tend broods of children smaller than those their mothers bore.

Yet what the family lost in economic value it gained in moral prestige, coming (in the antebellum period) to stand as the center for instruction in virtue. Gamaliel Bailey, echoing his contemporaries' sentiments, declared the family to be "the great primal institution, established by the Creator himself, as the first and best school for training men for all social relations and duties." There were good reasons why abolitionists like Bailey, and others eager for moral guidance in a time of flux, would look so fervently at the family—no other social institution seemed half so reliable. American Protestantism was busily dividing into rival denominations, the fragments cooperating briefly during revivals, then going their separate, bickering paths. Unlike the old days, no one clergyman served the community, no one church dominated the landscape. Jacksonian America's political system was even more bewildering because, so moralists thought, it played to the basest instincts of the voter, encouraging demagoguery rather than respectability and virtue. Changing though the family was, there was no other safe haven for morality in such tempestuous times.

And so, in yet another way, southern sexuality focused what was a matter of immediate concern among abolitionists—the nature of household relationships. Since the slaveholder lacked restraint on his erotic energy, antislavery propaganda assumed he "totally annihilates the marriage institution." Not only did the master fail to sanction or respect marriage among slaves, his uninhibited lustfulness also meant he did not honor his own marriage vows, destroying family relations among whites as well as blacks. Everything converged to deprive the South of a stable family life, robbing that section of the basic mechanism of social control, confirming its status as antithesis of order and civilization. There is no particular evidence that southern family instability was increasing in the 1830s, nor did abolitionists claim it was. The difference was that by 1830 the family itself was a matter both of anxiety and hope, anxiety found nightmarish confirmation in the southern way of life, with its ostensible eroticism and its disdain for the one reasonably dependable moral guardian.

Sexual attitudes, merging with objective conditions and with ideas about power and civilization, guided abolitionists as they looked fretfully southward. But in many of their particular beliefs abolitionists were hardly unique. Antislavery, in fact, moved to much larger rhythms of public concern. If abolitionists worried about licentiousness and the decline of order, then so did men who opposed them in anti-antislavery mobs, fearful that emancipation would upset conventional social relations and promote miscegenation. If abolitionists threw much of their faith for moral training upon the family then, it has to be said, so did defenders of slavery, who portrayed their supposedly patriarchal institution as an alternative to decay of personal ties in the North. It would be a mistake, nevertheless, to dismiss patterns of thought as unimportant because they appeared among otherwise very different people, utilized for different purposes. Concern for human sexuality and equation of civilization with its suppression were too general to be a direct cause for the rise of antislavery. Rather than make abolitionism inevitable, it made inevitable a certain *kind* of abolitionism; it ensured that some Northerners enmeshed in change would be able to see certain things in the South that earlier generations either had not seen or had taken far more lightly. There was, moreover, another kind of importance to assumptions abolitionists applied to southern behavior, particularly to southern sexuality: these were threads radi-

ating outward, forming a web of reform commitment much larger than antislavery alone, finally extending beyond the death of slavery.

Abolitionists seem crankish, or quaint, for the various fads and reforms they drifted into. Yet many of these auxiliary causes fit the same mold as antislavery, indicating that abolitionists were driven as much by a generalized desire to control the "animal nature" standing between man and civilization as they were by a specific quarrel with the South, which was only the worst of offenders, the logical extension of human depravity. Time after time abolitionists turned their guns toward the same lack of restraint in the North, or in individuals, as they imagined in the South. In numerous and occasionally subtle ways they betrayed how much of their vehemence stemmed from a pervasive fear that man was giving in too easily to his passionate self. The most frequent attacks of this sort probably were reserved for tyranny of the bottle. But despite near universality of temperance sentiment among abolitionists, they found their most spectacular examples of sin in presumably prevalent northern sexual immorality, a more literal surrender of man's "higher" qualities (his civilization) to the body's claims than alcoholism.

Abolitionists devoted themselves to sweeping back "the wild sea of prostitution, which swells and breaks and dashes against the bulwarks of society." In fact almost coincident with the rise of antislavery was a Moral Reform movement designed to curb prostitution and to promote purity. It had appeal at antislavery centers such as Oberlin and Western Reserve, and many abolitionists became involved in the efforts of one of Moral Reform's chief promoters, the Reverend John McDowall. McDowall's spicy account of sexual depravity in New York City brought tremendous criticism on his sponsor, the local Magdalen Society, and particularly on Arthur Tappan, a prominent member as well as a future president of the American Anti-Slavery

Society. A successor to the Magdalen Society, called the American Society for Promoting the Observance of the Seventh Commandment, drew upon abolitionists for its officers. Beriah Green was president; three abolitionists, including Weld, were vice-presidents; others, Joshua Leavitt and William Goodell among them, were on the executive committee. Lucretia Mott's support of an organization to redeem fallen women was dampened only by her discovery that it did not offer its services to blacks.

Some abolitionists were convinced that things were drastically wrong even with the institution designed to contain erotic impulses. "The right idea of marriage is at the foundation of all reforms," Elizabeth Cady Stanton decided in 1853. Amidst her suggestions for change was the complaint that "Man in his lust has regulated long enough this whole question of sexual intercourse." Henry C. Wright produced a work on *Marriage and Parentage,* which attacked "THE UN-NATURAL AND MONSTROUS EXPENDITURE OF THE SEXUAL ELEMENT, FOR MERE SENSUAL GRATIFICATION" within marriage. He presented as ideal two husbands able to "control all their passional expressions." Stephen Pearl Andrews preached an individualism which bordered on Free Love—except he argued that a liberalization of marriage and divorce practices would actually "moderate the passions instead of inflaming them, and so . . . contribute, in the highest degree, to a general Purity of life. . . ."

So sinister seemed man's erotic nature that it would not be satisfied with brothel and marriage bed, and abolitionists grasped odd times to warn against the "secret vice" of auto-eroticism. Lewis Tappan interrupted a biography of his brother to urge readers to warn their children that "youthful lusts" could lead to "idiocy, insanity, disfigurement of body, and imbecility of mind." Garrison used the *Liberator* to review a book entitled *Debilitated Young Men,* taking occasion to rail against "the dreadful vice of Masturbation." The vice apparently was prevalent enough, and dreadful enough, to call forth veiled words of warning from Harriet Beecher Stowe and her sister in a book for homemakers they coauthored.

All of this put a terrible burden on the erotic offender. The prostitute spread disease and misery; [T]he lustful husband blighted his wife and transmitted sins to his unborn child; and the masturbator faced self-destruction. One did not even have to be consciously lustful to be harmed by his sexuality. Theodore Dwight Weld badgered his son, suffering both from a mysterious lethargy and an apparently unstimulated loss of semen, by warning "All authorities agree that this drain upon the seminal fluid will . . . lead ultimately to *insanity* or *idiocy.*"

Such beliefs may have bordered on being conventional wisdom; certainly abolitionists were not the only people to think that sexual excess caused insanity and other frightening ills. But abolitionists fit such attitudes into a pattern of social concern, characterized by anxiety over eroticism, North and South. A major part of the pattern resulted from an antebellum turn to find the key to reform within man—not just within man (for others had done that too), but in man's physical nature. A feeling in Jacksonian reform that man's animal self had to be conquered in favor of his immaterial being came around, in circular fashion, to the body once more. Control and liberation were to be found in the same place. Victory lay in the enemy's camp after all.

Still, some ways of reaching that camp were more promising than others. Controlling man's sensual nature implied certain strategies, if one accepted the terms of antebellum culture literally. For one thing, the path cleared for women to participate more openly in reform causes than they had previously. As the middle-class women retreated from direct and obvious economic support of the family, it became common to invest her with other virtues: she was, it seemed, also removed from worldly crassness, more spiritual by nature and by position than man, less sensual. Sarach Grimké, late in life, made explicit what had more commonly been implicit in the antislavery crusade from the beginning. Woman is innately man's "superior," Miss Grimké thought, a fact related to her feeling that "the sexual passion in man is ten times stronger than in woman." Under the right order of things, William Goodell believed, woman serves man as "the chastizer of his desires." Sarah Grimké's sister, Angelina, knew where this argument led, writing of women that "it is through their instrumentality that the great and glorious work of reforming the world is to be done." Of course it can be a dubious blessing to be presumed morally superior—it places shame on sexual impulses and guilt on failure to affect social change. (Sarah Grimké, for instance, felt that female asexuality made women more culpable in sexual transgressions than men, and other abolitionists concluded from woman's moral power that "American mothers are responsible for American slavery.") Yet there was a powerful justification for female activity here, and the point that women had a special role in the drama of redemption was conceded by male abolitionists, even relatively conservative ones who never brought themselves to support the Woman's Rights Movement which grew out of antislavery agitation.

But a drive to control man's animal nature had other implications for antebellum reform besides awakening middle-class women to their obligations and their very real grievances. Virtually simultaneous with the rise of antislavery were still more attempts to subdue licentiousness—less obvious than the Moral Reform movement and less rooted in genuine social evils than antislavery and Woman's Rights. Chief among these peripheral causes was health reform, exemplified by Sylvester Graham, whose memory lives decadently in the Graham cracker. Graham, and men like him, sought to purify the body, to heal it of infirmities, through proper diet. Graham's regimen, which seemed laughable or repulsive to many Americans at the time, found adherents among abolitionists, and not just among Garrisonians (who had a susceptibility to fads). Non-Garrisonians like Henry B. Stanton and Lewis Tappan also found the Graham system enchanting and Oberlin greeted Graham and a fellow dietary reformer, William A. Alcott, with initial enthusiasm. In its heyday the Graham system secured fierce loyalty from such staunch immediate emancipationists as the Welds, Sarah Grimké, and William Goodell. LaRoy Sunderland went so far as to claim he owed his life to Graham's diet; Amasa Walker merely achieved regularity from it.

There was also a considerable interest among abolitionists in exercise and gymnastics, programs which, like proper diet, helped in bringing the body under control and in preventing it from interfering with man's spiritual nature. Theodore Dwight Weld had been a missionary for the manual labor school idea before he turned to antislavery. This was a plan designed to mix education and work, both for financial reasons and to put body and spirit into right relation. After his career as an abolitionist had virtually ended, Weld taught in Dio Lewis' gymnastic institute—where William Lloyd Garrison sent at least some of his children and where the Welds themselves sent the son who exhibited signs of excessive loss of seminal fluid. Charles Follen, an early and beloved abolitionist, had been among the first to bring German physical culture ideas to the United States. Although Follen died tragically before Thomas Wentworth Higginson entered the movement, Higginson proved to be his spiritual heir, managing (in New England culture) to glide from antebellum reform to the late 19th century's "vigorous life." So persuasive was Higginson's campaigning for exercise that his efforts, according to one abolitionist, produced an outburst of ice-skating in Worcester, Massachusetts, which earned the title of "Higginson's Revival."

Such activities seem innocent—and innocuous—enough, and, like dietary reform, they appear to have been aimed at an improvement in the quality of life. All that they were. But connected with dietary reform and advocacy of exercise was the familiar drive to subdue man's physical, particularly his sexual, aspects. Health reformers like Graham and William A. Alcott wrote extensively on the terrible effects of sexual excess and presented proper diet as a means of suppressing erotic impulses. Propagandists for physical culture such as Dio Lewis and Russell Trall likewise counseled sexual control and likewise saw their programs as a way of achieving it. "A vigorous life of the senses not only does not tend to sensuality in the objectionable sense," Higginson claimed in an essay on gymnastics, "but it helps to avert it." Dietary reform and the cult of exercise, like antislavery, fastened upon man's erotic nature in order to overcome it.

*   *   *

Abolitionism began, and ended, with man. It began with a call for individual outrage and repentance and ended with the Yankee schoolmar'm carrying civilization southward. It sought to liberate men and, at the same time, to control man, to make him moral, eventually to direct his most fearful energies toward his salvation. Abolitionists were not alone in their preoccupations; they were, instead, very much children of antebellum America, less unique in their anxieties and hopes than in the embodiment they found for those anxieties and hopes. The problem of why certain individuals became abolitionists while others, of similar backgrounds, did not is a task for those who can untangle personal motivation. Equally important to understand is the function antislavery played for those captivated by it. For abolitionists slavery summed up discontents which were social, personal and far more general than the South's peculiar institution. The erotic South, like the inhuman and exploitative North of proslavery propaganda, was less a real place than an organizing principle, a culturally planted reference point measuring the dreadful rush of antebellum change.

Beauty, the Beast, and the Militant Woman: Sex Roles and Social Stress in Jacksonian America

Carroll Smith-Rosenberg

On a spring evening in May 1834, a small group of women met at the revivalist Third Presbyterian Church in New York City to found the New York Female Moral Reform Society. The Society's goals were ambitious indeed; it hoped to convert New York's prostitutes to evangelical Protestantism and close forever the city's numerous brothels. This bold attack on prostitution was only one part of the Society's program. These self-assertive women hoped as well to confront that larger and more fundamental abuse, the double standard, and the male sexual license it condoned. Too many men, the Society defiantly asserted in its statement of goals, were aggressive destroyers of female innocence and happiness. No man was above suspicion. Women's only safety lay in a militant effort to reform American sexual mores—and, as we shall see, to reform sexual mores meant in practice to control man's sexual values and autonomy. The rhetoric of the Society's spokesmen consistently betrayed an unmistakable and deeply felt resentment toward a male-dominated society.

Few if any members of the Society were reformed prostitutes or the victims of rape or seduction. Most came from middle-class native American backgrounds and lived quietly respectable lives as pious wives and mothers. What needs explaining is the emotional logic which underlay the Society's militant and controversial program of sexual reform. I would like to suggest that both its reform program and the anti-male sentiments it served to express reflect a neglected area of stress in mid-19th-century America—that is, the nature of the role to be assumed by the middle-class American woman.

American society from the 1830s to the 1860s was marked by advances in political democracy; by a rapid increase in economic, social, and geographic mobility; and by uncompromising and morally relentless reform movements. Though many aspects of Jacksonianism have been subjected to historical investigation, the possibly stressful effects of such structural change upon family and sex roles have not. The following pages constitute an attempt to glean some understanding of women and women's role in antebellum America through an analy-

"Beauty, the Beast and the Militant Woman: A Case Study in Sex Roles and Social Stress in Jacksonian America" by Carroll Smith-Rosenberg, *American Quarterly,* Vol. 23, No. 4, December 1972. Copyright © 1972, American Studies Association. Reprinted by permission of the American Studies Association and Carroll Smith-Rosenberg. This essay appears in the collection *Disorderly Conduct: Visions of Gender in Nineteenth Century America* by Carroll Smith-Rosenberg (New York: Alfred A. Knopf, 1985).

sis of a self-consciously female voluntary association dedicated to the eradication of sexual immorality.

Women in Jacksonian America had few rights and little power. Their role in society was passive and sharply limited. Women were, in general, denied formal education above the minimum required by a literate early industrial society. The female brain and nervous system, male physicians and educators agreed, were inadequate to sustained intellectual effort. They were denied the vote in a society which placed a high value upon political participation; political activity might corrupt their pure feminine nature. All professional roles (with the exception of primary school education) were closed to women. Even so traditional a female role as midwife was undermined as male physicians began to establish professional control over obstetrics. Most economic alternatives to marriage (except such burdensome and menial tasks as those of seamstress or domestic) were closed to women. Their property rights were still restricted and females were generally considered to be the legal wards either of the state or of their nearest male relative. In the event of divorce, the mother lost custody of her children—even when the husband was conceded to be the erring party. Women's universe was bounded by their homes and the career of father or husband; within the home it was woman's duty to be submissive and patient.

Yet this was a period when change was considered a self-evident good, and when nothing was believed impossible to a determined free will, be it the conquest of a continent, the reform of society or the eternal salvation of all mankind. The contrast between these generally accepted ideals and expectations and the real possibilities available to American women could not have been more sharply drawn. It is not implausible to assume that at least a minority of American women would find ways to manifest a discontent with their comparatively passive and constricted social role.

Only a few women in antebellum America were able, however, to openly criticize their socially defined sexual identity. A handful, like Fanny Wright, devoted themselves to overtly subversive criticism of the social order. A scarcely more numerous group became pioneers in women's education. Others such as Elizabeth Cady Stanton, Lucretia Mott, and Susan B. Anthony founded the women's rights movement. But most respectable women—even those with a sense of ill-defined grievance—were unable to explicitly defy traditional sex-role prescriptions.

I would like to suggest that many such women channeled frustration, anger, and a compensatory sense of superior righteousness into the reform movements of the first half of the 19th century; and in the controversial moral reform crusade such motivations seem particularly apparent. Although unassailable within the absolute categories of a pervasive evangelical world-view, the Female Moral Reform Society's crusade against illicit sexuality permitted an expression of anti-male sentiments. And the Society's "final solution" —the right to control the mores of men—provided a logical emotional redress for those feelings of passivity which we have suggested. It should not be surprising that between 1830 and 1860 a significant number of militant women joined a crusade to establish their right to define—and limit—man's sexual behavior.

Yet adultery and prostitution were unaccustomed objects of reform even in the enthusiastic and millennial America of the 1830s. The mere discussion of these taboo subjects shocked most Americans; to undertake such a crusade implied no ordinary degree of commitment. The founders of the Female Moral Reform Society, however, were able to find both legitimization for the expression of grievance normally unspoken and an impulse to activism in the moral categories of evangelical piety. Both pious activism and sex-role anxieties shaped the early years of the Female Moral Reform Society. This conjunction of motives was hardly accidental.

The lady founders of the Moral Reform Society and their new organization represented an extreme wing of that movement within American Protestantism known as the Second Great Awakening. These women were intensely pious Christians, convinced that an era of millennial perfection awaited human effort. In this fervent generation, such deeply felt millennial possibilities made social action a moral imperative. Like many of the abolitionists, Jacksonian crusaders against sexual transgression were dedicated activists, compelled to attack sin wherever it existed and in whatever form it assumed—even the unmentionable sin of illicit sexuality.

New Yorkers' first awareness of the moral reform crusade came in the spring of 1832 when the New York Magdalen Society (an organization which sought to reform prostitutes) issued its first annual report. Written by John McDowall, their missionary and agent, the report stated unhesitatingly that 10,000 prostitutes lived and worked in New York City. Not only sailors and other transients, but men from the city's most respected families, were regular brothel patrons. Lewdness and impurity tainted all sectors of New York society. True Christians, the report concluded, must wage a thoroughgoing crusade against violators of the Seventh Commandment.

The report shocked and irritated respectable New Yorkers—not only by its tone of righteous indignation and implied criticism of the city's old and established families. The report, it seemed clear to many New Yorkers, was obscene, its author a mere seeker after notoriety. Hostility quickly spread from McDowall to the Society itself; its members were verbally abused and threatened with ostracism. The society disbanded.

A few of the women, however, would not retreat. Working quietly, they began to found church-affiliated female moral reform societies. Within a year, they had created a number of such groups, connected for the most part with the city's more evangelical congregations. These pious women hoped to reform prostitutes, but more immediately to warn other God-fearing Christians of the pervasiveness of sexual sin and the need to oppose it. Prostitution was after all only one of many offenses against the Seventh Commandment; adultery, lewd thoughts, and language, and bawdy literature were equally sinful in the eyes of God. These women at the same time continued unofficially to support their former missionary, John McDowall, using his newly established moral reform newspaper to advance their cause not only in the city, but throughout New York State.

After more than a year of such discreet crusading, the women active in the moral reform cause felt sufficiently numerous and confident to organize a second citywide moral reform society and renew their efforts to reform the city's prostitutes. On the evening of May 12, 1834, they met at the Third Presbyterian Church to found the New York Female Moral Reform Society.

Nearly four years of opposition and controversy had hardened the women's ardor into a militant determination. They proposed through their organization to extirpate sexual license and the double standard from American society. A forthright list of resolves announced their organization:

> Resolved, That immediate and vigorous efforts should be made to create a public sentiment in respect to this sin; and also in respect to the duty of parents, church members and ministers on the subject, which shall be in stricter accordance with . . . the word of God.
>
> Resolved, That the licentious man is no less guilty than his victim, and ought, therefore, to be excluded from all virtuous female society.
>
> Resolved, That it is the imperious duty of ladies everywhere, and of every religious denomination, to co-operate in the great work of moral reform.

A sense of urgency and spiritual absolutism marked this organization meeting, and indeed all of the Society's official statements for years to come. "It is the duty of the virtuous to use every consistent moral means to save our country from utter destruction," the women warned. "The sin of licentiousness has made fearful havoc . . . drowning souls in perdition and exposing us to the vengeance of a holy God." Americans hopeful of witnessing the promised millennium could delay no longer.

The motivating zeal that allowed the rejection of age-old proprieties and defied the criticism of pulpit and press was no casual and fashionable enthusiasm. Only an extraordinary set of legitimating values could have justified such commitment. And this was indeed the case. The women moral reformers acted in the conscious conviction that God imperiously commanded their work. As they explained soon after organizing their society: "As Christians we must view it in the light of God's word—we must enter into His feelings on the subject—engage in its overthrow just in the manner he would have us. . . . We must look away from all worldly opinions or influences, for they are perverted and wrong; and individually act only as in the presence of God." Though the Society's pious activism had deep roots in the evangelicalism of the Second Great Awakening, the immediate impetus for the founding of the Moral Reform Society came from the revivals Charles G. Finney conducted in New York City between the summer of 1829 and the spring of 1834.

Charles Finney, reformer, revivalist, and perfectionist theologian from western New York State, remains a pivotal figure in the history of American Protestantism. The four years Finney spent in New York had a profound influence on the city's churches and reform movements, and upon the consciences generally of the thousands of New Yorkers who crowded his revival meetings and flocked to his churches. Finney insisted that his disciples end any compromise with sin or human injustice. Souls were lost and sin prevailed, Finney urged, because men chose to sin—because they chose

not to work in God's vineyard converting souls and reforming sinners. Inspired by Finney's sermons, thousands of New Yorkers turned to missionary work; they distributed Bibles and tracts to the irreligious, established Sunday schools and sent ministers to the frontier. A smaller, more zealous number espoused abolition as well, determined, like Garrison, never to be silent and to be heard. An even smaller number of the most zealous and determined turned—as we have seen—to moral reform.

The program adopted by the Female Moral Reform Society in the spring of 1834 embraced two quite different, though to the Society's founders quite consistent, modes of attack. One was absolutist and millennial, an attempt to convert all of America to perfect moral purity. Concretely the New York women hoped to create a militant nationwide women's organization to fight the double standard and indeed any form of licentiousness—beginning of course in their own homes and neighborhoods. Only an organization of women, they contended, could be trusted with so sensitive and yet monumental a task. At the same time, the Society sponsored a parallel and somewhat more pragmatic attempt to convert and reform New York City's prostitutes. Though strikingly dissimilar in method and geographic scope, both efforts were unified by an uncompromising millennial zeal and by a strident hostility to the licentious and predatory male.

The Society began its renewed drive against prostitution in the fall of 1834 when the executive committee appointed John McDowall their missionary to New York's prostitutes and hired two young men to assist him. The Society's three missionaries visited the female wards of the almshouse, the city hospital and jails, leading prayer meetings, distributing Bibles and tracts. A greater proportion of their time, however, was spent in a more controversial manner, systematically visiting—or, to be more accurate, descending upon—brothels, praying with and exhorting

TEMPTING TO RUIN!

HOW GOTHAM'S PALACES OF SIN ARE GARRISONED OUT OF THE HOVELS—
THE GAUDY SPIDER SPREADING HER WEBS FOR THE FLIES WHO
MAKE HER LOATHSOME TRADE PROFITABLE.

*The Female Moral Reform Society embarked in 1834
on a program aimed at eliminating prostitution
and reforming New York City's "fallen women."*

then hastily walking past. Closed coaches, they also reported, were observed to circle suspiciously for upwards of an hour until, the missionary remaining, they drove away.

The Female Moral Reform Society did not depend completely on paid missionaries for the success of such pious harassment. The Society's executive committee, accompanied by like-thinking male volunteers, regularly visited the city's hapless brothels. (The executive committee minutes for January 1835, for example, contain a lengthy discussion of the properly discreet makeup of groups for such "active visiting.") The members went primarily to pray and to exert moral influence. They were not unaware, however, of the financially disruptive effect that frequent visits of large groups of praying Christians would have. The executive committee also aided the concerned parents (usually rural) of runaway daughters who, they feared, might have drifted to the city and been forced into prostitution. Members visited brothels asking for information about such girls; one pious volunteer even pretended to be delivering laundry in order to gain admittance to a brothel suspected of hiding such a runaway.

In conjunction with their visiting, the Moral Reform Society opened a House of Reception, a would-be refuge for prostitutes seeking to reform. The Society's managers and missionaries felt that if the prostitute could be convinced of her sin, and then offered both a place of retreat and an economic alternative to prostitution, reform would surely follow. Thus they envisioned their home as a "house of industry" where the errant ones would be taught new trades and prepared for useful jobs—while being instructed in morality and religion. When the managers felt their repentant charges prepared to return to society, they attempted to find them jobs with Christian families—and, so far as possible, away from the city's temptations.

Despite their efforts, however, few prosti-

both the inmates and their patrons. The missionaries were specially fond of arriving early Sunday morning—catching women and customers as they awoke on the traditionally sacred day. The missionaries would announce their arrival by a vigorous reading of Bible passages, followed by prayer and hymns. At other times they would station themselves across the street from known brothels to observe and note the identity of customers. They soon found their simple presence had an important deterring effect; many men, with doggedly innocent expressions, pausing momentarily and tutes reformed; fewer still appeared, to their benefactresses, to have experienced the saving grace of conversion. Indeed, the number of inmates at the Society's House of Reception was always small. In March 1835, for instance, the executive committee reported only fourteen women at the House. A year later, total admissions had reached but thirty—only four of whom were considered saved. The final debacle came that summer when the regular manager of the House left the city because of poor health. In his absence, the executive committee reported unhappily, the inmates seized control, and discipline and morality deteriorated precipitously. The managers reassembled in the fall to find their home in chaos. Bitterly discouraged, they dismissed the few remaining unruly inmates and closed the building.

The moral rehabilitation of New York's streetwalkers was but one aspect of the Society's attack upon immorality. The founders of the Female Moral Reform Society saw as their principal objective the creation of a woman's crusade to combat sexual license generally and the double standard particularly. American women would no longer willingly tolerate that traditional—and role-defining—masculine ethos that allotted respect to the hearty drinker and the sexual athlete. This age-old code of masculinity was as obviously related to man's social preeminence as it was contrary to society's explicitly avowed norms of purity and domesticity. The subterranean mores of the American male must be confronted, exposed, and rooted out.

The principal weapon of the Society in this crusade was its weekly, *The Advocate of Moral Reform.* In the fall of 1834, when the Society hired John McDowall as its agent, it voted as well to purchase his journal and transform it into a national women's paper with an exclusively female staff. Within three years, the *Advocate* grew into one of the nation's most widely read evangelical papers, boasting 16,500

subscribers. By the late 1830s the Society's managers pointed to this publication as their most important activity.

Two themes dominated virtually every issue of the *Advocate* from its founding in January 1835, until the early 1850s. The first was an angry and emphatic insistence upon the lascivious and predatory nature of the American male. Men were the initiators in virtually every case of adultery or fornication—and the source, therefore, of that widespread immorality that endangered America's spiritual life and delayed the promised millennium. A second major theme in the *Advocate's* editorials and letters was a call for the creation of a national union of women. Through their collective action such a united group of women might ultimately control the behavior of adult males and of the members' own children, particularly their sons.

The founders and supporters of the Female Moral Reform Society entertained several primary assumptions concerning the nature of human sexuality. Perhaps most central was the conviction that women felt little sexual desire; they were in almost every instance induced to violate the Seventh Commandment by lascivious men who craftily manipulated not their sensuality, but rather the female's trusting and affectionate nature. A woman acted out of romantic love, not carnal desire; she was innocent and defenseless, gentle and passive. "The worst crime alleged against [the fallen woman] in the outset," the *Advocate's* editors explained, "is . . . 'She is without discretion.' She is open-hearted, sincere, and affectionate. . . . She trusts the vows of the faithless. She commits her all into the hands of the deceiver."

The male lecher, on the other hand, was a creature controlled by base sexual drives . . . he neither could nor would control. He was, the *Advocate's* editors bitterly complained, powerful and decisive; unwilling (possibly unable) to curb his own willfullness, he callously used it to coerce the more passive and submissive female. This was an age of rhetorical expansiveness, and the *Advocate*'s editors and correspondents felt little constraint in their delineation of the dominant and aggressive male. "Reckless," "bold," "mad," "drenched in sin" were terms used commonly to describe erring males; they "robbed," "ruined" and "rioted." But one term above all others seemed most fit to describe the lecher—"The Destroyer."

A deep sense of anger and frustration characterized the *Advocate*'s discussion of such all-conquering males, a theme reiterated again and again in the letters sent to the paper by rural sympathizers. Women saw themselves with few defenses against the determined male; his will was far stronger than that of woman. Such letters often expressed a bitterness which seems directed not only against the specific seducer, but toward all American men. One representative rural subscriber complained, for example: "Honorable men; they would not plunder; . . . an imputation on their honour might cost a man his life's blood. And yet they are so passingly mean, so utterly contemptible, as basely and treacherously to contrive . . . the destruction of happiness, peace, morality, and all that is endearing in social life; they plunge into degradation, misery, and ruin, those whom they profess to love. O let them not be trusted. Their 'tender mercies are cruel.'"

The double standard seemed thus particularly unjust; it came to symbolize and embody for the Society and its rural sympathizers the callous indifference—indeed at times almost sadistic pleasure—a male-dominated society took in the misfortune of a passive and defenseless woman. The respectable harshly denied her their friendship; even parents might reject her. Often only the brothel offered food and shelter. But what of her seducer? Conventional wisdom found it easy to condone his greater sin: men will be men and right-thinking women must not inquire into such questionable matters.

But it was just such matters, the Society contended, to which women must ad-

dress themselves. They must enforce God's commandments despite hostility and censure. "Public opinion must be operated upon," the executive committee decided in the winter of 1835, "by endeavoring to bring the virtuous to treat the guilty of both sexes alike, and exercise toward them the same feeling." "Why should a female be trodden under foot," the executive committee's minutes questioned plaintively, "and spurned from society and driven from a parent's roof, if she but fall into sin—while common consent allows the male to habituate himself to this vice, and treats him as not guilty. Has God made a distinction in regard to the two sexes in this respect?" The guilty woman too should be condemned, the Moral Reform Society's quarterly meeting resolved in 1838: "But let not the most guilty of the two—the deliberate destroyer of innocence—be afforded even an 'apron of fig leaves' to conceal the blackness of his crimes."

Women must unite in a holy crusade against such sinners. The Society called upon pious women throughout the country to shun all social contact with men suspected of improper behavior—even if that behavior consisted only of reading improper books or singing indelicate songs. Churchgoing women of every village and town must organize local campaigns to outlaw such men from society and hold them up to public judgment. "Admit him not to your house," the executive committee urged, "hold no converse with him, warn others of him, permit not your friends to have fellowship with him, mark as an evildoer, stamp him as a villain and exclaim, 'Behold the Seducer.'" The power of ostracism could become an effective weapon in the defense of morality.

A key tactic in this campaign of public exposure was the Society's willingness to publish the names of men suspected of sexual immorality. The *Advocate*'s editors announced in their first issue that they intended to pursue this policy, first begun by John McDowall in his *Journal.* "We think it proper," they stated defiantly, "even to expose names, for the same reason that the names of thieves and robbers are published, that the public may know them and govern themselves accordingly. We mean to let the licentious know, that if they are not ashamed of their debasing vice, we will not be ashamed to expose them. . . . It is a justice which we owe each other." Their readers responded enthusiastically to this invitation. Letters from rural subscribers poured into the *Advocate,* recounting specific instances of seduction in their towns and warning readers to avoid the men described. The editors dutifully set them in type and printed them.

Within New York City itself the executive committee of the Society actively investigated charges of seduction and immorality. A particular target of their watchfulness was the city's employment agencies—or information offices as they were then called; these were frequently fronts for the white-slave trade. The *Advocate* printed the names and addresses of suspicious agencies, warning women seeking employment to avoid them at all costs. Prostitutes whom the Society's missionaries visited in brothels, in prison or in the city hospital were urged to report the names of men who had first seduced them and also of their later customers; they could then be published in the *Advocate.* The executive committee undertook as well a lobbying campaign in Albany to secure the passage of a statute making seduction a crime for the male participant. While awaiting the passage of this measure, the executive committee encouraged and aided victims of seduction (or where appropriate their parents or employers) to sue their seducers on the grounds of loss of services.

Ostracism, exposure, and statutory enactment offered immediate, if unfortunately partial, solutions to the problem of male licentiousness. But for the seduced and ruined victim such vengeance came too late. The tactic of preference, women moral reformers agreed, was to educate children, especially young male children, to a literal adherence to the Sev-

enth Commandment. This was a mother's task. American mothers, the *Advocate*'s editors repeated endlessly, must educate their sons to reject the double standard. No child was too young, no efforts too diligent in this crucial aspect of socialization. The true foundations of such a successful effort lay in an early and highly pietistic religious education and in the inculcation of a related imperative—the son's absolute and unquestioned obedience to his mother's will. "Obedience, entire and unquestioned, must be secured, or all is lost." The mother must devote herself whole-heartedly to this task for self-will in a child was an ever-recurring evil. "Let us watch over them continually. . . . Let us . . . teach them when they go out and when they come in—when they lie down, and when they rise up. . . ." A son must learn to confide in his mother instinctively; no thought should be hidden from her.

Explicit education in the Seventh Commandment itself should begin quite early, for bitter experience had shown that no child was too young for such sensual temptation. As her son grew older, his mother was urged to instill in him a love for the quiet of domesticity, a repugnance for the unnatural excitements of the theater and tavern. He should be taught to prefer home and the companionship of pious women to the temptations of bachelor life. The final step in a young man's moral education would come one evening shortly before he was to leave home for the first time. That night, the *Advocate* advised its readers, the mother must spend a long earnest time at his bedside (ordinarily in the dark to hide her natural blushes) discussing the importance of maintaining his sexual purity and the temptations he would inevitably face in attempting to remain true to his mother's religious principles.

Mothers, not fathers, were urged to supervise the sexual education of sons. Mothers, the Society argued, spent most time with their children; fathers were usually occupied with business concerns and found little time for their children. Sons were naturally close to their mothers, and devoted maternal supervision would cement these natural ties. A mother devoted to the moral reform cause could be trusted to teach her son to reject the traditional ethos of masculinity and accept the higher—more feminine—code of Christianity. A son thus educated would be inevitably a recruit in the women's crusade against sexual license.

The Society's general program of exposure and ostracism, lobbying, and education depended for effectiveness upon the creation of a national association of militant and pious women. In the fall of 1834, but a few months after they had organized their Society, its New York officers began to create such a woman's organization. At first they worked through the *Advocate* and the small network of sympathizers John McDowall's efforts had created. By the spring of 1835, however, they were able to hire a minister to travel through western New York State "in behalf of Moral Reform causes." The following year the committee sent two female missionaries, the editor of the Society's newspaper, and a paid female agent, on a thousand-mile tour of the New England states. Visiting women's groups and churches in Brattleboro, Deerfield, Northampton, Pittsfield, the Stockbridges, and many other towns, the ladies rallied their sisters to the moral reform cause and helped organize some forty-one new auxiliaries. Each succeeding summer saw similar trips by paid agents and managers of the Society throughout New York State and New England. By 1839, the New York Female Moral Reform Society boasted some 445 female auxiliaries, principally in greater New England. So successful were these efforts that within a few years the bulk of the Society's membership and financial support came from its auxiliaries. In February 1838, the executive committee voted to invite representatives of these auxiliaries to attend the Society's annual meeting. The following year the New York Society voted at its annual convention to reorganize as a national

society—the American Female Moral Reform Society; the New York group would be simply one of its many constituent societies.

This rural support was an indispensable part of the moral reform movement. The local auxiliaries held regular meetings in churches, persuaded hesitant ministers to preach on the Seventh Commandment, urged Sunday school teachers to confront this embarrassing but vital question. They raised money for the executive committee's ambitious projects, convinced at least some men to form male moral reform societies, and did their utmost to ostracize suspected lechers. When the American Female Moral Reform Society decided to mount a campaign to induce the New York State legislature to pass a law making seduction a criminal offense, the Society's hundreds of rural auxiliaries wrote regularly to their legislators, circulated petitions, and joined their New York City sisters in Albany to lobby for the bill (which was finally passed in 1848).

In addition to such financial and practical aid, members of the moral reform society's rural branches contributed another crucial, if less tangible, element to the reform movement. This was their commitment to the creation of a feeling of sisterhood among all morally dedicated women. Letters from individuals to the *Advocate* and reports from auxiliaries make clear, sometimes even in the most explicit terms, that many American women experienced a depressing sense of isolation. In part, this feeling merely reflected a physical reality for women living in rural communities. But since city- and town-dwelling women voiced similar complaints, I would like to suggest that this consciousness of isolation also reflected a sense of status inferiority. Confined by their non-maleness, antebellum American women lived within the concentric structure of a family organized around the needs and status of husbands or fathers. And such social isolation within the family—or perhaps more accurately a lack of autonomy both embodied in and symbolized by such isolation—not only dramatized, but partially constituted, a differentiation in status. The fact that social values and attitudes were established by men and oriented to male experiences only exacerbated women's feelings of inferiority and irrelevance. Again and again the Society's members were to express their desire for a feminine-sororial community that might help break down this isolation, lighten the monotony and harshness of life, and establish a countersystem of female values and priorities.

The New York Female Moral Reform Society quite consciously sought to inspire in its members a sense of solidarity in a cause peculiar to their sex and demanding total commitment, to give them a sense of worthiness and autonomy outside woman's traditionally confining role. Its members, their officers forcefully declared, formed a united phalanx twenty thousand strong, "A UNION OF SENTIMENT AND EFFORT AMONG . . . VIRTUOUS FEMALES FROM MAINE TO ALABAMA." The officers of the New York Society were particularly conscious of the emotional importance of female solidarity within their movement—and the significant role that they as leaders played in the lives of their rural supporters. "Thousands are looking to us," the executive committee recorded in their minutes with mingled pride and responsibility, "with the expectation that the principles we have adopted, and the example we have set before the world will continue to be held up & they reasonably expect to witness our *united onward* movements till the conflict shall end in Victory."

For many of the Society's scattered members, the moral reform cause was their only contact with the world outside farm or village—the *Advocate* perhaps the only newspaper received by the family. A sense of solidarity and of emotional affiliation permeated the correspondence between rural members and the executive committee. Letters and even official reports inevitably began with the salutation, "Sisters," "Dear Sisters," or "Beloved Sisters." Almost every letter and report expressed

the deep affection Society members felt for their like-thinking sisters in the cause of moral reform—even if their contact came only through letters and the *Advocate*. "I now pray and will not cease to pray," a woman in Syracuse, New York, wrote, "that your hearts may be encouraged and your hands strengthened." Letters to the Society's executive committee often promised unfailing loyalty and friendship; members and leaders pledged themselves ever ready to aid either local societies or an individual sister in need. Many letters from geographically isolated women reported that the Society made it possible for them for the first time to communicate with like-minded women. A few, in agitated terms, wrote about painful experiences with the double standard which only their correspondence with the *Advocate* allowed them to express and share.

Most significantly, the letters expressed a new consciousness of power. The moral reform society was based on the assertion of female moral superiority and the right and ability of women to reshape male behavior. No longer did women have to remain passive and isolated within the structuring presence of husband or father. The moral reform movement was, perhaps for the first time, a movement within which women could forge a sense of their own identity.

And its founders had no intention of relinquishing their new-found feeling of solidarity and autonomy. A few years after the Society was founded, for example, a group of male evangelicals established a Seventh Commandment Society. They promptly wrote to the Female Moral Reform Society suggesting helpfully that since men had organized, the ladies could now disband; moral reform was clearly an area of questionable propriety. The New York executive committee responded quickly, firmly—and negatively. Women throughout America, they wrote, had placed their trust in a female moral reform society and in female officers. Women, they informed the men, believed in both their own right and ability to combat the problem; it was decidedly a woman's, not a man's issue. "The paper is now in the right hands," one rural subscriber wrote: "This is the appropriate work for *women*. . . . Go on Ladies, go on, in the strength of the Lord."

In some ways, indeed, the New York Female Moral Reform Society could be considered a militant woman's organization. Although it was not overtly part of the woman's rights movement, it did concern itself with a number of feminist issues, especially those relating to woman's economic role. Society, the *Advocate*'s editors argued, had unjustly confined women to domestic tasks. There were many jobs in society that women could and should be trained to fill. They could perform any light indoor work as well as men. In such positions—as clerks and artisans—they would receive decent wages and consequent self-respect. And this economic emphasis was no arbitrary or inappropriate one, the Society contended. Thousands of women simply had to work; widows, orphaned young women, wives and mothers whose husbands could not work because of illness or intemperance had to support themselves and their children. Unfortunately, they had now to exercise these responsibilities on the pathetically inadequate salaries they received as domestics, washerwomen, or seamstresses—crowded, underpaid, and physically unpleasant occupations. By the end of the 1840s, the Society had adopted the cause of the working woman and made it one of their principal concerns—in the 1850s even urging women to join unions and, when mechanization came to the garment industry, helping underpaid seamstresses rent sewing machines at low rates.

The Society sought consciously, moreover, to demonstrate woman's ability to perform successfully in fields traditionally reserved for men. Quite early in their history they adopted the policy of hiring only women employees. From the first, of course, only women had been officers and managers of the Society. And after a few years, these officers began to

hire women in preference to men as agents and to urge other charitable societies and government agencies to do likewise. (They did this although the only salaried charitable positions held by women in this period tended to be those of teachers in girls' schools or supervisors of women's wings in hospitals and homes for juvenile delinquents.) In February 1835, for instance, the executive committee hired a woman agent to solicit subscriptions to the *Advocate*. That summer they hired another woman to travel through New England and New York State organizing auxiliaries and giving speeches to women on moral reform. In October of 1836, the executive officers appointed two women as editors of their journal—undoubtedly among the first of their sex in this country to hold such positions. In 1841, the executive committee decided to replace their male financial agent with a woman bookkeeper. By 1843 women even set type and did the folding for the Society's journal. All these jobs, the ladies proudly, indeed aggressively stressed, were appropriate tasks for women.

The broad feminist implications of such statements and actions must have been apparent to the officers of the New York Society. And indeed the Society's executive committee maintained discreet but active ties with the broader woman's rights movement of the 1830s, 1840s, and 1850s; at one point at least, they flirted with official endorsement of a bold woman's rights position. Evidence of this flirtation can be seen in the minutes of the executive committee and occasionally came to light in articles and editorials appearing in the *Advocate*. As early as the mid-1830s, for instance, the executive committee began to correspond with a number of women who were then or were later to become active in the woman's rights movement. Lucretia Mott, abolitionist and pioneer feminist, was a founder and secretary of the Philadelphia Female Moral Reform Society; as such she was in frequent communication with the New York executive committee. Emma Willard, a militant advocate of women's education and founder of the Troy Female Seminary, was another of the executive committee's regular correspondents. Significantly, when Elizabeth Blackwell, the first women doctor in either the United States or Great Britain, received her medical degree, Emma Willard wrote to the New York executive committee asking its members to use their influence to find her a job. The Society did more than that. The *Advocate* featured a story dramatizing Dr. Blackwell's struggles. The door was now open for other women, the editors urged; medicine was a peculiarly appropriate profession for sensitive and sympathetic womankind. The Society offered to help interested women in securing admission to medical school.

One of the most controversial aspects of the early woman's rights movement was its criticism of the subservient role of women within the American family and of the American man's imperious and domineering behavior toward women. Much of the Society's rhetorical onslaught upon the male's lack of sexual accountability served as a screen for a more general—and less socially acceptable—resentment of masculine social preeminence. Occasionally, however, the *Advocate* expressed such resentment overtly. An editorial in 1838, for example, revealed a deeply felt antagonism toward the power asserted by husbands over their wives and children. "A portion of the inhabitants of this favored land," the Society admonished, "are groaning under a despotism, which seems to be modeled precisely after that of the Autocrat of Russia. . . . We allude to the tyranny exercised in the HOME department, where lordly man, 'clothed with a little brief authority,' rules his trembling subjects with a rod of iron, conscious of entire impunity, and exalting in his fancied superiority." The Society's editorialist continued, perhaps even more bitterly: "Instead of regarding his wife as a help-mate for him, an equal sharer in his joys and sorrows, he looks upon her as

a useful article of furniture, which is valuable only for the benefit derived from it, but which may be thrown aside at pleasure." Such behavior, the editorial carefully emphasized, was not only commonplace, experienced by many of the Society's own members—even the wives of "Christians" and of ministers—but was accepted and even justified by society; was it not sanctioned by the Bible?

At about the same time, indeed, the editors of the *Advocate* went so far as to print an attack upon "masculine" translations and interpretations of the Bible, and especially of Paul's epistles. This appeared in a lengthy article written by Sarah Grimké, a "notorious" feminist and abolitionist. The executive committee clearly sought to associate their organization more closely with the nascent woman's rights movement. Calling upon American women to read and interpret the Bible for themselves, Sarah Grimké asserted that God had created woman the absolute equal of man. But throughout history, man, being stronger, had usurped woman's natural rights. He had subjected wives and daughters to his physical control and had evolved religious and scientific rationalizations to justify this domination. "Men have endeavored to entice, or to drive women from almost every sphere of moral action." Miss Grimké charged: "'Go home and spin' is the . . . advice of the domestic tyrant. . . . The first duty, I believe, which devolves on our sex now is to think for themselves. . . . Until we take our stand side by side with our brother; until we read all the precepts of the Bible as addressed to woman as well as to man, and lose . . . the consciousness of sex, we shall never fulfil the end of our existence." "Those who do undertake to labor," Miss Grimké wrote from her own and her sister's bitter experiences, "are the scorn and ridicule of their own and the other sex." "We are so little accustomed *to think for ourselves,*" she continued,

that we submit to the dictum of prejudice, and of usurped authority, almost without an effort to redeem ourselves from the unhallowed shackles which have so long bound us; almost without a desire to rise from that degradation and bondage to which we have been consigned by man, and by which the faculties of our minds, and the powers of our spiritual nature, have been prevented from expanding to their full growth, and are sometimes wholly crushed.

Each woman must reevaluate her role in society; no longer could she depend on husband or father to assume her responsibilities as a free individual. No longer, Sarah Grimké argued, could she be satisfied with simply caring for her family or setting a handsome table. The officers of the Society, in an editorial comment following this article, admitted that she had written a radical critique of woman's traditional role. But they urged their members, "It is of immense importance to our sex to possess clear and *correct* ideas of our rights and duties."

Sarah Grimké's overt criticism of woman's traditional role, containing as it did an attack upon the Protestant ministry and orthodox interpretations of the Bible, went far far beyond the consensus of the *Advocate*'s rural subscribers. The following issue contained several letters sharply critical of her and of the managers, for printing her editorial. And indeed the *Advocate* never again published the work of an overt feminist. Their membership, the officers concluded, would not tolerate explicit attacks upon traditional family structure and orthodox Christianity. Anti-male resentment and anger had to be expressed covertly. It was perhaps too threatening or—realistically—too dangerous for respectable matrons in relatively close-knit semi-rural communities in New York, New England, Ohio, or Wisconsin so openly to question the traditional relations of the sexes and demand a new and ominously forceful role for women.

The compromise the membership and the officers of the Society seemed to find most comfortable was one that kept the American woman within the home—but which greatly expanded her powers as pious wife and mother. In rejecting Sarah Grimké's feminist manifesto, the Society's members implicitly agreed to accept the role traditionally assigned woman: the self-sacrificing, supportive, determinedly chaste wife and mother who limited her "sphere" to domesticity and religion. But in these areas her power should be paramount. The mother, not the father, should have final control of the home and family—especially of the religious and moral education of her children. If the world of economics and public affairs was his, the home must be hers.

And even outside the home, woman's peculiar moral endowment and responsibilities justified her in playing an increasingly expansive role, one which might well ultimately impair aspects of man's traditional autonomy. When man transgressed God's commandments, through licentiousness, religious apathy, the defense of slavery, or the sin of intemperance—woman had both the right and duty of leaving the confines of the home and working to purify the male world.

The membership of the New York Female Moral Reform Society chose not to openly espouse the woman's rights movement. Yet many interesting emotional parallels remain to link the moral reform crusade and the suffrage movement of Elizabeth Cady Stanton, the Grimké sisters and Susan B. Anthony. In its own way, indeed, the war for purification of sexual mores was far more fundamental in its implications for woman's traditional role than the demand for woman's education—or even the vote.

Many of the needs and attitudes, moreover, expressed by suffragette leaders at the Seneca Falls Convention and in their efforts in the generation following are found decades earlier in the letters of rural women in the *Advocate of Moral Reform*. Both groups found woman's traditionally passive role intolerable. Both wished to assert female worth and values in a heretofore entirely male world. Both welcomed the creation of a sense of feminine loyalty and sisterhood that could give emotional strength and comfort to women isolated within their homes—whether in a remote farmstead or a Gramercy Park mansion. And it can hardly be assumed that the demand for votes for women was appreciably more radical than a moral absolutism that encouraged women to invade bordellos, befriend harlots, and publicly discuss rape, seduction, and prostitution.

It is important as well to reemphasize a more general historical perspective. When the pious women founders of the Moral Reform Society gathered at the Third Free Presbyterian Church, it was fourteen years before the Seneca Falls Convention—which has traditionally been accepted as the beginning of the woman's rights movement in the United States. There simply was no woman's movement in the 1830s. The future leaders were either still adolescents or just becoming dissatisfied with aspects of their role. Women advocates of moral reform were among the very first American women to challenge their completely passive, home-oriented image. They were among the first to travel throughout the country without male chaperones. They published, financed, even set type for their own paper, and defied a bitter and long-standing male opposition to their cause. They began, in short, to create a broader, less constricted sense of female identity. Naturally enough, they were dependent upon the activist impulse and legitimating imperatives of evangelical religion. This was indeed a complex symbiosis, the energies of pietism and the grievances of role discontent creating the new and activist female consciousness that characterized the history of the American Female Moral Reform Society in antebellum America. Their experience, moreover, was probably shared, though less overtly, by the thousands of women who devoted time and money to the great number of reform causes which multiplied in Jacksonian America. Women in the abolition and the temperance movements (and to a less extent in more narrowly evangelical and religious causes) also developed a sense of their ability to judge for themselves and of their right to publicly criticize the values of the larger society. The lives and self-image of all these women had changed—if only so little—because of their new reforming interests.

Part Nine

Masters and Slaves in the Southern Slave System

During the past twenty years or so, the study of slavery has been transformed. Previously, historians had fixed their attention on the material aspects of the South's "peculiar institution," that is, the conditions of slave life and labor and the kind of treatment the bondsmen received at the hands of their masters. Under the heading of conditions, matters such as the quality of food, clothing, shelter, and medical care were considered, along with the amount and terms of the work the slaves had to perform. Discussions of treatment usually addressed the nature of the punishment and discipline imposed by the master as well as the material rewards he made available to his slaves.

This emphasis on the physical and material features of the slave's life shifted quite dramatically in the 1960s and 1970s as historians began to look into the cultural experience and personal attitudes of the slaves themselves. Rather than seeing slaves as victims and unthinking toilers within a system that was prescribed for them by their owners, students of slavery now realized that they were able to influence their surroundings and that, in fact, they managed to forge a life in the quarters independent of the master's control and oversight.

Arising from the changing political and racial climate at the time, this new perspective and awareness enabled historians to unearth and explore aspects of the slave experience previously overlooked. Books began to appear whose authors probed in immense detail and with considerable perceptiveness subjects such as slave religion, the slave family, slave music and folklore, the existence of which had scarcely been acknowledged earlier. As the slave's vantage point assumed increasing importance, so too did documentary evidence that originated with the slaves themselves. Instead of relying exclusively on plantation records and other evidence compiled by the owners, historians now mined three sources in particular that slaves and ex-slaves had produced. These were, first, the autobiographies, or narratives, of slaves who had escaped to the North. With the encouragement of abolitionists these were written by fugitive slaves for use as propaganda in the movement to abolish slavery. A second source consisted of the interviews given by former slaves, by then in their old age, to researchers of the New Deal's Federal Writers' Project in the 1930s. And, finally, there were the spirituals and secular songs handed down by the slaves themselves after emancipation or collected by interested whites.

These records had existed all along, but, though it is hard to believe, few historians had thought to consult them. They had simply presumed that sources left by uneducated and inarticulate slaves were likely to be of marginal utility and little interest. Such is the power that elitist and racist assumptions have over the minds of even the most educated and intelligent people. Yet, once these suppositions were challenged and changed, then the history itself began to change.

The selections for this topic are both products of this new climate in slavery studies. The insightful essay by Willie Lee Rose of Johns Hopkins University highlights two facets of the institution that had not been sufficiently noticed previously. The first is that the relationship between master and slave was a dynamic and interactive one, and the second is that the institution itself, like the relations within it, was not static but undergoing continual change. In her essay, Professor Rose draws attention to a significant alteration in the slaveholders' attitudes toward their task of slave management that occurred in the early nineteenth century. Having done that, she then shows how the slaves were affected by this new situation.

The companion piece is by Drew Gilpin Faust of the University of Pennsylvania, who is the author of a prize-winning biography of Senator James H. Hammond, an antebellum South Carolina statesman and large slaveholder who actually obtained his lands and slaves by an astute marriage. Her article is a case study of how the master and his slaves dealt with each other on one particular plantation. Because of this, it approaches the question of master-slave relations from a microcosmic perspective, unlike the preceding piece. Moreover, Professor Faust emphasizes that the relationship between the master and his slaves was not just attitudinal, but also involved a contest over power. In this tug-of-war, the slaves had an occasional advantage—in the example she discusses at Hammond's Silver Bluff plantation, the slaves might even have won.

QUESTIONS TO CONSIDER

1. What aspects of Rose's essay do you find most fascinating or surprising?

2. How did the slaves manage to exert so much leverage in their struggle at Silver Bluff? Since this is, after all, just one plantation, is it possible to draw any conclusions from the episode that are applicable to master-slave relations in general and the slave system as a whole?

3. Explain the differences in the ways that Rose and Faust approach the problem of master-slave relations.

The Domestication of Domestic Slavery

Willie Lee Rose

Soon after Christmas in the year 1847, an aging Virginia planter named John Hartwell Cocke left his estate, Bremo Bluff in Fluvanna County, Virginia, to journey to his distant plantation in Alabama. He was off to check on his interesting human experiment involving preparation of certain chosen slaves for self-government and colonization in Liberia. Cocke was a staunch colonizationist, a religious evangelical, and a late child of the Revolutionary era. More important for our purposes, his life interests span the most crucial generation in the evolution of slavery in the United States.

By late January 1848, General Cocke's journey ended at his estate near Greensboro. In his private diary, Cocke revealed dismay at the state of affairs on his plantation and described measures taken to mend matters. The entry reveals much about Cocke and much about his class in the late antebellum era:

> A few days looking into the state of my plantation . . . disclosed a shocking state of moral depravity. . . . Two of my Foreman's Daughters had bastard white children. A state of almost indiscriminate sexual intercourse among them—not a marriage since I was last there—3 years ago. The venereal disease has

been prevalent—And to crown this mass of corruption—my Foreman with a wife and 10 living Children was keeping a young girl on the place. While his eldest daughters were the kept mistresses (there was strong reason to believe by his consent) of two of the young Southern Gentlemen of the vicinity—Another man hitherto regarded as next in respectability to the Foreman also with a wife and 10 children, had had the venereal—and these two both members of the Baptist Church. . . . My School for ultimate Liberian freedom had become a plantation Brothel headed by my Foreman. . . .

> I now commanded, that which I had formerly requested and advised—"that they should be married forthwith or be punished and sold" —they chose the first alternative. I allowed one week for them to make matches among themselves—but what was not agreed upon, at the expiration of that time—I should finish by my own authority—until every single man and woman were disposed of and united in marriage. The consequence was nine couples reported themselves as willing to marry forthwith. And I commenced building 4 new rooms required to accommodate the parties—which requiring two weeks afforded time to procure and make up a dress for each bride and some articles of simple furniture for the Chambers. To give solemnity to the matter—I engaged a respectable Baptist clergyman . . . to preach a Sermon upon the marriage relation—and unite the Nine Couples in the holy State of wedlock. . . . On Saturday the 12th of March the Ceremony was performed, . . . [preceded by]

From *Slavery and Freedom* by Willie Lee Rose, edited by William W. Freehling. Copyright © 1982 by Willie Lee Rose. Reprinted by permission of Oxford University Press, Inc.

suitable corporal punishment inflicted upon the Foreman and his brother of the Baptist Church. Having received abundant promises of amendment and confessions—I left with the hope of doing better in the future.

Such concern for slaves' domestic relations may surprise some readers. But I'd like to dispose of one question right away. Even if a scholar is latitudinarian in his definition of hypocrisy (and I am not), and wishes to question the sincerity of even material in the privacy of a diary, Cocke *was* sincere in his experiment. As long as the law had permitted, he had maintained a northern schoolteacher in residence at Bremo Bluff, charged with instructing his slaves to read and write. He had sent slaves to Liberia at his own expense and had sent them funds on request after they arrived. Knowing his religious views of the sanctity of "domestic relations," as well as his hostility to alcohol and tobacco, it seems most *improbable* that the desire to foster slave family life was prompted primarily by the consideration so often expressed by more acquisitive planters, that monogamous families were "favorable to increase" and promiscuity was not.

No, Cocke sincerely wished to elevate the character of "his people" to the presumed standard of Liberia, a word meaning, significantly, the land of freedom. Hundreds of planters who had no notion of freeing human property were also concerned, for whatever reasons, to establish among their slaves their own religious and social views, especially their view of domestic life. In fact their domesticating mission became for planters who bothered to justify slaveholding in the nineteenth century the main excuse for retaining what they very significantly entitled their "domestic institution."

It is a fascinating sidelight on slavery and on nineteenth-century ideas of domestic morality that when slaveholders, travelers, or abolitionists attempted to assess slaves' social "progress" they tended to gravitate sooner or later to the subject of sex on the plantation and the regularity (or lack) of family stability. But

this was distinctly a nineteenth-century phenomenon. Until the late eighteenth century, planters and their womenfolk seldom referred either to slave marriages or to slave religion. Nothing better illustrates the folly of treating an institution that existed for nearly 250 years as the same institution from start to finish. Slavery had to *become* "the Domestic Institution." How this took place requires a backward look.

Even the word "domestic," when applied to chattel slavery in the eighteenth century, carried a non-nineteenth-century connotation. In 1794, for example, St. George Tucker, a distinguished Virginia jurist, made careful use of the word when writing a disquisition on emancipation. Tucker distinguished between three types of bondage: political, civil, and domestic slavery. Merely political slavery Tucker illustrated by the example of the American colonial relation to England before the Revolution. Civil slavery he illustrated by the example of blacks freed but lacking such civil rights as power to vote. *Domestic* slavery was the legal position of enslaved blacks. Domestic slavery, then, was political slavery, plus civil slavery, plus the "numerous calamities" involved in one man being "subject to be directed by another in all his actions."

Whether this pleasant little word "domestic" came into style during the Revolutionary epoch as a means of avoiding the blatant contradiction that property in human beings implied for the natural rights philosophy, and/or from the need to distinguish between black chattel servitude and lesser forms of political servitude, is not clear. It is nevertheless a supreme irony that the phrase "domestic slavery" should have become in the nineteenth century the most frequent designation of an institution that was supposed, then and now, to have had a particularly devastating effect on family life—on homes of enslavers as well as the enslaved. Certainly in time defenders of slavery had so distinct a preference for the term "domestic slavery" that when they referred to their "domestic institution" the phrase absorbed the color of a euphemism, and was more often enunciated with pride than apology. Proslavery, philosophers intended to suggest a benign institution that encouraged between masters and slaves the qualities so much admired in the Victorian family: cheerful obedience and gratitude on the part of children (read slaves), and paternalistic wisdom, protection, and discipline on the part of the father (read master). An organic world was implied, the world of St. Paul's twelfth chapter to the Corinthians, in which feet, head, hands, and heart performed distinct but essential functions in the ongoing good of the whole. So, in the nineteenth century, the phrase "domestic institution" came to mean slavery idealized, slavery translated into a fundamental and idealized Victorian institution, the family. Of the hundred paradoxes set by the contradiction of property in man, none more teases the imagination.

Even in the eighteenth century some masters liked to think of themselves as "fathers." As early as 1726 William Byrd of Westover gave an engaging domestic picture of life in Virginia in a letter to the Earl of Orrery: "I have a large Family of my own," he wrote. "Like one of the Patriarchs, I have my Flocks and my Herds, my Bonds-men and Bond-women." He had to "take care to keep all my people to their Duty, to set all the springs in motion, and make everyone draw his equal share to carry the Machine forward."

But Byrd's attempt to identify himself with Father Abraham is somewhat vitiated by accounts in his famous private diary of times when his lady took a hot poker to an obstreperous maid, or when he made his eighteen-year-old slave Eugene (to use Byrd's inimitable language) "drink a pint of piss" as a correction for chronic bedwetting. Even in a day when parents occasionally horsewhipped their offspring, Byrd's "corrections" torture his analogy. Compared with their nineteenth-century descendants, eighteenth-century planters were decidedly poor patriarchs, if patriarchs at all.

Even the enlightened Robert Carter of Nomini Hall was accused by his children's tutor, Philip Fithian, of feeding his slaves inadequately, an accusation which has the ring of sincerity because the young teacher had otherwise favorable judgments on the character of his employer.

For the most part planters of eighteenth-century Virginia appear to have been more concerned with the state of their crops than with paternal relations with their chattels. George Washington, though opposed to slavery, was under no illusion about the essentially exploitative nature of "domestic slavery." He was a notably rigorous manager of slaves. No small details escaped his eagle eye. Once he learned how many shirts his seamstresses could make per week, he instructed their supervisor to inform them that "what *has* been done *shall* be done," adding ominously, "by fair means or foul." Certainly Dr. Benjamin West, traveling in the back country, seeing slaves half-clothed or naked, and noticing that white women took no more notice of naked male adults than if they had been horses, had no idea that eighteenth-century Virginia slaveowners thought of themselves as patriarchal providers. Nor could the Reverend Francis Le-Jau, sent to South Carolina by the Society for the Propagation of the Gospel in Foreign Parts, have been favorably impressed by his experience with masters who would castrate their slaves or invent diabolical punishment for trivial offenses. LeJau reported that these non-patriarchs denied slaves religion either because they wished labor on Sunday, or because they were afraid that slaves who became Christians might fancy themselves free men.

Of course instances of such abuse could be found throughout the slaveholding period. But the very frequency and casual nature of these eighteenth-century revelations indicates more pervasive suffering and brutality. There was neither sentiment nor sentimentality in eighteenth-century slaveholding. Slave codes were unspeakably harsh, permitting punishment by dismemberment and allowing any-one to kill slaves declared outlaws by masters. Slaveholders had no specific and enforceable obligations for housing, food, or clothing. Few appeared to have taken pride in physical ar-rangements for chattel property. Most never underestimated slaves' capacity or desire to resist and were distinctly frightened of what these "children" might take it into their heads to do. One seldom finds mention of slave mar-riages in early eighteenth-century accounts, and there is a great deal of hostility to the idea that religion could mean anything to slaves.

Developments of far-reaching importance occurred by the third decade of the nineteenth-century. These changes are clearly registered in personal letters and diaries and in the le-gal system that protected slaves. The meaning of these changes has been much harder for historians to assess than identifying them has been. The easiest and most fashionable course has been to assume that there could be no im-provement in the physical or moral condition of victims of so barbarous an institution. The horror was too absolute to admit of changes in degrees. But to do this is to overlook the evolutionary nature of all institutions. It is to denounce history as unnecessary.

The northern legal scholar James Codman Hurd, writing in the 1850s of southern laws on slavery, observed that every legal responsibility assigned to the master tended to establish the slave as a legal person. Every legal recognition of slaves' "rights, independent of the will of the owner or master, . . . diminishes in some degree the essence of that slavery by changing it into a relation between legal persons." These tendencies were gaining ground in all southern states in the first decades of the nineteenth century.

In time slave codes were altered to re-quire decent provisioning by slaveowners, and to curtail once-unbounded power to chastise slaves. Dismemberment and other cruel and unusual punishments became illegal. Killing a slave with malice was murder, and slaves were defined as persons at law, in spite of crip-pling civil disabilities. Humane judges extended by interpretation laws defending slaves' right to life and limb. Life assumed greater regu-larity, as the frontier retreated further to the West. Travelers in slaveholding states seldom reported seeing slaves half-clothed and under-fed. Reports of witnessing outrageous beat-ings are also much less frequent. Undoubtedly there was much, very much, that travelers did not see, on remote plantations where strangers never came. But remembering that in the eigh-teenth century planters had taken small pains to hide from view pitiable conditions of plan-tation life, it is apparent that in the nineteenth century a new social ideal, however imperfectly realized, had taken root. The new law, even if merely window dressing and unenforceable, had become, as always, a social artifact, a kind of cultural fist-hatchet indicating what a major-ity believed to be correct or desirable or nec-essary at the given time.

What was left undone in law was also sig-nificant. Aside from the responsibility for de-cent care and a limitation on indecent punish-ment, no part of a master's awful power was reduced. He could buy or sell slaves at will without regard for their family connections or wishes. Only social opinion could control him. He could punish, short of life and limb, as he saw fit. In fact society at large seemed bent on forcing the master to assume ever *more* re-sponsibility to police a population that could, if not carefully watched, create grave public danger. Tighter provisions were enacted for patrol duty, and laws restricting the associa-tion of slaves with free blacks became a reg-ular feature of the new codes. Harsh punish-ments were still assigned to rebels against the system. To prevent the master from shielding the slave from the law because of personal fi-nancial interest, the master was in most states awarded part or all of the cost of any slave the state condemned to death. Even meetings of slaves for religious exercises and funerals were tightly regulated. These opposing tendencies in

Wilson Chinn, a branded slave from Louisiana; also exhibiting instruments of torture used to punish slaves.
PHOTOGRAPHED BY KIMBALL, 477 BROADWAY, N. Y.
Ent'd accord'g to act of Congress in the year 1863, by Geo. H. Hanks, in the Clerk's Office of the U.S for the So. Dist. of N. Y.

A master exercised absolute power over his slaves, including the right to buy or sell them without regard to their wishes and to punish them with instruments of torture.

the changing slave law produced equivocal results, and one more fascinating paradox. They caused abolitionists to assert that slavery was becoming harsher with each passing year, and enabled southern apologists to state, with equal confidence, that slavery was becoming milder.

In fact, both sides were right, and both were wrong. As physical conditions improved, the slave's essential humanity was being recognized. But new laws restricting chattels' movement and eliminating their education indicate blacks were categorized as *a special and different kind of humanity,* as lesser humans in a dependency assumed to be perpetual. In earlier, harsher times, they had been seen as luck-

less, unfortunate barbarians. Now they were to be treated as children expected never to grow up.

The changing position of the nineteenth-century free black completes this portrait of a regime becoming tighter as it became softer. Manumission was made vastly more difficult, and petitioners all over the South made known their wish to keep freed blacks at a distance from their slaves by getting them out of the state wherever possible. Adult freedmen did not fit into a new scheme for humanizing treatment of perpetual children.

The Old South was actually engaged in a process of rationalizing slavery, not only in an economic sense, but also in emotional and psychological terms. The South was "domesticating" slavery, taming it, so to speak, for the new century. Of course domesticating laws were always flouted by passionate, sadistic, insane, or miserly masters. But the evolving attitudes and the changed law register an important choice made by the white South at the turn of the nineteenth century.

To explain how this change was brought about requires an understanding of the intellectual challenge slavery posed for the Revolutionary generation, and the eventual solution, partly progressive, partly reactionary, to that crisis. It also requires a look at the demographic changes among the slave population resulting from a liberalized emancipation policy in Virginia, the suppression of the slave trade, and from the increasing proportion of slaves born in America.

How close the older South came to general emancipation during the Revolutionary epoch is not a settled question. Considering all economic and social factors, it was probably not very close. And yet strong ideological pressures toward emancipation existed. An appreciable number of slaveowners were ready to take that step, either because they sensed that for the time slavery was no longer as profitable as it had been before the Revolution, or because slaves were dangerous, or because the Revolution had taught them that all men should be free.

Certainly important changes were called for even if the change from slavery to freedom should be rejected. If slavery should remain, it had to be made safe; and bondage did not seem to be safe at all, largely because bondsmen too seemed to be deciding whether slavery should remain. The prolonged struggle of Haitian blacks to be free had raised alarms that had not yet subsided when the mammoth plot of Gabriel Prosser, involving possibly thousands of Virginia slaves, was uncovered. Newspapers were peppered from this time forward with demands that black watermen's free movement on the Chesapeake Bay and up the rivers be curtailed. The black population had mounted steeply in proportion to the white through the eighteenth century, and by 1790 had come to constitute nearly half the total population. Blacks were recognized as a dangerous element.

This fear was further enhanced by the process of Afro-American acculturation. Newly imported Africans had been less able to resist slavery because of their ignorance of English and of regional geography. As they gained knowledge of their owners, however, and especially if they became skilled artisans, opportunities to resist or run away vastly enlarged. Many were able to escape slavery altogether by passing for free men in towns.

The phenomenon was the fruit of a serious dilemma eighteenth-century planters had faced. They had felt compelled to train slaves to diversify their economy. But steps taken to develop slaves' skills and to acculturate ex-Africans had made the captive population more dangerous.

The rise of *free* blacks in proportion to slaves during the Revolutionary era greatly increased this sense of danger. Laws were passed emancipating slaves who had served in the Revolutionary army. In 1776 a law was enacted forbidding further importation of slaves and emancipating those entered illegally. And in 1782 a policy in force for over fifty years prohibiting private emancipation was overturned. Emancipation was made as simple as a master's willingness. The response was enthusiastic, and before this policy was effectively neutralized by a law of 1806 requiring manumitted slaves to leave the state, the free black population rose from 2000–3000 in 1782 to over 30,000 by 1810.

Popular reaction to this increase in free blacks was almost immediate. Petitions objecting to emancipation by will or deed poured into the legislature. The discovery in 1800 of Gabriel Prosser's plot for insurrection gave force to this reactionary trend. Whether fear of free blacks or the economic motive of conserving slavery after the close of the slave trade was more important in this development is still a question. But the result was the same. The Virginia legislature opted, in the first twenty years of the new century, for a course designed to make slavery a safe and profitable institution, and one that did the private conscience of slave owners as little violence as possible. Other southern states followed suit. The domesticating process was on.

Domestication proceeded to feed on itself. New laws consolidating the regime, by reducing society's fears allowed masters to heed those other new laws requiring more humane treatment. The result was a more regular and systematic labor system, obtained more often by the threat of force than its employment. On well-managed plantations, just as in the home or in school, the use of violence was considered to be a failure of diplomacy. Selling slaves apart from their immediate families incurred a social stigma, and masters when they did this had to find a reasonable excuse for doing so, if they meant to save face. To retain the reputation of a good master, a "patriarch," as he liked to call himself, had to provide decently for "his people," as he liked to call them. To be known as a Christian master, he had to provide religious instruction for his slaves.

The role of evangelical religion in the South

was an important element in planters' changing notions of familial responsibility. It was
as though, once having made the decision to
retain slavery (by means of the hundreds of
small constituent decisions that class movements comprise), they required some omni-
scient plan on the part of the deity to explain
it to themselves. Slavery, most of them were
ready to admit, was an evil system, but God has
His purposes. In this instance His purpose was
the extension of Christianity to the slave population. Some even joined John Hartwell Cocke
in reasoning that intelligent slaves would and
should then be returned to Africa as missionaries.

It is an interesting and significant sidelight
on the religious influence that most attacks
launched later within the South against laws
forbidding anyone to teach slaves to read were
based on the Protestant idea that to save their
souls men had to read and interpret the Bible
for themselves: salvation was an individual matter. The same religious reason was advanced by
those who wanted slave marriages to carry the
same civil effects as marriages among whites.
Neither drive won numerous converts, however, because each flew in the face of social
control and endangered foundations of the social order.

Even with its many hardships and its total
injustice, the plantation system had become a
"domestic" institution, with the economic and
social divisions of labor that suggest a patriarchy that could be benevolent or cruel, according to the disposition of the patriarch. As
master, the slaveholder presided over not one,
but three interlocking domesticities—his blood
family, the slave families, and the larger family of the plantation community. The effects of
each of these upon the other two has been the
subject of endless speculation and too little dis-
passionate inquiry, but it is important, because
it is as clear a register as historians have available of what the new domesticity was like in
practice and of how white "fathers" and black
"children" saw "familial" roles.

The master gave himself star billing at the
apex of this domestic hierarchy, and he had
the same self-indulgent vision of his role in
the lives of his retainers that many novelists
and some historians have thought he had. With
the help of a virtuous and industrious wife,
whose price (in the Old Testament phrase)
was "above rubies," he strove to create on his
plantation an orderly world, where slaves were
well-fed and properly cared for, and to see that
they worked hard enough to raise his crops,
keep him solvent, and provide the entire plantation with essentials of life. He was stern, but
not unnecessarily so. In her inimitable diary
that records this world collapsing under the
impact of the Civil War, Mary Boykin Chestnut
turned a beady eye on her aging father-in-law,
a stately old man who was, in her words, "partly
patriarch, partly *grand seigneur*," a ruler of
men, under whose "smooth exterior" lay "the
grip of a tyrant whose will has never been
crossed." He might have stood for a portrait
for George Balcombe, the fictional creation of
Beverley Tucker, who is given to say, "I am well
pleased with the established order of things. I
see subordination everywhere. And when I find
the subordinate content with his actual conditions, and recognizing his place in the scale of
being, . . . I am content to leave him there."

But the domestic world men like Chestnut
ruled and Tucker described was more complex
than a "patriarchy," despite the planter's awesome legal power. The planter's blood family
was actually more of a matriarchy, because of
the paramount role of his wife in child-rearing,
in household management, and in religious
and social matters. Dispensing medicine and
comfort, the matriarch kept the keys to the
larder, insisted on order and morality at the
quarters, and kept a sharp eye on the deportment of her growing sons in the seductive am-
bience of her nubile maids.

To make the "domestic institution" still
more complicated, while the plantation community was a patriarchy and the planter's family a matriarchy, the domesticity in the en-

slaved cabin at the quarters was, ironically, about as close an approximation to equality of the sexes as the nineteenth century provided. An androgynous world was born, weirdly enough, not of freedom, but bondage.

Actually each human creature was involved in an economic and social way in at least two of these conflicting domesticities. Such an interlocking system of colliding conceptions of "family" invited love-hate relationships, a certain nervous stability, a discernable atmosphere of tension, and a pervading sense of incongruities locked in interminable suspension. Witness the many instances where slaveholders were thrown into conflict between demands of their blood families and the plantation family's welfare. These conflicts were not always resolved in the interest of the planter's pocketbook, or even his own family's affluence. Every decision to emancipate, or to enable a slave to purchase his own freedom, was a decision of this sort, and so would have been any decision not to deprive slaves of some customary or anticipated treat.

But because the slave and not the slaveholder had the most to lose when domestic arrangements became tense, the "dependent's" ambivalent attitude toward the "familial" regime more challenges the imagination. Ambivalence about "patriarchs" is registered in every category of the source materials of slavery, from the planters' private records to the songs and stories of slaves, their narratives, and travelers' accounts. Former slaves told about how sometimes old mistress' kindness helped when master was mean. Sometimes travelers told how it worked the other way. Harriet Martineau, for instance, learned of the young bride groom whose new wife was so cruel to the house servants, and so reluctant to curb her temper and reform, that he sent them out of the house and helped her do the chores himself.

Very often slaves complained to the master about the abuse they received from overseers. Sometimes masters sided with their "people" rather than overseers. The result, slaves' sometime sense of living in a caring domesticity, helps explain the rarity of organized political revolt on southern plantations. Hard as life was, it appears that few slaves really wanted to massacre the entire white domestic establishment.

There were even stronger supports for the domestic system within the slave family. Undoubtedly many a slave parent put off running away interminably because of attachment to wife, husband, or children. In this sense complex interdependencies of the plantation "family" became a most significant bulwark of slavery as a working system, even for slaves who wanted desperately to be free.

Some historians have futilely tried to deny the significance of slave treatment. But it obviously makes the greatest difference to slaves, prisoners, and children *how* and *whether* the necessities of life are provided. It makes a difference in physical security, personality development, emotional health, and in interpersonal relations. Because the plantation was indeed a personal affair, examples can be found of every conceivable kind of handling of slave property, from outrages to relative order and kindness. It is almost too obvious to mention that the same spectrum exists in the behavior of parents to their children, or prison guards to their inmates; it is also obvious that there are more kind parents than prison guards or plantation owners. But logic demands that historians face squarely the problem of assessing the kind of plantations *most* slaves lived on, for this would have had approximately everything to do with the result for most slaves, for the slave family, and for the eventual prospects a slave had as a successful free citizen.

Judgments are fraught with hazards. Some matters may in time yield to statistical analysis: provision of clothing, food allowances, hours of work, even the extent of family disruption resulting from the interstate slave trade. Punishment and discipline probably never will, unless they may be deduced from other care provided.

Nor will subjective and affective human relationships. But until further developments on the statistical front are brought to bear on this problem, the historian will have to deal with the evidence he has, with all the common sense he can command.

Because the slave had the same human emotional needs and biological urges all others have, the historian has got to remember that if these needs had not been met at least halfway, irreparable damage would have ensued, and disorder would have proliferated. Some historians have tried to have it both ways, describing a totally dehumanizing institution that dehumanized nobody. This won't do, logically speaking. Then historians have got to stop undervaluing the role of the Christian religion in the lives of slaves and masters alike, and recapture its dominant influence on nineteenth-century people, especially rural people. Then he must consider overriding facts. The rate of the black population growth in this country almost kept pace with the growth of the white population, one of the most phenomenal population explosions in world history. No other slaveholding country in the Western Hemisphere could show anything like this record. There was less slave suicide in this country by far than in Brazil, Carl Degler tells us in his comparative study of the two slave societies.

There was also relatively little overt resistance to slavery in the American South, as compared with other nations. Most running away, the most common form of resistance, was short-term, and to the nearby woods and swamps, and it was most often a work strike, or a demonstration against unwanted or unjustified discipline. When opportunities developed during the Civil War for organized revolt, those who expected insurrection were disappointed.

There can be little doubt that most slaves, nearly all, one assumes, deeply desired to be free. But their typical forms of resistance were passive rather than violent, individual rather than organized, involving malingering much more than murdering. Such resistance

was usually provoked by slavery perverted, by domestic bondage become undomesticated by some outrageously antifamilial instance of treatment or by some master's breach of unspoken patriarchal obligation. Such resistance successfully lived up to one of its key objectives: it forced masters to live up more regularly to prevailing standards. Unless one employs theories unconnected with demonstrable facts of behavior, one is forced to conclude that the "domestic institution" had more regularity than current portraits would indicate, and that most slaves thought they had something to lose by slaying patriarchs.

Most intelligent planters attempted to see that slaves *would* have something to lose, by introducing some incentives and accommodations into a system that was at bottom based on force. Most intelligent masters, whether harsh or liberal, understood that although force was the basis of their system, it had distinct limits in application. The slave had too many annoying means at his disposal to pay the master back. Let us note some of those slave reprisals. In the effort to discredit a bad overseer, slaves on an Alabama plantation got together to cover up the weeds in the cotton instead of chopping them out. The object was simple. Lose the crop, and see that the overseer is fired. In South Carolina six brothers threatened to run away in a group when one was threatened with a whipping. None of these brothers was whipped. Of two men who appeared well enough, but who were claiming to be ill, the master said in his diary, "I give up; they will have their time out." A master in Mississippi enjoined his overseer to give his slaves all they needed to eat, lest they steal.

Perhaps a closer examination of an extended crisis on a plantation that has enjoyed no very good reputation for "paternalism" may prove illuminating. Ever since Fanny Kemble denounced her husband's South Georgia estate, in a published form of her diary that came out during the Civil War, Butler's Island and its overseer, Roswell King, have been synonymous with hard use. In fact this little world of overseer King and absentee owner Thomas P. Butler and Sambo and Sampson and all the other "people" was a difficult family circle, controllable, if at all, only by a master diplomat.

In 1829, a slave preacher and plantation fiddler named Sampson put overseer King's diplomacy to a severe test. Sampson accused King of killing Sampson's son, Emanuel. Emanuel had allegedly been given a "cold shower" either for punishment or as treatment for an ailment. On this point King is rather vague, but he had secured the plantation doctor's note assigning the cause of death to worms, a grave affliction among the island's child population.

Sampson was angry. We must suppose that he really believed the overseer to be an unfamilial tyrant, responsible for his son's death. But Sampson was also engaged in a more elaborate political maneuver. With the aid of another influential plantation leader, an African named Icy, Sampson wanted to undermine the influence of the head slave driver, a man named Sambo.

Overseer King had himself at first distrusted Sambo. He remembered that Sambo's father had in his term as head driver organized a combination of slaves against King's father, when the elder King had been overseer for Pierce Butler's father. But after a period of watchful waiting, King understood that Sambo was as loyal as a man named Sambo ought to be. The overseer then did everything he could to bolster the driver's authority.

Before the dispute was settled, Sampson had attacked Sambo with an axe and was threatening to run off with more than thirty slaves. Explaining his difficulties to Butler, far away in Philadelphia, and excusing himself for failing to punish Sampson for his violence on Sambo, King also illuminated some basic plantation strategies. "It would not do," King wrote, "to have" Sampson "taken by our people. Years hence it would be a source of dispute, between family connections and friends on either side, which must be avoided on a plantation." Sambo

at last outgeneraled Sampson by calling the constable, who took the culprit to jail. King told Butler that Sampson remained the "most awful fellow in the country, who can play forcefully on the minds of others."

Throughout his service King showed the same caution before punishing those who could influence others. "The great art of managing negroes is to outmaneuver them," he said. Explaining to Butler why he had not followed instructions to sell a pair of troublemakers, King wrote that "unless done in such a way as to be productive of good, it would be an injury." As a manager of men and women as distinct from animals, King saw fit to consult public opinion in the plantation community. During the extended struggle with Sampson and Icy nothing disturbed King more than the charge Sampson circulated that he (King) and Sambo had divided between themselves the money raised from a part of the rice crop that was traditionally used to buy dried fish for the slaves themselves.

Over this point, and Sampson's assertion of his responsibility for little Emanuel's death, and other alleged ill use of the plantation people, overseer King eventually offered his resignation as manager of Butler's estate. It appears that the word of a slave could in some instances mortify a white man by endangering his reputation. Whether Sampson or King and Sambo were telling the truth is not the point here. It is not even the point whether King was the beast he appeared to be in Fanny Kemble's diary, or the good neighbor he seems to be in the Charles Colcock Jones family papers (published as *The Children of Pride*), or simply the harassed driver of men he reveals himself to be in his letters to Butler. The point is that plantation life was populated by people, not animals. Slaves had leaders who had to be negotiated with, allied with, cajoled, or isolated. King ultimately hung onto Sambo because he considered that driver the most useful slave on the entire place, clever enough to do anything from helve an axe to mend a rice mill. It also appears that family relationships would ultimately determine the side a person took in a quarrel, that people's memories were long, and that punishment when applied was supposed to have constructive purpose.

King's story also reveals considerable variety in slave talent and that this particular overseer liked to develop divergent abilities. Perhaps one reason why modern writers have difficulty seeing past the very real monotony and drudgery of agricultural labor, and particularly slave labor, into the complexity of that life is that we tend to associate it with modern mass production. In any event, even the most cursory list of slaves on any inventory reveals a wider variety of training and function than we have been ready to recognize. This complexity was not just a characteristic of good or bad plantations, but a plantation characteristic.

Still another characteristic of a domesticated regime was that plantations less harmful to the body could be more afflicting to the soul. Much can be learned about the patriarchy by examining what was left once it was destroyed. During the Civil War a young teacher who was working with freedmen in South Carolina, an area of high concentration of slaves, observed that all slaves in the neighborhood knew who the good masters were, and who were the cruel ones, and that they all agreed. The teacher offered his own opinion that slaves who had been harshly treated had many "faults" of character, being licentious, dishonest, irresponsible, and hard to work with, but he thought they were more independent, on the whole, than those who had had extremely benevolent masters.

If we grant the teacher his insight, we may also note that he observed, in the first moments of freedom, an unconscious reaching backward on the part of his more pliable students and their parents for the order of the plantation world, in which master was ultimately responsible for all manner of provisions and decisions for which nobody now seemed responsible. There must have been very few freedmen who regretted the passing of slavery. But many were discontent with the disorderliness of freedom, which took a little getting used to. By their subconscious efforts to thrust teachers and new plantation superintendents into old master's role, they revealed something of the part the patriarch had played in their lives.

It would appear that the time has come when historians of slavery should be more inquisitive about interpersonal relations in individual communities to determine what "normal" conditions were during the era of "domestic" servitude. Such an approach provides a way to determine some matters that quantifiers may never disclose, and may serve better to explain some matters they do disclose. The "domestic institution" must be studied in its full social, legal, religious, and material context.

Further advances also dictate that we approach slavery from the historian's true perspective, which is evolutionary, chronological (if you will), changing. In time we may know the relative weight to assign to social and religious factors as compared with material ones in the changes that gradually occurred in the nineteenth century: the way slavery became "domesticated," in the forlorn hope of the master class that it might be retained to their profit and as a social control. Such an evolutionary approach can illuminate as well how a strong and resilient people survived an institution designed to retain them in a perpetual state of childhood—how they endured and understood that slavery was a wretched institution, whether they were beaten and abused every day or not. The study of slavery can illuminate the spirit of freedom, which is of the mind as well as the body. I suggest we do not drop it.

The Meaning of Power on an Antebellum Plantation

Drew Gilpin Faust

A dozen miles south of Augusta, Georgia, the Savannah River curves gently, creating two bends that were known to antebellum steamboat captains as Stingy Venus and Hog Crawl Round. Nearby, on the South Carolina shore, a cliff abruptly rises almost thirty feet above the water. Mineral deposits in the soil give the promontory a metallic tinge, and the bank and the plantation of which it was part came as early as colonial times to be called Silver Bluff.

In 1831, an opportune marriage placed this property in the hands of twenty-four-year-old James Henry Hammond. An upwardly mobile lawyer, erstwhile schoolmaster and newspaper editor, the young Carolinian had achieved through matrimony the status the Old South accorded to planters alone. When he arrived to take possession of his estate, he found and carefully listed in his diary 10,800 acres of land, a dwelling, assorted household effects, and 147 bondsmen. But along with these valued acquisitions, he was to receive a challenge he had not anticipated. As he sought to exert his mastery over the labor force on which the prosperity of his undertaking depended, he was to discover that his task entailed more than simply directing 147 individual lives. Hammond had to dominate a complex social order already in existence on the plantation and to struggle for the next three decades to control what he called a "system of roguery" amongst his slaves.

Hammond astutely recognized that black life on his plantation was structured and organized as a "system," the very existence of which seemed necessarily a challenge to his absolute control—and therefore, as he perceived it, a kind of "roguery." Because Hammond's mastery over his bondsmen depended upon his success at undermining slave society and culture, he established a carefully designed plan of physical and psychological domination in hopes of destroying the foundations of black solidarity. Until he relinquished management of the estate to his sons in the late 1850s, Hammond kept extraordinarily detailed records. Including daily entries concerning the treatment, work patterns, and vital statistics of his slaves, they reveal a striking portrait of slave culture and resistance and of the highly structured efforts Hammond took to overpower it. The existence of such data about one master and one community of slaves over a considerable period of time makes possible a tracing of the dialectic of their interaction as one not so much among individuals, but between two loci of power and two opposing systems of belief. While Hammond sought to assert both dominance and legitimacy, the slaves at Silver Bluff strove to maintain networks of communication

"Culture, Conflict and Community: The Meaning of Power on an Antebellum Plantation" by Drew Gilpin Faust, *Journal of Social History,* Fall 1980, Vol. 14, No. 1. Reprinted by permission.

and community as the bases of their personal and cultural autonomy. This struggle, which constantly tested the ingenuity and strength of both the owner and his slaves, touched everything from religion to work routines to health, and even determined the complex pattern of unauthorized absences from the plantation.

A master-slave relationship is never static, but of necessity evolutionary. Each participant confronts the other with demands and expectations, seeking continually to enhance his own power within the framework of their interaction. In the emotional and ideological context of paternalism, this dialectic of oppression, challenge, and concession produces the interdependence of lord and bondsman that Eugene Genovese has so arrestingly described. But because of the comprehensive nature of *Roll, Jordan, Roll,* Genovese has dealt with this relationship in necessarily general terms. A detailed examination of the development of patterns of mutual response between a single master and his slaves thus promises an opportunity to supplement and refine some of Genovese's insights about the sources of that "reciprocity" he has urged as a defining feature of the South's slave system.

When Hammond took possession of Silver Bluff, he assumed a role and entered a world largely unfamiliar to him. His father had owned a few slaves and even deeded two to young James Henry. But Hammond was entirely inexperienced in the management of large numbers of agricultural and domestic workers. The blacks at Silver Bluff, for their part, confronted a new situation as well, for they had become accustomed to living without a master in permanent residence. Hammond's wife's father, Christopher Fitzsimons, had been a prominent Charleston merchant who visited this upcountry property only intermittently. Upon his death in 1825, the plantation was left to his daughter Catherine and came under the desultory management of Fitzsimons' sons, who had far less interest than would their future

brother-in-law in making it a profitable enterprise. In 1831, therefore, both Hammond and his slaves faced new circumstances. But it was Hammond who was the outsider, moving into a world of established patterns of behavior and interaction in the community at Silver Bluff. Although by law all power rested with Hammond, in reality the situation was rather different.

As a novice at masterhood, Hammond received advice and enouragement from his friends. "Be kind to them make them feel an obligation," one acquaintance counselled, ". . . and by all means keep all other negroes away from the place, and make yours stay at home—and Raise their church to the ground—keep them from fanaticism for God's sake as well as for your own. . . ." Hammond took this exhortation to heart, seeking within a week of his arrival at the Bluff to enhance his power by extending control over the very souls of his slaves. "Intend to break up negro preaching & negro churches," he proclaimed in his diary. "Refused to allow Ben Shubrick to join the Negro Church . . . but promised to have him taken in the church . . . I attended . . . Ordered night meetings on the plantation to be discontinued."

The desire to control black religious life led Hammond to endeavor to replace independent black worship with devotions entirely under white direction. At first he tried to compel slaves into white churches simply by making black ones unavailable and even sought to prevent his neighbors from permitting black churches on their own lands. But soon he took positive steps to provide the kind of religious environment he deemed appropriate for his slaves. For a number of years he hired itinerant ministers for Sunday afternoon slave services. By 1845, however, Hammond had constructed a Methodist Church for his plantation and named it St. Catherine's after his wife.

The piety of the Hammond slaves became a source of admiration even to visitors. A house guest on the plantation in the 1860s found the services at St. Catherine's "solemn and impressive," a tribute, she felt, to Hammond's beneficient control over his slaves. "There was a little company of white people," she recalled, "the flower of centuries of civilization, among hundreds of blacks but yesterday . . . in savagery, now peaceful, contented, respectful and comprehending the worship of God. . . . By reason of Senator Hammond's wise discipline," the visitor assured her readers, there was no evidence of "religious excesses," the usual "mixture of hysteria and conversion" that she believed characterized most black religion. These slaves, it appeared to an outsider, had abandoned religious ecstasy for the reverential passivity prescribed for them by white cultural norms.

Hammond had taken great pains to establish just such white standards amongst his slaves, and the visitor's description of the behavior he has succeeded in eliciting from his bondsmen would undoubtedly have pleased him. But even Hammond recognized that the decorous behavior of his slaves within the walls of St. Catherine's was but an outward compliance with his directives. He seemed unable to eradicate black religious expression, evidences of which appeared to him like tips of an iceberg indicating an underlying pattern of independent belief and worship that persisted among his slaves. Twenty years after his original decision to eliminate the slave church, Hammond recorded in his plantation diary, "Have ordered all church meetings to be broken up except at the Church with a white preacher." Hammond's slaves had over the preceding decades tested their master's initial resolve, quietly asserting their right to their own religious life in face of his attempt to deny it to them.

In the course of these years, they had reestablished their church, forcing Hammond to accept a level of black religious autonomy and to permit the slaves to hold as many as

James Henry Hammond's slaves continued to hold prayer meetings despite Hammond's attempts to suppress religious expression.

four different prayer meetings in the quarters each week. Hammond returned to his original commitment to "break up negro preaching" only when the intensity of black religious fervor seemed to threaten that compromise level of moderation he and his slaves had come tacitly to accept. "Religious troubles among the negroes"—as in 1851 he described his sense of the growing disorder—revived his determination to control the very emotional and ideational sources of unruliness among his slaves. "They are running the thing into the ground," he remarked, "by being allowed too much organization—too much power to the head men & too much praying and Church meeting on the plantation." Black religious life reemerged as an insupportable threat when it assumed the characteristics of a formal system, with, as Hammond explicitly recognized, organization and leadership to challenge his own power. The recurrent need for Hammond to act against the expanding strength of the black church indicates his failure either to eliminate this organization or to control his slaves' belief and worship.

The struggle for power manifested in the conflict over religious autonomy was paralleled in other areas of slave life on the Hammond domain. Just as Hammond sought from the time of his arrival in 1831 to control religious behavior, so too he desired to supervise work patterns more closely. "When I first began to plant," he later reminisced, "I found my people in very bad subjection from the long want of a master and it required of me a year of severity which cost me infinite pain." The slaves, accustomed to a far less rigorous system of management, resented his attempts and tried to undermine his drive for efficiency. "The negroes are trying me," Hammond remarked in his diary on more than one occasion during the early months of his tenure. In response, he was firm, recording frequent floggings of slaves who refused to comply with his will. When several bondsmen sought to extend the Christmas hol-

iday by declining to return to work as scheduled, Hammond was unyielding, forcing them back to the fields and whipping them as well.

As the weeks passed, the instances of beatings and overt insubordination noted in plantation records diminished; a more subtle form of conflict emerged. Over the next decade, this struggle over work patterns at Silver Bluff fixed on the issue of task versus gang labor. The slaves clearly preferred the independent management of their time offered by the task system, while Hammond feared the autonomy it provided the bondsmen. "They do much more" in a gang, Hammond noted, and "are not so apt to strain themselves." Task work, he found, encouraged the blacks to complete required chores too rapidly, with "no rest until 3 or 4 o'clock," and then gave them the opportunity for hours of unsupervised recreation. But despite what owners generally tended to see as its wholesomeness and security, gang work had the significant disadvantage of displeasing the laborers, who at Silver Bluff performed badly in a calculated effort to restore the task system. "Negroes dissatisfied to work in a gang & doing badly," Hammond observed in 1838. Almost exactly a year later he made a similar remark, noting that hoers were leaving "all the weeds and bunches of grass" growing around the cotton plants. "Evidently want to work task work which I will not do again."

Although at this time Hammond succeeded in establishing the gang as the predominant form of labor at Silver Bluff, the victory was apparently neither final nor total. Indeed, it may simply have served to regularize the pattern of poorly performed work Hammond had viewed as a form of resistance to the gang system. He continued to record hoeing that ignored weeds, picking that passed over bulging cotton bolls, and cultivating that destroyed both mule and plough. But eventually the slaves here too won a compromise. By 1850, Hammond was referring once again in his correspondence and in his plantation diary to task work, although he complained bitterly about continuing poor performance and the frequent departure of many bondsmen from the fields as early as midafternoon.

Hammond seemed not so much to master as to manipulate his slaves, offering a system not just of punishments, but of positive inducements, ranging from picking contests to single out the most diligent hands, to occasional rituals of rewards for all, such as Christmas holidays; rations of sugar, tobacco, and coffee; midsummer barbecues; or even the pipes sent all adult slaves from Europe when Hammond departed on the Grand Tour. The slaves were more than just passive recipients of these sporadic benefits; they in turn manipulated their master for those payments and privileges they had come to see as their due. Hammond complained that his bondsmen's demands led him against his will to countenance a slave force "too well fed & otherwise well treated," but he nevertheless could not entirely resist their claims. When after a particularly poor record of work by slaves in the fall of 1847 Hammond sought to shorten the usual Christmas holiday, he ruefully recorded on December 26 that he had been "persuaded out of my decision by the Negroes."

Hammond and his slaves arrived at a sort of accommodation on the issue of work. But in this process, Hammond had to adjust his desires and expectations as significantly as did his bondsmen. His abstract notions of order and absolute control were never to be fully realized. He and his slaves reached a truce that permitted a level of production acceptable to Hammond and a level of endeavor tolerable to his slaves.

Like his use of rewards and punishments, Hammond's more general instructions for plantation management reveal his understanding of the process of mastery as consisting in large measure of symbolic and psychological control. The necessity of resorting to physical punishment, he maintained, indicated a failure in ideal management. Hammond con-

stantly tried to encourage the bondsmen to internalize their master's definition of their inferiority and thus willingly come to acknowledge his legitimacy. Yet Hammond recognized that to succeed in this aim, he had necessarily to mask his own dependence upon them. Hammond was well aware that the black driver Tom Kollock was a far more experienced agriculturist than his master or than the plantation overseers. "I wish you to consult him [Tom]," Hammond instructed a new overseer, "on all occasions & in all matters of doubt take his opinion wh. you will find supported by good reasons." But, he warned, Kollock must be kept "in ignorance of his influence. . . . I would not have Tom injured by the supposition that he was the head manager any more than I would have you mortified by such a state of things." Yet Kollock knew more than he showed, for Hammond found two decades later that the driver had long exploited the power of which the master had presumed him ignorant. While pretending to effective management of both crops and personnel, Kollock had instead worked to undermine productivity by demanding the minimum of his workers. Kollock had fooled Hammond, who in a fury of discovery proclaimed him a "humbug." "I now see," Hammond declared in 1854, "that in him rests the fault of my last . . . crops. He has trained his hands to do very little & that badly."

Unaware how transparent and easily manipulable he must have appeared to slaves, Hammond sought continually to refine and perfect his system of management. A devoted disciple of scientific agriculture and administration, he developed in the 1840s a formal set of rules for treatment and supervision of slaves, allocating carefully defined areas of responsibility to master, overseer, and driver.

Nearly every detail of these regulations indicates a conscious desire to impress the bondsmen with their total dependence upon their master, and, simultaneously, with the merciful beneficence of his absolute rule. Lest the overseer's power seem to diminish the master's own authority, Hammond defined the role of the black driver to serve as check upon him. Because he could only be whipped by the master, the driver was removed from the overseer's control and his status enhanced amongst his fellow slaves. In addition, the driver had the explicit right to bypass the overseer and to appeal directly to the master with suggestions or complaints about plantation management—or the overseer's behavior. Hammond invested the driver with enough power to encourage the slaves to accept as their official voice the leader Hammond had chosen and, he hoped, co-opted. It was Hammond's specific intention, moreover, to use administrative arrangements to set the overseer and driver at odds and thus to limit the power of each in relation to his own. One of his greatest fears was that the two would cooperate to conspire against him.

Such divisions of authority were clearly designed to emphasize the master's power, but all the same time were meant to cast him as a somewhat distant arbiter of justice, one who did not involve himself in the sordidness of daily floggings. Instead, Hammond sought to portray himself as the dispenser of that mercy designed to win the grateful allegiance of the slave and to justify the plantation's social order. He constantly tried to make himself appear not so much the creator of rules—which of course in reality he was—but the grantor of exceptions and reprieves.

At Silver Bluff, the distribution of provisions was an occasion for Hammond to display this paternalistic conception. The event assumed the form and significance of a cultural ritual, a ceremony in which Hammond endeavored to present himself to his slaves as the source from whom all blessings flowed. Once a week, the bondsmen were required to put on clean clothes and appear before the master to receive their food allowance. "They should," he recorded in his plantation regulations, "be brought into that contact with the master at least once a week of receiving the means of subsistence from him." Although the overseer

could perfectly well have executed such a task, the ceremonial importance of this moment demanded the master's direct participation. The special requirement for fresh apparel set the occasion off from the less sacred events of daily life, and underlined the symbolic character of this interaction between lord and bondsmen. The event illustrated Hammond's most idealized conception of the master-slave relationship and represented his effort to communicate this understanding to the slaves themselves, convincing them of his merciful generosity and of their own humble dependence and need. The interaction was a statement designed to help transform his power into legitimized authority.

But Hammond's slaves were not taken in by this ritual; they remained less dependent on his dispensations of food and far more active in procuring the necessary means of subsistence than their master cared to admit. Slaves tended their own garden plots and fished for the rich bounty of the Savannah River. And to Hammond's intense displeasure, they also stole delicacies out of his own larder. Pilfering of food and alcohol at Silver Bluff did not consist simply of a series of random acts by slaves seeking to alleviate hunger or compensate for deprivation. Instead, theft assumed the characteristics of a contest between master and slave. Indeed, the prospect of winning the competition may have provided the organized slaves with nearly as much satisfaction as did the actual material fruits of victory; it was clearly a battle over power as well as for the specific goods in question. Although Hammond began immediately in 1831 to try to reduce the level of depredations against his hogs, flogging suspected thieves made little impact. He could not prevent the disappearance of a sizeable portion of his pork or break what he saw as the "habit" of theft among his slaves. Over the years, his supply of livestock consequently diminished, and he found himself compelled to buy provisions to feed his slaves. Hammond recorded with grim satisfaction that the resulting reduction of the meat allowance would be just retribution for the slaves' conspiracy against his herds. Theirs would be, he consoled himself, a hollow victory. "The negroes," he noted in 1845, "have for years killed about half my shoats and must now suffer for it." But the impact of black theft was perhaps even greater on other plantation products. Hammond was resigned to never harvesting his potato crop at all, for the slaves stole the entire yield before it was even removed from the ground.

Alcohol, however, was the commodity that inspired the most carefully designed system of slave intrigue. When Hammond began to ferment wines from his own vineyards, slaves constantly tapped his bottles, then blamed the disappearance of the liquid on leaks due to miscorking. But the slave community's most elaborate assault on Hammond's supplies of alcohol went well beyond such crude tactics to call upon a unique conjunction of engineering skill with the power of voodoo. In 1835, Hammond found that several of his slaves had dug tunnels beneath his wine cellar. Other house servants had provided aid, including necessary keys and information and some spiritual assistance as well. A female domestic, Urana, Hammond recorded, used " 'root work' " and thus "screened" the excavators by her "conjuration." Hammond determinedly "punished all who have had anything to do with the matter far or near." But his response could not replace the lost wine, nor compensate for the way the incident challenged the literal and figurative foundations of his plantation order. The force of voodoo lay entirely outside his system of domination and his efforts to establish cultural hegemony. The slaves were undermining his power as well as his house.

Folk beliefs flourished in other realms of slave life as well. Hammond's bondsmen succeeded in perpetuating African medical ideas and customs, even though their master's commitment to scientific plantation management necessarily included an effort to exercise close medical supervision over slave lives, in times of sickness and of health. The blacks of Silver Bluff may well have been encouraged in their resistance to Hammond's therapeutics by his record of dismal failure: he had great difficulty in achieving a slave population that reproduced itself. For the first twenty years of his management, slave deaths consistently exceeded slave births at the Bluff, despite Hammond's sincere and vigorous efforts to reverse these disheartening statistics. Hammond continually purchased new bondsmen, however, in order to offset a diminution in his labor supply probably caused as much by the low, damp, and unhealthy location of much of his property as by any physical mistreatment or deprivation of his slaves.

In part, these difficulties arose from the shortcomings of medical knowledge in antebellum white America more generally. Initially, Hammond and the physicians he consulted employed a series of those heroic treatments that characterized accepted 19th-century medical practice—compelling the slaves to submit to disagreeable purges, bleedings, and emetics. When these failed to cure, and seemed often to harm, Hammond gave up in disgust on conventional medicine and turned first to "Botanic Practice," then in 1854 to homeopathy, a medical fad that in its misguidedness at least had the virtue of advocating tiny dosages and thus minimizing the damage a practitioner might inflict.

Although Hammond never faltered in his certainty that Western science would eventually provide the solution to his dilemmas, his slaves retained an active skepticism, resisting his treatments by hiding illness and continuing to practice their own folk cures and remedies. In 1851, Hammond recognized that an entire alternative system of medical services thrived on his plantation. "Traced out the negro Doctors . . . who have been giving out medicine for years here & have killed I think most of those that have died. Punished them and also their patients very severely." Hammond was even able to use the existence of black medicine as a justification for the failures of his own methods. Although he did not refer to these doctors again, it seems likely that he achieved no greater success in controlling them than in eliminating black preaching or voodoo.

For most of Hammond's slaves, insubordination served to establish cultural and personal autonomy within the framework of plantation demands. Resistance was a tool of negotiation, a means of extracting concessions from the master to reduce the extent of his claims over black bodies and souls. At Silver Bluff, such efforts often were directed more at securing necessary support for black community life than at totally overwhelming the master's power. Hammond learned that he could to a certain degree repress, but never eliminate black cultural patterns; his slaves in turn concealed much of their lives so as not to appear directly to challenge their master's hegemony.

For some Silver Bluff residents, however, there could be no such compromise. Instead of seeking indirectly to avoid the domination inherent to slavery, these individuals confronted it, turning to arson and escape as overt expressions of their rebelliousness. Throughout the period of his management, Hammond referred to mysterious fires that would break out in the gin house on one occasion, the mill house, or the plantation hospital the next. Although these depredations could not be linked to specific individuals and only minimally affected the operation of the plantation, running away offered and the angry slave a potentially more effective means of immediate resistance to the master's control. Between 1831 and 1855, Hammond recorded fifty-three attempts at escape by his bondsmen. Because he was sometimes absent from the plantation for months at a time during these decades, serving in political office or travelling in Europe, it seems unlikely that this list is complete. Nevertheless, Hammond's slave records provide sufficient information about the personal attributes of the runaways, the circumstances of their departure, the length of their absence, and the nature of their family ties to demonstrate the meaning and significance of the action within the wider context of plantation life.

The most striking—and depressing—fact about Silver Bluff's runaways is that Hammond records no instance of a successful escape. A total of thirty-seven different slaves were listed as endeavoring to leave the plantation. Thirty-five percent of these were repeaters, although no slave was recorded as making more than three attempts. Newly purchased slaves who made several efforts to escape were often sold; those with long-term ties to the Silver Bluff community eventually abandoned the endeavor.

Runaways were 84 percent male, averaged thirty-three years of age, and had been under Hammond's dominance for a median period of two years. Hammond's initial assumption of power precipitated a flurry of escapes, as did subsequent changes in management. When the owner departed for long summer holidays or for business elsewhere, notations of increased numbers of slave escapes appeared in plantation records. This pattern suggests that slavery was rendered minimally tolerable to its victims by the gradual negotiation between master and slave of the kinds of implicit compromises earlier discussed. A shift in responsibility from one master to another or from master to overseer threatened those understandings and therefore produced eruptions of overt rebelliousness.

Although the decision to run away might appear to be a rejection of the ties of black community as well as the chains of bondage, the way in which escape functioned at Silver Bluff shows it usually to have operated somewhat differently. Because there were no runaways who achieved permanent freedom and because most escapees did not get far, they remained in a very real sense a part of the slave community they had seemingly fled. Forty-three percent of the runaways at the Bluff left with others. The small proportion—16 percent of the total—of females were almost without exception running with husbands or joining spouses who had already departed. Once slaves escaped, they succeeded in remaining at large an average of forty-nine days. Sixty-five percent were captured, and the rest returned voluntarily. The distribution of compulsory and elective returns over the calendar year reveals that harsh weather was a significant factor in persuading slaves to give themselves up. Seventy-seven percent of those returning in the winter months did so voluntarily, whereas in the spring and summer 80 percent were brought back against their will. Weather and workload made summer the runaway season, and 58 percent of all escape attempts occurred in June, July, and August.

Although certain individuals—notably young males, particularly those without family ties—were most likely to become runaways, the slave community as a whole provided these individuals with assistance and support. Hammond himself recognized that runaways often went no farther than the nearby Savannah River swamps, where they survived on food provided by those remaining at home. The ties between the escapees and the community were sufficiently strong that Hammond endeavored to force runaways to return by disciplining the rest of the slave force. On at least one occasion Hammond determined to stop the meat allowance of the entire plantation until the runaways came in. In another instance, he severely flogged four slaves harboring two runaways, hoping thereby to break the personal and communal bonds that made prolonged absences possible.

In the isolation of Silver Bluff, real escape seemed all but hopeless. Some newly arrived slaves, perhaps with family from whom they had been separated, turned to flight as a rejection of these new surroundings and an effort permanently to escape them. Individuals of this sort were captured as far as a hundred miles away. The majority of runaways, however, were part of the established black community on Hammond's plantation. Recognizing the near certainty of failure to escape the chains of bondage forever, they ran either in pursuit of a brief respite from labor or in response to uncontrollable anger. One function of the black community was to support this outlet for frustration and rage by feeding and sheltering runaways either until they were captured or until they were once again able to operate within the system of compromise that provided the foundation for the survival of black culture and identity at Silver Bluff.

Two examples demonstrate the way runaways eventually became integrated into the plantation order. Cudjo was returned to the Bluff as a plough hand in 1833 after a year of being hired out in Augusta. Thirty-two years old, he perhaps missed urban life or had established personal relationships he could not bear to break. In any case, he began to run away soon after his return. He first succeeded in departing for two weeks but was seized in Augusta and imprisoned. Hammond retrieved him and put him in irons, but within days he was off again with his fetters on. Captured soon on a nearby plantation, Cudjo tried again a few days later and remained at large for ten months. In March of 1834, Hammond recorded in his diary, "Cudjo came home. Just tired of running away." Although Cudjo was still on the plantation two decades later, there appeared no further mention of his attempting to escape.

Alonzo had been with Hammond only eight months when he first fled in 1843. Thirty-four years old, he had not yet developed settled family ties on the plantation, and he ran away alone. Captured in this first attempt, he escaped twice more within the year, disappearing, Hammond recorded, "without provocation." His second absence ended when he was caught in Savannah after thirty-two days and placed in irons. After less than two months at home, he was off again, but this time he returned voluntarily within two weeks. Reironed,

Alonzo did not flee again. After 1851, Hammond recorded an ever-growing family born to Alonzo and another Silver Bluff slave named Abby. But while he stopped trying to run away and became increasingly tied to Silver Bluff, Alonzo was by no means broken of his independence. In 1864 he provoked Hammond with a final act of resistance, refusing to supply his master with any information about the pains that were to kill him within a month. "A hale hearty man," Hammond remarked with annoyance, "killed by the negro perversity."

In the initial part of his tenure at the Bluff, Hammond recorded efforts to round up runaway slaves by means of extensive searches through the swamps on horseback or with packs of dogs. After the first decade, however, he made little mention of such vigorous measures and seems for the most part simply to have waited for his escapees to be captured by neighbors, turn up in nearby jails, or return home. In order to encourage voluntary surrender, Hammond announced a policy of punishment for runaways that allotted ten lashes for each day absent to those recaptured by force and three lashes per day to those returning of their own will. The establishment of this standardized rule integrated the problem of runaways into the system of rewards and punishments at Silver Bluff and rendered it an aspect of the understanding existing between master and slaves. Since no one escaped permanently, such a rule served to set forth the cost of unauthorized absence and encouraged those who had left in irrational rage to return as soon as their tempers had cooled. When the respected fifty-three-year-old driver John Shubrick was flogged for drunkenness, he fled in fury and mortification, but within a week was back exercising his customary responsibility in plantation affairs.

For some, anger assumed a longer duration and significance. These individuals, like Alonzo or Cudjo, ran repeatedly until greater age or change circumstances made life at home more bearable. Occasionally Hammond found himself confronted with a slave whose rage seemed so deep-rooted as to be incurable. When Hudson escaped soon after his purchase in 1844, he was not heard of for seven months. At last, Hammond was notified that the slave was in Barnwell, on trial for arson. To protect his investment, Hammond hired a lawyer to defend him. But when Hudson was acquitted, Hammond sold him immediately, determining that this individual was an insupportable menace to plantation life.

Although runaways disrupted routine and challenged Hammond's system of management, his greatest anxieties about loss of control arose from the fear that slave dissatisfaction would be exploited by external forces to threaten the fine balance of concession and oppression he had established. From the beginning of his tenure at the Bluff, he sought to isolate his bondsmen from outside influences, prohibiting their trading in local stores, selling produce to neighbors, marrying off the plantation or interacting too closely with hands on the steamboats that refuelled at the Bluff landing. Despite such efforts, however, Hammond perceived during the 1840s and 1850s an ever-growing threat to his power arising from challenges levelled at the peculiar institution as a whole. To Hammond's horror, it seemed impossible to keep information about growing abolition sentiment from the slaves. Such knowledge, Hammond feared, might provide the bondsmen with additional bases for ideological autonomy and greater motivation to resist his control. In an 1844 letter to John C. Calhoun, Hammond declared himself "astonished and shocked to find that some of them are aware of the opinions of the Presidential candidates on the subject of slavery and doubtless most of what the abolitionists are doing & I am sure they know as little of what is done off my place as almost any set of Negroes in the State. I fancy . . . there is a growing spirit of insubordination among the slaves in this section. In the lower part of this district they have fired several houses recently. This is fearful—horrible.

A quick and potent remedy must be applied. *Disunion* if *needs* be."

Yet when disunion came, it provided less a remedy than a further exacerbation of the problem. Both the possibility of emancipation by Union soldiers and the resort to slave impressment by the Confederates intervened to disrupt the established pattern of relationship between master and bondsmen. Hammond seemed almost as outraged by southern as by Yankee challenges to his power. He actively endeavored to resist providing workers to the Confederate government and proclaimed the impressment system "wrong every way & odious."

At the beginning of the war, Hammond was uncertain about the sympathies of his slaves. In 1861, he noted that they appeared "anxious," but remarked "Cant tell which side." As the fighting grew closer, with the firing of large guns near the coast audible at Silver Bluff, Hammond began to sense growing disloyalty among his slaves, and to confront intensifying problems of control. "Negroes demoralized greatly. Stealing right and left," he recorded in 1863. By the middle of that year, it seemed certain that the slaves expected "some great change." Despite his efforts, they seemed at all times "well apprised" of war news, sinking into "heavy gloom" at any Union reverse. Hammond observed the appearance of "a peculiar furtive glance with which they regard me & a hanging off from me that I do not like." They seemed to "shut up their faces & cease their cheeful greetings." Hammond felt the war had rendered his control tenuous, and he believed that even though his slaves sought to appear "passive . . . the roar of a single cannon of the Federal's would make them frantic—savage cutthroats and incendiaries."

Hammond never witnessed the Union conquest of the South nor the emancipation of his slaves, for he died in November of 1864. Despite his dire prophecies, however, the people of Silver Bluff did not rise in revolution against those who had oppressed them for so long. Unlike many slaves elsewhere who fled during the war itself, the Hammond bondsmen did not depart even when freedom was proclaimed. "We have not lost many negroes," Hammond's widow complained in September 1865 as she worried about having too many mouths to feed. "I wish we could get clear of many of the useless ones."

Given the turbulent nature of the interaction between Hammond and his slaves in the antebellum years, it would be misguided to regard the blacks' decision to remain on the plantation as evidence either of docility or of indifference about freedom. Instead, it might better be understood as final testimony to the importance of that solidarity we have seen among bondsmen on the Hammond estate. These blacks were more concerned to continue together as a group than to flee Hammond's domination. In the preoccupation with the undeniable importance of the master-slave relationship, historians may have failed fully to recognize how for many bondsmen, the positive meaning of the web of slave interrelationships was a more central influence than were the oppressive intrusions of the power of the master. Silver Bluff had been home to many of these slaves before Hammond ever arrived; the community had preceded him, and now it had outlived him. Its maintenance and autonomy were of the highest priority to its members, keeping them at Silver Bluff even when any single freedman's desire for personal liberty might have best been realized in flight. The values central to this cultural group were more closely associated with the forces of tradition and community than with an individualistic revolutionary romanticism.

On South Carolina's Sea Islands, blacks whose masters had fled perpetuated plantation boundaries as geographic definitions of black communal identity that have persisted to the present day. Although the ex-slaves at Silver Bluff never gained the land titles that would have served as the legal basis for such

long-lived solidarity, they, like their Sea Island counterparts, chose in 1865 to remain
on the plantation that in a powerful emotional
way they had come to regard as their own.
These freedmen saw themselves and their aspirations defined less by the oppressions of slavery than by the positive accomplishments of
autonomous black community that they had
achieved even under the domain of the peculiar institution.

Part Ten

Sectional Conflict and Civil War

The Civil War was the most traumatic event in American history. It lasted four long years, resulted in over 600,000 deaths, and caused massive physical destruction. Over and above its human and material toll, it carried a meaning of devastating significance to the nation's self-esteem: America's rather brief experiment in self-government had failed. The attempt to unify the thirty-three far-flung and diverse states under a decentralized federal system had come to grief. Furthermore, if the struggle to establish a separate Confederate nation had succeeded, the United States would have been split into two different countries. Then the war would have been referred to, not as a civil war, but as the War for Confederate Independence, rather like the war for American independence from Britain eighty years earlier.

If these were the stakes, why did the southern states take such a drastic step? Were the differences between the two sections so great and the threat to the South so immense that an undertaking of such risk was worth the attempt? Equally, if those differences were so irreconcilable, why did the North want to continue trying to coexist with the southern region? Had the North concluded that the differences were absolutely irreconcilable and decided to abandon the effort to harmonize them, then the South would have seceded without a struggle and there would have been no war.

This is all counterfactual speculation, of course. Presumably, the differences were great enough to cause conflict but not so imponderable that one side at least presumed they could, at some stage, be reconciled. Exactly what these points at issue were and how they came to be so problematic are the questions that any explanation of the outbreak of the war has to examine. At one time, a group of historians suggested instead that the problems were actually capable of solution but unfortunately became exaggerated and blown out of proportion. The culprits in this scenario were the extremists on both sides, namely the abolitionists and the fire-eating secessionists who agitated the issues until they were beyond negotiation and adjustment. Also blameworthy, it was thought, were the politicians of the time who failed to reduce the intersectional differences to politically manageable proportions. But, of course, arguments like these are based on the questionable assumption that, had people been more reasonable and skillful, the war could then have been avoided. The fact is, however, the war was *not* avoided, so these kinds of assertions are also counterfactual. They involve speculation about what might have happened if things had been different. As we have already seen, thinking about historical events in this way is valuable for the insight and perspective it can provide, but it does not, of itself, explain why particular events actually occurred.

Nowadays, historians do not dwell on the question of avoidability. Instead, they focus on the differences between the sections and how they became intractable. Although they stress how fundamentally antagonistic were the protaganists' respective positions on the questions that precipitated the conflict, some versions of what the antagonism was about are no longer accepted. For example, no one now supports the assertion that the war was fought because one side thought that slavery was right and the other thought it was wrong; the issue in the dispute was never posed in such clear-cut moral terms. Nor do historians currently believe that the two sections were utterly distinctive societies, even separate civilizations or nations, that had, through sheer bad luck, found themselves in the same political unit when governed by Britain. And finally, historians rarely suggest now that the two sections had totally different, and therefore incompatible, economies—one exclusively agricultural, the other industrial—since both were predominantly agricultural in the 1850s. These neat polarities simply do not fit the facts. The points of difference, although very real and hard to reconcile, were just not that sharp. Complicating the situation, moreover, is a renewed awareness of the similarities and shared characteristics between the two sections, most notably a common language and religion and similar cultural beliefs and political practices. With fewer features in common than this, many other contemporary nation-states were able to maintain their unity and viability. But, in the United States, this proved impossible. Instead, two parts of the same country that were very similar and wanted to coexist found that there were nevertheless vital questions on which they could not agree.

The anomalousness of the situation and the complexity of the disagreement are well illustrated by the two articles that follow. Eric Foner of Columbia University is one of the most perceptive among current historians of the coming of the Civil War. In his study of the newly emerging Republican party of the 1850s, called *Free Soil, Free Labor, Free Men* (1970), he argues that an understanding of the belief system of the Republicans—what he refers to as their ideology—provides the best clue as to why the North saw slavery as an institution it could not live with. To the Republicans, slavery represented a form of labor and a set of values that were the antithesis of "free labor." This idea of "free labor" was a firmly held belief that America could be socially progressive and economically dynamic only if labor were free to make its own terms with its employer and, over time, to rise and prosper—something that, needless to say, was precluded under slavery. Professor Foner's essay distills this argument and suggests that it was the development of two mutually contradictory ideologies, based on the ideas of free labor and slave labor, that created the conflict. These world views were so complete and so tenaciously held that the political system could not accommodate them both. Beset by such pressures, politics became so sectionalized that the party system was unable to function as a national institution whose purpose was to reconcile domestic conflicts.

James McPherson of Princeton University offers a rather different approach. A distinguished historian of the Civil War era who has just published a best-selling military history of the war, he examines the nature of southern distinctiveness. This is a perennial problem in American history that was, of course, most acute in the 1850s, when the South saw itself as so different that it seceded from the rest of the country. Unlike Professor Foner, he focuses on the material and institutional differences, that is, those that were physical rather than attitudinal. Furthermore, the conclusion he reaches regarding their significance is quite startling. He suggests that these features put the South more in tune than the North with contemporary economic and social developments in the rest of the world. So, if North-South differences are taken out of the American domestic context and placed in an international setting, it is the North that is really out of step, not the South. Thus, the South is less of an anomaly and its predicament more understandable than it might otherwise appear.

■

QUESTIONS TO CONSIDER

1. How does Foner make the argument that the Civil War was evidence of the failure of the governmental and political system to forge a nation? Do you agree with him?

2. Foner's account offers an explanation of why the war came; McPherson's does not. Why is this so?

3. Compare the way in which both historians deal with the question of the differences between the two protaganists in the Civil War.

Politics, Ideology, and the Origins of the American Civil War

Eric Foner

It has long been an axiom of political science that political parties help to hold together diverse, heterogeneous societies like our own. Since most major parties in American history have tried, in Seymour Lipset's phrase, to "appear as plausible representatives of the whole society," they have been broad coalitions cutting across lines of class, race, religion, and section. And although party competition requires that there be differences between the major parties, these differences usually have not been along sharp ideological lines. In fact, the very diversity of American society has inhibited the formation of ideological parties, for such parties assume the existence of a single line of social division along which a majority of the electorate can be mobilized. In a large, heterogeneous society, such a line rarely exists. There are, therefore, strong reasons why, in a two-party system, a major party—or a party aspiring to become "major"—will eschew ideology, for the statement of a coherent ideology will set limits to the groups in the electorate the party can hope to mobilize. Under most circumstances, in other words, the party's role as

a carrier of a coherent ideology will conflict with its role as an electoral machine bent on winning the widest possible number of votes.

For much of the seventy years preceding the Civil War, the American political system functioned as a mechanism for relieving social tensions, ordering group conflict, and integrating the society. The existence of national political parties, increasingly focused on the contest for the presidency, necessitated alliances among political elites in various sections of the country. A recent study of early American politics notes that "political nationalization was far ahead of economic, cultural, and social nationalization"—that is, that the national political system was itself a major bond of union in a diverse, growing society. But as North and South increasingly took different paths of economic and social development and as, from the 1830s onwards, antagonistic value systems and ideologies grounded in the question of slavery emerged in these sections, the political system inevitably came under severe disruptive pressures. Because they brought into play basic values and moral judgments, the competing sectional ideologies could not be defused by the normal processes of political compromise, nor could they be contained within the existing inter-sectional political system. Once parties began to reorient themselves on sectional lines, a fundamental necessity of democratic

"Politics, Ideology, and the Origins of the American Civil War" by Eric Foner from *A Nation Divided: Problems and Issues of the Civil War and Reconstruction,* edited by George M. Fredrickson (Minneapolis: Burgess Publishing Company, 1975). Reprinted by permission of Eric Foner.

politics—that each party look upon the other as a legitimate alternative government—was destroyed.

When we consider the causes of the sectional conflict, we must ask ourselves not only why civil war came when it did, but why it did not come sooner. How did a divided nation manage to hold itself together for as long as it did? In part, the answer lies in the unifying effects of inter-sectional political parties. On the level of politics, the coming of the Civil War is the story of the intrusion of sectional ideology into the political system, despite the efforts of political leaders of both parties to keep it out. Once this happened, political competition worked to exacerbate, rather than to solve, social and sectional conflicts. For as Frank Sorauf has explained:

> The party of extensive ideology develops in and reflects the society in which little consensus prevails on basic social values and institutions. It betokens deep social disagreements and conflicts. Indeed, the party of ideology that is also a major, competitive party accompanies a politics of almost total concern. Since its ideology defines political issues as including almost every facet of life, it brings to the political system almost every division, every difference, every conflict of any importance in society.

"Parties in this country," wrote a conservative northern Whig in 1855, "heretofore have helped, not delayed, the slow and difficult growth of a consummated nationality." Rufus Choate was lamenting the passing of a bygone era, a time when "our allies were everywhere . . . there were no Alleghenies nor Mississippi rivers in our politics." Party organization and the nature of political conflict had taken on new and unprecedented forms in the 1850s. It is no accident that the breakup of the last major inter-sectional party preceded by less than a year the breakup of the Union or that the final crisis was precipitated not by any "overt act," but by a presidential election.

From the beginning of national government, of course, differences of opinion over slavery constituted an important obstacle to the formation of a national community. "The great danger to our general government," as Madison remarked at the Constitutional Convention, "is the great southern and northern interests of the continent, being opposed to each other." "The institution of slavery and its consequences," according to him, was the main "line of discrimination" in convention disputes. As far as slavery was concerned, the Constitution amply fulfilled Lord Acton's dictum that it was an effort to avoid settling basic questions. Aside from the Atlantic slave trade, Congress was given no power to regulate slavery in any way—the framers' main intention seems to have been to place slavery completely outside the national political arena. The only basis on which a national politics could exist—the avoidance of sectional issues—was thus defined at the outset.

Although the slavery question was never completely excluded from political debate in the 1790s, and there was considerable Federalist grumbling about the three-fifths clause of the Constitution after 1800, the first full demonstration of the political possibilities inherent in a sectional attack on slavery occurred in the Missouri controversy of 1819–21. These debates established a number of precedents that forecast the future course of the slavery extension issue in Congress. Most important was the fact that the issue was able for a time to completely obliterate party lines. In the first votes on slavery in Missouri, virtually every Northerner, regardless of party, voted against expansion. It was not surprising, of course, that northern Federalists would try to make political capital out of the issue. What was unexpected was that northern Republicans, many of whom were aggrieved by Virginia's long dominance of the Presidency and by the Monroe administration's tariff and internal improvements policies, would unite with the Federalists. As John Quincy Adams observed, the debate "disclosed a secret: it revealed the basis for a new organization of parties. . . . Here was a new party really formed . . . terrible to the whole Union, but portentously terrible to the South." But the final compromise set another important precedent: enough northern Republicans became convinced that the Federalists were making political gains from the debates and that the Union was seriously endangered to break with the sectional bloc and support a compromise which a majority of northern Congressmen—Republicans and Federalists—opposed. As for the Monroe administration, its semiofficial spokesman, the *National Intelligencer,* pleaded for a return to the policy of avoiding sectional issues, even to the extent of refusing to publish letters which dealt in any way with the subject of slavery.

The Missouri controversy and the election of 1824, in which four candidates contested the presidency, largely drawing support from their home sections, revealed that in the absence of two-party competition, sectional loyalties would constitute the lines of political division. No one recognized this more clearly than the architect of the second-party system, Martin Van Buren. In his well-known letter to Thomas Ritchie of Virginia, Van Buren explained the need for a revival of national two-party politics on precisely this ground: "Party attachment in former times furnished a complete antidote for sectional prejudices by producing counteracting feelings. It was not until that defense had been broken down that the clamor against southern Influence and African Slavery could be made effectual in the North." Van Buren and many of his generation of politicians had been genuinely frightened by the threats of disunion which echoed through Congress in 1820; they saw national two-party competition as the alternative to sectional conflict and eventual disunion. Ironically, as Richard McCormick has made clear, the creation of the second-party system owed as much to sectionalism as to national loyalties. The South, for example, only developed an organized, competitive Whig party in 1835 and 1836 when

it became apparent that Jackson, the southern President, had chosen Van Buren, a Northerner, as his successor. Once party divisions had emerged, however, they stuck, and by 1840, for one of the very few times in American history, two truly inter-sectional parties, each united behind a single candidate, competed for the Presidency.

The 1830s witnessed a vast expansion of political loyalties and awareness and the creation of party mechanisms to channel voter participation in politics. But the new mass sense of identification with politics had ominous implications for the sectional antagonisms the party system sought to suppress. The historian of the Missouri Compromise has observed that "if there had been a civil war in 1819–21 it would have been between the members of Congress, with the rest of the country looking on in amazement." This is only one example of the intellectual and political isolation of Washington from the general populace James Young has described in *The Washington Community.* The mass, non-ideological politics of the Jackson era created the desperately needed link between governors and governed. But this very link made possible the emergence of two kinds of sectional agitators: the abolitionists, who stood outside of politics and hoped to force public opinion—and through it, politicians—to confront the slavery issue, and political agitators, who used politics as a way of heightening sectional self-consciousness and antagonism in the populace at large.

Because of the rise of mass politics and the emergence of these sectional agitators, the 1830s was the decade in which long-standing, latent sectional divisions were suddenly activated, and previously unrelated patterns of derogatory sectional imagery began to emerge into full-blown sectional ideology. Many of the antislavery arguments which gained wide currency in the 1830s had roots stretching back into the eighteenth century. The idea that slavery degraded white labor and retarded economic development, for example, had been voiced by Benjamin Franklin. After 1800, the Federalists, increasingly localized in New England, had developed a fairly coherent critique, not only of the social and economic effects of slavery, but of what Harrison Gray Otis called the divergence of "manners, habits, customs, principles, and ways of thinking" which separated Northerners and Southerners. And, during the Missouri debates, almost every economic, political, and moral argument against slavery that would be used in the later sectional debate was voiced. In fact, one recurring argument was not picked up later—the warning of northern Congressmen that the South faced the danger of slave rebellion if steps were not taken toward abolition. (As far as I know, only Thaddeus Stevens of Republican spokesmen in the 1850s would explicitly use this line of argument.)

The similarity between Federalist attacks on the South and later abolitionist and Republican arguments, coupled with the fact that many abolitionists—including Garrison, Philips, the Tappans, and others—came from Federalist backgrounds, has led James Banner to describe abolitionism as "the Massachusetts Federalist ideology come back to life." Yet there was a long road to be travelled from Harrison Gray Otis to William H. Seward, just as there was from Thomas Jefferson to George Fitzhugh. For one thing, the Federalist distrust of democracy, social competition, the Jeffersonian cry of "equal rights," their commitment to social inequality, hierarchy, tradition, and order prevented them from pushing their antislavery views to their logical conclusion. And New England Federalists were inhibited by the requirements of national party organization and competition from voicing antislavery views. In the 1790s, they maintained close ties with southern Federalists, and after 1800 hope of reviving their strength in the South never completely died. Only a party which embraced social mobility and competitive individualism, rejected the permanent subordination of any "rank" in society, and was unburdened

by a southern wing could develop a fully coherent antislavery ideology.

An equally important reason why the Federalists did not develop a consistent sectional ideology was that the South in the early part of the nineteenth century shared many of the Federalists' reservations about slavery. The growth of an antislavery ideology, in other words, depended in large measure on the growth of proslavery thought, and, by the same token, it was the abolitionist assault which brought into being the coherent defense of slavery. The opening years of the 1830s, of course, were ones of crisis for the South. The emergence of militant abolitionism, Nat Turner's rebellion, the Virginia debates on slavery, and the nullification crisis suddenly presented assaults to the institution of slavery from within and outside the South. The reaction was the closing of southern society in defense of slavery, "the most thorough-going repression of free thought, free speech, and a free press ever witnessed in an American community." At the same time, Southerners increasingly abandoned their previous, highly qualified defenses of slavery and embarked on the formulation of the proslavery argument. By 1837, as is well known, John C. Calhoun could thank the abolitionists on precisely this ground:

> This agitation has produced one happy effect at least; it has compelled us at the South to look into the nature and character of this great institution, and to correct many false impressions that even we had entertained in relation to it. Many in the South once believed that it was a moral and political evil; that folly and delusion are gone; we see it now in its true light, and regard it as the most safe and stable basis for free institutions in the world.

The South, of course, was hardly as united as Calhoun asserted. But the progressive rejection of the Jeffersonian tradition, the suppression of civil liberties, and the increasing stridency of the defense of slavery all pushed the South further and further out of the inter-sectional mainstream, setting it increasingly apart from the rest of the country. Coupled with the Gag Rule and the mobs which broke up abolitionist presses and meetings, the growth of proslavery thought was vital to a new antislavery formulation which emerged in the late 1830s and had been absent from both the Federalist attacks on slavery and the Missouri debates—the idea of the slave power. The slave power replaced the three-fifths clause as the symbol of southern power, and it was a far more sophisticated and complex formulation. Abolitionists could now argue that slavery was not only morally repugnant, it was incompatible with the basic democratic values and liberties of white Americans. As one abolitionist declared, "We commenced the present struggle to obtain the freedom of the slave; we are compelled to continue it to preserve our own." In other words, a process of ideological expansion had begun, fed in large measure by the sequence of response and counter-response between the competing sectional outlooks. Once this process had begun, it had an internal dynamic which made it extremely difficult to stop. This was especially true because of the emergence of agitators whose avowed purpose was to sharpen sectional conflict, polarize public opinion, and develop sectional ideologies to their logical extremes.

As the 1840s opened, most political leaders still clung to the traditional basis of politics, but the sectional, ideological political agitators formed growing minorities in each section. In the South, there was a small group of outright secessionists and a larger group, led by Calhoun, who were firmly committed to the Union but who viewed sectional organization and self-defense, not the traditional reliance on inter-sectional political parties, as the surest means of protecting southern interests within the Union. In the North, a small radical group gathered in Congress around John Quincy Adams and Congressmen like Joshua Giddings, William Slade, and Seth Gates—men who represented areas of the most intense

abolitionist agitation and whose presence confirmed Garrison's belief that, once public opinion was aroused on the slavery issue, politicians would have to follow step. These radicals were determined to force slavery into every Congressional debate. They were continually frustrated but never suppressed, and the reelection of Giddings in 1842 after his censure and resignation from the House proved that in some districts party discipline was no longer able to control the slavery issue.

The northern political agitators, both Congressmen and Liberty party leaders, also performed the function of developing and popularizing a political rhetoric, especially focused on fear of the slave power, which could be seized upon by traditional politicians and large masses of voters if slavery ever entered the center of political conflict.

In the 1840s, this is precisely what happened. As one politician later recalled, "Slavery upon which by common consent no party issue had been made was then obtruded upon the field of party action." It is significant that John Tyler and John C. Calhoun, the two men most responsible for this intrusion, were political outsiders, men without places in the national party structure. Both of their careers were blocked by the major parties but might be advanced if tied to the slavery question in the form of Texas annexation. Once introduced into politics, slavery was there to stay. The Wilmot Proviso, introduced in 1846, had precisely the same effect as the proposal two decades earlier to restrict slavery in Missouri—it completely fractured the major parties along sectional lines. As in 1820, opposition to the expansion of slavery became the way in which a diverse group of Northerners expressed their various resentments against a southern-dominated administration. And, as in 1821, a small group of northern Democrats eventually broke with their section, reaffirmed their primary loyalty to the party, and joined with the South to kill the Proviso in 1847. In the same year, enough Southerners rejected Calhoun's call for united sectional action to doom his personal and sectional ambitions.

But the slavery extension debates of the 1840s had far greater effects on the political system that the Missouri controversy had had. Within each party, they created a significant group of sectional politicians—men whose careers were linked to the slavery question and who would therefore resist its exclusion from future politics. And in the North, the 1840s witnessed the expansion of sectional political rhetoric—as more and more Northerners became familiar with the "aggressions" of the slave power and the need to resist them. At the same time, as antislavery ideas expanded, unpopular and divisive elements were weeded out, especially the old alliance of antislavery with demands for the rights of free blacks. Opposition to slavery was already coming to focus on its lowest common denominators—free soil, opposition to the slave power, and union.

The political system reacted to the intrusion of the slavery question in the traditional ways. At first, it tried to suppress it. This is the meaning of the famous letters opposing the immediate annexation of Texas issued by Clay and Van Buren on the same spring day in 1844, probably after consultation on the subject. It was an agreement that slavery was too explosive a question for either party to try to take partisan advantage of it. The agreement, of course, was torpedoed by the defeat of Van Buren for the Democratic nomination, a defeat caused in part by the willingness of his Democratic opponents to use the Texas and slavery questions to discredit Van Buren—thereby violating the previously established rules of political conduct. In the North from 1844 onwards, both parties, particularly the Whigs, tried to defuse the slavery issue and minimize defection to the Liberty party by adopting anti-southern rhetoric. This tended to prevent defections to third parties, but it had the effect of nurturing and le-

gitimating anti-southern sentiment within the ranks of the major parties themselves. After the 1848 election in which northern Whigs and Democrats vied for title of "free soil" to minimize the impact of the Free Soil party, William H. Seward commented, "Antislavery is at length a respectable element in politics."

Both parties also attempted to devise formulas for compromising the divisive issue. For the Whigs, it was "no territory"—an end to expansion would end the question of the spread of slavery. The Democratic answer, first announced by Vice President Dallas in 1847 and picked up by Lewis Cass, was popular sovereignty or nonintervention: giving to the people of each territory the right to decide on slavery. As has often been pointed out, popular sovereignty was an exceedingly vague and ambiguous doctrine. It was never precisely clear what the powers of a territorial legislature were to be or at what point the question of slavery was to be decided. But politically such ambiguity was essential (and intentional) if popular sovereignty were to serve as a means of settling the slavery issue on the traditional basis—by removing it from national politics and transferring the battleground from Congress to the territories. Popular sovereignty formed one basis of the compromise of 1850, the last attempt of the political system to expel the disease of sectional ideology by finally settling all the points at which slavery and national politics intersected.

That compromise was possible in 1850 was testimony to the resiliency of the political system and the continuing ability of party loyalty to compete with sectional commitments. But the very method of passage revealed how deeply sectional divisions were embedded in party politics. Because only a small group of Congressmen—mostly northwestern Democrats and southern Whigs—were committed to compromise on every issue, the "omnibus" compromise measure could not pass. The compromise had to be enacted se-

Henry Clay argues in the Senate Chamber for the passage of the Compromise of 1850.

rially with the small compromise bloc, led by Stephen A. Douglas of Illinois, aligned with first one sectional bloc, then the other, to pass the individual measures.

His role in the passage of the compromise announced the emergence of Douglas as the last of the great Unionist, compromising politicians, the heir of Clay, Webster, and other spokesmen for the center. And his career, like Webster's, showed that it was no longer possible to win the confidence of both sections with a combination of extreme nationalism and the calculated suppression of the slavery issue in national politics. Like his predecessors, Douglas called for a policy of "entire silence on the slavery question," and throughout the 1850s, as Robert Johannsen has written, his aim was to restore "order and stability to American pol-

itics through the agency of a national, conservative Democratic party." Ultimately, Douglas failed—a traditional career for the Union was simply not possible in the 1850s—but it is equally true that in 1860 he was the only presidential candidate to draw significant support in all parts of the country.

It is, of course, highly ironic that it was Douglas' attempt to extend the principle of popular sovereignty to territory already guaranteed to free labor by the Missouri Compromise which finally shattered the second-party system. We can date almost exactly the final collapse of that system—February 15, 1854—the day a caucus of southern Whig Congressmen and Senators decided to support Douglas' Nebraska bill, despite the fact that they could have united with northern Whigs in opposition both to the repeal of the Missouri Compromise and the revival of sectional agitation. But in spite of the sectionalization of politics which occurred after 1854, Douglas continued his attempt to maintain a national basis of party competition. In fact, from one angle of vision, whether politics was to be national or sectional was the basic issue of the Lincoln-Douglas debates of 1858. The Little Giant presented local autonomy—popular sovereignty for states and territories—as the only "national" solution to the slavery question, while Lincoln attempted to destroy this middle ground and force a single, sectional solution on the entire Union. There is a common critique of Douglas' politics, expressed perhaps most persuasively by Allan Nevins, which argues that, as a man with no moral feelings about slavery, Douglas was incapable of recognizing that this moral issue affected millions of northern voters. This, in my opinion, is a serious misunderstanding of Douglas' politics. What he insisted was not that there was no moral question involved in slavery but that it was not the function of the politician to deal in moral judgments. To Lincoln's prediction that the nation could not exist half slave and half free, Douglas replied that it had so existed for seventy years and could continue to do so if Northerners stopped trying to impose their own brand of morality upon the South.

Douglas' insistence on the separation of politics and morality was expressed in his oft-quoted statement that—in his role as a politician—he did not care if the people of a territory voted slavery "up or down." As he explained in his Chicago speech of July, 1858, just before the opening of the great debates:

> I deny the right of Congress to force a slave-holding state upon an unwilling people. I deny their right to force a free state upon an unwilling people. I deny their right to force a good thing upon a people who are unwilling to receive it. . . . It is no answer to this argument to say that slavery is an evil and hence should not be tolerated. You must allow the people to decide for themselves whether it is a good or an evil.

When Lincoln, therefore, said the real purpose of popular sovereignty was "to educate and mould public opinion, at least northern public opinion, to not care whether slavery is voted down or up," he was, of course, right. For Douglas recognized that moral categories, being essentially uncompromisable, are unassimilable in politics. The only solution to the slavery issue was local autonomy. Whatever a majority of a state or territory wished to do about slavery was right—or at least should not be tampered with by politicians from other areas. To this, Lincoln's only possible reply was the one formulated in the debates—the will of the majority must be tempered by considerations of morality. Slavery was not, he declared, an "*ordinary* matter of domestic concern in the states and territories." Because of its essential immorality, it tainted the entire nation, and its disposition in the territories, and eventually in the entire nation, was a matter of national concern to be decided by a national, not a local, majority. As the debates continued, Lincoln increasingly moved to this moral level of the slavery argument: "Everything that emanates from [Douglas] or his coadjutors, carefully excludes the thought that there is anything wrong with slavery. All their arguments, if you will consider them, will be seen to exclude the thought. . . . If you do admit that it is wrong, Judge Douglas can't logically say that he don't care whether a wrong is voted up or down."

In order to press home the moral argument, moreover, Lincoln had to insist throughout the debates on the basic humanity of the black; while Douglas, by the same token, logically had to define blacks as subhuman, or at least, as the Dred Scott decision had insisted, not part of the American "people" included in the Declaration of Independence and the Constitution. Douglas' view of the black, Lincoln declared, conveyed "no vivid impression that the Negro is a human, and consequently has no idea that there can be any moral question in legislating about him." Of course, the standard of morality which Lincoln felt the nation should adopt regarding slavery and the black was the sectional morality of the Republican party.

By 1860, Douglas' local majoritarianism was not more acceptable to southern political leaders than Lincoln's national and moral majoritarianism. The principle of state rights and minority self-determination had always been the first line of defense of slavery from northern interference, but Southerners now coupled it with the demand that Congress intervene to establish and guarantee slavery in the territories. The Lecompton fight had clearly demonstrated that Southerners would no longer be satisfied with what Douglas hoped the territories would become—free, Democratic states. And the refusal of the Douglas Democrats to accede to southern demands was the culmination of a long history of resentment on the part of northern Democrats, stretching back into the 1840s, at the impossible political dilemma of being caught between increasingly anti-southern constituency pressure and loyalty to an increasingly pro-southern national party. For their part, southern Democrats viewed their northern allies as too weak at home and too tainted with anti-southernism after the Lecompton battle to be relied on to protect southern interests any longer.

As for the Republicans, by the late 1850s they had succeeded in developing a coherent ideology that, despite internal ambiguities and contradictions, incorporated the fundamental values, hopes, and fears of a majority of Northerners. As I have argued elsewhere, it rested on a commitment to the northern social order, founded on the dignity and opportunities of free labor, and to social mobility, enterprise, and "progress." It gloried in the same qualities of northern life—materialism, social fluidity, and the dominance of the self-made man—which twenty years earlier had been the source of widespread anxiety and fear in Jack-

sonian America. And it defined the South as a backward, stagnant, aristocratic society, totally alien in values and social order to the middle-class capitalism of the North.

Some elements of the Republican ideology had roots stretching back into the eighteenth century. Others, especially the Republican emphasis on the threat of the slave power, were relatively new. Northern politics and thought were permeated by the slave power idea in the 1850s. The effect can perhaps be gauged by a brief look at the career of the leading Republican spokesman of the 1850s, William H. Seward. As a political child of upstate New York's burned-over district and anti-Masonic crusade, Seward had long believed that the Whig party's main political liability was its image as the spokeman of the wealthy and aristocratic. Firmly committed to egalitarian democracy, Seward had attempted to reorient the New York State Whigs into a reformist, egalitarian party, friendly to immigrants and embracing political and economic democracy, but he was always defeated by the party's downstate conservative wing. In the 1840s, he became convinced that the only way for the party to counteract the Democrats' monopoly of the rhetoric of democracy and equality was for the Whigs to embrace antislavery as a party platform.

The slave power idea gave the Republicans the anti-aristocratic appeal with which men like Seward had long wished to be associated politically. By fusing older antislavery arguments with the idea that slavery posed a threat to northern free labor and democratic values, it enabled the Republicans to tap the egalitarian outlook which lay at the heart of northern society. At the same time, it enabled Republicans to present antislavery as an essentially conservative reform, an attempt to reestablish the antislavery principles of the founding fathers and rescue the federal government from southern usurpation. And, of course, the slave power idea had a far greater appeal to northern self-interest than arguments based on the plight of black slaves in the South. As the black abolitionist Frederick Douglass noted, "The cry of Free Man was raised, not for the extension of liberty to the black man, but for the protection of the liberty of the white."

By the late 1850s, it had become a standard part of Republican rhetoric to accuse the slave power of a long series of transgressions against northern rights and liberties and to predict that, unless halted by effective political action, the ultimate aim of the conspiracy—the complete subordination of the national government to slavery and the suppression of northern liberties—would be accomplished. Like other conspiracy theories, the slave power idea was a way of ordering and interpreting history, assigning clear causes to otherwise inexplicable events, from the Gag Rule to Bleeding Kansas and the Dred Scott decision. It also provided a convenient symbol through which a host of anxieties about the future could be expressed. At the same time, the notion of a black Republican conspiracy to overthrow slavery and southern society had taken hold in the South. These competing conspiratorial outlooks were reflections, not merely of sectional "paranoia," but of the fact that the nation was every day growing apart and into two societies whose ultimate interests were diametrically opposed. The South's fear of black Republicans, despite its exaggerated rhetoric, was based on the realistic assessment that at the heart of Republican aspirations for the nation's future was the restriction and eventual eradication of slavery. And the slave power expressed Northerners' conviction, not only that slavery was incompatible with basic democratic values, but that to protect slavery, Southerners were determined to control the federal government and use it to foster the expansion of slavery. In summary, the slave power idea was the ideological glue of the Republican party—it enabled them to elect in 1860 a man conservative enough to sweep to victory in every northern state, yet radical enough to trigger the secession crisis.

Did the election of Lincoln pose any real danger to the institution of slavery? In my view, it is only possible to argue that it did not if one takes a completely static—and therefore ahistorical—view of the slavery issue. The expansion of slavery was not simply an issue; it was a fact. By 1860, over half the slaves lived in areas outside the original slave states. At the same time, however, the South had become a permanent and shrinking minority within the nation. And in the majority section, antislavery sentiment had expanded at a phenomenal rate. Within one generation, it had moved from the commitment of a small minority of Northerners to the motive force behind a victorious party. That sentiment now demanded the exclusion of slavery from the territories. Who could tell what its demands would be in ten or twenty years? The incoming President had often declared his commitment to the "ultimate extinction" of slavery. In Alton, Illinois, in the heart of the most proslavery area of the North, he had condemned Douglas because "he looks to no end of the institution of slavery." A Lincoln administration seemed likely to be only the beginning of a prolonged period of Republican hegemony. And the succession of generally weak, one-term Presidents between 1836 and 1860 did not obscure the great expansion in the potential power of the presidency which had taken place during the administration of Andrew Jackson. Old Hickory had clearly shown that a strong-willed President, backed by a united political party, had tremendous power to shape the affairs of government and to transform into policy his version of majority will.

What was at stake in 1860, as in the entire sectional conflict, was the character of the nation's future. This was one reason Republicans had placed so much stress on the question of the expansion of slavery. Not only was this the most available issue concerning slavery constitutionally open to them, but it involved the nation's future in the most direct way. In the West, the future was a tabula rasa, and the future course of western development would gravely affect the direction of the entire nation. Now that the territorial issue was settled by Lincoln's election, it seemed likely that the slavery controversy would be transferred back into the southern states themselves. Secessionists, as William Freehling has argued, feared that slavery was weak and vulnerable in the border states, even in Virginia. They feared Republican efforts to encourage the formation of Republican organizations in these areas and the renewal of the long-suppressed internal debate on slavery in the South itself. And, lurking behind these anxieties, may have been fear of antislavery debate reaching the slave quarters, of an undermining of the masters' authority, and, ultimately, of slave rebellion itself. The slaveholders knew, despite the great economic strength of King Cotton, that the existence of slavery as a local institution in a larger free economy demanded an inter-sectional community consensus, real or enforced. It was this consensus Lincoln's election seemed to undermine, which is why the secession convention of South Carolina declared, "Experience has proved that slaveholding states cannot be safe in subjection to non-slaveholding states."

More than seventy years before the secession crisis, James Madison had laid down the principles by which a central government and individual and minority liberties could coexist in a large and heterogeneous Union. The very diversity of interests in the nation, he argued in the Federalist papers, was the security for the rights of minorities, for it ensured that no one interest would ever gain control of the government. In the 1830s, John C. Calhoun recognized the danger which abolitionism posed to the South—it threatened to rally the North in the way Madison had said would not happen—in terms of one commitment hostile to the interests of the minority South. Moreover, Calhoun recognized, when a majority interest is organized into an effective political party, it can seize control of all the branches of government, overturning the system of constitutional checks and

balances which supposedly protected minority rights. Only the principle of the concurrent majority—a veto each major interest could exercise over policies directly affecting it—could reestablish this constitutional balance.

At the outset of the abolitionist crusade, Calhoun had been convinced that, while emancipation must be "resisted at all costs," the South should avoid hasty action until it was "certain that it is the real object, not by a few, but by a very large portion of the non-slaveholding states." By 1850, Calhoun was convinced that "Every portion of the North entertains views more or less hostile to slavery." And by 1860, the election returns demonstrated that this antislavery sentiment, contrary to Madison's expectations, had united in an interest capable of electing a President, despite the fact that it had not the slightest support from the sectional minority. The character of Lincoln's election, in other words, completely overturned the ground rules which were supposed to govern American politics. The South Carolina secession convention expressed secessionists' reaction when it declared that once the sectional Republican party, founded on hostility to southern values and interests, took over control of the federal government, "the guarantees of the Constitution will then no longer exist."

Thus the South came face to face with a conflict between its loyalty to the nation and loyalty to the South—that is, to slavery, which, more than anything else, made the South distinct. David Potter has pointed out that the principle of majority rule implies the existence of a coherent, clearly recognizable body of which more than half may be legitimately considered as a majority of the whole. For the South to accept majority rule in 1860, in other words, would have been an affirmation of a common nationality with the North. Certainly, it is true that in terms of ethnicity, language, religion—many of the usual components of nationality—Americans, North and South, were still quite close. On the other hand, one important element, community of interest, was not present. And perhaps most important, the preceding decades had witnessed an escalation of distrust—an erosion of the reciprocal currents of good will so essential for national harmony. "We are not one people." declared the New York *Tribune* in 1855. "We are two peoples. We are a people for Freedom and a people for Slavery. Between the two, conflict is inevitable." We can paraphrase John Adams' famous comment on the American Revolution and apply it to the coming of the Civil War—the separation was complete, in the minds of the people, before the war began. In a sense, the Constitution and national political system had failed in the difficult task of creating a nation—only the Civil War itself would accomplish it.

Was the Antebellum South Different?

James M. McPherson

The notion of American Exceptionalism has received quite a drubbing since the heyday of the exceptionalist thesis among the consensus school of historians in the 1950s. Interpreters of the American experience then argued that something special about the American experience—whether it was abundance, free land on the frontier, the absence of a feudal past, exceptional mobility and the relative lack of class conflict, or the pragmatic and consensual liberalism of our politics—set the American people apart from the rest of mankind. Historians writing since the 1950s, by contrast, have demonstrated the existence of class and class conflict, ideological politics, land speculation, and patterns of economic and industrial development similar to those of Western Europe, which placed the United States in the mainstream of modern North Atlantic history, not on a special and privileged fringe.

If the theme of American Exceptionalism has suffered heavy and perhaps irreparable damage, the idea of Southern Exceptionalism still flourishes—though also subjected to repeated challenges. In this essay, *Southern*

Exceptionialsm refers to the belief that the South has "posessed a separate and unique identity . . . which appeared to be out of the mainstream of American experience." Or as Quentin Compson (in William Faulkner's *Absalom, Absalom!*) expressed it in a reply to his Canadian-born college roommate's question about what made Southerners tick: "You can't understand it. You would have to be born there."

The questions of whether the South was indeed out of the mainstream and if so, whether it has recently been swept into it, continue to be vital issues in southern historiography. The clash of viewpoints can be illustrated by a sampling of titles or subtitles of books that have appeared in recent years. On one side we have: *The Enduring South; The Everlasting South; The Idea of the South; The Lasting South;* and *The Continuity of Southern Distinctiveness*—all arguing, in one way or another, that the South was and continues to be different. On the other side we have: *The Southerner as American; The Americanization of Dixie; Epitaph for Dixie; Southerners and Other Americans; The Vanishing South;* and *Into the Mainstream*. Some of these books insist that "the traditional emphasis on the South's differentness . . . is wrong historically." Others concede that while the South may once have been different, it has ceased to be or is ceasing to be so. There is no unanim-

"Antebellum Southern Exceptionalism: A New Look at an Old Question" by James M. McPherson from *Civil War History: A Journal of the Middle Period,* Vol. 29, No. 3, September 1983, pp. 220-244. Copyright © 1983 by The Kent State University Press. Reprinted by permission.

ity among this latter group of scholars about precisely when or how the South joined the mainstream. Some emphasize the civil rights revolution of the 1960s; others the bulldozer revolution of the 1950s; still others the Chamber of Commerce Sabbittry of the 1920s; and some the New South crusade of the 1880s. As far back as 1869 the Yankee novelist John William DeForest wrote of the South: "We shall do well to study this peculiar people, which will soon lose its pecularities." As George Tindall has wryly remarked, the Vanishing South has "staged one of the most prolonged disappearing acts since the decline and fall of Rome."

Some historians, however, would quarrel with the concept of a Vanishing South because they believe that the South as a separate, exceptional entity never existed—with of course the ephemeral exception of the Confederacy. But a good many other historians insist that not only did a unique "South" exist before the Civil War, but also that its sense of a separate identity that was being threatened by the North was the underlying cause of secession. A few paired quotations will illustrate these conflicting interpretations.

In 1960 one southern historian maintained that "no picture of the Old South as a section confident and united in its dedication to a neo-feudal social order, and no explanation of the Civil War as a conflict between two civilizations,' can encompass the complexity and pathos of the antebellum reality." But later in the decade another historian insisted that slavery created "a ruling class with economic interests, political ideals, and moral sentiments" that included an "aristocratic, antibourgeois spirit with values and mores emphasizing family and status, a strong code of honor, and aspirations to luxury, ease, and accomplishment" which "set it apart from the mainstream of capitalist development." This ruling class possessed "the political and economic power to impose their values on [southern] society as a whole." Since submission to the hegemony of Northern free-soilers would have

meant "moral and political suicide" for this "special civilization" of the South, a "final struggle [was] so probable that we may safely call it inevitable." The first historian was Charles Sellers; the second, Eugene Genovese.

Or let us examine another pair of quotations, the first published in 1973 by a southern historian who asserted that the thesis of a "basically divergent and antagonistic" North and South in 1861 is "one of the great myths of American history." Almost as if in reply, a historian wrote a few years later that such an assertion "belies common sense and the nearly universal observation of contemporaries. We submit a single figure that . . . attests to the irrelevance of all [statistical manipulations] purporting to show similarities between North and South. The figure is 600,000—the number of Civil War graves." The first of these quotations is from Grady McWhiney. The second is from—Grady McWhiney.

Finally, let us look at another pair of statements, the first from one of the South's most eminent historians writing in 1958: "The South was American a long time before it was Southern in any self-conscious or distinctive way. It remains more American by far than anything else, and has all along." The second is from an equally eminent historian writing in 1969: "A great slave society . . . had grown up and miraculously flourished in the heart of a thoroughly bourgeois and partly puritanical republic. It had renounced its bourgeois origins and elaborated and painfully rationalized its institutional, legal, metaphysical, and religious defenses. . . . When the crisis came [it] chose to fight. It proved to be the death struggle of a society, which went down in ruins." The first historian was C. Vann Woodward; the second—it should come as no surprise by now—was C. Vann Woodward.

If given the opportunity, McWhiney and Woodward might be able to reconcile the apparent inconsistencies in these statements. Or perhaps they really changed their minds. After all, as Ralph Waldo Emerson told us more than a century ago, "a foolish consistency is the hob-goblin of little minds." In any case, the more recent vintage of both McWhiney and Woodward has a fuller, more robust, and truer flavor.

Many antebellum Americans certainly thought that North and South had evolved separate societies with institutions, interests, values, and ideologies so incompatible, so much in deadly conflict that they could no longer live together in the same nation. Traveling through the South in the spring of 1861, London *Times* correspondent William Howard Russell encountered this Conflict of Civilizations theme everywhere he went. "The tone in which [Southerners] alluded to the whole of the Northern people indicated the clear conviction that trade, commerce, the pursuit of gain, manufacture, and the base mechanical arts, had so degraded the whole race" that Southerners could no longer tolerate association with them, wrote Russell. "There is a degree of something like ferocity in the Southern mind [especially] toward New England which exceeds belief." A South Carolinian told Russell: "We are an agricultural people, pursuing our own system, and working out our own destiny, breeding up women and men with some other purpose than to make them vulgar, fanatical, cheating Yankees." Louis Wigfall of Texas, a former U.S. senator, told Russell: "We are a peculiar people, sir! . . . We are an agricultural people. . . . We have no cities—we don't want them. . . . We want no manufactures: we desire no trading, no mechanical or manufacturing classes. . . . As long as we have our rice, our sugar, our tobacco, and our cotton, we can command wealth to purchase all we want. . . . But with the Yankees we will never trade—never. Not one pound of cotton shall ever go from the South to their accursed cities."

Such opinions were not universal in the South, of course, but in the fevered atmosphere of the late 1850s they were widely shared. "Free Society!" exclaimed a Georgia newspaper. "We sicken at the name. What is it but a conglomeration of greasy mechanics, filthy operatives, small-fisted farmers, and moon-struck theorists . . . hardly fit for association with a southern gentleman's body servant." In 1861 the *Southern Literary Messenger* explained to its readers: "It is not a question of slavery alone that we are called upon to decide. It is free society which we must shun or embrace." In the same year Charles Colcock Jones, Jr.—no fire-eater, for after all he had graduated from Princeton and from Harvard Law School—spoke of the development of antagonistic cultures in North and South: "In this country have arisen two races [i.e., Northerners and Southerners] which, although claiming a common parentage, have been so entirely separated by climate, by morals, by religion, and by estimates so totally opposite to all that constitutes honor, truth, and manliness, that they cannot longer exist under the same government."

Spokesmen for the free-labor ideology—which had become the dominant political force in the North by 1860—reciprocated these sentiments. The South, said Theodore Parker, was "the foe to Northern Industry—to our mines, our manufactures, and our commerce. . . . She is the foe to our institutions—to our democratic politics in the State, our democratic culture in the school, our democratic work in the community, our democratic equality in the family." Slavery, said William H. Seward, undermined "intelligence, vigor, and energy" in both blacks and whites. It produced "an exhausted soil, old and decaying towns, wretchedly neglected roads . . . an absence of enterprise and improvement." Slavery was therefore "incompatible with all . . . the elements of the security, welfare, and greatness of nations." The struggle between free labor and slavery, between North and South, said Seward in his most famous speech, was "an irrepressible conflict between two opposing and enduring forces." The United States was therefore two nations, but it could not remain forever so: it "must and will, sooner or later, become either entirely a slaveholding nation, or entirely a free-labor nation." Abraham Lincoln expressed exactly the same theme in his House Divided speech. Many other Republicans echoed this argument that the struggle, in the words of an Ohio congressman, was "between systems, between civilizations."

These sentiments were no more confined to fire-breathing northern radicals than were southern exceptionalist viewpoints confined to fire-eaters. Lincoln represented the mainstream of his party, which commanded a majority of votes in the North by 1860. The dominant elements in the North and in the lower South believed the United States to be composed of two incompatible civilizations. Southerners believed that survival of their special civilization could be assured only in a separate nation. The creation of the Confederacy was merely a political ratification of an irrevocable separation that had already taken place in the hearts and minds of the people.

The proponents of an assimilationist rather than exceptionalist interpretation of southern history might object that this concept of a separate and unique South existed *only* in hearts and minds. It was a subjective reality, they might argue, not an objective one. Objectively, they would insist, North and South were one people. They shared the same language, the same Constitution, the same legal system, the same commitment to republican political institutions, an interconnected economy, the same predominantly Protestant religion and British ethnic heritage, the same history, the same shared memories of a common struggle for nationhood.

Two recent proponents of the objective similarity thesis are Edward Pessen and the late David Potter. In a long article entitled "How Different from Each Other Were the Antebellum North and South?" Pessen concludes that they "were far more alike than the conventional scholarly wisdom has led us to believe." His evidence for this conclusion consists mainly of quantitative measures of the distribution of wealth and of the socioeconomic status of political officeholders in North and South. He finds that wealth was distributed in a similarly unequal fashion in both sections, that voting requirements were similar, and that voters in both sections elected a similarly disproportionate number of men from the upper economic strata to office. The problem with this argument, of course, is that it could be used to prove many obviously different societies to be similar. France and Germany in 1914 and in 1932 had about the same distribution of wealth and similar habits of electing men from the upper strata to the Assembly or the Reichstag. England and France had a comparable distribution of wealth during most of the 18th century. Turkey and Russia were not dissimilar in these respects in the 19th century. And so on.

David Potter's contention that commonalities of language, religion, law, and political system outweighed differences in other areas is more convincing than the Pessen argument. But the Potter thesis nevertheless begs some important questions. The same similarities prevailed between England and her North American colonies in 1776, but they did not prevent the development of a separate nationalism in the latter. It is not language or law alone that are important, but the uses to which they are put. In the United States of the 1850s, Northerners and Southerners spoke the same language, to be sure, but they were increasingly using this language to revile each other. Language became an instrument of division, not unity. The same was true of the political system. So also of the law: Northern states passed personal liberty laws to defy a national Fugitive Slave Law supported by the South; a Southern-dominated Supreme Court denied the right of Congress to exclude slavery from the territories, a ruling that most Northerners considered an infamous distortion of the Constitution. As for a shared commitment to Protestantism, this too had become a divisive rather than unifying factor, with the two largest denominations—

Methodist and Baptist—having split into hostile southern and northern churches over the question of slavery, and the third largest—Presbyterian—having split partly along sectional lines and partly on the question of slavery. As for a shared historical commitment to republicanism, by the 1850s this too was more divisive than unifying. Northern Republicans interpreted this commitment in a free-soil context, while most Southerners continued to insist that one of the most cherished tenets of republican liberty was the right of property—including property in slaves.

There is another dimension of the Potter thesis—or perhaps it would be more accurate to call it a separate Potter thesis—that might put us on the right track to solving the puzzle of southern exceptionalism. After challenging most notions of southern distinctiveness,

Potter concluded that the principal characteristic distinguishing the South from the rest of the country was the persistence of a "folk culture" in the South. This gemeinschaft society, with its emphasis on tradition, rural life, close kinship ties, a hierarchical social structure, ascribed status, patterns of deference, and masculine codes of honor and chivalry, persisted in the South long after the North began moving toward a gesellschaft society with its impersonal, bureaucratic meritocratic, urbanizing, commercial, industrializing, mobile, and rootless characteristics. Above all, the South's folk culture valued tradition and stability and felt threatened by change; the North's modernizing culture enshrined change as progress and condemned the South as backward.

A critic of this gemeinschaft-gesellschaft dichotomy might contend that it was more myth

The impressive growth and prosperity of towns like Rochester, N.Y. were thought by Northerners to provide tangible proof of the superiority of free labor over slavery.

than reality. One might respond to such criticism by pointing out that human behavior is often governed more by myth—that is, by people's perceptions of the world—than by objective reality. Moreover, there *were* real and important differences between North and South by the mid-19th century, differences that might support the gemeinschaft-gesellschaft contrast.

The North was more urban than the South and was urbanizing at a faster rate. In 1820, 10 percent of the free-state residents lived in urban areas compared with 5 percent in the slave states; by 1860 the figures were 26 percent and 10 percent respectively. Even more striking was the growing contrast between farm and non-farm occupations in the two sections. In 1800, 82 percent of the southern labor force worked in agriculture compared with 68 percent in the free states. By 1860 the northern share had dropped to 40 percent while the southern proportion had actually increased slightly, to 84 percent. Southern agriculture remained traditionally labor-intensive while northern agriculture became increasingly capital-intensive and mechanized. By 1860 the free states had nearly twice the value of farm machinery per acre and per farm worker as the slave states. And the pace of industrialization in the North far outstripped that in the South. In 1810 the slave states had an estimated 31 percent of the capital invested in manufacturing in the United States; by 1840 this had declined to 20 percent and by 1860 to 16 percent. In 1810 the North had two and a half times the amount per capita invested in manufacturing as the South; by 1860 this had increased to three and a half times as much.

A critic of the inferences drawn from these data might point out that in many respects the differences between the free states east and west of the Appalachians were nearly or virtually as great as those between North and South, yet these differences did not produce a sense of separate nationality in East and West. This point is true—as far as it goes. While the western free states at midcentury did have a higher proportion of workers employed in non-farm occupations than the South, they had about the same percentage of urban population and the same amount per capita invested in manufacturing. But the crucial factor was *the rate of change*. The West was urbanizing and industrializing more rapidly than either the Northeast or the South. Therefore while North and South as a whole were growing relatively farther apart, the eastern and western free states were drawing closer together. This frustrated southern hopes for an alliance with the Old Northwest on grounds of similarity of agrarian interests. From 1840 to 1860 the rate of urbanization in the West was three times greater than in the Northeast and four times greater than in the South. The amount of capital invested in manufacturing grew twice as fast in the West as in the Northeast and nearly three times as fast as in the South. The same was true of employment in non-farm occupations. The railroad-building boom of the 1850s tied the Northwest to the Northeast with links of iron and shifted the dominant pattern of inland trade from a North-South to an East-West orientation. The remarkable growth of cities like Chicago, Cincinnati, Cleveland, and Detroit with their farm machinery, food-processing, machine-tool, and railroad equipment industries foreshadowed the emergence of the industrial Midwest and helped to assure that when the crisis of the Union came in 1861 the West joined the East instead of the South.

According to the most recent study of antebellum southern industry, the southern lag in this category of development resulted not from any inherent economic disadvantages—not shortage of capital, nor low rates of return, nor non-adaptability of slave labor—but from the choices of Southerners who had money to invest it in agriculture and slaves rather than in manufacturing. In the 1780s Thomas Jefferson had praised farmers as the "peculiar deposit for substantial and genuine virtue" and warned against the industrial classes in cities as sores on the body politic. In 1860 many southern leaders still felt the same way; as Louis Wigfall put it in the passage quoted earlier, "we want no manufactures; we desire no trading, no mechanical or manufacturing classes."

Partly as a consequence of this attitude, the South received only a trickle of the great antebellum stream of immigration. Fewer than one eighth of the immigrants settled in slave states, where the foreign-born percentage of the population was less than a fourth of the North's percentage. The South's white population was ethnically more homogeneous and less cosmopolitan than the North's. The traditional patriarchal family and tight kinship networks typical of gemeinschaft societies, reinforced in the South by a relatively high rate of cousin marriages, also persisted much more strongly in the 19th-century South than in the North.

The greater volume of immigration to the free states contributed to the faster rate of population growth there than in the South. Another factor in this differential growth rate was out-migration from the South. During the middle decades of the 19th century, twice as many whites left the South for the North as vice versa. These facts did not go unnoticed at the time; indeed, they formed the topic of much public comment. Northerners cited the differential in population growth as evidence for the superiority of the free-labor system; Southerners perceived it with alarm as evidence of their declining minority status in the nation. These perceptions became important factors in the growing sectional self-consciousness that led to secession.

The most crucial demographic difference between North and South, of course, resulted from slavery. Ninety-five percent of the country's black people lived in the slave states, where blacks constituted one third of the population in contrast to their one percent of the northern population. The implications of this for the economy and social structure of the two sections, not to mention their ideologies and politics, are obvious and require little elaboration here. Two brief points are worth emphasizing, however. First, historians in recent years have discovered the viability of Afro-American culture under slavery. They have noted that black music, folklore, speech patterns, religion, and other manifestations of this culture influenced white society in the South. Since the Afro-American culture was preeminently a folk culture with an emphasis on oral tradition and other non-literate forms of ritual and communication, it reinforced the persistence of a traditional, gemeinschaft, folk-oriented society in the South.

Second, a number of recent historians have maintained that Northerners were as committed to white supremacy as Southerners. This may have been true, but the scale of concern with this matter in the South was so much greater as to constitute a different order of magnitude and to contribute more than any other factor to the difference between North and South. And of course slavery was more than an institution of racial control. Its centrality to many aspects of life focused southern politics almost exclusively on defense of the institution—to the point that, in the words of the *Charleston Mercury* in 1858, "on the subject of slavery . . . the North and South . . . are not only two Peoples, but they are rival, hostile Peoples."

The fear that slavery was being hemmed in and threatened with destruction contributed to the defensive-aggressive style of Southern political behavior. This aggressiveness sometimes took physical form. Southern whites were more likely to carry weapons and to use them against other human beings than Northerners were. The homicide rate was higher in the South. The phenomenon of dueling persisted longer there. Bertram Wyatt-Brown attributes this to the unique southern code of honor based on traditional patriarchal values of courtesy, status, courage, family, and the symbiosis of shame and pride. The enforcement of order through the threat and practice of violence also resulted from the felt need to control a large slave population.

Martial values and practices were more pervasive in the South than in the North. Marcus Cunliffe has argued to the contrary, but the evidence confutes him. Cunliffe's argument is based mainly on two sets of data: the prevalence of militia and volunteer military companies in the free as well as in the slave states; and the proportion of West Pointers and regular army officers from the two sections. Yet the first set of data do not support his thesis, and the second contradict it. Cunliffe does present evidence on the popularity of military companies in northern cities, but nowhere does he estimate the comparative numbers of such companies in North and South or the number of men in proportion to population who belonged to them. If such comparative evidence could be assembled, it would probably support the traditional view of a higher concentration of such companies in the South. What northern city, for example, could compare with Charleston, which had no fewer than twenty-two military companies in the late 1850s—one for every two hundred white men of military age? Another important quasi-military institution in the South with no northern counterpart escaped Cunliffe's attention—the slave patrol, which gave tens of thousands of Southerners a more practical form of military experience than the often ceremonial functions of volunteer drill companies could do.

As for the West Point alumni and regular army officers it is true, as Cunliffe points out, that about 60 percent of these were from the North and only 40 percent from the South in the late antebellum decades. What he fails to note is that the South had only about 30 percent of the nation's white population during this era, so that on a proportional basis the South was overrepresented in these categories. Moreover, from 1849 to 1861 all of the secretaries of war were Southerners, as were the general in chief of the army, two of the three brigadier generals, all but one commander of the army's geographical departments on the eve of the Civil War, the authors of the two manuals on infantry tactics and of the artillery manual used at West Point, and the professor who taught tactics and strategy at the military academy.

Other evidence supports the thesis of a significant martial tradition in the South contrasted with a concentration in different professions in the North. More than three fifths of the volunteer soldiers in the Mexican War came from the slave states—on a per capita basis, four times the proportion of free-state volunteers. Seven of the eight military "colleges" (not including West Point and Annapolis) listed in the 1860 census were in the slave states. A study of the occupations of antebellum men chronicled in the *Dictionary of American Biography* found that the military profession claimed twice the percentage of Southerners as of Northerners, while this ratio was reversed for men distinguished in literature, art, medicine, and education. In business the per capita proportion of Yankees was three times as great, and among engineers and inventors it was six times as large. When Southerners labeled themselves a nation of warriors and Yankees a nation of shopkeepers—a common comparison in 1860—or when Jefferson Davis told a London *Times* correspondent in 1861 that "we are a military people," they were not just whistling Dixie.

One final comparison of objective differences is in order—a comparison of education and literacy in North and South. Contemporaries perceived this as a matter of importance. The South's alleged backwardness in schooling and its large numbers of illiterates framed one of the principal free-soil indictments of slavery. This was one area in which a good many Southerners admitted inferiority and tried to do something about it. But in 1860, after a decade of school reform in the South, the slave states still had only half the North's proportion of white children enrolled in public and private schools, and the length of the annual school term in the South was only a little more than half as long as in the North. Of course education did not take place solely in school. But other forms of education—in the home, at church, through lyceums and public lectures, by apprenticeship, and so on—were also more active in North than South. According to the census of 1860, per capita newspaper circulation was three times greater in the North, and the number of library volumes per white person was nearly twice as large.

The proportion of illiterate white people was three times greater in the South than in the North; if the black population is included, as indeed it should be, the percentage of illiterates was seven or eight times as high in the South. In the free states, what two recent historians have termed an "ideology of literacy" prevailed—a commitment to education as an instrument of social mobility, economic prosperity, progress, and freedom. While this ideology also existed in the South, especially in the 1850s, it was much weaker there and made slow headway against the inertia of a rural folk culture. "The Creator did not intend that every individual human being should be highly cultivated," wrote William Harper of South Carolina. "It is better that a part should be fully and highly educated and the rest utterly ignorant." Commenting on a demand by northern workingmen for universal public education, the *Southern Review* asked: "Is this the way to produce producers? To make every child in the state a literary character would not be a good qualification for those who must live by manual labor."

The ideology of literacy in the North was part of a larger ferment that produced an astonishing number of reform movements, which aroused both contempt and fear in the South. Southern whites viewed the most dynamic of these movements—abolitionism—as a threat to their very existence. Southerners came to distrust the whole concept of "progress" as it seemed to be understood in the North. *DeBow's Review* declared in 1851: "Southern life, habits, thoughts, and aims, are

so essentially different from those of the North, that here a different character of books . . . and training is required." A Richmond newspaper warned in 1855 that Southerners must stop reading northern newspapers and books and stop sending their sons to colleges in the North, where "every village has its press and its lecture room, and each lecturer and editor, unchecked by a healthy public opinion, opens up for discussion all the received dogmas of faith," where unwary youth are "exposed to the danger of imbibing doctrines subversive of all old institutions." Young men should be educated instead in the South "where their training would be moral, religious, and conservative, and they would never learn, or read a word in school or out of school, inconsistent with orthodox Christianity, pure morality, the right of property, and sacredness of marriage."

In all of the areas discussed above—urbanization, industrialization, labor force, demographic structure, violence and martial values, education, and attitudes toward change—contemporaries accurately perceived significant differences between North and South, differences that in most respects were increasing over time. The question remains: were these differences crucial enough to make the South an exception to generalizations about antebellum America?

This essay concludes by suggesting a tentative answer to the question: Perhaps it was the *North* that was "different," the North that departed from the mainstream of historical development; and perhaps therefore we should speak not of southern exceptionalism but of northern exceptionalism. This idea is borrowed shamelessly from C. Vann Woodward, who applied it, however, to the post–Civil War United States. In essays written during the 1950s on "The Irony of Southern History" and "The Search for Southern Identity," Woodward suggested that, unlike other Americans but like most people in the rest of the world, Southerners had experienced poverty, failure, defeat, and had a skepticism about "progress" that grows out of such experiences. The South thus shared a bond with the rest of humankind that other Americans did not share. This theme of northern exceptionalism might well be applied also to the antebellum United States—not for Woodward's categories of defeat, poverty, and failure, but for the categories of a persistent folk culture discussed in this essay.

At the beginning of the republic the North and South were less different in most of these categories than they became later. Nearly all northern states had slavery in 1776, and the institution persisted in some of them for decades thereafter. The ethnic homogeneity of northern and southern whites was quite similar before 1830. The proportion of urban dwellers was similarly small and the percentage of the labor force employed in agriculture similarly large in 1800. The northern predominance in commerce and manufacturing was not so great as it later became. Nor was the contrast in education and literacy as great as it subsequently became. A belief in progress and commitments to reform or radicalism were no more prevalent in the North than in the South in 1800—indeed, they may have been less so. In 1776, in 1800, even as late as 1820, similarity in values and institutions was the salient fact. Within the next generation, difference and conflict became prominent. This happened primarily because of developments in the North. The South changed relatively little, and because so many northern changes seemed threatening, the South developed a defensive ideology that resisted change.

In most of these respects the South resembled a majority of the societies in the world more than the changing North did. Despite the abolition of legal slavery or serfdom throughout much of the western hemisphere and western Europe, much of the world—like the South—had an unfree or quasi-free labor force. Most societies in the world remained predominantly rural, agricultural, and labor-intensive; most, including even several European countries, had illiteracy rates as high or higher than the South's 45 percent; most like the South remained bound by traditional values and networks of family, kinship, hierarchy, and patriarchy. The North—along with a few countries in northwestern Europe—hurtled forward eagerly toward a future that many Southerners found distasteful if not frightening; the South remained proudly and even defiantly rooted in the past.

Thus when secessionists protested in 1861 that they were acting to preserve traditional rights and values, they were correct. They fought to protect their constitutional liberties against the perceived northern threat to overthrow them. The South's concept of republicanism had not changed in three quarters of a century; the North's had. With complete sincerity the South fought to preserve its version of the republic of the founding fathers—a government of limited powers that protected the rights of property and whose constituency comprised an independent gentry and yeomanry of the white race undisturbed by large cities, heartless factories, restless free workers, and class conflict. The accession to power of the Republican party, with its ideology of competitive, egalitarian, free-labor capitalism, was a signal to the South that the northern majority had turned irrevocably toward this frightening, revolutionary future. Indeed, the Black Republican party appeared to the eyes of many Southerners as "essentially a revolutionary party" composed of "a motley throng of Sans culottes . . . Infidels and freelovers, interspersed by Bloomer women, fugitive slaves, and amalgamationists." Therefore secession was a preemptive counterrevolution to prevent the Black Republican revolution from engulfing the South. "*We* are not revolutionists," insisted James B. D. De Bow and Jefferson Davis during the Civil War. "We are resisting revolution. . . . We are not engaged in a Quixotic fight for the rights of man; our struggle is for inherited rights. . . . We are upholding the true doctrines of the Federal Constitution. We are conservative."

Union victory in the war destroyed the southern vision of America and ensured that the northern vision would become the American vision. Until 1861, however, it was the North that was out of the mainstream, not the South. Of course the northern states, along with Britain and a few countries in northwestern Europe, were cutting a new channel in world history that would doubtless have become the mainstream even if the American Civil War had not happened. But it did happen, and for Americans it marked the turning point. A Louisiana planter who returned home sadly after the war wrote in 1865: "Society has been completely changed by the war. The [French] revolution of '89 did not produce a greater change in the 'Ancien Regime' than has this in our social life." And four years later George Ticknor, a retired Harvard professor, concluded that the Civil War had created a "great gulf between what happened before in our century and what has happened since, or what is likely to happen hereafter. It does not seem to me as if I were living in the country in which I was born." From the war sprang the great flood that wrenched the stream of American history into a new channel and transferred the burden of exceptionalism from North to South.

Part Eleven

Why the North Won and the South Lost

When hostilities began in 1861, each side expected to win, and both expected the contest to be brief. What followed instead was a long, destructive struggle and the loss of 600,000 lives. Ever since, this most cataclysmic episode in American history has been examined with intense scrutiny and commemorated and romanticized to a degree unmatched by any other war in modern times. Those aspects of the war that have been pored over in closest detail have been the battles and campaigns, the generals and armies of both the Federal and Confederate sides. Perhaps the best known historian to most Americans, the late Bruce Catton, has written voluminously and skillfully about the military history of the conflict.

Although the battlefield may be the place where the actual fighting occurred and where the outcome was formally decided, it was not necessarily where the result of the struggle was determined. Modern warfare involves societies, not just armies. Consequently, the decisive factor is how a society wages war, not simply how its soldiers fight battles. What happens behind the lines is probably more significant. Thus, accounting for why one side prevailed over the other requires the historian to move beyond the military aspects of the contest to engage in a wider ranging and more complex analysis. This will involve consideration of, for example, the material resources of the rival protaganists, their respective ability to mobilize the assets they already possess, the nature of the cause they are fighting for, and the effectiveness of their political leadership. All these elements play a critical, perhaps decisive, role.

The task of the historian therefore becomes increasingly difficult as the scope of his inquiry fans out from the field of carnage at Antietam and the grim siege of Vicksburg. And, as in any other topic of historical analysis, the historian has to consider all these contributory factors and then generalize about them. This act of generalization is called a *historical explanation,* and it will probably be reached in one of two ways. The historian may arrange all the various and often conflicting elements into a formulation that will tie them together and make sense of the relationships among them. Alternatively, one of the factors in the equation may seem to be so overridingly important that it proves to be determinative. Thus, the historian might conclude that one side had such an overwhelming superiority or deficiency in a particular area that, no matter what its other capabilities were, this single aspect suffices to explain the outcome.

The two selections on this topic deal with this larger question that goes beyond the purely military in explaining the result of the Civil War. Interestingly, they also offer explanations based on the two different kinds of generalizations just described. The reader, however, will have to determine which one is which.

George Fredrickson of Stanford University focuses his attention on the North and discusses the resources available to it in the form of manpower and material assets. But he does not stop there and claim simply that the North had a decisive quantitative advantage. Instead, he suggests that such a superiority did not in itself adequately explain the northern victory. He concludes that something more was involved, namely, that the Northerners had an attitude of mind and a set of values that enabled the section to build on its assets in a fashion that was, in effect, exponential. This outlook meant that, as the war continued, the North actually grew stronger.

Professor Fredrickson engages the question of why the North won, but Kenneth Stampp of the University of California at Berkeley investigates the flip side of the coin—why the South lost. Although seeking an explanation in the South rather than in the North, Professor Stampp nevertheless follows the same path as George Fredrickson by concentrating on the attitudes of the Southerners. He finds, however, that there was a particular feature that was crucial to the southern war effort. This was a widespread ambivalence about fighting a war to preserve slavery. Nonslaveholders as well as many slaveholders themselves seemed not to be thoroughly committed to the enterprise and appeared unwilling to sacrifice for it. Toward the end of his article, he expands his analysis into the post-war era when the slaves were emancipated and the South placed under Reconstruction. He then suggests that, after the war, when the struggle was over white supremacy rather than slavery, the white South was far more invested and prepared to resist to the bitter end. This is an observation to be borne in mind when the scene shifts to Reconstruction in the next topic.

QUESTIONS TO CONSIDER

1. Why does Fredrickson think that the North's material superiority is an insufficient explanation for its victory in the war?

2. How convincing do you consider Stampp's account of why the South failed to win?

3. Which do you think is the more effective and revealing approach to explaining the outcome of the Civil War—to ask why the North won or why the South lost?

Blue Over Gray:
Why the North Won

George M. Fredrickson

Historians have expended vast amounts of time, energy, and ingenuity searching for the causes and consequences of the Civil War. Much less effort has been devoted to explaining the outcome of the war itself. Yet the question is obviously important. One only has to imagine how radically different the future of North America would have been had the South won its permanent independence. It is also possible that a full comparison of how the two sides responded to the ultimate test of war will shed reflex light on both the background and legacy of the conflict. If northern success and southern failure can be traced to significant differences in the two societies as they existed on the eve of the war, then we may have further reason for locating the origins of the war in the clash of divergent social systems and ideologies. If the relative strengths of the North in wartime were rooted in the character of its society, then the sources of northern victory would foreshadow, to some extent at least, the postwar development of a nation reunited under northern hegemony.

A number of plausible explanations of "why the North won" have been advanced. The problem with most of them is not that they are wrong but that they are partial or incomplete. What is needed is not the unearthing of new "factors" propelling the South down the road to Appomattox but a broader frame of reference allowing for a synthesis of these familiar explanations into a more comprehensive interpretation.

*   *   *

Since both societies faced unprecedented challenges, success would depend to a great extent on which side had the greater ability to adjust to new situations. Key elements in such an adjustment would be the readiness to innovate and the capacity to organize. Lincoln summed up a characteristic northern attitude in his Annual Message to Congress on December 1, 1862: "The dogmas of the quiet past, are inadequate to the stormy present. The occasion is piled high with difficulty, and we must rise with the occasion. As our case is new, we must think anew. We must disenthrall ourselves, and then we shall save our country."

Lincoln himself set the pattern for precedent-breaking innovation. Whenever he felt obligated to assume extra-constitutional powers to deal with situations unforeseen by the Constitution, he did so with little hesitation. After the outbreak of the war and before

From "Blue Over Gray: Sources of Success and Failure in the Civil War" by George M. Fredrickson in *A Nation Divided: Problems and Issues of the Civil War and Reconstruction,* edited by George M. Fredrickson (Minneapolis: Burgess Publishing Company, 1975). Reprinted by permission of the author.

Congress was in session to sanction his actions, he expanded the regular army, advanced public money to private individuals, and declared martial law on a line from Washington to Philadelphia. On September 24, 1862, again without Congressional authorization, he extended the jurisdiction of martial law and suspended the writ of habeas corpus in all cases of alleged disloyalty. The Emancipation Proclamation can also be seen as an example of extra-constitutional innovation. Acting under the amorphous concept of "the war powers" of the President, Lincoln struck at slavery primarily because "military necessity" dictated new measures to disrupt the economic and social system of the enemy. There was bitter opposition in some quarters to such unprecedented assertions of executive power, but a majority in Congress and in the country accepted the argument of necessity and supported the President's actions.

The spirit of innovation was manifested in other areas as well. In Grant and Sherman the North finally found generals who grasped the nature of modern war and were ready to jettison outworn rules of strategy and tactics. "If men make war in slavish observance of rules, they will fail. . . ," said Grant in summing up his military philosophy. "War is progressive, because all the instruments and elements of war are progressive." In his march from Atlanta to the sea in the fall of 1864, Sherman introduced for the first time the modern strategy of striking directly at the enemy's domestic economy. The coordinated, multipronged offensive launched by Grant in 1864, of which Sherman's march was a critical component, was probably the biggest, boldest, and most complex military operation mounted anywhere before the 20th century. Grant, like Lincoln, can be seen as embodying the North's capacity for organization and innovation.

The necessity of supplying and servicing the massive Union army also led to some startling departures from traditional practices. When necessary, railroads were seized and operated by the government. (Some were even built by the government.) Federal administration of the railroads not only facilitated the movement of men and materials but also helped unify the nation's system by connecting separated lines and standardizing gauges. The need to care for hordes of wounded men led to a number of innovations and improvements in medical services. The building and operation of great military hospitals both encouraged the rapid development of new therapeutic methods and helped revolutionize hospital administration. Major advances in the science of sanitation as well as aid in the distribution of medical supplies took place under the auspices of the United States Sanitary Commission, an extraordinary instrument of private philanthropy operating on a national scale.

Businessmen also responded to the crisis and found that what was patriotic could also be highly profitable. There were the inevitable frauds perpetrated on the government by contractors, but more significant was the overall success of the industrial system in producing the goods required. Since manufacturers in many lines now had a guaranteed national market, they had every incentive to expand operations and increase efficiency. A new kind of large-scale industrial enterprise began to come into existence as entrepreneurial energies responded vigorously to new opportunities. Military demand encouraged expansion and consolidation in such industries as iron and steel, ready-to-wear clothing, shoes, meat packing, and even pocket watches. The reaper industry underwent a huge expansion, as farmers, adjusting to a wartime labor shortage, mechanized their operations and actually increased production of grains to such an extent that they not only met the domestic need but exported enough to make up for the slack in American exports caused by the blockade of southern cotton. On the whole, the northern economy adapted so successfully to war that the nation enjoyed increasing prosperity on the home front in the very midst of civil war.

Matthew Brady's photograph, taken at City Point, Virginia, in 1864, shows the amount of arms and equipment available to General U. S. Grant in his campaign through northern Virginia to take Richmond, the Confederate capital.

No small part of this success was due to the willingness of businessmen, farmers, and government procurement officials to "think and act anew" by organizing themselves into larger and more efficient units for the production, transportation, and allocation of goods.

It would be an understatement to say that the South demonstrated less capacity than the North for organization and innovation. In fact, the South's most glaring failures were precisely in the area of coordination and collective adaptation to new conditions. The Confederacy did, of course, manage to put an army in the field that was able to hold the North at

bay for four years. And it kept that army reasonably well supplied with arms, mainly as a result of the prodigious efforts of Josiah Gorgas, chief of the Confederate Bureau of Ordnance. Gorgas, a Pennsylvanian by birth, was probably the South's boldest and most effective organizer and innovator. From nothing, he personally built up a modern munitions industry sufficient to meet the needs of the Confederate army. But Gorgas was quite exceptional; there were few others like him in the Confederacy. Southern successes on the battlefield were in no real sense triumphs of organization or innovation. Before the rise of Grant and Sherman, most Civil War battles were fought according to the outdated tactical principles that generals on both sides had learned at West Point. In these very conventional battles, the South had the advantage because it had the most intelligent and experienced of the West Pointers. Since everyone played by the same rules, it was inevitable that those who could play the game best would win. When the rules were changed by Grant and Sherman, the essential conservatism and rigidity of southern military leadership became apparent.

Besides being conventional in their tactics, southern armies were notoriously undisciplined; insubordination was an everyday occurrence and desertion eventually became a crippling problem. There were so many men absent without leave by August 1, 1863, that a general amnesty for deserters had to be declared. For full effectiveness, southern soldiers had to be commanded by generals such as Robert E. Lee and Stonewall Jackson, charismatic leaders who could command the personal loyalty and respect of their men. The idea of obeying an officer simply because of his rank went against the southern grain.

Although the army suffered from the excessive individualism of its men and the narrow traditionalism of its officers, these defects were not fatal until very late in the war, mainly because it took the North such a long time to apply its characteristic talent for organization and innovation directly to military operations. But on the southern home front similar attitudes had disastrous consequences almost from the beginning. In its efforts to mobilize the men and resources of the South, the Confederate government was constantly hamstrung by particularistic resistance to central direction and by a general reluctance to give up traditional ideas and practices incompatible with the necessities of war.

Particularism was manifested most obviously in the refusal of state governments to respond to the needs of the Confederacy. The central government was rudely rebuffed when it sought in 1861 to get the states to give up control over the large quantity of arms in their possession. The states held back for their own defense most of the 350,000 small arms that they held. The Confederacy, initially able to muster only 190,000 weapons, was forced to turn down 200,000 volunteers in the first year of the war because it could not arm them. The states also held back men. In 1862, when McClellan was threatening Richmond, the approximately 100,000 men held in state service were unavailable for defending the Confederate capital or for any other significant military operations. When manpower problems forced the adoption of conscription in 1862, some southern governors worked openly and successfully to obstruct it. Governor Brown of Georgia came close to resorting to the old southern tactic of nullification in his efforts to prevent Georgians from being drafted to fight for the Confederacy. After his stance of outright defiance was declared unconstitutional by the state Supreme Court, Brown resorted to more devious tactics. Noting that the Confederate conscription law exempted public officials and militia officers, Brown proceeded to appoint men of draft age in large numbers to nominal public offices and made wholesale promotions from enlisted to officer rank in the militia. In 1864 when Sherman was besieging Atlanta, Brown still refused to place his 10,000-man state army under Confederate command and thus withheld it from the defense of his own capital. State governments also hindered Confederate efforts to provide the army with adequate supplies of food and clothing. Some states insisted on provisioning only their own troops. North Carolina, the center of the southern cotton industry, reserved the production of its mills almost exclusively for North Carolina regiments. In the last days of the war when Lee's army was fighting in rags, North Carolina was still holding in its warehouses 92,000 uniforms, along with thousands of blankets, tents, and shoes.

It would be misleading, however, to attach too much importance to the states' rights philosophy per se as a source of difficulties of this kind. In much the same way that states' rights had been used as a facade for the social and economic interests of slaveholders before the war, it was utilized during the war by local interests that wished to avoid effective regulation. These interests found it easier to manipulate state governments than to deal with Richmond. A case in point is the history of attempts to regulate the shippers engaged in running the Union blockade. Blockade runners made their greatest profits when they imported luxury goods for the open market and exported privately owned cotton. The vital interests of the Confederacy demanded, on the other hand, that priority be given to the importation of war materials and the export of cotton the government had acquired through loans and taxation "in kind." The blockade runners, with the connivance of state governments, had great success in foiling Confederate efforts to control their cargoes. In 1863, shipowners were finally pressured into an agreement to rent one third of the space on every vessel to the Conferate government. But they quickly nullified this arrangement by allowing themselves to be chartered by the states, a device that effectively froze out Confederate goods. In 1864, Richmond made another attempt to gain control of shipping, this time passing a law that enabled President Davis to reserve one half the cargo space on all outgoing and incoming ships. The result was a strike of the blockade runners lasting several weeks, which did serious damage to an already crumbling economy. The state governments condoned and even supported the strike because they regarded the shippers as local interests to be regulated, if at all, by the states rather than the central government. In this instance, states' rights and laissez faire economic attitudes combined to favor private interests over public needs.

The South's strong commitment to economic laissez faire hindered the Confederate cause even more dramatically in railroad policy. Although the Confederacy had a more pressing need than the North to make effective use of its limited rail facilities, it was slower to assert direct control over the system. For most of the war, the government tried ineffectually to control the railroads through a series of voluntary agreements. Not until February 1865 was it given the right to seize and operate the lines. Thus shipping and railroads, the external and internal lifelines of the Confederacy, resisted effective control and coordination until the war was already lost—striking examples of how economic particularism impeded the South's struggle for independence.

The southern interest that might have been expected to make the greatest sacrifices for the cause was the interest for which many believed the war was being fought. But the slaveholding planters, taken as a group, were no more able to rise above narrow and selfish concerns than other segments of southern society. Because of their influence, the Confederacy was unable to adopt a sound financial policy; land and slaves, the main resources of the South, remained immune from direct taxes. As a result, the government was only able to raise about 1 percent of its revenue from taxation; the rest came from loans and the printing of vast quantities of fiat paper money. The inevitable consequence was the catastrophic runaway inflation that made Confederate money almost worthless even before the government went out of existence. Besides resisting the taxation of their wealth, planters fought bitterly against efforts to regulate what they raised on their land, battled and obstructed attempts to impress their food crops to meet the urgent needs of the Confederate commissary, and vehemently refused to cooperate in plans to make use of slaves for public purposes. Strong planter opposition to the impressment of slaves was a principal factor in the failure of the Confederacy to gain control over a third of its manpower. Had planters not feared the loss of immediate control over their bondsmen or suspected that they might be "damaged" in government service, the Confederacy could have drawn on a large pool of forced labor for the construction of railroads, the building of fortifications, and even the production of goods. One of the South's most damaging manpower shortages was the lack of sufficient factory workers, too many of whom had been drafted into the army. Slaves were not conscripted to fill this void despite the fact that prewar experience had provided ample evidence that slaves could be used successfully in manufacturing. Without giving up slavery as an institution or taking the desperate gamble of arming blacks in the hope that they would fight for the South, the Confederacy could have made substantial use of slaves as a flexible and mobile labor force capable of being allocated to those sectors of the war economy that most needed labor. As it was, planters kept too many of their slaves at home, where, because of a shortage of overseers and the impending approach of northern armies, they became increasingly unproductive and difficult to control. It was not devotion to slavery per se that accounts for this situation but rather a peculiarly limited and narrow-minded concept of slavery as an institution necessarily linked to agriculture and a plantation environment.

Southern particularism and rigidity were also manifested in the area of public safety and internal security. Although the South had a much more severe disloyalty problem than the North, Davis resorted to martial law and suspension of the writ of habeas corpus more sparingly than Lincoln. Unwilling to declare martial law on his own authority, as Lincoln had done, Davis awaited Congressional authorization, which was given only reluctantly and in small doses. The Confederate President was allowed to suspend the writ during three brief periods totaling sixteen months and then only in limited geographical areas. As a result of this cautious use of executive power, Unionist guerrilla movements were able to thrive in the mountainous backcountry of the South, and large numbers of conscripts were released from military service by state judges who registered their belief in the unconstitutionality of the draft by freely issuing writs of habeas corpus to inductees. Thus, while the Lincoln administration was arresting and holding without trial thousands of allegedly disloyal northerners and also surpressing unfriendly newspapers, the Confederate government made little effort to counter even the most flagrant manifestations of dissent, divisiveness, and sedition. This contrast can scarcely be attributed to a greater southern devotion to civil liberties. Prewar critics of slavery had learned how narrow the limits of southern tolerance could be. The southern majority did not object to the forcible suppression of unpopular individuals, groups, and opinions, but its strong commitment to localism made it reluctant to see such powers exercised by a central government. In staunchly pro-Confederate areas, outright disloyalty could be dealt with by time-honored vigilante methods. But local pressures were unavailing against whole districts, such as portions of eastern Tennessee and western North Carolina, where a majority of the population had remained loyal to the Union.

Taking all the evidence into account, it seems safe to conclude that the South lost the war primarily because it had fewer sources of cohesion then the North and less aptitude for innovation. In political, economic, social, and even military spheres, the North demonstrated a greater capacity for organization and creative adaptation. The North fought the war progressively, readily making major adjustments and accepting new policies whenever change promised to bring results. The South fought on the whole regressively, learning little and compounding its errors. It was hampered and eventually defeated by a particularistic ethos that made it difficult and sometimes impossible for Southerners to discard traditional habits and attitudes even when they were obviously detrimental to the cause.

The description of these behavioral patterns might seem to provide a sufficient answer to our initial question. But there is the further problem of explaining precisely why the North and South responded so differently to the challenges they faced. What was there about the culture and social structure of the North that made possible the kinds of organizational initiatives and daring innovations that have been described? What was there about southern society and culture that explains the lack of cohesiveness and adaptability that doomed the Confederacy? Answers to such questions require some further understanding of the differences in northern and southern society on the eve of the war, especially as these differences related to war-making potential.

A fuller comprehension of what social strengths and weaknesses the two sides brought to the conflict can perhaps be gained by borrowing a well-known concept from the social sciences—the idea of modernization. Sociologists and political scientists often employ this term to describe the interrelated changes that occur when a whole society begins to move away from a traditional agrarian pattern toward an urban-industrial system. There is a growing tendency, however, to see modernization as an open-ended and relative process rather than as the stereotyped evolution from one fixed state to another. According to this formulation, societies can be relatively modernized or nonmodernized, but there are no existing models of either perfect modernity, or, in recent history at least, of societies organized on a large scale that totally lack modernizing tendencies.

One recent student of the subject describes the concept as follows:

> Modernization . . . refers to the dynamic form that the age-old process of innovation has assumed as a result of the explosive proliferation of knowledge in recent centuries. It owes its special significance both to its dynamic character and to the universality of its impact on human affairs. It stems initially from an attitude, a belief that society can and should be transformed, that change is desirable. If a definition is necessary, "modernization" may be defined as the process by which historically evolved in-

stitutions are adapted to the rapidly changing functions that reflect the unprecedented increased in man's knowledge, permitting control over his environment, that accompanied the scientific revolution.

Another theorist has provided a simple rule of thumb to gauge the extent of modernization in various societies: the higher the proportion of energy derived from inanimate sources, as opposed to the direct application of human and animal strength, the more modernized the society. Modernization therefore has its intellectual foundations in a rationalistic or scientific world view and a commitment to technological development; it comes to fruition in the industrialization of production, the increase of the urban sector relative to the rural, the centralization or consolidation of political, social, and cultural activity, the recruitment of leadership on a basis of merit and efficiency rather than ascribed or hereditary characteristics, and the mobilization of the general population to serve collective ends as defined by a dominant elite.

By any definition of this process, the North was relatively more modernized than the South in 1861. To apply one of the most important indices of modernization, thirty-six percent of the northern population was already urban as compared to the South's nine and six-tenths percent. As we have already seen, there was an even greater gap in the extent of industrialization. Furthermore, the foundations had been laid in the northern states for a rapid increase in the pace of modernization. The antebellum "transportation revolution" had set the stage for economic integration on a national scale, and the quickening pace of industrial development foreshadowed the massive and diversified growth of the future. Because of better and cheaper transportation, new markets, and a rise in efficiency and mechanization, midwestern agriculture was in a position to begin playing its modern role as the food-producing adjunct to an urban-industrial society. Literacy was widespread and means of mass communication, such as inexpensively produced newspapers, pamphlets, and books, were available for mobilizing public opinion. The opening up of the political system and the increase of economic opportunities had made rapid social mobility possible, especially in newly developing areas, and had increased the chances that leadership would be based on achievement rather than social background. As the socioeconomic system became more complex, greater specialization of individual and institutional functions was occurring. Organizational skills, developed on the local level in small enterprises and in the numerous voluntary organizations that dominated community life, were ready to be tapped for larger tasks of national integration. In short, given the necessary stimulus and opportunity, the North was ready for a "great leap forward" in the modernization process.

The South, on the other hand, had little potentiality for rapid modernization. Overwhelmingly agricultural and tied to the slave plantation as its basic unit of production, it had many of the characteristics of what today would be called "an underdeveloped society." Like such societies, the Old South had what amounted to a "dual economy": a small modern or capitalistic sector, profitably producing cotton and other commodities for export, coexisted with a vast "traditional" sector, composed of white subsistence farmers and black slaves. The subsistence farmers had no role at all in the market economy, and slaves contributed to it only as a source of labor. Compared with the North, the South relied much more heavily on animate sources of energy, especially the work of slaves using primitive implements. Without substantial urban, commercial, and industrial centers of its own, the southern economy was almost completely dependent on the outside world for the utilization of its products. Large-scale economic diversification and technological progress were inconceivable without revolutionary changes in its social and economic system.

Besides lacking the foundations for the kind of unified and self-sustaining modern economy that was developing in the North, the South was also characterized by a fragmented social order. Most obvious was the radical disjunction between the conditions of life and fundamental interests of white masters and black slaves; but even among whites the dual economy was probably paralleled by something approaching a dual society. It is at least arguable that the outlook and way of life of the rich planters diverged significantly from the folk culture of the backcountry farmers who owned no slaves or only a few. In the North—because of the growing interdependence and diffused prosperity caused by improved communications and market facilities—midwestern farmers, eastern manufacturers, and, to some extent at least, skilled artisans and industrial workers not only felt they had common interests but could also partake of a common culture rooted in the Protestant ethic. Central to their world view was the myth of equal and unlimited opportunity generated by a rapidly growing capitalistic economy in which gross and unfair differences in wealth and privilege had not yet become palpable. The two main segments of the white South were united neither by a sense of common economic interests nor by a complete identity of social and political values. But the presence of millions of black slaves did make possible a perverse kind of solidarity. Fear of blacks, and more specifically of black emancipation, was the principal force holding the white South together. Without it, there could have been no broadly based struggle for independence.

The planter and the non-slaveholding farmer had one other characteristic in common besides racism; in their differing ways, they were both extreme individualists. The planter's individualism came mainly from a lifetime of commanding slaves on isolated plantations. Used to unquestioned authority in all things and prone to think of himself as an aristocrat, he commonly exhibited an indomitable sense of personal independence. The non-slaveholder, on the other hand, was basically a backwoodsman who combined the stiff-necked individualism of the frontier with the arrogance of race that provided him with an exaggerated sense of his personal worth. Southern whites in general, therefore, were conditioned by slavery, racism, and rural isolation to condone and even encourage quasi-anarchic patterns of behavior that could not have been tolerated in a more modernized society with a greater need for social cohesion and discipline. W. J. Cash has provided a graphic description of this syndrome in *The Mind of the South:*

> In focusing the old backcountry pride upon the ideas of the superiority to the Negro and the peerage of the white man, and thereby (fully in the masses, and in some basic way in the planters) divorcing it from the necessity for achievement, [this individualism] inevitably shifted emphasis back upon and lent new impulsion to the purely personal and puerile attitude which distinguishes the frontier outlook everywhere. And when to that was added the natural effect on the planters of virtually unlimited sway over their bondsmen, and the natural effect on the whites of the example of these planters, it eventuated in this: that the individualism of the plantation world would be one which, like that of the backcountry before it, would be far too concerned with the bald, immediate, unsupported assertion of the ego, which placed too great stress on the inviolability of personal whim, and was full of the chip-on shoulder swagger and brag of a boy—one, in brief, by which the essence was the boast, voiced or not, on the part of every Southerner, that he could knock hell out of whoever dared cross him.

Such an attitude was obviously incompatible with the needs of a modernizing society for cooperation and collective innovation. Furthermore, the divorce of status from achievement made it less likely that competent leaders and organizers would emerge. Particularism, localism, and extreme individualism were the natural outgrowth of the South's economic and social system. So was resistance to any changes that posed a threat to slavery and racial domination. A few southern spokesmen of the 1850s did call for collective action to diversify agriculture and promote industrialization. Most of them were militant southern nationalists, deeply committed to the preservation of slavery, who acknowledged the South's vulnerability in any struggle with the more developed North and perceived that the successful establishment of southern independence required a greater degree of modernization. More specifically, they believed that slavery could be combined with urban, commercial, and industrial development. But they probably underestimated the objective barriers to economic diversification and, in any case, made relatively little headway against traditional southern attitudes.

In one category of modernization, it might appear that the South had kept reasonably abreast of the North. If a characteristic of modernizing societies is an increase in the actual or symbolic participation of the general population in the political process, then the upsurge of democratic activity among whites beginning in the age of Jackson might be taken as a sign of southern modernity. Yet southern politics, despite its high level of popular involvement, remained largely the disorganized competition of individual office seekers. Those who won elections usually did so either because they were already men of weight in their communities or because they came off better than their rivals in face-to-face contact with predominantly rural voters. In the North by 1861, politics was less a matter of personalities and more an impersonal struggle of well-organized parties. In urban areas, the rudiments of the modern political machine could already be perceived.

The fact that the South was economically, socially, and politically less "developed" or modernized than the North in 1861 may not by itself fully explain why war had to come, but it does provide a key to understanding why the war had to turn out the way it did. The northern successes and southern failures recounted earlier were not mysterious or accidental. They were predetermined largely by the essential nature of the two societies. The Civil War, despite its insurrectionary origins, rapidly took on the character of a conventional war between two independent nations. In such a war, a relatively modernized society has certain inherent advantages over a relatively undeveloped society. Since the essence of modernization is the acceptance of change as normal and desirable, it follows that the more modernized party in a conflict will be more likely to make radical adjustments and welcome innovations. It can also apply its more highly developed technology to the instruments of warfare. Its greater social mobility and emphasis on achievement will bring to the fore more effective leaders, and its more highly differentiated structure of social and occupational roles will make possible a more efficient allocation of tasks. Finally, and most significantly, its greater political and economic integration gives it a superior ability to exert centralized control over the mobilization of men and resources.

Such a model would appear to account for all or most of the patterns of wartime behavior that have been described. But there is one possible objection to this explanation that must be confronted. Just as the stronger side, as measured in crude physical terms, has not always won in wars of national independence, neither has the more modernized society always emerged triumphant. The recent American experience in Viet Nam provides fresh and dramatic evidence of this possibility. But the war in Viet Nam was essentially a guerrilla war; whenever the Viet Cong attempted to engage in conventional warfare, it was relatively unsuccessful. Had the South chosen at some point to change from conventional to guerrilla warfare, it might have stood a better chance of wearing down the North and gaining its independence. In partisan or guerrilla conflicts, the advantages of relative modernization are greatly diminished. The Anglo-Boer

War of 1899–1902 might be taken as a case in point. The Boers, with their lack of advanced technology and their relatively primitive social and economic system, were no match for the British on the battlefield. After the conventional war was over, however, fewer than 40,000 Boer guerrillas were able to hold their own for two years against British forces eventually numbering half a million and possessing a much greater technological superiority than the North ever enjoyed in the Civil War. In order to win, the British had to scorch the countryside and intern a large proportion of the Afrikaner population. The South, despite a greater physical capability than the Boers to engage in extensive guerilla warfare, chose not to do so. Perhaps southern nationalism was made of less stern stuff than that of the Afrikaners. But a more likely explanation for the southerners' refusal to revert to partisan war was their awareness of what effects such a policy would have on their social system. Above all things, Southerners feared loss of control over the black population; their ultimate nightmare was a black uprising or "race war." To accept the inevitable chaos and disorder of a guerrilla war was also to accept the end of effective white supremacy. And this was something that white Southerners were unwilling to contemplate even after the end of slavery itself had become inevitable.

As it was, the only course open to southern leaders during the war was in effect a crash program of modernization in an attempt to neutralize the immense advantages of the North. When we consider the cultural heritage and economic resources they had to work with, their achievements went beyond what might have been expected. But the South had far too much ground to make up, and persisting rigidities, especially as manifested in the die-hard commitment to localism, racism, and plantation slavery, constituted fatal checks on the modernizing impulse.

The North, on the other hand, not only capitalized on its initial advantages during the war

but was able to multiply them. In fact, the conflict itself served as a catalyst for rapid development in many areas. Modernizing trends that
had begun in the prewar period came to un-
expectably rapid fruition in a way that both
compounded the North's advantage in the conflict and helped set the pattern for postwar
America. The war saw the transformation of
the federal government into a modern state,
with a new revenue structure based partly
on direct taxation, a national currency and
banking system, the first active involvement of
government agencies in the promotion of agriculture and technology, and the increased
bureaucracy that all this entailed. Most significantly, the national government, through protective tariffs, subsidies, and land grants, began
to play a more positive role in economic development. In the private sphere, the war gave
impetus to the organization of business, philanthropy, and the professions on a broader
scale. Hence the very tendencies toward consolidation and integration that gave the North a
decisive advantage at the outset of the Civil War
were accelerated by the exigencies and opportunities of the conflict. The very situation that
led to northern victory made it possible for the
war to propel the nation into a new and more
advanced stage of modernization.

The Southern Road to Appomattox

Kenneth M. Stampp

Not long ago one of America's best political commentators made an observation about the problem of causation in history that every responsible historian would surely endorse:

> I hold a kind of Tolstoyan view of history and believe that it is hardly ever possible to determine the real truth about how we got from here to there. Since I find it extremely difficult to uncover my own motives, I hesitate to deal with those of other people, and I positively despair at the thought of ever being really sure about what has moved whole nations and whole generations of mankind. No explanation of the causes and origins of any war—of any large happening in history—can ever be for me much more than a plausible one, a reasonable hypothesis.

This is a position to which I fully subscribe, and I believe that it is as valid for explanations of why a war was won or lost as for explanations of why a war began.

With this cautionary statement in mind, I am going to suggest one of the conditions, among several, that may help to explain why the South lost the Civil War. I think there is reason to believe that many Southerners—how many I cannot say, but enough to affect the outcome of the war—who outwardly appeared to support the Confederate cause had inward doubts about its validity, and that, in all probability, some unconsciously even hoped for its defeat. Like all historical explanations, my hypothesis is not subject to definitive proof; but I think it can be established as circumstantially plausible, because it is a reasonable explanation for a certain amount of empirical evidence.

All interpretations of the defeat of the Confederacy fall into two broad categories: those that stress the South's physical handicaps and those that stress human failings. Explanations in the first category emphasize the overwhelming preponderance of northern manpower and economic resources. To some historians it is enough to note that the North had four times as many men of military age as the South, ten times as productive an industrial plant, three times as many miles of railroads in operation, and far greater supplies of raw materials. Moreover, the North had a large merchant marine and sufficient naval power to establish an effective blockade of southern ports, whereas the South had virtually no merchant marine and no navy at all. "The prime cause [of Confederate defeat] must have been economic," argues Richard N. Current. "Given the vast superiority of the North in men and materials, in instruments of production, in communication facilities, in business organization and skill—and assuming for the sake of the argument no more than rough equality in statecraft and generalship—the final outcome seems all but inevitable."

And yet, as Professor Current observes, "the

"The Southern Road to Appomattox" by Kenneth M. Stampp, *Cotton Memorial Papers,* No. 4 (February 1969), 3–22. Reprinted by permission of Kenneth M. Stampp.

victory is not always to the rich," for history provides some striking examples of wealthy nations losing to economically poorer adversaries. "In terms of economic logic," David M. Potter writes, "it can perhaps be demonstrated that the Confederacy, hopelessly overmatched by almost every measure of strength, was doomed to defeat. But history not only shows that in war the lighter antagonist sometimes defeats the heavier, it also shows that what seems logically certain often fails to happen." Professor Potter believes that for at least the first two years of the war the outcome was in doubt; therefore the analysis of Confederate defeat must "go beyond the *a priori* arguments of economic determinism," for "other countervailing factors" might possibly have offset northern economic superiority. He thus introduces the second category of explanations for Confederate defeat: those that compare and evaluate the behavior of Northerners and Southerners under the stresses of war.

The behavioral factor that Potter has in mind is political leadership. He suggests that superior Confederate leadership might have counterbalanced the North's economic power, but he finds instead another area of decisive Confederate weakness. Potter emphasizes Abraham Lincoln's brilliant record as a war leader and compares it to the dismal record of Jefferson Davis—a discrepancy "as real and as significant as the inequality in mileage between Union and Confederate railroad systems." Indeed, Potter believes that Lincoln contributed so much to the ultimate Union victory that "if the Union and the Confederacy had exchanged Presidents with one another, the Confederacy might have won its independence." Moreover, because the South failed to develop a two-party system, no constructive leadership emerged from the opposition to Davis in Congress or in the state governments. Instead, the "petulant, short-sighted, narrow-gauge, negativistic, vindictive quality of the criticism of Davis made him seem, with all his shortcomings, a better man than most of those who assailed him."

Professor Potter argues the political fail-

ure of the Confederacy so convincingly that, for the purposes of my own argument, I need make only one additional point: It is odd that the South, with its long tradition of leadership in political affairs, should have thus given the appearance of political bankruptcy during the four years of the Civil War. Among the politicians who created the Confederate States of America were men of superior talent, and many of them had considerable legislative and administrative experience. One wonders what happened to them. A study of the political history of the Confederacy leaves one with the impression that the South was afflicted with what Roy F. Nichols has described as "an undefined and stultifying force of some sort which inhibited effective statesmanship." Political failure does help to explain Confederate defeat, but it also raises some questions that need to be answered.

The theme of political failure has several variations. According to one of them, the widespread assertion of the constitutional doctrine of state rights during the war crisis made southern defeat certain. Frank L. Owsley maintains that "if the political system of the South had not broken down under the weight of an impracticable doctrine put into practice in the midst of a revolution, the South might have established its independence." He suggests that on the gravestone of the Confederacy should be carved these words: "Died of State Rights." Owsley provides ample illustrations of the extremes to which some Confederate politicians went in defense of the sovereignty of the states.

Unquestionably the state-rights doctrinaires helped to paralyze the hands of the Confederate government and thus grievously injured their own cause. But this explanation of Confederate defeat also raises questions, because before the war most southern politicians had not been consistent state-rights doctrinaires. Instead, like Northerners, they had shown a good deal of flexibility in their constitutional theories, and they had been willing to tolerate a relatively vigorous federal government as long as it heeded southern needs. They had not objected to a federally subsidized transcontinental railroad—along a southern route; they had not objected to federal appropriations for internal improvements—if the appropriations were for the improvement of transportation along southern rivers; and they showed no fear of creeping federal tyranny when they demanded effective federal action to recover fugitive slaves or to protect slavery in the territories. Indeed, some southern politicians seemed to show less constitutional flexibility in dealing with a government of their own creation than they had in dealing with the federal government before 1861.

David Donald offers another variation on the theme of Confederate political failure. He argues that the basic weakness of the Confederacy was that "the Southern people insisted upon retaining their democratic liberties in wartime. If they were fighting for freedom, they asked, why should they start abridging it? As soldiers, as critics of the government, and as voters they stuck to their democratic, individualistic rights." In the North civil rights were more severely compromised, the soldier was better disciplined, and regimentation was more readily accepted. Therefore, Professor Donald concludes, "we should write on the tombstone of the Confederacy: 'Died of Democracy.'"

Before the Civil War, needless to say, the South had not been notably more democratic than the North; and at some points Donald seems to equate democracy with poor organization, political ineptitude, and chaos. But there is truth in his generalization, which raises still another question: Why was it that Northerners, who were every bit as democratic and almost as individualistic as Southerners, by and large were willing to tolerate more regimentation for the sake of their cause than Southerners appeared ready to tolerate for the sake of theirs? The question, of course, is one of degree, for many Northerners also resisted war measures such as conscription and encroachments on civil liberties.

Bell I. Wiley adds a final touch to the behavioral approach to Confederate defeat. "Perhaps the most costly of the Confederacy's shortcomings," he suggests,

> was the disharmony among its people. A cursory glance at the Confederacy reveals numerous instances of bitter strife. . . . Behind the battle of bullets waged with the invaders was an enormous war of words and emotions among Confederates themselves which began before secession and which eventually became so intense that it sapped the South's vitality and hastened northern victory.

In a recent study of Confederate politics, Eric L. McKitrick was also struck by the bickering "that seeped in from everywhere to soften the very will of the Confederacy."

Collectively, all these behavioral problems—the failure of political leadership, the absurd lengths to which state rights was carried, the reluctance of Southerners to accept the discipline that war demanded, and the internal conflicts among the southern people—point to a Confederate weakness that matched in importance its phycial handicaps. This was a weakness of morale. Assuming rough equality in military training and similar military traditions, a country with inferior resources and manpower can hope to defeat a more powerful adversary only if it enjoys decidedly superior morale in its civilian population. High morale is the product of passionate dedication to a cause, which creates a willingness to subordinate personal interests to its success. This is what has sometimes enabled small states to resist successfully the aggression of stronger neighbors, and nationalist movements to succeed against colonial powers. In such cases the fires of patriotism, fed by a genuine national identity, burned fiercely, and the longing for political freedom produced a spirit of self-sacrifice. When the partisans of a cause have no doubts about its validity, when they view the consequences of defeat as unbearable, morale is likely to be extremely high.

Such was not the case in the Confederacy, as numerous historians have observed. "The collapse of the Confederacy," Charles H.

Wesley concludes, "was due in part to a lack of resources, but more directly to the absence of a wholehearted and sustained resistance, . . . without which no revolution has been successful." E. Merton Coulter, though admitting physical handicaps, insists that "the Confederacy never fully utilized the human and material resources it had," because it "never succeeded in developing an *esprit de corps,* either in its civil or military organization." The reason for this, according to Coulter, was that the Confederacy "was not blessed with an 'one for all and all for one' patriotism with which future generations of sentimental romancers were to endow it." Coulter concludes succinctly: "The forces leading to defeat were many but they may be summed up in this one fact: The people did not will hard enough and long enough to win."

The problem of morale to which I am referring here should not be confused with another persistent but separate Confederate problem:

that of disloyalty among southern Unionists. Nor should it be confused with the defeatism and demoralization that grew out of military reverses, shortages of civilian supplies, and financial collapse during the closing stages of the war. In the Confederacy weak morale was not simply the ultimate consequence of war weariness, for the problem was there at its birth. It was the product of uncertainty about the South's identity, of the peculiar circumstances that led to secession and the attempt at independence, and of widespread doubts and apprehensions about the validity of the Confederate cause. The problem was obscured for a time by the semi-hysteria that swept the Deep South in the months after Lincoln's election, and to some extent by early military successes. But it was always there and soon began to make itself felt, for the South was ill-equipped for a long war not only physically but spiritually and ideologically as well.

That southern morale was not high enough

Ruins in Richmond, Virginia, 1865. Grim evidence of the defeat and collapse of the Confederacy.

and dedication to the cause fierce enough to offset the Confederacy's physical handicaps has sometimes been attributed to the failure of its leaders to perform their duties as propagandists and morale builders. Charles W. Ramsdell holds the politicians responsible for failing to build an efficient propaganda organization or to portray some compelling issue for which the southern people would have made great sacrifices. Similarly, Bell I. Wiley blames both Jefferson Davis and the Confederate Congress for not realizing "the necessity of winning the hearts and minds of the people." To David M. Potter the prime responsibility for the failure to dramatize the southern cause belonged to President Davis. One of his major shortcomings was his inability to "communicate with the people of the Confederacy. He seemed to think in abstractions and to speak in platitudes."

If Davis had a penchant for abstract and platitudinous discourse, most other Confederate politicians and publicists, when upholding the Confederate cause, seemed to suffer from the same defect. Yet the South had more than its share of able speakers and editors, who exploited as best they could the available issues: the menace of a ruthless northern invader, the need to defend the constitutional principles of the Founding Fathers, and the threat to southern civilization posed by northern abolitionists and their doctrine of racial equality. Significantly, however, only occasionally did they identify the Confederacy with slavery. "Our new Government," Vice President Alexander H. Stephens once boldly proclaimed,

> is founded upon . . . the great truth that the negro is not equal to the white man; that slavery, subordination to the superior race, is his natural and moral condition. This, our new Government, is the first, in the history of the world, based upon this great physical, philosophical and moral truth.

In his message to Congress, April 29, 1861, President Davis declared that "the labor of African slaves was and is indispensable" to the South's economic development. "With interests of such overwhelming magnitude imperiled, the people of the Southern States were driven by the conduct of the North to the adoption of some course of action to avert the danger with which they were openly menaced." This rhetoric was hardly inspiring, but, more important, neither was the cause it supported. Confederate propagandists apparently found the defense of slavery a poor tool with which to build southern morale, and they usually laid stress on other issues.

This reluctance of southern propagandists candidly to identify the Confederacy with slavery helps to explain their sterile rhetoric and their dismal failure; for, in my opinion, slavery was the key factor that gave the antebellum South its distinct identity, and the supposed northern threat to slavery was the basic cause of secession. To understand why southern propagandists failed, one must, in addition to evaluating their skill and techniques, compare the issues at their disposal with those at the disposal of their antagonists. Northern propagandists exploited all the historic traditions associated with the federal Union; reaffirmed America's mission and manifest destiny; proclaimed that democracy and self-government were on trial; above all, identified their cause with the principles of the Declaration of Independence. These were the themes that Lincoln developed in the letters, speeches, and state papers which we remember a century later. It is of the utmost significance that no southern leader, even if he had had Lincoln's skill with words, could have claimed for the Confederacy a set of war aims that fired the nineteenth-century imagination as did those described in the Gettysburg Address. One wonders what Lincoln could have done with the issues available to him in the South, what even Jefferson Davis might have done with those that every northern politician had available to him.

When southern propagandists found it expedient, for reasons of domestic policy as well as foreign, to soft-pedal the very *cause* of the war, the Confederacy was at a considerable disadvantage as far as its moral position was concerned. This may help to explain why the Confederate Congress contained no group as fiercely dedicated to the southern cause as the Radical Republicans were to the northern cause. It illuminates Roy F. Nichols' impression that southern leaders were "beset by psychological handicaps." In short, it locates one of the fundamental reasons for the weakness of southern morale. It was due not only to the failure of those who tried to uphold the cause, important as that may have been; but, viewed as an appeal to the minds and emotions of nineteenth-century Americans, it was also due to the inherent frailty of the cause itself.

At this point, keeping the southern morale problem in mind, I would like to introduce my hypothesis that many seemingly loyal Confederates lacked a deep commitment to the southern cause and that some unconsciously even desired to lose the war. In the study of human behavior we frequently encounter cases of persons involved in conflicts which outwardly they seem to be striving to win, when, for reasons of which they are hardly conscious, they are in fact inviting defeat. I believe that there is considerable circumstantial evidence indicating that an indeterminate but significant number of Southerners were behaving in this manner, and I would like to suggest two reasons why unconsciously they might have welcomed defeat, or at least declined to give that "last full measure" which might have avoided it.

The first reason is related to the circumstances of southern secession. Fundamentally this movement was not the product of genuine southern nationalism; indeed, except for the institution of slavery, the South had little to give it a clear national identity. It had no natural frontiers; its white population came from the same stocks as the northern population; its political traditions and religious beliefs were not significantly different from those of the North; and the notion of a dis-

tinct southern culture was largely a figment of the imaginations of proslavery propagandists. Few of the conditions that underlay 19th- and 20th-century nationalist movements in other parts of the world were present in the antebellum South. As Charles G. Sellers, Jr., has observed: "No picture of the Old South as a section confident and united in its dedication to a neo-feudal social order, and no explanation of the Civil War as a conflict between 'two civilizations' can encompass the complexity and pathos of the antebellum reality." Southerners, notwithstanding the paradox of slavery, shared the ideals of other Americans. From the Revolution on, for Northerners and Southerners alike,

> liberty was the end for which the Union existed, while the Union was the instrument by which liberty was to be extended to all mankind. Thus the Fourth of July . . . became the occasion for renewing the liberal idealism and the patriotic nationalism which united Americans of all sections at the highest levels of political conviction.

Even after a generation of intense sectional conflict over slavery, the South was still bound to the Union by a heritage of national ideals and traditions. Nothing was more common in southern political rhetoric than boasts of the South's manifold contributions to the building of the nation and of the national heroes it had produced. Southerners knew that the American dream was to have its fulfillment not in a regional confederacy but in the federal Union. Few could resist the appeal of American nationalism; few found a viable substitute in that most flimsy and ephemeral of dreams: southern nationalism.

This is not to say that the people of the Deep South were dragged out of the Union against their will. In all probability secession had the approval of the overwhelming majority, but most of them were driven to secession not by some mystical southern nationalism but by fear and anger, feeling that secession was not so much a positive good as a painful last resort. At his inauguration as provisional President, Jefferson Davis spoke of the "sincerity" with which Southerners had "labored to preserve the government of our fathers" and explained that they had turned finally to secession as "a necessity not a choice." A New Orleans editor believed that many left the Union "with feelings akin to those they would experience at witnessing some crushing national calamity." Nearly all the public celebrations in the seceded states during the dismal winter of 1860–61 had about them a quality of forced gaiety, and much of the flamboyant oratory had a slightly hollow sound. Whatever was to be gained from independence, Southerners knew that some priceless things would inevitably be lost. They could hate the Yankees, but that was not quite the same as hating the Union.

They hated the Yankees for questioning their fidelity to American traditions and for denying them a share of the American dream; and they held the Yankees responsible for driving them out of the Union. As they departed, Southerners announced their determination to cherish more faithfully than Northerners the sacred heritage of the Founding Fathers. In the Confederate Constitution, said Alexander H. Stephens, "all the essentials of the old Constitution, which have endeared it to the hearts of the American people, have been preserved and perpetuated." By 1861 Southerners could no longer escape this heritage, and rather than seeking to escape it they claimed it as their own. But in doing so they confessed rather pathetically the speciousness of southern nationalism.

This being the case, it may well be that for many Southerners secession was not in fact the ultimate goal. Roy F. Nichols suggests that even among the active secessionists "it may be doubted if all had the same final objective—namely, an independent republic, a confederacy of slave states." Nichols believes that some southern politicians were looking for a device that would enable them to ne-

gotiate for a better and stronger position in the old Union and that they thought of secession in these terms. "The real motive and object of many . . . was the creation of the Confederacy as a bargaining agency more effective than a minority group negotiating within the Union. As Thomas R. R. Cobb expressed it, better terms could be secured out of the Union than in it." John Bell of Tennessee described the secession movement as a strategem to alarm the North, force it to "make such concessions as would be satisfactory and therefore the seceding states would return to the fold of the Union." In fact, an argument repeatedly used by some secessionists was that an independent Confederacy would be the first step toward a reconstructed Union on southern terms. On December 5, 1860, the New Orleans *Bee* reported:

> Moderate men . . . are now forced painfully, reluctantly, with sorrow and anguish, to the conclusion that it is wholly impossible for the South tamely to tolerate the present, or indulge the slightest hope of an improvement in the future. They now see clearly that there are but two alternatives before the South, . . . either a final separation from the section which has oppressed and aggrieved her, or a new compact under which her rights will be amply secured. The one may take place, and still eventually prepare for the other.

Southerners who went out of the Union in anguish hoping for negotiations and peaceful reunion were bitterly disappointed by events. The Union did not negotiate with the Confederacy, and two months after its birth the Confederacy was involved in a war for which it was poorly equipped both physically and morally. Those who had expected reunion through negotiation found themselves trapped in a war they had not anticipated, fighting for an independence they had never sought; and, in spite of their indignation at northern "aggression," they may well have turned now unconsciously to reunion through defeat. The game had to be played out, the war had to be fought—and the men who served in the Confederate armies displayed their share of gallantry—but a contestant suffering from a lack of national identity and a serious morale problem, as well as from inferior resources, was involved in a lost cause from the start. Defeat restored to the South its traditions, its long-held aspirations, and, as part of the federal Union, the only national identity it ever had. It is instructive to contrast the myth of a special southern national identity with the reality of, say, Polish nationalism, which survived more than a century of occupation, partition, and repression. After Appomattox the myth of southern nationalism died remarkably soon.

Defeat gave Southerners another reward: a way to rid themselves of the moral burden of slavery. This is the second reason why I think that some of them, once they found themselves locked in combat with the North, unconsciously wanted to lose. To suggest as I do that slavery gave the South such identity as it had, caused secession and war, and at the same time gave some Southerners a reason for wanting to lose the war will, I admit, take some explaining.

Let me begin with what I believe to be a fact, namely, that a large number of white Southerners, however much they tried, could not persuade themselves that slavery was a positive good, defensible on Christian and ethical principles. In spite of their defense of slavery and denial of its abuses, many of them, as their unpublished records eloquently testify, knew that their critics were essentially right. In saying this, I do not think I am judging 19th-century men by 20th-century standards, for among the romanticists of the 19th century there was no greater moral good than individual liberty. Hence, the dimensions of the South's moral problem cannot be appreciated unless one understands that slavery was, by the South's own values, an abomination. The problem would not have been nearly as serious for Southerners if abolitionist criticism, strident and abrasive though it often was, had not been a mere echo of their own consciences.

No analysis of the Old South, writes Professor Sellers, "that misses the inner turmoil of the antebellum Southerner can do justice to the central tragedy of the southern experience. . . . Southerners were at least subconsciously aware of the 'detestable paradox' of 'our every-day sentiments of liberty' while holding beings in slavery." Their general misgivings about slavery "burrowed beneath the surface of the southern mind, where they kept gnawing away the shaky foundations on which Southerners sought to rebuild their morale and self-confidence as a slave-holding people." Wilbur J. Cash insists that the Old South

in its secret heart always carried a powerful and uneasy sense of the essential rightness of the 19th century's position on slavery. . . . This Old South, in short, was a society beset by the specters of defeat, of shame, of guilt—a society driven by the need to bolster its morale, to nerve its arm against waxing odds, to justify itself in its own eyes and in those of the world.

To be sure, a basic purpose of the proslavery argument, with its historical, biblical, philosophical, and scientific defenses, was to soothe the troubled consciences of slaveholders. This is evident in the frequency with which they recited the argument to themselves and to each other in their diaries and letters. But it did not seem to be enough. No people secure in their conviction that slavery was indeed a positive good and unaware of any contradictions between theory and practice would have quarreled with the outside world so aggressively and reassured themselves so often as the slaveholders did. "The problem for the South," William R. Taylor believes,

was not that it lived by an entirely different set of values and civic ideals but rather that it was forced either to live with the values of the nation at large or—as a desperate solution—to invent others, others which had even less relevance to the southern situation. . . . More and more it became difficult for Southerners to live in peace with themselves: to accept the aspirations and the ideals of the nation and, at the same time, accept the claims and rationalizations produced by the South's special pleaders. Almost invariably they found themselves confronted with contradictions of the most troubling and disquieting kind.

I do not mean to suggest that every slaveholder was guilt-ridden because of slavery. The private papers of many of them give no sign of such a moral crisis—only a nagging fear of slave insurrections and bitter resentment at outside meddling in the South's affairs. Countless slaveholders looked upon Negroes as subhuman, or at least so far inferior to whites as to be suited only for bondage, and some showed little sensitivity about the ugly aspects of slavery. On the other hand, many slaveholders, perhaps most, were more or less tormented by the dilemma they were in. They could not, of their own volition, give up the advantages of slavery—a profitable labor system in which they had a $2 billion capital investment. They dreaded the adjustments they would have to make if they were to live in the same region with four million free Negroes, for their racial attitudes were much like those of most other white Americans, North and South. Yet they knew that slavery betrayed the American tradition of individual liberty and natural rights and that the attack on it was in the main valid.

In their extremity sensitive Southerners joined their less sensitive neighbors in angry attacks on their tormentors, until, finally, driven by their inner tensions, they were ready to seek an escape from their problems by breaking up the Union, or at least by threatening to do so. Professor Sellers argues persuasively that this moral crisis eventually converted Southerners into an "aggressive slavocracy." "The almost pathological violence of their reaction to northern criticism indicated that their misgivings about their moral position on slavery had become literally intolerable under the mounting abolitionist attack." Slavery was doomed, Sellers concludes, but Southerners were so caught in its contradictions "that

they could neither deal with it rationally nor longer endure the tensions and anxieties it generated. Under these circumstances the Civil War or something very like it was unavoidable."

Indeed, I believe that under these circumstances not only the Civil War but the outcome as we know it was unavoidable. Southerners, many of whom were unsure of their goals and tormented by guilt about slavery, having founded a nation on nothing more substantial than anger and fear, were in no position to overcome the North's physical advantages. Moreover, at least some of them must have been troubled, at some conscious or unconscious level, by the question of what precisely was to be gained from winning the war—whether more in fact might be gained from losing it. For it soon became evident that, in addition to restoring the South to the Union, defeat would be the doom of slavery. Thus President Lincoln and the Union Congress would do for the slaveholders what even the more sensitive among them seemed unable to do for themselves—resolve once and for all the conflict between their deeply held values and their peculiar and archaic institution.

What circumstantial evidence is there to suggest that Southerners lost the Civil War in part because a significant number of them unconsciously felt that they had less to gain by winning than by losing? There is, first of all, the poor performance of some of the South's talented and experienced political leaders; the uninspiring record of the Confederate Congress; the aggressive assertion of state rights even though it was a sure road to defeat; and the internal bickering and lack of individual commitment that would have made possible the discipline essential to victory. The history of the Confederacy is not that of a people with a sense of deep commitment to their cause—a feeling that without victory there is no future—for too many of them declined to make the all-out effort that victory would have required.

Equally significant was the behavior of Confederate civilians in areas occupied by Union military forces. One must be cautious in the use of historical analogies, but it is worth recalling the problems that plagued the German Nazis in the countries they occupied during the second World War. Everywhere they met resistance from an organized underground that supplied information to Germany's enemies, committed acts of sabotage, and made life precarious for collaborators and German military personnel. At the same time, bands of partisans gathered in remote places to continue the war against the Nazis. The French had a similar experience in Algeria after the second World War. The Algerian nationalists struggled with fanatical devotion to their cause; every village was a center of resistance, and no Frenchman was safe away from the protection of the French army. The country simply could not be pacified, and France, in spite of its great physical superiority, had to withdraw.

In the Confederate South, apart from border-state bushwhacking, there was only one example of underground resistance even remotely comparable to that demonstrated in Nazi-occupied Europe or French-occupied Algeria. This example was provided not by southern nationalists but by East Tennessee Unionists against the Confederacy itself. The counties of East Tennessee had been strongly opposed to secession, and so great was the disaffection that by the fall of 1861 some 11,000 Confederate infantry, cavalry, and artillery occupied them. In response some 2000 Union partisans fled to Kentucky to begin training as an army of liberation, while others drilled in mountain fastnesses in preparation for the arrival of federal forces. Still other East Tennesseans organized an underground and engaged in such activities as cutting telegraph wires and burning bridges. The most strenuous Confederate efforts at pacification failed to suppress these dedicated Unionists, and East Tennessee remained a cancer in the vitals of the Confederacy.

Nowhere in the South was there impressive resistance to the federal occupation, even making allowance for the fact that most able-bodied men of military age were serving in the Confederate armies. In 1862 Middle Tennessee, West Tennessee, part of northern Mississippi, and New Orleans fell under federal military occupation, but no significant underground developed. In 1864, General Sherman marched through Georgia and maintained long lines of communication without the semblance of a partisan resistance to trouble him. In commenting on this remarkable phenomenon, Governor Zebulon Vance of North Carolina wrote:

> With a base line of communication of 500 miles in Sherman's rear, through our own country, not a bridge has been burnt, a car thrown from its track, nor a man shot by our people whose country has been desolated! They seem everywhere to submit. . . . It shows what I have always believed, that the great *popular heart* is not now and never has been in this war!

The absence of civilian resistance was quite as remarkable when, early in 1865, Sherman's army turned northward from Savannah into South Carolina. In the spring, when the Confederate armies surrendered, there were no partisans to take refuge in the mountains for a last desperate defense of southern nationalism. The Confederate States of America expired quietly, and throughout the South most people were reconciled to its death with relative ease. We hear much of unreconstructed southern rebels, but the number of them was not very large; the great majority of Southerners made haste to swear allegiance to the Union.

Finally, and to me most significant of all, was the readiness, if not always good grace, with which most Southerners accepted the abolition of slavery—a readiness that I do not think is explained entirely by the circumstances of defeat. Probably historians have given too much emphasis to the cases of recalcitrance on this matter in the months after Appomattox, when, actually, slavery collapsed with remarkably little resistance. Just a few years earlier it had been impossible publicly to oppose slavery in all but the border slave states, and southern politicians and publicists had aggressively asserted that slavery was a positive good; yet soon after the Confederate surrender no Southerner except an occasional eccentric would publicly affirm the validity of the proslavery argument. Indeed, I believe that even in the spring of 1866, if Southerners had been permitted to vote for or against the reestablishment of slavery, not one southern state would have mustered a favorable majority. Only two weeks after Appomattox, when a group of South Carolina aristocrats looked to the years ahead, though one of them could see only "poverty, no future, no hope," another found solace in the fact that at least there would be "no slaves, thank God!" In July another South Carolinian said more crudely: "It's a great relief to get rid of the horrid negroes."

Very soon, as a matter of fact, white Southerners were publicly expressing their satisfaction that the institution had been abolished and asserting that the whites, though perhaps not the blacks, were better off without it. Many were ready now to give voice to the private doubts they had felt before the war. They denied that slavery had anything to do with the Confederate cause, thus decontaminating it and turning it into something they could cherish. After Appomattox Jefferson Davis claimed that slavery "was in no wise the cause of the conflict," and Alexander H. Stephens argued that the war "was not a contest between the advocates or opponents of that Peculiar Institution." The speed with which white Southerners dissociated themselves from the cause of slavery is an indication of how great a burden it had been to them before Appomattox.

The acceptance of emancipation, of course, did not commit Southerners to a policy of racial equality. Rather, they assumed that the free Negroes would be an inferior caste, exposed to legal discrimination, denied political rights, and subjected to social segregation. They had every reason to assume this, because these, by and large, were the politics of most of the northern states toward their free Negro populations, and because the racial attitudes of the great majority of Northerners were not much different from their own. White Southerners were understandably shocked, therefore, when Radical Republicans, during the Reconstruction years, tried to impose a different relationship between the races in the South—to give Negroes legal equality, political rights, and, here and there, even social equality. Now for the first time white Southerners organized a powerful partisan movement and resisted more fiercely than they ever had during the war. The difference, I think, was that in rejecting Radical race policy they felt surer of their moral position, for they were convinced that Northerners were perpetrating an outrage that Northerners themselves would not have endured. Thus the moral problem was now on the other side; and the North, in spite of its great physical power, lacked the will to prevail. Unlike slavery, racial discrimination did not disturb many nineteenth-century white Americans, North or South. Accordingly, in a relatively short time, chiefly because of the unrelenting opposition of white Southerners, Radical Reconstruction collapsed.

The outcome of Reconstruction is significant: it shows what a people can do against overwhelming odds when their morale is high, when they believe in their cause, and when they are convinced that defeat means catastrophe. The fatal weakness of the Confederacy was that not enough of its people really thought that defeat would be a catastrophe; and, moreover, I believe that many of them unconsciously felt that the fruits of defeat would be less bitter than those of success.

Part Twelve

The Problem
of Reconstruction

The coming of peace in 1865 brought with it the defeat of secession and the abolition of slavery. But the settlement of these two issues did not preclude the emergence of yet other problems stemming directly from them. Despite all that had been achieved up until then, the victorious federal government had now to decide how and on what terms the South would be restored to the Union as well as what protection and rights were to be afforded to the former slaves.

These were extremely complicated questions, and it took three years of trial and debate to arrive at a final formula and then implement it. The struggle within Congress to decide on the specifics of the terms for the South was exacerbated by opposition from the executive branch, where President Andrew Johnson defiantly challenged the legislature's authority and criticized its proposals as being too demanding. Even after the South was politically reorganized and readmitted under the Reconstruction Act of 1867, the problem was still unresolved. The terms of the act required that new governments be set up in each southern state, with all black males able to vote and leading Confederates denied the suffrage and, in some cases, the right to hold office as well. The trouble was, however, that these Republican-controlled administrations rested on a precarious, mainly black, base of electoral support, and their survival was therefore far from assured. Yet, only if they could stay in power would the experiment of southern reconstruction continue, take hold, and expand its scope. Since these governments soon found themselves in great difficulties, the federal authorities' involvement in southern affairs continued into the late 1870s, at which point they abandoned the attempt to maintain the Reconstruction governments they had striven so manfully to establish earlier.

The reaction of historians to the Era of Reconstruction has been, almost universally, to proclaim it a failure. But the reasons for failure have varied. At one time, it was attributed, by conservative historians with a sympathy for the South, to the unreasonableness and foolishness of attempting to force humiliating and excessive terms on the former rebels, and especially of trying to enfranchise black men who had only a few years earlier been slaves. More recently, historians have taken a quite different stance, finding the cause of Reconstruction's failure in the leniency of its provisions and their ineffective enforcement. Although black suffrage may have been a more radical step than any other slave society in the Americas ever took after emancipation, these historians argue that it was insufficient without greater military force or more adequate political machinery and support than was in fact provided. Some even assert that, without the enforced break up of the plantations and the provision of land to the freedmen, no amount of political manipulation would have been enough to bring about the social and economic reconstruction that was needed in the postwar, postemancipation South.

So there is a great deal of criticism of Reconstruction and it is invariably expressed with vigor and passion. The two selections on this topic are not chosen for the purpose of representing the two divergent explanations outlined here. Instead, they each present a different aspect of the difficulties confronted by the proponents and supporters of Reconstruction. The first is by C. Vann Woodward of Yale University, who is the foremost southern historian of the past generation or so. In this essay, he points out how pervasive were racist attitudes even in the North. Since one of Reconstruction's primary considerations was the protection and empowerment of the freed slaves, the ability of the Congressmen and others in the North to act firmly on their behalf was bound to be severely constrained.

The Republicans in the South who controlled the state governments there after 1868 were also faced with a vexing dilemma, whose essential characteristics are depicted in the accompanying selection by Ted Tunnell of Virginia Commonwealth University. In this chapter from his book on the Republican party in Louisiana, entitled *Crucible of Reconstruction: War, Radicalism and Race in Louisiana, 1862–1877* (1984), Professor Tunnell shows how the Reconstruction government in that state, headed by Governor Henry Clay Warmoth, pursued political strategies that proved to be contradictory and ultimately self-defeating. Although the contrast between these conflicting courses of action was greater in Louisiana than elsewhere, every Republican administration in the South was beset by cross-pressures and adopted similarly incompatible policies. Whether the southern Republicans could have resolved the dilemma by pursuing just one of the possible options rather than both is a question to debate. Nevertheless, the two selections presented here deal with the Republicans' dilemma—in formulating policy in the North and in implementing it in the South. Before rushing to judgment about the shortcomings of Reconstruction and its advocates, perhaps an appreciation of the agonizing problems involved may provide perspective and understanding.

QUESTIONS TO CONSIDER

1. Could an argument be made that policymakers in Congress deserve credit for their policies toward the freedman, in view of the restraints imposed on them by their own and their constituents' racial prejudice?

2. Why did the Warmoth administration in Louisiana try to pursue policies that were simultaneously conciliatory and coercive in its attempt to stay in power?

3. Was Reconstruction's lack of success attributable primarily to the inadequacy of Congressional policy or to the ineffectiveness of its implementation in the South after 1868? Or should the question be reformulated to take into account the successes achieved by Reconstruction?

Seeds of Failure in Republican Race Policy

C. Vann Woodward

The Republican leaders were quite aware in 1865 that the issue of Negro status and rights was closely connected with the two other great issues of Reconstruction—who should reconstruct the South and who should govern the country. But while they were agreed on the two latter issues, they were not agreed on the third. They were increasingly conscious that in order to reconstruct the South along the lines they planned they would require the support and the votes of the freedmen. And it was apparent to some that once the reconstructed states were restored to the Union, the Republicans would need the votes of the freedmen to retain control over the national government. While they could agree on this much, they were far from agreeing on the status, the rights, the equality, or the future of the Negro.

The fact was that the constituency on which the Republican congressmen relied in the North lived in a race-conscious, segregated society devoted to the doctrine of white supremacy and Negro inferiority. "In virtually every phase of existence," writes Leon Litwack with regard to the North in 1860, "Negroes found themselves systematically separated from whites. They were either excluded from railway cars, omnibuses, stage coaches, and steamboats or assigned to special 'Jim Crow' sections; they sat, when permitted, in secluded and remote corners of theatres and lecture halls; they could not enter most hotels, restaurants, and resorts, except as servants; they prayed in 'Negro pews' in the white churches. . . . Moreover, they were often educated in segregated schools, punished in segregated prisons, nursed in segregated hospitals, and buried in segregated cemeteries." Ninety-four percent of the northern Negroes in 1860 lived in states that denied them the ballot, and the 6 percent who lived in the five states that permitted them to vote were often disfranchised by ruse. In many northern states, discriminatory laws excluded Negroes from interracial marriage, from militia service, from the jury box, and from the witness stand when whites were involved. Ohio denied them poor relief, and Indiana, Illinois, and Iowa had laws carrying severe penalties against Negroes settling in those states. Everywhere in the free states, the Negro met with barriers to job opportunities and in most places . . . encountered severe limitations to the protection of . . . life, liberty, and property.

One political consequence of these racial attitudes was that the major parties vied with each other in their professions of devotion to the dogma of white supremacy. Republicans were especially sensitive on the point be-

"Seeds of Failure in Radical Race Policy" by C. Vann Woodward from *Proceedings of the American Philosophical Society,* CX, February 1966, 1–9. Reprinted by permission of the American Philosophical Society.

cause of their antislavery associations. Many of them, like Senator Lyman Trumbull of Illinois, found no difficulty in reconciling antislavery with anti-Negro views. "We are for free white men," said Senator Trumbull in 1858, "and for making white labor respectable and honorable, which it can never be when negro slave labor is brought into competition with it." Horace Greeley the following year regretted that it was "the controlling idea" of some of his fellow Republicans "to prove themselves 'the white man's party,' or else all the mean, low, ignorant, drunken, brutish whites will go against them from horror of 'negro equality.'" Greeley called such people "the one-horse politicians," but he could hardly apply that name to Lyman Trumbull, nor for that matter to William H. Seward, who in 1860 described the American Negro as "a foreign and feeble element like the Indians, incapable of assimilation," nor to Senator Henry Wilson of Massachusetts, who firmly disavowed any belief "in the mental or the intellectual equality of the African race with this proud and domineering white race of ours." Trumbull, Seward, and Wilson were the front rank of Republican leadership, and they spoke the mind of the Middle West, the Middle Atlantic. . . , and New England. There is much evidence to sustain the estimate of W. E. B. Du Bois that "At the beginning of the Civil War probably not one white American in a hundred believed that Negroes could become an integral part of American democracy."

When the war for Union began to take on the character of a war for Freedom, northern attitudes toward the Negro, as demonstrated in the previous chapter, paradoxically began to harden rather than soften. This hardening process was especially prominent in the middle western states where the old fear of Negro invasion was intensified by apprehensions that once the millions of slaves below the Ohio River were freed they would push northward—this time by the thousands and tens of thousands, perhaps in mass exodus, instead of in driblets of one or two who came

furtively as fugitive slaves. The prospect filled the whites with alarm and their spokesmen voiced these fears with great candor. "There is," Lyman Trumbull told the Senate, in April 1862, "a very great aversion in the West—I know it to be so in my state—against having free negroes come among us." And about the same time, John Sherman, who was to give his name to the Radical Reconstruction acts five years later, told Congress that in Ohio "we do not like negroes. We do not disguise our dislike. As my friend from Indiana [Congressman Joseph A. Wright] said yesterday, the whole people of the northwestern States are, for reasons whether correct or not, opposed to having many negroes among them, and the principle or prejudice has been engrafted in the legislation of nearly all the northwestern States."

So powerful was this anti-Negro feeling that it almost overwhelmed antislavery feeling and seriously imperiled the passage of various confiscation and emancipation laws designed to free the slave. To combat the opposition Republican leaders such as George W. Julian of Indiana, Albert G. Riddle of Ohio, and Treasury Secretary Salmon P. Chase advanced the theory that emancipation would actually solve northern race problems. Instead of starting a mass migration of freedmen northward, they argued, the abolition of slavery would not only put a stop to the entry of fugitive slaves but would drain the northern Negroes back to the South. Once slavery were ended, the Negro would flee northern race prejudice and return to his natural environment and the congenial climate of the South.

The official answer of the Republican party to the northern fear of Negro invasion, however, was deportation of the freedmen and colonization abroad. The scheme ran into opposition from some Republicans, especially in New England, on the ground that it was inhumane as well as impractical. But with the powerful backing of President Lincoln and the support of western Republicans, Congress overcame the opposition. Lincoln was committed to colonization not only as a solution to the race problem but as a means of allaying northern opposition to emancipation and fears of Negro exodus. To dramatize his solution, the President took the unprecedented step of calling Negro leaders to the White House and addressing them on the subject. "There is an unwillingness on the part of our people," he told them on August 14, 1862, "harsh as it may be, for you free colored people to remain with us." He told them that "your race suffer very greatly, many of them by living among us, while ours suffer from your presence. . . . If this be admitted, it affords a reason at least why we should be separated."

The fall elections following the announcement of the Emancipation Proclamation were disastrous for the Republican party. And in his annual message in December the President returned to the theme of northern fears and deportation. "But it is dreaded that the freed people will swarm forth and cover the whole land?" he asked. They would flee the South, he suggested, only if they had something to flee from. "*Heretofore,*" he pointed out, "colored people to some extent have fled North from bondage; and *now,* perhaps, from both bondage and destitution. But if gradual emancipation and deportation be adopted, they will have neither to flee from." They would cheerfully work for wages under their old masters "till new homes can be found for them in congenial climes and with people of their own blood and race." But even if this did not keep the Negroes out of the North, Lincoln asked, "in any event, can not the North decide for itself, whether to receive them?" Here the President was suggesting that the Northern states might resort to laws such as several of them used before the war to keep Negroes out.

During the last two years of the war northern states began to modify or repeal some of their anti-Negro and discriminatory laws. But the party that emerged triumphant from the crusade to save the Union and free the slave was not in the best political and moral position to expand the rights and assure the equality of the freedman. It is difficult to identify any dominant organization of so-called "Radical Republicans" who were dedicated to the establishment of Negro equality and agreed on a program to accomplish their end. Both southern conservatives and northern liberals have long insisted or assumed that such an organization of radicals existed and determinedly pursued their purpose. But the evidence does not seem to support this assumption. There undoubtedly *did* emerge eventually an organization determined to overthrow Johnson's policies and take over the control of the South. But that was a different matter. On the issue of Negro equality the party remained divided, hesitant, and unsure of its purpose. The historic commitment to equality it eventually made was lacking in clarity, ambivalent in purpose, and capable of numerous interpretations. Needless to say, its meaning has been debated from that day to this.

The northern electorate that the Republicans faced in seeking support for their program of reconstruction had undergone no fundamental conversion in its wartime racial prejudices and dogmas. As George W. Julian told his Indiana constituents in 1865, "[T]he real trouble is that *we hate the negro.* It is not his ignorance that offends us, but his color."

In the years immediately following the war every northern state in which the electorate was given the opportunity to express its views on issues involving racial relations reaffirmed, usually with overwhelming majorities, its earlier and conservative stand. This included the states that reconsidered—and reaffirmed—their laws excluding Negroes from the polls, and others that voted on such questions as office holding, jury service, and school attendance. Throughout these years, the North remained fundamentally what it was before—a society organized upon assumptions of racial privilege and segregation. As Senator Henry Wilson of Massachusetts told his colleagues in 1867, "There is today not a square mile in the

United States where the advocacy of the equal rights of those colored men has not been in the past and is not now unpopular." Whether the Senator was entirely accurate in his estimate of white opinion or not, he faithfully reflects the political constraints and assumptions under which his party operated as they cautiously and hesitantly framed legislation for Negro civil and political rights—a program they knew had to be made acceptable to the electorate that Senator Wilson described.

This is not to suggest that there was not widespread and sincere concern in the North for the terrible condition of the freedmen in the South. There can be no doubt that many northern people were deeply moved by the reports of atrocities, peonage, brutality, lynchings, riots, and injustices that filled the press. Indignation was especially strong over the Black Codes adopted by some of the Johnsonian state legislatures, for they blatantly advertised the intention of some Southerners to substitute a degrading peonage for slavery and make a mockery of the moral fruits of northern victory. What is sometimes overlooked in analyzing northern response to the Negro's plight is the continued apprehension over the threat of a massive Negro invasion of the North. The panicky fear that this might be precipitated by emancipation had been allayed in 1862 by the promises of President Lincoln and other Republican spokesmen that once slavery was abolished, the freedmen would cheerfully settle down to remain in the South, that northern Negroes would be drawn back to the South, and that deportation and colonization abroad would take care of any threat of northern invasion that remained. But not only had experiments with deportation come to grief, but southern white persecution and abuse combined with the ugly Black Codes had produced new and powerful incentives for a Negro exodus while removal of the shackles of slavery cleared the way for emigration.

The response of the Republican Congress to this situation was the Civil Rights Act of

A cartoon by Thomas Nast in Harper's Weekly *illustrating the Democrats' vehement opposition to Reconstruction. It depicts the Democratic party as a lawless alliance of the former Confederates with the northern city bosses* (right) *and their ignorant supporters from the slums of New York and elsewhere* (left). *Under their feet are the U.S. flag and the newly enfranchised southern blacks; behind them, in flames, are the schools and other public institutions that had begun to arise in the South after emancipation. In Nast's view, the Democrats represented the forces of rebellion, violence, and corruption.*

1866, later incorporated into the Fourteenth Amendment. Undoubtedly part of the motivation for this legislation was a humanitarian concern for the protection of the Negro in the South, but another part of the motivation was less philanthropic and it was concerned not with the protection of the black man in the

South but the white man in the North. Senator Roscoe Conkling of New York, a member of the Joint Committee of Fifteen who helped draft the Civil Rights provisions, was quite explicit on this point. "Four years ago," he said in the campaign of 1866, "mobs were raised, passions were roused, votes were given, upon the idea that emancipated negroes were to burst in hordes upon the North. We then said, give them liberty and rights at the South, and they will stay there and never come into a cold climate to die. We say so still, and we want them let alone, and that is one thing that this part of the amendment is for."

Another prominent member of the Joint Committee who had a right to speak authoritatively of the meaning of its racial policy was George Boutwell of Massachusetts. Addressing his colleagues in 1866, Boutwell said: "I bid the people, the working people of the North, the men who are struggling for subsistence, to beware of the day when the southern freedmen shall swarm over the borders in quest of those rights which should be secured to them in their native states. A just policy on our part leaves the black man in the South where he will soon become prosperous and happy. An unjust policy in the South forces him from home and into those states where his rights will be protected, to the injury of the black man and the white man both of the North and the South. Justice and expediency are united in indissoluble bonds, and the men of the North cannot be unjust to the former slaves without themselves suffering the bitter penalty of transgression." The "bitter penalty" to which Boutwell referred was not the pangs of a Puritan conscience. It was an invasion of southern Negros. "Justice and expediency" were, in the words of a more famous statesman of Massachusetts, "one and inseparable."

The author and sponsor of the Civil Rights Act of 1866 was Senator Lyman Trumbull, the same man who had in 1858 described the Republicans as "the white man's party," and in 1862 had declared that "our people want noth-

ing to do with the negro." Trumbull's bill was passed and, after Johnson's veto, was repassed by an overwhelming majority. Limited in application, the Civil Rights Act did not confer political rights or the franchise on the freedmen.

The Fourteenth Amendment, which followed, was even more equivocal and less forthright on racial questions and freedmen's rights. Rejecting Senator Sumner's plea for a guarantee of Negro suffrage, Congress left that decision up to the southern states. It also left northern states free to continue the disfranchisement of Negroes, but it exempted them from the penalties inflicted on the southern states for the same decision. The real concern of the franchise provisions of the Fourteenth Amendment was not with justice to the Negro but with justice to the North. The rebel states stood to gain some twelve seats in the House if all Negroes were counted as a basis of representation and to have about eighteen fewer seats if none were counted. The Amendment fixed apportionment of representation according to enfranchisement.

There was a great deal of justice and sound wisdom in the Fourteenth Amendment, and not only in the first section conferring citizenship on the Negro and protecting his rights, but in the other three sections as well. No sensible person could contend that the rebel states should be rewarded and the loyal states penalized in apportionment of representation by the abolition of slavery and the counting of voteless freedmen. That simply made no sense. Nor were there many, in the North at least, who could object to the temporary disqualification for office and ballot of such southern officeholders of the old regime as were described in the third section. The fourth section asserting the validity of the national debt and avoiding the Confederate debts was obviously necessary. As it turned out these were the best terms the South could expect—far better than they eventually got—and the South would have been wise to have accepted them.

The tragic failure in statesmanship of the Fourteenth Amendment lay not in its terms but in the equivocal and pusillanimous way it was presented. Had it been made a firm and clear condition for readmission of the rebel states, a lot of anguish would have been spared that generation as well as later ones, including our own. Instead, in equivocal deference to states rights, the South was requested to approve instead of being compelled to accept. In this I think the moderates were wrong and Thaddeus Stevens was right. As W. R. Brock put it, "The onus of decision was passed to the southern states at a moment when they were still able to defy Congress but hardly capable of taking a statesmanlike view of the future." It was also the fateful moment when President Johnson declared war on Congress and advised the South to reject the Amendment. Under the circumstances, it was inevitable that the South should reject it, and it did so with stunning unanimity. Only thirty-two votes were cast for ratification in all the southern legislatures. This spelled the end of any hope for the moderate position in the Republican leadership.

After two years of stalling and fumbling, of endless committee work and compromise, the First Reconstruction Act was finally adopted in the eleventh hour of the expiring Thirty-ninth Congress. Only after this momentous bill was passed, was it realized that it had been drastically changed at the last moment by amendments that had not been referred to or considered by committees and that had been adopted without debate in the House and virtually without debate in the Senate. In a panicky spirit of urgency, men who were ordinarily clear-headed yielded their better judgment to the demand for anything-better-than-nothing. Few of them liked what they got, and fewer still understood the implications and the meaning of what they had done. Even John Sherman, who gave his name to the bill, was so badly confused and misled on its effect that he underestimated by some 90 percent the number

who would be disqualified from office and disfranchised. And this was one of the key provisions of the bill. It was, on the whole, a sorry performance and was far from doing justice to the intelligence and statesmanship and responsibility of the men who shaped and passed the measure.

One thing was at least clear, despite the charges of the southern enemies and the northern friends of the act to the contrary. It was not primarily devised for the protection of Negro rights and the provision of Negro equality. Its primary purpose, however awkwardly and poorly implemented, was to put the southern states under the control of men loyal to the Union or men the Republicans thought they could trust to control those states for their purposes. As far as the Negro's future was concerned, the votes of the Congress that adopted the Reconstruction Act speak for themselves. Those votes had turned down Stevens' proposal to assure an economic foundation for Negro equality and Sumner's resolutions to give the Negro equal opportunity in schools, in homesteads, and full civil rights. As for the Negro franchise, its provisions, like those for civil rights, were limited. The Negro franchise was devised for the passage of the Fourteenth Amendment and setting up the new southern state constitutions. But disfranchisement by educational and property qualifications was left an available option, and escape from the whole scheme was left open by permitting the choice of military rule. No guarantee of proportional representation for the Negro population was contemplated, and no assurance was provided for Negro officeholding.

A sudden shift from defiance to acquiescence took place in the South with the passage of the Reconstruction Act of March 2, 1867. How deep the change ran it would be hard to say. The evidence of it comes largely from public pronouncements of the press and conservative leaders, and on the negative side from the silence of the voices of defiance. The mood of submission and acquiescence was experimental, tentative, and precarious at best. It can not be said to have predominated longer than seven months, from spring to autumn of 1867. That brief period was crucial for the future of the South and the Negro in the long agony of Reconstruction.

Southerners watched intently the forthcoming state elections in the North in October. They were expected to reflect northern reactions to Radical Reconstruction and especially to the issue of Negro suffrage. There was much earnest speculation in the South. "It may be," said the Charleston *Mercury,* "that Congress but represents the feelings of its constituents, that it is but the moderate mouthpiece of incensed Northern opinion. It may be that measures harsher than any . . . that confiscation, incarceration, banishment may brood over us in turn! But all these things will not change our earnest belief—that *there will be a revulsion of popular feeling in the North.*"

Hopes were aroused first by the elections in Connecticut on April 1, less than a month after the passage of the Reconstruction Act. The Democrats won in almost all quarters. The radical *Independent* taunted the North for hypocrisy. "Republicans in all the great states, North and West, are in a false position on this question," it said. "In Congress they are for impartial suffrage; at home they are against it." In only six states outside the South were Negroes permitted to vote, and in none with appreciable Negro population. The *Independent* thought that "it ought to bring a blush to every white cheek in the loyal North to reflect that the political equality of American citizens is likely to be sooner achieved in Mississippi than in Illinois—sooner on the plantation of Jefferson Davis than around the grave of Abraham Lincoln!" Election returns in October seemed to confirm this. Republican majorities were reduced throughout the North. In the New England states and in Nebraska and Iowa, they were sharply reduced, and in New York, New Jersey, and Maryland, the party of Reconstruction went down to defeat. Democrats scored

striking victories in Pennsylvania and Ohio. In Ohio, Republicans narrowly elected the Governor by 8000 votes but overwhelmed a Negro suffrage amendment by 40,000. In every state where the voters expressed themselves on the Negro suffrage issue, they turned it down.

Horace Greeley read the returns bluntly, saying that "the Negro question lies at the bottom of our reverses. . . . Thousands have turned against us because we purpose to enfranchise the Blacks. . . . We have lost votes in the Free States by daring to be just to the Negro." The *Independent* was quite as frank. "Negroes suffrage, as a political issue," it admitted, "never before was put so squarely to certain portions of the northern people as during the late campaigns. The result shows that the Negro is still an unpopular man." Jay Cooke, the conservative financier, wrote John Sherman that he "felt a sort of intuition of coming disaster—probably growing out of a consciousness that other people would feel just as I did—disgust and mortification at the vagaries into which extremists in the Republican ranks were leading the party."

To the South, the northern elections seemed a confirmation of their hopes and suspicions. The old voices of defiance and resistance, silent or subdued since March, were lifted again. They had been right all along, they said. Congress did not speak the true sentiment of the North on the Negro and Reconstruction. President Johnson had been the true prophet. The correct strategy was not to seek the Negro vote but to suppress it, not to comply with the Reconstruction Acts but to subvert them. The New York *Times* thought that "the Southern people seem to have become quite beside themselves in consequence of the *quasi* Democratic victories" in the North, and that there was "neither sense nor sanity in their exultations." Moderates such as Governor James W. Throckmorton of Texas, who declared he "had advocated publicly and privately a compliance with the Sherman Reconstruction Bill," were now "determined to defeat" compliance and to leave "no stone unturned" in their efforts.

The standard southern reply to northern demands was the endlessly reiterated charge of hypocrisy. Northern radicals, as a Memphis conservative put it, were "seeking to fasten what they themselves repudiate with loathing upon the unfortunate people of the South." And he pointed to the succession of northern states that had voted on and defeated Negro suffrage. A Raleigh editor ridiculed Republicans of the Pennsylvania legislature who voted twenty-nine to thirteen against the franchise for Negroes. "This is a direct confession, by Northern Radicals," he added, "that they refuse to grant in Pennsylvania the *'justice'* they would enforce on the South. . . . And this is Radical meanness and hypocrisy—this their love for the negro."

There was little in the Republican presidential campaign of 1868 to confute the southern charge of hypocrisy and much to support it. The Chicago Platform of May on which General Grant was nominated contained as its second section this formulation of the double standard of racial morality: "The guaranty by Congress of equal suffrage to all loyal men at the South was demanded by every consideration of public safety, of gratitude, and of justice, and must be maintained; while the question of suffrage in all the loyal [i.e., northern] States properly belongs to the people of those States." Thus Negro *dis*franchisement was assured in the North along with enfranchisement in the South. No direct mention of the Negro was made in the entire platform, and no mention of schools or homesteads for freedmen. Neither Grant nor his running-mate Schuyler Colfax was known for any personal commitment to Negro rights, and Republican campaign speeches in the North generally avoided the issue of Negro suffrage.

Congress acted to readmit seven of the reconstructed states to the Union in time for them to vote in the presidential election and contribute to the Republican majority. In at-

taching conditions to readmission, however, Congress deliberately refrained from specifying state laws protecting Negroes against discrimination in jury duty, officeholding, education, intermarriage, and a wide range of political and civil rights. By a vote of thirty to five, the Senate defeated a bill attaching to the admission of Arkansas the condition that "no person on account of race or color shall be excluded from the benefits of education, or be deprived of an equal share of the moneys or other funds created or used by public authority to promote education. . . ."

Not until the election of 1868 was safely behind them did the Republicans come forward with proposals of national action on Negro suffrage that was to result in the Fifteenth Amendment. They were extremely sensitive to northern opposition to enfranchisement. By 1869, only seven northern states had voluntarily acted to permit the Negro to vote, and no state with a substantial Negro population outside the South had done so. Except for Minnesota and Iowa, which had only a handful of Negroes, every postwar referendum on the subject had gone down to defeat.

As a consequence moderates and conservatives among Republicans took over and dominated the framing of the Fifteenth Amendment and very strongly left their imprint on the measure. Even the incorrigibly radical Wendell Phillips yielded to their sway. Addressing other radicals, he pleaded, ". . . for the first time in our lives we beseech them to be a little more *politicians* and a little less *reformers.*" The issue lay between the moderates and the radicals. The former wanted a limited, negative amendment that would not confer suffrage on the freedmen, would not guarantee the franchise and take positive steps to protect it, but would merely prohibit its denial on the grounds of race and previous condition. Opposed to this narrow objective were the radicals who demanded positive and firm guarantees, federal protection, and national control of suffrage. They would take away state control, North as well as South. They fully anticipated and warned of all the elaborate devices that states might resort to—and eventually did resort to—in order to disfranchise the Negro without violating the proposed amendment. These included such methods— later made famous—as the literacy and property tests, the understanding clause, the poll tax, as well as elaborate and difficult registration tricks and handicaps. But safeguards against them were all rejected by the moderates. Only four votes could be mustered for a bill to guarantee equal suffrage to all states, North as well as South. "This amendment," said its moderate proponent Oliver P. Morton, "leaves the whole power in the State as it exists, now, except that colored men, shall not be disfranchised for the three reasons of race, color, or previous condition of slavery." And he added significantly, "They may, perhaps, require property or educational tests." Such tests were already in existence in Massachusetts and other northern states, and the debate made it perfectly apparent what might be expected to happen later in the South.

It was little wonder that southern Republicans, already faced with aggression against Negro voters and terribly apprehensive about the future, were intensely disappointed and unhappy about the shape the debate was taking. One of their keenest disappointments was the rejection of a clause prohibiting denial or abridgment of the right of officeholding on the ground of race. It is also not surprising that southern white conservatives, in view of these developments, were on the whole fairly relaxed about the proposed Fifteenth Amendment. The shrewder of them, in fact, began to realize that the whole thing was concerned mainly, not with the reconstruction of the South, but with maneuvers of internal politics in the northern states. After all, the Negroes were already fully enfranchised and voting regularly and solidly in all the southern states, their suffrage built into state constitutions and a condition of readmission to the Union.

Were there other motives behind the Fif-

teenth Amendment? The evidence is somewhat inferential, but a recent study has drawn attention to the significance of the closely divided vote in such states as Indiana, Ohio, Connecticut, New York, and Pennsylvania. The Negro population of these states was small, of course, but so closely was the white electorate in them divided between the two major parties that a small Negro vote could often make the difference between victory and defeat. It was assumed, of course, that this potential Negro vote would be reliably Republican. Enfranchisement by state action had been defeated in all those states, and federal action seemed the only way. There is no doubt that there was some idealistic support for Negro enfranchisement, especially among antislavery people in the North. But it was not the antislavery idealists who shaped the Fifteenth Amendment and guided it through Congress. The effective leaders of legislative action were moderates with practical political considerations in mind—particularly that thin margin of difference in partisan voting strength in certain northern states. They had their way, and they relentlessly voted down all measures of the sort the idealists, such as Senator Sumner, were demanding.

For successful adoption the amendment required ratification by twenty-eight states. Ratification would therefore have been impossible without support of the southern states, and an essential part of that had to come by requiring ratification as a condition of readmission of Virginia, and perhaps of Mississippi and Georgia as well.

The Fifteenth Amendment has often been read as evidence of renewed notice to the South of the North's firmness of purpose, as proof of its determination not be cheated of its idealistic war aims, as a solemn rededication to those aims. Read more carefully, however, the Fifteenth Amendment reveals more deviousness than clarity of purpose, more partisan needs than idealistic aims, more timidity than boldness.

Signals of faltering purpose in the North,

such as the Fifteenth Amendment and state elections in 1867, were not lost on the South. They were assessed carefully and weighed for their implications for the strategy of resistance. The movement of counter-reconstruction was already well under way by the time the amendment was ratified in March 1870, and in that year, the reactionary movement took on new life in several quarters. Fundamentally it was a terroristic campaign of underground organizations, the Ku Klux Klan and several similar ones, for the intimidation of Republican voters and officials, the overthrow of their power, and the destruction of their organization. Terrorists used violence of all kinds, including murder by mob, by drowning, by torch; they whipped, they tortured, they maimed, they mutilated. It became perfectly clear that federal intervention of a determined sort was the only means of suppressing the movement and protecting the freedmen in their civil and political rights.

To meet this situation, Congress passed the Enforcement Act of May 30, 1870, and followed it with the Second Enforcement Act and the Ku Klux Klan Act of 1871. These acts on the face of it would seem to have provided full and adequate machinery for the enforcement of the Fifteenth Amendment and the protection of the Negro and white Republican voters. They authorized the President to call out the army and navy and suspend the writ of habeas corpus; they empowered federal troops to implement court orders; and they reserved the federal courts' exclusive jurisdiction in all suffrage cases. The enforcement acts have gone down in history with the stereotypes "infamous" and "tyrannical" tagged to them. As a matter of fact, they were consistent with tradition and with democratic principle. Surviving remnants of them were invoked in recent years to authorize federal intervention at Little Rock and at Oxford, Mississippi. They are echoed in the Civil Rights Acts of 1957 and 1960, and they are greatly surpassed in the powers conferred by the Civil Rights Act of 1964 and the Voting Rights Act of 1965.

Surely this impressive display of federal power and determination, backed by gleaming steel and judicial majesty, might be assumed to have been enough to bring the South to its senses and dispel forever the fantasies of southern intransigents. And in fact, historians have in the main endorsed the assumption that the power of the Klan was broken by the impact of the so-called Force Bills.

The truth is that, while the Klan was nominally dissolved, the campaign of violence, terror, and intimidation went forward virtually unabated, save temporarily in places where federal power was displayed and so long as it was sustained. For all the efforts of the Department of Justice, the deterioration of the freedman's status and the curtailment and denial of his suffrage continued steadily and rapidly. Federal enforcement officials met with impediments of all sorts. A close study of their efforts reveals that "in virtually every Southern state . . . federal deputy marshals, supervisors of elections, or soldiers were arrested by local law-enforcement officers on charges ranging from false arrest or assault and battery to murder."

The obvious course for the avoidance of local passions was to remove cases to federal courts for trial, as provided under a section of the First Enforcement Act. But in practice this turned out to be "exceedingly difficult." And the effort to find juries that would convict proved often to be all but impossible, however carefully they were chosen, and in whatever admixture of color composed them. The most overwhelming evidence of guilt proved unavailing at times. Key witnesses under intimidation simply refused to testify, and those that did were known to meet with terrible reprisals. The law authorized the organization of the *posse comitatus* and the use of troops to protect juries and witnesses. But in practice the local recruits were reluctant or unreliable, and federal troops were few and remote and slow to come, and the request for them was wrapped in endless red tape and bureaucratic frustration.

All these impediments to justice might have

been overcome had sufficient money been made available by Congress. And right at this crucial point, once again, the northern will and purpose flagged and failed the cause they professed to sustain. It is quite clear where the blame lies. Under the new laws, the cost of maintaining courts in the most affected districts of the South soared tremendously, quadrupled in some. Yet Congress starved the courts from the start, providing only about a million dollars a year—far less than was required. The Attorney General had to cut corners, urge economy, and in 1873 instruct district attorneys to prosecute no case "unless the public interest imperatively demands it." An antiquated judicial structure proved wholly inadequate to handle the extra burden and clear their dockets. "If it takes a court over one month to try five offenders," asked the Attorney General concerning 420 indictments in South Carolina, "how long will it take to try four hundred, already indicted, and many hundreds more who deserve to be indicted?" He thought it "obvious that the attempt to bring to justice even a small portion of the guilty in that state must fail" under the circumstances. Quite apart from the inadequacy and inefficiency of the judicial structure, it is of significance that a majority of the Department of Justice officers in the South at this time, despite the carpetbagger infusion, were southern-born. A study by Everette Swinney concludes that "some marshals and district attorneys were either sensitive to southern public opinion or in substantial agreement with it." The same has been found true of numbers of federal troops and their officers on duty in the South. Then in 1874 an emasculating opinion of the Supreme Court by Justice Joseph P. Bradley in *United States* v. *Cruikshank et al.* cast so much doubt on the constitutionality of the enforcement

acts as to render successful prosecutions virtually impossible.

There is also sufficient evidence in existence to raise a question about how much the Enforcement Acts were intended all along for application in the policing of elections in the South, as against their possible application in other quarters of the Union. As it turned out, nearly half of the cost of policing was applied to elections of New York City, where Democratic bosses gave the opposition much trouble. Actually the bulk of federal expenditures under the Enforcement Acts was made in the North, which leads one student to conclude that their primary object from the start was not the distraught South under reconstruction, but the urban strongholds of the Democrats in the North. Once again, as in the purposes behind the Fifteenth Amendment, one is left to wonder how much Radical Reconstruction was really concerned with the South and how much with the party needs of the Republicans in the North.

Finally, to take a longer view, it is only fair to allow that if ambiguous and partisan motives in the writing and enforcing of Reconstruction laws proved to be the seeds of failure in American race policy for the earlier generations, those same laws and constitutional amendments eventually acquired a wholly different significance for the race policy of a later generation. The laws outlasted the ambiguities of their origins. The logic that excuses and vindicates the failures of one generation by reference to the successes of the next has always left something to be desired. It is, nevertheless, impossible to account fully for such limited successes as the Second Reconstruction can claim without acknowledging its profound indebtedness to the First.

Republican Rule in the South: The Contradictions of Power

Ted Tunnell

Henry Clay Warmoth celebrated his nineteenth birthday less than a month after the first shots of the Civil War lit up the early morning darkness of Charleston Harbor. He entered the army as a lieutenant colonel in the 32d Missouri, served on the staff of General John A. McClernand, commanded his regiment at Lookout Mountain, and hastened to the relief of General Banks during the ill-fated Red River campaign. His attachment to McClernand involved him in the bitter rivalry between that general and the rising star of the Union army, Ulysses S. Grant. Wounded at Vicksburg, Warmoth returned home on leave, which was subsequently extended (or so he believed). During his absence Grant ordered his dishonorable discharge, alleging that the young officer, absent without leave, had spread exaggerated accounts of Union losses in the North. Only an appeal to President Lincoln saved Warmoth's career. In later years, President Grant and Governor Warmoth probably never spoke of the incident, but neither man could have forgotten.

In 1864 General Banks appointed Warmoth judge of the provost court in New Orleans,

a position that proved important to his postwar career. As provost judge, he "became acquainted with all the members of the Bar and a great many of the residents of the city." He left the army in early 1865 and joined the small but influential class of Crescent City lawyers specializing in the legal problems of the occupation regime: courts-martial, military commissions, the federal bureaucracy, and claims against the government. His practice took him to Washington, and he was in the capital city the night of Lincoln's assassination.

Unlike most northern migrants of the war era, Warmoth pursued a political career from the start. Active in the organization of the state Republican party, he went to Washington in late 1865 as Louisiana's unofficial "territorial" delegate. Though his public speeches from this early period were quite ordinary (he stood for universal suffrage, loyal government, the return of General Butler, and the ex-soldier), his contemporaries marked him as a comer. Louisiana abounded with ex-brigadiers and major generals: yet the former lieutenant colonel emerged as the leader of the Grand Army of the Republic. Warmoth easily formed friendships with influential older men of widely varying views and backgrounds: Thomas J. Durant, the Reverend John P. Newman, General McClernand, George S. Denison, his law partner John F. Deane, William L. McMillen, and later Henry S. McComb. A tall, strikingly hand-

Reprinted by permission of Louisiana State University Press from *The Crucible of Reconstruction: War, Radicalism, and Race in Louisiana, 1862–1877* by Ted Tunnell. Copyright © 1984 by Louisiana State University Press.

some man, Warmoth's appearance was one of his strongest political assets. Like Banks, he looked the part of the statesman. In fact, Mrs. Banks had informed him at a wartime ball that he spoke and acted like young General Banks. Warmoth blushed and danced with the lady. Several days later, Banks offered him the judgeship of the provost court.

In his autobiography Warmoth described the condition of Louisiana in July 1868, when he took over as governor. New Orleans and the state government were bankrupt. The value of assessed property had fallen from $470 million in 1860 to only $250 million. Taxes were in arrears for every year since 1859. The state's agriculture had been ravaged by war, flood, and infestation. The longest piece of railroad track stretched a mere sixty miles; the only canal extended six miles from New Orleans to Lake Pontchartrain. The levees of the Mississippi and other waterways remained in a deplorable state. Almost no extractive or manufacturing industries marred the landscape. The public roads were little more than mud trails. Epidemics of yellow fever and malaria visited the state yearly. Of New Orleans, whatever romantic images it usually evokes, Warmoth recorded that it had only four paved streets, and "the slaughter-houses were so located that all of their offal and filth were poured into the Mississippi River, just about the mains that supplied the people with their drinking water." Overrun with gamblers, prostitutes, and thugs: ruled by corrupt and ignorant officials; the Crescent City was "a dirty, impoverished, and hopeless place." In sum, the state foundered in a veritable sea of troubles, but the paramount concern of the new regime was survival.

The response of the white South to the onset of Radical Reconstruction has been aptly described as "Counter Reconstruction." Rejecting the legitimacy of Republican governments based on Negro suffrage, white Southerners organized secretly and massively to destroy them. By the fall of 1868 there existed in Louisiana, as in other southern states,

a vast shadowland of secret paramilitary political clubs and societies: Knights of the White Camellia, Swamp Fox Rangers, Innocents, Seymour Knights, Hancock Guards, and the seldom seen but widely rumored Ku Klux Klan. The Knights of the White Camellia ranked as the largest and most important of these. Led by the "best" citizens and organized statewide, in many parishes its membership claimed half or more of the white males. The veil of secrecy shrouding these organizations concealed a fantasy world, where respectable citizens, like the heroes of a Thomas Dixon novel, guarded the "nest of the White Eagle" against the "black Vulture." In this paranoid realm, Negro uprisings were always imminent, and the carpetbagger and scalawag stereotypes of Reconstruction legend took on a sinister reality. The need to restore white rule justified every means, every sadistic impulse, every enormity.

A few instances of intimidation and fraud marred the April elections of 1868. On the upper Red River and a few other places, whites kept Negroes from the polls, destroyed Republican tickets, and tampered with the returns. None of this, though, prepared the new regime for the terrible ordeal of the presidential election. Starting in May and continuing through November, gangs of armed whites rode by day and night, spreading terror across the state. Among the first casualties was William R. Meadows, the literate ex-slave who had represented Claiborne Parish in the constitutional convention. Assassins murdered him in his yard. In a neighboring parish whites pulled a black leader from his home, shot him, and cut off his head. In St. Mary Parish disguised whites entered a hotel in the town of Franklin and publicly murdered the sheriff and judge with knives and pistols. A white Republican warned a colleague that unless the "almost daily" murders of Union men in north-central Louisiana could be stopped and stopped soon, "the Republican Party is at an end." Unprecedented murders and outrages in Franklin Parish convinced local Unionists that their enemies in-

This cartoon indicates the immense obstacles that southern blacks encountered when they tried to vote during Reconstruction. When they reached the polling place, after much struggle, they often found that their white Democratic opponents had managed to gain control of even the election machinery itself.

white mobs roamed the city and its suburbs, robbing, beating, and killing Negroes; breaking up Republican clubs and processions; and ambushing and so intimidating the police that patrolmen feared to leave their station houses. The violence spread to neighboring St. Bernard Parish where a series of clashes over four days left many people dead. Throughout the strife hundreds of Federal troops stood by passively, unable or unwilling to act. Estimates of deaths vary widely; clearly, however, at least sixty people, mostly black Republicans, died violent deaths between September 22 and election day in St. Bernard, Jefferson, and Orleans parishes.

*   *   *

State officials reported that the terrorists of 1868 killed 784 people and wounded or mistreated 450 more. A subsequent federal report estimated the dead alone at over a thousand. Election day revealed the full political effect of the violence. Warmoth had received 65,000 votes in April; in November Grant obtained only 33,000. In twenty-four parishes the Republican tally declined by over 27,000; in seven parishes Grant received not a single vote; in nine others he obtained a total of nineteen.

Had the voters that November chosen a state government, Radical Reconstruction in Louisiana would have ended almost before it started. The lesson was not lost on Warmoth and his party. Over the next three years they adopted an extraordinary legislative program. Like Republicans in other southern states, they organized a state militia. They feared, however, that a militia made up largely of blacks would prove inadequate; the massacres of 1868 had demonstrated all too vividly that nothing inflamed whites more than Negroes with guns. The regime badly needed dependable law officers in those parishes where the sheriffs were unreliable. Hence, they set up a constabulary force in the rural parishes directly under the governor. The constables and their deputies

tended to drive them out of the country or exterminate them. In an unsuccessful appeal to President Johnson for more Federal troops, Warmoth estimated on August 1 that 150 persons had been killed in Louisiana since the middle of June. Two weeks later an investigator informed him that his estimate erred by half and that "authentic evidence" indicated "double the number of Murders stated by you in your letter to the President."

The violence crested in the fall in a series of bloody massacres. In the Crescent City the first serious clash occurred on September 22 when white Democrats attacked a Republican procession. The last week in October New Orleans resembled a major European city in the throes of violent revolution. By day and night would guard the voting precincts on election day and arrest people who committed violent crimes. In time of trouble, the constabulary could be expanded indefinitely. In subsequent years Republican constables proved extremely effective in solidly Republican parishes, but much less so in Democratic or contested areas.

The Republican organization had taken a severe beating at the local level in 1868. All over the state party leaders had fled to New Orleans, perhaps 200 from St. Landry Parish alone. To break the Democratic hold over the countryside and reestablish their own position, the Republicans created eight new parishes, securing at least temporary dominance through the simple expedient of letting Warmoth appoint the new officials who then served until the next general election. This plan proved extremely effective in places. In Red River, for example, Marshall Harvey Twitchell built up such a base that it took the massed power of the White League in the Coushatta Massacre to tear it down. A ninth parish, Lincoln, organized in 1873 under Kellogg, emerged as the bailiwick of the Unionist Allen Greene and his family. Overall, however, parish reorganization did not significantly alter the balance of power in the countryside.

New Orleans ranked high on the Republican agenda. Nearly half the white males in the city belonged to the Knights of the White Camellia and other secret societies. The preelection riots there and in the adjacent parishes of Jefferson and St. Bernard not only cost the Republicans nearly 16,000 votes, they paralyzed the seat of government and mocked the authority of the new regime. The crux of the problem lay with the immense white majority in the Crescent City. Even in an honest election, the Republicans could rarely hope to elect the city government. They could, however, reorganize it, or transfer its powers to the state. In 1869–70 the legislature gave New Orleans a new charter, joined part of Jefferson Parish to Orleans, and combined the cities of New Orleans and Jefferson. Under this re-organization, Warmoth temporarily appointed the city government. Thus, from 1870 until the 1872 election, for the only time during Reconstruction, the top officials of New Orleans were Republicans. Even more important, the legislature combined Orleans, Jefferson, and St. Bernard parishes into the Metropolitan Police District, administered by a board of commissioners appointed by the governor. It also made the mayor of New Orleans and the sheriffs of all three parishes strictly subservient to the Metropolitan Police in matters of law enforcement. Although normally fixed at 500 patrolmen, the governor could expand the force indefinitely in special circumstances. Much more so than the state militia or the constabulary, the Metropolitan Police served as the military arm of both Governor Warmoth and Governor Kellogg [his successor from 1872 to 1876] throughout Reconstruction.

Finally, in the election law of 1870, the legislature gave the governor broad authority over the conduct of elections and, most important, created the state Returning Board. The Returning Board compiled the official results of every election; the law empowered it to discard the polls of any precinct in which violence or intimidation occurred; and the governor, lieutenant governor, and secretary of state served as ex officio members. In the political wars that followed, the Returning Board proved the most feared weapon in the Radical arsenal. The Returning Board cheated the Democrats in 1872, lamented one disgruntled member of that party, and robbed them a second time in 1874, "and we all believed that we would be cheated again in 1876 if the returning board dared to do it."

Considering the provocation, the Republican response was entirely logical. Nonetheless, it entrapped Warmoth and his party in the first of a series of fateful contradictions. The Republicans set out, as they believed, to democratize a land corrupted by the tyranny of slavery and, in fact, created the most democratic government the state had ever seen or would see again for a hundred years. But to protect themselves from those who would destroy them with violence, they constructed a police and election apparatus the internal logic of which subverted democratic government as surely as the tactics of their opponents. What leaders in American history could be trusted with a Returning Board legally authorized to alter election returns at will? Whether they fully realized it or not, the Republicans had created the instruments of one-party rule for the simple, compelling reason that the new implements of power could never be permitted to fall into the hands of the opposition. To lose one election, after all, meant surrendering the police and the Returning Board to Democratic control. Forced to use these powerful tools to remain in power, the Republicans employed them for that purpose in every election after 1870. They then found themselves caught in still another contradiction. Dependent on support from Washington, each time they employed their election apparatus to stave off the Democrats, they lost support in the nation's capital. Weary of the whole Reconstruction question, influential northerners listened with renewed interest to southern talk of home rule and the evils of carpetbag government.

At the start, though, all this lay in the future, and Warmoth never attempted to rule by such means alone. His strategy for consolidating Republican strength was twofold: Side by side with the policy of force, he pursued a policy of peace, a conciliatory approach intended to soften white resistance to Republican rule and win white converts to the Republican party. He used his patronage liberally, appointing prominent white conservatives to the bench and other state and local offices. His chief state engineer was a former Confederate general; as adjutant general of the state militia, he chose James A. Longstreet, distinguished corps commander of the Army of Northern Virginia, and he chose Penn Mason, a former officer on Robert E. Lee's staff, as major general. He divided the 5000-man militia force equally between whites, who were mostly ex-Rebel soldiers, and blacks. Depicting

himself as a fiscal conservative, Warmoth obtained a constitutional amendment limiting the state debt to $25,000,000. He vetoed thirty-nine bills, many of them pork barrel projects favored by Republican politicos. The governor also obtained the repeal of Article 99, the disfranchisement clause of the Radical constitution. Campaigning at Shreveport in 1870, the Illinoian boasted that his great-grandfather was a Virginian, his father a Tennessean, and that "every drop" of his own blood was southern. He claimed that he and President Grant "wanted every old 'Rebel' and every young 'Rebel,' to come in and join the Republican Party." He also stressed his efforts to hold down the public debt and promised a railroad to connect the former Confederate capital with New Orleans and Houston; afterwards the band played "Dixie."

Although they were opportunistic, these actions were not steeped in hypocrisy. Unlike many carpetbaggers, Warmoth, who was a prewar Democrat, remained comparatively free of sectional prejudice. Although outraged by southern atrocities, he expressed his anger against specific acts committed by specific people. He never concluded, as Ephraim S. Stoddard did, that the South was a "political fungus upon the body politic." Nor does one find him, like Marshall Harvey Twitchell, describing southern chivalry as a savage and barbaric "remnant of the dark ages." Stoddard and Twitchell, of course, were New Englanders, whereas Warmoth came from southern Illinois and boasted of his southern blood, probably with genuine pride. The young governor was plainly uncomfortable as the head of a mostly Negro party; whitening the party would have increased his personal self-esteem. Above all he held fast to the hope that expanding the Republican party's support among white voters would gain the respectability and acceptance that would make a repetition of the 1868 terror unthinkable.

Warmoth's policy achieved its most notable success among the state's foreign population. By the 1870 census, 113,486 of Louisiana's

726,915 people had either been born abroad or came from families in which both parents were foreign born. Eighty-two percent of this predominantly German and Irish population was strategically located in New Orleans. The employment rolls of the federal bureaucracy show that the Republicans recruited for members heavily among these people: Of 393 jobholders in 1875 whose nativity is listed, 108 were foreign born. Many other federal employees almost certainly came from immigrant families. If the Republicans could combine enough immigrant votes with black votes, they might challenge Democratic control of the Crescent City.

The Germans of New Orleans revealed divided loyalties during the Civil War and Reconstruction. At least several thousand had entered the Confederate armies; and on the other hand, Governor Michael Hahn, Max F. Bonzano, and other Germans contributed vitally to Free State Louisiana. Both of the German-language newspapers of wartime New Orleans took Unionist stands. One of these, the *German Gazette,* survived through Reconstruction and loyally supported Warmoth, although it broke with Kellogg. German Republican clubs existed in the city at least as early as the spring of 1867, and under Warmoth they were organized in the German sections of the city. The New Orleans *Republican,* the official mouthpiece of the Warmoth administration, described a club meeting in July 1870. In revival fashion the club's officers appealed for new members: "About eighteen men came forward and signed, . . . making the strength of this club eighty-one members."

Unfortunately, the Republicans proved less successful with the Irish. The Germans were conservative, the Irish even more so. A prominent leader resigned from the Irish Republican Club in 1870, according to the secretary, because the club was "to[o] radical." He departed advising the members "to be more Democratic." The crux of the matter, of course, was race. The New Orleans *Tribune* observed in 1869 that, unlike the Germans, the Irish

"have for the most part sided with the Democratic party against us."

Beyond the foreign population, the interim elections of 1870 revealed the Warmoth administration attempting to embrace a broad spectrum of white Louisianians. In the Florida parishes, a predominantly small farming region, the governor asserted that staple of Republican doctrine that held slavery had oppressed "the poor white man" almost as much as the Negro. The Republican party, he therefore concluded, had done as much for southern whites as for blacks. Too often in the past, he said, yeoman whites had spurned the party of emancipation, but all that had not changed; every day brought new recruits as white Southerners saw the truth. The "old line Whigs" represented another recruitment target; they "are abandoning the ranks of the Democracy and joining the Republican clubs all through the northern portion of the State," asserted the *Republican.* The newspaper also predicted that "scores of the best citizens" in Shreveport and "leading Democratic merchants" in New Orleans intended to vote Republican. The official journal even placed faith in "that large and intelligent class of citizens who vote for the best men without regard to politics." Indeed, wherever the *Republican* looked it discovered unhappy whites deserting the Democratic standard.

The 1870 returns, moreover, seemed to justify optimism. In the freest election of the decade, the Republicans won their most sweeping victory, cementing their hold on the legislature, controlling New Orleans, and sending five carpetbaggers to Congress. In the statewide races for auditor and treasurer, an Irishman, James Graham, and a free man of color, Antoine Dubuclet, rolled up 24,000-vote majorities, sweeping the Crescent City with a 6000-vote edge, carrying the white-dominated rural parishes, Sabine, Cameron, Tangipahoa, Catahoula and finishing close in others. Warmoth's goal of a Republican party "in which the conservative and honest white people of the State should have a share," appeared on the verge of reality. But the appearance was deceptive. Graham and Dubuclet received only about 300 more votes than Warmoth had obtained in 1868. In other words, Louisiana whites, instead of converting to Radicalism, simply failed to vote.

Despite victory, the Republicans were a troubled party. Many Radicals failed to share the governor's vision of their future; more fundamentally, the policy of peace, like the policy of force, entrapped Warmoth and his party in damaging contradictions. There was, to begin with, the patronage dilemma. In a patronage-hungry party, every job the governor gave a Democrat took a job away from a Republican, arousing resentment in the Radical party. One disgruntled man asked state superintendent of education Thomas W. Conway, if Warmoth "is the staunch Republican you take him to be, why is it, that he invariably appoints the most ultra democrats to offices of trust & emolument?" In East Feliciana Parish, the man claimed, Warmoth appointed a Confederate colonel who tried "to have me snobbed" by the "leading rebel families." Among those most alarmed was Lieutenant Governor Oscar J. Dunn, who, before his death in November 1871, was among the most influential Negro leaders in the South. Pointing to Warmoth's Democratic appointments, he warned a black leader in Opelousas that "an effort is being made to sell us out to the Democrats . . . and we must nip it right in the bud." In a widely published letter to Horace Greeley, Dunn charged that Warmoth "has shown an itching desire . . . to secure the personal support of the Democracy at the expense of his own party, and an equally manifest craving to obtain a cheap and ignoble white respectability by the sacrifice of . . . the masses of that race who elected him." Warmoth, Dunn alleged, was "the first Ku Klux Governor" of the Republican party.

The patronage controversy climaxed in a vicious fight over the collectorship of the port of New Orleans. Under President Johnson the United States Custom House remained notoriously conservative. For three years Kellogg carefully trimmed his sail to the Johnsonian breeze. When Kellogg resigned the collectorship to enter the United States Senate, a coterie of lame-duck Democratic officials put in motion a clever scheme to ensure their position and influence under a Republican President. The interim collector, Perry Fuller, resigned, and President Johnson then recommended President-elect Grant's brother-in-law James F. Casey, a Kentucky Democrat, as his replacement. Grant walked into the trap. Louisiana Republicans found themselves saddled with a Democratic collector of the port, and they were soon up in arms, demanding that either Casey get rid of the Democrats in the Custom House or that Grant remove him. This movement peaked in the spring of 1870 and appeared on the verge of success when Warmoth abruptly deserted a united front and swung over to the collector's support. He probably hoped to bring Casey and the Custom House into alliance with himself, at the same time cementing his relations with the President, who was plainly reluctant to fire his wife's brother. He saved Casey, but Kellogg, Packard, and a legion of powerful Republicans never forgave him. And, prophetically, a carpetbagger friend warned him that Casey was faithless to his word: "He will not stand by you one week unless for his interest." Sure enough, the following year Casey abandoned Warmoth and went over to Kellogg and Packard. Warmoth now found the whole of federal officialdom arrayed against him and his once cordial relations with Grant suddenly grown cold.

To blacks, conciliation was not simply a matter of jobs; jobs involved race, and race emerged as the central contradiction in Warmoth's policy. Few words revealed the conflict more fully than those the *German Gazette* wrote about the new editor of the New Orleans *Republican,* Michael Hahn in 1869. Under Hahn, a German and a Southerner, the

Gazette observed approvingly, the *Republican* had abandoned its ultra-Radical, anti-southern bias. Most important, the new editor was not addicted to the "nigger-question." He believed that the Negro had received his due, and the country should now turn to other matters; nothing would be gained by abasing white Southerners for the benefit of Africa.

Warmoth and the official press strove to subordinate the race issue in the 1870 election. At Shreveport the governor stressed that he had not pressed the Negro question on white Louisiana. The party supported the political equality of all men, said the *Republican,* but "we have denounced social equality, for that is neither beneficent nor practical." The official journal looked forward to the day when "the grave of caste and color will be sealed up irrevocably, and our only issues will be as to good men and correct principles." A parish newspaper argued that the Republican party "has got to rise superior to a white man's party or a black man's party." The Negro, it claimed had to resist being "the tool of men who would make him . . . vote as a black man and not as a Republican." Another rural Republican paper asserted that promoting individuals to public office merely because they were black "is not the principle of the Republican party." Intelligence and integrity, it argued, ought to be the qualifications for office, regardless of color.

The conflicts in Warmoth's policy showed up most clearly in the long controversy over civil rights in Louisiana Reconstruction. As set forth in the Radical constitution, the legal and political equality of all men was the keystone of the new order, Warmoth asserted in his inaugural address. Yet he recognized that a significant portion of the population, "not wanting in intelligence and virtue," resisted this doctrine. "Let our course," then, "while resolute and manly, be also moderate and discreet." Better, he added, that our laws should lag behind popular opinion than outrun it. Two months later the legislature gave him a chance to demonstrate this manly discretion; it adopted a bill to enforce Article 13 of the constitution, making it a criminal offense for steamboats, railroads, and places of public resort to discriminate against Negroes. Warmoth resolutely vetoed it. Public opinion, he maintained, was not ready for such measures, and "we can not hope by legislation to control questions of personal association." He also observed that the eve of the 1868 election was notably bad timing for "what is practically class legislation." The bill's author, Robert H. Isabelle, a free man of color, and other black legislators fumed.

When the legislature convened again a few months later, P. B. S. Pinchback sponsored a second bill to enforce Article 13. The election was past, and Pinchback, after Dunn, ranked as the most powerful black leader in the state. During his entire governorship Warmoth worked to keep him on his side. In 1871, for example, the New Orleans, Mobile and Chattanooga Railroad denied Pinchback sleeping car accommodations, resulting in a $25,000 lawsuit by the Negro senator. Behind the scenes, Warmoth tried to get the railroad's policy reversed. "Just tell your ticket agents," he advised Henry S. McComb, "to give tickets to those who apply without regard to color and it will be soon forgotten entirely that whites and negroes had not been sleeping together always (as indeed they have in this country)." When Dunn died, Warmoth secured Pinchback's election in his place, or, probably more accurately, Pinchback, controlling the balance of power in the senate between rival factions of the Republican party and the Democrats, secured his own election. Pinchback the realist perceived what Dunn never did: that Negroes would not attain their rights to any greater degree under Kellogg and Packard than under Warmoth. In any event, Warmoth signed the civil rights act of 1869.

Under the new law segregation in Louisiana remained virtually unchanged. The Negro sheriff of Orleans Parish won a lawsuit against a tavern owner, but apart from that race relations continued as they had before. When Senator William Butler demanded equal accommodations on the steamer *Bannock City,* white passengers clubbed him with an iron bar and threw him out of his cabin onto the deck. It was a measure of black frustration that in 1870 the legislature adopted yet a third bill "forbidding unjust discrimination" in places of public accommodation "on account of race or color." It was passed in the last five days of the session, and under Louisiana law Warmoth had until the next legislature met to sign or reject it. It was an election year, and Warmoth waited, his delay coinciding exactly with his turnabout in the Casey controversy. When the annual state convention of the Republican party met in August, a coalition of indignant carpetbaggers and blacks skillfully ambushed him. The convention first nominated both Warmoth and Dunn for President, and then humiliated Warmoth by choosing his lieutenant governor. His enemies then stacked the central executive committee against him and started a heated debate over the unsigned civil rights bill. Packard and Charles W. Lowell denounced Warmoth as "the great stumbling-block" to Negro rights in the state. Despite the uproar, the governor vetoed the held-over civil rights bill early in 1871.

Warmoth pursued an equally equivocal policy on mixed schools. Under the education act of 1869, Warmoth and Superintendent Conway, a loyal supporter, controlled the state board of education, which in turn controlled the school directors of New Orleans. Thus, the ultimate responsibility for the limited desegregation instituted in New Orleans in 1870 belonged with the governor, who probably felt compelled to satisfy the demands of the *gens de couleur* for enforcement of the constitution. On the other hand, Warmoth and Conway made no effort to desegregate rural schools, and it is clear that they cooperated secretly with officials at Louisiana State Seminary in preserving that institution's lily-white policy. The seminary's president, David F. Boyd, talked with Warmoth and Conway soon after they took office. The governor and the state superintendent would leave the seminary alone, he informed friends, "because they are fully impressed with the belief that if they materially interfere with the school, they will *kill* it, which (for *political* reasons, if no other) they are anxious not to do." Warmoth and Conway adhered to this course throughout their term of office.

By mid-1871 the policy of peace had permanently destroyed the unity of the Radical party. And in a moral climate set by the night riders of 1868, Republican tactics against one another increasingly resembled the terrorists' tactics against them. In August, United States Marshal Packard used the army and federal deputy marshals to control the Republican state convention. Five months later the warring Republicans turned the streets of New Orleans into a scene reminiscent of 1868. On January 4, Packard's deputies arrested Warmoth, Pinchback, and seventeen members of the legislature. The governor obtained bail, proclaimed a conspiracy existed to overthrow the government, and seized the State House with militia and Metropolitan Police. Only the presence of federal troops prevented a pitched battle. These episodes made headlines all over the nation and had far-reaching repercussions. In New York and "everywhere through the north, there is but one feeling," an ally informed Warmoth. "They know little & care less about our fight among ourselves but they won't stand bayonets."

The crisis came to a head in the 1872 election. The party became divided into three separate factions led by Warmoth, Kellogg-Packard, and Pinchback. The Kellogg-Packard and Pinchback groups eventually united, while, as a Liberal Republican, Warmoth tried to lead a fusion party of conservative Republicans, Democrats, and "Reformers." Privy to the inner councils of the Democratic party, David F. Boyd explained what happened to William T. Sherman. Numerous Democrats, he claimed, saw in Warmoth and *"his Republican influence* their only chance . . . for freeing our

State from Carpet-bag and negro rule. I was one of them, and . . . wished to run him for Governor." The Democratic majority, however, "said *no*" to Warmoth leading the ticket and resolved instead to "get '*his influence,*' with the understanding that we send him to the U.S. Senate! This policy prevailed. Warmoth was left off the ticket, but still *his influence* was counted upon, with his election law . . . as the *mainspring* of the Liberal and Democratic movement." Warmoth accepted the bargain because he could not again be elected Republican governor of Louisiana; even if he had won the nomination, which was a doubtful proposition, the Kellogg-Packard forces would have run against him, dividing the party and ensuring a Democratic victory.

Both the Fusionists and the Republicans defrauded one another, although there was no repetition of the horrors of 1868. The Fusionists had more to work with and probably won, but the actual returns mattered little, for this was an extraordinary affair, even by the standards of Reconstruction. For weeks after the election Warmoth and his enemies maneuvered like wild men in some bizarre political theater of the absurd. In a development that its creators never foresaw, the state Returning Board split into two different panels: One proclaimed victory for Kellogg (though it never looked at the returns), the other declared victory for the Fusionist-Democratic candidate John D. McEnery. The house impeached Warmoth in December, and, although he was never convicted, Pinchback acted as governor for the few weeks that remained in his term. The evening before his impeachment, the governor attempted to strike some desperate bargain with his lieutenant governor. I have slept on the proposition you made to me last night," Pinchback replied, "and have resolutely determined to do my duty to my state, party, and race, by declining. . . . I am truly sorry for you but cannot help you."

On January 14, 1873, William Pitt Kellogg took the oath of office as Governor of Louisiana. On the same hour of the same day John D. McEnery swore the same oath at Lafayette Square. That winter and spring rival governors, legislatures, and, in many places, parish officials claimed power in Louisiana. A reign of violence descended on the state. On March 5 the Metropolitan Police, supported by Federal troops, bloodily repulsed white mobs that attacked police stations in the Crescent City. The Metropolitans struck back the next day, seizing Odd Fellows Hall and arresting the members of the McEnery legislature, who were inside. In April a conflict between rival officials in Grant parish resulted in the bloody Colfax Massacre. The disputants carried the controversy to Washington, where with evident distaste for the fruits of Radical Reconstruction in Louisiana, the Republican-dominated Congress adjourned without resolving the conflict. Finally, in May President Grant upheld the Kellogg regime, but it proved a costly and barren victory. Kellogg would rule the corpse of Republican Louisiana.

The debacle of the Warmoth years resulted from a failure to resolve a crisis of legitimacy. Louisiana Republicans, as did their counterparts elsewhere in the South, confronted enemies who challenged not only Radical policies but the very existence of the Radical regime, enemies who held Warmoth and all his party to be criminal usurpers. The Warmoth administration met the threat with a twofold strategy: the policy of force and the policy of peace. The strategy failed. The policy of force helped protect the regime, but at an unacceptable cost. The Republican election apparatus was so patently undemocratic that it made northern voters as well as Southerners question the legitimacy of the Republican government. By the end of 1872 the crisis of legitimacy was fast emerging as a national, not just a regional, problem. The policy of peace, on the other hand, not only failed, on any significant scale, to conciliate white Louisianians, it destroyed the Republican party from within. The Warmoth strategies were in fact mutually contradictory; they negated each other and demolished his government.

Suggestions for Further Reading

Part One   The Encounter Between the Indians and the Europeans

Some of the most fascinating studies arising from the renewed interest in native American history can be sampled through James Axtell's *The European and the Indian: Essays in the Ethnohistory of British America, 1607–1789* (1985); his *The Invasion Within: The Contest of Cultures in Colonial North America* (1985); Francis Jennings, *The Invasion of America: Indians, Colonialism and the Cant of Conquest* (1975); William Cronon, *Changes in the Land: Indians, Colonists and the Ecology of New England* (1983); Neal Saulsbury, *Manitou and Providence: Indians, Europeans and the Making of New England* (1982).

Also helpful are Robert Berkhofer, *The White Man's Indian: Images of the Indian from Columbus to the Present* (1978); Gary B. Nash, *Red, White, and Black: The Peoples of Early America* (1982); Karen Ordahl Kupperman, *Settling with the Indians: The Meeting of English and Indian Cultures in America, 1580–1640* (1980); Bernard Sheehan, *Savagism and Civility: Indians and Englishmen in Colonial Virginia* (1980); and the anthropologist, Anthony F. C. Wallace, *The Death and Rebirth of the Seneca* (1969). An examination of how Indians have been treated in textbooks is Frederick E. Hoxie, *The Indians Versus the Textbooks: Is There Any Way Out?* (1984).

Part Two   The Origins of Slavery

Readers wishing to pursue this topic further should naturally consult Edmund Morgan, *American Slavery, American Freedom: The Ordeal of Colonial Virginia* (1975) and Peter Kolchin, *Unfree Labor: American Slavery and Russian Serfdom* (1987).

The earlier debate about the origins of race prejudice can be followed through Oscar and Mary Handlin, "Origins of the Southern Labor System," *William and Mary Quarterly,* 1950; Carl Degler, "Slavery and the Genesis of American Race Prejudice," *Comparative Studies in Society and History,* 1959; and Winthrop Jordan, *White Over Black: American Attitudes toward the Negro, 1550–1812* (1968), chapter 2.

On colonial slavery, see Peter Wood, *Black Majority: Negroes in Colonial South Carolina from 1670 through the Stono Rebellion* (1974); Gerald Mullin, *Flight and Rebellion: Slave Resistance in Eighteenth Century Virginia* (1972); Timothy H. Breen and Stephen Innes, *"Myne Owne Ground:" Race and Freedom on Virginia's Eastern Shore, 1640–1676* (1980); and Daniel C. Littlefield, *Rice and Slaves: Ethnicity and the Slave Trade in Colonial South Carolina* (1981).

On the economics and demographics of the Chesapeake labor force, see Russell Menard, "From Servants to Slaves: The Transformation of the Chesapeake Labor System," *Southern Studies,* 1977, and David W. Galenson, *White Servitude in Colonial America* (1981). Allan Kulikoff, *Tobacco and Slaves: The Development of Southern Cultures in the Chesapeake, 1680–1800* (1987) is a study of Virginia and Maryland after slavery was established.

Part Three   Culture and Society in Seventeenth-Century New England

Many books have been written about the Puritans and the Massachusetts Bay colony. In fact, until recently, seventeenth-century colonial history was almost entirely focused on New England. Edmund Morgan has produced two of the most influential books on the Puritans in recent years, and both are brief and very readable. They are *The Puritan Family* (1966) and *The Puritan Dilemma: The Story of John Winthrop* (1958). Also worthwhile is Timothy Breen and Stephen Foster, "The Puritans' Greatest Achievement: Social Cohesion in 17th Century Massachusetts," *Journal of American History,* 1973.

In the 1960s and 1970s, a spate of books on New England village communities appeared, three of which might be consulted; they are Kenneth Lockridge, *A New England Town: The First Hundred Years, Dedham, Mass., 1636–1736* (1970); Sumner C. Powell, *Puritan Village: The Formation of a New Town* (1963); and John Demos, *A Little Commonwealth: Family Life in Plymouth Colony* (1970). A different view can be found in Christine Heyrman, *Community and Culture: the Maritime Communities of Colonial Massachusetts, 1690–1750* (1984). An earlier evaluation is John Murrin's "Review Essay" in *History and Theory* (1972).

Perry Miller's studies of Puritan thought are most important, and perhaps the most accessible is a collection of essays, entitled *Errand into the Wilderness* (1964). On the crisis at Salem in the 1690s, see Paul Boyer and Stephen Nissenbaum, *Salem Possessed: The Social Origins of Witchcraft* (1974). Finally, a collection of perceptive essays by Timothy Breen, entitled *Puritans and Adventurers: Change and Persistence in Early America* (1980), discusses the transmission of English ideas and experiences to America in both the New England and the southern colonies.

Part Four   The Great Awakening

The most extensive treatment of the ideas of the Awakening and their impact is Alan Heimert, *Religion and the American Mind: From the Great Awakening to the American Revolution* (1966). Also exploring the broader implications of the revivals are Richard L. Bushman, *From Puritan to Yankee: Character and the Social Order in Connecticut, 1690–1765* (1967); Sidney Mead, "From Coercion to Persuasion: Another Look at the Rise of Religious Liberty and the Emergence of Denominationalism," *Church History,* 1956 (reprinted in his *The Lively Experiment: The Shaping of Christianity in America,* 1963); Cedric B. Cowing, *The Great Awakening and the American Revolution: Colonial Thought in the Eighteenth Century* (1971); and Richard Hofstadter, *America at 1750: A Social Portrait* (1973), chapters 7 and 8. See also Rhys Isaac, *The Transformation of Virginia, 1740–1790* (1982).

Valuable collections of texts and documents from the Awakening are J. M. Bumsted and John E. Van de Wetering, eds., *What Must I Do To Be Saved?* (1976); Richard L. Bushman, ed., *The Great Awakening: Documents on the Revival of Religion, 1740–1745* (1970); and Alan Heimert and Perry Miller, eds., *The Great Awakening: Documents Illustrating the Crisis and Its Consequences* (1967).

Biographies of figures in the revivals are Perry Miller, *Jonathan Edwards* (1958); Patricia Tracy, *Jonathan Edwards, Pastor: Religion and Society in Eighteenth Century Northampton* [*Mass.*] (1979); and William G. McLoughlin, *Isaac Backus and the American Pietistic Tradition* (1967).

Perry Miller's classic essay "The Great Awakening from 1740 to 1750" in his *Errand into the Wilderness* (1956) should be consulted.

Part Five   The Origins and Nature of the American Revolution

Readers should first consult the books by Bailyn and Nash mentioned in the introduction to the readings. In addition, there is a fascinating collection of essays by a number of leading historians, including the three chosen for this topic, in Stephen G. Kurtz and James H. Hutson, eds., *Essays on the American Revolution* (1973).

A pivotal moment in the widening breach with Britain is analyzed in Edmund S. and Helen M. Morgan, *The Stamp Act Crisis: Prologue to Revolution* (1953). Robert Gross, *The Minutemen and Their World* (1976) is a local but revealing study of how the war came to Concord, Massachusetts. An interesting angle on the Revolution is Thomas C. Barrow, "The American Revolution Considered as a Colonial War for Independence," *William and Mary Quarterly,* 1968. A discussion of rival interpretations is Ian R. Christie and Benjamin W. Labaree, *Empire or Independence, 1760–1776* (1976).

The social implications of the crisis are discussed in J. Franklin Jameson's pioneering *The American Revolution Considered as a Social Movement* (1926); in a collection of essays edited by Alfred F. Young, *The American Revolution: Explorations in the History of American Radicalism* (1976); in Jack P. Greene, "The Social Origins of the American Revolution: An Evaluation and an Interpretation," *Political Science Quarterly,* 1973; and in Edward Countryman's interpretative survey, *The American Revolution* (1985).

The war itself is analyzed in a collection of essays by John Shy, entitled *A People Numerous and*

Armed (1976) and in Charles Royster, *A Revolutionary People at War: The Continental Army and American Character, 1775–1783* (1979).

Part Six   The Federal Constitution and Its Political Significance

More about Murrin's view on the Englishness of Revolutionary America can be found in John Murrin and Rowland Berthoff, "Feudalism, Communalism, and the Yeoman Freeholder: The American Revolution Considered as a Social Accident," in Stephen G. Kurtz and James H. Hutson, eds., *Essays on the American Revolution* (1973). And more on Banning's approach is in Lance Banning, *The Jeffersonian Persuasion: Evolution of a Party Ideology* (1978).

The political ideas of the Revolutionary generation are discussed in Bernard Bailyn, *The Ideological Origins of the American Revolution* (1967) and Gordon S. Wood, *The Creation of the American Republic, 1776–1787* (1969). The opponents of the Constitution are investigated in Jackson T. Main, *The Anti-Federalists: Critics of the Constitution* (1961); Cecilia M. Kenyon, "Men of Little Faith: The Anti-Federalists on the Nature of Representative Government," *William and Mary Quarterly,* 1955; and Herbert J. Storing and Murray Dry, *What the Anti-Federalists Were For* (1981). Two other articles of interest are Stanley Elkins and Eric McKitrick, "The Founding Fathers: Young Men of the Revolution," *Political Science Quarterly,* 1961, and Martin Diamond, "Democracy and *The Federalist,*" *American Political Science Review,* 1959. The thought and attitudes of the Founders are discussed in a recent collection of essays, edited by Richard Beeman and others, called *Beyond Confederation: Origins of the Constitution and American National Identity* (1987), which includes the essay by John Murrin.

A critique of Banning's views about republicanism is in Joyce Appleby, "What is Still American in the Political Philosophy of Thomas Jefferson?" *William and Mary Quarterly,* 1982, and also in her *Capitalism and a New Social Order: The Republican Vision of the 1790's* (1984).

Of course, students who want to delve into the debate on the Constitution should read Madison, Hamilton and Jay, *The Federalist Papers,* especially Madison's celebrated Tenth, and also Herbert J. Storing, ed., *The Anti-Federalist* (1985).

Part Seven   Political Parties in the Age of Jackson

The dominating figure in the politics of the era was Andrew Jackson, of course, and Robert V. Remini's *The Life of Andrew Jackson* (1988), a distillation of his prize-winning biography in three volumes, is the place to start. Also valuable are John William Ward, *Andrew Jackson: Symbol for an Age* (1955) and Richard Hofstadter's chapter on Jackson in his *The American Political Tradition* (1948). Richard P. McCormick's *The Second American Party System: Party Formation in the Jacksonian Era* (1966) suggests how the new parties came into being. With the exception of Remini, these historians tend to see the parties as similar and not primarily concerned about issues.

Examples of a different viewpoint can be found in Herbert Ershkowitz and William G. Shade, "Consensus or Conflict? State Legislatures during the Jacksonian Era," *Journal of American History,* 1971; Marc W. Kruman, *Parties and Politics in North Carolina, 1835–1865* (1983); and Major Wilson, "The Concept of Time and the Political Dialogue in the United States, 1828–1848," *American Quarterly,* 1967.

Also relevant are Sydney Nathans, *Daniel Webster and Jacksonian Democracy* (1973); Peter Temin, *The Jacksonian Economy* (1969); James R. Sharp, *The Jacksonians Versus the Banks: Politics in the States After the Panic of 1837* (1970); and William R. Brock, *Parties and Political Conscience, 1840–1850* (1979). A diverse collection of interpretations has been assembled in *New Perspectives on Jacksonian Parties and Politics* (1969), edited by Edward Pessen.

Part Eight   A Ferment of Reform, 1830–1860

Insightful essays offering differing interpretations of the galaxy of reforms of this era are John L. Thomas, "Romantic Reform in America, 1815–1865," *American Quarterly,* 1965, and Arthur E. Bestor, Jr., "Patent-Office Models of the Good Society," *American Historical Review,* 1953. Books covering all aspects of reform are Alice Felt Tyler, *Freedom's Ferment: Phases of American Social History from the Colonial Period to the Outbreak of the Civil War* (1944) and Ronald Walters, *American Reformers, 1815–1860* (1978).

On abolition, which became the predominant reform by the 1840s and which was also brought to a successful conclusion after the war, see Ronald Walters, *The Antislavery Appeal: American Abolitionism after 1830* (1976); James B. Stewart, *Holy Warriors: The Abolitionists and American Slavery* (1976); Aileen Kraditor, *Means and Ends in American Abolitionism: Garrison and His Critics on Strategy and Tactics* (1967); and two collections of essays, Martin Duberman, ed., *The Anti-slavery Vanguard* (1965) and Lewis Perry and Michael Fellman, eds., *Anti-slavery Reconsidered: New Perspectives on the Abolitionists* (1979).

On other reforms, consult David Rothman, *The Discovery of the Asylum: Social Order and Disorder in the New Republic* (1971); Michael Katz, *The Irony of Early School Reform: Education and Innovation in Mid-Nineteenth Century Massachusetts* (1968); Carroll Smith-Rosenberg, *Religion and the Rise of the American City: The New York City Mission Movement, 1812–1870* (1971); Michael Fellman, *The Unbounded Frame: Freedom and Community in Nineteenth Century American Utopianism* (1973); Mary P. Ryan, *Cradle of the Middle Class: The Family in Oneida County, New York, 1790–1865* (1981); and Whitney Cross, *The Burned-over District; The Social and Intellectual History of Enthusiastic Religion in Western New York, 1800–1850* (1950). The intense opposition to the abolitionists in the North is revealed in Leonard L. Richards, *"Gentlemen of Property and Standing:" Anti-Abolition Mobs in Jacksonian America* (1970).

Part Nine   Masters and Slaves in the Southern Slave System

There are two books that offer a synthesis of the new findings on slavery; they are Nathan I. Huggins, *Black Odyssey* (1977) and John Blassingame, *The Slave Community* (1979). Eugene D. Genovese, *Roll, Jordan, Roll: The World the Slaves Made* (1974) is a demanding but rewarding treatment. An insightful essay on several aspects of the master-slave relationship is his "American Slaves and Their History," in Eugene D. Genovese, *In Red and Black: Marxian Explorations in Southern and Afro-American History* (1972).

On slave religion, see Albert Raboteau, *Slave Religion: The "Invisible" Institution in the Antebellum South* (1978). On slave songs and folklore, consult Lawrence Levine, *Black Culture and Black Consciousness* (1970), chapters 1 and 2. And, for the

slave family, see Herbert Gutman, *The Black Family in Slavery and Freedom, 1750–1925* (1976). The experience of a particular slave population is portrayed in Charles Joyner, *Down By the Riverside: A South Carolina Slave Community* (1984). A thoughtful qualification of the thrust of most of these studies is Peter Kolchin, "Reevaluating the Antebellum Slave Community: A Comparative Perspective," *Journal of American History,* 1983.

Also to be considered, of course, are Willie Lee Rose's essays in *Slavery and Freedom* (1982), from which the selection was taken, and Drew Gilpin Faust, *James Henry Hammond and the Old South: A Design For Mastery* (1982), especially chapters 5 and 6.

Part Ten   Sectional Conflict and Civil War

The best single volume on the coming of the Civil War is David M. Potter, *The Impending Crisis, 1848–1861* (1976). Another account that is insightful is David H. Donald, *Liberty and Union: The Crisis of Popular Government* (1978). Barrington Moore, Jr., "The American Civil War: Last Capitalist Revolution," a chapter in his *Social Origins of Dictatorship and Democracy* (1966), is a stimulating analysis. Kenneth M. Stampp, "The Irrepressible Conflict," in his collected essays, *The Imperiled Union* (1980), offers a judicious assessment of the cause of the war. Two interesting pieces on the interpretative debate over the war's origins and meaning are Arthur Schlesinger, Jr., "The Causes of the Civil War: A Note On Historical Sentimentalism," *Partisan Review,* 1949, and Eric Foner, "The Causes of the Civil War: Recent Interpretations and New Directions," *Civil War History,* 1974.

The politics of the 1850s are treated in Eric Foner, *Free Soil, Free Labor, Free Men: The Ideology of the Republican Party Before the Civil War* (1970); Michael Holt, *The Political Crisis of the 1850s* (1978); and William Gienapp, *The Origins of the Republican Party, 1852–1856* (1987).

On the antebellum South, see Edward Pessen, "How Different from Each Other Were the Antebellum North and South?" *American Historical Review,* 1980; Eugene D. Genovese, *The Political Economy of Slavery* (1965), especially chapter 1; James Oakes, *The Ruling Race: A History of American Slaveholders* (1982); Michael Johnson, *Toward a Patriarchal Republic: The Secession of*

Georgia (1977): J. Mills Thornton III, *Politics and Power in a Slave Society: Alabama, 1800–1860* (1978); and several of the essays in David Potter, *The South and the Sectional Conflict* (1968).

Part Eleven   Why the North Won and the South Lost

The military history of the war can be followed in great detail through Bruce Catton's *The Centennial History of the Civil War* (1961–1965) in three volumes and James McPherson's *Battle Cry of Freedom: The Civil War* (1988). Also helpful is T. Harry Williams, *Lincoln and His Generals* (1967).

A recent study by Richard E. Beringer, Herman Hattaway et al., called *Why the South Lost the Civil War* (1986) is very valuable, as is an earlier collection of essays edited by David Donald, entitled *Why the North Won the Civil War* (1962), that contains provocative contributions by T. Harry Williams, David Potter, Richard Current, David Donald and Norman Graebner. Eric L. McKitrick's "Party Politics and the Union and Confederate War Efforts, in William N. Chambers and Walter Dean Burnham, eds., *The American Party Systems* (1967) is particularly insightful.

A challenging interpretation of the Confederacy is Emory Thomas, *The Confederacy as a Revolutionary Experience* (1971). See also his *The Confederate Nation* (1979) and Peter Parish's *The American Civil War* (1975), along with William L. Barney's *Flawed Victory* (1975). The latest biography of Lincoln is Stephen B. Oates, *With Malice Toward None* (1979).

Part Twelve   The Problem of Reconstruction

Vann Woodward's piece has since been republished in a book of his essays, entitled *American Counterpoint: Slavery and Racism in the North-South Dialogue* (1976). He also has a very perceptive essay emphasizing the radical features of the post-emancipation experience of the United States, called "The Price of Freedom," in David Sansing, ed., *What Was Freedom's Price?* (1978).

A brief synthesis of the history of the period that has appeared recently is Michael Perman's *Emancipation and Reconstruction, 1862–1879* (1987). Also covering the entire period is Eric Foner's *Reconstruction: America's Unfinished Revolution, 1863–1877* (1988).

Discussion of the Federal government's formulation of Reconstruction policy can be found in W. R. Brock, *An American Crisis: Congress and Reconstruction, 1865–1867* (1963); M. Les Benedict, *A Compromise of Principle: Congressional Republicans and Reconstruction, 1863–1869* (1974); and M. Les Benedict, "Preserving the Constitution: The Conservative Basis of Radical Reconstruction," *Journal of American History,* 1974. Andrew Johnson is best approached through James E. Sefton, *Andrew Johnson and the Uses of Constitutional Power* (1980). Also valuable is William Gillette, *Retreat from Reconstruction, 1869–1879* (1979).

Developments in the South are treated in Michael Perman, *The Road to Redemption: Southern Politics, 1869–1879* (1984); Thomas Holt, *Black Over White: Negro Political Leadership in South Carolina During Reconstruction* (1977); Carl Moneyhon, *Republicanism in Reconstruction Texas* (1980); a collection of essays, *Southern Black Leaders of the Reconstruction Era* (1982), edited by Howard Rabinowitz; and a set of essays focusing on the Republican party in several states, edited by Otto H. Olsen and entitled *Reconstruction and Redemption in the South* (1978). A sensitive and detailed account of how the freedmen experienced emancipation is Leon Litwack, *Been in the Storm So Long: The Aftermath of Slavery* (1979).

Photo Credits